A

COMPARATIVE DICTIONARY

OF THE

BIHARI LANGUAGE

A COMPARATIVE DICTIONARY OF THE BIHARI LANGUAGE.

COMPILED BY

A. F. RUDOLF HOERNLE,

AND

GEORGE A. GRIERSON

PART I. PART II.

GYAN

Published by

Gyan Publishing House
5, Ansari Road
Daryaganj, New Delhi-110002
Phone: 011-47034999, 9811692060
E-mail: books@gyanbooks.com

Distribution Network
gyanbooks.com
India, USA, Canada, UK, Australia

ISBN: 978-93-6280-142-5 (HB)
First Published, 1885-1889

2nd Impression 2024

Printed at: Gyan Press, Delhi.

A COMPARATIVE DICTIONARY OF THE BIHARI LANGUAGE, PART I. PART II.

Compiler: A. F. RUDOLF HOERNLE AND GEORGE A. GRIERSON

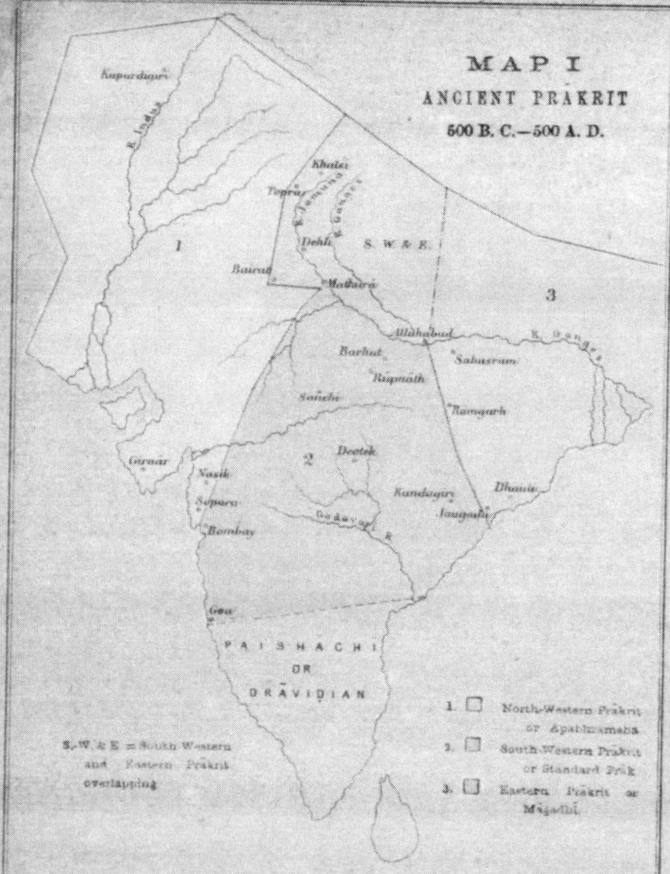
MAP I
ANCIENT PRĀKRIT
500 B. C.—500 A. D.
Kapurdagiri
R. Indus
Khalsi
Topra
Dehli
S. W. & E.
Bairat
Mathura
Allahabad
R. Ganges
Barhut
Sahasram
Rupnath
Sanchi
Ramgarh
Girnar
Nasik
Deotek
Sopara
Khandagiri
Dhauli
Jaugada
Bombay
Goa
PAISHACHI
OR
DRĀVIDIAN
S.-W. & E. = South-Western and Eastern Prākrit overlapping
1. North-Western Prākrit or Apabhramsha
2. South-Western Prākrit or Standard Prāk.
3. Eastern Prākrit or Māgadhī.

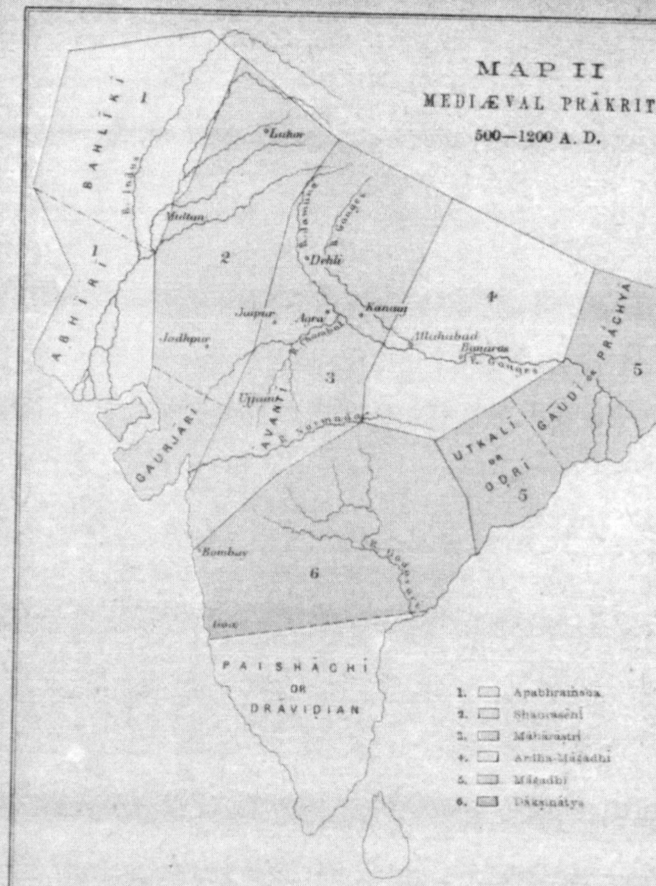
MAP II
MEDIÆVAL PRĀKRIT
500—1200 A. D.
BAHLIKI
ABHIRI
Lahor
R. Indus
Multan
Dehli
Kanauj
Jaipur
Agra
Jodhpur
Allahabad
Banaras
R. Ganges
Ujjain
AVANTI
GAURJARI
PRACHYA
GAUDI
UTKALI
OR
ODRI
Bombay
Goa
PAISHACHI
OR
DRĀVIDIAN
1. Apabhramsha.
2. Shaurasenī
3. Māhārāṣṭrī
4. Ardha-Māgadhī
5. Māgadhī
6. Dākṣiṇātya

MAP III
MODERN PRĀKRIT
OR
GAUDIAN
from 1200 A. D.
Lahor
Multan
Bikaner
Dehli
Agra
Kanauj
Audh
Jaipur
Jodhpur
Allahabad
Darbhanga
Banaras
Gaya
Kotah
Jabalpur
Ujjain
Bombay
Goa
DRAVIDIAN
DIALECTS
Br = Braj
Mr = Marwari
Rj. = Rajputani
K = Kanauji
Hindi.
Ko. = Konkani-Marathi
Bw., Bh., Mg., Mth. see Map IV
1. Sindhī
2. Panjābi
3. Hindi
4. Gujarati
Western Gaudian
5. Bihari
6. Bengali
7. Oriya
Eastern Gaudian
8. Marathi — Southern Gaudian
9. Naipali — Northern Gaudian.

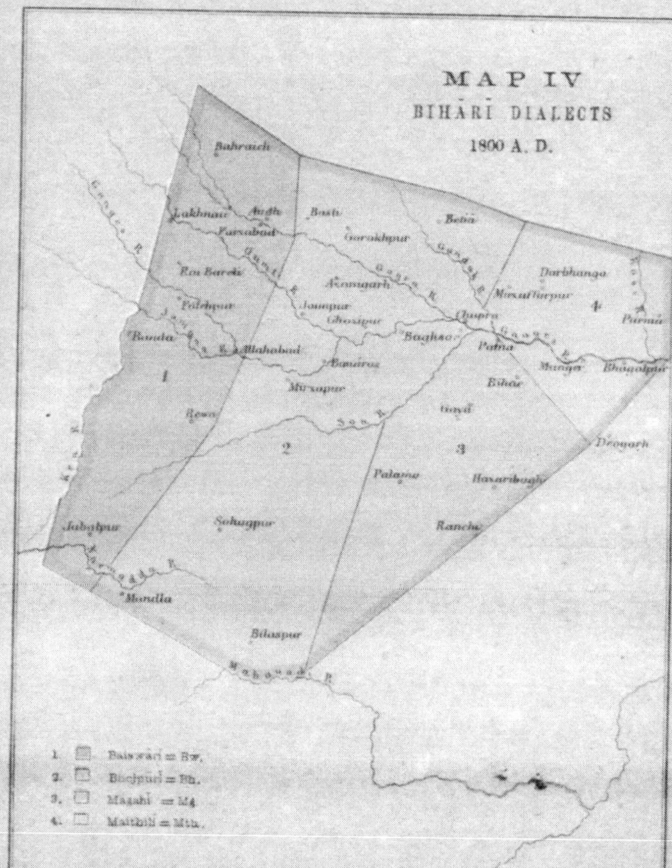
MAP IV
BIHARĪ DIALECTS
1800 A. D.
Bahraich
Lakhnau
Audh
Basti
Betia
Faizabad
Gorakhpur
Darbhanga
Rai Bareli
Azamgarh
Muzaffarpur
Fatehpur
Jaunpur
Ghazipur
Chapra
Banda
Allahabad
Baghsar
Patna
Banaras
Bihar
Mirzapur
Rewa
Gaya
Deogarh
Palamau
Hazaribagh
Jabalpur
Sohagpur
Ranchi
Mandla
Bilaspur
1. Baiswārī = Bw.
2. Bhojpurī = Bh.
3. Magahī = Mg.
4. Maithilī = Mth.

A
COMPARATIVE DICTIONARY
OF THE
BIHĀRĪ LANGUAGE.

COMPILED BY

A. F. RUDOLF HOERNLE,

OF THE BENGAL EDUCATIONAL SERVICE,

AND

GEORGE A. GRIERSON,

OF HER MAJESTY'S BENGAL CIVIL SERVICE.

[Published under the Patronage of the Government of Bengal.]

CALCUTTA:
AT THE BENGAL SECRETARIAT PRESS.
SOLD BY
TRÜBNER & CO., 57 AND 59, LUDGATE HILL, LONDON;
BREITKOPF & HÆRTEL, LEIPZIG;
AND
W. NEWMAN & CO., 4, DALHOUSIE SQUARE, CALCUTTA.
1885.

To

THE HONORABLE SIR ASHLEY EDEN, K.C.S.I., C.I.E.

Sir,

When you, being then Lieutenant-Governor of these provinces, consented more than three years ago to allow us to dedicate this work to you, we little thought that so great a delay would have occurred before this, the first part of it, was published. Nevertheless, we cannot altogether regret that delay, which has resulted, we venture to hope, in making our Dictionary more worthy of your acceptance.

There is a peculiar fitness in dedicating the first Dictionary of the Bihārī language to you; for it was you who, when ruling over these provinces, succeeded in making the national character of the country current in the law-courts, and who first officially recognised the existence of a national language in Bihār.

To you, Sir, therefore, in grateful remembrance of the beneficent reform which you introduced, this work is dedicated by

THE AUTHORS.

Calcutta,

Bankipore,

1885.

INTRODUCTION.

CONTENTS.

INTRODUCTION.

(Ad interim.)

In issuing the first part of our Dictionary, it will be convenient briefly to explain the method observed by us in its compilation.

I.—SYSTEM OF TRANSLITERATION.

We shall make use of transliteration in the following two cases only:—

(1) The first word or words of every article (*i.e.*, up to the term Tbh. or Ts., see Chap. 11) in the Dictionary will be transliterated, immediately after its Nāgarī form: thus अउत *aüt*, ऊत *ūt*, औतिया *autiyā*, Tbh. These transliterations will always be printed in *italics*.

(2) Generally in the Introduction, and occasionally in the Dictionary, transliteration will be employed where it may serve to elucidate our meaning more clearly. In this case italic or roman type will be used according to circumstances.

The systems of transliteration at present in use unfortunately still differ in several important points. It becomes necessary, therefore, to explain clearly the system adopted by ourselves.

(1) Long vowels are usually indicated in three different ways—thus *á* or *â* or *ā*. We have adopted the last sign, the horizontal stroke, because it combines most easily with the sign (˜) of nasalisation, which so commonly occurs with long vowels: thus आँ *ā̃*, ईं *ī̃*, ऊँ *ū̃*, etc. The circumflex we shall only employ in the exceptional case of आ̂ *â*, mentioned in Chapter 4, *e*. The acute accent we shall reserve to indicate, when necessary, the tonic accent or stressed syllable of a word: thus छोटक्का *chhoṭákkā* 'small.'

(2) As regards the vowels *e, o, ai, au*, we shall, in order to preserve uniformity, indicate them when they are long, instead of, as it has been usual hitherto, when they are short: thus we spell *e, ē; o, ō; ai, āi; au, āu*; (not *ĕ, e; ŏ, o; ăi ai; ău, au*); the short vowels being the ones without diacritical marks.

(3) The imperfect vowel (see Chap. 2) we indicate by the *apostrophe*: thus देखलहुँ *dekh'láhŭ* 'I saw,' चारि *chāri* 'four,' किछु *kichhŭ* 'something.'

(4) The *anunāsika* (ँ) or nasalisation of a vowel we indicate by the *circumflex* (˜): thus अँ *ã*, इँ *ĩ*. In combination with the sign (–) of length, it is placed above the latter: thus आँ *ā̃*, ईँ *ī̃*, etc. The *anuswāra* (ं) we transcribe by *ṁ*.

(5) For the guttural nasal ङ, we have adopted the 'phonetic' type *ŋ*, which is coming into fashion and has the advantage of getting rid of the inconvenient dots or strokes.

(6) For the hard palatals we have retained the old-fashioned, though somewhat unscientific, signs *ch* (च) and *chh* (छ). They are so well known and so generally used, at least in English, that the inconvenience of discarding them would have greatly overbalanced any advantage that might accrue from the use of a little more scientifically accurate signs, even supposing there were any general agreement as to what the latter should be. The palatal nasal ञ is indicated by *ñ*, the sign now almost universally adopted.

(7) The whole of the cerebral series is indicated by a subscribed dot, according to a well-known and nearly universal practice. We extend it, however, as some have done before us, to the cerebral sibilant ṣ (ष), transcribing the palatal sibilant श by *sh*. This for two reasons—(1) because it preserves theoretical uniformity, and (2) because it conforms to the universal usage of using *sh* to signify the modern sibilant, which is not a cerebral but a palatal sound, as in *Krish'n* क्रिश्न (कृष्ण), *Shām Lāl* शाम लाल, etc.

For convenient reference we append a table exhibiting our system of transliteration. The letters are arranged in the order explained below in Chapter 5.

Vowels.*

	Dēvanāgarī.		Transliteration.		Dēvanāgarī.		Transliteration.
	Initial.	Medial.			Initial.	Medial.	
1	—	ऽ†	'	4	ए†	े	*e*
	अ	ऽ† (final)	*a*		एँ†	ेँ	*ẽ*
	अँ	ँ	*ã*		ए	े	*ē*
	अं†	ॅ	*á*		एँ	ेँ	*ē̃*
	अ††	†	*ă*	5	ऐ†	ै	*ai*
	अँ†	†̃	*ã̆*		ऐँ†	ैँ	*ãi*
	आ	ा	*ā*		ऐ	ै	*āi*
	आँ	ाँ	*ā̃*		ऐँ	ैँ	*ā̃i*
2	—	ि	*i̓*	6	ओ†	ो	*o*
	इ	ि	*i*		ओँ†	ोँ	*õ*
	इँ	िँ	*ĩ*		ओ	ो	*ō*
	ई	ी	*ī*		ओँ	ोँ	*ō̃*
	ईँ	ीँ	*ī̃*	7	औ†	ौ	*au*
3	—	ु	*u̓*		औँ†	ौँ	*ãu*
	उ	ु	*u*		औ	ौ	*āu*
	उँ	ुँ	*ũ*		औँ	ौँ	*ā̃u*
	ऊ	ू	*ū*				
	ऊँ	ूँ	*ū̃*				

* The vowel ऋ and anuswāra (ं), when they occur in Sanskrit words, will be transliterated by *ṛi* and *ṃ* respectively.

† These are new signs. See Chap. 4, *e* and *f*.

Consonants.

Dēvanāgarī.	Trans-literation.	Dēvanāgarī.	Trans-literation.	Dēvanāgarī.	Trans-literation.	Dēvanāgarī.	Trans-literation.
1 क	*k*	3 ट	*ṭ*	5 प	*p*	7 श	*sh*
ख	*kh*	ठ	*ṭh*	फ	*ph*	ष	*ś*
ग	*g*	ड	*ḍ*	ब	*b*	स	*s*
घ	*gh*	ड़	*ṛ*	भ	*bh*	8 ह	*h*
ङ	*ŋ*	ढ	*ḍh*	म	*m*		
		ढ़	*ṛh*				
		ण	*ṇ*				
2 च	*ch*	4 त	*t*				
छ	*chh*	थ	*th*	6 य	*y*		
ज	*j*	द	*d*	र	*r*		
झ	*jh*	ध	*dh*	ल	*l*		
ञ	*ñ*	न	*n*	व	*w**		

As we shall have occasionally to translate Arabic and Persian words, when quoted as such (*e.g.*, in the comparative portions of our Dictionary), it may be well to state that we follow the system adopted in the dictionaries of Shakespear and Forbes; with one exception, viz. that of using *q* instead of *ḳ* to indicate ق. For the sake of convenience we give here a list of the signs appropriated for those consonantal sounds which are peculiar to Arabic and Persian :—

Ar. Prs.	Roman.	Ar. Prs.	Roman.	Ar. Prs.	Roman.
ا	*a*	ز	*z*	ظ	*z̤*
ث	*s̤*	ژ	*zh*	ع	‘
ح	*ḥ*	ص	*ṣ*	غ	*g͟h*
خ	*k͟h*	ض	*ẓ*	ق	*q*
ذ	*ẕ*	ط	*t̤*	ة	*h*

2.—THE IMPERFECT VOWEL.

The imperfect vowel being a sound frequently met with in the Bihārī (and more or less in the Gauḍians generally), and its occurrence not having been sufficiently recognised or noticed, hitherto, it becomes necessary to explain the subject as fully as possible.

By the 'imperfect vowel' we mean what is called the 'voice-glide' by the English phonetists,† that is the shortest possible vocal utterance, like *o* in the word *Brighton* (*Bright'n*) or the obscure vowel sound in the final syllable of *amiable*, *centre* (*amiab'l*, *cent'r*). It occurs in a threefold variety,

* Or *v* in Sanskrit and Prakrit words.

† See Mr. Sweet's Handbook of Phonetics, § 200.

according as it partakes of the nature of *a* (guttural), *i* (palatal), or *u* (labial). Practically it may be said to be a very slightly pronounced sound of *a*, or *i*, or *u*.

In this Dictionary we shall indicate the transliterated imperfect vowel by the apostrophe, under which we shall place the vowels *i* and *u*, whenever it is intended to signify the palatal (ỉ) and labial (ủ) variety respectively. In Nāgarī it is only convenient to indicate the medial imperfect vowel, which we do by means of a dot (॰), as explained below. In the comparative portion of an article we shall not indicate an imperfect vowel in order to avoid any misleading conclusions regarding cognate Gauḍian forms of a word.

An imperfect vowel may occur in the middle of a word, or at the end of a word. In the former case it can only occur between two consonants, in the latter case only after a consonant. It can therefore never occur after or before any vowel; nor does it ever commence a word.

The *guttural* imperfect vowel (') is very often found in the middle of a word, as in घर॰वा *ghar'wā* 'house,' मिठ॰कवा *míṭh'kawā* 'sweet.' The cases when it occurs in this position must be learned by practice; no general workable rules on the subject can be given. At the end of a word it only occurs in poetry, where the final sound of every word which according to Sanskrit usage would end in *a* is pronounced as the imperfect vowel ('). In prose and conversation, with a few exceptions, this final sound becomes altogether silent, that is, all words containing it are pronounced as if they ended in a consonant; thus घर 'house' is pronounced *ghar* in prose and *ghar'* in poetry, but never, as in Sanskrit, *ghara*. There are, however, a few cases in which the final *a*-sound is not silent, but is pronounced either as the full vowel *a* or as the imperfect vowel ('); thus देख॰बँ * 'you will see' is pronounced *dekh'bá*, terminating with the full vowel, and दत्त 'given' is pronounced *datt'*, terminating with the imperfect vowel (not *dēkh'b* and *datt* respectively). These exceptional cases will be found enumerated in the Dictionary article अ *a*. Hitherto it has not been customary to distinguish between the final *a* when it is silent and when it is pronounced. This practice, however, is rendered all the more inconvenient and misleading by the fact that according to the well-known rule of Sanskrit phonetics the final *a* of every word thus spelt should be pronounced (thus, घर and देखब would be pronounced alike *ghara* and *dekh'ba*). The Sanskrit method of indicating the absence of *a* from any consonant is to append the so-called *virāma* (्) to the consonant. This would at first sight have seemed the best plan to adopt in writing Bihārī, and to spell *ghar* घर्, but *dekh'bá* देखबँ.† But there are two great objections to it. In the first place, the *virāma* would express too much; for the final *a*, though silent in all ordinary speech, is not really *absent*. In poetry it must be always read, and must be counted in scanning, if the metre is to be preserved. In the second place, the *virāma* is apt to create difficulties in printing. Hence we have thought it better to invent a new sign to indicate the final *a* when it is pronounced, instead of using the *virāma* to indicate *a* when it is not pronounced. We have adopted for this purpose a small circle (॰), placed after the consonant, below the top line, to indicate the full sound of *a*, and a dot (॰), placed in the same position, to indicate its imperfect sound. In this Dictionary, therefore, a final *a* is never to be pronounced except when indicated by ॰ or ॰: thus घर *ghar*, but देख॰बँ॰ *dekh'bá* and दत्त॰ *datt'*.

The occurrence of the *palatal* and *labial* imperfect vowels (ỉ and ủ) is, in prose, almost entirely limited to the Maithilī dialect of Bihārī. In this dialect, with a few exceptions, the final sound of every word ending in *i* or *u* is pronounced (in prose and poetry alike) as the imperfect vowel ỉ or ủ respectively.‡ Thus अछि 'he is,' देखथु 'let him see,' are pronounced *achhỉ*, *dēkhathủ* respectively, not *achhi*, *dēkhathu*. There are to this rule only three exceptions, in which a final *i* is always

* For an explanation of the sign (ँ), see Chap. 4, *e*.

† This system of spelling is followed in Dr. Hœrnle's Gauḍian Grammar.

‡ See Mth. Gr., p. 6, § 7; also B. Gr., I (Introd.), p. 26, § 43.

pronounced as a full vowel. These are—(1) the final *i* of the plural termination अनि *ani*, as in लोकनि *lokani* (not *lōkanĭ*), plural of लोक *lōk* 'people;'* (2) the final *i* of masc. nouns, as in पानि *pāni* 'water,' मानि *māni* 'proud' (not *pānĭ*, *mānĭ*); † (3) a final *i* preceded by a vowel, as in हलुकाइ *halukāi* 'lightness' (not *halukāĭ*). In this respect the other Bihār dialects differ from Maithilī. In them, with a few exceptions, every final *i* and *u* become silent, that is, all words containing them are pronounced as if they ended in a consonant. Hence in these dialects, in respect to their Nāgarī spelling no difference is made between such words and those which end in a silent *a*; that is, both classes of words are spelt alike as ending in silent अ *a*. Thus, while Maithilī has सुन्दरि (fem.) 'beautiful,' मारि 'beating,' pronounced *sundarĭ*, *mārĭ*, the other dialects have सुन्दर *sundar*, मार *mār*, etc. There are, however, a few isolated cases of the occurrence of these imperfect vowels in Bhoj'pūrī and Magahī, especially in the former, though even in these cases the use of the imperfect vowel is always optional and is, in fact, less usual. The more prominent cases are the following :—(1) the plural termination of substantives, which in Mth. is अनि *ani*, in Bh. अनि *ani*, अनि *anĭ* or अन *an*, in Mg. अन *an*; *e.g.*, Mth. लोकनि *lokani*, Bh. लोकनि *lokani* or लोकनि *lōkanĭ* or लोकन *lōkan*, Mg. लोकन *lōkan*; (2) feminine terminations like that of the 3rd pers. sg. pret. ind., which in Mth. is अलि *alĭ*, in Bh. अलि *alĭ* or अल *al*,‡ *e.g.*, Mth. गिरलि *giralĭ*, Bh. गिरलि *giralĭ* or गिरल *giral*; (3) the poetical termination of the conjunctive participle, which in all Bihār dialects, including Bais'wārī, is इ *ĭ*; *e.g.*, Mth., Bh., Mg., Bw., देखि *dēkhĭ* 'having seen;'§ (4) in pronominal forms like Bh. एहि *ehĭ* or एह *eh* 'this,' but Mg. एह *eh* only; (5) the numeral 'four,' which is Mth. चारि *chārĭ*, Bh. चारि *chārĭ* or चार *chār*,‖ but Mg. चार *chār*; (6) the 2nd pers. sg. imp., which in Bh. may end in *ŭ*; ¶ *e.g.*, देखु *dēkhŭ* or देख *dēkh* 'see thou,' but Mg. only देख *dēkh*; (7) the indefinite pronoun, which in Mth. is किछु *kichhŭ*, in Bh. किछु *kichhŭ* or किछ *kichh*, in Mg. कछु *kachhŭ*.** It may be added that in the old Bais'wārī poetry of the Rāmāyan, etc., every final इ and उ, if preceded by a consonant, is pronounced with the imperfect sound.

It should be particularly noted, with regard to these imperfect vowels (ᵃ, *ĭ*, *ŭ*) that, on the one hand, for the purpose of scanning they are counted as full vowels (*a*, *i*, *u*,) while, on the other hand, for the purpose of shortening the antepenultimate (on which see Chap. 6) a medial one (ᵃ) counts, but a final one (*ĭ* and *ŭ*) does not count.

3.—ANUSWĀRA AND ANUNĀSIKA.

There is no sign in the treatment of which there prevails greater uncertainty and confusion in the existing dictionaries than the symbol (ं) of the so-called *anuswāra*. It is necessary therefore to explain briefly the subject and justify our treatment of it.

In Sanskrit the sign (ं) of the *anuswāra* is used for two entirely distinct purposes :—

(1) It is employed—and this is its proper use—to signify a peculiar nasal sound, intermediate between a vowel and a consonant, which is not a mere nasalisation of a vowel, but an independent sound following a vowel, just as any other sound (vowel or consonant) might follow a vowel : thus, हंस *haṁsa*, वनं *vanaṁ*.

(2) It is employed—in an improper fashion—to signify the nasalised consonants ङ *ṅ*, ञ *ñ*, ण *ṇ*, न *n*, म *m*, when conjunct with a non-nasalised consonant of their own classes : thus, अंगं *aṅgaṁ*, अंजनं *añjanaṁ* (for अङ्गं, अञ्जनं).

---

* See Mth. Gr., p. 10, § 25.

† See Mth. Gr., pp. 17, 20, §§ 40, 47.

‡ See Gḍ. Gr., p. 350, § 504 ; B. Gr. II (Bh.), p. 71, § 83.

§ See B. Gr., II (Bh.), pp 68, 69, §§ 78, 79.

‖ See Gḍ. Gr., p. 251, §§ 391, 392.

¶ See Gḍ. Gr., p. 331, § 495.

** See B. Gr., II (Bh.), pp. 26, 27, § 29.

In addition to these two, the *anuswāra* is used in Hindī dictionaries for a third purpose, viz., to indicate the *anunāsika* or the nasalisation of a vowel. This *anunāsika* is the same as the nasal sound in the Swābian and other South German dialects, as in *ũmöglich* (for *unmöglich* 'impossible'), *wohĩ* (for *wohin* 'whereto'); it is something like, though not quite the same as, the nasal sound of the French, as in *bon.** What makes the practice of the Hindī dictionaries still more confusing is that the second mode of employing the *anuswāra* is resorted to very capriciously, some nasal consonants being represented by the *anuswāra*, others by their proper symbols. All this confusion is avoided by adhering to the simple and obvious principle of rigorously limiting each symbol to its own proper use. Accordingly, the system followed in our Dictionary is the following :—

(1) As in the Bihārī (and Gauḍian generally) the proper *anuswāra* sound does not exist, its sign (ं) has been discarded altogether, except in the case of a few words, such as हंस *haṁs* 'goose,' सिंह *siṁh* 'lion,' the *tatsama* spelling of which it was thought convenient to give in addition to their Bihārī spellings (हन्स *hans*, सिङ्ह *siŋgh*).†

(2) The nasal consonants, when in conjunction with their class consonants, are always indicated by their proper symbols, viz., ङ *ŋ*, ञ *ñ*, ण *ṇ*, न *n*, म *m*, never by the *anuswāra*: thus we always spell गङ्गा *gaŋgā*, चन्दन *chandan*, not गंगा *gaṁgā*, चंदन *chaṁdan*, etc.

(3) The nasalisation of a vowel is indicated by its proper sign, the *anunāsika* (ँ): thus we spell आँखि *ā̃khi* 'eye,' नीँद *nī̃d* 'sleep' (not आंखि *āṁkhi*, नींद *nīṁd*).

In order to determine whether a word which according to the prevalent practice is spelt with the *anuswāra* should in our Dictionary be looked for under a class-nasal or the *anunāsika*, the following rule should be observed :—

If the nasal occurs in a syllable containing a long vowel, it is the *anunāsika;* but in a syllable with a short vowel, it is the nasal consonant of the class to which the following (muṭe) consonant belongs: *e.g.*, आँकुर *ā̃kur* 'sprout,' आँगन *ā̃gan* 'courtyard,' हाँस *hā̃s* 'goose,' नीँद *nī̃d* 'sleep,' ऊँच *ū̃ch* 'high,' बेँत *bē̃t* 'rattan,' भैँस *bhaĩs* buffalo,' मोँछ *mõchh* 'moustache,' मौँसी *maũsī* 'maternal aunt;' but अङ्कुर *aŋkur* 'sprout,' निन्दा *nindā* 'abuse,' उञ्च *uñch* 'high,' etc.

There is only one important exception to this rule. If the nasal occurs in the antepenultimate syllable of a tadbhava word, especially in long and strong forms of nouns, and in causal verbs where an original long vowel is made short,‡ the nasal always is the *anunāsika*: thus, अँकनि *ãkani*, 'having heard,' अँठये *ãṭhayē*, 'they set,' and अँधियार *ãdhiyār*, 'darkness;' strong form अँकुरा *ãkurā* (or आँकुरा *ā̃kurā*), अँगना *ãg'nā* 'courtyard' and long forms अँकुरवा *ãkur'wā* (or आँकुरवा *ā̃kur'wā*) 'sprout,' हँसवा *hãs'wā* (from tadbh. हाँस *hā̃s*) goose, निँदवा *nĩd'wā* (from tadbh. नीँद *nī̃d*) 'sleep,' बेँतवा *bĕ̃t'wā* 'rattan,' भैँसवा *bhaĩs'wā* 'buffalo,' मोँछवा *mŏ̃chh'wā* 'moustache,' मौँसिया *maũsiyā* 'maternal aunt;' causal verbs भिँजाएब *bhĩjāeb*, 'to cause to be wet' (from भीँजब *bhī̃jab*), फेँकाएब *phĕ̃kāeb*, 'to cause to throw' (from फेँकब *phē̃kab*). But in the antepenultimate of a tatsama word it is the class-nasal; *e.g.*, अङ्कुरे *aŋkurē*, 'they spring up,' अङ्गना *aŋg'nā* 'woman,' and अन्धकार *andhakār*, 'darkness,' long forms हन्सवा *hans'wā* 'goose' (from tats. हन्स *hans*), निन्दवा *nind'wā* 'abuse' (from tats. निन्दा *nindā*).

---

* See Mr. Sweet's Handbook of Phonetics, § 22.

† It should be noted that such *tatsama* forms are a mere matter of spelling, not of pronunciation; हंस is never pronounced *haṁs*, but *hans*

‡ By the peculiar rule of shortening the antepenultimate. See below, Chap. 6.

There are some other isolated exceptions, such as मुँह *mũh* 'face' and कान्ह *kānh* 'Krishna,' etc., but they are so rare as to render the above given rule a practically safe one.

4.—SYSTEM OF SPELLING.

(*a*) The main principle followed in our Dictionary is to spell every word as nearly as possible as it is pronounced. This principle is so obvious, both in regard to its scientific correctness and its practical utility, that it needs no defence. Since, however, it has been carried out in our Dictionary more rigorously and uniformly than is usually the practice, it may be well to observe that customary unphonetic spellings have been discarded in all cases except where practical considerations seemed to render that course inexpedient. But even in these exceptional cases the words have always been given both in their phonetic and in their customary unphonetic shapes, arranged in their respective alphabetical order, and accompanied by cross-references; the main article being reserved for the word in its phonetic spelling. Thus the term for 'flower' is commonly spelt, in Sanskrit fashion, पुष्प *puṣp*. It is, however, pronounced पुस्प *pusp* or पुश्प *pushp* or पुह्फ *puh'ph*. All four spellings have been given, the main article being under पुस्प *pusp*, to which the reader is referred under पुह्फ *puh'ph*, पुश्प *pushp*, and पुष्प *puṣp*. Again, the usual spelling of Krishna's name is कृष्ण *Kṛiṣṇa*, pronounced क्रिश्न *Krish'n*. The latter forms the main article, to which a cross-reference is given under कृष्ण *Kṛiṣṇa*. So again ग्रांझ्य *grãjhy'*, which represents the pronunciation of what is usually written ग्राह्य *grāhy*, is the main article, with a cross-reference to the latter. In the great majority of cases, however, where the phonetic spelling adopted by us can cause no practical inconvenience, because it is not altogether unknown to already existing practice, the words are only given in their phonetic shapes. In order to minimise the risk of inconvenience as far as possible, a table of the phonetic spellings adopted by us in this Dictionary is here inserted.

Unphonetic.	Phonetic.	Examples.				
ऋ *ṛi*	रि *ri*	ऋतु *ṛitu*	spelt	रितु *ritu*		
ण *ṇ*	न *n*	रण *raṇ*	„	रन *ran*		
श *sh*	स *s*	शरण *sharaṇ*	„	सरन *saran*		
ष *ṣ*	ख *kh*	भाषा *bhāṣā*	„	भाखा *bhākhā*,	आकर्षण *ākarṣan* spelt	आकर्खन *ākarkhan*
क्ष *kṣ*	छ *chh* or ख *kh**	क्षमा *kṣamā*	„	छमा *chhamā*, or राक्षस *rākṣas*	„	राखस *rākhas*
ज्ञ *jñ*	ग्य *gy*	ज्ञान *jñān*	„	ग्यान *gyān*		
ंस *ṁs*	न्स *ns*	हंस *haṁs*	„	हन्स *hans*		
ंह *ṁh*	ङ्घ *ŋgh*	सिंह *siṁh*	„	सिङ्घ *siŋgh*		

It seems hardly necessary to mention, as a practical rule, that if a word is not found under one spelling, it should be looked up under the other.

(*b*) Sometimes a word is pronounced, at pleasure, in two different ways. Of the two phonetic spellings possible in these cases, as a rule only that which expresses the more usual pronunciation has been adopted. In order, however, to facilitate the finding of such a word by those who may be more accustomed to the rejected spelling, a list of alternative spellings

* The more usual pronunciation is छ *chh*. If ख *kh* or छ *chh* are medial, they may, after a short vowel, be spelt क्ख *kkh* or च्छ *chchh*, *e.g.*, दखिन *dakhin* or दक्खिन *dakkhin* for दक्षिण *dakṣiṇ*, रछा *rachhā* or रच्छा *rachchhā* for रक्षा *rakṣā*.

is herewith given. Those in the first column have been usually adopted; but if any word is not given in that spelling, it will be found in the other.

Adopted.	Rejected.	Examples.	Adopted.	Rejected.	Examples.
आय	आए or आइ	परआय and परआए or परआइ	र	ड़	√पर or √पड़
āy	āe ,, āi	parāy ,, parāe ,, parāi	r	ṛ	par ,, paṛ
आव	आओ or आउ	चढ़आव ,, चढ़आओ ,, चढ़आउ			
āw	āo ,, āü	chaṛhāw ,, chaṛhāo ,, chaṛhāü	र	ल	फर ,, फल
इया	इआ	बेटिया ,, बेटिआ	r	l	phar ,, phal
iyā	iā	beṭiyā ,, beṭiā			
उआ	उवा	बहुआ ,, बहुवा	ग्य	गे	ग्यान ,, गेआन
uā	uwā	bahuā ,, bahuwā	gy	ge	gyān ,, geān
ऐ or अँए	अँइ	अघैला or अघँएला and अघँइला			
ai ,, ăe	ăi	aghailā ,, aghăelā ,, aghăilā	पर'	प्र	पर'भु ,, प्रभु
औ ,, अँओ	अँउ	पौला ,, पँओला ,, पँउला	par'	pra	par'bhu ,, prabhu
au ,, ăo	ăü	paulā ,, păolā ,, păülā			

(c) There is one case in which there are two graphic ways of expressing the same sound; viz., the nasal consonants ङ ŋ, ञ ñ, ण ṇ, न n, म m, when conjunct with a following consonant of their own class, may be either written in full (ङ, ञ, ण, न, म), or simply indicated by the *anuswāra* (ं). In the latter case, accordingly, the *anuswāra* must be understood to have, not its proper sound (of the Sanskrit *anuswāra*), but to be a sort of stenographic representation of the nasal sound of the class of consonant which it precedes. As this use of the *anuswāra*, however, is not only unscientific, but also (as explained in Chap. 6) productive of much confusion, it has been altogether discarded by us, and the nasal consonants are always represented by their own proper symbols. A list of these is herewith given :—

Rejected.				Adopted.				Examples.					
ंक,	ंख,	ंग,	ंघ,	ङ्क,	ङ्ख,	ङ्ग,	ङ्घ,	अंक,	सिंघ	spelt	अङ्क	सिङ्घ	(for सिंह)
ṁk,	ṁkh,	ṁg,	ṁgh,	ŋk,	ŋkh,	ŋg,	ŋgh,	aṁk,	siṁgh	,,	aŋk,	siŋgh	(,, siṁh)
ंच,	ंछ,	ंज,	ंझ,	ञ्च,	ञ्छ,	ञ्ज,	ञ्झ,	कुंजी,	संजम	,,	कुञ्जी,	सञ्जम	(for संयम)
ṁch,	ṁchh,	ṁj,	ṁjh,	ñch,	ñchh,	ñj,	ñjh,	kuṁjī,	saṁjam	,,	kuñjī,	sañjam	(,, saṁyam)
ंट,	ंठ,	ंड,	ंढ,	ण्ट,	ण्ठ,	ण्ड,	ण्ढ,	पंडित		,,	पण्डित		
ṁṭ,	ṁṭh,	ṁḍ,	ṁḍh,	ṇṭ,	ṇṭh,	ṇḍ,	ṇḍh,	paṁḍit		,,	paṇḍit.		
ंत,	ंथ,	ंद,	ंध,	न्त,	न्थ,	न्द,	न्ध,	चंद		,,	चन्द		
ṁt,	ṁth,	ṁd,	ṁdh	nt,	nth,	nd,	ndh,	chaṁd		,,	chand.		
ंप,	ंफ,	ंब,	ंभ,	म्प,	म्फ,	म्ब,	म्भ,	बिंब,	दंभ	,,	बिम्ब,	दम्भ	
ṁp,	ṁph,	ṁb,	ṁbh,	mp,	mph,	mb,	mbh,	biṁb,	daṁbh		bimb,	dambh.	

(d) There is one case in which there is one graphic way of expressing two distinct sounds, viz., the so-called semi-vowels य and व. The former of these may express the sound of *y* or of *j*, the latter of *w* or of *b*. This practice is both unscientific and confusing, and as there are, in the alphabet, already the separate symbols ज and ब for the sounds of *j* and *b* respectively, we shall employ the latter signs, ज and ब, in every case in which the sounds of *j* and *b* are to be pronounced, and reserve the signs of य and व for those cases only in which they really signify the sounds of *y* and *w* respectively. At the same time, it should be carefully noted, with regard to the hard sound of व, that it is not exactly a mute sound like our common *b*, nor quite so liquid as our common *v*. It is a very peculiar sound, neither distinctly *b* nor *v*. Of the two it is nearer to *b*; but in many cases it is very difficult, for European ears, to say which it is. Bihārīs, however, when questioned, in most cases declare it to be *b*, that is, the sound of ब. This being so, we have thought it best to abide by the judgment of the native ear; and accordingly we invariably spell व *b*, whenever the hard sound of व is to be pronounced. It is difficult to give exact rules to distinguish the cases in which the two sets of sounds (*y*, *w* and *j*, *b* respectively) occur; but the following directions, founded on the practice of the standard Maithilī, will be found to be approximately correct.

(1) य is pronounced as ज *j* whenever it is the initial sound of a simple word, as जात्री (unphon. यात्री)* *jātrī* 'traveller,' or of the parts of a compound word, as मनोजोग (unphon. मनोयोग) *manōjōg*, 'desire,' अजोग (unphon. अयोग) *ajōg*, 'unsuitable.' There is only one exception to this practice; viz., when the initial य is inorganic or euphonic,† as in यह *yah* 'he' (not *jah*), for एह *eh*. It is also pronounced ज when it occurs in the conjuncts य्य, र्य ंय, as सज्या (unphon. शय्या) *sajyā* 'bed,' आचार्ज (unphon. आचार्य) *āchārj* 'preceptor,' सञ्जम (unphon. संयम) *sañjam* 'continence.' In all other cases it is pronounced as *y*; *e.g.*, समय *samay* 'season,' रामायण *rāmāyan* 'the Rāmāyan,' पयोधर *payodhar* 'bosom,' आद्य *ādya* 'to-day,' व्यतीत *byatīt* 'passed,' etc. In the case of words compounded with prefixes, there is some uncertainty. After सं *saṁ*, initial य is always *j*, as in सञ्जोग (unphon. संयोग) *sañjōg* 'junction,' सञ्जुक्त *sañjuk't* 'joined;' after परऽ (प्र) *par'* it is always *y*, as in परऽयोग *par'yōg* 'application,' परऽयुक्त *par'yuk't* 'applied;' after नि *ni* it may be *y* or *j*, as in नियोग *niyōg* 'appointment,' but निजुक्त *nijuk't* or नियुक्त *niyuk't* 'appointed.'

(2) व is pronounced as *b* as a general rule, of which there are only a few exceptions. Thus व is *b* in बेद (unphon. वेद) *bēd* 'Veda,' निब्रित्ति (unphon. निवृत्ति) *nibritt'* 'ceased,' अबगाह (unphon. अवगाह) *abagāh* 'ablution,' पबन (unphon. पवन) *paban* 'wind,' भाबिनी (unphon. भाविनी) *bhābinī* 'wife,' पाबथि (unphon. पावथि) *pābathi* 'if they obtain,' आबि कँ (unphon. आवि कँ) *ābi-kā̃* 'having come,' दरब (unphon. दरव or द्रव) *darab* 'substance,' सिब (unphon. शिव) *sib* 'Shiva,' देब (unphon. देव) *dēb* 'god,' पूरऽब (unphon. पूर्व) *pūr'b* 'former,' सम्बत (unphon. संवत) *sambat* 'year.' In भाव, being the final element of a word, व may be pronounced *b* or *w*; *e.g.*, भाब *bhāb* or भाव *bhāw* 'condition.' The exceptions are: in the termination of the long and redundant forms of nouns, as घरऽवा *ghar'wā* 'house,' माँलियवा *mā̆liyawā* 'gardener,' in the √ हँव *hā̃w* and its derivatives, and in words like गाँव *gā̃w* 'village,' भँवर *bhā̃war* 'humblebee,' वह *wah* 'he' (for ओह *oh*). Generally speaking व is pronounced *w* when it is an inorganic or euphonic element. But even in that case, it may sometimes be pronounced *b*; thus in the termination of the long and redundant forms (*e.g.*, घोरऽबा *ghor'bā* for घोरऽवा *ghor'wā* 'horse') and in certain inflections of such roots as पी *pi* 'drink,' चू *chū* 'drip,' धो *dhō* 'wash' (*e.g.*, चूबि *chūbi* for चूवि *chūwi* 'dripping,' B. Gr. I, p. 36, fable 13;—पिबँह *pibā̃h* for पिवँह *piwā̃h* 'drink ye,' B. Gr. I, p. 38, fable 16;—धोबू *dhōbū* for धोवू *dhōwū* 'wash thou,' Mth. Gr., p. 92). It should be noted that this rule in its entirety only holds good in Maithilī. In Bhoj'pūrī and Magahī there is a distinct tendency towards pronouncing व as *w* (not *b*).

(*e*) There remains one case to which we must invite special attention, as it is one which has hitherto been nearly altogether overlooked. In Bihārī (and, more or less, in all Eastern Gauḍians) there are two different *a*-sounds,—one close, the other open. Each of these may be long or short; so that there are two pairs: (1) the close *a* (short) and the close *ā* (long);

---

* The examples are spelt phonetically, their unphonetic forms being added in brackets.

† Regarding this term see footnote * on page 13.

(2) the open *ă* (short) and the open *ā* (long). The former pair are pronounced something like *ăw* (short) in the English 'hot' and *āw* (long) in the English 'law.' The long sound of the latter pair is pronounced like the long *ā* in the English or, nearer still, the Scotch 'father;' the short sound does not exist in English, but it may be noticed in the Italian *ballo.* The present method among natives of expressing the two different sounds is to write अ for the close *a*-sound, and आ for the open *a*-sound ; and when they wish to be accurate and to distinguish the quantity of the two sounds, they indicate the long close sound of *a* by अ̄ (*i.e.*, अ *plus* the prosodic mark of length), reserving the simple अ for its short close sound ; on the other hand, they indicate the short open sound of *a* by आ̆ (*i.e.*, आ *plus* the prosodic mark of shortness), reserving the simple आ for its long open sound. This is a point of much importance, for it practically amounts to the fact that the two ancient graphic signs अ and आ have changed their signification. While originally they indicated different quantities (*ă* and *ā*) of the same sound, they now primarily signify two different sounds (*aw* and *a*), and secondarily (with the help of prosodic marks) the quantities of those two sounds. In our Dictionary we have adopted the native system of spelling in its more accurate form, that is, we uniformly spell the close pair of the *a*-sound by अ (short) and अ̄ (long) respectively, and the open pair of it by आ̆ (short) and आ (long) respectively. In transliteration we distinguish the former pair by *a* (short) and *â* (long), the latter by *ă* (short) and *ā* (long). Accordingly the graphic representation, in our Dictionary, of the *a*-sounds, both in Nāgarī and Roman, will stand thus :—

Close *a* ...	Short अ *a* *(= *ăw.*)	Open *a* ...	Short आ̆ *ă*.
	Long अ̄ *â* (= *āw.*)		Long आ *ā*.

The following examples will illustrate this system : न *na* 'not,' मरलौं *mar'lõ*, 'I died' (pronounced something like *năw*, *măwr'lõ*), and देखबँ *dekh'bâ*, 'you will see,' देखलें *dēkhâlâ*, 'you see.' Again बाँतिया *bătiyā*, 'word,' माँरलौं *măr'lõ*, 'I beat,' and बात *bāt*, 'word,' मारल *māral*, 'beating.' For an enumeration, as far as it is in our power, of the various cases in which the two *a*-sounds (short or long) occur, we must refer the student to the Dictionary articles अ and आ.

(*f*) For the medial imperfect vowel (॒), the final audible *a* and the short vowels *e*, *ai*, *o*, *au*, we have been obliged to invent special Nāgarī symbols. These are fully explained in Chapters 2 and 5.

(*g*) In spelling Arabic or Persian words incorporated into Bihārī, we have discarded the usual practice of employing diacritical marks (dots) to indicate those sounds which are foreign to the Bihārī alphabet. Thus we spell जरूर *jarūr*, 'necessary,' अरजी *ar'jī*, 'petition,' खुस *khush*, 'happy,' गरीब *garīb*, 'poor,' not ज़रूर (Ar. ضرور), अरज़ी (Ar.-Prs. عرضي), ख़ुश (Prs. خوش), ग़रीब (Ar. غريب). The reason is that these foreign sounds are never pronounced in Bihārī (except by educated Musalmāns), the nearest indigenous sound being always substituted. And since we give the words in a Bihārī Dictionary as integral parts of the Bihārī vocabulary, we prefer spelling them in their adopted Bihārī garb. To this may be added that the usual system is both inaccurate and useless. All the dots in the world will never make a Bihārī pronounce the foreign sounds, and in some cases the same dotted letter is made to do duty for several different sounds, *e.g.*, ज़ for ز, ذ, ض, ظ, so that it is impossible to know which sound it indicates, as well as to which language the word originally belonged.† We supply the latter information, useful for many purposes, by adding 'Arabic, Persian,'

---

* It is more convenient to retain *a* for the short close *a*-sound, because this sound is the most common one, and its transliteration by *a*, therefore, least interferes with the already existing practice of using *a*, as may be seen from the above given examples.

† See Dr. Hœrnle's Gauḍian Grammar, p. 25, and Mr. Beames' Comparative Grammar, vol. I, p. 71.

etc., as the case may be, together with the original spelling in Arabic characters in the comparative portion of the article. As a matter of convenience we here append a list of the foreign sounds, including English, and their Bihārī equivalents.

Ar., Prs.	Bihārī.	Examples.	Ar., Prs.	Bihārī.	Examples.
ا or ع	अ *a*	اصل असल *asal*, مرضي अरजी *ar'ji*	ش	स or श *sh* or *s*	خوشي खुसी *khushī* or खुसी *khusī*
ث or ص	स *s*	ثابت साबित *sābit*, صاحب साहिब *sāhib*	غ	ग *g*	غريب गरीब *garīb*
ح or ه	ह *h*	حكم हुकुम *hukum*, هزار हजार *hajār*	ف‡	फ *ph*	فايده फैदा *phaidā*
خ*	ख *kh*	خالي खाली *khālī*	ق	क *k*	اقرار एकरार *ek'rār*
ذ† or ز or ض or ظ	ज *j*	كاغذ कागज *kāgaj*, زمين जमीन *jamīn*, حاضر हाजिर *hājir*, ظاهر जाहिर *jāhir*			

Initial آ, § final ا or ه, and medial ع and ا, are represented by आ *ā*; *e.g.*, آخر आखिर *ākhir*, بنده or بندا बन्दा *bandā*, معلوم मालूम *mālūm*, موافق माफिक *māphik*.

English.	Bihārī.	Examples.	English.	Bihārī.	Examples.
d, t	ड *ḍ*, ट *ṭ*	lord लाड *lāḍ* (Mth. Ch. 28, 56), London लण्डन *lanḍan*, ticket टिकट *ṭikaṭ*,	f	फ *ph*	office आफिस *āphis*.
			qu	क्व *kw*	queen क्वीन *kwīn*.
th	थ *th*, द *d*	thin थिन *thin*, the दी *dī*.	du	जु *ju*	education एजुकेशन *ajukēshan*.

Sometimes, in the process of incorporation into Bihārī, foreign words suffer curious and apparently arbitrary alterations, especially with regard to vowels; thus जिमिदार *jimidār* for زميندار *zamīndār*, अनतकाल *antakāl* for انتقال *intiqāl*, कुमेटी *kumeṭī* for *committee* (Mth. Ch. p. 27, verse 49), इस्टीसन *istīsan* for *station* (Mth. Ch., p. 27, verse 55), &c.

5.—ALPHABETICAL ORDER.

It has been usual hitherto, in dictionaries of the modern Indian languages, to follow the order of the Sanskrit alphabet.‖ This practice has the advantage of observing a well-known system of alphabetic arrangement; we have, therefore, adopted it. But we have been obliged to introduce some modifications, necessitated by two most important differences between the phonetic systems of the Gauḍian and the Sanskrit.¶ These differences are the following:—

(1) Sanskrit possesses no short sounds of *e*, *ai*, *o*, *au*, nor any imperfect vowel, while Gauḍian has these sounds.

---

* خ is sometimes turned into क *k*; *e.g.*, बकसीस *bak'sīs* for بخشش 'gift,' see Mag. 63.

† ذ is also sometimes turned into द *d* or even त *t*; *e.g.*, कागद *kāgad* or कगता *kagatā* for كاغذ 'paper.' See Mars., ii, ६.

‡ ف is sometimes turned into प *p*; *e.g.*, सुपेती *supētī* for سفيدي 'whiteness' (in the Rāmāyan).

§ When आ *ā* is in the antepenultimate, it is, as usual, shortened and represented by अॅ *ă*; *e.g.*, अॅयना *ăyana* or ऐना *ainā* for آينه, 'mirror.'

‖ Unless when printed in the Persian or Arabic characters.

¶ This, of course, refers only to the established Pāṇinian phonetic system.

(2) Gauḍian makes a very extensive use of the *anunāsika*, or the nasalisation of vowels, but none at all of the proper *anuswāra*, or pure nasal sound; while in Sanskrit the opposite practice prevails.

In the existing dictionaries there is nothing to show these differences, the long and the short sounds of *e, ai, o, au*, and the *anunāsika* and *anuswāra*, being respectively represented by the same symbols. In this Dictionary an attempt has been made, while interfering as little as possible with the accustomed Sanskrit order of letters, to indicate the peculiar Gauḍian sounds by distinctive signs.

For the *anunāsika* and *anuswāra* (as stated in Chap. 3) we have adopted the symbols ँ and ं respectively, both being already used for this purpose in Sanskrit. For the short *e, ai, o, au*, as well as for the imperfect vowel, it was necessary to invent new symbols; and in so doing we have endeavoured to adhere as closely as possible to the already current forms of the letters that are nearest in sound. For the short *ai, o, au*, we have adopted the signs ऐ, ओ, औ, *i.e.*, the established signs for the long *āi, ō, āu*, merely giving the slanting top-strokes a serpentine instead of a straight form. For short *e* we have invented the sign ऎ, *i.e.*, the sign for long *ē* (ए) reversed. For the imperfect vowel we have adopted a point (॰) placed in the position of the accustomed stroke (ा) of the long *ā*. In transliterating it is indicated by the *apostrophe*: thus क॰ *k'*, क *ka*, का *kā*.

With regard to the alignment of these new symbols into the usual Sanskrit alphabetic order, we have, following out the principle indicated by that order, placed the new short vowels *e, ai, o, au*, severally, immediately before their corresponding long sounds, while, with regard to the imperfect vowel and the nasalisation of vowels, we have, after careful consideration, decided to set them aside altogether as principles of arrangement. Accordingly, neither the *anunāsika* nor the imperfect vowel is allowed to affect the order of the words in our Dictionary. In other words: each of the sets ॰, अ, अँ, — आ, आँ, — इ, इँ, — ई, ईँ, — उ, उँ, — ऊ, ऊँ, — ऎ, ऎँ, — ए, एँ, — ऐ, ऐँ, — ऐ, ऐँ, — ओ, ओँ, — ओ, ओँ, — औ, औँ, — औ, औँ, so far as dictionary order is concerned, constitutes one letter only. Accordingly, we shall first give all words containing the sound *a*, irrespective of that sound being imperfect, or short, or nasalised, and simply arrange them according to their consonants; next will come all words containing the sound *ā*, similarly arranged; next, in similar order, those containing the sounds *i* or *ī*, or *u* or *ū*, and so forth.

This method, no doubt, is a considerable innovation on an existing general practice; but it would have been impossible to do justice to the peculiar Gauḍian sounds, on a practical and at the same time scientific plan, without resorting to some kind of innovation: and after a full consideration of the difficulties surrounding the subject, we have come to the conclusion that the innovation adopted in this work is the most advantageous and least inconvenient that could have been selected. With any other arrangement any one ignorant of, or unfamiliar with, the peculiar Gauḍian sounds and their symbols would have experienced no little difficulty in identifying the place where any particular word containing those sounds might be found. With the plan adopted by us, it is hoped no difficulty will be felt in this respect, if only the obvious rule is kept in mind,—that if a word is not found under long *ē, āi, ō, āu*, it should be looked up under short *e, ai, o, au*, and that words containing a nasalised vowel (*e.g.*, चाँद *chăd*) must be looked up under that vowel (viz., आँ *ăĩ*), while words containing a nasal consonant (*e.g.*, चन्द *chand*) must be found under that consonant (viz., न्द *nd*). The observation of the latter distinction is facilitated by our system of discarding the equivocal anuswāra (ं), and using the anunāsika (ँ) and the nasal letters (ङ *ṅ*, ञ *ñ*, ण *ṇ*, न *n*, म *m*) to indicate a nasalised vowel and a nasal consonant respectively (*e.g.*, चाँद *chăd* and चन्द *chand*, not चांद *chāṁd* and चंद *chaṁd*).

As regards the alignment of the peculiar* Gauḍian semivowels ड़ *ṛ* and ढ़ *ṛh*, we have thought it best to adhere to the customary practice of placing them after ड *ḍ* and ढ *ḍh* respectively—a practice

* See, however, Dr. Hœrnle's Gḍ. Gr., §§ 15, 16. ड़ *ṛ* is a cerebral semivowel, while र *r* is dental.

which is recommended by considerations of convenience, though perhaps not absolutely defensible scientifically.

6.—SHORTENING OF THE ANTEPENULTIMATE VOWEL.

The genius of the Bihārī language is adverse to the existence of a long vowel or diphthong in a tadbhava word (see Chap. 11), when it would occupy a position removed more than two syllables from the end of the word. In counting syllables, it must be clearly understood that neither a final silent अ *a* nor a final imperfect इ *ĭ* or उ *ŭ* counts as a syllable, while the medial imperfect *a* (ऺ) does. (See Chap. 2.) Thus घर *ghar*, 'a house,' is a word of one syllable; देखब *dēkhab*, 'I shall see,' आओरि *āorĭ* 'and,' सुतथु *sūtathŭ* 'let him sleep,' are words of two syllables: while देखबॆंह *dekh'bå*, 'you will see,' and देखल्हूँ *dekh'lū̃*, 'I saw,' are words of three syllables.

This practice of shortening a vowel or diphthong is subject to the following rules, to which careful attention is invited:—

(*a*) Whenever the vowel आ *ā* finds itself in the antepenultimate syllable, *i.e.*, in the third from the end of the word, it is shortened to आॅ *ă*; *e.g.*, नॅाउआ *năūwā* (or, contracted नौआ *naūā*), long form* of नाउ *nāū*, 'barber'; ऑगिया *ăgiyā*, long form of आगि *āgi*, 'fire'; पॅाउल *păūlā* (or, contracted, पौल *paūlā*), 2nd plur. pret. ind. of पाएब *pāeb*, 'to obtain' (√ पाब *pāb*).

(*b*) Similarly any other vowel or diphthong, finding itself in the antepenultimate, is shortened, provided a consonant which is not euphonic† य *y* or व *w* follows it; thus सिखल्हूँ *sikh'lū̃*, 'I learned,' from √ सीख *sīkh*, देखइत *dekhaït*, 'if he saw,' from √ देख *dēkh*. On the other hand, चूअलूँ *chūalū̃* or चूअल्हूँ *chūw'lū̃*, 'I dripped,' पीयल्हूँ *pīy'lū̃*, 'I drank,' from √ चू *chū* and √ पी *pī*.

(*c*) Any vowel or diphthong whatever, finding itself removed more than three syllables from the end of the word, is shortened, whether it is followed by a consonant or not; thus चुइत्हू *chuït'hū*, '(if) you dripped,' from √ चू *chū*, होअइ *hoïaï*, '(it) he become,' from √ हो *hō*, देखैतिऔं *dekhaitiaū̃* or देखइतिअउ *dekhaïtiaü*, '(if) I had seen,' from √ देख *dēkh*.

There is an isolated exception in the Bhoj'pūrī present indicative where the final syllable (लों *lõ*, etc.) may not be counted for the purposes of these rules. Thus 'I see' is in Bhoj'pūrī देखेलों *dēkhålõ* or देखैलों *dēkhailõ*; 'we see' is देखीला *dēkhīlā*. This, however, is merely an apparent exception, as the final syllable (लों *lõ*, ला *lā*) is really a separate, enclitic word. It may be added that the antepenultimate vowel is never shortened in verbs in the Rāmāyan; *e.g.*, *Ut.*, *do.* 42, देखिअहि *dēkhiahi* with long *ē*, as shown by the metre.

It should be remarked (though the remark does not apply to the Maithilī dialect) that when, according to the rules of optional spelling (see Chap. 4, *b*), the number of syllables is lessened by the contraction of two adjunct vowels, the long vowel retains its length. Thus Magahī होअइ *hoïaï*, '(if) we become,' and देखइत *dekhaït*, '(if) he saw,' may also be spelt होऐ *hōaĩ* and देखैत *dēkhaĩt*; but Maithilī होऐ *hoaĩ*, देखैत *dekhaĩt*.

With regard to the pronunciation of the (long open) आ *ā* when shortened in the antepenultimate, it should be observed that it naturally becomes the corresponding (short open) आॅ *ă*. (See Chap. 4, *e*). But there is a tendency, (optional in Maithilī, Magahī, and Eastern Bhoj'pūrī, but imperative in

* For an explanation of this term, see below, Chap. 7.

† When इ *i* or उ *u* is followed by अ *a* or आ *ā*, the letters य *y* and व *w* may be inserted respectively. These inserted letters are called euphonic य and व: thus, मॉलिआ *măliā* or मॉलिया *măliyā*, 'gardener;' ऑँसुआ *ăsuā*, or ऑँसुवा *ăsuwā*, 'tear.' See B. Gr., I, p. 22; Gd. Gr., p. 16. They may also be inserted after अ *a*, as in मॉलियवा *măliawā*, ऑँसुववा *ăsuawā*.

Western Bhoj'pūrī and Bais'wārī), though in the case of long forms only, to substitute the short close अ *a* for the short open आ *ă*. Thus, while the Bihārī throughout has मारलों *mār'lō̃*, 'I beat,' (never मरलों *mar'lō̃*), on the other hand, the Maithilī, Magahī, and Eastern Bhoj'pūrī have बतिया *bătiyā* or बतिया *batiyā* 'word,' but the Western Bhoj'pūrī and Bais'wārī have only बतिया *batiyā*.*

Among the Bihārīs no fixed usage has as yet established itself regarding the graphic representation of the shortened antepenultimate. Though it is always *pronounced* short, it is frequently *written* long. Following our principle of phonetic spelling, we shall uniformly write it short; and any word, found elsewhere spelt wrongly after the uncertain Bihārī fashion, should be looked up as containing a short vowel. Thus, बतिया *bătiyā* or बतिया *batiyā* 'word,' पिढ़िया *piṛhiyā* 'stool,' बुढ़वा *buṛh'wā* 'old man' (long forms of बात *bāt*, पीढ़ी *pīṛhī*, बूढ़ा *būṛhā*) are frequently, though incorrectly, written बातिया *bātiyā*, पीढ़िया *pīṛhiyā*, बूढ़वा *būṛh'wā*.

It will be seen from the examples given in illustration of these rules how intimately the latter are connected with many processes of derivation and inflexion. Careful attention to them alone will enable the student to determine the dictionary form of many words which in literature or conversation may be met with in some derived (see Chap. 7) or inflected form.

7.—EQUIVALENT FORMS OF NOUNS.

All nouns, whether substantives or adjectives, admit of various equivalent forms, *i.e.*, of various forms which do not differ appreciably in meaning. These forms are the *short*, *long*, and *redundant*.

The short form is the primary form, by which the word is generally known. It is also in most cases the only one admissible in good and literary language. Accordingly, as a rule, the short forms only will be given in this Dictionary. We shall occasionally add to them, in brackets, their corresponding long and redundant forms; but we shall not devote separate articles to the latter, except in those special cases where they are of equal or even greater currency than the short forms, or have acquired any distinct meaning. Hence, whenever they are not found specially mentioned, they should be looked up under their corresponding short forms. The following rough directions will enable the student to do this without any difficulty.

(*a*) The long forms of substantives are made by adding one of the suffixes आ *ā*, या *yā*, or वा *wā* (vulg. sometimes ए *ẽ*, यें *yẽ*, वें *wẽ*) to the short form, the vowels of which, if long, are shortened. The short form, therefore, is found by detaching these suffixes, and, if necessary, lengthening the vowels. Thus the short forms of मलिया *măliyā* 'gardener,' घोरवा *ghor'wā* 'horse,' घरवा *ghar'wā* 'house,' पोथिया *pothiyā* or पोथिआ *pothiā* 'book,' अँसुवा *ăsuwā* or अँसुआ *ăsuā* 'tear,' are respectively माली *mālī*, घोरा *ghōrā*, घर *ghar*, पोथी *pōthī*, आँसू *ãsū*.

(*b*) The long forms of adjectives are made similarly by adding the suffixes का *kā* or क्का *kkā* (*fem.* की *kī* or क्की *kkī*) to their short forms. Thus the short forms of बड़का *baṛ'kā*, मिठक्का *miṭhákkā*, भरिका *bhărikā*, छोटकी *chhoṭ'kī* or छोटक्की *chhoṭákkī*, are respectively बड़ *baṛ* or बड़ा *baṛā*, मीठ *mīṭh* or मीठा *mīṭhā*, भारि *bhāri* or भारी *bhārī*, छोट *chhōṭ* or छोटी *chhōṭī*.

---

* It is easy to see that the reason why the pronunciation *a* is not extended to other cases is the avoidance of ambiguity. If causal verbs were pronounced with *a*, they could not be distinguished from the corresponding primary verbs, which are rightly pronounced with *a*; *e.g.*, the causal मारलों *mār'lō̃* 'I beat,' if pronounced मरलों *mar'lō̃*, would be indistinguishable from the primary verb मरलों *mar'lō̃*, 'I died.' Similarly, if गिरलाह *gir'lāh* 'they fell' (see Chap. 9, A, 2) were pronounced गिरलह *gir'lah*, it might be confounded with गिरलह *gir'lah* (or rather गिरलहँ *gir'lăh*), 'you fell.'

(*c*) The redundant forms of substantives and adjectives are formed from their long forms precisely as long forms of substantives are formed from their short forms, viz., by adding आ *ā*, या *yā* or वा *wā* to the long form. Thus the long forms of मालियवा *mălíyawā* or (contracted) मालीवा *mălīwā*, घोरौवा *ghorāūwā* (contracted for घोरववा *ghor'wawā*), घरौवा *gharāūwā*, पोथियवा *pothiyawā* or (contracted) पोथीवा *pothīwā*, आँसुअवा *ăsuawā*, are मालिया *mălíyā*, घोरवा *ghor'wā*, घरवा *ghar'wā*, पोथिया *pothiyā*, आँसुवा *ăsuwā*, and the long forms of बड़कवा *baṛ'kawā* 'large,' मिठक्कवा *miṭhákk'wā* 'sweet,' भारिकवा *bhărikawā* 'heavy,' छोटकिया *chhoṭ'kiyā* or छोटक्किया *chhoṭákkiyā* 'small,' are respectively बड़का *baṛ'kā*, मिठक्का *miṭhákkā*, भारिका *bhărikā*, छोटकी *chhoṭ'kī* or छोटक्की *chhoṭákkī*.

Of the short form of nouns ending in a silent अ *a* there are again two equivalent kinds, viz., a weak and a strong form. In Bihārī most nouns occur usually in the weak form only; a few, however, occur in the strong form only, and some in both the weak and strong forms. This Dictionary, of course, will follow herein the Bihārī usages; but as theoretically all nouns may take both forms, and as it can only be learnt by practice which of the two forms is used in the case of any particular noun, the following easy direction may be given:—

The strong form is made by substituting आ *ā* (*fem.* ई *ī*) in the place of the final silent अ *a* of the weak form. The latter form, therefore, is found by detaching the final आ *ā* or ई *ī* of the strong form. Thus—

	Weak.	*Meaning.*	*Strong.*
MASC. ...	घोर *ghōr* ...	... 'horse' ...	... घोरा *ghōrā*.
	बड़ *baṛ* ...	... 'large' ...	... बड़ा *baṛā*.
FEM. ...	घोर *ghōr* ...	... 'mare' ...	... घोरी *ghōrī*.
	छोट *chhōṭ* ...	... 'small' ...	... छोटी *chhōṭī*.

A similar remark may be made regarding certain nouns ending in an imperfect इ *ĭ* or short इ *i*, which in the Maithilī dialect admit of a weak and a strong form. These are: (1) verbal nouns in इ *ĭ*; (2) abstract nouns in आइ *āi*, and (3) nouns of agency in इ *i*. The strong form is made by substituting ई *ī* in the place of the final इ *ĭ* or इ *i* of the weak form. Both forms may be used indifferently, but the weak form is the more usual one. In this Dictionary we shall, as a rule, give both forms. Thus—

	Weak.	*Meaning.*	*Strong.*
VERBAL NOUN	मारि *mārĭ*	'beating'	मारी *mārī*.
ABSTRACT "	हलुकाइ *halukāi*	'lightness'	हलुकाई *halukāī*.
NOUN OF AGENCY	मानि *māni*	'proud'	मानी *mānī*.

It should be noted here that many speakers nasalise the final syllable of long and redundant forms, so that we can have घोरवाँ *ghor'wā̃* as well as घोरवा *ghor'wā*, घोरौवाँ *ghorāūwā̃* as well as घोरौवा *ghorāūwā*, and so on.

In order to make the above perfectly plain, the following tables, which explain themselves, are here printed. A reference to them will enable the learner, when any one of the three forms (short, long, or redundant) are given, to find the other two.

Table showing the corresponding Long and Redundant Forms of all possible Short Forms of Nouns and Adjectives in Bihārī.

Classification of Short Form.	Short Form.	Long Form.	Redundant Form.
Strong masculine noun in आ *ā* ...	घोरा *ghōrā*, 'a horse'	घोरवा *ghor'wā*	घोरौआ *ghorāūwā*. घोरौआ *ghorāūā*.
Tatsama masc. or fem. noun in आ *ā* ...	राजा *rājā*, 'a king'	राँजवा *rāj'wā*	राँजौआ *rājāuwā*. राँजौआ *rājāūā*.
	सभा *sabhā*, 'an assembly'	सभवा *sabh'wā*	सभौआ *sabhāuwā*. सभौआ *sabhāūā*.
Weak masculine noun in अ *a* silent ...	घर *ghar*, 'a house'	घरवा *ghar'wā*	घरौआ *gharāuwā*. घरौआ *gharāūā*.
Weak feminine noun in अ *a* silent ...	बात *bāt*, 'a word'	बँतिया *bătiyā* or बँतिआ *bătiā* ...	बँतियवा *bătiyawā* or बँतीआ *bătiwā*.
Any masc. or fem. noun in इ *i* or ई *ī* ...	माली *mālī*, 'a gardener'	मँलिया *măliyā* or मँलिआ *măliā* ...	मँलियवा *măliyawa* or मँलीआ *măliwā*.
	पोथी *pōthī*, 'a book'	पोथिया *pothiyā* or पोथिआ *pothiā* ...	पोथियवा *pothiyawā* or पोथीआ *pothiwā*.
Any masc. or fem. noun in उ *u* or ऊ *ū* ...	नाऊ *nāū*, 'a barber'	नँउवा *năūwā*, नँउआ *năūā*, or नौआ *nāūā* ...	नँउअवा *năūawā* or नौअवा *nāūawā*.
Any masculine adjective	मीठ *mīṭh* or मीठा *mīṭhā*, 'sweet' ...	मिठका *miṭh'kā*	मिठकवा *miṭh'kawā*.
		मिठक्का *miṭhákkā*	मिठक्कवा *miṭhákk'wā*.
Any feminine adjective	मीठ *mīṭh* or मीठी *mīṭhī*, 'sweet' ...	मिठकी *miṭh'kī*	मिठकिया *miṭh'kiyā*. मिठकिआ *miṭh'kiā*.
		मिठक्की *miṭhákkī*	मिठक्किया *miṭhákkiyā*. मिठक्किआ *miṭhákkiā*.

Table showing the corresponding Short Forms of all possible Long Forms of Nouns and Adjectives in Bihārī.

Termination of Long Form.	Long Form.	Short Form.	Classification of Short Form.
वा *'wā* … … …	घोड़वा *ghor'wā* … …	घोड़ा *ghōrā*, 'a horse' … …	Strong masculine noun in आ *ā*.
	राँजवा *rāj'wā* … …	राजा *rājā*, 'a king' … …	Tatsama noun, masculine or feminine, in आ *ā*
	सभवा *sabh'wā* … …	सभा *sabhā*, 'an assembly' … …	
	घरवा *ghar'wā* … …	घर *ghar*, 'a house' … …	Weak masculine noun in अ *a* silent.
इया *iyā* or इआ *iā* … …	बतिया *bātiyā* … …	बात *bāt*, 'a word' … …	Weak feminine noun in अ *a* silent.
	बतिआ *bātiā* … …		
	मलिया *māliyā* … …	माली *mālī*, 'a gardener' … …	Any noun, masculine or feminine, in इ *i* or ई *ī*.
	मलिआ *māliā* … …		
	पोथिया *pothiyā* … …	पोथी *pōthī*, 'a book' … …	
	पोथिआ *pothiā* … …		
उवा *uwā*, उआ *uā*, or आ *ā*. …	नउवा *nāüwā* … …	नाऊ *nāū*, 'a barber' … …	Any noun, masculine or feminine, in उ *u* or ऊ *ū*.
	नउआ *nāüā* … …		
	नौआ *nāuā* … …		
का *'kā* … … …	मिठका *mīṭh'kā* … …	मीठ *mīṭh* or मीठा *mīṭhā*, 'sweet' …	Any masculine adjective.
क्का *kkā* … … …	मिठक्का *miṭhākkā* … …		
की *'kī* … … …	मिठकी *mīṭh'kī* … …	मीठ *mīṭh* or मीठी *mīṭhī*, 'sweet' ..	Any feminine adjective.
क्की *kkī* … … …	मिठक्की *miṭhākkī* … …		

Table showing the corresponding Short Forms of all possible Redundant Forms of Nouns and Adjectives in Bihārī.

Termination of Redundant Form.	Redundant Form.	Short Form.	Classification of Short Form.
	घोड़ौवा *ghorăuwă*	घोड़ा *ghōrā*, 'a horse'	Strong masculine noun in आ *ā*.
	घोड़ौआ *ghorăuā*		
औवा *ăuwā* or औआ *ăuā*	राजौवा *rājăuwā*	राजा *rājā*, 'a king	Tatsama noun, masculine or feminine, in आ *ā*.
	राजौआ *rājăuā*		
	सभौवा *sabhăuwā*	सभा *sabhā*, 'an assembly'	
	सभौआ *sabhăuā*		
	घरौवा *gharăuwā*	घर *ghar*, 'a house'	Weak masculine noun in अ *a* silent.
	घरौआ *gharăuā*		
इयवा *iyawā* or ईवा *īwā*	बतियवा *bătiyawā*	बात *bāt*, 'a word'	Weak feminine noun in अ *a* silent.
	बतीवा *bătīwā*		
	मलियवा *măliyawā*	माली *mālī*, 'a gardener'	Any noun, masculine or feminine, in इ *i* or ई *ī*.
	मलीवा *mălīwā*		
	पोथियवा *pothiyawā*	पोथी *pōthī*, 'a book'	
	पोथीवा *pothīwā*		
उअवा *uawā* or अवा *awā*	नाउअवा *năüawā*	नाउ *nāū*, 'a barber'	Any noun, masculine or feminine, in उ *u* or ऊ *ū*.
	नौअवा *năuawā*		
कवा *'kawā* or क्कवा *kk'wā*	मिठकवा *miṭh'kawā*	मीठ *mīṭh* or मीठा *mīṭhā*, 'sweet'	Any masculine adjective.
	मिठक्कवा *miṭhakk'wā*		
किया *'kiyā*, किआ *kiā* or क्किया *kkiyā*, क्किआ *kkiā*.	मिठकिया *miṭh'kiyā*	मीठ *mīṭh* or मिठी *miṭhī*, 'sweet'	Any feminine adjective.
	मिठकिआ *miṭh'kiā*		
	मिठक्किया *miṭhakkiyā*		
	मिठक्किआ *miṭhakkiā*		

8.—FEMININE GENDER OF ADJECTIVES.

Our treatment of the feminine gender of adjectives (including participles used as adjectives) requires a word of explanation. The matter is not entirely free from difficulties, and the methods of treatment hitherto adopted are in some respects calculated to mislead the student.

Adjectives may be used in three different ways: either *attributively*, as in सुन्दर नारी *sundar nārī* 'a fair woman;' or *predicatively*, as in ई नारी सुन्दर बा *ī nārī sundar bā* 'this woman is fair;' or *substantively*, as in हे सुन्दरी *hē sundarī* 'oh fair one'! In the two first cases the adjective is used in its proper adjectival sense; in the third case it has become, to all intents and purposes, a substantive, and it should be added that in this substantival sense an adjective is only used when it expresses a person.

Besides this three-fold usage, there is another circumstance which affects the question of the gender of adjectives; namely its origin, whether it is a tatsama (*i.e.* Sanskritic) or a tadbhava (*i.e.* Prākritic) word (see Chap. 11).

For all practical purposes the following five rules will accurately represent the whole state of the matter:—

(1) All adjectives, whether tatsama or tadbhava, when used as substantives, must be inflected in the feminine form whenever they refer to a female person or personification.

Thus, tadbh., हे पियारी *hē piyārī* or पियारि *piyāri* 'O beloved one,' अकली *akalī* or अकलि *akali* 'a foolish one' (*e.g.*, Chan. अकलिक बिपति *akalik bipati* 'the distress of the foolish woman;' see s.v.), परोसिनी *parosinī* or परोसिनि *parōsini* 'a female neighbour'; tats., सुन्दरी *sundarī* or सुन्दरि *sundari* 'a fair one' (Bid. 12, 1), सुमुखी *sumukhī* or सुमुखि *sumukhi* 'a friendly one' (Bid. 7, 1), मानिनी *māninī* or मानिनि *mānini* 'a proud one' (Bid. 50, 1), बुधिमती *budhimatī* or बुधिमति *budhimati* 'a wise one.' These correspond, respectively, to the masculine tadbh. पियारा *piyārā* or पियार *piyār*, अकल *akal*, परोसी *parōsī*; tats. सुन्दर *sundar*, मानी *mānī* or मानि *māni*, बुधिमान *budhimān*. It will be noticed that the feminines are most variously formed. We shall therefore add the substantive feminine form (printed *subst. f.*) in every case in which the nature of the adjective admits of its being used as a substantive. At the same time the following broad rules may be given :— tatsama adjectives form their feminine as in Sanskrit; tadbhava adjectives in आ *ā* and in silent अ *a* have a feminine in ई *ī*; tadbhava adjectives in ई *ī* form as a rule their feminine in इनी *inī*; tadbhava adjectives in ऊ *ū*, as a rule, remain the same in the feminine; finally in Maithilī, and in poetry generally, any feminine may end in इ *i* instead of ई *ī*.

(2) All tatsama adjectives, when used as proper adjectives (whether attributively or predicatively), are not inflected in the feminine; but their masculine form is used, whether the noun to which they refer be masculine or feminine.

Thus, attributively, सुन्दर चुनरी *sundar chun'rī* 'a beautiful veil' (Hb., 5, 44, masc. सुन्दर *sundar*), रसमय बानी *ras'may bānī* 'a sweet word' (Bid. 33, 6, masc. रसमय *ras'may*), हरखित रानी *har'khit rānī* 'the happy queen' (Hb. 3, 3, masc. हरखित *har'khit*, Skr. हर्षित *harṣita*), कोमल कामिनी *kōmal kāminī* 'a pretty woman' (Bid. 22, 8, masc. कोमल *komal*); predicatively, रङ्ग-भूमि भेल अति परचण्ड *rang-bhūmi bhel ati par'chaṇḍ* 'the arena was very vast' (Hb. 9, 5, masc. परचण्ड *par'chaṇḍ*), अधिक भेल लाज *adhik bhel lāj* 'great was the shame' (Bid. 27, 1, masc. अधिक *adhik*). Exceptionally (especially in Maithilī) instances of the use of the feminine form of tatsama adjectives do occur; *e.g.*, attributively, गुनमति नारि *gun'mati nāri* 'a virtuous woman' (Bid. 64, 7), and predicatively, धरनी बेआकुलि भेलि *dhar'nī beākuli bhēli* 'the earth was distressed' (Hb. 1, 6). But they are so rare that they may safely be disregarded for the purposes of the above given practical rule.* In this Dictionary, therefore, we shall mark all tatsama adjectives as being of common gender (printed *com. gen.*), at the same time noting in brackets the occurrence of any exceptional feminine form.

(3) All tadbhava adjectives ending in आ *ā*, when used as proper adjectives, (whether attributively or predicatively), must form their feminine in ई *ī*.

Thus attributively छोटी नारी *chhōṭī nārī* 'a little woman' (masc. छोटा *chhōṭā*), जनक-सुता अकेली *janak-sutā akēlī* 'the daughter of Janak alone' (Rām., Ar., ch. 26, 2; masc. अकेला *akēlā*); predicatively, ई बात बड़ मीठी बा *ī bāt baṛ mīṭhī bā* 'this thing is very pleasant' (masc. मीठा *mīṭhā*). The following passage of the Gītābalī (*A.* 82, 1) contains an example of both the second and third rules:— राम-भगति करत सुगम, सुनत मीठी लगति *Rām-bhagati karat sugam* (tats.), *sunat mīṭhī* (tadbh.) *lagati* 'devotion to Rām is easy to exercise and pleasant to be told.' It should be added, however, that owing to the fact that in the dialects of Bihārī (especially in Maithilī) these adjectives are more commonly used in their weak form terminating in silent अ *a*, their feminine (as will be noticed below) usually ends in इ *i*. Thus in the place of the strong form masculine छोटा *chhōṭā*, अकेला *akēlā*, the Bihārī commonly has छोट *chhōṭ*, अकेल *akēl*, with the feminines छोटि *chhōṭi*, अकेलि *akēli* (*e.g.*, Bid. 30, 3, बिलासिनि छोटि *bilāsini chhōṭi* 'the little bride,' Rām., Ut., chh. 5, 19, बेलि अकेलि *bēli akēli* 'a single creeper').

(4) All tadbhava adjectives ending in इ *i* or ई *ī*, and in उ *u* or ऊ *ū*, are of common gender.

Thus, masc. भारी पथल *bhārī pathal* 'a heavy stone,' or fem. भारी बात *bhārī bāt* 'an important matter'; again masc. झगड़ालू जन *jhag'ṛālū jan* 'a quarrelsome person,' or fem. झगड़ालू नारी *jhag'ṛālū nārī* 'a quarrelsome woman.'

(5) The tadbhava adjectives terminating with a silent अ *a* are now commonly treated as being of common gender.

Originally they always possessed a feminine form in इ *i*, whether they were used attributively or predicatively; and this usage prevails almost uniformly in the older literature of all the Bihārī dialects; *e.g.*, in the Bais'wāṛī Rāmāyan of Tul'sī Dās, in the Maithilī songs of Bidyāpati, and Haribans of Man'bōdh, etc. Indeed in the Maithilī dialect the use is exceptionally extended even to tatsama adjectives in silent अ *a* (see footnote*). Thus, tadbhava, attributively, बड़ि अगलहि नारि *baṛi ag'lahi nāri* 'a very vicious woman' (Hb. 2, 30, masc. बड़ अगलह *baṛ ag'lah*), बड़ि अनुमनि सखि *baṛi anumani sakhi* 'a very melancholy (female) friend' (Bid. 34, 1, masc. बड़ अनुमन *baṛ anuman*); बिलासिनि छोटि *bilāsini chhōṭi* 'little bride' (Bid. 30, 3, masc. छोट *chhoṭ*), बेलि अकेलि *bēli akēli* 'a single creeper' (Rām., Ut., chh. 5, 19, masc. अकेल *akēl*), ऐसनि झपट *aisani jhapaṭ* 'such a swoop' (Sal. 7, masc. ऐसन *aisan*), टेढ़ि चालि *ṭēṛhi chāli* 'false step' (B. Gr., I, Introd., fable 11, masc. टेढ़ *ṭeṛh*); again tatsama, दुष्टि जाति *dushṭi jāti* 'a vile caste' (Hb. 9, 33, masc. दुष्ट *dushṭ*); and predicatively, सुमुखि न होइ *sumukhi na hōi* 'she was not friendly' (Bid. 30, 2, masc. सुमुख *sumukh*), परापति अस्ति नारि *parāp'ti asti nāri* 'the woman had arrived' (Hb. 10, 1, masc. परापत *parāp't*).† The practice, however, is not uniform; exceptions of the use of the masculine instead of the feminine occasionally occur; *e.g.*, एहन रमनि *ehan ramani* 'such a woman' (Bid. 17, 5), केहन सुरखी *kehan sur'khī* 'what a beauty!' (Sal. 7). The latter fashion of dropping the use of the feminine form extended more and more in later times, till in the present day the feminine form is almost entirely abandoned, the masculine form

* A rough calculation of the occurrence of tatsama adjectives in the songs of Bidyāpati and the Haribans of Man'bōdh shows that among a total of 45 cases of such adjectives in construction with feminine nouns, the feminine form is only used nine times, while the masculine occurs 36 times.

† It should be noted that some of the feminines of tatsama adjectives are not tatsama feminines, as they should be; thus, Maithilī has दुष्टि *dushṭi* for Skr. दुष्टा *dushṭā*. This hybridism of such Maithilī forms shows that the latter are anomalous forms made by a false analogy.

being used equally with reference to masculine and feminine nouns.* It is only in the Maithilī dialect that the feminine is still occasionally used both in prose and poetry, but in the other Bihārī dialects it may now be said to be practically unknown except in poetry. In any case, it should be noted that whenever the feminine form is used, its final ई has the sound of the imperfect ǐ (see Chap. 2, and Mth. Gr. §§ 7, 43, 44). Under these circumstances, we shall, in this Dictionary, describe the tadbhava adjectives which terminate with silent अ *a* as being of common gender. At the same time we shall note in brackets any feminine in ई ǐ which we may have met with in literature.

For convenient reference we here add a list of typical examples illustrating our system of treating the feminine gender of adjectives:—

(1) *Tats. adj.*, (rules 1 and 5); *e.g.*—

अकृत *akrit*, *adj. com. gen.*, not done.

अकलंक *akalaŋk*, *adj. com. gen.*, (*subst. f.* अकलंका *akalaŋkā*), blameless.

बिमुख *bimukh*, *adj. com. gen.*, (*old Mth. and poet. f.* बिमुखि *bimukhǐ*, *subst. f.* बिमुखी *bimukhī or Mth. and poet.* बिमुखि *bimukhǐ*), unfriendly.

(2) *Tadbh. adj. in* आ (rules 1 and 3); *e.g.*—

अकरा *ak'rā*, (*f.* अकरी *ak'rī*), *adj.*, dear.

(3) *Tadbh. adj. in* ई or अ (rules 1 and 4); *e.g.*—

भारी *bhārī*, (*Mth. and poet.* भारि *bhārǐ*), *adj. com. gen.*, heavy.

परोसी *parōsī*, *adj. com. gen.*, (*subst. f.* परोसिनी *parosinī or Mth. and poet.* परोसिनि *parōsinǐ*), neighbouring.

(4) *Tadbh. adj. in* अ (rules 1 and 5); *e.g.*—

अकेल *akēl*, *adj. com. gen.*, (*old poet. f.* अकेलि *akēlǐ*), alone.

अकल *akal*, *adj. com. gen.*, (*subst. f.* अकली *akalī or Mth. and poet.* अकलि *akalǐ*), foolish.

9.—CONJUGATIONAL TERMS AND TABLES.

As there are considerable differences between the names given to the tenses of verbs by the various grammarians, it has been necessary to adopt one system for ourselves. We therefore give below the verb of √ देख *dēkh* 'see,' conjugated throughout all its various forms with the name which we have adopted for each tense prefixed to each.

The radical tenses are conjugated in full, and after them is given a list of the principal parts of all the various auxiliary verbs used in Bihārī. Then follow the various periphrastic tenses, the first person singular of each being given as sufficient for all practical purposes.

It will be observed that there are six columns for each tense. The first gives the forms current in Maithilī, then follow in order Magahī, Eastern Bhoj'pūrī, Western Bhoj'pūrī, the old Western Bihārī or Bais'wārī of the Rāmāyan, and finally the corresponding forms in Hindī for the sake of comparison and ready reference.

There are in all these dialects (especially in Maithilī and Magahī) many optional forms, which for want of space are not here given. These can all be learned, so far as Western Bhoj'pūrī is concerned, from Dr. Hœrnle's Gauḍian Grammar, and for the other dialects from Mr. Grierson's Maithilī Grammar published by the Asiatic Society of Bengal, and from the same author's Seven Grammars of the Bihār Dialects published by the Government of Bengal.

* Strictly speaking, the process was this: the final ई *i* of the fem. form became at first the imperfect sound of ǐ, and lastly it was indistinguishable from a silent अ *a*, and thus the feminine of an adjective became practically identical with its masculine form (see Chap. 2). It will thus be seen that though an adjective ending in silent *a*, when it qualifies a feminine noun, is in outward appearance masculine, yet originally it was, and *in intention* it still is, feminine.

A.—RADICAL AND PARTICIPIAL TENSES.

INDICATIVE MOOD.

1. Present: '*I see,*' &c.

Number.	Person.	Maithilī.	Magahī.	East Bhoj'pūrī.	West Bhoj'pūrī.	Rāmāyan.	High Hindī.
Singular ...	1st	*Wanting.*	*Wanting.*	देखँलौं *dēkhâlõ̃.*	देखँलौं *dēkhâlõ̃.*	*Wanting.*	*Wanting.*
	2nd			देखँले *dēkhâlē.*	देखँले *dēkhâlē.*		
	3rd			देखँला *dēkhâlā.*	देखँला *dēkhâlā.*		
Plural ...	1st			देखीला *dēkhīlā.*	देखीला *dēkhīlā.*		
	2nd			देखँलँऽ *dēkhâlâ.*	देखँलँऽ *dēkhâlâ.*		
	3rd			देखँलन *dēkhâlan.*	देखँलेन *dēkhâlen.*		

2. Preterite: '*I saw,*' &c.

Number.	Person.	Maithilī.	Magahī.	East Bhoj'pūrī.	West Bhoj'pūrī.	Rāmāyan.	High Hindī.
Singular ...	1st	*Wanting.*	देखलूँ *dekh'lũ.*	देखलौं *dekh'lõ*, देखेऊँ *dekheũ.*	देखलौं *dekh'lõ̃*, देख्यौं *dēkhyõ̃.*	देखेऊँ *dēkheũ.*	देखा *dēkhā.*
	2nd	देखलेँ *dekh'lẽ.*	देखलेँ *dekh'lẽ.*	देखले *dekh'lē*, देखुए *dekhuē.*	देखले *dekh'lē*, देखिस *dēkhis.*	देखेउ *dēkheu*, देखेसि *dēkhesi.*	देखा *dēkhā.*
	3rd	देखलक *dekh'lak.*	देखलक *dekh'lak.* देखिस *dēkhis.*	देखलस *dekh'las*, देखुए *drkhuē.*	देखलेस *dekh'les*, देखिस *dēkhis.*	देखेउ *dēkheu*, देखेसि *dēkhesi*, देखल *dēkhal.*	देखा *dēkhā.*
Intr. 'he fell'	3rd sing.	गिरल *giral*; 3rd pl. गिरलाह *gir'lāh.*	3rd sing. गिरल *giral.*	3rd sing. गिरल *giral*	3rd sing. गिरल *giral.*	गिरेउ *gireu.*	sing. गिरा *girā*, pl. गिरे *girē.*
Plural ...	1st	देखल *dēkhal*, देखलहुँ *dekh'lahũ.*	देखलीं *dekh'lī̃.*	देखलीं *dekh'lī̃*, देखुईं *dekhuī̃.*	देखली *dekh'lī*, देखा *dēkhā.*	देखेन्हि *dēkhenhi.*	देखा *dēkhā.*
	2nd	देखलँह *dekh'lâh.*	देखलँऽ *dekh'lâ.*	देखलँऽ *dekh'lâ*, देखुअँ *dekhuâ.*	देखलऽ *dekh'lâ*, देख्याँ *dēkhyā̃.*	देखेहु *dēkhehu.*	देखा *dēkhā.*
	3rd	देखलन्हि *dekh'lanhi.*	देखलन *dekh'lan.*	देखलन *dekh'lan*, देखुअन *dekhuan.*	देखलेन *dekh'len*, देखिन *dēkhin.*	देखेन्हि *dēkhenhi.*	देखा *dēkhā.*

3. **Future**: '*I shall see,*' &c.

Singular ...	1st	*Wanting.*	देखब्यौं *dekh'bau̐.*	देखब्यों *dekh'bõ.*	देखब्यों *dekh'bõ.*	देखबौं* *dēkhabau̐*, देखिहौं [*dēkhihau̐.*	देखूँगा *dekhū̃gā.*
	2nd	देखब्यें *dekhabẽ.*	देखब्यें *dekh'bẽ.*	देखब्ये *dekh'bē.*	देखब्ये *dekh'bē.*	देखबै *dēkhabā̃i*, देखिहहि [*dēkhihahi.*	देखेगा *dekhēgā.*
	3rd	देखत *dēkhat.*	देखत *dēkhat*, देखी *dēkhī.*	देखी *dēkhī.*	देखी *dēkhī.*	देखबै *dēkhabā̃i*, देखिहहि [*dēkhihahi.*	देखेगा *dēkhēgā.*
Plural ...	1st	देखब *dēkhab*, देखिअहु [*dekhiáhů.*	देखब *dēkhab.*	देखब *dēkhab*, देखब्यी [*dekh'bī.*	देखब *dēkhab.*	देखबि *dēkhabi*, देखबैं *dēkha-*[*bā̃i*, देखिहहिं *dēkhihahĩ.*	देखेंगे *dekhẽgē.*
	2nd	देखब्यौह *dekh'bâh*, देखिअहु [*dekhiáhů.*	देखब्यौ *dekh'bâ.*	देखब्यौ *dekh'bâ.*	देखब्यौ *dekh'bâ.*	देखबौ *dēkhabau̐*, देखिहहु [*dēkhihahů.*	देखोगे *dekhōgē.*
	3rd	देखब्यांह *dekh'tâh.*	देखब्यन *dekh'tan*, देखिहें [*dekhihẽ.*	देखिहें *dekhihẽ.*	देखिहैं *dekhihā̃i.*	देखबैं *dēkhabā̃i*, देखिहहिं [*dēkhihahĩ.*	देखेंगे *dekhẽgē.*

* Or देखब *dekhab* throughout.

CONJUNCTIVE MOOD.

4. **Present**: '(*If*) *I see,*' rarely '*I see,*' '*I shall see,*' &c.

Also **Present Imperative** *and* **Simple Present Indicative.**

Singular ...	1st	देखू *dēkhū*, देखौ *dēkhi.*	देखूँ *dekhū̃.*	देखौं *dēkhõ.*	देखौं *dēkhõ.*	देखेऊँ *dēkheū̃.*	देखूँ *dēkhū̃.*
	2nd	देख *dēkh.*	देखें *dēkhẽ.*	देखे *dēkhē*, देखस *dēkhas.*	देखु *dēkhů*, देख *dēkh.*	देखसि *dēkhasi*, देखै *dēkhā̃i.*	देखे *dēkhē*, (imperat.) देख *dēkh.*
	3rd	देखै *dēkhā̃i*, देखौ *dēkhau̐.*	देखै *dēkhā̃i*, देखस *dēkhas.*	देखे *dēkhē*, देखस *dēkhas.*	देखै *dēkhā̃i.*	देखसि *dēkhasi*, देखै *dēkhā̃i*	देखे *dēkhē.*
Plural ...	1st	देखी *dēkhi*, देखू *dēkhū.*	देखीं *dekhī.*	देखीं *dēkhī.*	देखीं *dēkhī.*	देखहिं *dēkhahi.*	देखें *dēkhẽ.*
	2nd	देखौह *dēkhâh.*	देखौ *dēkhâ.*	देखौ *dēkhâ.*	देखौ *dēkhâ.*	देखहु *dēkhahů.*	देखो *dēkhō.*
	3rd	देखथु *dēkháthů*, देखथि [*dēkháthi.*	देखथू *dekh'thū*, देखथी [*dekh'thī*, देखथ *dēkhath.*	देखन *dēkhan.*	देखैं *dēkhā̃i.*	देखहिं *dēkhahĩ.*	देखें *dēkhẽ.*

5. Preterite: '(*If*) *I had seen*, &c.

Number.	Person.	Maithilī.	Magahī.	East Bhoj'pūrī.	West Bhoj'pūrī.	Rāmāyan.	High Hindī.
Singular ...	1st	*Wanting.*	देखितूँ *dekhitū̃.*	देखितोँ *dekhitõ.*	देखन्तोँ *dekh'tõ.*	देखतेउँ *dēkhateũ.*	देखता *dēkh'tā.*
	2nd	देखितेँ *dekhitẽ.*	देखितेँ *dekhitẽ.*	देखिते *dekhitē*, देखितस [*dekhitas.*	देखन्ते *dekh'tē*, देखन्तेस [*dekh'tes.*	(?) देखतेउ *dēkhateu.*	देखता *dēkh'tā.*
	3rd	देखैत *dekhāit.*	देखैत *dēkhāit.*	देखिते *dekhitē*, देखितस [*dekhitas*, देखैत *dēkhāt.*	देखत *dēkhat.*	(?) देखतेउ *dēkhateu.*	देखता *dēkh'tā.*
Plural ...	1st	देखितहुँ *dekhitāhũ.*	देखितीँ *dekhitī̃.*	देखितीँ *dekhitī̃.*	देखन्ती *dekh'tī.*	(?) देखतेन्हि *dēkhatenhi.*	देखते *dēkh'tē.*
	2nd	देखितह *dekhitāh.*	देखितँह *dekhitā.*	देखितँह *dekhitā.*	देखन्तँह *dekh'tā.*	देखतेहु *dēkhatehu.*	देखते *dēkh'tē.*
	3rd	देखितथि *dekhitāthi.*	देखितथी *dekhit'thi*, [देखितन *dekhitan.*	देखितन *dekhitan.*	देखन्तेन *dekh'ten.*	(?) देखतेन्हि *dēkhatenhi.*	देखते *dēkh'tē.*

IMPERATIVE MOOD.

6. Precative Forms: '*be good enough to let me see.*'

Number.	Person.	Maithilī.	Magahī.	East Bhoj'pūrī.	West Bhoj'pūrī.	Rāmāyan.	High Hindī.
Singular ...	2nd	*Wanting.*	*Wanting.*	देखिहे *dekhihē.*	देखिहे *dekhihē.*	*Wanting.*	*Wanting.*
Plural ...	2nd	देखिहँह *dehhihā.*	देखी *dēkhi*, देखिहँह *dekhihā.*	देखीं *dēkhī*, देखिहँह *dekhi*-[*hā.*	देखिहँह *dekhihā.*	देखिअ *dēkhij*, देखिअँ *dēkhiā*, [देखी *dēkhi.*	देखिये *dēkhiyē.*

B.—AUXILIARY VERBS

√ अह *ahw* or हव *haw.*

PRESENT INDICATIVE.

Number.	Person.	Maithilī.	Magahī.	East Bhoj'pūrī.	West Bhoj'pūrī.	Rāmāyan.	High Hindī.
Singular ...	1st	हौँ *hau̐.*	(pl.) ही *hī.*	हवोँ *hawõ.*	हौवोँ *hauwõ.*	अहेउँ *aheũ.*	हूँ *hū̃.*
	3rd	अछि *ahi*, हौ *hau.*	है *hai*, हौ *hau*, हँ *hā*, हकै [*hakai*, हस *has.*	है *hai*, हउ *hā*, हवे *hawē*, [हवस *hawas.*	हौ *hau.*	अहै *ahai*, अहहि *ahahi*, [अहसि *ahasi.*	है *hai.*

PRETERITE INDICATIVE.

Singular ...	1st 3rd	Wanting.	हलूँ *halŭ.* हल *hal.*	Wanting.	Wanting.	Wanting.	Wanting.

FUTURE INDICATIVE.

Singular ...	1st 3rd	हैब *hãib.* ह्वैत *hwãit,* हैत *hãit.*	Wanting.	Wanting.	Wanting.	Wanting. ह्वैहै *hwaihai.*	Wanting.

√ हो *ho.*

FUTURE INDICATIVE.

Singular ...	1st	होएब *hōeb.*	होब *hōb.*	होइबों *hōibō̃.*	होइबों *hōibō̃.*	(?) होउब *hōüb,* होबौं *hōbāũ,* होइहौं *hōihāũ.*	होऊँगा *hōŭgā.*
	3rd	होत *hōt.*	होत *hōt,* होइ *hōi.*	होइ *hōi.*	होइ *hōi.*	(?) होबै *hōbāi,* होइहहि *hōihahi.*	होएगा *hōēgā.*

PRESENT CONJUNCTIVE.

Singular ...	1st	होउ *hōu,* होइ *hōi.*	होऊँ *hōŭ.*	होवों *hōõ.*	होंहूँ *hõhū̃.*	होऊँ *hōŭ.*	होऊँ *hōŭ.*
	3rd	होऐ *hōāi,* होअ *hōa.*	होऐ *hōāi,* होअस *hōas.*	होए *hōĕ,* होअस *hōas.*	होय *hōy.*	होऐ *hōāi,* होहि *hōhi,* होसि *hōsi.*	हो *hō.*

PRETERITE CONJUNCTIVE.

Singular ...	1st	होइतहुँ *hoitáhŭ.*	होइतूँ *hōitŭ.*	होइतों *hōitõ.*	होतों *hōtõ.*	होतेऊँ *hōteŭ.*	होता *hōtā.*
	3rd	होइत *hōit.*	होइत *hōit.*	होइत *hōit,* होइतस *hōitas.*	होत *hōt,* होतै *hōtāi.*	? होतेउ *hōteu.*	होता *hōtā.*

PAST PARTICIPLE.

		भेल *bhēl.*	होइल *hōil,* भेल *bhēl.*	भैल *bhāil.*	भैल *bhāil.*	भयउ *bhayaü.*	हुआ *huā.*

अछ *achh.*

PRESENT INDICATIVE.

Number.	Person.	Maithilī.	Magahī.	East Bhoj'pūrī.	West Bhoj'pūrī.	Rāmāyan.	High Hindī.
Singular ...	1st 3rd	छी *chhī.* अछि *achhi,* छै *chhai.*	*Wanting.*	*Wanting.*	*Wanting.*	*Wanting.*	*Wanting.*

Pres. Part. in Mth. & Bh. अछैत *achhait*; in Rām. अछत *achhat.*

PRETERITE INDICATIVE.

Number.	Person.	Maithilī.	Magahī.	East Bhoj'pūrī.	West Bhoj'pūrī.	Rāmāyan.	High Hindī.
Singular ...	1st 3rd	छलहुँ *chhaláhũ.* छल *chhal.*	*Wanting.*	*Wanting.*	*Wanting.*	*Wanting.*	*Wanting.*

√ थि *thi.*

PRESENT INDICATIVE.

Number.	Person.	Maithilī.	Magahī.	East Bhoj'pūrī.	West Bhoj'pūrī.	Rāmāyan.	High Hindī.
Singular ...	1st 3rd	थिकहुँ *thikáhũ.* थिकाह *thikāh.*	*Wanting.*	*Wanting.*	*Wanting.*	*Wanting.*	*Wanting.*

PRETERITE INDICATIVE.

Number.	Person.	Maithilī.	Magahī.	East Bhoj'pūrī.	West Bhoj'pūrī.	Rāmāyan.	High Hindī.
Singular ...	1st 3rd	*Wanting.*	*Wanting.*	*Wanting.*	*Wanting.*	*Wanting.*	था *thā.* था *thā.*

√ रह *rah.*

PRETERITE INDICATIVE.

Number.	Person.	Maithilī.	Magahī.	East Bhoj'pūrī.	West Bhoj'pūrī.	Rāmāyan.	High Hindī.
Singular ...	1st 3rd	रही *rahī.* रहौं *rahaũ.*	*Wanting.*	रहलों *rah'lõ,* रहों *rahõ.* रहल *rahal,* रहे *rahē.*	रहलों *rah'lõ.* रहल *rahal.*	रहेउँ *raheũ.* रह *rah.*	*Wanting as an auxiliary.*

√ बाट *bāṭ*.

PRESENT INDICATIVE.

Singular ...	1st 3rd	*Wanting.*	*Wanting.*	बाटों *bāṭō̃.* बाटे, बा *bāṭē, bā.*	बाटों *bāṭō̃.* बाटे *bāṭā̃.*	*Wanting.*	*Wanting.*	

C.—PERIPHRASTIC TENSES.

INDICATIVE MOOD.

7. **Indefinite Present: '*I see,*' &c.**

Singular ...	1st	*Wanting.*	देखछ बो *dēkha hī,* [देखे बो *dēkhe hī.*	*Wanting.*	*Wanting.*	*Wanting.*	*Wanting.*

8. **Indefinite Past: '*I saw,*' &c.**

Singular ...	1st	*Wanting.*	देखछ चहूँ *dēkha halū̃,* [देखे चहूँ *dēkhe halū̃.*	*Wanting.*	*Wanting.*	*Wanting.*	*Wanting.*

9. **Definite Present: '*I am seeing,*' &c.**

Singular ...	1st	Open ...	देखैत बो *dekhãıt chhī* (3rd sing. देखैत अछि) (*dekhãıt achhi*).	देखैत बो *dēkhãıt hī.*	देखत बाटों *dēkhat bāṭō̃.*	देखत बाटों *dēkhat bāṭō̃.*	देखत अहेऊँ *dēkhat aheū̃.*	देखता हूँ *dēkh'tā hū̃.*
		Contracted ...	देखैछी *dēkhãichhī* (3rd sing. देखैछि *dekhaï-chhi*).	*Wanting.*	देखतारों *dekh'tārō̃.*	*Wanting.*	*Wanting.*	*Wanting.*

10. Imperfect: '*I was seeing*,' *&c.*

Number.	Person.		Maithilī.	Magahī.	East Bhoj'pūrī.	West Bhoj'pūrī.	Rāmāyan.	High Hindī.
Singular ...	1st	Open ...	देखैत छलहुँ *dekhāt chhaláhŭ̃.*	देखैत हलूँ *dēkhāt halū̃.*	देखत रहलों (रहों) *dēkhat rah'lō̃ (rahō̃).*	देखत रहलों *dēkhat rah'lō̃.*	देखत रहेउँ *dēkhat raheũ.*	देखता था *dēkh'tā thā.*
		Contracted ...	देखैछलहुँ *dekhāchhaláhŭ̃.*	*Wanting.*	*Wanting.*	*Wanting.*	*Wanting.*	*Wanting.*
11. Durative Future: '*I shall be seeing*,' *&c.*								
Singular ...	1st	...	देखैत होएब *dekhāt hōeb.*	देखैत होब *dēkhāt hōb.*	देखत होइबों *dēkhat hōibō̃.*	देखत होबों *dēkhat hōbō̃.*	? देखत होउब *dēkhat hōüb.*	देखता होऊँगा *dēkh'tā hōŭ̃gā.*
12. Perfect: '*I have seen*,' *&c.*								
Singular ...	1st	Trans. direct	देखलों छी *dekh'lō̃ chhī.*	*Wanting.*	देखले बाटों *dekh'le bāṭō̃.*	देखले बाटों *dekh'lē bāṭō̃.*	?	देखा है *dēkhā hā̃.*
		Intrans. direct	गिरल छी *giral chhī.*	*Wanting.*	गिरल बाटों *giral bāṭō̃.*	गिरल बाटों *giral bāṭō̃.*		गिरा हूँ *girā hū̃.*
		Trans. and intrans. indirect.	देखलहुँ अछि *dekh'láhŭ̃ achhī.*	देखलूँ हें *dekh'lū̃ hā̃.*	देखलों हाँ *dekh'lō̃ hā̃.*	*Wanting.*		*Wanting.*
13. Pluperfect: '*I had seen*,' *&c.*								
Singular ...	1st	Direct ...	देखलौं छलहुँ *dekh'lō̃ chhaláhŭ̃.*	*Wanting.*	देखले रहलों *dekh'le rah'lō̃.*	देखले रहलों *dekh'lē rah'lō̃.*	?	देखा था *dēkhā thā.*
		Indirect ...	*Wanting.*	देखलूँ हल *dekh'lū̃ hal.*	*Wanting.*	*Wanting.*		*Wanting.*
14. Future Exact: '*I shall have seen*' or '*I may have seen*,' *&c.*								
Singular ...	1st	(Direct) ...	देखलौं होएब *dekh'lō̃ hōeb.*	देखले होब *dekh'le hōb.*	देखले होइबों *dekh'le hōibō̃.*	देखले होबों *dekh'lē hōbō̃.*	?	देखा होगा *dēkhā hōgā.*

CONJUNCTIVE MOOD.

15. **Future Conditional**: (*If*) '*I be seeing*,' *&c.*

Singular ...	1st ...	देखैत होउ *dekhāit hōū.*	देखैत होऊँ *dēkhāit hōū̃.*	देखत होयौं *dēkhat hōō̃.*	देखत होऊँ *dēkhat hōhū.*	?	देखता होऊँ *dēkh'tā hōū̃.*

16. **Durative Present Conditional**: '(*If*) *I were seeing*,' *&c.*

Singular ...	1st ...	देखैत होइतहुँ *dekhāit* [*hoïtáhū̃.*	देखैत होतूँ *dēkhāit hōtū̃*	देखत होइतौं *dēkhat* [*hōïtō̃.*	देखत होतौं *dēkhat hōtō̃.*	?	देखता होता *dēkh'tā hōtā.*

17. **Future Exact Conditional**: '(*If*) *I have seen*,' *&c.*

Singular ...	1st. ...	देखलेँ होउ *dekh'lẽ hōū.*	देखले होऊँ *dekh'le hōū̃.*	देखले होयौं *dekh'le hōō̃.*	देखले होऊँ *dekh'le hōhū.*	?	देखा हो *dēkhā hō.*

18. **Second Preterite Conditional**: '(*If*) *I had seen*,' *&c.*

Singular ...	1st ...	देखलेँ होइतहुँ *dekh'lẽ* [*hoïtáhū̃.*	देखले होतूँ *dekh'le hōtū̃.*	देखले होइतौं *dekh'le* [*hōïtō̃.*	देखले होतौं *dekh'lē* [*hōtō̃.*	?	देखा होता *dēkhā hōtā.*

D.—PARTICIPLES.

1. **Present**: '*seeing.*'

Singular ...	Masculine ...	देखैत *dekhāit.*	देखैत *dēkhāit*, देखित [*dēkhit.*	देखत *dēkhat.*	देख *dēkhat.*	देखत *dēkhat.*	देखता *dekh'tā.*

2. **Past**: '*seen.*'

Singular ...	Masculine ...	देखल *dēkhal.*	देखल *dēkhal.*	देखल *dēkhal.*	देखल *dēkhal*, देखिल [*dēkhil.*	देखल *dēkhal*, देख *dēkh.*	देखा *dēkhā.*

E.—VERBAL NOUNS AND THEIR DERIVATIVES.

1. First Verbal Noun : '*the act of seeing.*'

Number.	Person.	Maithili.	Magahī.	East Bhoj'pūrī.	West Bhoj'pūrī.	Rāmāyan.	High Hindī.
Singular ...	Direct ...	देखि *dēkhi̐*, देख *dēkh.*	देख *dēkh.*	देख *dēkh.*	देखे *dēkhe*, देख *dēkh.*	देखि *dēkhi̐*, देख *dēkh.*	देखी *dēkhī*, देखि *dēkhi*, [देख *dēkh.*
	Oblique ...	देखै *dēkhai*, देखऽ *dēkha.*	देखे *dēkhe.*	देखे *dēkhe.*	देखै *dēkhai.*	देखे *dēkhē*, देखैं *dēkhai̐.*	देखा *dēkhā.*

2. Second Verbal Noun : '*the act of seeing.*'

Number.	Person.	Maithili.	Magahī.	East Bhoj'pūrī.	West Bhoj'pūrī.	Rāmāyan.	High Hindī.
Singular ...	Direct ...	देखल *dēkhal.*	देखल *dēkhal.*	देखल *dēkhal.*	देखल *dēkhal.*	*Wanting.*	*Wanting.*
	Oblique ...	देखला *dekh'lā.*	देखला *dekh'lā.*	देखला *dekh'lā.*	देखले *dekh'le.*	*Wanting.*	*Wanting.*

3. Third Verbal Noun : '*the act of seeing.*'

Number.	Person.	Maithili.	Magahī.	East Bhoj'pūrī.	West Bhoj'pūrī.	Rāmāyan.	High Hindī.
Singular ...	Direct ...	देखब *dēkhab.*	देखब *dēkhab.*	देखब *dēkhab.*	देखब *dēkhab.*	देखब *dēkhab.*	*Wanting.*
	Oblique ...	देखबा *dekh'bā.*	*Wanting.*	*Wanting.*	देखबे *dekh'be*, देखबै [*dekh'bai.*	देखिबे *dēkhibē.*	*Wanting.*

4. Conjunctive Participle : '*having done the act of seeing,*' '*having seen.*'

		Maithili.	Magahī.	East Bhoj'pūrī.	West Bhoj'pūrī.	Rāmāyan.	High Hindī.
		देखि *dēkhi̐* or देख *dēkh* { कहँ *kahā̐*, (काँ *kā̃*, के *kē*, कँ *kă*, के *ke*).	देख के *dēkh ke*, (कर) [(*kar*).	देख के *dēkh ke.*	देखे *dēkhe* } के *ke.* देख *dēkh* }	देखि (कैं) *dēkhi̐* (*kā̃*).	देख कर के *dēkh* [*kar kē.*

5. Noun of Agency : '*a doer of the act of seeing,*' '*one who sees.*'

		Maithili.	Magahī.	East Bhoj'pūrī.	West Bhoj'pūrī.	Rāmāyan.	High Hindī.
		देखिनहार *dekhin'hār.*	देखिनहार *dekhin'hār.*	देखनिहार *dekh'nihār.*	देखनिहार *dekh'nihār.*	देखनिहार *dēkhanihār.*	देखनेहारा *dēkh'nēhārā.*

10.—TREATMENT OF THE SO-CALLED ROOTS IN आ.

There is a large number of roots* which it has been customary to treat as ending in आ *a*. By far the largest number of these roots belong to causal verbs; *e.g.*, करा *karā* 'cause to do,' बना *banā* 'make.' But a few of them are primitive roots; such as पा *pā* 'get,' गा *gā* 'sing,' खा *khā* 'eat,' etc.

These roots are divided into two classes by a very characteristic difference, namely that, when inflected, some roots insert ब *b* (in Maithilī, or व *w* in the other dialects, see Chap. 4, *d*, 2), while others interpose य *y*, between the root and its inflectional termination. The reason of this difference is a simple one. The element ब *b* of one class of roots is organic, representing an ancient प *p*, which in the Sanskrit or Pāli formed part of the root; on the other hand the element य *y* of the other class of roots is inorganic, being a modern—merely euphonic—insertion. The influence of this difference on the inflection of the two classes of roots is very important, causing as it does nearly the whole of the inflections of one class to differ considerably from those of the other class. It becomes, therefore, very desirable to distinguish the two classes by some outward mark. Accordingly we have, in this Dictionary, adopted the following system: all roots which take the organic ब *b* we shall spell with a final ब *b*, while all roots which insert the euphonic य *y* will be spelt with final आ *ā*. To the former class belong all causal roots and the three primitive roots आब *āb* 'come,'† गाब *gāb* 'sing,' and पाब *pāb* 'get.' To the latter class belong all other primitive roots, such as अघा *aghā* 'be satiated,' खा *khā* 'eat,' घबरा *ghab'rā* 'be confused,' etc. Thus the final ब *b* of the √पाब *pāb* 'get' corresponds to the final radical प *p* of the Sanskrit √प्राप् *prāp*, and the final ब *b* of the causal √कराब *karāb* 'cause to do,' to the suffixal प *p* of the Pāli causal √कारापि *kārāpi*. On the other hand the √खा *khā* 'eat' is not spelt with ब *b*; for it corresponds to the Sanskrit √खाद् *khād*, Prākrit √खा *khā*, where the final organic द *d* is elided by a Prākrit phonetic law and, for the sake of euphony, replaced by the semivowel य *y* before certain inflexional terminations.

It may be here explained that the element ब (which, it should be remembered, is a semiconsonant, its sound being intermediate between *b* and *v*, see Chap. 4, *d*), has a tendency to be vocalised into ओ *o* or उ *u*. Similarly the element य *y* has a tendency to be vocalised into ए *e* or इ *i*, or even to be elided altogether. It is this circumstance which mainly gives rise to the wide divergence between the inflections of the two classes of roots. It may also be added that owing to the action of false analogy there is a tendency in certain tenses (notably in the future indicative) to assimilate the inflection of the *b*-class of roots to that of the *y*-class. This is, however, not the place to enter into grammatical details, for a statement of which we must refer the reader to Mr. Grierson's Bihārī Grammars, especially to Chapters VIII, X, and XI of Part II, Bhoj'pūrī dialect.

---

* We have adopted the now not uncommon practice of indicating a language root by the mathematical radical symbol √. We use the term 'root' in the sense of the constant element in any series of sense-related words. Thus in the Bihārī words *bōl-i*, 'speech,' *bōl-dhaṭ*, 'calling,' *bōl-ab*, 'speaking,' *bōl-at*, 'speaking,' *bōl-al*, 'spoken,' *bōl-ai*, 'he speaks,' etc., the constant element *bōl* is the root; the remainder are suffixes, and vary according to the meaning which is to be expressed by the root. (See Dr. Hœrnle's H. R., p. 33, Reprint, p. 1.)

† The root आब *āb* is peculiar, inasmuch as its ब *b* is not organic. It probably comes from the Skr. √पा + आ (see Dr. Hœrnle's H. R, p. 41, Reprint, p. 9). It is evidently formed by false analogy with the √पाब *pāb*, the inflection of which it generally follows, except in the past participle and in the tenses derived therefrom, in which it has आएल *āel*, thus reverting to its original character of a √आ *ā*. The case of the √गाब *gāb* is similar. It may correspond to a Skr. denominative (or causal) √गापि *gāpi*, but it is more probably another instance of false analogy, √गाब *gāb* being formed after √पाब *pāb*, the inflection of which it follows throughout.

The following examples will illustrate both the radical difference of the two classes and the importance of its bearing on their inflection :—

Root Form.		Regular Inflection.			Irregular.
Modern.	Ancient.	3rd Pers. Pres. Sing.	Pres. Part.	Past. Part.	1st Pers. Fut.
पाब *pāb*	Skr. प्राप् *prāp*	पाबथि *pābathi*	पाँबैत *pǎbāit*	पाओल *pāol*	पाएब *pāēb*
करब *karāb*	Pā. कारापि *kārāpi*	करबथि *karābathi*	करबैत *karăbāit*	करओल *karāol*	करएब *karāēb*
खा *khā*	Pr. खा *khā*	खाथि *khāthi*	खाइत *khāït* (for खायत *khayat*)	खाएल *khāēl*	खाएब or खाब *khāēb* or *khāb*

II.—THE TERMS TATSAMA AND TADBHAVA.

Omitting words of entirely foreign origin which have been adopted into the Gauḍian languages, such as the English words टिकट *ṭikaṭ* 'ticket,' रेल *rēl* 'railway,' or the Arabic जुलम *julam*, *i.e.* ظلم, 'oppression,' the Persian जलदी *jal'dī*, *i.e.* جلدي, 'quickly,' the vocabularies of those languages are of Aryan origin.* All foreign words will, in this Dictionary, be indicated by the collective term *Anyadēshaja*.

The Aryan portion of the vocabulary may be divided into two, on the whole, very clearly distinguishable classes, which are now commonly known by the names of *tatsama* and *tadbhava*, given to them by the native grammarians. Tadbhava words are those which have descended into the modern vernaculars from Prākrit sources, while tatsama words are those which have been borrowed direct from the Sanskrit to supply real or fancied deficiencies in the vocabulary.

Tatsama means 'having the same form as in Sanskrit,' *tadbhava* means 'being essentially, though not in form, the same as in Sanskrit.' These meanings of the two terms afford a rough and ready test for distinguishing the two classes of words. Thus राय *rāy* 'king,' भाइ *bhāï* 'brother,' खेत *khēt* 'field,' दहिन *dahin* 'right,' आन *ān* 'command,' are *tadbhavas* ; while राजा *rājā* 'king,' भ्राता *bhrātā* 'brother,' खेत्र *khēt'r* 'field,' दक्खिन *dakhin* 'right,' आग्या *āgyā* or अग्या *agyā* 'command,' are *tatsamas*, the latter set being in Sanskrit राजा *rājā*, भ्राता *bhrātā*, क्षेत्रम् *kshētram*, दक्षिणः *dakshiṇaḥ*, आज्ञा *ājñā*.

A similar division of words of Latin origin may be made in the English language; for example, *honour*, *ransom*, are *tadbhavas* derived from Latin through French, while *honor*, *redemption*, are *tatsamas* borrowed direct from the Latin.†

It should not be thought that a *tatsama* must be absolutely the same as in Sanskrit. On the contrary, *tatsamas* exhibit the most various grades of divergence from their Sanskrit equivalents, and only a small number of them are really absolutely the same as in Sanskrit. To the latter class, *e.g.*,

* We leave aside the question whether any and what portion of the Aryan element is Aboriginal or Drāviḍian.

† See Mr. Grierson's B. Gr., Part I, page 8. The existence of such a division of words is even more conspicuous in the Romance languages. For examples from the French, the student may consult M. Auguste Brachet's *Historical Grammar of the French Tongue* (Mr. Kitchin's Translation, p. 32), *e.g.*, 'popular' (tadbhava) words are—*ange, blâme, porche*, etc., while the corresponding 'learned' (tatsama) words are—*angelus, blasphème, portique*, etc.

belong the above-mentioned राजा *rājā* and भ्राता *bhrātā ;* while खेलर *khēl'r*, दखिन *dakhin*, and आग्या *āgyā* or अग्या *agya*, as will be noticed, differ, in an increasing scale, from their Sanskrit prototypes. It will readily be understood that there may occur cases in which, owing to this circumstance, it may be doubtful in which class a particular word should properly be placed. Thus there is the word जग *jag* 'sacrifice,' for the Sanskrit यज्ञ *yajña.* The real *tadbhava* form of the latter is जन *jan* (Prakrit जण्ण *jaṇṇa* or जञ्ञ *jañña*), which, however, *now* only occurs in the compound word जनेवो *janco* (Sanskrit यज्ञोपवीत: *yajñopavītaḥ*), 'sacrificial thread.' But the word जग *jag* is so different from its Sanskrit original, that it might be thought to be a *tadbhava* also; yet there cannot be much doubt that it is more properly classed with the *tatsamas*, because it is a (*technical*) term adopted direct into the Gauḍian from the Sanskrit in early times. The fact is, the real test of classification is a historico-philological one. *Tadbhavas* are those words which have come to the Gauḍian through the Prākrit, while *tatsamas* are those which have been adopted into it from the Sanskrit. And according as that adoption occurred at an earlier or later point in the history of the Gauḍian, the Sanskrit words exhibit greater or smaller changes in their form.* It may be well, therefore, in order to elucidate still further the meaning and object of the two terms *tatsama* and *tadbhava,* to add a brief historical sketch of the course of descent of the Gauḍians or modern vernaculars of North India.

The earliest glimpse of the Aryan vernacular we obtain in the older hymns of the Rig Veda, composed perhaps as early as 2000 B.C. Like every other language, this Vedic language changed, or developed, in the course of time; and another glimpse of it, in a somewhat less antique form, we obtain in the hymns of the Atharva Veda, referable perhaps to about 1000 B.C.† As the Aryan immigration gradually extended over the north of India, their vernacular, in the course of its development, naturally differentiated into several more or less distinct branches. From about 500 B.C. we receive, partly from extant literature, partly from inscriptions on rocks, pillars, etc., information of the existence of three different languages—one current in the north-western, another in the south-western, and the third in the eastern portion of the northern half of the Indian peninsula. Their areas may be roughly indicated by two lines—one touching Khāl'sī, Bairāt, Mathurā, Nāsik, the other joining Mathurā, Allāhābād, Rām'gaṛh, Jaugaḍa; the southern boundary of the whole Aryan area being a west-easterly line commencing near Goa.‡ This is shown on the accompanying Map I.

At this time Buddhism had arisen and spread over the whole of the northern portion of India. Everywhere it adopted the vernaculars of India, in order to propagate its doctrines, in speech and in writing. Thus these vernaculars rose to the dignity of literary languages, with its attendant characteristics of grammatical fixedness and artificialness. Henceforth, therefore, these languages co-existed in a twofold form—the vernacular and the literary. Contemporaneously with, and perhaps in opposition to, the adoption of the vernaculars by the Buddhists for their heterodox compositions, the Brahmanical schools, in which the use and the study of the Vedas and their ancient language had been handed down, elaborated and established,§ for the purpose of their own orthodox compositions, another literary language, drawn on the lines of the ancient Vedic

---

* For this reason Mr. Beames (Cp. Gr., vol. I, p. 13 ff) divides *tadbhavas* into 'early and late *tadbhavas*,' and Dr. Hœrnle (Gḍ. Gr., Introd., p. xxxviii ff) divides *tatsamas* into '*tatsamas* and *semi-tatsamas*,' the two terms 'late *tadbhavas*' and '*semi-tatsamas*' being intended to distinguish those *tatsamas* which, having been early adopted into Gauḍian, have more or less widely diverged from their Sanskrit prototypes. In this Dictionary we have thought it better to limit ourselves to the simpler classification into *tatsamas* and *tadbhavas* only.

† See Professor Whitney's Sanskrit Grammar, pp. xiii, xiv.

‡ For the grounds of this determination, see the Introduction to Dr. Hœrnle's editions of the *Prākṛita Lakṣaṇa* and of the *Bakhshālī Manuscript*.

§ The process culminated in the grammarian Pāṇini, probably in the third or fourth century B.C.

language, and thus possessing a character at once archaic and artificial. This language they designated the *Sanskrit* (संस्कृत *saṁskṛita*, *i.e.*, elaborated, perfected),* in opposition to which the vernaculars were called by them *Prākrit* (प्राकृत *prākṛita*, *i.e.*, natural, unelaborated).† It will be understood from this that while the Prākrits existed, as already stated, both in a vernacular (or spoken) and a literary form, the Sanskrit was only a literary language, but never a spoken one in the sense of a vernacular.

It has already been mentioned that at this period there existed three Prākrits—a north-western, a south-western, and an eastern. The first of these was called the *Apabhraṁsha*, (*i.e.*, corrupt); the second, the Prākrit simply; and the third was named the Māgadhī.‡ The literary form of the first may be seen in the Buddhist works written in the so-called '*Gāthā* dialect' (a sort of *Apabhraṁsha* Sanskrit, to speak from the Sanskrit point of view); that of the second is preserved in the Buddhist works written in the so-called 'Pāli';§ of the third there is no literature extant, though some evidence of its literary form is afforded by certain ancient inscriptions; and this last remark applies to the two other Prākrits also.‖

Some centuries later, perhaps from the fifth century of our era, a new state of things is disclosed to us in Prākrit literature.¶ The three great Prākrits are now seen to have differentiated into a still

---

* Indian grammarians, when speaking of the Vedic language *technically*, do not call it Sanskrit, but *Chhandas* (छन्दस्). The former is their technical term for the scholastic language elaborated on the lines of the Vedic. The two terms Sanskrit and Prākrit, however, are of comparatively late origin, the date of which it would be desirable to determine accurately. Lassen (Ind. Ant., Vol. II, p. 1151) places it vaguely some time within the first three centuries A.D. At the time of Pāṇini the Vedic language was called *Chhandas*, while the vernacular language of his time, which formed the groundwork of what we now call Sanskrit, was simply designated by the general term *bhāṣā* (भाषा). The latter term, therefore, does not show, as some appear to think, that Sanskrit itself was a *vernacular* language. It may be well perhaps, to prevent any misconception of the theory set forth in this Chapter, to state distinctly that we use the term *Sanskrit* exclusively in its strict and accurate sense, as denoting the scholastic language, elaborated (to follow a convenient tradition) by Pāṇini. We, therefore, never understand by that term, or include under it, either the Vedic language or the so-called Gāthā dialect, but only (what is sometimes called the 'classical') Sanskrit. The Vedic is not uncommonly said to be 'ancient' Sanskrit, and the Gāthā dialect, a 'corrupt' Sanskrit. They may be so designated in a loose way, and by way of speaking from the point of view of Sanskrit proper (or 'classical' Sanskrit). But for the purpose of the present Chapter it appeared desirable to avoid an inaccurate and misleading terminology. To call the so-called Gāthā dialect a corrupt Sanskrit is as little appropriate as it would be to call the Vedic language a corrupt Sanskrit. Both do not conform to Pāṇini's rules, and may be 'corrupt' as judged by that standard; but intrinsically neither of them is corrupt, as little as any other vernacular language is so. It should be added, however, that the so-called Gāthā dialect is, strictly speaking, that literary form of the North-Western vernacular (the *Apabhraṁsha* Prākrit of Chaṇḍ) which the latter received at the hands of Buddhist writers. A purer vernacular form of it is preserved in the Indo-Scythic and other inscriptions of North-Western India and Afghanistan. It is not improbable that it was this same vernacular that was the *bhāṣā* of (or spoken by) Pāṇini, and that, in his hands and with his brahmanic knowledge of the Vedic language (*Chhandas*), led to the creation of that far more thoroughly methodic and antique literary form of it which we now call the Sanskrit. In Pāṇini's age there were three great vernaculars in India,—the north-western, the south-western, and the eastern. Pāṇini himself is said to have been a native of the extreme north-west of India. This would tend to show that the north-western vernacular was probably his *bhāṣā*. On the other hand, other traditions connect the elaboration of his grammar with Bad'rī Nāth, where Shiva is said to have inspired him. This would point to that vernacular as his *bhāṣā*, which was spoken in the overlapping portion of the eastern and south-western vernaculars (see Map I). It should be also remembered that probably Pāṇini is only the most prominent representative of what was really a line of grammarians that gradually accomplished the elaboration of Sanskrit, by eliminating from the vernacular all more decayed forms in favour of less decayed ones preserved in the Vedic, by preferring, of two optional forms, that which happened to be favoured by the Vedic, and by other such or similar processes.

† Best expressed by the German 'naturwüchsig.'

‡ Under these names they are treated of by the ancient native grammarian Chaṇḍa (चण्ड) in his *Prākṛita Lakṣaṇa*. See Introduction to Dr. Hœrnle's edition of that work in the *Bibliotheca Indica*.

§ Strictly the Pāli represents only the Prākrit of the southern portion of the south-western area.

‖ The Ashōka inscriptions, the Nāsik inscriptions, etc. See Dr. Hœrnle's Introduction to his edition of the *Bakhshālī Manuscript*.

¶ At the commencement of the fifth century Fa Hian, the Chinese traveller (399—413 A.D.), tells us:—"Crossing the river we arrive at the country of *Ouchang* (or *Udyāna*). This is the most northern part of India. The language of middle India is everywhere used. Middle India is that which is called the middle country (*madhya dēsha*). The clothes and food of the ordinary people are likewise just the same as in the middle country." (See Beales' Translation, ch. VIII, p. 26.) This seems to show that at that time the ancient distribution of the Prākrits was still prominent, though possibly the passage means no more than that Fa Hian was struck with the wide western extent of the language and manner of life of India *proper*.

larger group. Beginning at the farthest north-west, we have first the *Apabhramsha*, and next to it a Prākrit, called *Shāurasēnī* ; these two forming the new subdivisions of what was hitherto called the *Apabhramsha* or the north-western Prākrit. Going still westwards, comes now a Prākrit called *Māhārāṣṭrī*, corresponding to the major portion of the old south-western or standard *Prākrit* ; and in the east we find the *Māgadhī*, having preserved the ancient name of the old eastern or *Māgadhī* Prākrit. But between the *Māhārāṣṭrī* and the *Māgadhī* there appears a new Prākrit, called the *Ardha-Māgadhī* (*i.e.*, half-Māgadhī), which consists of the eastern and western portions respectively of the old south-western or standard Prākrit and the old eastern or Māgadhī Prākrit.* This distribution of the mediæval Prākrits is shown in the accompanying Map II.

None of these five mediæval Prākrits received any literary cultivation except the Māhārāṣṭrī.† The latter, indeed, as a literary language, soon came to acquire a character fully as inflexible and artificial as Sanskrit, if not even more so. There were two varieties of it, however, which may be called respectively the Jain and the Brahmanic Māhārāṣṭrī.‡ Of these, the former was rather less artificial, and more nearly approached the vernacular, or spoken, form of that Prākrit. The other four mediæval Prākrits, so far as known, never rose above the state of a mere vernacular.§

Again a few centuries later, about 1200 A.D., the process of disintegration is shown a step further advanced. The mediæval Prākrits now already appear in the incipient stage of that division into the modern Prākrits or (as we briefly call them) Gauḍians, which we see fully developed in the present day. In the accompanying Map III this modern distribution is shown. Thus the mediæval Shāurasēnī becomes divided into a *Gurjarī* and *Shāurasēnī proper*, the modern Gujarātī and Mār'wāṛī. To the south of the mediæval Māhārāṣṭrī and Ardha-Māgadhī, corresponding respectively to the modern Hindī and Bihārī, comes into view the *Dākṣiṇātyā* (*i.e.*, southern) or *Vāidarbhī*, the modern Marāṭhī.‖ The mediæval Māgadhī divides into the *Gāuḍī*¶ (or *Prāchyā*) and *Utkalī* (or *Ōḍrī*), which are the modern Bangālī and Ōṛīyā.

There is yet a fourth step—the modern division of the Gauḍian languages into their dialects. For the present purpose, however, it will suffice to refer only to the distribution of the dialects of the Bihārī (or the mediæval Ardha-Māgadhī), which are the special subject of this Dictionary. In the accompanying Map IV this distribution is shown. Proceeding from west to east, the Bihārī possesses four principal dialects, the Bais'wārī, Bhoj'pūrī, Magahī (or Māgadhī), and Maithilī, the last named of which, being the most highly developed, and possessing a literature dating from the 14th century, may be considered as the standard.**

---

* These are the Prākrit divisions named by the native Prākrit grammarians Hēma Chandra and (though less fully) Vararuchi.

† The occasional employment, in a few mediæval Sanskrit dramas, of the other Prākrits does not affect this statement.

‡ They differ mainly in two points: (1) the use of the euphonic *y* and *w*, and (2) the preservation of the dental *n*, in the Jain Māhārāṣṭrī, while the Brahmanic variety carefully avoids both. See Dr. Hœrnle's edition of the *Prākṛita Lakṣaṇa*, Introd., pp. lx ff; also his *Sketch of the History of Prākrit Philology* in the *Calcutta Review* of October 1880.

§ This difference between the Māhārāṣṭrī and the other Prākrits is strikingly shown by the fact that in Sanskrit literature the term 'Prākṛita' is commonly used as a synonym of *Māhārāṣṭrī* when the latter is contrasted with Sanskrit. The literary cultivation of the Māhārāṣṭrī was most probably due to its happening to be the vernacular of the Jain community, who continued to use the vernacular for their literary compositions when everywhere else it had become customary to use the Sanskrit for this purpose.

‖ The leading dialect of Marāṭhī is still called *Dakhinī* or Southern. The far extent of the ancient Māhārāṣṭrī, towards the south, is still shown by the existence of the *Kōnkaṇī* dialect of the Marāṭhī in the country round Goa. The Kōnkaṇī has strong affinities with the Hindī, the direct representative of the ancient Māhārāṣṭrī. (See Rev. F. Maffei's and Mr. Da Cunha's Kōnkaṇī Grammars.) This, the proper Kōnkaṇī, should not be confounded with the Marāṭhī, spoken in the northern part of the coast-line, which is also, though improperly, called Kōnkaṇī.

¶ The terms Gāuḍī and Prāchyā appear to be also sometimes used to denote what we now call the Bais'wāṛī, the westernmost dialect of Bihārī.

** For further information on these dialects, their areas, etc., see the Introduction to Mr. Grierson's Bihārī Grammars, Part I, pp. 14-17; also J. A. S. B., vol. LII, pt. I, p. 119.

It will be seen at once from this historical sketch of the origin of the Gauḍians or modern vernaculars of North India that they are not descended from the Sanskrit in any true sense whatever. Their line of descent, starting from the Vedic, runs through the Prākrits, and, of course, not through the literary, but through the vernacular Prākrits. Hence it will be understood that the origin of the whole of their grammatical structure, and the main portion of their vocabulary, must be looked for in the successive stages of Prākrit development. At the same time, it is easy to conceive that the Indian vernaculars must at all times have drawn some portion of their vocabulary from the literary Sanskrit, especially whenever they happened to be made use of for literary purposes; for it would have been impossible to find in the vernaculars adequate means of expressing many thoughts and things of a higher order. These Sanskritic portions constitute now, as they did always, the *tatsamas* of the vernacular vocabulary, while their *tadbhavas*, which are much the most numerous, are made up by their Prākritic portions.

There is, however, notwithstanding, a sense in which Sanskrit may be said to be the source of the modern vernaculars, to which their words may be ultimately traced up through the Prākrits. For Sanskrit, though not older than the oldest known Prākrit, and though not in the direct line of descent of the Gauḍians, yet, in the main, conserves a form of the Indian Aryan language which is older than the oldest Prākrit and the direct source of the latter, namely the Vedic; and for the present purpose Sanskrit thus affords a convenient means of carrying up the historical investigation of the origin of modern words to its legitimate conclusion.

With regard to the maps which accompany the foregoing remarks, it is perhaps hardly necessary to add that they "pretend to be no more than rough exemplifications, by means of definite lines, of our present knowledge regarding a state of affairs essentially indefinite; for languages are not separated by straight lines, but insensibly merge into each other."*

It should also be noted that the distribution of the aboriginal, or the so-called Kolarian, languages in Central India has not been indicated in these maps. For the purpose now in hand, it was scarcely necessary to do so. Their area is extensively encroached upon by settlers from the surrounding tracts occupied by the Gauḍian languages, Bangālī, Bihārī, Marāṭhī, and Uṛiyā, the boundaries of which thus become, in a rough way, coterminous.

12.—DERIVATIONS, AFFINITIES, &c.

We have attempted, as far as possible, to trace the derivation of every Bihārī word to its Prākrit and Sanskrit sources. It must be understood, however, that in some cases the derivation suggested is merely a tentative one. In order to enable students to judge for themselves the accuracy or probability of our derivations, we shall quote, wherever possible, the work in which any given Pāli or Prākrit form can be verified; it being understood in the case of Pāli that, unless otherwise specified, the word is taken from Childers' Dictionary. Any form which we are unable to support by a quotation, and which we simply give as a more or less probable conjecture, we shall indicate by an asterisk (*). All forms, however—and they are the majority—which, though not at present quotable, have been made by us in strict accordance with the rules of derivation from Sanskrit laid down by Pāli and Prākrit grammarians, will be given without any special indication. Thus the Prākrit equivalents अंकवाली *aṁkawālī*, एक्कसरिअं *ekkasariaṁ*, एकल्लो *ēkallō* or एक्कल्लो *ekkallō*, of the Bihārī words अँकवार *ãk'wār* 'embrace,' अकसर *ak'sar* or एकसर *ek'sar* 'alone,' and अकेल *akēl* or एकल *ekal* 'alone,' respectively, are all supported by quotations. On the other hand, the Prākrit equivalent of the Bihārī अखारा *akhārā* 'palæstra'

* See Mr. Grierson's Bihārī Grammars, Introduction, page 6.

being simply conjectural, is marked with an asterisk. And again the Pāli and Prākrit equivalents अकम्मिको *akammikō*, अकम्मिओ *akammiō*, of the Bihārī अकामी *akāmī* 'useless,' are given without any special mark or note, because they are perfectly regular and undoubtedly correct forms, though at present we are not able to verify them by actual quotations. Of some words we have found ourselves quite unable to offer even a tentative derivation, and we shall in such cases simply write 'Der. ?' (*i.e.*, derivation unknown).

With regard to the equivalent forms of Bihārī words, which we adduce from the other Gauḍian languages, it should be understood that, unless otherwise mentioned, they are quoted from the dictionaries of those languages; and in all these cases, therefore, it was not thought necessary to add any special reference to the respective dictionary. We have always had recourse to the best dictionaries available, a list of which will be found in the table of abbreviations. In those few cases, however, where the cognate Gauḍian word was not taken from a dictionary but from some other work, a reference to the latter, to allow of verification, is always added.

If a word which is inserted in any of the Hindī dictionaries is not found in our Dictionary, it must be understood that the word in question, so far as we have been able to ascertain from literature or personal intercourse, does not exist in Bihārī. With this view, every word occurring in any of the existing Hindī dictionaries has been carefully scrutinised by us.

We may add that we shall always be glad to receive communications on these and other points, which will be duly acknowledged. Such communications will receive our fullest consideration, and, if adopted, will be inserted in their proper places, or, if necessary, in a supplement which will be published at the conclusion of the work.

13.—STRUCTURE OF THE ARTICLES.

First a word, spelt both in Nāgarī and Roman, is given, with its cognate forms (if any) in the various Bihārī dialects. If the word is an adjective, its feminine (printed *f.*) form (if different from the masculine), or, if it is a verb, its principal parts* (printed *pr. pts.*) are also noted; and it is further distinguished as *tadbhava* or *tatsama* or *anyadēshaja* (printed Tbh., Ts., Any.): thus अकेल *akēl*, (*f.* अकेल *akēl or Mth.* अकेलि *akēli*), Tbh.

This is followed by an enumeration of the different meanings of the word, which are distinguished from one another by means of raised numbers and semicolons, while synonyms are merely separated by commas: thus under अकास *akās* we have [1]sky; [2]air; [3]ether; [4]cypher; [5]nose.

Immediately after the meanings are given any compounds (printed Comp.) or peculiar phrases (printed Phr.) in which the word may occur.

The compounds or phrases are next followed by examples (printed Exam.) to illustrate the various meanings, the object of the compilers being as far as possible to cite one, or several, examples in support of each meaning given (especially of *tadbhavas*);† and to facilitate reference, raised numbers have been added to the examples, corresponding to the raised numbers of the meanings which they are intended to illustrate. Thus under अकास *akās* several examples are cited in illustration of the five meanings of the word. In every case an example has been accompanied by a translation. Whenever possible, an example has been quoted by us from the Bihārī literature known to us (see Chap. 14), and in every such case an exact reference has been given to the place where the passage may be found and the meaning, in support of which the example is

---

* The 'principal parts' of a verb are—present participle, past participle, verbal noun in *b*, and oblique verbal noun in *ai*.

† In the case of examples quoted by Fallon in his Hindūstānī Dictionary, as being ostensibly in some dialect of Bihār, we have, in reproducing them in our Dictionary, sometimes been obliged to alter their spelling or grammar, in order to render them in their real Bihārī shape. Such cases we specify by adding 'after Fallon.'

cited, verified. In a few cases, however, (*e.g.*, अकरा *ak'rā* 'costly') in which the word also occurs in Hindī with the same meaning, we have quoted examples from Hindī literature. When literature failed to supply us with an example, we have given one (distinguished by *Coll.*, *i.e.*, colloquial) from our personal intercourse with the people. This was thought by us better than omitting all illustration by example, because examples serve not only to throw further light on a given meaning, but also to show the idiomatic way of applying it. In cases in which a meaning given by us is not borne out by either existing literature or our personal experience, we always quote the source from which it is obtained.

Sometimes a word is used in two different 'parts of speech:' thus अकट *akat* occurs both as an adjective (*adj.*) and as an adverb (printed *adv.*). In such cases the various parts of speech are treated separately and consecutively; each part of speech, with its meanings, examples, and phrases, forming a distinct set, and being distinguished in separate paragraphs and by large Roman numbers. Thus in the article अकट *akat* we have it, first, as an adjective (I. *adj.*), with its meaning, example, and phrases; then we have it, secondly, as an adverb (II. *adv.*), with its meaning and corresponding example.

If there is anything peculiar to be remarked regarding a word, it is now given, enclosed within round brackets and forming a separate paragraph: thus under अकास *akās* there is a long note after the examples.

This concludes the first portion of an article, which treats of the word as used in Bihārī. The second portion, which immediately follows, forming a fresh paragraph, always contains the comparative matter of the Dictionary, and not only gives all the cognate forms of the word that occur in the various Gauḍian languages, but also traces its derivation from its antecedent forms in Prākrit, Pāli, and Sanskrit. This second, or comparative, portion is distinguished from the first by being enclosed in angular brackets.

It should further be noted as a general rule that with the exception of the meanings and translations, which are printed in Roman, the whole of the (English) matter of an article is printed in *Italics*. This shows at a glance what is translation and what is commentary.

14.—BIHĀRĪ LITERATURE.

The following is a list of all the Bihārī literature with which we are acquainted. A large portion of it does not yet exist in print, but is only to be met with in manuscript. The two portions are indicated in the subjoined list by the addition of *PR.* and *MS.* respectively. As some of the printed works have been issued from various presses, we have always added in brackets the needful notices to identify the particular edition which has been consulted by us in the preparation of this Dictionary. Similar notices, where necessary, have been added to the manuscripts, nearly all of which are in our own possession.

Though the list contains all the existing literature known to us at present, it must not be supposed that we have been able to read the whole, or even that we have seen every portion of it. Most portions, especially of the larger and more important kind, like the Rāmāyan and Bidyāpati's poems, we have worked through carefully; others we have only been able to go over cursorily; others, again, especially of the smaller compositions, we have had no opportunity of seeing. The three classes will be indicated in the following list by *Read*, *Seen*, and *Unknown* respectively.

As far as possible within the limited time at our command, we have carefully indexed all those works which we have *read* or *seen*. This was done, in the first place, for our own convenience in preparing the Dictionary, but also with a hope that the indexes when printed may prove acceptable to other students of Bihārī literature. They will be found very useful for the purpose of verifying the numerous statements and quotations in our Dictionary, as well as, generally, for any comparative study in the field of North-Indian literature and languages. The word 'Index' has been added to every work to which one has been made; and when it exists in print, the needful reference is given.

In Maithilī.

(1) Bidyāpati Ṭhākur's Poems, in old Maithilī. Text and English translation by G. A. Grierson. *PR.* (J. A. S. B., Extra Number for 1880, Part II, Maithil Chrestomathy.) *Read.* Index (issued in parts with the Bihārī Dictionary).

(2) Two plays in old Maithilī, said to be by the same author, viz. Pārijāt Haran and Rukminī Swayambar. They are said still to exist in MS., though we have not succeeded in tracing them. *Unknown.*

(3) Kabi Lāl's Gaūrī Parinay, a small play in Sanskrit, Prākrit, and old Maithilī. *MS. Seen.* Index (in *MS*).

(4) Man'bodh's Haribans, in old Maithilī verse. Text and English translation by G. A. Grierson. *PR.* (J. A. S. B., vol. LI, Part I, for 1882, and vol. LIII, Part I, for 1884.) *Read.* Index. (J. A. S. B., vol. LIII, Part I, Special Number for 1884.)

(5) Song of King Salhēs, in modern Maithilī prose. Text and English translation by G. A. Grierson. *PR.* (J. A. S. B., Extra Number for 1880, Part II, Maithil Chrestomathy.) *Read.* Index (in *MS.*)

(6) Song of the Famine, by Phatūrī Lāl (a living poet), in modern Maithilī verse. Text and English translation by G. A. Grierson. *PR.* (J. A. S. B., Extra Number for 1880, Part II, Maithil Chrestomathy.) *Read.* Index (in *MS.*)

(7) Ukhāharan, a play in modern Maithilī, by Harkh Nāth (a living poet). *MS.* (not in our possession.) *Unknown.*

(8) Some poems by the same, in modern Maithilī verse. Text and English translation by G. A. Grierson. *PR.* (J. A. S. B., Extra Number for 1880, Part II, Maithil Chrestomathy.) *Read.* Index (in *MS.*)

(9) Prabhābatī Haran, a Sanskrit and Prākrit drama interspersed with eighteen Maithilī songs, by Bhānu Nāth Jhā (a living poet). Date: beginning of the present century. *MS.* (A copy, corrected by the author himself, in Mr. G. A. Grierson's possession.) *Read.* Index (in *MS.*)

(10) Bātā-hbān, a metrical incantation for wind, one verse being devoted to each letter of the alphabet; by the same. (See article मस *mūs* in the vocabulary to Maithil Chrestomathy, Part II of Extra Number for 1880, J. A. S. B.) *MS. Read.* Index (in *MS.*)

(11) Gīt Nebārak, a song in modern Maithilī. Author and date unknown. *MS. Seen.* Index (in *MS.*)

(12) Gīt Dīnā Bhadrīk, a song in the modern Maithilī of the Nēpāl Tarāi. *MS. Read.* Index (in *MS.*)

(13) Gīt Dīnā Bhadrī Kawand, a song in the modern Maithilī of the Nēpāl Tarāi. *MS. Read.* Index (in *MS.*)

(14) Numerous songs by the following poets:—

a. Umāpati.	*e.* Mahīpati.	*i.* Jayadēb.	*n.* Chakrapāni.
b. Nandīpati.	*f.* Jayānand.	*k.* Kēshab.	*o.* Lakshmīpati.
c. Mod Nārāyan.	*g.* Chaturbhuj.	*l.* Shēkhar.	*p.* Chandra Kabi.
d. Ramāpati.	*h.* Saras Rām.	*m.* Bhanjan.	

All in *MS.* Mostly *unknown;* but specimens of the songs of most of these poets, with English translations, by G. A. Grierson, have been published in J. A. S. B., vol. LIII, Part I, Special Number for 1884. Index (in *MS.*) Lakshmīpatí died about ten years ago; he was a very prolific writer, but wrote mostly in the Bais'wārī dialect. Chandra Kabí is a living poet, and has supplied us with many examples. Regarding the other poets no information was obtainable.

(15) Miscellaneous writings in modern Maithilī; *e.g.*—

(*a*) Chaūkīdārī Nīyamābalī, by G. A. Grierson and Srī Nārāyan Singh. *PR.* *Read.*

(*b*) Translation of portions of the Bible and some Tracts, by Baptist Missionaries. *PR.* *Seen.* Index. (English concordance may be used for the purpose.)

(*c*) Fables and Dialogues, by Srī Nārāyan Singh, in modern Northern Maithilī. Text and English translation by G. A. Grierson. *PR.* (J. A. S. B., Extra Number for 1880, Part I, Maithil Grammar, Appendix II; and Bihārī Grammars, Part I, Introduction, Appendix). *Read.* Index (in *MS.*)

In Bhoj'pūrī.

(1) Song of Ālhā, in a mixture of Bhoj'pūrī and Magahī. *MS.* The relation of this version to another in Hindī, usually, though probably erroneously, ascribed to Chand Bar'dāī, is still uncertain. *PR.* (ed. G. A. Grierson in Ind. Ant. for 1885). *Read.* Index (in *MS.*)

(2) Gīt Bijaī Mal, a song in old Bhoj'pūrī. *PR.* (J. A. S. B., vol. LIII, Part I, Special Number for 1884). *Read.* Index (in *MS.*)

(3) Gīt Rājā Gōpī Chand, a ballad in old Bhoj'pūrī (apparently a fragment). *PR.* (ed. G. A. Grierson in J. A. S. B., vol. LIV, Part I, for 1885). *Read.* Index (in *MS.*)

(4) Folklore from Eastern Gorakh'pur, in modern Bhoj'pūrī verse. Text and English translation by Hugh Fraser. *PR.* (J. A. S. B., vol. LII, Part I, for 1883.) *Read.* Index (in *MS.*)

(5) Folksongs, in modern Bhoj'pūrī. Text and English translation by G. A. Grierson. *PR.* (J. R. A. S., vol. XVI (N.S.), Part II, 1884.) *Read.* Index (in *MS.*)

(6) Bhoj'pūrī Songs, from the Shāhābād district. Text and English translation by G. A. Grierson. *PR.* (Bihārī Grammars, Part II, Bhoj'pūrī, Appendix II.) *Read.* Index (in *MS.*)

(7) Agricultural Songs, in Western Bhoj'pūrī. *PR.* (In detached portions; in Carnegy's Kachahrī Technicalities *s.v.* *NAKHAT*, and in Fallon's Hindūstānī Dictionary; also all in Grierson's Bihār Peasant Life.) *Read.* Index (in *MS.*)

(8) Fables and Dialogues, in the Sāran Bhoj'pūrī, by Bisēsar Parshād. Text and English translation by G. A. Grierson. *PR.* (Bihārī Grammars, Part II, Bhoj'pūrī, Appendix I.) *Read.* Index (in *MS.*)

(9) A number of miscellaneous songs. *MS.* (to be ed. by A. F. Rudolf Hoernle in J. A. S. B.) *Read.* Index (in *MS.*)

(10) Sudhābund, a collection of sixty Kajalīs by Maharājādhirāj Kumār Lāl Kharg Bahādur Mall. *PR.* (1884, by S. P. Sinha, Khadgbilas Press, Bankipore). *Seen.* Index (in *MS.*)

(11) Dēvākṣara Charitra, a serio-comic drama in the vernacular, by Paṇḍit Ravidatta Shukla. *PR.* (Benares, Light Press, 1884). *Read.* Index (in *MS*). The third and fourth scenes are in the Bhoj'pūrī dialect.

In Magahī.

(1) A few songs, in *MS. Read.*

(2) A large collection of songs, in impure Magahi, *i.e.*, in the dialect of the borderland between Magahī and Bhōj'pūrī. *MS.* (Procured from a man who had been one of Fallon's assistants.) *Read.* Index (in *MS.*)

(3) Fables and Dialogues, in the dialects of Gayā and South Patna. Text and English translation by G. A. Grierson. *PR.* (Bihārī Grammars, Part III, Māgadhī, Appendix I.) *Read.* Index (in *MS.*)

(4) Gīt Rājā Gōpī Chand, a ballad in Magahī. *PR.* (ed. G. A. Grierson in J. A. S. B., vol. LIV, Part I, for 1885). *Read.* Index (in *MS.*)

In Bais'wārī.

(1) Rāmāyan (also called the Chaūpāī Rāmāyan), in old Bais'wārī, by Tul'sī Dās. *PR.* (Medical Hall Press, Benares, 1869; ed. Rām Jasan). *Read.* Index (issued in parts with the Bihārī Dictionary).

(2) Various smaller works by the same author, the most important of which are the following:—

(*a*) Kabit Rāmāyan or Kabittābalī. *PR.* (Benares, Light Press, 1879 (S. 1936); ed. Gōpī Nāth Pāṭhak. *Read.* Index (in *MS.*)

(*b*) Sat Saī. *PR.* (Benares, Light Press; complete without commentary; ed. Gōpī Nāth Pāṭhak; also selected portions with commentary, ed. the same). *Seen.* Index (in *MS.*)

(*c*) Gītābalī. *PR.* (Benares, Light Press, 1869.) *Read.* Index (in *MS.*)

(*d*) Jānakī Maṅgal, Pārbatī Maṅgal, Baīrāgya Sandīpinī, Rām Lalākar Nah'chhū, Bar'wē Rāmāyan. *PR.* (All in one volume, ed. by Prayāg Datt' Siṅgh, at the Braj Chandra Press, Benares.) *Read.* Index (in *MS.*)

(*e*) Rām Salākā. *MS. Unknown.*

(*f*) Srī Rām Agyā, also called Rām Sagunābalī; *PR.* (ed. Prayāg Datt' Siṅgh at the Braj Chandra Press). *Seen.* Index (in *MS.*)

(*g*) Dohābalī. *PR.* (1882, Lucknow, Nawal Kishor Press). *Seen.* Index (in *MS.*)

(*h*) Chhandābalī or Chhand Rāmāyan. *Unknown.*

(*i*) Kuṇḍalīyā Rāmāyan. *Unknown*

(*k*) Saṅkaṭ Mōchan. *PR.* (1879 or S. 1936 at Lucknow, by Munshī Bēnī Prasād). *Seen.* Index (in *MS.*)

(*l*) Hanumān Bāhuk. *PR.* (in the same volume with the Kabit Rāmāyan). *Seen.* Index (in *MS.*)

(*m*) Krishṇābalī. *PR.* (1882 or S. 1939, by Braj Chandra, at the Braj Chandra Press. Benares). In Braj, not Bais'wārī. *Seen.* Index (in *MS.*)

(*n*) Kaṛ'kā Chhand. *Unknown.*

(*o*) Rōlā Chhand. *Unknown.*

(*p*) Jhūl'na Chhand. *Unknown.*

(*q*) Binay Patrikā. *PR.* (ed., with a commentary, by Bābū Shiv Prakāsh of Ḍum'rāō, at Lucknow, Nawal Kishor Press, 1878.) *Seen.* Index (in *MS.*)

(*r*) Chhappāī Rāmāyan. *PR.* (ed. Kāshī Nāth Siṅgh, Dinapore, Central Press, 1884). *Seen.* Index (in *MS*).

N.B.—Extracts from most of the above-named smaller works are contained in Professor Bihārī Lāl Chaūbē's Anthology, called the Bihārī Tul'sī Bhūshan Bōdh; also in Shiv Siṅgh's Anthology, called Shiva Siṁha Sarōja (2nd ed., Lucknow, Nawal Kishor Press, 1881).

(3) **Sundarī Tilak.** *PR.* (Benares, Light Press.) *Seen.*

(4) **Lāl Jhā's Battle of Kanarpī Ghāt, by a Maithil Brāhman at the end of the last century.** *PR.* (J. A. S. B., vol. LIV, Part I, for 1885.) *Read.* Index (in *MS.*)

(5) **Padmāwat, by Malik Mohammad Jāy'sī.** *PR.* (Chandra Prabhā Press, Benares, 1884; ed. Rām Jasan). *Read.* Index (in *MS.*)

15.—RESUMÉ OF INSTRUCTIONS FOR FINDING WORDS IN THIS DICTIONARY.

In order to reduce the labour of finding words in this Dictionary to a minimum, the following *resumé* of the instructions as to the principles to be followed is appended. The want of such instructions in other dictionaries has been much felt.

(1) Neither *anunāsika* nor the imperfect vowel is allowed to influence the alphabetical order. (See Chap. 5, p. 12.)

(2) If a word containing an *anuswāra* has to be looked up in the Dictionary, note that—

(*a*) If the nasal occurs in a syllable containing a long vowel, it must be considered as *anunāsika*. Example: for आंकुर *āṁkur*, look up आँकुर *ā̃kur*.

(*b*) If it occurs in a syllable with a short vowel, and is followed by a mute consonant, it must be considered as the nasal of the class to which the following consonant belongs. Example: for अंकुर *aṁkur* look up अङ्कुर *aṅkur*. For isolated exceptions, see Chapter 3, page 7.

(*c*) When (occurring in a syllable with a short vowel) *anuswāra* comes before य *y*, the two together must be considered as ञ *ñj*. Example: for संयम *saṁyam*, look up सञ्जम *sañjam*.

(*d*) When (occurring in a syllable with a short vowel) it comes before व *v*, the two together must be considered as म्ब *mb*. Example: for संवत *saṁvat*, look up सम्बत *sambat*.

(*e*) When (occurring in a syllable with a short vowel) it comes before स *s*, it must be considered as न *n*. Example: for हंस *haṁs*, look up हन्स *hans*.

(*f*) When (occurring in a syllable with a short vowel) it comes before ह *h*, the two together must be considered as ङ्घ *ṅgh*. Example: for सिंह *siṁgh*, look up सिङ्घ *siṅgh*. (See Chap. 4, pp. 7, 8.)

(3) Words containing the following letters must be looked up under the spelling shown in the following table as the adopted one. (See Chap. 4, pp. 7—9.)

Rejected.		Adopted.	Examples.			
ऋ *ṛi*		रि *ri*	For	ऋतु *ṛitu*,	look up	रितु *ritu*.
ल *l*	When non-initial.	र *r*	„	फल *phal*,	„	फर *phar*.
ड़ *ṛ*	When non-initial.	र *r*	„	√पड़ *paṛ*,	„	√पर *par*.
ण *ṇ*		न *n*	„	रामायण *rāmāyaṇ*,	„	रामायन *rāmāyan*.
य *y*	When organic and initial of a simple or compound word.	ज *j*	„	यात्री *yātrī*,	„	जात्री *jātrī*.
			„	मनोयोग *manōyōg*,	„	मनोजोग *manōjōg*.
व *v*	When organic.	ब *b*	„	वेद *vēd*,	„	बेद *bēd*.
			„	निवृत्त *nivṛitt'*,	„	निबित्त *nibritt'*.

Rejected.	Adopted.	Examples.			
श *sh*	स *s*	For	शरण *sharaṇ*,	look up	सरन *saran*.
ष *ṣ*	ख *kh*	„	भाषा *bhāṣā*,	„	भाखा *bhākhā*.
क्ष *kṣ*	छ *chh* or	„	क्षमा *kṣamā*,	„	छमा *chhamā*.
	ख *kh* or (when medial and preceded by a short vowel)	„	राक्षस *rākṣas*,	„	राखस *rākhas*.
	च्छ *chchh* or	„	रक्षा *rakṣā*,	„	रच्छा *rachchhā*.
	क्ख *kkh*	„	दक्षिण *dakṣiṇ*,	„	दक्खिन *dakkhin*.
ज्ञ *jñ* or गे *ge*	ग्य *gy*	„	ज्ञान *jñān* or गेआन *geān*,	„	ग्यान *gyān*.
प्र *pr*	पर॰ *par’*	„	प्रभु *prabhu*.	„	पर॰भु *par’bhu*.
य्य *yy*	ज्य *jy*	„	शय्या *sayyā*,	„	सज्या *sajyā*.
र्य *ry*	र्ज *rj* or र॰ज *r’j*	„	आचार्य *āchārya*,	„	आचार्ज *āchārj* or आचार॰ज *āchār’j*
र्व *rv*	र्ब *rb* or र॰ब *r’b*	„	पूर्व *pūrv*,	„	पूर्ब *pūrb* or पूर॰ब *pūr’b*.
र्ष *rṣ*	र्ख *rkh*	„	आकर्षण *ākarṣaṇ*,	„	आकर्खन *ākarkhan*.
ष्ण *ṣṇ*	श्न *shn* or श॰न *sh’n*	„	कृष्ण *kriṣṇ*,	„	क्रिश॰न *krish’n*.
		„	कृष्णौतार *kṛiṣṇāutār*	„	क्रिश्नौतार *krishnāutār*.
ष्प *ṣp*	स्प *sp*	„	पुष्प *puṣp*,	„	पुस्प *pusp*.
ह्य *hy*	झ॰ *jhy’* with shortening of preceding long vowel.	„	ग्राह्य *grāhya*,	„	ग्रांझ॰ *grā̃jhy’*.
अइ *aï*	ऐ *āi* or अए *aë*	„	अघइलॅ *aghaïlā*,	„	अघैलॅ *aghāilā* or अघएल॰ *aghaëlā*.
अउ *aü*	औ *āu* or अओ *aö*	„	पउलॅ *paülā*	„	पौलॅ *pāulā* or पओलॅ *paölā*.
आए *āë* or आइ *āï*	आय *āy*	„	पराए *parāë*, पराइ *parāï*,	„	पराय *parāy*.
आओ *āö* or आउ *āü*	आव *āw*	„	चढ़ाओ *chaṛhāö* or चढ़ाउ *chaṛhāü*,	„	चढ़ाव *chaṛhāw*.
इआ *iā*	इया *iyā*	„	बेटिआ *beṭiā*,	„	बेटिया *beṭiyā*.
उवा *uwā*	उआ *uā*	„	बहुवा *bahuwā*,	„	बहुआ *bahuā*.

(4) Long and redundant forms of nouns are not usually given. Their short forms can be found on consulting the tables in Chapter 7. As a rule, only these short forms will be found in the Dictionary. In looking them up, it must be remembered that short forms containing long vowels shorten these vowels in certain cases in long and redundant forms. (See Chap. 6, pp. 13, 14.) Hence, if a long or redundant from contains a short antepenultimate vowel, its short form may possibly contain a long one.

(5) Many verbs the roots of which contain long vowels shorten these vowels when they fall in the antepenultimate. (See Chap. 6, pp. 13, 14.) Hence verbal forms containing short radical vowels may have to be looked up under the head of a root containing a long vowel.

(6) Attention is called to the treatment of verbal roots in आ ā, as explained in Chapter 10.

(7) Verbs are given under their root forms, the radical sign ✓ being prefixed in each case, and not in the form of the infinitive, as is usual in Hindī dictionaries.

16.—LIST OF ABBREVIATIONS EMPLOYED IN THE DICTIONARY.

I.—*Names of Languages and Titles of Works.*

A.	Assamese.
A. Dy.	Dictionary in Assamese and English. By M. Bronson. (Sibsagor, 1867.)
Ā. G.	Trumpp's Translation of the Ādi Granth.
Ag.	Rām Agyā, by Tul'sī Dās, (ed. Prayāg Datt' Siŋgh, Braj Chandra Press).
Any.	Anyadēshaja, *i.e.*, foreign (Arabic, Persian, English, etc.).
Ap. Pr.	Apabhraṁsha Prakrit.
Ar.	Arabic.
Ār. Pr.	Arṣa Prākrit.
Ardh. Mg. Pr.	Ardha Māgadhī Prākrit.
Ath.	Index Verborum to the published Text of the Atharva Veda. By W. D. Whitney. In the Journal of the American Oriental Society (Vol XII.)
Ath.	The Ālha Kaṇḍ, a Bhoj'pūrī ballad (in Ind. Ant. for 1885).
As. Res.	The Asiatic Researches.
Aup.	Das Aupapātika Sūtra (ed. E. Lenmann, in Collection of G. O. S., vol. VIII, No. 2).
Av.	Avery's Contributions to the History of Verb Inflection in Sanskrit (in Journal of the American Oriental Society, vol. X).
Āz. Gy.	Glossaries in Āzam'gaṛh Settlement Report, Appendix III.
B.	Bihārī.
B. Gr.	Grierson's Seven Grammars of the Dialects and Subdialects of the Bihārī Language. (Calcutta, Bengal Secretariat Press, 1883.)
B. Rām.	The Bar'wē Rāmāyan of Tul'sī Dās (ed. Prayāg Datt' Siŋgh: Braj Chandra Press, Benares.)
Bais.	Bais'wārī folksongs collected by Bābū J. N. Rae (in J. A. S. B., vol. LIII).
Bg.	Bangālī.
Bg. Dy.	Dictionary of the Bangālī and Sanskrit. By Sir G.C. Haughton. (London 1833.)
Bg. Gr.	Shama Churn Sircar's Bangālī Grammar. (Calcutta, 1861.)
Bh.	Bhoj'pūrī.
Bh. Mā.	The Bhakti Mālā, (printed by Gan'pat Krishnajī in Bombay).
Bhag.	Bhagavatī (ed. Weber).
Bid.	Bidyāpati.
Bin.	Binay Patrikā, by Tul'sī Dās; (ed. with comm. by Shiv Prashād, Lucknow, Nawal Kishor Press, 1878.)
Bih.	Bihārī Songs (ed. G. A. Grierson, in J. R. A. S., vol. XVI, 1884.)
Bij.	Gīt Bijaī Mal, a Bhoj'pūrī Song, (ed. G. A. Grierson, in J. A. S. B., vol. LIII, Part I, Special Number for 1884).
Br.	Braj.
Bw.	Bais'wārī (and Bundēl'khaṇḍī).
Chan.	Chandra Kabi's poems, in MS.
Chh. Rām.	The Chhappaī Ramāyan of Tul'sī Dās; (ed. Kāshī Nāth Siŋgh, Dinapore, 1884.)
Cp. Gr.	Beames' Comparative Grammar of the Modern Aryan Languages of India.
Cr.	Materials for a Rural and Agricultural Glossary of the N.-W. P. and Oudh. By William Crooke, B.C.S. (*N.B.*, on p. 4 in the vernacular index the word 'glossary' means the work itself. The page numbers after 39, however, are all incorrect; they should be read as follows:—

Pp.	40 or 41	for pp.	41
„	42, 43	„	41, 42
„	45—89	„	43—87
„	91—111	„	88—108
„	113—115	„	109—111
„	117—to end	„	112 to end.)

Dac. Kōnkaṇī Language and Literature. By J. Gerson Da Cunha. (Bombay, 1881.)

Del. Delius' Radices Pracriticæ.

Dēc. Dēvākṣara Charitra, a drama by Paṇḍit Ravi Datta Shukla, (Light Press, Benares).

Din. Gīt Dīnā Bhadrī, a Maithilī song of the Nēpāl Tarāi (in MS.)

Din. K. Gīt Dīnā Bhadrī Kawand, a Maithilī song of the Nēpāl Tarāi (in MS.)

Dk. Pr. Dākṣiṇātya Prākrit.

Dōh. Dōhābalī, by Tul'sī Dās, (Lucknow Nawal Kishor Press, 1882).

E. English: or, in conjunction with language initials = Eastern: *e.g.*, E. Gḍ. = Eastern Gauḍian.

Ell. Sir H. Elliot's Races of the N. W. Provinces (ed. J. Beames, London, 1869.)

Fam. Famine Song (ed. Grierson, in J. A. S. B., Extra Number for 1882.)

G. Gujarātī.

G. Dy. Shahpurji Edalji's Gujarātī Dictionary.

G. Gr. Shahpurji Edalji's Gujarātī Grammar (Bombay, 1867.)

G. Gr. C. Grammar of the Gujarātī Language. By William Clarkson. (Bombay, 1847.)

Gā. Gāthā.

Gā. Gr. Der Dialect der Gāthās des Lalita Vistara. By Eduard Müller.

Garh. Gaṛhwālī.

Gḍ. Gauḍian.

Gḍ. Gr. Hœrnle's Comparative Grammar of the Gauḍian Languages. (London, 1880.)

Gip. Gipsy.

Gīt. The Gītābalī of Tul'sī Dās (Benares, Light Press, 1869). (N.B.—The Gīt. is quoted by the numbers of the verses and stanzas of each Kāṇḍ; thus, Gīt., Bā. 6, 2, means the second verse of the sixth stanza of the Bāla Kāṇḍ. The pages on which the several Kāṇḍs begin are the following: Bā. on p. 1, A. on p. 170, Ki. on p. 181, Su. on p. 182, Ln. on p. 218, Ut. on p. 234. It should be noted that the numbering of the *mūl* or text is wrong, being carried from the Araṇya Kāṇḍ, straight through the Ki., Su., Ln., and Ut. Kāṇḍs, to the end. The numbering of the Ṭīkā or commentary, however, is correct, and has been followed in all quotations in this Dictionary. Accordingly to find a reference to the Mūl of the Sundar, Laṅkhā and Uttar Khāṇḍs, the numbers 19, 269 (or in the earlier verses 70) and 292 respectively must be added to those given in this Dictionary.)

Gōp. Gīt Rājā Gōpī Chand, a ballad in Bhoj'-pūrī and Magahī (in J. A. S. B., vol. LIV, 1885).

Gor. Folklore from Eastern Gorakh'pūr. By Hugh Fraser, C.S., in J. A. S. B., vol. LII.

Grs. Grierson's Bihār Peasant Life. (Calcutta, Bengal Secretariat Press, 1885.)

H. Hindī; or, in conjunction with other language initials = High: *e.g.*, *H.H.* = High Hindī; *H. Bg.* = High Bangālī.

H. Dy. Bate's Hindī Dictionary.

H. Gr. Kellogg's Hindī Grammar.

H. R. Hœrnle's Collection of Hindī Roots (in J. A. S. B., vol. XLIX). (Those who have the separate reprint, in order to find a reference, must deduct 32 from the figures given in this Dictionary.)

Ham. Popular Songs of the Hamīr'pur district, in Bundēl'khaṇḍ, N.-W.P. (ed. V. A. Smith, in J. A. S. B., vols. XLIV and XLV.)

Han. Hanumān Bāhuk, by Tul'sī Dās (ed. Gōpī Nāth Pāṭhak, Benares, Light Press, 1879).

Hās. Hāsya Pañch Ratna, an Anthology in various languages, by Mahārāj jī Krişņa Lāla, (Benares Añjuman Press, Benares).

Hb. Man'bōdh's Haribans (ed. Grierson, in J. A. S. B., Vol. LI, transl. in vol. LIII).

Hd. Hindūstānī.

Hd. Dy. Fallon's Hindūstānī Dictionary.

Hd. Prov. A dictionary of Hindūstanī Proverbs, by the late S. W. Fallon; (ed. Capt. R. C. Temple. Benares, 1884.)

Hēm. Hēma Chandra's Prākrit Grammar (ed. Pischel).

Hēm. Dy. Hēma Chandra's Dēshīshabdamālā (ed. Pischel).

Hn. Harkh Nāth's Poems (ed. Grierson, in J. A. S. B., Extra Number for 1882).

Ind. Ant. The Indian Antiquary, a Journal of Oriental Research, ed. Jas. Burgess.

J. Jāipūrī.

J. A. S. B. Journal, Asiatic Society of Bengal.

J. G. O. S. Journal, German Oriental Society.

J. R. A. S. Journal, Royal Asiatic Society.

Jan. The Jānakī Maṇgal of Tul'sī Dās, (ed. Prayāg Datt' Siṇgh: Braj Chandra Press, Benares).

Jt. Jātaka (ed. Fausböll).

K. Kanaujī.

K. Rām. The Kabit Rāmāyan of Tul'sī Dās (ed. Gōpī Nāth Pāṭhak, Light Press, Benares, 1879). (It should be noted that the numbering in the Uttar Khaṇḍ is incorrect. The numbers up to 100 are correct, after which they recommence with 1. Accordingly, to find a reference to the latter portion of the Uttar Khaṇḍ, 100 must be deducted from the numbers given in this Dictionary.)

Kalp. Kalpasūtra (ed. Jacobi; in Collection of German Oriental Society, vol. VII, No. 1).

Kan. Lāl Jhā's battle of Kanarpī Ghāṭ (ed. Shrī Nārāyan Siṇgh, in J. A. S. B., vol. LIV, Part I, for 1885).

Kās. Kāsī ke Chhayāchitrā, a drama by Harishchandra, (Hari Prakāsh Press, Benares).

Kch. Kachchayana's Pāli Grammar (ed. Senart; the references are to the separate edition, Paris, 1881).

Kf. Kafirī.

Km. Kumaonī.

Kn. Kōnkaṇī.

Kn. Dy. English-Kōnkaṇī and Kōnkaṇī-English Dictionary, by A. F. X. Maffei. (Mangalore, Basel Mission Press, 1883.)

Kn. Gr. Maffei's Kōnkaṇī Grammar. (Mangalore, 1882.)

Kram. Kramadīshvara's Prākrit Grammar.

Krish. Shrī Krishnagītāvalī, (ed. Munshī Mahāvīr Prasād, Lakhnau, Nawal Kishōr Press, 1884.)

Krishnab. Krishnābalī of Tul'sī Dās (Braj Chandra Press, Benares, 1882).

Ksh. Kāshmīrī.

Ksh. Vy. Elmslie's Kāshmīrī Vocabulary.

L. L. Borrow's Romano Lavo Lil (ed. 1874.)

L. V. Lalita Vistara (ed. R. Mitra, in Bibliotheca Indica).

Ln. Lanman's Statistical Account of Noun Inflection in the Veda. (In Journal of American Oriental Society, vol. X.)

Ls. Lassen's Institutiones Linguæ Pracriticæ.

Lt. Latin.

M. Marāṭhī; or, in conjunction with other language initials = Modern: *e.g.*, *M. Gḍ.* = Modern Gauḍian; *M. M.* = Modern Marāṭhī.

M. Dy. Molesworth's Marāṭhī Dictionary.

M. Gr. Student's Manual of Marāṭhī Grammar (2nd ed., 1880).

Ma. V. Mahāvastu (ed. Senart, in Oriental Collection of Société Asiatique).

Mag. A collection of songs in impure Magahı (in MS.)

Mars. Marsīā (ed. Grierson, in J. A. S. B., Extra Number for 1882).

Mcch. Mṛichchhakaṭikā (ed. Stenzler).

Mḍ. Mārkaṇḍēya's Prākrit Grammar.

Mg. Magahī (dialect of Bihārī).

Mg. Pr. Māgadhī Prākrit.

Mh. Pr. Māhārāṣṭrī Prākrit.

Misc. A collection of miscellaneous folksongs in Bhoj'pūrī, Bais'wāṛī, and Hindı (in MS.)

Mik. Ueber die Mundarten und die Wanderungen der Zigeuner Europa's. By Dr. Franz Miklosich (Vienna, 1872–1880.)

Ml. Multānī (dialect of Panjābī).

Ml. Gy. O'Brien's Glossary of the Multānī Language, compared with the Panjābī and Sindhī. (Lahore 1881.)

Mr. Mār'wāṛī (and Mewāṛī).

Mth. Maithilī.

Mth. Ch. Grierson's Maithil Chrestomathy (in J. A. S. B., Extra Number for 1882).

Mth. Gr. Grierson's Maithil Grammar (in J. A. S. B., Extra Number for 1880).

Muh. Muhammadan.

N. Naipālī: or, in conjunction with language initials = Northern: *e.g., N. Gḍ.* = Northern Gauḍian.

N. Acts. The Acts of the Apostles in Naipālī.

N. Gr. Grammar of the Nepalese Language. By Lieut. J. A. Ayton. (Calcutta, 1820.)

N. L. S. Luke's Gospel in Naipālī.

Nāg. Nāg Songs (ed. Grierson, in J. A. S. B., Extra Number for 1882).

Nah. The Rām Lalākar Nah'chhū of Tul'sī Dās (ed. Prayāg Datt' Siṅgh: Braj Chandra Press, Benares).

Nām. The Pāiyalachchhı Nāmamāla, a Prakrit Kosha by Dhanapāla (ed. G. Bühler, Göttingen, 1879).

Nāy. Specimen of the Nāyā Dhamma Kahā (ed. Steinthal, Leipzig, 1881).

Neb. Gīt Nebārak, a modern Maithilī song (in MS.)

Nir. Nirayāvaliyā Suttam (ed. Warren).

O. Oṛiyā: or, in conjunction with language initials = Old: *e.g., O. H.* = Old Hindī; *O. Bg.* = Old Bangālī.

O. Dy. Sutton's English and Oṛiyā Dictionary.

O. Gr. Sutton's Oṛiyā Grammar. (Cuttack, 1872.)

O. Vy. Mohunpersaud Takoor's Vocabulary, Oṛiyā and English. (Serampore 1811.)

P. Panjābī.

P. Dy. Panjābī Dictionary, printed in Lodiāna.

P. Dy. St. Dictionary of English and Panjābī. By Captain Starkey. (Calcutta, 1849.)

P. Gr. Panjābī Grammar, printed in Lodiāna.

Pā. Pāli.

Pā. Dy. Childers' Pāli Dictionary.

Pā. Gr. Minayef's Pāli Grammar (tr. Guyard).

Pā. Gr. K. Beiträge zur Pāli Grammatik. By E. Kuhn. (Berlin, 1875.)

Padm. Padmāwat, by Malik Mohammad Jāy'sī (ed. Rām Jasan; Chandra Prabhā Press, Benares, 1884.)

Pārb. The Pārbatī Maṅgal of Tul'sī Dās (ed. Prayāg Datt' Siṅgh; Braj Chandra Press, Benares.)

Port. Portuguese.

Pr. Prākrit.

Pr. L. Prākṛita Lakṣaṇa (ed. Hœrnle, in Bibliotheca Indica.)

Prabh. Prabhābatı Haran, a drama by Bhānu Nāth Jhā, in MS.

Prop. A dissertation on the proper names of Panjābīs, by Captain R. C. Temple. (Bombay, 1883.)

Prs. Persian.

Psh. Pr. Paiśhāchī Prākrit.

Psh. Pashtu.

Psp. Paspati's Études sur les Tchingianés.

Psp. M. Paspati's Memoir on the Language of the Gypsies (in Journal of the American Oriental Society, vol. VII, pp. 143—270). (Those who have the separate reprint, in order to find a reference, must deduct 142 from the figures given in this Dictionary.)

Rām. The Rāmāyan of Tul'sī Dās (ed. Rām Jasan: Benares, 1869; transl. F. S. Growse, C.S., 2nd ed., with illustrations: Allahabad, 1883).

Rāv. Rāvaṇavaho or Setubandha (ed. S. Goldschmidt).

Rg. Raŋg'pūrī.

Rg. Gr. Notes on the Raŋgpūrī Dialect, by G. A. Grierson (in J. A. S. B., vol. XLVI).

Rig. Wörterbuch zum Rig-Veda, by H. Grassmann (Leipzig).

Rj. Rāj'pūtānī.

S. Sindhī: or, in conjunction with language initials = Southern: *e.g., S. Gḍ.* = Southern Gauḍian, &c.

S. Dy. Shirt, Thavurdas, and Mirza's Dictionary; (Kurrachee, Commissioner's Printing Press, 1879.)

S. Gr. Trumpp's Sindhī Grammar (London and Leipzig, 1872).

S. Vy. Eastwick's Sindhī Vocabulary.

Sal. Song of Salhēs (ed. Grierson, in J. A. S. B., Extra Number for 1882).

San. The Bairāgya Sandīpinī of Tul'sī Dās (ed. Prayāg Datt' Siŋgh: Braj Chandra Press, Benares.)

Saŋk. Saŋkat Mōchan, by Tul'sī Dās (Lucknow, 1879).

Sapt. Sapta Shataka (ed. Weber, in Collection of German Oriental Society, vol. VII, No. 4.)

Sat. The Sat'saī of Tul'sī Dās (ed. Gōpī Nāth Pāṭhak, Benares, Light Press).

Sgh. Singhalese.

Shr. Pr. Shaurasēnī Prākrit.

Siv. Siva Siŋgha Sarōja, or Notices of Vernacular Poets, by Siv Siŋgh, Inspector of Police. (Lucknow, Nawal Kishōr Press, 1883.)

Skr. Sanskrit.

Skr. Dy. Bœhtlingk's Sanskrit Dictionary (being the smaller edition of the Petersburg Dictionary).

Skr. Dy. P. Petersburg Sanskrit Dictionary.

Skr. Dy. W. Monier Williams' Sanskrit Dictionary.

Sudh. Sudhābund, a collection of sixty Kajalīs, by Kumār Lāl Kharg Bahādur. (Bankipore, Khadgbilas Press, 1884.)

Sun. Sundarī Tilak (Benares, Light Press edition).

T. Türkī.

Tv. Trivikrama's Prākrit Grammar.

Vaish. Twenty one Vaishṇava Hymns; ed. and transl. by G. A. Grierson (in J. A. S. B., vol. LIII, Part I, Special Number for 1884).

Ved. Vedic.

Vr. Vararuchi's Prākrit Grammar (ed. Cowell).

W. In conjunction with other language initials = Western: *e.g., W. Gḍ.* = Western Gauḍian.

Wat. Watson's Index to Names of Eastern Plants and Products (London, 1868).

Wil. Glossary of Judicial and Revenue Terms and of useful words occurring in Official Documents of British India. By H. H. Wilson. (London, 1855.)

Z. Zend.

Zach. Beitræge zur Indischen Lexicographie von Theodor Zachariæ (Berlin, 1883).

II.—*Grammatical and other Terms.*

abbr.	abbreviated.
abl.	ablative.
abs.	abstract.
acc.	accusative.
act.	active (case *or* voice *or* verb).
adj.	adjective.
adv.	adverb.
aff.	affix.
agric.	agricultural.
anon.	anonymous.
art.	article.
auxil.	auxiliary.
caus.	causal.
cf.	confer, compare.
ch.	chaupai.
chap.	chapter.
cl.	class.
coll.	colloquial.
com.	commonly.
com. gen.	common gender.
comm.	commentary.
comp.	compound.
con.	concrete.
cond.	conditional.
conj.	conjunct *or* conjugation *or* conjunctive.
cons.	consonant.
constr.	construction.
cont.	contemptuous.
contr.	contracted *or* contraction.
cor.	corrupt.
corr.	correct.
correl.	correlative *or* correlative pronoun.
dat.	dative.
dem.	demonstrative pronoun.
den.	denominative.
der.	derivation *or* derivative.
dim.	diminutive.
dir.	direct.
do.	dōhā, a Hindū metre.
du.	dual.
emph.	emphatic.
esp.	especial.
euph.	euphonic.
exam.	example.
exc.	except *or* exception.
f. or *fem.*	feminine.
fac.	facetious.
fig.	figurative.
fut.	future.
gen.	genitive *or* general.
geog.	geographical.
gram.	grammatical.
imp.	imperfect tense.
imper.	imperative mood.
incorr.	incorrect.
ind.	indicative mood.
indef.	indefinite *or* indefinitive.
inf.	infinitive.
instr.	instrumental.
intens.	intensitive.
inter.	interrogative pronoun *or* interrogative.
intr.	intransitive.
introd.	introduction.
l.	line.
lg. f.	long form.
lit.	literally.
loc.	locative.
m. or *masc.*	masculine.
m.c.	metri causa, *or* 'for the sake of metre.'
med.	medical.
met.	metaphorical.
myth.	mythological.
n. or *neut.*	neuter.
neg.	negative.
nom.	nominative.
num.	numeral.
obl.	oblique.
obs.	obsolete.
obsc.	sensu obscœno.
opp.	opposite.
orig.	original.
p.	page.
p.p.	past participle.
part.	participle.
pt.	particle.
pass.	passive.
pers.	person *or* personal.
phon.	phonetic.
phr.	phrase.
pl. or *plur.*	plural.
pleon.	pleonastic.
poet.	poetical.
postpos.	postposition.
pphr.	periphrastic.
pr. pts.	principal parts of a verb, *i.e.* the present participle, the past participle, the verbal noun in *b*, and the oblique verbal noun in *ai*.

prec.	precative.
pref.	prefix.
prep.	preposition.
pres.	present.
pret.	preterite.
prim.	primary.
pron.	pronoun *or* pronominal.
prop.	properly.
prov.	proverb.
q.v.	quod vide, *or* 'which see.'
qual.	quality *or* qualitative.
quant.	quantity *or* quantitative.
red.	redundant.
red. f.	redundant form.
redupl.	reduplication *or* reduplicated.
refl.	reflexive.
rel.	relative.
resp.	respective.
s.v.	sub voce.
sc.	scene (in a drama).
scl.	scilicet *or* to be understood.
sec.	secondary.
sg. or *sing.*	singular.
sh. f.	short form.
st.	stem.
str. f.	strong form.
subst.	substantive.
suff.	suffix.
tbh. or *tadbh.*	tadbhava.
tech.	technical.
term.	termination.
tr.	transitive.
transl.	translated *or* translation.
ts. or *tats.*	tatsama.
unphon.	unphonetic.
v.	verb.
v. intr.	verb intransitive.
v. tr.	verb transitive.
voc.	vocative.
vr. l.	varia lectio.
vs.	verse.
vulg.	vulgar.
wom.	used by women.
wk. f.	weak form.
√	root.

N.B.—Abbreviations of adjectives may also be used as abbreviations of the corresponding adverbs.

III.—*In Quotations from the Rāmāyan.*

A.	*Ajōdhyā Kāṇḍ.*
Ar.	*Aranya Kāṇḍ.*
Bā.	*Bāl Kāṇḍ.*
Ki.	*Kis'kindā Kāṇḍ.*
Ln.	*Laṅkā Kāṇḍ.*
Su.	*Sundar Kāṇḍ.*
Ut.	*Uttar Kāṇḍ.*
ch.	chaupāī.
chh.	chhand.
do.	dōhā.
so.	sor'ṭhā.
toṭ.	tōṭak.

A

COMPARATIVE DICTIONARY

OF THE

BIHĀRĪ LANGUAGE.

अ a

अ *a* (1), *the first letter of the* Bihārī *alphabet, represents three distinct vowels. First, it indicates* [1]*a short vowel, which we, for the sake of convenience (see Introd.), transliterate with* a, *but which really has, as a rule, the sound of short* ăw *(or short broad* ŏ), *as in the English* '*hot,*' '*not,*' *though not quite so deep as the corresponding* Bangālī ăw. *Secondly, it sometimes indicates* [2]*a long vowel, the sound of which is a long* āw *(or long broad* ō, *see Introd.), as in the English* '*awe,*' '*law.*' *In this case it is distinguished in this Dictionary by placing the prosodic mark of length* (ॅ) *over it and transliterating it by* â, *thus* हॅ *hâ. Thirdly, it sometimes indicates* [3]*a mere imperfect vowel (see Introd.), the sound of which is a very short* ĕ, *as in the English* '*bigger*' *(see Sweet's Handbook of Phonetics,* § 200). *In this case it is distinguished, in this Dictionary, by a dot* (॰) *placed in line after the consonant, and transliterated by the apostrophe; thus* क॰ *k*', ग्य॰ *gy*'.

With regard to the use of the sign अ *and its new substitutes, it should be noted that the former* (अ) *is never used except at the beginning of a word or after another vowel, as* अगा *agâ* before, नौअवा *naũawâ* barber. *In the middle of a word, after a cons., it is always omitted, its absence indicating the presence of the vowel it represents, according to the native grammarians' theory that the sound of* a *inheres in every consonant unless otherwise specified; thus* कली *kalī* bud, हॅवीं *hâwī* I am, घर॰वा *ghar'wâ* house. *The last two examples illustrate the use of the new signs, which practically serve as substitutes for the omitted* अ *when it is either a long or an imperfect vowel. At the end of a word, also, it has been the common practice hitherto to omit the sign* अ. *This practice has a very serious inconvenience. There are but very few cases in which any of the three sounds of* अ *is pronounced at the end of a word after a consonant, whereas the omission of the sign* अ, *according to the already-mentioned grammatical theory, would indicate the necessity of pronouncing an inherent* a *after every final consonant. For this reason the sign* ऽ *or* ॰ *(see Introd.) is adopted in this Dictionary to replace the sign* अ *whenever any of its sounds are pronounced at the end of a word; the sign* ऽ *signifying the full (short or long) sound of* अ, *and the sign* ॰ *its imperfect sound. Hence when any word is spelt without* ऽ *or* ॰, *it must be read as ending in a consonant. The principal cases when there is a final audible sound are given below; and it will be noticed that the short sound* a *occurs in the first case, the long sound* â *in the second, and the imperfect sound in the two remaining cases. With the exception of these cases, no word is ever pronounced with a final* a; *thus* अङ्ग *ayg* limb, घर *ghar* house, कमल *kamal* lotus, *etc. It should be noted, however, that this rule is only applicable to prose. In poetry every final* a *is pronounced as the imperfect vowel; and hence in verse quotations the substitutes* ऽ *or* ॰ *will not be used, the absence of the vowel sign being understood to be, as usual, an indication of the vowel pronunciation.*

With regard to the occurrence of the various sounds of अ, *the following rules may be given.* [1]*The short* ăw*-sound is the regular and most common one. It is not the Sanskrit open* a, *nor the common* Hindī a *(which sounds less hollow), nor is it like the English* u *in* '*nut,*' '*but.*' *It is something between the* u *in* '*nut*' *and the* (Bangālī) ŏ *or* ăw *in* '*not,*' *but exactly agrees with neither. It may occur in any syllable, whether open or closed, stressed or unstressed, whether initial or medial or final; thus* घर *ghăwr* house, अमर *ăwmăwr* immortal, कमल *kăwmăwl* lotus,

करल्वक *kǎwr'lǎwk* he did, नउ *nǎw* not. [2]*The long* ǎw-*sound has been observed by us in the following cases:*—(1) *the auxiliary verb* √ हैव *hǎw* be (*e.g.*, हैवीं *hǎwī* I am); (2) *the Bhoj'pūrī pres. ind.* (*e.g.*, देखैलों *dēkhǎlō̃* I see); (3) *the termination of the 2nd pers. plur. of any tense* (*e.g.*, देखैऽ *dēkhǎ* may ye see, *Bh.* देखैलैऽ *dēkhǎlǎ* you see, *Bh.* देखल्बैऽ *dekh'bǎ* or *Mth.* देखल्बैह *dekh'bǎh* you will see); (4) *in the Maithilī abl. postpos.* सैं *sǎ̃* (*e.g.*, मुख सैं *mukh sǎ̃* from the mouth, *Bid.* 6, 2); (5) *in the Magahī termination of the obl. form of nouns in silent* a (*e.g.*, घरैऽ कैं *gharǎ kǎ̃ī* to a house, देखैऽ कैं *dēkhǎ kǎ̃ī* to see, *J. A. S. B., vol.* LII, *pp.* 151, 154). *The Bihārīs have no special graphic sign for this peculiar long sound, but, when necessary, they sometimes indicate it by placing the prosodic mark of length* (ˉ) *over* अ (*thus* हैवौं); *or, though incorrectly, write it as* औ (*e.g.*, हौवौं, *or, as in the Āzamgaṛh Settlement Report*, *p.* 20A, हौवे); *or, still less correctly, they express it by adding the visarga* (*e.g.*, देखःलों I see, देखःऽ you see, *see Gd. Gr.*, *p.* 26, *footnote*). *It is, however, clearly nothing else but the long sound corresponding to the common short sound* ǎw, *these two forming an exact pair of short and long vowels.* [3]*The imperfect a-sound never occurs in the beginning of a word. In the middle of a word it is not uncommon, though no exact rules as to its occurrence can be given, except that* (1) *it is usually met with between two syllables, the second of which contains a long vowel, as in* घरल्वा *ghar'wǎ* house, सुतल्लै *sut'lǎ̃i* he slept; *and* (2) *it always occurs between or after two consonants which originally formed a conjunct consonant, as in* सबल्द *sab'd* word, जतल्न *jat'n* purpose, किरल्पा *kir'pǎ* grace, परल्योजन *par'yōjan* need (*from Skr.* शब्द, यत्न, कृपा, प्रयोजन). *At the end of a word it never occurs in prose, except in the two last cases, mentioned below, of the final audible* अ. *In poetry, as already mentioned, every final* अ *is pronounced as the imperfect vowel.*

At the end of a word the vowel अ *is audible in the following cases:*—(1) *in monosyllables, as* नउ *na* not; (2) *in the 2nd pers. plur., as* देखैऽ *dēkhǎ* may ye see; (3) *after a double consonant, as* रिच्छऽ *richchh'* bear, दत्तऽ *datt'* given; (4) *after* य, *or a conjunct consonant the latter part of which is* य, *as* अकथल्नीयऽ *akath'nīy'* unspeakable, अजोग्यऽ *ajogy'* unworthy, ग्राह्यऽ *grǎjhy'* acceptable. *In the case of most other conjunct consonants their component parts are pronounced separately with the interposition of the imperfect vowel, so that the word practically ends in a single consonant, without any inherent* a; *thus* जुकल्त *juk't* joined (*Skr.* युक्त), सबल्द *sab'd* word (*Skr.* शब्द), जनल्म *jan'm* birth (*Skr.* जन्म), पुतल्र *put'r* son (*Skr.* पुत्र), सुकल्ल *suk'l* white (*Skr.* शुक्ल), किरसल्न *Krish'n* Krishna (Skr. कृष्ण), *etc.*; *but if the conj. cons. consists of a nasal or a sibilant followed by a mute, it is treated like a single cons., that is, it is pronounced without any inherent* a; *thus* अङ्ग *ayg* limb, अन्त *ant* end, दण्ड *daṇḍ* staff, *and* समस्त *samast* whole, गिहस्त *grihast* (*Mth.*) *or* गिरल्हस्त *gir'hast* (*Bh.*) householder (*Skr.* गृहस्थ), पुस्प *pusp or* पुश्प *pushp* flower (*Skr.* पुष्प).

It may be added that in Bais'wārī the letter अ, *inherent in a preceding* य y *or* व w, *is sometimes written to express the short vowels* ए e *and* ओ o *respectively; thus in the pron. forms* ज्यहि, ज्यन, *and* म्वहि, स्वइ, *pronounced* jehi, jen, *and* mohi, soï, *for* जेहि, जेन, *and* मोहि, सोइ, *etc. On the same principle the Skr.* व्यक्ति *vyakti* person *becomes* बेकत *bekat in Bihārī* (*cf. Bid.* 8, 2).

[*The ancient Indo-aryan language possessed a pair of short and long sounds of* a, *pronounced clear and open, like* a *in the German 'mǎnn' and 'māhl,' Italian 'bǎllo' and 'bāco.' The short sound of* ǎ *does not occur in English, but the long* ā *is met with in words like 'far', 'star.' In Sanskrit these were graphically represented by* अ ǎ *and* आ ā. *The sound of* अ, *however, began to undergo changes from very early times. These changes took two different directions. On the one hand, the sound* a *tended to be obscured into a short* ĕ, *on the other, into a short* ŏ (*compare the analogous change of* a *in Greek to* ε *and* ο), *by which two sounds are not to be understood a clear* ĕ *and* ŏ, *but obscure sounds like German* ĕ (*or* æ) *short and English* ǎw *short, pronounced something like* ĕ *in 'error' and* ŏ *in 'hot.'* (*Cf. Sweet's Phonetics*, §§ 31, 66, 71–74.) *The former sound is best represented by the common* अ *of the Hindī, the latter by the common* अ *of the Bangālī; thus* घर *ghar, pronounced H. ghĕr, Bg. ghŏr. The tendency of* a *to change to short* ĕ *is already noticed by the most ancient native grammarians* (*Prātishākyas and Pāṇini in the 3rd cent. B.C.; see Whitney's Skr. Gr.*, § 21, *p.* 9), *who call the vowel so changed* संवृत *saṁvṛita or 'dimmed.' The tendency of* a *to change to short* ŏ *probably also declared itself very early, though no similar testimony on this point seems to be available. The evidence of the modern Gauḍians, however, shows that the former tendency affected more the centre and west of India, while the latter was active in the east and extreme south. Thus* अ *is pronounced as short* ĕ *in all Western Gauḍians* (*Hindī, Panjābī, Sindhī, Gujarātī*) *and in the Southern Gauḍian* (*or Marāṭhī*) *with the exception of the Kōnkaṇī dialect of the Marāṭhī, in the extreme south, near Goa. On the* other hand, अ is pronounced as short ŏ (or ăw) in all Eastern Gauḍians (Bihārī, Bangālī, Oṛiyā) and in the Kōnkaṇī. In Bangālī the ŏ-sound is most clearly developed (see Bg. Gr., pp. 7, 8), less so in Oṛiyā (O. Gr., p. 1., Op. Gr., p. 67) and Kōnkaṇī (Kn. Gr., p. 5), and also less so in Bihārī, in the westernmost dialects of which (Bais'wārī, Western Bhoj'pūrī) the ĕ-sound already predominates. In the Gipsy both changes, ĕ and ŏ, are found in different words; thus desh, 'ten,' but shov, 'six;' see Psp. M., pp. 230, 231 (Skr. दश and षट्). The result of the process thus far explained was to give to the Gauḍian two a-sounds. One was short (ĕ or ŏ), and was the obscure close representative of the ancient short open a, while the other was long and identical with the ancient long open ā. But by the side of this process there gradually developed in the Eastern Gauḍians another, which consisted in creating on the one hand a long counterpart of the short close a, and on the other hand a short counterpart of the long open ā. Thus the final result of the two processes was to produce two pairs of a-sounds, one being open, the other close, and each pair consisting of a short and long sound. Moreover, the second process led to a further important result in the Eastern Gauḍians. The fact that the two initial sounds were the short close a and the long open ā, and were graphically represented by अ and आ respectively, had practically the effect of causing these two graphic signs to be looked upon as serving to distinguish not so much the quantity as the tone of those two a-sounds. In other words, अ became the sign, not of the short a-sound, but of the close a-sound, while similarly आ became the sign, not of the long, but of the open a-sound. When this result had been attained, it obviously became necessary to devise some new marks to distinguish the quantities of the new pair of a-sounds, whenever such distinction appeared to be desirable. In the ordinary converse of life, indeed, this necessity was not much felt; it is a common observation that people will continue, without much practical inconvenience, a system of spelling which no longer conforms to the realities of pronunciation; and thus at the present day natives as a rule use the signs अ and आ for the close and open sounds without distinction of quantity. Still occasionally there is need of defining quantity, and then, as already explained, various means are resorted to. One of these, the system of using prosodic marks, has been adopted in this Dictionary, as being the simplest and most consistent. According to this system the long close a-sound (i.e., āw) is represented by अ̄ (i.e., अ plus the prosodic mark of length), and the short open a-sound (i.e., ă) is indicated by आ̆ (i.e., आ plus the prosodic mark of shortness). The system of E. Gd. a-sounds and their graphic representations may then be thus tabularly shown :—

Close a-sound ... { Short, अ a (= ŏw).
{ Long, अ̄ ā (= āw).

Open a-sound ... { Short, आ̆ ă.
{ Long, आ ā.

The creation of a short counterpart to the long open ā in the E. Gd. appears in every case to be due to the shortening of an original long open ā, and is most frequently the result of the law of shortening the antepenultimate (see Introd.). Thus, B. खाटिया khăṭiyā bed (lg. f. of खाट khāt); B. खाइलों khăilō̃, Bg. खाइलाम khăilām, O. खाइलुँ khăilū̃ I ate (from √ खा khā); B. मारलों măr'lō̃, Bg. मारिलाम mărilām, O. मारिलुँ mărilū̃ I beat; Bg. मारिया măriyā having beaten, खाइया khăiyā having eaten, आसिया ăsiyā having come, etc. (The short pronunciation of आ in all these cases is strikingly shown by the contraction of आ + इ ăi to ē in Bangālī (colloquially, see Bg. Gr., p. 330) and to ăi in Bihārī; thus Bg. खेलाम khēlām, B. खेलों khăilō̃ I ate; Bg. मेरे mērē having beaten, etc.) It should be observed, however, that in the case of the shortening the antepenultimate of long forms (but of no others) there is a tendency (imperative in Western Bhoj'pūrī and Bais'wārī, but optional in the other dialects of Bihārī) to substitute the short close a for the short open ă; thus in Bw. and W. Bh. only खटिया khaṭiyā, but खटिया khaṭiyā or खाटिया khăṭiyā in Mth., Mg., and E. Bh. But besides the case of the antepenultimate, the short open ă occurs also in other cases; e.g., in tatsamas which originally contained a long open ā before a conj. cons.; thus, B., Bg., and O. न्याय्य nyăjy' just (Skr. न्याय्य), वाक्य băky' sentence (Skr. वाक्य), ग्राह्य grăjhy' acceptable (Skr. ग्राह्य), बाह्य băjhy' external (Skr. बाह्य), etc. For some other cases, see the Art. आ ā. The existence of the long counterpart (āw) of the short close a in Bangālī and Oṛiyā has not as yet been specially noticed by grammarians; but in Bangālī it occurs, for example, in the vocative term. of such nouns as पिता father, माता mother (e.g., हे पिताः he pitā! oh father!). It is now usual in Bangālī to spell these forms with the visarga (पिताः, माताः), a practice which has led to the mistaken notion that they are identical with the Sanskrit vocatives thus spelt (see Bg. Gr., p. 65), but which is none else than the erroneous practice already noticed as being also found in Bihārī writers. The creation of this long āw appears in most, if not all, cases to be due to the curtailment of a syllable which in the preceding stage of the Ap. Pr. contained an उ u. Thus 2nd pers. plur. B. देखह dekhā = Ap. Pr.

देखलउ; *Bh.* देखैलैंह *dēkhâlâ* = *Ap. Pr.* देखलउ + अहउ (*see Gḍ. Gr.*, §§ 497, 501); *voc.*, *Bg.* पितैंह *pitâ* = *Ap. Pr.* पितअउ *or* पितअहो (*see Gḍ. Gr.*, § 369); *pres. ind.*, *Bh.* देखैलौं *dēkhâlō̃* = *Ap. Pr.* देखलवं + अहवं (*see Gḍ. Gr.*, §§ 497, 501); *auxil. verb* हैव *hâw is contracted from Ap. Pr.* हविच *or* अविच (*Gḍ. Gr.*, § 514); *abl. postpos.* सैं *sẫ is a contraction of the alternative form* सौं *sâũ*; *obl. sing.* घरैंह = *Ap. Pr. gen. sg.* घरह (*see Gḍ. Gr.*, *p.* 195, *J. A. S. B.*, *vol.* LII, *p.* 163). *Respecting the Western and Southern Gauḍians, it remains to be added that in them the ancient short open ă has often survived, in words like* गन *găn* multitude (*Skr.* गण), *etc.*, *especially in onomatopœic words like* झन झन *jhăn jhăn* jingling, *and frequently in stressed syllables, like* कमल *kămal*, *but E. Gḍ. kăwmal*.

With regard to the Bais'wārī practice of expressing ए *e by* अ, *it may be noted that the same use is also sometimes observed in Bangālī; e.g.*, देखाजाय he is seen, *pronounced dekhăjăi*, व्यक्ति individual, *pronounced bekti.*]

अ *a* (2), (*f.* अ *a or* इ *i*; *str. f.*, *m.* आ *ā*, *f.* ई *ī*), **Ts.**, *a prim. der. suff. used to form nouns of action.* **Exam.**, खेल *m.*, *and* खेल *or* खेलि *f.* play, *from* √ खेल play; *sh. f.* हँस *m.*, हँस *or* हँसि *f.*, *str. f.* हँसा *m.*, हँसी *f.* laughter, *from* √ हँस laugh; मार *or* मारि *f.* beating, *from* √मार beat; *wk. f.* बोल *f.*, *and str. f.* बोली *f.* language, *from* √ बोल speak. *See art.* आ *ā* (2) *and art.* इ *i* (2).

(*It should be remembered that this suff. becomes silent in prose, though not in poetry, according to the ordinary rule regarding a final* अ, *as explained in art.* अ *a* (1). *The fem. gender is the more usual one in words formed with this suff. The fem. form in* इ *i is common in the poetry of all dialects, but in prose it is almost entirely limited to the Mth. dialect, the corresponding fem. form in the other dialects ending in silent* अ *a. The complete set, consisting of masc. and fem., short and long forms, does not exist in every instance. Practice alone can supply the needful information on this point*).

[*The original of this suff. is the Skr. suff.* अ, *which* (*in the nom. sg.*) *forms m.* अः, *f.* आ. *In Pr. the fem. suff.* ई *may be substituted for* आ (*see Hēm.* iii, 32, *Vr.* v, 24), *the Pr. set of the suff. thus becoming m.* ओ, *f.* आ *or* ई. *In Gḍ.*, *according to its usual phon. laws, this set changes to m.* अ, *f.* अ *or* इ; *see Gḍ. Gr.*, *p.* 155, § 329; *also* §§ 41-51. *The lg. f. of this suff. is made by the addition of the pleon. suff.* क; *see the art.* आ *ā* (2) *and* क *ka.*]

अ *a* (3), **Tbh.**, *pref. euph.*, *added to words beginning with a conj. cons. the first part of which is* स; *thus* अस्नान bathing (*Rām.*, *Ut.*, *ch.* 30, 2; *Skr.* स्नान), अस्तुति praise (*Rām.*, *Bā.*, *ch.* 93, 8; *Skr.* स्तुति), अस्थान place (*San.*, *vs.* 39; *Skr.* स्थान). *Sometimes the conj. cons. is dissolved; e.g.*, असनान *Gōp.* 13; असतुति *Bih.* iii, 9. *Optionally, and perhaps preferably,* इ *is prefixed to such words, e.g.*, इस्कोल school (*B. Gr.* II (*Bh.*), *conversation* 20), इस्थिर firm (*Padm.*, *ch.* 618, 7; *Skr.* स्थिर); *see art.* इ *i* (4).

[*That the euph. use of the pref.* अ *was not entirely unknown in mediæval and ancient India may be conjectured from such instances as Skr.* कुप्य *or* अकुप्य, base metal, *Skr.* अनेडमूक *or* एडमूक, dumb (*see Goldstücker's Skr. Dy.*, *s.v.* अ); *and the existence of the Gā.* इत्थी, इत्थिआ (*L. V.*, *p.* 269, *l.* 10; *Gā. Gr.*, *p.* 14), *Pā.* इत्थी, इत्थिका (*Pā. Dy.*), *Pr.* इत्थी, इत्थिआ (*Hēm.* ii, 130; *according to Vr.* xii, 22 *only Shr. Pr.*), *for Skr.* स्त्री, *seems to point in the same direction. On the other hand, instances like the Skr. astronomical terms* कौर्प scorpion (*Greek* σκορπίος), कोण 'kronos' (*Greek* κρόνος)—*see Weber's History of Indian Literature, p.* 254, *footnote—indicate an alternative treatment of initial conj. cons. In all Gḍs. the euph. use of the pref.* अ *prevails.*]

अ *a* (4), **Ts.**, *pref. neg.*, *added to words* (*subst.*, *adj.*, *part.*, *num.*, *or adv.*) [1]*to negative their meaning, like the E.* in-, un-, dis-, *or* [2]*to depreciate it; thus* [1]अज्ञान ignorance (*Rām.*, *B.*, *ch.* 64, 1; *from* ज्ञान knowledge), अचल immoveable (*Rām.*, *Bā.*, *ch.* 2, 11; *from* चल moveable); अविशेषे without distinction (*Bid.* 29, 3; *from* विशेषे specially); *again* [2]अदिन an unlucky day (*Padm.*, *ch.* 419, 3; *from* दिन day). *It becomes* अन *an, if the word begins with a vowel; thus* अनादर disrespect (*Vaish.* iv, 2, *from* आदर respect), अनुचित improper (*Bid.* 51, 4, *from* उचित proper), अनेक many, *lit.* not one (*Bid.* 45, 1, *from* एक one). *Not unfrequently it is pleonastically reduplicated* अन *an* + अ *a*, *in which form it occurs both before words beginning with a consonant and words beginning with a vowel; thus, before cons.*, अनचिन्ह unnoticed (*Sal.* 18; *from* चिन्ह mark), अनभयउ not having become (*Rām.*, *Bā.*, *ch.* 176, 2, अनभयउ बिहाना when it had not yet become morning, *from* भयउ having become, *past part.* = *Skr.* भूतः); *again before vowels*, अनअधिकारी *an'adhikārī* uninitiated (*Rām.*, *Bā.*, *ch.* 118, 1, *from* अधिकारी initiated), अनइच्छित *an'ichchhit* undesired (*Rām.*, *Ut.*, *ch.* 116, 4, *from* इच्छित desired). *If thus used pleonastically,* अन *is practically treated as a separate word.*

[अ, *before vowels* अन, *is well known in Skr. as a neg. pref. There are even a few, though doubtful and mostly vedic cases of its reduplication;*

e.g., अकाकाल famine (अ not + अकाल inauspicious time, famine, *there is no real word* आकाल), *ved.* अभाभयिन् fearless (अ not + अभयिन् fearless, *there is no real word* आभयिन्); *see Goldstücker's Skr. Dy., s. vv. In Pr. also it is well known, both in its simple and reduplicated forms; examples of the latter are* अअचिंतिअं unconsidered (*from* चिंतिअं considered, *Hēm.* ii, 190), अईईर freedom from calamity (*from* ईति calamity, *Aup.* § 4). *The same remark applies to all Gḍs.*]

अ *a* (5), **Tbh.**, *pref. intens.*, very, excessively, *sometimes added to words to emphasise their meaning; thus* अकोप great destruction (*Hb.* v, 35, *for* कोप), अचपल very unsteady (*for* चपल), अदूर very difficult (*Āz. Gy. for* दूर); *occasionally in compounds, as* अकाय *or* अकाए very great, huge (*Hb.* iii, 10, *lit.* having a large body, *from* काय body).

[*Skr.* अति, *Pr.* अइ; *hence Gḍ.* ऐ *and shortened* अ; *see the remarks on derivation under the art.* अकाय. *The origin of this pref.* अ, *however, is now lost sight of, and it is added, at pleasure, to tats. as well as tadbh. words.*]

अ *a* (6), **Tbh.**, *pref. pleon., added to many words without modifying their meaning, as in* अघरघु destroyer (*Pārv. dq.* 13), अनन्द *happiness* (*Jan., ch.* 12), असीस *blessing* (*Jan., ch.* 5, *Nah., vs.* 17), अधार support, food (*San., vs.* 53), अकाश *sky* (*Hb.* i, 36), *etc.*

[*Skr.* आ; *in Pā. and Pr. generally* आ, *but occasionally shortened to* अ *with doubling of the succeeding cons.; thus Pr.* अघग्घओ (*Nām., vs.* 23) destroyer (= *Skr.* आघातकः), *Pr.* अल्लवालं (*Nām., vs.* 203) pond (= *Skr.* आलवालं), *Pā.* अविद्धो removed (= *Skr.* आविद्धः), *Pā.* अल्लीणो *or Pr.* अल्लीणो (*Hēm.* iv, 54, *Nāy.* 117) *attached* (= *Skr.* आलीनः), *Pr.* अच्छायणं (*Kalp.* § 95) *clothes* (= *Skr.* आच्छादनं). *In Gḍ. the latter process became much more general, hence B.* अकाश *or* अकास = *Pr.** अक्कासो, *Skr.* आकाशः; *B.* अघघघु, *Pr.* अग्घग्घओ, *Skr.* आघघकः, *etc.*]

अ *a* (7), **Ts.**, *interjection of pity*, ah!

[*Skr.* अ; *so possibly in all Gḍs.*]

अ *a* (8), **Tbh.**, *voc. pt., only occurring in the compounds* अरे, अरी, *etc.; a shortened form of* ऐ *ai, q.v.*

अ *a* (9), **Ts.**, [1]a name of Vishnu (*see* अोम्); [2]a name of Brahma. *Only occurring in fanciful usages, e.g., in riddles, etc.* **Exam.**, *Sat.*, (*with comm.*) p. 1, l. 3, जनक-सुता, दसजान-सुत, उरग, ईस, अ, स आर, तुलसिदास दस पद परसि भव-सागर भव पार, Having put together Sitā, Rām, Lachhman, Bharat, and Satrugh'n, Tul'sī Dās touching (*their*) ten feet crossed over the sea of existence. (*Here* जनक-सुता daughter of Janak *is Sitā;* दसजान *or* दसयान *stands for* दसरथ, जान *and* रथ *both meaning* vehicle: दसजान-सुत son of Das'jān *is Rām;* उरग snake *signifies the Nāg king Sheṣ, who became incarnate as Lachhman;* अ *signifies Vishnu, who became incarnate as Bharat; and* स *signifies Sib, who became incarnate as Satrugh'n.*)

[*Skr.* [1]अः : [2]अं; *so in all Gḍs.*]

अइ *aï* (1), *for words commencing thus and not mentioned below, see under* ऐ *ai. It should also be noted that certain words, beginning with* अइ॰ *aï°*, अइत॰ *aït°*, अइल॰ *aïl°*, अइब॰ *aïb°*, ऐ॰ *ai°* *or* ऐत॰ *ait°*, ऐल॰ *ail°*, ऐब॰ *aib°*, *etc.*, (*e.g.*, अइहै *aïhai* he will come, *Padm., ch.* 175, 3; अइतों *aïtõ* I should have come, *Misc.* 79; अइलें *aïlẽ* they came, *Bais.* 7, *etc.*) *are inflections of the* √आव *āb* come, *and must be looked up under that root.*

अइ *aï* (2), *a verbal termination*, = ऐ *ai*, *q.v.*

अइसन *aïsan* = ऐसन *aisan*, *q.v.* **Exam.**, *Bais.* 7, अइसन देवरवा के फँसिया दे दिहतीं, रामा, I would have got such a brother-in-law hanged, O Ram!

अइसा *aïsā*, (*f.* अइसी *aïsī*) = ऐसा *aisā*, *q.v.* **Exam.**, *Bais.* 27, अइसी ओयनी टाम समम को जाने ना देती, Working such an (*efficacious*) magic, I should not let my lover depart.

अई *aī* = आई *āi* (1), आई *āī* (1), *a sec. der. suff. used to form abstract nouns from adjectives, as* हलुआई lightness, *from* हलुक light; भलाई goodness, *from* भला good.

[*Skr.* ता, *Shr. Pr.* दा, *or Mh. Pr.* आ (*Hēm.* ii, 154), *with pleon.* क *superadded, it is Skr.* तिका, *Pr.* दिआ *or* इआ, *or, including the final* अ *of the base,* अइआ, *and Gḍ.* आई; *with pleon.* अ (= क) *added again to the base, we have Pr.* अअइआ *contracted to Gḍ.* आई. *See Gḍ. Gr.*, § 220.]

अउ *aü* (1); *for words commencing thus, and not mentioned below, see under* औ *au.*

अउ *aü* (2), *a verbal termination*, = औ *au*, *q.v.*

अउर *aür* = आओर *āor*, *q.v.*

अउत *aüt*, अत *ūt*, अउतिया, *autiyā*, **Tbh.**, *subst. m.*; [1]a man who dies without leaving issue; [2]a bachelor, [3]a blockhead, fool.

(*Properly Hindī, but occasionally used by educated Bihāris.*)

[*Skr.* [1]अयुक्त: *or* [2]अयुक्तक; *Pā.* [1]अयुत्तो, [2]अयुत्तको; *Pr.* [1]अउत्तो, [2]अउत्तओ; *Ap. Pr.* [1]अउत्तु, [2]अउत्तउ, *or* [3]अउत्तउ; —*H.* [1]अउत, अत, [2]अतिया; *Garh.* [2]औता; *P.* [1]औत, औंत (*Ml. Gy.*), अत, (*f.*) अतरी; *Ml.* [3]औतरउ (*m.*), [3]औतरी (*f.*); *M. has* अउत *in the sense of* plough, plough-boy.]

अए *aë ; for words commencing thus, see under* **ऐ** *ai.*

अओ *aö ; for words commencing thus, see under* **औ** *au.*

अंश *aṁsh,* **अंस** *aṁs ; for words commencing thus, see under* **अन्स** *ans.*

अक *ak* (1), **Tbh.,** *a der. suff. occurring in a certain number of sec. roots. Sometimes the original root (generally with a slightly different meaning) occurs side by side with the sec. root thus formed ; but in most cases the former is no longer in use.* **Exam.,** √फटक be separated *and* √फट be split; √कसक be painful *and* √कस tighten ; *again* √दरक split, √कड़क rumble, *from the disused* √दृ *or* दर *and* √कड़ *respectively; similarly* √चमक glitter, √झलक shine, *and many others, see H. R.,* 63.

(*It may be noted that these sec. roots, just like prim. roots, may be used as nouns of action, which are generally feminine in their weak form; while their strong forms end in* अका *masc. and* अकी *fem.*; *e.g.,* कसक *f.* pain, चमक *f.* glitter, झलकी *f.* glance. *See the art.* अ *a* (2) *and* इ *i* (2), *both prim. der. suff.*)

[*The original of this suffix most probably is the Skr.* √कृ *kri, which in construction with any noun (generally in the acc. sing.) may form a sort of periphrastic root. Thus Skr.* फुत् + √कृ blow (*lit.* make puff), चम् + √कृ hinder (*lit.* make hindrance, *from* चम्), कड़ं + √कृ rumble (*lit.* make a rumbling noise), कसं + √कृ pain (*lit.* make torment). *In Pr. the* √कृ *coalesces with the noun, so as to form an indivisible compound root ending in* अ, *which last element is in Gḍ. further reduced to a single* क. *Thus the abovementioned Skr. periphrastic roots become in Pr. the compound roots* √फुक्क (*pres. part. act.* फुक्कंतो, *Sapt., vs.* 176; *pres. part. pass.* फुक्किज्जंत *Hēm.* iv, 422), √चमक, √कड़क्क, √कसक, *and in Gḍ.,* √फूक, √रोक, √कड़क, √कसक. *It will thus be seen that the initial* अ *of the suffix* अक *is really the termination of what was originally a noun, while the element* क *represents what was originally the root* कृ. *For further information on the nature and origin of such comp. roots, see Gḍ. Gr.,* § 353, *p.* 173.]

अक *ak* (2), (*f.* इका), **Ts.,** *a prim. der. suff., used only in tats. words to form adjectives and nouns of agency.* **Exam.,** कारक, (*f.* कारिका), a doer, *from* √कृ.

[*Skr.* अक:, *f.* इका; *met with in all Gḍs. In all probability this suff. is a compound of the prim. der. suff.* अ *a* (2), *q.v., and the pleon. suff.* क, *q.v.*; *thus, m.* अक: = अ + क:, *f.* इका = इ + का. *The tadbh. form of the suff. is m.* आ *ā* (2), *f.* ई *ī, q.v.*]

अक *ak* (3), **Tbh.,** *a shortened form of* एक *ek or* एक *ēk* one, *occurring only in compounds, such as* अकला *ak'lā,* अकसर *ak'sar,* अकहत्तरि *ak'hattari,* अकोतर-सो *akōtar'sō, etc.* (*q.v.*).

[*Skr.* एक, *Ap. Pr.* एक्क (*Hēm.* iv., 371), *B.* एक *or* अक.]

अकन्टङ *ak'ṭaṅ,* **अकटङ** *akṭaṅ,* **इकन्टङ** *ik'ṭaṅ,* **इकटङ** *ikṭaṅ,* **Any.,** *adj. com. gen.,* acting, being temporarily in charge of an office in the place of another officer.

[*E.* acting, *a tech. term of the Indian Administration.*]

अकट-बकट *akaṭ'bakaṭ,* **Tbh.,** *subst. m.,* [1]trifles, things worth nothing (= चाको-बाको) ; *hence* [2]the minor portions of a composite whole. **Exam.,** [1]*Chan.,* अकट-बकट बक जे मन आव, दुर्जन कौं निज सहज सुभाव, To speak trifles as they come into the mind, is the natural disposition of evil men. [2]*Hb.* 2, 59, सकडक अकट-बकट सब छूटल, All the pegs and pins of the cart came loose. *See* अगड़-बगड़ *agaṛ'bagaṛ.*

[*Perhaps connected with* अगड़ *or* अगड़ (1), *q.v.,* बकट *being a reduplication of* अकट ; *or the latter might itself be a reduplication of* बकट, *q.v. Cf. M.* अकट-विकट rigorously minute, *and* अकट-विकट hideously large.]

अँकन्टा *ăk'ṭā* (1), *the same as* अँकरा *ăk'rā* (1), *q.v.*

अँकन्टा *ăk'ṭā* (2), *the same as* अँकड़ा *ăk'ṛā, q.v.*

अँकन्टी *ăk'ṭī, fem. of* अँकटा *ăk'ṭā* (2), *q.v.*

अकन्टोबर *ak'ṭōbar,* **अकोबर** *akṭōbar, the same as* अकतूबर *ak'tūbar, q.v.*

अकाठी *akaṭhī,* **Tbh.,** *adj. com. gen.,* mischievous, noxious, injurious. **Exam.,** *Chan.,* अन्याबी अजबै (= अजबै + सौ) दूषन, अकाठी अब अवगह दिढ़ दूषन, To an unreasonable man defects alone are visible: a mischievous person sees them very deftly.

[*Probably from Skr.* अतिकष्ट, *Pā.* अतिकट्ठ ; *with the intens.* अ *a* (5), *q.v.*]

√ अकाड़ akaṛ, (pr. pts. अकड़ैत ak'ṛait, Bh. अकड़त ak'ṛat, अकड़ित ak'ṛit; अकड़ल ak'ṛal; अकड़ब ak'ṛab; अकड़ै ak'ṛai), **Tbh.**, v. intr., [1]to become hard, stiff; [2]to writhe, become distorted, cramped; [3]to strut affectedly, swagger, give oneself airs; [4]to challenge to fight. **Phr.**, अकड़ जाएब (lit. to become stiff, hence) to come to the end of one's resources (as in a lawsuit or struggle.) **Exam.**, [1]Coll. मुरदवा अकड़ि गेल, The corpse has got stiff; Coll. (Bh.), एतनहीं में अकड़ गेलहो? अब कछु नहिं करबऽ, Have you come to the end of your resources already? Now you are powerless. [2]Coll. (Bh.), घोड़ा के गोड़ अकड़ल बाटे, The horse's legs are distorted or crooked; Coll. (Bh.), हमार हाथ गोड़ अकड़ के लकड़ी सन होए गेल बा, My arms and legs, being stiff and distorted, have become like sticks. [3]B. Gr., I (Introd.), Fable 11, हम अकड़ि चलत गहना कपड़ाक सुन्दरताई आओर मुँहक ढबक छिमक देखाएब, Swaggering along, I shall show off the finery of my ornaments and clothes and the beauty of my countenance. [4]Coll. (Bh.), ऊ अकड़ के खड़ा होख चाहत, He stands up swaggeringly, challenging to fight.

[Der. uncertain; but cf. Skr. √कड़ be hard, also Skr. कठिन and कठोर hard, stiff, which are probably prākritising derivations from Skr. कठ or क्रथ, both derivatives of Skr. √क्रथ्. The most common representative of the latter root in Pā. and Pr. is कड्ड, properly a der. root, for Pā. or Pr. कड्डइ = Skr. क्रथति (see Hēm. iv, 187; ड्ड standing for थ as in Pr. √वेड्ड for Skr. वेष, Hēm. iv, 51, 221). Thence comes Pā. and Pr. √आकड्ड, representing Skr. √आकृष् (lit. आकर्ष) draw up, cramp. This might change in Gḍ. to √अकड़ or √आकड़ or √अकड़ or अकड़ (for अकड्ड). The process of loss or transfer of aspiration is not uncommon in Gḍ. (see remarks on derivation of अकारण), or even in Pr., see Gḍ Gr., p. 82, and possibly the prākritising Skr. √कड़ is due to it. Or perhaps the √अकड़ may be related to the adj. खड़ा standing, which is a modification of Pr. खड्ड, Skr. खात, p.p.p. of √खन (see Cp. Gr. iii, 60). In this case the initial अ of the √अकड़ would be the intens. pref. (see art. अ a (5)). H. √अकड़ or अकड़ाव (Hd. Dy.) with adj. अकड़ or अकड़, P. √अकड़ or √आकड़, G. अकड़ with numerous derivatives, S. अकिड़ण (properly a pass. form अकिड़ + ण, see S. Gr., p. 258); wanting, apparently, in the other Gḍs., in which only derivatives of it occur (see art. अकड़ि akaṛi), adopted from the Hindī.]

अकाड़ akaṛ, also (Mth.) अगड़ agaṛ (1), the same as अकड़ि akaṛi, q.v.

अकड़वाई akaṛ'bāi, अकड़बाई akaṛ'bāi, **Tbh.**, subst. f., (Bh.) the cramps, rheumatism. **Exam.**, Coll. (Bh.), ओकरा अकड़बाइ भेल बा, He has got rheumatism.

[Properly 1st verb. noun of the double-causal √अकड़वाव, made with the prim. suff. ई ī (2), q.v. This double causal root does not otherwise occur in B., the simple causal √अकड़ाव (q.v.) being ordinarily used. From this latter root the corresponding words P. अकड़ाउ or अकड़ाव, G. अकड़ाट, are derived. H., like B., has अकड़वाई. It should be noted that in such derivatives the causal or double causal root has the same meaning as the prim. root, i.e., it is properly a pleon. root, formed with the pleon. suff. आवि, see Gd. Gr., p. 170, § 349. See art. आइ āi (2), अबाइ abāi, बाइ bāi. See also art. अकड़ि akaṛi. Or the word may be explained as a compound of अकड़ (q.v.) and बाइ wind, the latter word being an usual term for rheumatism.]

अँकड़ा ā̃k'ṛā, आँकरा ā̃k'ṛā (2), **Tbh.**, subst. m., (Bh.) [1]a calcareous nodular limestone, found in the soil in many parts of India, used in making roads, lime, etc.; [2](S. Bh.) coarse gravel (Grs., § 794), pebbles. See आँकड़ा ā̃k'ṛā (2), आँकड़ी ā̃k'ṛī (2), अङ्कट aṅkaṭ.

(When it appears in large blocks, it is आँकड़ा; the small pieces for road-metal are कांकड़, or आँकड़ी, or आँकड़ी; when used for lime-burning, it is कंकड़.)

[This word does not appear to occur in any of the other dialects of B., nor in any of the other Gds.; it is in all probability merely a mutilated form of कँकड़ा, कंकड़, q.v. The latter are the forms occurring in all other Gd. languages and B. dialects, and also occur in Bh. by the side of आँकड़ा. Compare, however, the first part of अकड़बकड़, q.v.]

√ अकड़ाव ak'ṛāb, (pr. pts. अकड़वैत akaṛ'bāit, Bh. & Mg., अकड़ावत ak'ṛāwat, अकड़ावित ak'ṛāwit, अकड़ाइत ak'ṛāit; अकड़ाओल ak'ṛāol; अकड़ाएब ak'ṛāeb; अकड़ावै ak'ṛābai, अकड़ाए ak'ṛāe), **Tbh.**, v. tr., to distress, impede. **Exam.**, Coll. (Bh.), तूं ओकरा अकड़ाव दिहलऽ? नहीं? You have impeded him, haven't you?

[Causal of √अकड़, q.v.]

अकाड़ि akaṛi, अकड़ akaṛ, **Tbh.**, subst. f., (Bh.) [1]cramps, crookedness, contortedness, stiffness; [2]pride, swagger, strut, airs, conceit; [3]parade, pomp, show. **Comp.**, अकड़-बकड़, अकड़-धकड़, अकड़म-बकड़म, m., pomp, stateliness, affected airs; अकड़-बाज, com. gen., an affected person, a fop; अकड़-बाजी, f., swaggering, strutting, foppishness, airs. **Phr.**, अकड़ देखाएब, to swagger. **Exam.**, [1]Coll. (Bh.), ओकरा डाँड़ में अकड़ि धारि गेल बा, He has got cramps or stiffness in the loins. [2]Coll. (Bh.), हमरा लोगों का अकड़

देखावताड़ँऽ, What airs are you giving yourself before me! ²*Coll.* (*Bh.*), ई बड़ अकड़नाकड़ के बरियात बा, This is a wedding procession of great pomp. *See* अगड़ *agaṛ*.

[*Properly* 1*st verb. noun of* √ अकड़ (*q.v.*), *formed with prim. suff.* इ ĭ (2), *q.v.* *H. same as B.*; *P.* आकड़ *or* अकड़ (*subst.*), अकड़बाज (*adj.*), अकड़बाजी (*subst.*); *S.* आकिड़णी (*subst., as in* आकिड़णी वहणु to walk affectedly, to strut); *G.* अकड़ (*subst.*), अकड़ा-अकड़ी (*subst.*, rivalry, contest, *cf.* 4*th meaning of* √अकड़), अकड़बाज (*adj.*), अकड़बाजु (*subst.*), *probably also* आँकड़ी (*subst.*, cramps). *In the other Gds. it is adopted from H. or B.; thus Bg.* आँकड़ि (*subst.*, a spasm); *M.* अकड़ *or* अकड़ (*subst.*), अकड़बाज *or* अकड़बाज (*adj.*), अकड़बाजी *or* अकड़बाजी (*subst.*)]

अँक॰ड़ी *ãk'ṛī* (1), अँकरी *ãk'rī* (1), **Tbh.**, *subst. f.*, *a rarely used Mth. form for* अँकुरी *ãkurī*, *q.v.*

[*The simplest derivation* (*suggested already in Molesworth's M. Dy.*) *is from Skr.* अङ्क hook, *with the Ap. Pr. pleon. suff.* ड (*Hēm.* iv, 429); *thus Ap. Pr.* अंकडउ *m.*, अंकडिआ *f.*, *contracted into* अँकड़ा, अँकड़ी. *It may, however, be simply a corruption of* अँकुरी, *which would explain the appearance of* उ *u in the O.* अँकुड़ा *and of* ओ *in the G.* अकोरी (*G.* अकोर = अंकुर), *and on the other hand the disappearance of* उ *u in B.* अँकरी (*q.v.*), *M.* आँकरी shoot. *H.* अँकड़ी, *G.* आँकडी *and* अकोरी, *M.* अकडा *and* आँकडा *m.*, आँकडी *f.* (*the fem. meaning, as in B.*, a forked stick for pulling down fruit), *O.* आँकुड़ा *m.*, आँकुड़ी *f.*, *Bg.* आँकड़ा; *but S.* कुड़ो *m.*, कुड़ी *f.*]

अँक॰ड़ी *ãk'ṛī* (2), अँकरी *ãk'rī* (2), अँकटी *ãk'ṭī*, (*also in Mth. and N. Bh.* ईकड़ी *īk'ṛī or* इकड़ी *ik'ṛī*), **Tbh.**, *subst. f.*, ¹ (*Bh.*) small pieces of limestone, *used as road-metal* (*Grs.* § 1266); ² (*S. Bh.*) fine gravel (*Grs.* § 794). *See* अँकड़ा *ãk'ṛā and* अँकरोरी, *ãk'rōrī*.

[*Properly fem. of* अँकड़ा *ãk'ṛā*, *q.v.*]

अक॰ड़ैत *ak'ṛāit*, **Tbh.**, *adj. com. gen.*, (*Mth. f.* अकड़ैति *ak'ṛāiti*), swaggering, foppish. **Exam.**, *Chan.*, दुसह दुख सज्जन कौं देत, मन का डेर न, चल अकड़ैत, It causes insufferable pain to good people not to think of others and to walk swaggeringly; *Coll.* (*Bh.*), साँड़ अकड़ैत बा, The bull is wallowing and roaring.

(*The word is principally used of bulls and the like, and thence also applied to men.*)

[*Properly* (*Mth*). *pres. part. of* √अकड़ (*q.v.*); *H.* अकड़ैत, *P.* अकड़ैन्द (*or corrupt* अकड़ैत, *from P. pres. part. in* न्द *nd*) *subst. f.*, swagger.]

अँक॰ड़ैल *ãk'ṛāil*, **Tbh.**, *adj. com. gen.*, (*Bh.*) gravelly, *said espec. of certain soils*, (*Grs.* § 794). *See* अँकड़ौर *ãk'ṛāur*.

[*Der. from* अँकड़ा *by means of the sec. der. suff.* ऐल; *see Gd. Gr.* § 245.]

अँक॰ड़ौर *ãk'ṛāur*, *a synonym of* अँकड़ैल *ak'ṛāil*, *q.v.* (*Grs.* § 794).

[*Der. from* अँकड़ा *by means of the sec. der. suff.* और; *see Gd. Gr.* § 245.]

अकण्टक *akanṭak*, **Ts.**, *adj. com. gen.*, *lit.* free from thorns; *hence met.* ¹free from annoyance, trouble; ²free from enemies. **Exam.**, ¹*Rām.*, *Bā.*, *ch.* 96, 8, भये अकण्टक तापस जोगी, Saints and hermits felt relieved of an annoyance. ²*Ib.*, *A.*, *ch.* 182, 5, करौं अकण्टक राज तुम्हारो, I will reign at ease and free from enemies.

(*The word is never used in its literal sense.*)

[*Skr.* अकण्टकः, *Bg.* अकण्टक, *and so in all Gds.*]

अकत *akat*, **Ts.**, (I) *adj. com. gen.*, thorough, utter, perfect (*in a bad sense*). **Exam.**, *Mg. ballad*, पहिल कवर जब सरवन खाए, अकत महुरवा जैसे बुझाए, When Sar'wan ate the first mouthful, it seemed as it were utter poison (*after Fallon*); *Coll.* (*Mth.*), ओहि कूँआक पानी अकत माहुर थी, The water of that well is thorough poison; *Coll.* (*Mth.*), ई जहर के अकत गाँठ थिक, *lit.* he is a perfect knot of poison, *i.e.*, he is a thoroughly wicked person; *similarly* अकत नीम a perfect nīm, *i.e.*, as bitter as the juice of the nīm-tree.

(II) *adv.*, thoroughly, intensely (*in a bad sense*), (*practically serving as a superlative particle*). **Exam.**, *Coll.* (*Bh.*), ई फल अकत तीता बा, This fruit is intensely bitter; *so also* अकत करुआ, thoroughly bitter.

[*Skr.* अकृत: *lit.* not made, not artificial; *hence* eternal, natural; *hence* thorough; *Pā.* अकतं the eternal (*an epithet of the Nirvāna*); *not met with in the other Gds. The tadbh. equivalent is Pr.* अकअ *or* अकिअ (*cf.* अकअए *Sapt.*, *vs.* 920, *and* अकिआ *Hēm.* iv, 396, *meaning, in both instances,* thoroughly); *cf. M.* अकित the uncreate (*an epithet of God*). *An analogous case is that of* सहज, *which also properly means* natural, *and hence* thorough, *e.g.*, *Jan.*, *ch.* 12, सहज मनोहर, thoroughly charming. *The word might, however, also be derived from Skr.* अक्षत, *Pr.* अक्खत, uncut, unimpaired; *hence*, entire, whole, thorough; *analogously to* अखिल, अखण्ड, *q.v.*]

अक॰तूबर *ak'tūbar*, अक्टोबर *ak'ṭobar*, **Any.**, *subst. m.*, the month of October.

[E. October.]

अकत्थ *akatth* (*old Bw.*) = अकथ *akath*, *q.v.*

अकथ *akath*, *old Bw.* अकत्थ *akatth*, **Ts.**, *adj. com. gen.*, what cannot be spoken or described, unspeakable, unutterable, inexpressible, indescribable. **Exam.**, *Rām.*, *Bā.*, *ch.* 2, 13, अकथ अलौकिक तीरथ-राउ, An unspeakable, spiritual chief Tīrtha; *ibid.*, *ch.* 25, 7, नाम रूप-गति अकथ (*fem.*) कहानी. The mystery of name and form cannot be told; *K. Rām.*, *Ut.* 145, सब बिधि समत्थ, अमिता अकत्थ (*fem.*), तुलसी संदेह सन्तय समन, (*Sib*) powerful in every way, of unutterable greatness, the appeaser of Tul'sī Dās' doubts; *Dōh.* 199, वाम-सरूप तुम्हार बचन, अगोचर, बुद्धि-पर, अबिगत, अकथ, अपार; नेति नेति नित निगम कह, (*Wise*) like Saraswatī is thy speech, incomprehensible, past understanding, indeterminable, unutterable, impenetrable; the sacred scriptures can speak of it only in negatives, (वाम *or* वामा *is Saraswatī*, *the goddess of speech and learning*; नेति *is Skr.* न + इति; *lit.*, *the scriptures always say* 'no, no'); *Padm.*, *do.* 229, 1, मसि नयना लिखनी बरुन रोय रोय लिखा अकत्थ, (*The tears of her*) eyes were her ink, and her eyelashes the pen, and bitterly weeping she wrote unutterable (*words*). *See* अकथ्य *akathy'* *and* अकथनीय *akath'nīy'*.

[*Properly a fut. part. pass.*, *Skr.* अकथ्यः, *Pā.* अकथ्यो (*cf. pass.* कथ्यते *Pā. Dy.*), *Pr.* अकत्थो (*cf. pass.* कत्थइ, *Hēm.* iv, 249), *Ap. Pr.* अकत्थु; *S.* अकथु *or* अकथ (*S. Dy.*; *on the change of* थ *to* त्थ, *cf. Gd. Gr.*, §§ 116-120, 145), *H.* अकथ; *apparently wanting in the other Gḍs. The form of the word is noteworthy on account of its irregularity. As a rule the Skr. conj. cons.* थ्य *changes to* च्छ *in Pā. and Pr.* (*Hēm.* ii, 21; *e.g.* पच्छा = *Skr.* पथ्या road, *fem. fut. part. pass. of* √पथ); *in order to avoid this inconvenient change in pass. inflexion, it was usual to employ the alternative phon. change of dissolving the conj. cons.* थ्य *into* थिज्ज *or* थीय (*Pā.* थीय), *cf. Hēm.* iii, 160; *thus Skr.* कथ्यते, = कहिज्जइ (*Hēm.* iv, 249) *or* कथीयइ, *Pā.* कथीयति (*Pā. Dy.*) *The change of* थ्य *to* त्थ *or* थ, *therefore, is quite irregular. The irregularity is clearly an old one, as it is already noticed by Pā. and Pr. grammarians* (*Hēm.* ii, 174). *In all probability the word is really an ancient tatsama, being preserved from the Skr. as a sort of technical term, applicable to 'things transcending the human mind.' Other similar instances are* पत्थ *or* पथ dietetic food (*a medical techn. term, also in Pr.*, *see Sapt.*, *vs.* 814, *for* पच्छ = *Skr.* पथ्य), मज्झ *or* मझ *poet.* within (*for* मज्झ, = *Skr.* मध्य).]

अकथनीय॰ *akath'nīy'*, **Ts.**, *adj. com. gen.*, (*subst. f.* अकथनीया *akath'nīyā*), [1]unspeakable, unutterable, inexpressible, indescribable; [2]unsuitable to be spoken or described. **Exam.**, [1]*Rām.*, *Bā.*, *ch.* 70, 1, अकथनीय दारुन दुख भारी, A heavy, grievous, and unutterable pain. [2]*Coll.* (*Bh.*), उनकर भाइ अबकी बेर काम बैसन है के अकथनीय था, His brother has this time done such a thing as is unsuitable to be described.

[*From* अ + कथनीय, *fut. pass. part. of* √कथ, *Skr.* अकथनीयः, *a pure tats.*, *which may be used in all Gḍs.*]

अकथ्य॰ *akathy'*, **Ts.**, *adj. com. gen.*, *the same as* अकथनीय॰ *akath'nīy'*, *q.v.*

[*From* अ + कथ्य, *fut. pass. part. of* √कथ, *Skr.* अकथ्यः, *a pure tats.*, *which may be used in all Gḍs.*]

अकद *akad*, **Any.**, *subst. m.*, the marriage contract amongst Musalmāns (*Grs.* §§ 1273, 1279).

[*Ar.* عقد *'aqd.*]

अकन *akan* = √अँकन *ãkan*, *q.v.*

अँकन *ãkan*, अकन *akan*, (*pr. pts.* अँकनैत *ãk'nait*, अँकनल *ãk'nal*, अँकनब *ãk'nab*, अँकनै *ãk'nai*), (*Bw.*), **Tbh.**, *v. tr.*, [1]to give ear, hear, hearken, listen, attend; *hence* [2]to attend to information, to learn, to come to know; *and* [3]to attend to music, to keep time to music, to march in accordance with musical time; *also* [4]to attend to the sound of money, test money (*Grs.* § 1489). **Exam.**, [1]*Rām.*, *Bā.*, *ch.* 349, 3, पुरजन आवत अकनि बराता, When the citizens heard the marriage procession coming; *Rām.*, *A.*, *ch.* 44, 1, अब निप अकनि राम पगु धारे, When the king heard the fall of the footsteps of Rām; *Gīt.*, *Bā.*, 37, 5. प्रेम सनिलित बर बचन रचना अकनि राम राजीव लोचन उघारे, Hearing the arrangement of excellent words filled with affection (*the allusion is to a number of songs*), Rām opened his lotuslike eyes; *K. Rām.*, *Bā.* 19, रोष माखे लखन अकनि अनखोही बातैं, Lakhan, hearing these unpleasant words (*of Parasurām*), felt enraged. [2]*Bin.* 220, अकनि या के कपट करतब अमित अनय अपाय, सुखी हरि-पुर बसत होत परिछितहि पछिताय, Learning that the object of its (*i.e.*, *Kalikāl's*) deceptions was (*to do*) countless (*deeds of*) injustice and destruction, Parichhit, when residing happily in Haripur (*i.e. Baikunṭh or Bishnu's heaven*), repented (*of having spared it*). [3]*Rām.*, *Bā.*, *do.*, 309, 1, तुरग नचावहिं कुँवर बर, अँकनि मिरदङ्ग निसान, Noble princes cause horses to prance, keeping time to drums and kettle-drums. [4]*Coll.*, ई रुपैया अँकनैं, Sound this rupee. *See* √अकान *akān*.

(*The conj. part.* अकनि *is the only form in which this verb has been met with by us in B. literature.*)

[*Skr.* √आकर्ण, 10*th cl.* आकर्णयति; *Pr.* [1]आकण्णेइ *or* [2]अकण्णेइ *or* [3]आअण्णेइ (*Rāv.* xi, 7, *Sapt.*, *vs.* 365);

B. ¹अकबे or अँकबे or अकावे; H. same as B.; S. ¹ओवारब (inf.; perhaps a pleon. √ओवार, contr. from आवमार (with euph. व) = Pr. √आववावि, Skr. √*आवबोधि); apparently wanting in the other Gḍs. All Gḍs. also use the equivalent tats. √आकंब.]

अकंनून ak'nūn, Any., adv., now, at present.
[Prs. اکنون aknūn.]

अकंफक ak'phak, सकफक sak'phak, (Bh.), the same as अकसक ak'sak, q.v.

अकंबक ak'bak, Tbh., subst. m., nonsensical talk.
[Redupl. of बक, q.v.]

अकंबर ak'bar, अकबर akbar, (poet. अकब्बर akabbar), Any., subst. m., a man's name, the emperor Akbar. He was the second emperor of Hindūstān of the Mughul house of Tīmūr. His full name and title, as given on his coins, was Jalālu-d-dīn Muhammad Akbar Pādshāh Ghāzī, i.e., Jalālu-d-dīn Muhammad, the Great, the Victorious Emperor. He reigned at Agra (see art. अकंबराबाद) from A.D. 1542—1605. See Beale's Oriental Biographical Dictionary, s.v. Some detached Hindī verses are commonly ascribed to him, among which is the following dōhā. Exam., Siv., p. 375, जा को जस है जगत मैं, जगत सराहै जाहि। ता को जीवन सफल है, कहत अकब्बर साहि। Whose fame is (spread) in the world, whom the world praises, his life is successful, (so) says Akbar Shāh.
[Ar. اکبر akbar, lit. the Great.]

अकंबराबाद ak'barābād, अकबराबाद akbarābād, Any., subst. m., the name of the capital of the emperor Akbar, Āgrā.
[Ar. اکبرآباد akbarābād, lit. the ābād or settlement of Akbar. He built a fort at Āgrā, made it his principal residence, and named it Akbarābād after himself.]

अकंबरी ak'barī, अकबरी akbarī, Any., (I) adj. com. gen., relating to Akbar. Phr., अकंबरी ओंवर subst. m., fac., a one-eyed man (Hd. Dy.). Exam., आईन अकंबरी the Aīn-i-Akbarī or the Institutes of Akbar, the name of the third volume of Abū'l Fazl's celebrated history of the reign of the emperor Akbar, called the Akbar-nāmah; अकंबरी असरफी or असरफी a gold coin of Akbar, worth variously, 9, 10, 12, 27, or 30 (but not 16) rupees (see Prinsep's Useful Tables, p. 5).

(II) subst. f., a sweetmeat of rice-flour and sugar formed into balls, and, after being fried in ghī or clarified butter, encrusted with clarified sugar.
[From Ar. اکبر akbar, with Prs. suff. ی ī.]

अकंमा ak'mā, Any., adj. com. gen., born blind. (Properly Urdū; used only by educated Muhammadans of Bihār.)
[Ar. اکمه akmah.]

आँकंमाल ãk'māl, Tbh., subst. f., embrace, hug. Phr., आँकंमाल देब, to embrace. Exam., K. Rām., Su. 29, बूड़त जहाज बाचा पथिक-समाज मानो आजु आए जानि, सब आँकमाल देत चैं, Like a company of travellers, escaped from a sinking ship and considering themselves as being born (anew) that day, they all embraced (one another). See आँकंवार ãk'wār.
[Skr. अङ्कपालिः, Pr. अँकवालि (Sapt., vs. 996), hence B. आँकंमाल, with the not uncommon change of व to म through an intermediate Ap. Pr. ˜व. See Gḍ. Gr., § 134, p. 74.]

अकामित akamit, Tbh., adv., suddenly, unexpectedly. Exam., Vaish. x, 3, अकमित, चो रे, कोकिल पञ्चम कल सुनि, Suddenly, alas! (she hears) the song of the cuckoo in the fifth scale.
[Perhaps a corruption of Skr. अकस्मात्, q.v. Compare also अकामिक.]

अकम्पन akampan, Ts., subst. m., (lit. free from trembling), name of a rākshasa or demon in the suite of Rāban, king of Ceylon. Exam., Rām., Ln., ch. 45, 10, भजिय अकम्पन अरु अतिकाया बिचलत सेन कीन्ह इन माया, When the line began to break, Akampan and Atikāya had recourse to jugglery; Han. 19, बारिदनाद अकम्पन कुम्भकरन से कुञ्जर केहरि-बारो, He (Hanumān) is the lion's cub (that killed) those elephants Bārid'nād, (i.e. Megh'nād), Akampan, and Kumbhakaran.
[Skr. अकम्पनः, a 'bahuvrīhi' compound of अ not and कम्पन trembling; Pr. अकम्पणो (Rāv. xiv, 70).]

अकर akar, Ts., adj., com. gen., exempt from taxes, duty-free, (tech.) one who does not pay Government revenue. Exam., Chan., अकर सकल कर लिअउँ कपाल, सकर भानु पर कर नहिँ लाव, While paying himself no revenue, he exacts it from every one; the sun, though possessed of rays, does not take any payment.
[Skr. अकरः; hence अकर in all Gḍs.]

अकरंनी akar'nī, Tbh., adj. com. gen., not to be done, wrong, unsuitable. Exam., Chan., अनुचित कर्म सबहि कैं भोल, मरने भल, न अकरनी भोल, (The performance of) good acts is (a duty) for every one; it is well to die; it is not good to do wrong (i.e. death is preferable to wrong-doing); Coll. (Bh.), तोहरे करनी अकरनी भेल, What was right in your eyes has turned out to be the reverse.

[*From* अ + करणीय, *fut. pass. part. of* √कृ do; *hence Skr.* अकरणीयः *m.*, अकरणीया *f.*, *Pr.* अकरणीओ *m.*, अकरणीआ *f.* (*cf. Hēm.* i, 248), *Ap. Pr.* अकरणीउ *m.*, अकरणीअ *f.*, *or* अकरणीउ *com. gen.* (*cf. Hēm.* iv, 329 330); *hence, contracted, Gḍ.* अकरनी *or* अकरणी. *The form with* ण ṇ *belongs to W. Gḍ. In M. it occurs shortened to* अकरन *in the comp.* अकरनकर *lit.* doing what is not to be done, perverse.]

अकारऽमल *akar'mal*, **Tbh.**, *adj. com. gen.*, (*Mth.*) unfortunate. **Exam.**, *Chan.* बेलक गाछ जाय बइसाउ, बेलआंच ग्रसांच रौद हैं चाँड। अकस्मात सिर अकसन्हि बेल, झड़कन्हि माथ, अभाद कि भेल। सिव सिव, असहि अकरमल जाय, स्रब अकर्मक फल अबुथाय ॥ A bald man went and sat down under the shade of a bēl-tree, being made uncomfortable by the sun shining on him. Suddenly a bēl fruit dropped on his head and his skull was broken. What an unlucky thing it was! O Sib, Sib, wherever an unfortunate man may go, the fruit of his sins will be preceding him.

[*Formed from* अकरम्म *or* अकर्म (*q.v.*) *with the Mth. suff.* ल, *which is only the past part. term., and is added in Mth. to make participial adj. of real or supposititious verbs.*]

अकारऽमार *akar'mār*, **Tbh.**, *subst. f.*, ground not properly cleaned for receiving seed.

[*A comp. of* आँकऽरा (1) *and* मार (*q.v.*), *lit.* infested with vetch. *Cf. H.* अकराया.]

अकऽरा *ak'rā* (1), (*f.* अकऽरी *ak'ri*), **Tbh.**, *adj.*, dear, costly, high-priced (*in a bad sense*). **Exam.**, (*Rj.*) मैं तो गोविन्द लीन्हो मोल, को कहे अकरा, को कहे सस्ता, लीन्हो तराजू तोल, I bought Gobind, some said dearly, others said cheaply, so I weighed him in the balances (*said by Mīrā Bāī, a celebrated poetess, wife of Rānā Kūmbhū of Chitōr, in the 15th cent. A.D., see Calcutta Review, vol. XLVIII, p. 7, and As. Res., vol.* XVI, *p.* 99). *See* अकऽरी *ak'ri* (3) *and* अकाल *akāl*.

[*Probably derived from Skr.* अकालः (= अ + काल) *or* आकालः (= आकाल-अ), *lit.* unseasonable, *hence* dear (*as in times of scarcity*), *and* (*with pleon. suff.* क) अकालकः *or* आकालकः, *Pr.* [1]अकालओ *or* [2]आकालओ *or* [3]अकलओ, *Ap. Pr.* [4]आकालउ *or* [1]*आकालउ; *S.* [5]आकिर, (र *being due to the influence of the lost* ल), *P.* [6]अकरो, *B. and H.* [7]अकरा. *Apparently wanting in the other Gḍs. This is an instance of the common B. change of* ल *to* र *extended to the W. Gḍs; in S., like B., it is usual; cf. S.* डुकार famine = *Skr.* दुष्काल:.]

अकऽरा *ak'rā* (2) = आँकऽरा *āk'rā* (3), *q.v.*

आँकऽरा *āk'rā* (1) *or* आँकड़ा *āk'ṛā*, **Tbh.**, *subst. f.*, a kind of grass or vetch (*vicia sativa, Wat.*); *it is a parasitic weed which grows in the wheat-fields under the spring crop and twines amongst the plants* (*Grs.* § 1075). *It is sometimes used as a fodder* (*Ell., vol. II, p.* 213); *also termed* आँकऽरी *āk'ri* (1), आँकुरी *ākurī*, *q.v.*

[*It may be a corruption of* आँकुरा (*cf. the fem.*), *derived from Skr.* अङ्कुर, *which lit. means* having a hook, *hence* (*with pleon. suff.* क) *Pr.* अंकुरओ *m.*, अंकुरिआ *f.*, *Gḍ.* आँकुरा *m.*, आँकुरी *f. Or it may be derived from Skr.* अङ्क hook, *with the Pr. suff.* ड, *which in Gḍ. may change to* र; *thus Pr.* अंकडओ *or* (*with pleon.* क) अंकडअओ, *Gḍ.* आँकरा. *In the latter case, however, there should be in B. an alternative form* आँकड़ा *āk'ṛā*; *and in the absence of it* (*though there is Mg.* आँकड़ा), *the former derivation is the more probable one. In any case, the B. word is undoubtedly connected in one way or the other with the Skr.* अङ्क hook. *Generally speaking, it may be noted that the derivatives of the Skr.* अङ्क *and* अङ्कुर *have been greatly confused in the modern languages, owing to interchanges of* उ u *and* अ a *and of* ड़ ṛ *and* र r. *See also the remarks on the derivation of* आँकड़ी (1), आँकुरा, *and the note on* आँकऽरी (1). *H. the same as B. In the other Gḍs., apparently, it occurs only in the fem. form, q.v.*]

आँकऽरा *āk'rā* (2) = आँकऽड़ा *āk'ṛā*, *q.v.*

आँकऽरा *āk'rā* (3), अकऽरा *ak'rā* (2), (*f.* आँकऽरी *āk'ri*, अकऽरी *ak'ri*), **Tbh.**, *adj.*, true, genuine, good. **Exam.**, *K. Rām., Ut.* 121, नाम-प्रताप महा-महिमा आँकरे किये खोटेउ, छोटेउ बाढ़े, Through the power of his name and his great renown, he (*Rām*) turned even the bad (*e.g., Ajāmil, &c.*) into good, and raised even the lowly (*e.g., Nikhāds and Bhīls; the encl.* उ *is a particle of emphasis*).

(*The word is said to be a synonym of* खरा, *q.v., and the opp. of* खोट *or* खोटा, *q.v.*)

[*Perhaps connected with Skr.* आकर, a mine; *hence* best, excellent.]

अकऽरार *ak'rār*, इकरार *ek'rār*, इकऽरार *ik'rār*, **Any.**, *subst. m.*, [1]an admission, confession (*in this sense also* करार *karār*); [2]a written bond *or* agreement. **Comp.** अकऽरार-नामा, *subst. m.*, a written agreement. **Exam.**, [1]*Coll.* (*Bh.*), ई पाप हम अकऽरार करऽतानी, हमऽरा से भेल बा, I confess this sin: it has been committed by me. [2]*Sal.*, 16, से दुहू तरफ अकऽरार भेल भेल, Thus on both sides an agreement was made; *B. Gr.*, II (*Bh.*), *p.* 32, ओकर अकऽरार लिखँ, Write a bond to that effect.

[*Ar.* اقرار *iqrār.*]

अकंराव *ak'rāw*, अकड़ाव *ak'ṛāw*, **Tbh.**, *subst. m.*, foot and mouth disease in cattle, *in which the feet and face swell and the stomach distends* (*Indian Cattle-Plague Report, Vocab. s.v. Ukrao*).

[*Derived by means of the prim. der. suff.* अ *a* (2), (*q.v.*), *from the causal* √अकड़ाव, *itself derived from the simple* √अकड़, *q.v. Literally the word means* stiffness, cramps.]

अँकरिया *ãkariyā*, **Tbh.**, *subst. f.*, (*South Bhagalpur*) a heifer ready for the bull (*Grs.* § 1118).

[*Prop. lg. f. of* अँकरी (*or* अँकुरी) *a possessive adj. derived from* अँकुर, *q.v., by means of the Gd. suff.* ई *i, see Gd. Gr.* § 252.]

अकंरी *ak'rī* (1) (*Mg.*), *also* (*S. Mth.-Mg.*) उकरी *uk'rī*, **Tbh.**, *subst. f.*, the funnel *or* cup at the top of the hollow bamboo tube of a seed-drill (*Grs.*, § 24). **Exam.**, *Coll.* (*Mg.*), अकरी डँरवा मेँ लगा दीहो रे, ले जाहो खेतवा पर रे, Fasten the funnel to the drill-plough (डाँर) and take it off to the field.

[*A corruption of* ओखरी (*with* ओ *reduced to* अ, *see Gd. Gr.*, § 26; *the long form* ओखरियँ *occurs in the example of the following article*), *a fem. diminutive of* ओखर *or* ओखल (*or* उखर, उखल), a mortar *or* pot for husking rice, *Pr.* उक्खलं (*Hēm.* ii, 90) *or* ओक्खलं (*Hēm.* i, 171), *Skr.* उदूखलं.]

अकंरी *ak'rī* (2), एकरी *ek'rī*, ऍकरी *ĕk'rī*, **Tbh.**, *subst. f.*, uncleaned rice (*Grs.* § 1272). **Exam.**, *Coll.* (*Bh.*), तम तीन दीन से अकरी चाउर खात बाटीं, ओखरियँ न मिलल, I have been three days eating unhusked rice, for I could not get a crushing-mortar.

[*Der.* ? *S. has* अखिड़ो.]

अकंरी *ak'rī* (3), **Tbh.**, *subst. f.*, high prices, scarcity.

(*Properly Urdū; only used by the educated in Bihār.*)

[*This word is properly the fem. of* अकरा (1), *q.v., used as a subst. In Skr.,* कालिका, *the fem. of* कालिक, *is used as a subst. in the sense of* price of a commodity payable at a fixed time, credit price. *Similarly the Skr.* कालिका, *fem. of* कालक, *might be used. Hence* अकालिका *or* अकालिका *would mean* want of credit prices, a time when no credit is given; *hence* scarcity.]

अकंरी *ak'rī* (4), *fem. of* अकरा *ak'rā* (1) *and* (2), *q.v.*

अँकंरी *ãk'rī* (1), **Tbh.**, *the same as* अँकड़ी *ãk'ṛī* (1) *and* अँकुरी *ãkurī*, *q.v.*

(*It may be noted that with the sense of* vetch *it admits a masc. form* अँकरा, *q.v., while apparently it does not admit the forms* अँकड़ा *and* अँकड़ी, *spelt with* ड़ *ṛ*. *But though not hitherto noticed, it is probable, from all the circumstances of the case, that they do exist.*)

[*For der. see art.* अँकड़ी (1), अँकरा (1), *and* अँकुरा.—*H. and M.* अकरी, *Bg.* आँकरी.]

अँकंरी *ãk'rī* (2) = अँकड़ी *ãk'ṛī* (2), *q.v.*

अकरुन *akarun*, **Tbh.**, *adj. com. gen.*, (*subst. f.* अकरुना *akarunā*), pitiless, merciless, relentless. **Exam.**, *Rām.*, *Bā.*, *ch.* 283, 6, कर कुठार मैं अकरुन कोही, Having axe in hand, I am pitiless in my wrath.

(*Rām Jasan's reading* अकरन *is an error. It has been adopted into Bate's Hindī Dictionary, where it is explained as equal to* अकारन.)

[*Skr.* अकरुण:, *Pr.* अकरुणो (*see Nām., vs.* 73), *all Gds.* अकरुण *or* अकरुन.]

अकंरूर *ak'rūr*, अकड़ूर *ak'rūṛ*, अकरुड़ *ak'ruṛ* = अक्रूर *akrūr*, *q.v.*

अकंरोट *ak'roṭ*, अक्रोट *akroṭ* = अखोट *akhroṭ*, *q.v.* (*Wat. akrot.*)

अँकंरोरी *ãk'rōrī*, **Tbh.**, *subst. f.*, small pebbles. **Exam.**, *Padm.*, *ch.* 137, 3, पायन पहिर लेहु सब पँवरी, काँट न चुभे, न गड़े अँकरोरी, Put slippers on your feet so that thorns may not pierce, nor pebbles wound them. *See* अँकरी *ãk'rī* (2) *and* अँकड़ी *ãk'ṛī* (2).

[*Derived from* अँकरा (2) *by means of the pleon. suff.* ओरा, *fem.* ओरी (*Gd. Gr.* § 209). *The fem. gender indicates diminutiveness.*]

अकर्कस *akarkas*, **Ts.**, *adj. com. gen.*, very hard, very difficult, very unpleasant. **Exam.**, *Coll.* (*Bh.*), ई बड़ अकर्कस बा, This is extremely unpleasant.

[*From Skr.* कर्कश, *with the intens. pref.* अ; *see art.* अ *a* (5). *The word is not uncommonly used in Bihār, but not in the negative sense,* 'not hard' *or* 'soft,' *given to it in the H. Dy.*]

अकर्म *akarm*, **Ts.**, *subst. m.*, [1] a bad *or* low action, sin, wickedness; [2] (*its result*) evil, misfortune, ill fate. **Exam.**, [1] *Coll.* (*Bh.*), ई कौन अकर्म करत रहँऽ, ऐसन नऽ करे के चाही, What wickedness are you committing? You should not act thus. *See another example under* अकरमल *akar'mal.* [2] *For an example see under* अकोल *akōl* (3).

[*Skr.* अकर्म, *and so in all Gds.*]

अकर्मक *akarmak*, **Ts.**, *adj. com. gen.*, (*gram.*) intransitive.

[*Skr.* अकर्मक: ; *hence* अकर्मक *in all Gds.*]

अकर्मन्य *akarmany'*, **Ts.**, *adj. com. gen.*, (*subst. f.* अकर्मन्या *akarmanyā*), useless, good for nothing, unprofitable. **Exam.**, *Coll.* (*Bh.*), ई मनई बड़ा अकर्मन्य बँवे, एकरा से किछु काम नाहिँ निकली, This is a most good-for-nothing fellow; no work can be got from him.

[*Skr.* अकर्मण्यः; *hence* अकर्मण्य *or* अकर्मन्य *in all Gds.*]

अकर्मि *akarmi*, (*f.* अकर्मिनि *akarmini*) = अकर्मी *akarmī*, *q.v.*

[*This form is peculiar to the Mth. dialect and to poetry. See Mth. Gr.*, § 47, *p.* 20.]

अकर्मी *akarmī*, **Ts.**, *adj. com. gen.*, (*subst. f.* अकर्मिनी *akarminī*), wicked, rascally, an evil-doer. **Exam.**, *Coll.* (*Bh.*), तोहरे भाई बड़ा अकर्मी बँवे, ओकरा नूँ समझावँऽ, नाँ? Your brother is a great rascal, you should remonstrate with him, won't you?

[*Skr. m.* अकर्मी, *f.* अकर्मिणी, *and so in all Gds.*]

अकल *akal* (1), **Ts.**, *adj. com. gen.*, [1]*lit.* not in parts, not divisible, not subject to increase or decrease, *used tech. as an epithet of* Brahma; *hence* [2]immeasurable, inconceivable, mysterious. **Exam.**, [1]*Rām.*, *Bā.*, *do.* 61, 1, ब्रह्म जो व्यापक बिरज अज अकल अनीह अभेद, Brahma, who is omnipresent, passionless, unbegotten, indivisible, desireless, undifferentiated; *Bin.* 49, ब्रह्म, व्यापक, अकल, सकल-पर, परम-हित-ग्यान, गोतीत, गुनबित्ति-बर्जित, (*Hari is*) like Brahma, omnipresent, indivisible, transcending all, (*the source of*) the knowledge of the highest good, imperceptible to the senses, excluding the existence of any quality. [2]*Sat.* iv, 38, बिनहि बीज तरु एक भो साखा दल फल फूल; को बरनै अतिसे अमित सब बिधि अकल अतूल, Without seed a tree has been produced (*i.e. the kalpa-tree*), with branches, twigs, fruit, and flowers. Who can describe it? It is thoroughly immeasurable, altogether mysterious and incomparable.

[*Skr.* अकलः, *Pr.* अकलो, *in all Gds* अकल.]

अकाल *akal* (2), **Tbh.**, (I) *adj. com. gen.*, (*subst. f.* अकली *akali or Mth.* अकलि *akali*), *lit.* [1]unskilled in conversation; *hence* [2]simple, foolish, silly; [3]befooled. **Exam.**, [1]*Chan.*, राज द्वार मेँ अकलक सहायता की, What assistance can one who is unskilled in conversation render in (*introducing another into*) a king's court? [2]*Chan.*, अकलक सरधि सकल निरवाह, सबहिक पालक धरनी-नाह; राजा अकल सकल दुरि जाय; सभ कौं राजा देव उपाय, The lord of the earth, the protector of all (*i.e. the king*), supplies all the necessities of a fool; (*but*) with a foolish king all goes wrong: kings and gods are the refuge of all; *Chan.*, ननद पठाओलि परस पओरि। औरि मखान मिसरी बोरि॥ अकलिक (*fem.*) बिपति सकल दुरि गेलि। भाग्यमान सुत माता भेलि॥ The sister-in-law sent (*to her brother's wife*) a delicious dish made of rice-milk with water-nuts mixed with sugar; all the distress of the foolish woman was removed; she became the mother of a fortunate son. [3]*Chan.*, तेल मध्य कारिख मिलाराय। डाड़ी डाबा देल पठाय॥ बाबक सभ अंग चढ़ लगाय। चटिकिरिनीक कपट नहिँ पाव॥ प्रात देखि पड़ जैसन भील। मधि व्याप्रल जनु मुसहड़ भील॥ अकल सकल बरियातक ठाठ। लाजक-लेल भेल जनु काठ॥ (*The bride's people*) mixed soot with the oil and sent it in large and small pots; all the (*bridegroom's*) people being weary rubbed it on their bodies without discovering the maid-servant's trick. In the morning they looked black like Bhils or Musahars coming away from the preparation of indigo. The whole company of the befooled wedding party became like blocks of wood through shame. (*Compare the story in the Kathā Sarit Sāgar, transl., vol.* I, *p.* 19).

[*Skr.* अकल्प, *Pā.* अकलो (*Pā. Dy.*), *Pr.* अकलो, *P.* अकल, *O.* अकळ, *M.* अकळ, *G.* अकळ *or* अकल, *B.*, *Bg.*, *and H.* अकल.]

अकल *akal* (3), **Tbh.**, *prop. wk. f. of* अकला *ak'lā*, *q.v.*, *occurring in comp. only, e.g., in* अकलखुरा *akal'khurā*, (*f.* °री *ri*), *adj.*, *lit.* eating alone; *hence* unsociable, greedy, selfish, jealous.

अकल *ak'l* = अकिल *akil*, *q.v.*

अकलङ्क *akalaŋk*, (*poet.* अकलङ्का *akalaŋkā*), **Ts.**, *adj. com. gen.*, *a religious and moral tech. term*, without spot, stain, *or* defect. **Exam.**, *Rām.*, *Bā.*, *ch.* 82, 4, अस बिचारि तुम तजि सब सङ्का, सबहि भाँति सङ्कर अकलङ्का, Thus do thou think and put away all doubt, that Saŋkar (*i.e.*, *Mahādeb*) is in every way without stain; *Gīt.*, *A.*, 43, 3, बिलसत मुनि-जन चकोर बैठे निज ठौर ठौर अच्छय अकलङ्क सरद चन्द चन्दिनी, The Munis sit like chakōrs (*a kind of partridge said to be enamoured of the moon*), each in his own place, beholding the imperishable spotless autumnal moon (*i.e.*, *Rām*) and its moonlight (*i.e.*, *Sītā*).

[*Skr.* अकलङ्कः; *in all Gds.* अकलङ्क.]

अकलङ्कता *ak'laŋk'tā*, **Ts.**, *subst. f.*, absence of spot or defect, fair fame. **Exam.**, *Rām.*, *Bā.*, *ch.* 275, 3, अकलङ्कता कि कामी लहई, As a gallant who would have no scandal.

[*Skr.* अकलङ्कता, *and so possibly in all Gds.*]

अकलङ्का *akalaŋkā*, *poet.* = अकलङ्क *akalaŋk*, *q.v.*

अकलल्वा akal'wā, अकलुआ akaluā, **Tbh.**, *subst. m.*, *lit.* famine, *hence often used as a* personal name *for the child of a person whose elder children have all died, the superstition being that calling a child by an unpleasant or disgusting object would cause it to live long. See Ind. Ant., vol.* VIII, *p.* 321; *Prop., p.* 22.

[*Properly the long form of* अकाल *akāl*, famine, *q.v.*]

अकल्ला *ak'lā, the same as* एकल्ला *ek'lā, q.v.*

अकलियान *ākaliyān*, अकल्यान *akalyān*, **Ts.**, (I) *adj. com. gen.*, (*subst. f.* अकलियानी *akaliyānī or Mth.* अकलियानि *akaliyānĭ*), [1]unpropitious, ill-omened, unlucky; [2]uncomfortable, disconsolate, unblessed. **Exam.**, [1]*Coll.* (*Bh.*), ए गोसाईं, ऐसन अकलियान बात मत बोलौं, O Gosāī! do not say such unpropitious words. [2]*Chan.*, जनि कौं द्रोह सुधमेक नाम, अकलियान तनि कौं सब ठाम, To whom the (*very*) name of virtue is an aversion, for him every place is unblessed.

(II) *subst. m.*, bad luck, misfortune. **Exam.**, *Coll.* (*Bh.*), तोहरा घर में आगि लगौलक हा, ओकर अकलियान बेरौं बोत, He has set fire to your house, he will certainly have bad luck.

[*Ved.* अकल्याणी *f.* (*Ath.* 20, 128, 8), *Skr.* अकल्याणः *m.*; *in all Gds.* अकल्याण *or* अकल्यान.]

अकलुआ *akaluā* = अकलल्वा *akal'wa, q.v.*

अकलेस *akalēs*, अकलेश *akalēsh*, **Tbh.**, *adv. com. gen., lit.* without trouble; *hence* [1](*physically*) without difficulty, easily; [2](*mentally*) without discomfort, comfortably, happily. **Exam.**, [1]*Hb.* viii, 32, धनि अकलेस देल धनु मोरि, बिस बिसतन्तु जस दे सह तोरि, Most easily he strung the bow and snapped it like the thread of the inner stalk of a lotus. [2]*Prabh., p.* 12, *l.* 20, रति-पति सम्पति लेल परवेस, जनिक सबल जग बस अकलेस, The attendants of Cupid entered, through whom the whole world lives happily.

[*Skr.* अ + क्लेश; *for the cognate forms of* क्लेश *in Pā., Pr., and Gd., see that article. On the origin of the adv. use, see the remarks under* अकारन. *The word appears to be never used as a subst. or adj.*]

अकल्यान *akalyān*, = अकलियान *akaliyān, q.v.*

अकल्वन *ak'wan*, **Tbh.**, *subst. m.*, curled, flowered, gigantic swallowwort, *celebrated among native practitioners for its many medicinal qualities*, calotropis gigantea, *also called* Mandār (मन्दार). *See* आक *āk* (2), *of which it is the more usual Mth. form.*

[*Skr.* अर्कपर्णः, *another name of the arka plant* (*Skr. Dy. P.*), *Pr.* अक्कवण्णो, *B.* आकन्द. *Another name is Skr.* अर्कपत्रः, *whence probably comes the H.* अकौड़ा (*Hd. Dy.*), *contr. from Pr.* अक्कवत्तो.]

अँकल्वरिया *ā̃k'wariyā* (1), **Tbh.**, *subst. f., lg. f. of* अँकल्वारि *ā̃k'wārĭ, q.v.* **Exam.**, *Mag.* 18, भरी अँकवरिया पीया के ले सुतबै, जिया मोर धड़कत जुरमाए, Tightly embracing (*lit.* taking a full hug of) my beloved I shall sleep, and my heart goes beating.

अँकल्वरिया *ā̃k'wariyā* (2), **Tbh.**, *subst. f.*, the rope by which the rudder of a country-boat is held up (*Grs.* § 236).

[*Skr.* अङ्कपाली, *Pr.* अंकवाली *or* (*with pleon. suff.* क) अंकवालिआ; *hence* (*with short antepenultimate*) *B.* अँकल्वरिया.]

अकल्वार *ak'wār* (*Grs.* § 886) = अँकल्वार *ā̃k'wār, q.v.*

अँकल्वार *ā̃k'wār*, अँकल्वारि *ā̃k'wārĭ*, अकल्वार *ak'wār*, अकल्वारि *ak'wārĭ*, **Tbh.**, *subst. f.*, [1]grasp, hug, embrace; [2]an armful, as much as can be taken between the two arms (= अँगा, *q.v., and* भर पाँजा, *Grs.* § 886), *or* as much as can be taken under one arm (*Cr., p.* 51). **Comp.**, अँकल्वार भेंट, *subst. f.*, (*wom.*), salutation by message (*Āz. Gy., where it is erroneously said to be masc.*). **Phr.**, अँकल्वार भरब or अँ॰ लेब to embrace, to hug to one's self (=अङ्क भरब); *hence fig.*, to take greedily, to take with all one's heart (*with the genitive of the thing desired*). **Exam.**, *Mg. song*, [1]जो मैं जनितौं फगुनि बहार, धन के धरितौं भरि भरि अँकवार, If I had known the festival of Phāgun (*the Hōlī*), I would have held my beloved fast with many embraces (*after Fallon*); *Coll.* (*Bh.*), हमार अँकल्वार-भेंट कह दिहलकि, She sent an affectionate salutation to me, (*lit. she sent 'a meeting with embraces' or 'her embraces' to me, as in French letters, 'je vous envoie mille embrassements,' or 'je vous embrasse mille fois'*); *Coll.* (*Bh.*), है वास के हम अँकल्वार लेलौं, I took that object with all my heart (*lit., I took a grasp of that object*). *See* अँकल्माल *ā̃k'māl*, अङ्कम *aykam*, कौल *kaul*, कौली *kaulī*.

[*Skr.* अङ्कपालिः *fem.*, *Pr.* अंकवाली (*Sapt., vs.* 996): *hence B.* अँकल्वारि, *turning* ल *into* र, *as usual; see Gd. Gr.*, § 30, *p.* 34. *In the other Gds. this word occurs only in a mutilated state, with loss of the initial* अ *and contraction of medial* अवा *to* औ; *thus M.* कवळ *f.*, कवळी *or* कौळी *f.*, कवळा *or* कौळा *m.*, *P.* कौली *f.* (*also* कौळा *m. in the sense* corner of a room), *H.* कौली *or lg. f.* कौलिया *f.*, कौला *m.*, *also* कोल *m.*, *B.* कोल, *O.* कोळ. *Most of these mutilated forms occur also in the sense of* lap, bosom; *hence* corner of a room, a lane or long passage. *With these may be compared the B.* कोर, *O.* कोड़, *H.* कोड़ *or* कोड़ा, lap, bosom, *M.* कोठ inlet, branch of a creek, *and in all Gds.* कोन *or* कोना corner; *the cons.* ड़, र, ल, न *being easily interchangeable in the Gds. On the other hand, Skr. has* क्रोड *m.*, lap, bosom, कोल *m.*, lap, embrace, कोण corner; *and there can be little doubt but that in the Gds. the derivatives of the Skr.* अङ्कपालि *and* क्रोड *have been to a great extent confused. It is, however, not impossible that some of the Skr. forms, such as* कोल, कोण, *and perhaps also* कवल mouthful (*M.* कवळ *or* कवठ), *may themselves be due to mutilations of* अङ्कपालि; *cf. the mutilated Skr. form* अङ्कोलिका.]

अँकन्वारि *ãk'wari*, अकन्वारि *ak'wari*, **Tbh.**, *subst. f.*, *the same as* अँकन्वार *ãk'war, q.v.* **Exam.**, *Krish.* 238, यह लालच अकन्वारि भरत सौ, हार तोरि, चोली मडकारि, From this desire you are embracing me, tearing my necklace and disordering my bodice.

अकस *akas*, इक्स *ikkas*, **Any.**, *subst. f.*, [1]spite, enmity (*Āz. Gy.*); [2]envy, jealousy. **Phr.**, अकस राखब *or* अ॰ करब, to bear enmity, to be jealous. **Exam.**, [1]*K. Rām.*, *Ut.* 94, एते मान अकस कौनै (= करिबे) को आहु आहि (= है) को, Who are you that you should act towards me with such pride and enmity? *Coll.* (*Bh.*), तूँ ओकरा बेटवा के मारले रहलँह, ओही से ऊ तोहरा से अकस राखेला, He bears you ill-will because you killed his son long ago (*with pluperf. in the sense of a very long time ago*); *see also under* अकन्सक. [2]*Gīt.*, *Bā.*, 84, 7, चालि चाउ चलत उछाउ चाउ-चल कहि कन्यौ कोहे बिरद अकस उपजाउ है, The heralds proclaimed the fame (*of Sītā's swayambar*), describing the loss, the gain, the rage (*at failing*), the joy (*at succeeding*), the power of arm (*in breaking the bow*), (*and thus*) rousing the envy (*of Rām's co-suitors*).

[Ar., عکس *aks*, *lit.* inversion; *hence*, opposition.]

अकन्सक *ak'sak*, (*Bh.*) अकन्फक *ak'phak or* सकन्फक *sak'phak*, **Tbh.**, *adj. com. gen.*, gorged so that one cannot rise from one's seat. **Exam.**, *Chan.*, काल अकस के अकसक टार, अवटिल काल दन्ड सँसार, What! can the gorged one turn aside Time's enmity? Time's punishment is certain in the world; *ibid.*, अकट-भोज मेँ बैसल्हि जाय, अलसैलाह सुतलाह अघाय। लेलकन्हि सभ चिकु चोर चोराय, अकसक अन काँ की बहुताय॥ Going to a great feast he ate, felt drowsy, and slept, well satiated: a thief stole away all his things: what (*remains*) for the gorged one but to rave like a tiger.

(*The form* अकसक *appears to be pure Maithilī. See Vocabulary in Mth. Ch.*)

[*The word is evidently an alliterative compound connected with the* √फाँक (*cf.* √फाँक, फँक, *Skr.* प्रेर *in H. R., p.* 80, *or* भखिर), to gobble, to toss food into the mouth, *and* फका *or* फक्का *or* फाका *or* फँका, a quantity of food taken to be chucked into the mouth, or the act of chucking such a quantity of food into the mouth. *The alliteration imparts an intensive force, implying* one who gobbles up many handfuls. *M. has* फकफक *or* फकाफक, one who repeatedly throws handfuls into the mouth. *Possibly the form of the B. word may be due to some confusion with* भक्षक, a glutton, *a bye-form of* भक्षक (*with* स *for* क्ष, *see Gd. Gr.*, § 11, *p.* 8), *Skr.* भक्षक.]

अकन्सर *ak'sar* (1), (*lg. f.* अकन्सरन्वा *ak'sar'wā or* अकसरुआ *ak'saruā*), **Tbh.**, *adj. com. gen.*, alone, solitary, single. **Exam.**, *Rām.*, *Ar.*, *do.* 20, 2, कवन हेतु मन व्यग्र अति अकसर आयेहु तात, For what reason have you come, (*my*) son, troubled in mind (*and*) quite alone? *Bij.*, *l.* 943, बाप! अब ले मैं रहलौं अकसर जियरवा, O father, up to now I have been but a single life (*i.e., I have been alone, see Bij., l.* 961). *See* एकन्सर *ek'sar.*

[*Skr.* एककता, *Pr.* एक्कसरिओ (*adv.* एक्कसरिअं *in Hēm.* ii, 213, *synonymous with* झगिति, सम्प्रति) *or* एक्कसरिअं (*Nām.*, *vs.* 17 = झगि एकदा); *the Pr.* सरिअं *becomes in Gd. shortened into* सरि, सर, *just as Pr.* करिअ *becomes Gd.* करि, कर; *see Gd. Gr.*, § 271, *p.* 128. *Hence B.* एकसर *or* अकसर, *H.* इकसर *or* अकसर, *O.* अकसर. *M.* एकसर. *M. has also a str. f. adj.* एकसरा (*fem.* री), *adv.* एकसरेँ. *Similar formations, common to all Gds., are—with the numeral* द्वि two, *B.* (*wk. f.*) दोसर, (*str. f.*) दोसन्रा second; *with the num.* त्रि three, *B.* (*wk. f.*) तेसर *or* (*str. f.*) तेसन्रा third; *with the num.* चतुर four, *B.* चोसरी a land four times ploughed. *Similarly* एकसरी *is* a land once ploughed; *see s. vv. The second and third members of this set are now used as ordinal numbers, replacing the proper forms* दूजा, तीजा. *The first and fourth members have no such specialised meaning. But the original equivalence of the whole set is strikingly shown in such sentences as the M.* तुका म्हणे देह दिधला एकसर, तयासी दुसरें नाहीं जन्म, Tukā Rām says a body he gave me once, hence I shall not be born twice. *M. has also a similar verb* चौसरणें, to perform for a fourth time.]

अकन्सर *ak'sar* (2), **Any.**, (I) *adj. com. gen.*, many, most, nearly all. **Exam.**, *Coll.* (*Bh.*), अकन्सर अदिमी कोग कहेलन, Many people say it.

(II) *adv.*, [1]often; [2]for the most part, usually, generally. **Exam.**, *Coll.* (*Bh.*), अदमी लोग अकन्सर कहेलन, People often say.

[*Ar.* اکثر *akṣar*, *comparative of* کثیر *kaṣīr.*]

अकन्सरन्वा *ak'sar'wā*, *lg. f. of* अकन्सर *ak'sar* (1), *q.v.*

अकसरुआ *ak'saruā* = अकसरवा *ak'sar'wā, q.v.* **Exam.,** *Coll.* (*Bh.*), दीहल घरमे घर है अकसरुआ बा, Dīhal is the only man in his house (*Āz. Gy.*); *i.e. he has no relations.*

अकसवा *akas'wā*, **Tbh.,** *subst. m., lg. f. of* अकास, *q.v.* **Exam.,** *Bij., l.* 818, हिच्छल उड़ि जाते भय अकसवा, Hichchhal (*name of horse*) now flew up into the air (*see also ibid., ll.* 551, 973).

अकसात *ak'sāt*, अक्सात *aksāt*, **Any.,** *subst. m.,* instalments of the annual revenue.

(*A term only used in the kachah'ries or magisterial courts of India.*)

[*Ar.* اقساط *aqsāṭ, properly plur.* of قسط *qisṭ*, an instalment.]

अकसाम *ak'sām*, अक्साम *aksām*, **Any.**, *adv.*, of various kinds, of every sort.

(*A term only used in the kachah'ries or magisterial courts of India.*)

[*Ar.* اقسام *aqsām, properly plur. of* قسم *qism, subst. fem.,* kind, sort.]

अकसीर *ak'sīr*, अक्सीर *aksīr*, **Any.**, *subst. f.,* [1]powder, dust, filings; *especially* [2]powder *or* mixture pretended to be capable of converting other metals to gold or silver, the philosopher's stone, elixir; *hence* [3]the science concerning such powders, alchemy, chemistry; *hence also colloquially used in the sense of an* [4]efficacious *or* beneficial remedy. **Exam.,** [2]*Coll.* (*Bh.*), जबकीम ओकरा हाथमें अकसीर सनि गेल, That doctor became like a philosopher's stone in his hand (*said of a Baniyā in Patna who prospered through the favour shown him by a certain native doctor*). [4]*Coll.* (*Bh.*), ई दवाई बड़ अकसीर होई, This medicine will do you a great deal of good.

[*Ar.* اکسیر *iksīr or* اکثیر *ikṡīr, also pronounced aksīr or akṡīr. Connected with* کسر *kasar* breaking, a fraction.]

अकस्मात *akasmāt*, (*poet.* आकस्मात *ākas'māt*), **Ts.,** *adv., lit.,* [1]without a wherefore, (*i.e., without the operation of any known cause*), perchance; *hence* [2]suddenly, abruptly, unexpectedly, unawares, instantaneously, immediately. **Exam.,** [1]*Sat.,* v, 62, जौं पै आकस्मात ते उपजे बुधि बिसाल, ता तो अति-छल-हीन जे गुर सेवन कछु काल, Although perchance an eminent intellect may be born, still the very guileless spend some time in serving their spiritual preceptor. [2]*Dēv., sc.* 3, जेहि गाँव में ई लोगन के डेरा डण्डा पड़ँचल, जहाँ के लोगन के पराने (= प्राण + हि) सुख जाता; जान पड़ैछा, मानो जम-राज के सैना अकस्मात मानुख-रूप धर के आइल हो, Into whatever village the tents and (*measuring*) rods of these people come, the souls of the people of that place dry up; it seems as if the army of Jam'rāj in human form had suddenly arrived. *For another example, see under* अकरमल *akar'mal.*

[*This word is rarely used. A more usual one is* अकामिक, *q.v., or* अचानक, *q.v.*]

[*Skr.* अकस्मात्; अकस्मात *in all Gds.*]

अकहत्तरि *ak'hattari*, (*Mth.*) = एकहत्तरि *ek'hattari, q.v.*

अकहरा *akah'rā* = एकहरा *ekah'rā, q.v.*

अका *akā*, (*fem.* अकी *akī*), *str. f. of* अक *ak* (1), *q.v.*

अकाए *akāē* = अकाय *akāy, q.v.*

अकाज *akāj*, (*poet.* अकाजा *akājā or* अकाजू *akājū*), **Tbh.,** *subst. m., lit.* what is not to be done; *hence* [1]wrong, sin, crime; [2]harm, injury, loss (*done to others or suffered by one's self*); [3]evil. **Exam.,** [1]*Rām., A., ch.* 203, 1, मुनि-समाज अरु तीरथ-राजू साँचेहु सपथ अघाइ अकाजू, In an assembly of saints and in such a holy place, an oath, even in (*speaking the*) truth, is a sin and a crime. [2]*Rām., A., ch.* 290, 9, पर अकाज प्रिय आपन काजू, Another's loss is dear (*to him and*) his own gain; *ibid., ch.* 285, 1, भरत हाथ सब काज अकाजू, In Bharat's hand is all gain and loss; *ibid., ch.* 72, 7, राम सनेह-बस करत अकाजू, Under the influence of her very love she will do me harm; *ibid., ch.* 23, 8, होइ अकाज, आजु निसि बीते, It will be our loss (*if*) this night pass away (*unutilised*); *ibid., Ba., ch.* 56, 8, जो न कहौं, बड़ होइ अकाजा, If I do not tell it, it will be a great loss (*to me*); *ibid., ch.* 170, 1, कहे कथा, तव परम अकाजा, If you tell your story, then (*you will do yourself*) exceeding harm; *Bin.* 76, तुलसी अकाज काज राम ही के रीझे खीझे; प्रीति की प्रतीति मन मुदित रहत हौं, Tul'sī Dās (*says*), (*the test of*) loss and gain is solely the pleasure and displeasure of Rām; through the experience of His love I remain happy in my heart; *K. Rām., Ut.* 49, जिनका जेहि जी कछु काज नहीं, न अकाज कछू जेहि के मुख मोरे, करे तिन की परवाहि को, From whose favour no gain results, nor any loss from whose displeasure (*lit.* turning away of the face), for him who has any respect? [3]*Ag.* iii, 4, अकरब, अपसुगुन, अघ, असुभ, अनभल, अखिल अकाज, Disappointments, inauspicious omens, mishaps, misfortunes, bad luck, (*and in short*) every evil; *Dōh.* 67. तुलसी हरि अपमान ते होइ अकाज समाज, Tul'sī Dās (*says*), from disrespect to Hari comes every evil.

(*The forms in* आ *ā*, ऊ *ū*, *are merely due to the exigencies of metre and rhyme.*)

[*Skr.* अकार्य, *Pā.* अकज्ज (*Kch.* 318), *Pr.* अकज्ज; *all Gḍs.* अकाज.]

अकाज *akāj*, (*pr. pts.* अकजैत *akajāit*, *Bh.* अकाजत *akājat*, अकाजित *akājit*; अकाजल *akājal*; अकाजब *akājab*; अकाजै *akājai*), **Tbh.**, (I) *v. tr.*, to render useless, inflict injury upon, spoil. **Exam.**, *Coll.* (*Bh.*), तोहर ई काज हम अकाजब, I will spoil this business of yours.

(II) *v. intr.*, *lit.* to be wasted; *hence* to die. **Exam.**, *Rām.*, *A.*, *ch.* 238, 6, मानहुँ राज अकाजेउ आजू, As if the king had died that very day.

[*Der. root made from* अकाज, *q.v.*]

अकाजा *akājā*, *poet.* = अकाज *akāj*, *q.v.*

अकाजि *akāji*, (*f.* अकाजिनि *akājini*), *Mth. and poet.* = अकाजी *akāji*, *q.v.*

अकाजी *akāji*, **Tbh.**, *adj. com. gen.*, (*subst. f.* अकाजिनी *akājini*), bad, injurious. **Exam.**, *Coll.* (*Bh.*), ऊ बड़ अकाजी आदिमी हवे, He is a very bad man.

[*Der. from* अकाज *by the Gḍ. suff.* ई; *see Gḍ. Gr.*, § 252. *Though not noted, it probably occurs in all Gḍs.*]

अकाजू *akājū*, *poet.* = अकाज *akāj*, *q.v.*

अकाथ *akāth*, **Tbh.**, *adv.*, unsuccessfully, vainly, profitlessly, uselessly. **Exam.**, *Bin.* 84, भयो है सुगम तो को अमर अगम तनु समुझि, धौं कत खोवत अकाथ, Knowing that there has been vouchsafed to you a body unattainable to the gods (*lit.* immortals), why (कत) then (धौं) do you lose it profitlessly?

[*Skr.* अकृतार्थ, *Pr.* अकयत्थ (*Sapt.*, *vs.* 516), *B. contr.* अकाथ; *apparently wanting in the other Gḍs.*]

अकान *akān*, (*pr. pts.* अकनैत *akanāit*, *Bh.* अकानत *akānat*, अकानित *akānit*; अकानल *akānal*; अकानब *akānab*; अकानै *akānai*) = *Bw.* √अकन *akan or* √आँकन *ākan*, *q.v.*

अँकाब *ākāb*, (*pr. pts.* अँकबैत *ākabāit*, *Bh. and Mg. also* अँकाबत *ākābat*, अँकाबित *ākābit*, अँकाइत *ākāit*; अँकाओल *ākāol*; अँकाएब *ākāeb*; अँकाबै *ākābai*, अँकाए *ākāe*), **Tbh.**, *caus. v.*, (*Bh.*) to cause to be valued *or* prized. **Exam.**, *Coll.* (*Bh.*), तूँ प्रकरना के कैसे अँकाबतारँ ह, How do you get this valued?

[*Skr.* √अङ्क, *caus.* अङ्कयति, *Pr.* अंकावेइ; *hence Gḍ.* अँकावे; *see Gḍ. Gr.* § 349.]

अँकाव *ākāb* = अँकाव *ākāw*, *q.v.*

अकाबीर *akābir*, **Any.**, *subst. m.*, people of rank, nobles, grandees, the upper ten.

[*Ar.* اکابر *akābir*, *plur. of* اکبر *akbar* great.]

अकाम *akām* (1), (*poet.* अकामा *akāmā*), **Ts.**, (I) *adj. com. gen.*, (*subst. f.* अकामा *akāmā*), without desire, without lust; *used technically as one of the epithets of the Supreme Being.* **Comp.** (*Rām.*, *Ar.*, *chh.* 9, 8) अकाम-प्रिय, The friend of the unsensual, (*i.e.*, *Rām*). **Exam.**, *Rām.*, *Bā.*, *do.* 77, 1, जोगी जटिल अकाम-मन नगन अमङ्गल-बेष, A mendicant recluse with matted hair, his soul free from lust, naked, with hideous accoutrements; *ibid.*, *ch.* 86, 2, जदपि अकाम, तदपि भगवाना भक्त-बिरह-दुख दुखित सुजाना, Though himself passionless, yet God sympathises (*lit.* is pained) with a pious man's pain of bereavement, knowing it well; *K. Rām.*, *Ut.* 144, सिव अकाम, अभिराम-धाम, नित राम नाम रमि, Sib (*is*) devoid of desire, the abode of (*moral*) beauty, always rejoicing in Rām's name.

(II) *subst. m.*, continence. **Exam.**, *Rām.*, *Ut.*, *ch.* 114, 13, परम धरममय पय दुहि, भाई, अवटै अनल अकाम बनाई, After drawing off the milk of sound religion, O brother, it is set to boil on (*lit.* having made) the fire of continence.

[*Ved.* अकामः (*Ath.* 10, 8, 44), *Skr.* अकामः, *Pā.* अकामो, *Pr.* अकामो (*cf. Bhag.*, *p.* 200); *all Gḍs.* अकाम.]

अकाम *akām* (2), **Ts.**, *adj. com. gen.*, not done with any intention of a reward. **Exam.**, *Coll.* (*Bh.*), ई काज अकाम बा, This act is done without wish for any reward.

(*The word is probably a tats. from Skr.* अकाम्य, *M.* अकाम्म, *though theoretically it might be derived as a tadbh. through Pr.* *अकम्मो.]

अकामा *akāmā*, *poet.* = अकाम *akām* (1), *q.v.*

अकामिक *akāmik*, **Ts.**, (I) *adj. com. gen.*, without cause or reason.

(II) *adv.*, causelessly.

[*Apparently a corruption of Sk.* आकस्मिक.]

अकामी *akāmi*, **Tbh.**, *adj. com. gen.*, bad, wrong, useless, profitless. **Exam.**, *Coll.* (*Bh.*), अकामी धन्धा से किछु फल नाहिँ होर, From profitless employment there will be no fruit.

[*Skr.* अ + कर्मिकः, *Pr.* अकम्मिओ, *B.*, *H.*, *and M.* अकामी; *wanting apparently in the other Gḍs. The subst.* अकाम uselessness *does not exist.*]

अकाय *akāy*, अकाए *akāĕ*, **Tbh.**, *adj. com. gen.*, huge, vast, dense. **Exam.**, *Hb.*, *Transl.*, *p.* 9, अकायबन, a vast forest, a dense forest; *Hb.* iii, 10, अलप रवय दुइ बिच अकाय, (*It went on to*) where two huge trees were standing.

[*Skr.* अतिकायः *lit.* having an excessive body, *Pr.* अइकाओ (*Rāv.* xii, 59); *the initial* अइ *contracts to* ऐ *or* ऐ *and afterwards shortens into* अ (*see Gḍ. Gr.* §26); *hence Gḍ.* अकाय (*with euph.* य, *for* अकाअ). *All the steps of this phon. process are still exhibited in the Ap. Pr.* अइसो such (*Hēm.* iv, 403), *H.* ऐस *or* अस. *Wanting in the other Gḍs.*]

अकार akār (1), **Ts.**, *subst. m.*, [1]the letter अ a; [2]*a symbolic name of the* Sun *and of* Brahmā. **Exam.**, *Sat.*, ii, 36, 37, बरनउ रकार अकार रवि आलु मकार मयङ्क। अरि रकार अकार विधि म महेस निसङ्क॥ बन अग्यानहि दहन कर अनल प्रबल रकार। रवि अकार वर मोह-तम तुलसी कयवि बिचार॥ The letter r you should understand (*to represent*) fire; the letter a, the sun; and the letter m, the moon. Without doubt, the letter r is Hari (*or Bishnu*), the letter a is Bidhi (*i.e. Brahmā*), and m is Mahēs (*or Sib*); the letter r is the fierce fire which burns the forest of (*man's*) ignorance; the letter a is the sun, which disperses the darkness of (*man's*) infatuation, so Tul'sī Dās says advisedly.

[*Skr.* अकारः; *all Gḍs.* अकार.]

अकार akār (2), (*poet.* अकारा akārā), **Ts.**, *subst. m.*, [1]form, shape, figure; [2]likeness, portrait (*sculptured or painted, etc.*); *hence derivatively* [3]appearance, sign, token. **Exam.**, [1]*Padm.*, *ch.* 322, 5, भौंह धनुक जो छिपा अकारा, बेनी बासुक छिपा पतारा, (*At the sight of*) her eyebrows the bow (*of the Zodiac*) felt ashamed of (*lit.* concealed) its (*curved*) form, and (*at the sight of*) her braided hair Basuki felt ashamed in the nether world; *Prabh.*, *p.* 19, *l.* 2, सिन्दुर रेख चिकुर मध रे, अनुपम अकारे, A line of vermilion is in her hair, and her figure is matchless. [2]*Sat.*, ii, 42, रामानुज सद्गुन विमल श्याम राम अनुहार, भरत भरत सो जगत को तुलसी धरम अकार, Bharat, Rām's younger brother, virtuous, pure, and dark-hued like Rām, he—so Tul'sī Dās says—was the pleasing likeness of the supporter of the world; *Coll.* (*Bh.*), मीयाँ-जी साहब के अकार अस्सू उतारलक, The Mīyā̃-jī has taken the gentleman's portrait exactly. [3]*Coll.* (*Bh.*), जाए के इनकरा अकार नैखे, He has not the appearance of going, *i.e.*, *it does not look as if he would go*; *Coll.* (*Bh.*), विधि के किछु अकार नैखे, There is no sign of rain.

[*Skr.* आकारः, *Pā.* आकारो, *Pr.* आकारो *or* अकारो, *hence B.* अकार, *and so probably in all Gḍs* *The form* आकार ākār, *usually given in the dictionaries as the 'proper' one, does not exist, and arose in the manner explained under the art.* अकास (*q.v.*). *The fact that the true Gḍ. form is* अकार *akar is clearly proved by the existence of the word* निरङ्कार *niraṅkār*, formless (*for Skr.* निराकार *nirākār*) *with the initial vowel* a *shortened, and the compensatory conjunct* ङ्क *ṅk* (*for* क्क *kk*). *The tadbh. Pr. form* आआरो (*Nām.*, *vs.* 249, *Aup.* §1) *has not survived in the Gḍs.*]

अकार akār (3) = अकाल *akāl*, *q.v.*

अँकार ā̃kār, **Tbh.**, *subst. m.*, (*Bh.*) assent (*Ās. Gy.*). **Exam.**, *Coll.* (*Bh.*), इनकरा अँकार नैखे, He objects.

[*S.* आँकार; *perhaps also in other Gḍs. It may be a contraction of Skr.* अङ्गीकार (*through* अङ्गिकार, अङ्कार, अककार, अङ्कार, आँकार; *the change of* ङ्ग *to* क *is not uncommon*); *or it may be derived from the phrase* हाँ करब, to say yes, assent, *with loss of the initial aspirate. Sindhī has both* हाँ *and* आँ *for* yes.]

अकारथ akārath, **Tbh.**, *adj. com. gen.*, *lit.*, not worth doing; *hence* useless, fruitless, aimless. **Phr.**, अकारथ जाएब, अकारथ होएब, to be lost, wasted, destroyed; अकारथ करब, to render useless, squander. **Exam.**, *Prov.*, चोरक माल सभ केओ खाए, चोरक जान अकारथ जाए, A thief's wealth every one enjoys, (*but*) a thief's life is wasted; *Gōp.*, *Introd.*, जनम अकारथ जाय, बचो सुन बाबो मेरी, Your life will be wasted: O listen to my advice!

[*Skr.* अ + कार्यार्थः, *Pā.* अकारियत्थो; *hence Gḍ.*, *with transposition of* य *y*, [1]अकारयथ; *or with loss of* य *y*, [2]अकारथ; *or with transfer of aspiration*, [3]अखारत; *or with loss of aspiration*, [4]अकारत. *All these forms actually occur: S.* (*str. f.*) अकारत्थो *or* अकारत्थो, *M.* (*wk. f.*) अकारथ (*Hd. Dy. wrongly* अक्कारथ), *B. and P.* अकारथ, *H.* अकारथ *or* अकारत, *Br.* अकारत (*Hd. Dy.*), *G.* अकारत. *Regarding the transposition of letters and the transfer or loss of aspiration, see Gḍ. Gr.*, §§ 130 ff, 145, *and H. R.*, *p.* 40.]

अकारन akāran, (*old obl.* अकारनहिँ *akāranahi̐*), **Tbh.**, (I) *subst. m.*, [1]absence of cause *or* reason; [2]freedom from necessity *or* constraint *or* bias, disinterestedness. **Exam.**, [2]*Bin.* 230, अकारन को हित और को है, Who else (*beside Rām*) is a disinterested friend (*lit.* friend of disinterestedness; *comm.* निःप्रयोजन हितकारी)? *ib.* 243, नाहिँ न नाथ अकारन को हित तुम समान पुरान श्रुति गायो, Both the Purāns and Bēds proclaim that there is no lord and disinterested friend like unto Thee (*i.e. Rām*; *ib.*, *opp.* स्वारथ-हित egotistic friend); *K. Rām.*, *Ut.* 9, प्रह्लाद-विषाद निवारन, वारन-तारन, मीत अकारन को, (*Rām*) the reliever of Prah'lād's sorrow, the salvation-giver of the elephant, a disinterested friend.

(II) *adj. com. gen.*, [1]causeless, groundless; [2]free, voluntary, disinterested. **Exam.**, [1]*Rām.*, *Ut.*, *ch.* 40,

6, सबर अकारन सब काहू सौं, (*Entertaining*) groundless enmity towards every one. [2]*Bin.* 206, का को सरल सुभाव सेवक सन, काहि प्रनत पर प्रीति अकारन, Who else (*beside Rām*) shows (*such*) genial disposition towards his servants or (*such*) disinterested love towards his devotees?

(III) *adv.*, [1]without cause *or* reason, groundlessly, causelessly; [2]without necessity *or* constraint, gratuitously, freely, disinterestedly. Exam., *Rām.*, *Bā.*, *ch.* 275, 2, जिमि चह कुसल अकारन कोही, Just as if one who is passionate without cause desires peace of mind; *ibid.*, *Ut.*, *ch.* 99, 3, अभिमान बिरोध अकारनहीँ, Self-conceit and wrangling without cause.

[*Skr.* अकारणः, *Pr.* अकारणो; *hence all Gḍs.* अकारन *or* अकारन. *In the instr. case it is used adverbially; Skr.* अकारणेन, *Pā.* अकारणेन, *Ap. Pr.* अकारणहिँ (*see Hēm.*, iv, 347, 342, *Gḍ. Gr.* § 376); *hence old Bw.* अकारनहिँ (*the final* हीँ *is lengthened in the example quoted above for the sake of metre and rhyme; see Hēm.*, iv, 330), *or, with loss of inflexion,* अकारन, *in which latter form it may occur in all Gḍs.*]

अकाल *akāl*, अकार *akār* (3), **Ts.**, (I) *subst. m.*, [1]unseasonableness; [2]a famine, scarcity. **Comp.**, अकाल-फल, fruit produced out of season; अकाल-बीर a kind of rice, sown broadcast (*Mth.*); अकाल-बिष्टि, untimely rain; अकाल-मौत *or* अकाल-मिरतु *f.*, premature death, sudden *or* unnatural death. Exam., [1]*Rām.*, *Ar.*, *ch.* 20, 8, खल-द्रावक बच कै प्रिय बानी, जिमि अकाल के कुसुम, The friendly speech of the wicked is portentous, like flowers that blossom out of season. [2]*Fam.*, *vs.* 1, सुनु एकासिक बरनन सुनो, चौदिस परल अकाल, Hear the tale of '81 (*i.e. Fasli year* 1281 = 1873-74 *A.D.*), on all sides fell a famine. *See* काल *kāl.*

(II) *adj. com. gen.*, unseasonable, untimely. Exam., *Ag.* vi, 30, बालक मौत अकाल (*fem.*) भइ राम राजा केहि पाप, Whose is the guilt, O King Rām, of the untimely death of the child?

[*Skr.* अकालः, *Pā.* अकालो, *Pr.* अकालो (अकाल-मेह untimely cloud, *Nāy.* § 59), *G. and O.* अकाळ, *M.* अकाल *or* अकाळ, *H. and B.* अकाल, *P.* अकाल *or* काळ, *S.* काळु; *in the two last forms the loss of the initial* अ *is probably due to a confusion with* काल death, destiny. *S. has also* डुकाळु *and* डुकर (*Skr.* दुष्कालः). *The tadbh. Pr. form* अआलो (*Spt.*, *vs.* 55) *has not survived in the Gḍs.*]

अकाल-बीर *akāl'bīr* (*Grs.* § 965), *see under* अकाल *akāl.*

अकाला *akālā*, **Any.**, *subst. m.*, cancelling *or* revocation of a sale (*Wil.*).

[*Ar.* اقالة *aqālah.*]

अकाली *akālī* (1), (*lg. f.* अकलिया *akaliyā*), **Tbh.**, *adj. com. gen.*, relating to a famine. *Sometimes used as a personal name, to indicate the time of birth, in the sense of* famine-born, born in a famine year (*Prop.*, *p.* 31), *like* अकलुआ *akaluā*, *q.v.* Exam., कबित अकाली, The famine song, *the name of Faturī Lāl's poem in Mth. Ch.*

[*Skr.* अकालिकः, *Pr.* अकालिओ, *Gḍ.* अकाली. *See Gḍ. Gr.*, §§ 252-55.]

अकाली *akālī* (2), (*fem.* अकालिनी *akālinī*), **Tbh.**, *subst.*, a believer in the Akāl *or* the Immortal (*God*), *the name of a kind of devotees in the Panjāb.*

[*A Gḍ. derivation from* अकाल *akāl*, *either by the Prs. suff.* ई *ī or by the Gḍ. suff.* ई, *corresponding to the Skr. suff.* इक. *See Gḍ. Gr.*, § 252.]

आँकाव *ā̃kāw*, आँकाब *ā̃kāb*, **Tbh.**, *subst. m.*, (*Bh.*) valuation, appraisement. Exam., *Coll.* (*Bh.*), हाथी कां दाम के आँकाव पैसन नाहिँ होत, The valuation of an elephant is not a matter of pice (*lit.* is not done by pice; पैसन *is the W. Bh. instr. of* पैसा).

[*First verb. noun, der. from the caus.* √आँकाव (*q.v.*), *by means of the prim. der. suff.* अ *a* (2), (*q.v.*).]

अकास *akās*, अकाश *akāsh*, (*poet.* अकासा *akāsā*, *lg. f.* अकसवा *akas'wā*, *old. dir.* अकासु *akāsu or poet.* अकासू *akāsū*, *old. obl.* अकासहिँ *akāsahi or poet.* अकासहीँ *akāsahī*, *mod. loc.* अकासे *akāsē or* अकासेँ *akāsē̃*), **Ts.**, *subst. m.*, [1]sky, heaven, visible firmament; [2]air, atmosphere; [3]ether *or* the fifth element of Hindū physics (*supposed to be one of the five component parts of the human body and the vehicle of sound; in this sense* समीर *is used as a synonym in Rām.*, *Ki.*, *ch.* 11, 4); [4](*poet.*) *a symbolical name for the* cypher; [5](*poet.*) *a symbolical name for the* nose (*owing to the fact that its synonym* नाक *has both meanings*, sky *and* nose; *cf. Rām.*, *Bā.*, *ch.* 273, 13). **Comp.**, अकास-कुसुम *m.*, flowers in the sky (*used as a synonym for an impossibility*); अकासग bird (*lit.*, going in the air); अकास-गङ्गा *f.*, the milky way (*lit.*, the Ganges of heaven); अकास-जान *or* अकास-बहन *m.*, a vehicle that proceeds through the air, balloon; अकास-दीयक *or* अकास-दीया *or* अकास-दीपा *m.*, any elevated lantern, a beacon (*esp. applied to a kind of lamp which the Hindūs hang aloft on a bamboo in the month of Kārtik* (*October–November*) *in honour of Lachhmī or Krish'n*); अकास-नगर *m.*, a visionary town in the sky, fata morgana; अकास-नीम *m.*, a certain plant (*a kind of epidendron*) which grows on the nīm-tree (*Bignonia suberosa*); अकास-पवन *m.*, *v.* अकास-बेल; अकास-पुहुप *m.*, *v.* अकास-कुसुम; अकास-फल *m.*, darling child (*lit.* fruit of heaven);

अकास-बर्न or अकास-बरन, sky-coloured, cærulean, azure; अकास-बानी *f.*, heavenly voice, a divine voice from heaven; अकास-बेल *f.*, *lit.* an air-plant, the name of various parasitic plants (*Cuscuta reflexa*, *Cassyta filiformis*, *Pistia stratiotes*, *see Ell.*, *vol.* II, *p.* 213); अकास-थिति or अकास-थिते *f.*, casual subsistence, living from hand to mouth (*lit.* living on air); अकास-थितो, *adj.* (*f.* अकास-थितिनी), a casual, cadger, one who lives from hand to mouth; अकास-मण्डल or अकास-मँडर *m.*, the atmosphere, the celestial sphere, firmament; अकास-मुखी *m.*, a certain kind of devotee of the Shaib sect (*so called from turning up the face towards the sky in the direction of the sun, till they become unable to hold it in its proper position*); अकास-मूली *m.*, *v.* अकास-बेल. Exam., [1]*Rām.*, *Su.*, *do.* 25, 2, अट्टहास करि गरजा कपि बढ़ि लाग अकास, The monkey shouted with roars of laughter and swelled (*so big*) that he touched the sky; *Hb.*, i, 36, अवशहि उड़ि तोहि लागब अकास, Thou shalt fly away from him to the skies; *Padm.*, *do.* 255, 2, नखत चहूँ दिसि रोवहिँ, अँधेर धरत अकास, The stars all around weep, and darkness covers the sky; *Kan.* 19, चढ़े कमान बान सेँ भयो अकास अन्तरा, Through the arrows (*shot*) from the bows a separation was made between heaven and earth (*i.e.*, *the arrows discharged from the bows were so exceedingly numerous that they hid the sky from the sight of men*); *Padm.*, *ch.*, 562, 1, भयो रैन ससि उआ अकासा, At nightfall the moon rose in the sky; *ib.*, *ch.*, 601, 5, जब लग सूर को दिस्टि अकासू, तब लग ससि नहिँ करै प्रकासू, So long as the sun looks upon (*i.e. governs*) the sky, the moon does not shed any light; *ib.*, *ch.* 562, 3, नखत अकासहिँ चढ़े दियारे, The stars rise in the sky to give light; *ib.*, *ch.* 135, 6, बायेँ अकासेँ धवरे आवे, लोवा दरस आव देखरवे, On the left, in the sky, white quails came, and a fox showed himself in front (*both are good omens at the commencement of a journey*); *Rām.*, *Bā.*, *ch.* 177, 5, भइ अकास-बानी तेहि काला, A voice came from heaven at that very time. [2]*Rām.*, *Ln.*, *ch.* 63, 6, गरजि अकास चलेउ, With a shout he ascended into the air; *ibid.*, *ch.* 70, 5, गहि गिरि तरु अकास कपि धावहिँ, (*Snatching up*) rocks and trees the monkeys sprang into the air; *Bid.* 1, 5, बाँधि धरिय उड़ि लागत अकासे, Hold them fast, (*else*) they will fly up into the air; *Bih.*, v, 6, दुख सुख राम साथे भँजेतौँ, दीपक बरितौँ अकासवौँ, I would endure pain and pleasure with Rām, and would have lit a beacon in the air (*alluding to the* अकास-दीपक, *q.v.*); *Alh.*, *l.* 380, घोड़ा खोल देल बघ रूदल के, घोड़ा उड़ के लागल अकास, She unloosened the horse of the tiger-like Rūdal, and the horse flew up into the air. [3]*Bw. do.*, *anon.*, सम्बत बिक्रम-भूप के जुग अकास नव चन्द, कासी-तारक देह तिज गयो देव दिव चन्द, In the year 1902 of King . Vikramāditya's era King Chand, the saviour of Kāshī, left his body to go to God, (*here* जुग = 2, अकास = 0, नव = 9, चन्द = 1). [4]*B. Rām.* 28, बेद नाम कहि, अँगुरिन खंडि अकास, पठयो सूपनखाहि लखन के पास, Mentioning the name of the 'ear,' and with his fingers (*making the sign of*) cutting off his nose, he (*Rām*) sent Sūp'nakhā to Lakhan (बेद *being a synonym of* श्रुति *signifies the* ear; *the sentence means that Rām, in sending Sūp'nakhā to Lakhan, warned her that her ears and nose would be cut off*).

(*Both forms* अकास *akās and* अकाश *akāsh are met with, varying with the circumstances and the speaker. On the whole, throughout Bihār* अकास *is the common, everyday pronunciation, while* अकाश *is considered affected and stylish. The forms* आकास *ākās or* आकाश *ākāsh, generally given in the dictionaries as the so-called 'correct' or 'proper' ones, have never been met with by us in B. literature except in one place, though the word itself is of very frequent occurrence. That single exception is in Rām., Bā., ch.* 206, 2, सुमन-बृष्टि आकास तेँ होई, ब्रह्मानन्द मगन सब कोई. *Here all copies that we have consulted agree in reading* आकास, *except one which reads* अंबर. *But the metre shows that here too the correct reading is probably* अकास. *The fact is that the form* आकाश (*or* आकास), *so much affected now-a-days, is a falsely restituted unphonetic spelling. The word certainly is never pronounced ākās or ākāsh, but always akās or akāsh. There are two other forms* अक्कास *akkās and* अगास *agās* (*see the respective articles*). *We have never met with them in B. literature, but they are true Gauḍian forms, and may be met with colloquially.*)

[*Ved.* आकाश (*Skr. Dy. P.*), *Skr.* आकाशः, *Pā.* आकासो, *Pr.* आआसो *or* *अआसो, *Mg. Pr.* आआशे *or* *अआशे (*see art.* अ *a* (6)); *hence B.* अकास *or* अकाश *or* अकाश, *H. as in B.*, *P.* अकास, आकास, *M.* आकाश, *G.* आकाश, *O.* अकाश (*O. Vy.*), आकाश, *B.* आकाश, *S.* आकासु, *Ksh.* आकाश. *The usual tadbh. Pr. form is* आगासो (*cf. Bhag.*, *p.* 207, *Aup.* § 22, *Nāy.* § 65), *which has survived in B., H., P., and M. in the form* अगास. *The other tadbh. Pr. form* आयासो *or* आवासो (*Sapt.*, *vs.* 571, *Rāv.* xv, 85), *however, has not survived in the Gḍs.*]

अकासी *akāsī*, अकाशी *akāshī*, Tbh., (I) *adj. com. gen.*, [1]appertaining to space, celestial, aerial, atmospherical; [2]suspended in the air. Phr., [1]अकासी बरन sky blue (*v.* अकास-बरन); [2]अकासी दीया a raised lantern, a beacon (*v.* अकास-दीया).

(II) *subst. m.*, [1]anything suspended in the air, *or* over one's head; *hence* [2](*Mth.*) the upper beam of a loom to which the levers are attached, *and which is above the head of the weaver* (*Grs.*, § 363); ²(*S.-E. Tirhut*) a scarecrow *pulled by a string and hung on a tree* (*Grs.*, § 68); ³*f.* (*in Chāiṅ' slang*) a head-dress (*Ās. Gy.*). **Exam.,** *Coll.* (*Bh.*, *in Kahārs' slang*), ¹अकासी धये के (*scl.* चलँड), Go stooping (*to avoid*) something over-head. *See also* अगासी *agāsī*.

अकिञ्चन *akiñchan* (1), **Ts.,** *adj. com. gen.*, (*subst. f.* अकिञ्चना *akiñchanā*), without anything, utterly destitute, poor, wretched, miserable. (*A tech. term of Indian asceticism; see Bhag., pp.* 175, 187.) **Exam.,** *Rām.*, *Bā.*, *ch.* 166, 3, परम अकिंचन प्रिय हरि केरे, The destitute is the most beloved of Hari; *ib.*, *Ar.*, *ch.* 40, 7, अचल अकिंचन सुचि सुखधामा, (*Saints are*) imperturbable, have no worldly goods, and live a life of chastity and contentedness.

[*Skr.* अकिंचन, *Pr.* अकिंचणो (*Nām.*, *vs.* 35) *or* अकिंचणो (*cf. Aup.* § 27); *in all Gds.* अकिंचन.]

अकिञ्चन *akiñchan* (2), **Ts.,** *subst. m.*, want of any possession, poverty. (*Tech. term for one of the vows of Indian asceticism; see Bhag., pp.* 175, 187.) **Exam.,** *Coll.* (*W. Bh.*), ओकरा घरे ऐसन अकिंचन बा कि मूस ओकस मरै, There is such poverty in his house that the very mice are dying.

[*Skr.* आकिंचनं, *Pr.* आकिंचणं, *H.* अकिंचन *or* आकिंचन; *all other Gds.* आकिंचन.]

अकिल *akil*, अकल *ak'l*, अक्कल *akkal*, **Any.,** *subst. f.*, sense, common sense, understanding, wisdom. **Phr.,** अकिल लगाएब, to exercise one's common sense, to act wisely; अकिल जोमब, (*lit.* to have one's senses congealed), to be astonished; अकिल दमाएब, to have one's mind bent, to consider, to think; (*Bh.*) अकिल के पढ पढ, perfect fool. **Exam.,** *Misc.* 6, तेरो अकिल भुलानो राम-दसिय, Thy senses are astray, O Rāmdas! *Dēv.*, *sc.* 3, जब से एह जिलन्वा में बन्दोबस्त जारी भइल है, तब से हमनी ऐसन अउझाइल बाडीं कि कौनो अकिलो काम नाहीं करत, Since the settlement has been begun in this district, we have become so entangled that our intellect even can do nothing (*i.e. we don't know what on earth to do*); *B. Gr.*, iii (*Mg.*), *Fable* 15, जौन बात अकिल में नइ घड़े, ओकरा मानै के नइ चाही, That which does not agree (*lit.* fit into) one's understanding, should not be regarded; *Mth. Ch.*, *p.* 2, एह बेकूब कें कखों मह जोक अकिल हैतैक, When will there be good common sense to this fool? *Coll.* (*Bh.*), तूं मड अकिल के पढ पढ चँऽ, You are a perfect fool!

[*Ar.* عقل *'aql.*]

अकिलमन्द *akil'mand*, **Any.,** *adj. com. gen.*, sensible, wise.

[*Ar. Prs.* عقلمند *'aqlmand; derived from Ar.* عقل *'aql with the Prs. suff.* مند *mand.*]

अकीक *akīk*, **Any.,** *subst. m.*, cornelian.

[*Ar.* عقيق *'aqīq.*]

अकीदा *akīdā*, **Any.,** *subst. m.*, ¹religious belief, profession of faith; ²confidence. **Exam.,** ¹*Coll.* (*Bh.*), रसूलन के अकीदा बोलँऽ, Say the Apostles' Creed; ²*Coll.* (*Bh.*), हमार एह पर अकीदा नैखे, I have no confidence in him.

(*Used among Musalmāns and native Christians.*)

[*Ar.* عقيدة *'aqīdah.*]

अकीरत *akīrat*, अकिरति *akīr'ti*, अकीर्ति *akīrti*, **Ts.,** *subst. f.*, disgrace, infamy, ill repute. **Exam.,** *Bw. do. anon.* अपनो कीरत जो चहै पर कीरत को खोय, ताकु अकीरत होत है, जग मह कहइ न कोय, One who wishes to gain reputation by destroying the repute of others gains only ill repute, and no one in the world calls him a good man.

[*Skr.* अकीर्तिः; *H. the same as in B.*; *other Gds.* अकीर्ति. *The tadbh. Pr. form is* अकित्ति (*Aup.* § 117), *which, however, has not survived in the Gds.*]

अकीर्ति *akīrti*, *the same as* अकीरत *akīrat*, *q.v.*

अँकुआ *ãkuā*, (*Mg.*), **Tbh.,** *subst. m.*, *cor. for* अँखुआ *ãkhuā*, *q.v.*

अँकुड़ा *ãkuṛā*, = अँकुरा *ãkurā in one of its fourth series of meanings*, *q.v.* (*Grs.* § 500.)

अँकुढ़ा *ãkuṛhā*, **Tbh.,** *subst. m.*, ¹(*N. Bh.*) the end of the pipe of a blacksmith's bellows which goes into the fire (*Grs.* § 414); ²(*N. Bh. and N. Mth.*) = अँकुरा *ãkurā*, *in two of its fourth series of meanings*, *q.v.* (*Grs.* §§ 376, 412.)

[*This is merely a corruption of* अँकुरा, *q.v. Regarding the aspiration, see Gd. Gr.*, § 131, *p.* 72.]

अकुण्ठ *akuṇṭh*, (*poet.* अकुण्ठा *akuṇṭhā*), **Ts.,** *adj. com. gen.*, *lit.* not blunted *or* worn out; *hence met.* keen, sharp, intense. **Exam.,** *Rām.*, *Ln.*, *ch.* 26, 8, सुनु अति-अन्ध, लोक बैकुण्ठ लाभ कि रघुपति-भगति अकुण्ठा, Hearken, O dull of understanding! is Baikuṇṭh (*merely*) a world (*like other worlds*) or intense faith in Rām (*merely*) a gain (*like other gains*)? *ib.*, *Ut.*, *ch.* 64, 1, मति अकुण्ठ (*fem.*) हरि-भक्ति अखण्डा, A man of keen understanding and indestructible faith in Hari.

[*Skr.* अकुण्ठः; *as above possibly in all Gds.*]

अकुताना *akutā*, (*pr. pts.* अकुतात *akutāt*; अकुताइल *akutāil*; अकुताब *akutāb*; अकुताय *akutāy*), **Tbh.**, (*Bh. and Mg.*), *v. intr.*, to be weary, tired, distressed, worried. **Exam.**, *B. Gr.*, II (*Bh.*), *Fable* 9, मुनस्सी को अकुता के कहले, The scribe being worried said; *Gōp.*, (*Mg.*), 11, उठि गोपी चन्द अकुताए, Gōpī Chand having arisen in distress of mind. *See* √अखुता *akhutā*, √अगुता *agutā, and* √औकता *auk'tā*.

[*Der. root from* अति + क्रम + अय *or* + आर्त, *lit.* pulled down *or* afflicted with great weariness, *Skr.* *अतिक्रमायति *or* अतिक्रमार्तयति, *Pr.* *अइक्कमावेइ, *hence contracted, Gd.* *ऐकौताऐ *or shortened* अकुताऐ. *Regarding the shortening see Gd. Gr.*, §§ 25, 26, *also art.* अ (5). *Skr.* क्रम *becomes Pr.* कम *or* किलम (*Hēm.* ii, 106). *Skr.* अय *becomes Pā.* आय (*Pā. Gr. K.*, *p.* 53); *Skr.* आर्त *becomes Pr.* अत्त (*Aup.* § 30, *p.* 41) *or* (*more usually*) अट्ट (*Aup.* § 30, *p.* 42, § 56, *p.* 63; *Nāy.* § 73, *Kalp.* § 92). *cf. Pr.* अत्त *or* अट्ट = *Skr.* आर्त (*Hēm.* ii, 33). *The Pr. p.p.p.* अट्टिय (= *Skr.* आर्तित) *of the den.* √आर्त *occurs in Aup.* § 56, *p.* 63. *The W. Bh. form of the root is* अखुता, *Mth.*. अगुता, *S. Mth.* औकता, *H.* उकता *or* उकताना, *P.* उकताव.]

अकुरा *akurā*, **Tbh.**, *subst. m.*, a hooked instrument *used by the glassmakers for turning the glass in, or for taking it out of, the crucible* (*Grs.* § 564). *See* अँकुरा *ãkurā*.

[*This is merely a bye-form of* अँकुरा, *q.v.*]

अँकुरा *ãkurā*, **Tbh.**, *subst. m.*, [1] sprout, shoot, plantlet; *hence particularly the* [2] *name of certain* sprouting plants, *such as the* large millet (*holcus sorghum*, *Grs.* § 986), the pea (*pisum sativum*, *Grs.* § 1001); [3] *in the various other meanings of* आँकुर *ãkur*, *q.v.*; [4] the name of various implements which have the form of a hook or are furnished with a hook; *thus* (*S. Mth.*) the iron bands *or* hooks *in a pony-carriage, by which the strengthening spokes* (मुखाना) *outside the wheel are fastened to the cross-pieces* (बाम *and* ढेकानी) *which run from side to side at the back* (*Grs.* § 222; *also* अँकुरी, *q.v.*); the hook *by which the pitcher is fastened to a toddy-seller's waist as he climbs the palm-tree* (*Grs.* § 376; *also* (*N.Bh.*) अँकुसा, (*Bh.*) अँकुसी, *and* (*S. Mth.-Bg.*) अँकोरा, *q.v.*); (*N. Bh.*) the hooked iron poker *by which a blacksmith stirs his fire* (*Grs.* § 412; *also* अँकुरी *or* अँकुसा, *q.v*, *or* (*S. Mth.-Bg.*) अँकोरा *or* आँकन्सा, *q.v.*); (*N. Bh.*, *S. Mth.*) the hooked pivot *on which a blacksmith's bellows work* (*Grs.* § 414); the iron hook with a ring *which goes round the toe of a fancy-silk or fringe-maker* (*Grs.* § 500; *also* अँकुसा, *q.v.*, *or* अँकुसा *or* अँकुसी, *q.v.*); (*N. Bh.*) the iron hook *for taking out the glass from the crucible of a glassmaker* (*Grs.* § 564; *also* अकुरा *or* अँकुरी, *q.v.*, *or* (*S. Mth.*) अकुरी *or* उकरी, *q.v.*)

[*Properly the str. f. of* आँकुर, (*q.v.*) = *Skr.* अङ्कुर *The latter word properly means a* sprout *or* shoot, *but is clearly a derivative of* अङ्क a hook. *The above given meanings, however, are probably due to a confusion of the three closely allied words* अँकन्सा (*see f.* अँकन्ही (1) *or* अँकन्री), अँकुरा, *and* अँकुसा, *which are all derivatives of* अङ्क hook. *See the remarks on derivation under art.* अँकन्ही (1) *and* अँकन्सा (1).]

अँकुराना *ãkurā*, (*pr. pts.* अँकुराइत *ãkurāit*, अँकुरात *ãkurāt*; अँकुराएल *ãkurāēl*; अँकुराएब *ãkurāēb or* अँकुराब *ãkurāb*; अँकुराए *ãkurāē*), **Tbh.**, *v. intr.*, to throw out a shoot, to sprout (*used esp. of sugar-cane*, *Grs.* § 1009.). *See* √अँखुआ *ãkhuā*.

[*A der. root derived from* आँकुर *or* अँकुरा, *q.v. See Gd. Gr.* § 352.]

अकुरी *akurī*, **Tbh.**, *subst. f.*, [1] the name of various implements which have the form of a hook or are furnished with a hook; *thus* a wooden goad for young elephants (*Grs.* § 102); (*S. Mth.*) the iron hook of a glassmaker (*Grs.* § 564; *also* अँकुरा *or* उकरी *uk'ri*, *q.v.*); [2] gram given to each of the female members of a household on the seventh day after a death in the house (*Grs.* § 1424).

[*This word is merely a bye-form of* अँकुरी, *q.v.*]

अँकुरी *ãkurī*, **Tbh.**, *subst. f.*, [1] a sprout; *hence* [2] unripe crop cut for food, *or* the cutting of such crop (*Grs.* § 877); *also* [3] a hook, tenter, catch; *hence* [4] the name of various implements which have the form of a hook or are furnished with a hook; *thus* the barb of an arrow; a fish-hook; a forked stick *for pulling down fruit from trees* (*Cr.*, *also* (*Mg.*) अँकुसी, *q.v.*), *also in some of the fourth series of meanings of* अँकुरा *ãkurā*, *q.v.* (*Grs.* §§ 222, 412, 564); *hence also* [5] a kind of grass *or* vetch (*Wat.*), = अँकरा *ãk'rā* (1), *q.v.* **Exam.**, *Coll.* (*Bh.*), एकर तऽ अँकुरी तूर देलँऽ, जामी कैसे, You have broken its sprout, how will it grow? [3] *Coll.* (*Bh.*), उनका मन के अँकुरी टूट गेल, The hook of his mind has broken (*i.e.*, *he has failed to succeed*). *See* अँकन्ही *ãk'ri* (1) *and* अँकन्री *ãk'rī* (1).

[*This word is merely the fem. of* अँकुरा, *q.v. The fem. form in such cases often indicates a diminutive sense, or a vulgar use.*]

अकुल *akul*, **Ts.**, (I) *adj. com. gen.*, (*subst. f.* अकुला *akulā*), *lit.* of no family; *hence* [1] not born of parents, beginningless, eternal (*a synonym of* अनादि *anādi*, *q.v.*); [2] of bad family, of low pedigree (*the same as* अकुली *akulī and* अकुलीन *akulīn*, *q.v.*); [3] outside of the Hindū social system, out of caste, etc. (*a synonym of Skr.* सर्वाश्रयत्वात्:). Exam., [1,2] *B. Rām., vs.* 35, कुजन-पाल, गुन-बरजित, अकुल, अनाथ, कहउँ, कृपा-निधि, राउर कस गुन-गाथ (*Thou who art*) the protector of (*even*) the wicked, devoid of all qualities (= निर्गुण), without a beginning (*or* of no good family) and without a superior, O thou treasury of grace (*i.e. Rām*), how shall I say the praises of thy excellencies! (*There is a play here on the word* अकुल; *the meaning is that one always praises those who protect good people, who are of good family, etc., but how can I praise him who is a protector of bad people, who is of no good family, etc.*). [2] *Rām., Bā., ch.* 89, 6, अकुल, अगेह, दिगम्बर, ब्याली, Casteless, houseless, naked, and necklaced with serpents (*epithets of Sib*).

(II) *subst. f.*, a prostitute, (*lit.* not belonging to a family). Exam., *Chan.*, अकुला नारि सकल धन खाय, बिन तजि अकुसल कहु कत जाय, The woman (*who is*) a prostitute eats up all wealth: where can (*one who wants to be*) an unlucky fellow go but to her?

[*Skr.* अकुलः; *as above in all Gds.*]

अकुलता *akulatā*, (*unphon.* आकुलता *ākulatā*), *subst. f.*, Ts., *subst. m.*, agitation, distress of mind.

[*Skr.* आकुलता; *as above in all other Gds.*]

अकुला *akulā*, उकन्ला *uk'lā*, (*pr. pts.* अकुलात *akulāt*; अकुलाएल *akulāel*, *Rām.* अकुलान *akulān*; अकुलाएब *akulāeb*; अकुलाए *akulāē*), Tbh., *v. intr.*, [1] to be agitated (*mentally*), confounded, perplexed, distressed, alarmed, hurried, anxious, worn out, wearied; [2] to be agitated (*physically*), confused, put out of order, tossed, disturbed, worn out, fatigued. Exam., *Hb.*, iv, 40, हलधर कें मति अति अकुलाएल, Hal'dhar's soul became agitated with anguish; *Gīt., Bā.*, 61, 1, जानि बड़े भाग, अनुराग अकुलाने हैं (*Janak*) learning his good fortune, became agitated with affection; *Rām., A., ch.* 57, 1, अति सुकुमारि देखि अकुलानी, Seeing her (*i.e. Sītā*) to be very tender, she (*Sītā's mother*) was distressed; *ib., do.* 56, 1, समाचार तेहि समय सुनि सीय उठि अकुलाइ, At that moment Sītā, hearing the news, rose in agitation; *ib., Ar., ch* 7, 19, सुनि अकुलाइ उठा मुनि, The saint thereupon rose in alarm; *ib., Bā., ch.* 260, 6, परिकर बाँधि उठे अकुलाई, Girding up their loins they arose in haste; *ib., A., ch.* 117, 7, सुनि सरूप पूछहिँ अकुलाई, When they heard of their beauty, they asked anxiously; *ib., Su., ch.* 13, 2, हरष बिषाद हृदय अकुलानी, She was confused in her heart by joy and sorrow; *K. Ram., Su.* 16, धूम अकुलाने, पहिचाने कौन काहि रे, Confounded by smoke, who indeed can recognise whom? *ib., Su.* 10, पानी, पानी, पानी, सब रानी अकुलानी कहैं, The queens all cry in dismay, 'water, water, water'! *ib., Su.* 8, भागे बीर धीर, अकुलाइ उठो रावनो, The great heroes run away, and in dismay Rāban arose; *ib., Su.* 15, नाम ले चिलात बिललात अकुलात अति, Calling (*Rāban*) by name, they are screaming, lamenting, and greatly distressed; *Coll.* (*W. Bh.*), काम करत करत जिउ अकुलाय गेल, He got weary as he went on doing the work. [2] *Rām., A., ch.* 266, 6, जनु उठेउ अम्बुधि अकुलाई, As though the ocean had risen and become tossed; *ib., Ar., ch.* 18, 1, सुनत सभासद उठे अकुलाई, When the assembly heard her word, they rose in confusion; *Padm., ch.* 534, 2, दुन्द धाव भा इन्द्र सकाना, डोला मेरु, सेस अकुलाना, At the din (*lit.* running) of the battle Ind'r cowers, Meru shakes, and Sēs is agitated; *Bih.* i, 11, बैसाख मैं सोषि जाम जागत, मैं मरौं अकुलाइ के, In Baisākh heat oppresses me: I die worn out by it.

[*Skr.* √आकुल (*der. root from adj.* आकुल), 10*th cl.* आकुलयति; *Pr.* आकुलावेइ (*cf. Sapt., vs.* 383) *or* अकुलावेइ, *hence Gd.* अकुलाई; *it only occurs in B. and H. The tadbh. Pr. form* आउल० (*cf. Sapt., vs.* 25, *Aup.* § 48, *Bhag., p.* 181) *does not survive in Gd. An analogon of the transposition of the vowels* उ *u and* अ *a in the form* उकन्ला *is the* √उकन्लाव *uk'tāv for* √अकुता *akutā* (*q.v.*).]

अकुलाई *akulāī*, अकुलाइ *akulāi*, Tbh., *subst. f.*, confusion, perplexity, distress, alarm, anxiety, weariness.

[*Either verbal noun derived from* √अकुला, *or abstr. noun derived from adj.* आकुल *by means of the Gd. sec. der. suff.* आइ *or* आई; *see Gd. Gr.*, § 220.]

अकुलि *akuli*, (*f.* अकुलिनि *akulini*), *Mth. or poet. form of* अकुली *akulī*, *q.v.*

अकुली *akulī*, Ts., *adj. com. gen.*, (*subst. f.* अकुलिनी *akulinī*), of low origin, mean pedigree, low, mean, base. Exam., *Prov. Mth.*, अकुलिनि बियाही कुलक उपहास, A marriage with a woman of low extraction brings ridicule on your own. *See* अकुल *akul and* अकुलीन *akulīn*.

[*Skr.* अकुली; *as above in all Gds.*]

अकुलीन *akulīn*, (*old obl.* अकुलीनहिँ *akulīnahi̐*), Ts., *adj. com. gen.*, (*subst. f.* अकुलीना *akulīnā*), *the same as* अकुली *akulī*, *q.v.* Exam., *Bin.* 69, कुल अकुलीन को; सुन्यौ है, बेद साखि है; पाँगुर को हाथ-पाँय, आँधरे को आँखि है, (*Rām is*) family to those who are of no family (*i.e.* of low family; *comm.* अधम); this is well-known by tradition, and the Bēds are witness; he is hand and foot to the paralytic, and eye to the blind; *Pārb., ch.* 7, कहहु काह सुनि रीझिहु बर अकुलीनहिँ, Say, what did you hear to make you so pleased with a bridegroom of (*such*) low pedigree; *Bw. do. anon.* (*song on Sib's marriage*) बनि अकुलीन अकुलीन सिव, तू कौं चाहे नारि, Sib is of mean pedigree and foul, why do you desire him?

[*Skr.* अकुलीन, *Pr.* अकुलीणो (*cf. Sapt., vs.* 253, *footnote*); *all Gds.* अकुलीन. *The tadbh. Pr. form* अकुलीणो (*Sapt., vs.* 253) *has not survived in Gḍ.*]

अकुलैया *akulạ̃iyā*, **Tbh.**, *adj., lg. f. of* अकुलाइ *akulāi, q.v.* **Exam.**, *Bij., l.* 851, बबुआ! एतने में अकुलैया, Prince! are you distressed at so little as this?

अकुसल *akusal*, **Ts.**, *adj. com. gen.*, (*subst. f.* अकुसल्ला *akus'lā*), unlucky, inauspicious. **Exam.**, *Coll.* (*Bh.*), उनकर खेम-कुसल नीमन सुनावँऽ, अकुसल मत सुनावँऽ, Tell me good, and not bad, news about his health and well-being. *For another example see under* अकुल *akul and* अकोल *akōl.*

[*Skr.* अकुशलः; *as above in other Gḍs.*]

अँकुसा *ãkusā*, **Tbh.**, *subst. m.*, the name of various implements which have the form of a hook or are furnished with a hook; *thus* [1]*in the several meanings of* आँकुस *ãkus, q.v.*; [2](*Mg.*) *in one of the fourth series of meanings of* आँकुरा *ãkurā, q.v.* (*Grs.* § 500.)

[*Properly str. f. of* आँकुस, *q.v.*]

अँकुसी *ãkusī*, **Tbh.**, *subst. f.*, the name of various implements which have the form of a hook or are furnished with a hook; *thus* (*Mg.*) [1]a hooked stick *for pulling down fruit from a tree* (*Grs.* § 41); [2](*Mg.*) *in one of the fourth series of meanings of* आँकुरा *ãkurā, q.v.* (*Grs.* § 500.)

[*This is merely the fem. of* आँकुसा, *q.v.*]

अँकूर *ãkūr*, (*old dir.* आँकूरु *ãkūru or poet.* आँकूरु *ãkūrū*), **Tbh.**, *subst. m., the same as* अङ्कुर *aṅkur, q.v.* **Exam.**, *Padm., ch.* 95, 5, पिरम कस न भा प्रेम आँकूरू, जो ससि सरग चढ़ैं होय सूरू, Why should not the germ of my love become like sunbeams, on which I, like the sun, may ascend to the heaven of my moon (*i.e. to Padmavatī*)? (*it is believed that the sun climbs the sky by the aid of its rays.*)

[*Skr.* अङ्कुरः, *Pr.* अंकुरो. *The Multānī has* आँकूरी (*Ml. Gy.*).]

अकेलवा *akel'wā*, (*f.* अकेलिया *akeliyā*), *lg. f. of* अकेल *akēl, q.v.* **Exam.**, *Bij., l.* 735, बने बने फिरेलु अकेलवा, You wander about alone from forest to forest.

अकेलापन *akelāpan*, **Tbh.**, *subst. m.*, [1]loneliness, solitude; [2]celibacy. **Exam.**, [1]*Coll.* (*Bh.*), अकेलापन में काम बहुत निकसेला, When a man is alone, he does a great deal of work, (*lit.* in solitude much work is produced). [2]*Coll.* (*Bh.*), अकेलापन में रहल नीक ना बा, काहे कि बेटा ना होवे त पिण्डा के दी, It is not good to remain a bachelor (*lit.* in celibacy), for who will offer a piṇḍa if there is no son? *See* अकेलेपन *akelēpan and* एकल्लापन *ek'lāpan.*

[*Der. from* अकेला *with Gḍ. suff.* पन *forming abstract nouns. See Gḍ. Gr.*, § 228.]

अकेलेपन *akelēpan*, **Tbh.**, *subst. m., the same as* अकेलापन *akelāpan, q.v.* **Exam.**, *Coll.* (*Bh.*), का करीं, हमरा केहु जान पहचान के बाड़िनो नैखे, अकेलेपन में जिनगी काट रहल बानी, What can I do? here I have no acquaintance; I pass my life in loneliness. *Coll.* (*Bh.*), ओकर का बियाह ना होई, उमर भर अकेलेपन में रही, He will never be married: he will remain a bachelor all his life.

अकेल *akēl*, **Tbh.**, *adj. com. gen.*, (*old Mth. and poet. f.* अकेलि *akēli*), alone, solitary (*used of individual beings or things, while* अकोल *is used of places*). **Phr.**, अकेल रहब, to live apart; अकेल सूतब, to sleep apart from one's husband *or* wife, be deserted *or* abandoned by one's husband; अकेलि कहानी, the explanation of one party to a case; अकेले (*loc., used adverbially*), alone; अकेले दुकेले (*an alliterative repetition*) entirely alone. **Exam.**, *Rām., Bā., ch.* 161, 6, जदपि अकेल बन बिपुल कलेसू, तदपि न मृग-मग तजै नरेसू, Though quite alone in the forest and greatly distressed, yet the king would not give up the chase of the deer; *Padm., ch.* 371, 3, रहौं अकेल (*fem.*) गहे एक पाटी, नयन पसार मरौं हिय फाटी, I remain alone and (*from fear of falling out*) catch hold of one of the side-planks of the bed, straining my eyes I die with a broken heart; *ib., ch.* 63, 8, बिपिन अकेलि फिरहु केहि हेतू, Why are you (*Satī*) wandering alone in the forest? *Prov.*, अकेलि कहानी गुड़ से मीठी, One's own story is sweeter than treacle; *Rām., Bā., ch.* 163, 3, को तुम, कस बन फिरहु अकेले, Who are you, and why do you roam alone in the forest? *B. Gr.*, II (*Bh.*), *Fable* 7, बाघ अकेले हरीन के खा गइल, The tiger by himself ate up the deer.

(*The word is seldom heard east of Bw.; in the other B. dialects the usual word is* एकल्लर, *q.v.*; अकेल *may be considered as borrowed from H.*)

[*Der. from Skr.* एक *by means of the Pr. pleon. suff.* ल; *hence Pr.* एक्कल्लो *or* एकल्लो (*Hem.* ii, 165), *Gḍ.* एकल, *q.v.*; *whence, by transposition of* अ *a and* ए *e, arises the form* अकेल. *Or the latter form might be derived from a Pr. form* एक्कइल्लो, *made with the pleon. suff.* इल्ल, *like Pr.* पढमइल्लो (*Bhag., pp.* 437, 198 = *Skr.* प्रथम first); *but the former derivation is more probable, because the corresponding forms in all other Gḍs. are derivatives of Pr.* एकल.]

अकेला *akēlā*, (*f.* अकेली *akēlī*), **Tbh.**, *adj.*, *str. f. of* अकेल *akēl, q.v.* **Exam.**, *Padm.*, *ch.* 139, 4, ठाँवहिँ ठाँव सब सोवहिँ चेला, राजा जागै आपु अकेला, All the pupils sleep in every place, the king himself alone wakes; *ib.*, *ch.* 134, 5, सुमिरहिँ राजा ओहि अकेला, जहिँ रे पन्थ खेल ओय चेला, The king—he alone remembers the path on which the pupil is accustomed to play; *Rām.*, *Ar.*, *ch.* 26, 2, जनक-सुता परिहरेउ अकेली, आयेउ तात बचन मम पेली, O brother, have you left Janak's daughter (*i.e. Sītā*) alone and come here against my order? *Bih.*, i, 6, अगहन मैं एक सेज सूनी, मैं अकेली ताकली, In Ag'han there is an empty bed, and alone I watch; *Sudh.* 42, एक तो अकेली, दूजी सङ्ग ना सहेली, रामा, In the first place I am alone (*without my husband*), secondly there is no confidante with me, O Rām.

[*Der. from Pr.* एकल्लओ (*with pleon. suff.* क). *See remarks on der. of* अकेल.]

अकैन *akāin* (*used in Gorakh'pūr, Cr., p.* 6), *the same as* अखैन *akhāin, q.v.*

अकोट *akōṭ*, **Ts.**, *subst. m.*, a kind of war-drum, *beaten with an iron drum-stick.* **Exam.**, *Padm.*, *ch.* 551, 3, बाजे तबल अकोट जुझाऊ, चढ़ा कोप सब राजा राऊ, Tabal and akoṭ (*two kinds of drums*) sounded the attack, fierce passion arose in all the kings and princes.

[*Skr.* अकोट?]

अँकोड़ा *ãkōṛā*, **Tbh.**, *subst.*, *m.*, (*Bh.*) a large hook, a kind of grapnel. **Exam.**, *Coll.* (*W. Bh.*), दरवाजा के अँकोड़ा लगा है, The hook of the door is fastened.

[*Apparently a bye-form of* अँकुरा *or* अँकुड़ा, *q.v.*; *the medial* ओ *ō is apparently a modification of* उ *u. Compare the G.* अँकोर *and* अँकोस, *bye-forms of* अङ्कुर *and* अङ्कुश. *G. has* अँकोड़ो.].

अकोतर-सो *akōtar'sō*, **Tbh.**, *num.*, one hundred and one. **Exam.**, *Padm.*, *ch.* 299, 4, कँदरा काँड जो बचे बचे, बरी अकोतर-सो करँ बचे, Lumps of sugar which were (*broken*) in pieces (*were given*) with one hundred and one dishes of barī (*a kind of dish made of pulse*).

[*Skr.* एकोत्तरशतं, *Pr.* एक्कोत्तरसयं, *Ap. Pr.* एक्कोत्तरसउ.]

अकोबिद *akōbid*, **Ts.**, *adj. com. gen.*, (*subst. f.* अकोबिदा *akōbidā*), ignorant, unlearned, unskilled. **Exam.**, *Rām.*, *Bā.*, *ch.* 123, 1, अग्य अकोबिद अन्ध अभागी, Ignorant, unlearned, and blind reprobates.

[*Skr.* अकोविदः; *as above possibly in all Gḍs.*]

अकोर *akōr*, (*poet* अकोरा *akōrā*), **Tbh.**, *subst. m.*, [1]bribe; *hence* [2]the coaxing of a cow or buffalo, which has lost its calf, to eat grain (*Ell. vol.* II, *p.* 213); [3]the refreshment which a labourer eats in the intervals of work in the open field, (*Ell.* II, 213). **Phr.**; अकोर खाब, to take a bribe. **Exam.**, [1]*Gīt.*, *Ut.* 3, 2 अहि सभीत है अकोर राखे जुग रुचिर मोर-कुण्डल, छबि निरखि चोर सकुचत अधिकाई, The thief (*i.e. the spreading curls on Rām's head which approach his face, and which are likened to snakes bent on stealing the nectar of his moon-like face*) is exceedingly afraid on seeing the beauty of the pair of bright, peacock-like earrings (*alluding to the traditional enmity of the peafowl towards a snake*) which (*the face of Rām*) being as it were afraid, has put on (*by way of*) giving a bribe; *Sudh.*, 37, अँगिया तोरी रे कचहरी, जोबन हाकिम जालिम जोर। नाय फँसी नायक लालच बस ते होय नैना चोर। छूटे प्यारी मन तुमही कौं है के प्रान अकोर, Thy bodice is like a court, thy full bosom like a tyrannous magistrate; mine eyes, overcome by covetousness, were unjustly kept in bonds (*before them*), like a thief; but, O beloved, they got free by offering the bribe of my life to thy soul (*which was*) the magistrate's clerk; *Padm.*, *ch.* 671, 2, जहँ अकोर तहँ नेक न राजू, ठाकुर केर बिनासहि काजू, Where bribes (*occur*) there is no good government; they ruin the actions of the king: *ib.*, *ch.* 670, 2, दसा लाख दस दीन्ह अकोरा, बिनती कीन्ह पाय गहि गोरा, The Gōrā gave ten lākhs of rupees as a bribe, and, falling at his (*i.e. Pat'nā's*) feet, made supplication.

[*Perhaps from Skr.* उत्कोचः, *Pā.* उक्कोचो, *Ap. Pr.* (*with pleon. suff.* क, *Hēm.* iv, 429) *उक्कोचअो, *whence* (*contr. and with change of* च *to* र *and of* उ *to* अ) *Gḍ.* अकोर. *H. as B. Apparently wanting in the other Gḍs.*]

अँकोरा *ãkōrā*, **Tbh.**, *subst. m.*, the name of various implements which have the form of a hook or are furnished with a hook; thus [1](*S. Mth.-Bg.*) the hooks of a harrow *by which it is attached to the traces* (*Grs.* § 32); [2](*ib.*) the piece of bamboo *tied on behind the main beam* (पाड) *in the rear of a country-cart and forming its tail* (*Grs.* § 172); [3](*ib.*) = अँकुरा *ãkurā*, *in some of its fourth series of meanings* (*Grs.* §§ 376, 412).

[*A bye-form of* अँकुरा, *q.v.*, *with the provincialism of changing* उ *u to* ओ (*cf.* अँकोड़ा *for* अँकुड़ा); *G.* अँकोर.]

अकोल *akōl* (1), (*str. f.* अकोला *akōlā*), **Tbh.**, *subst. m.*, a plant (*Alangium hexapetalum or decapetalum, Wat.*) the oil of the fruit of which is supposed to be useful in enchantments. (*The nut, however, is said to be very hard, so hard that oil cannot be expressed from it; hence magical properties might safely be ascribed to it!*).

[*Skr.* अङ्कोटः *or* अङ्कोठः *or* (*prākritising*) अङ्कोलः *or* अङ्कोलः, *Pā.* अंकोलो, *Pr.* अंकोल्लो (*Hēm.* i, 200, *Sapt.*, *vs.* 779, *et passim*); *G. and M.* अकोल, *H.* अकोल, *Bg.* अकोल (*akalo, Wat.*). *The oil made of the fruit is called in Pr.* अंकोल्लतेल्लं, *Hēm.* ii, 155.]

अकोल *akōl* (2), (*str. f.* अकोला *akōlā*), **Tbh.**, *subst. m.*, the top shoot of the sugar-cane plant (*Hd. Dy.*). *See synonyms under* अगौल *agin.*

[*Probably* = अकोर = अँकोर, *for* अङ्कुर, *cf.* अँकोरा *ãkōrā.*]

अकोल *akōl* (3), **Tbh.**, *adj. com. gen.*, lonely, solitary, (*used of places, syn.* एकान्त, *while* अकेल *is used of individuals*). **Exam.**, *Chan.*, बड़िया बरदक झूलत आँड़, संग संग फिरए अकेया आँड़। अब अकोल बैसल गोवार, अकुलल अकबहिँ ननि लकुर। उदय अकलेक की बुधिवार, चितु अधार चि अर सम्हार। The testicles of a bullock were swinging, and a jackal went along with him (*hoping that they would fall, so that he might eat them*); a cowherd sat in a lonely place and killed the unlucky (*jackal*) with a stick. In the presence of ill-fate, what (*advantage is there*) in being wise? The world says his very (*search of*) food was (*the cause of*) his death.

[*Perhaps from Skr.* एक, *Pr.* एक *with the pleon. suff.* उल; *analogous to the derivation of* अकेल, *q.v.*]

अकोला *akōlā* (1), **Tbh.**, *subst. m.*, a tree, *Aleuritis triloba* (*Wat.*).

[*Skr.* अक्षोटकः *or* आक्षोटकः *or* आखोटकः *or* अक्षोलकः *or* आक्षोलकः.]

अकोला *akōlā* (2), *str. f. of* अकोल *akōl* (1) *and* (2), *q.v.*

अकौता *akāutā*, **Tbh.**, *subst. m.*, an eruption in the leg. (*It is popularly supposed to be caused by stepping over a place where a dog has been eating and left some refuse, and to be cured by rubbing the place with curds and making a dog lick it.*)

[*Der.?* *Connected with* अक *or* आकाम? *H.* रकौता.]

अक्कन्द *akkand* = आकन्द *ākand, q.v.*

अक्कल *akkal* = अकिल *akil, q.v.*

अक्कास *akkās* (*Coll.*) = अकास *akās, q.v.*

अक्खन *akkhan*, **Tbh.**, *adj. com. gen.*, (*Coll.*, *Allāhābād*), blind. **Exam.**, *Coll.* तुम बड़े अक्खन हो, You are very blind.

(*The meanings* 'half-blind,' 'one-eyed,' *given by Fallon do not appear to be correct.*)

[*Perhaps connected with Skr.* अक्ष, *one of the meanings of which is said to be* 'born blind.']

अक्खर *akkhar* = अखर *akhar, q.v.* *See* अच्छर *achchhar.*

अक्खा *akkhā* = आँखा *ãkhā, q.v.*

अक्खी *akkhī*, **Tbh.**, *subst. f.*, the act of making water (*used by path'shālā or school boys*) = इक्की *ikkī.* *Cf.* दुक्खी *dukkhī.*

[*Deriv. doubtful. Probably a secondary formation from* एक one; दुक्खी, the act of easing, *being similarly formed from* दुइ two. *The idea is that the two acts consist of a single and a double operation respectively. A similar expression is in use amongst English children.*]

अक्खैं *akkhẽ* (*Coll.*) = आँखा *ãkhā, q.v.*

अक्टइ *aktay*, इक्टइ *iktay* = अकटइ *ak'tay, q.v.*

अक्तूबर *aktūbar* = अकतूबर *ak'tūbar, q.v.*

अक्बर *akbar* = अकबर *ak'bar, q.v.*

अक्बरी *akbarī* = अकबरी *ak'barī, q.v.*

अक्बराबाद *akbarābād* = अकबराबाद *ak'barābād, q.v.*

अक्रमातिशयोक्ति *akramātishayōkti*, **Ts.**, *subst. f.*, the name of a figure of rhetoric in which cause and effect are not shown in their natural order of sequence, but as occurring simultaneously. **Exam.**, *Git.*, *Ba.*, 90, 5, 6, गहि कर-तल मुनि पुलक सहित, कौतुकहि उठाइ लियो; नृप-गन मुखनि समेत नमित करि सजि, सुख सबहि दियो। आकरष्यो सिय मन समेत, हरि हरष्यौ जनक हियो; भंज्यो भृगु-पति गर्ब सहित, तिहु-लोक बिमोद कियो। Seizing (*the bow*) in his hand together with the thrilling of the sages (*i.e. while the sages thrilled with joy on seeing him seize it*), he (*i.e. Rām*) sportively raised it; stringing it, together with making low the faces of the (*competing*) princes, he gave happiness to all. Hari (*i.e. Rām*) pulled it, together with Sītā's soul (*i.e. winning her affection*), and rejoiced the heart of Janak; he broke it together with Bhrig'pati's (*i.e. Parasurām's*) pride, and caused delight in the three worlds. *Here the seizing, stringing, pulling, and breaking of the bow are the causes, of which the thrilling of the sages, the defeating of the princes, the winning of Sītā, and the humiliating of Bhrig'pati respectively, are the effects. The two sets are mentioned as occurring simultaneously. This figure should not be confounded with another called sahōkti* (सहोक्ति), *which consists in mentioning together a similitude and its real counterpart. (See Bihārī Tul'sī Bhūkhan Bōdh, a treatise on Hindī Rhetoric and Poetry, by Pandit Bihārī Lāl Chaūbē, Nos.* 77 *and* 84.)

अक्रित *ākrit*, **Ts.**, *adj. com. gen., lit.* not done *or* wrought; *hence* [1]unmanufactured, natural; [2]unfinished. **Exam.**, [1] *Coll. (Bh.)*, महादेव के ई पिण्डी अक्रित (*fem.*) छौ, This image (*lit.* cone) of Mahadeb is not made with hands (*referring to a natural conical lingam of stone*). [2] *Coll. (Bh.)*, ज मर गेल, और काम अक्रिते (अक्रित + ही) रह गेल, He died and his work remained unfinished.

[*Skr.* अकृतः; *as above in all Gds.*]

अक्रित्रिम *akritrim*, **Ts.**, *adj. com. gen.*, inartificial, unfeigned, natural. **Exam.**, *Coll. (Bh.)*, ई प्रिथिवी के अक्रित्रिम विभाग है, This is a natural division (*or continent*) of the earth.

[*Skr.* अकृत्रिमः; *as above possibly in all Gds.*]

अक्रिपाल *akripāl*, **Ts.**, *adj. com. gen.*, pitiless, merciless, unkind. **Exam.**, *Bin.* 232, प्रभु अक्रिपाल, क्रिपाल असमर्थ, जहँ जहँ चितहि डुलावौं, Wherever (*else, beside Rām*) I turn my thoughts, (*I see but*) a lord (*who is*) pitiless, (*or, if he be*) pitiful, (*he is*) powerless.

[*Skr.* अकृपालुः, *as above possibly in all Gds.*]

अक्रिबा *akribā*, **Any.**, *subst. com. gen.*, kinsman, relations within degrees recognised by law.

(*A word only used in kachah'rīs or magisterial courts.*)

[*Ar.* اقربا *aqribā, pl. of* قريب *qarīb* near; *also used in M.* (*Wil.*).]

अक्रूर *akrūr*, अकन्हूर *ak'rūr*, अकन्हूर *ak'rūṛ*, अकरूर *ak'ruṛ*, **Ts.**, *subst. m., name of a Jādab, the paternal uncle and friend of Krish'n. He was the son of Shwaphal'k and Gāndinī. It was he who took Krish'n and Bal'rām to Mathurā when the former broke the great bow and slew Kans. He is chiefly known as being the holder of the Syamantak gem, which yielded to its owner daily eight loads of gold. Man'bōdh calls him Dān'pati or 'master of liberality' on that account, e.g., Hb.* vi, 41, ओहि दिन दान-पति ओतहि रहल, जँजिहि ओहिठाँ सब कंसक कहल, For that day Dān'patī (*Akrūr*) remained there and agreed to all that Kans said.

The various forms of the name occur in the following passages of Man'bōdh's Haribans, viz. अकन्हूर, vi, 43, x, 24, 25; अकन्हूर, vi, 26, 49; vii, 17, 18, 27, 37, viii, 7, 35, 36; अकरूर, viii, 38, ix, 21.

[*Skr.* अक्रूरः; अक्रूर *in all Gds.*]

अक्रोट *akrōt*, अकन्रोट *ak'rōṭ* = अखोट *akhroṭ*, *q.v.*

अक्सर *aksar* = अकन्सर *ak'sar*, *q.v.*

अक्सात *aksāt* = अकन्सात *āk'sāt*, *q.v.*

अक्साम *aksām* = अकन्साम *ak'sām*, *q.v.*

अक्सीर *aksīr* = अकन्सीर *ak'sīr*, *q.v.*

अख *akh*; *for words beginning thus and not found below, see under the more proper form commencing with* अछ *achh or* अच्छ *achchh.*

अखउत *akhaüt*, अखाउत *akhāüt* = अकौत *akaūt*, *q.v.*

अँखगर *ākh'gar* = आँखिगर *ākhigar*. *See under* आँखि *ākhi.*

अखज *akhaj* (1), **Tbh.**, *adj. com. gen.*, [1]what is not to be eaten, indigestible, in excess of one's need of food; *hence generally* [2]what is not required, superfluous, a nuisance; *also substantively* [3]one who will eat even what is unwholesome *or* what is in excess of his requirements, a glutton. **Exam.**, [1] *Coll. (Bh.)*, हमार खाय के साथ अखज भो गेल, My dinner has not agreed with me. [2] *Coll. (Bh.)*, प्रभि तरह देब, अखज आ, I'll give it anyhow, 'tis of no use to me. [3] *Coll. (Bh.)*, ज बड़ अखज छंठ, He is a terrible glutton.

(*The first is the usual use of the word. The idea is that with the dinner something has been taken which ought not to have been eaten, and which caused indigestion. The meaning of* 'excess in eating,' 'indigestion,' *given in the Āz. Gy., is therefore only true in the above sense. The second use may be due to some confusion with* अखाज, *q.v.*)

[*Skr.* अखाद्यं, *Pr.* अखज्जं, *Gd.* अखज.]

अखज *akhaj* (2), **Any.**, *subst. f.*, [1](*lit.*) taking, seizing, intercepting; [2]objection, cavil; [3](*usually in this sense*) aversion (*Āz. Gy.*), hostility, a grudge. **Exam.**, [3] *Coll. (Bh.)*, हम से ज बड़ अखज राखेला, He has a great grudge against me; *Coll. (Bh.)*, मन मैं अखज पर गेल, Hostility came into his mind.

[*Ar.*, اخذ *akhz*; — *Bg.* आखज *ākhaj or* आखेज *ākhej.*]

अखड़ा *akharā, a corruption of the obl. f.* अखाड़ा *akhārā, see* अखाड़ *akhār*. **Exam.,** *Alh., l.* 130, **रूदल रोपाल अखड़ा मैं दूदल दन्ड बैठ नौ लाख,** Rūdal planted the palms of his hands (*on the ground*) in the arena and made nine times ten-thousand dands (*a kind of athletic exercise*).

अखढ़्वा *akharh'wā*, **Ts.,** *subst. m., lg. f. of* अखाड़ *akhārh* (2), *q.v.* **Exam.,** *Prov.,* **जैकर बनल अखढ़्वा रे, तेकर बारहो मास,** Whose (*fields*) are prepared in (*the month of*) Akhārh, his (*fields*) are so for all the twelve months (*Grs.* § 1086).

अखण्ड *akhand*, (*poet.* अखण्डा *akhandā*), **Ts.,** (I) *adj. com. gen.,* [1]unbroken, irrefragable, indivisible, indestructible (*used as an epithet of the Supreme Being*); *hence,* [2]whole, entire, complete, absolute. **Phr.,** **अखण्ड आँक,** an integer, a whole number. **Exam.,** [1] *Rām., Bā., ch.* 68, 8, **लागि समाधि अखण्ड अपारा,** commencing an unbroken unsurpassed trance; *ib., ch.* 149, 4, **अगुन अखण्ड अनन्त अनादि,** (*God*) without qualities or parts, without end or beginning. [2] *Rām., Su., do.* 49, 2, **जरत बिभीषन राखा दीन्हेउ राज अखण्ड** (*fem.*), To the burning Vibhīshan the king afforded complete protection; *ib., Ut., ch.* 64, 1, **मति अकुण्ठ हरि-भक्ति अखण्डा** (*final* आ *ā, m.c.*), (*A man of*) keen understanding and absolute faith in Hari; *ib., ch.* 115, 1, **सो ऽहमस्मि इति बृत्ति अखण्डा** (*final* आ *ā, m.c.*), The absolute persuasion that I am he.

(II) *adv.,* wholly, entirely, completely, thoroughly. **Exam.,** *Rām., Bā., do.* 213, 1, **दिखरावत मातहि निज अद्भुत रूप अखण्ड,** He showed to his mother his wondrous body completely.

(*This word also occurs in Rām., Ln., chh.* 36, 15, **अनवद्य, अखण्ड, अगोचरगो; सब रूप सदा, सब होइ नगो,** (*God is*) irreproachable, indivisible, not coming within the range of sense (= अगोचर); all forms (*are in him*) always, yet no (*form*) is abiding in him (*i.e., he is both immanent and transcendent in regard to the world*). *In Rām Jasan's edition the words are wrongly divided into* **अखण्डन गोचरगो.** *Another edition reads the passage thus*—**अनवद्य अखण्ड अगोचरगो अखरूप सदा सब होइ न सो,** *the meaning being the same.*)

[*Skr.* **अखण्डः**, *Pā.* **अखण्डो**, *Pr.* **अखण्डो** (*Aup.* § 16, **अखण्डदन्ते**, *p.* 29); *as above in all Gds.*]

अखण्डल *akhandal*, (*old nom. sg.* **अखण्डलु** *akhandalu*), **Tbh.,** *subst. m., lit.* breaker, destroyer, *used as an epithet of Sib.* **Exam.,** *Pārv., ch.* 13, **पुर कलरव उर हरखेउ अचल अखण्डलु,** The Destroyer (*Sib*), the Mountain King, rejoiced in his heart at the tumult in the city.

[*Skr.* **आखण्डलः**, *orig. an epithet of Ind'r* (*Rig.* viii, 17, 12), *in later times also of Sib* (*see Skr. Dy.*), *Pr.* **अखण्डलो** (*Nām., vs.* 23), *Ap. Pr.* **अखण्डलु** (*cf., Hēm.* iv, 331); *the Ap. Pr. form is nearly preserved in the old Bw. of Tul'sī Dās.*]

अखण्डा *akhandā, adj., poet. for* **अखण्ड** *akhand, q.v.*

अखण्डित *akhandit*, **Ts.,** *adj. com. gen., a synonym of* **अखण्ड** *akhand, q.v.* **Exam.,** [1] *Padm., ch.* 80, 1, **सुवै असीस दीन्ह बड़ साजू, बड़ परताप अखण्डित राजू,** The parrot gave a blessing with great ceremony, (*promising*) great power and an unbroken rule. [2] *Rām., Ut., ch.* 50, 7, **होइ गुन-गिरा बिग्यान अखण्डित,** He is thoroughly accomplished, (*and possessed*) of absolute knowledge.

[*Skr.* **अखण्डितः**; *as above possibly in all Gds. The tadbh. form* **अखण्डिय** *occurs in Sapt., vs.* 689.].

अखत *akhat*, **आखत** *ākhat*, **Ts.,** *subst. m., lit.* uncrushed, unbroken, whole; *hence variously employed as a tech. term for* whole grain; *thus* [1]a portion of the crop per plough paid to village artizans, *as the smith, carpenter, etc.* (*Hd. Dy.*); [2]grain placed on a sieve and given to servants, etc., at marriages and other ceremonies (*Āz. Gy.*); [3] consecrated rice used in religious ceremonies (*such as the sandhyā and dasha-karmānī*); [4]*also used figuratively of* pearls, etc. **Exam.,** [4] *Popular song, sung by women at the Nah'chhū ceremony at a marriage,* **सोनवा के ढका मैं बभनाँ के देबूँ, मोतिअन अखत नौनियाँ के रे, भडवा के घोरवा, सोनरवा के कड़वा, दरजिया के बगवा पहरैबूँ रे,** To the Brāhman I will give coins of gold, to the barber's wife whole (*grains of*) pearls, to the bard a horse, to the goldsmith an armlet, and the tailor I will dress in a suit of honour.

(*In the third meaning the more usual form of the word is* **अछत** *achhat or* **अच्छत** *achchhat, q.v.*)

[*Ved.* **अक्षत:** (*Rig.* v, 78, 9; x, 166, 2; *Ath.* xii, 1, 11), *Skr.* **अक्षतं**; *Pā.* **अक्खतं**; *Pr.* (*tech. ts.*) **अक्खतं**; *hence B. and H.* **अखत** *or* **आखत**, *M.* **अखत**, *Bg.* **अक्षत** (*written* **अखत**), *possibly in all Gds.* (*The Pr. form* **अक्खयं** *which occurs in Kalp.* § 16, *Nāy.* § 8, *Aup.* § 20, *Nām. vs.* 237, *Bhag. p.* 262, *is not a tadbh. of Skr.* **अक्षतं**, *as explained by the editors of Kalp. and Nām., but a tadbh. of Skr.* **अक्षय**, indestructible, *as shown by the context.*)]

अख़्तर *akh'tar*, **Any.,** *subst. m.,* [1]a star; [2]a kind of jewel made in the form of a star. **Exam.,** *Bais.* 23, **जब तू अखतर बेंदिया ना देबो, ता पर मारौं कटरिया,** If you do not give me the starry bēdiya (*or tikulī*), I will thereupon kill you with a dagger.

[*Prs.* اختر *akhtar.*]

अखन्ता *akh'tā*, **अखता** *akhtā*, **Any.**, *subst. m.*, a gelding. [*Prs.* اختہ *akhtah.*]

अखन्तियार *akh'tiyār*, **इखन्तियार** *ikh'tiyār*, **Any.**, *subst. m*, [1]choice, option, election; [2]will, discretion, pleasure; [3]control, power, authority. **Exam.**, [2]*Coll.* (*Bh.*), **आगे राउर अखन्तियार**, For the rest, you may do as you please. [3]*Coll.* (*Bh.*), **बिराना माल पर का अखन्तियार**, What power has any one over strange property? *B. Gr.*, II (*Bh.*), *Fable* 15, **जो दुसमन अपना अखन्तियार में आ जाए**, If your enemy fall into your power.
[*Ar.* اختیار *ikhtiyār*, *lit.* what is chosen, good.]

अखन्तीज *akh'tīj*, *the same as* **अखैतीज** *akhāitīj*, *q.v.*

अखनी *akhanī*, **अखन्नी** *akh'nī*, **Tbh.**, *adv.*, (*Mg. & Bh.*) [1]now, just now; [2]now a-days. **Exam.**, [2]*Coll.* (*Bh.*), **अखनी एकर चलन नैखे**, Now-a-days it is not the custom.
[*Skr.* **एतस्मिन्क्षणे** at this moment, *Pr.* **एअक्खणे** (*or* **एअक्खणे**, *cf. Nām. vs* 175 **एअम्मिर** = *Skr.* **एतस्मिन्**). *Ap. Pr.* **एक्खणहिँ** (*cf. Hēm.* iv, 399, *transl.*), *hence B.* **अखनी**, *the term.* **ई** *being a contraction of the Ap. Pr. loc. sg. term.* **अहिँ** (*see Gḍ. Gr.*, § 378 *and* § 367, *p.* 208) *and* **ए** *being shortened to* **अ** (*see Gḍ. Gr.* § 26).]

अखन्दा *akhandā*, **अखदा** *akh'dā*, **Tbh.**, *subst. m.*, (*Bh.*) a hole dug in the bottom of a pond or elsewhere for catching fish (*Āz. Gy.*, *where it is spelt* **अखंडा** *akhaṇḍā*).
[*Probably from* **Skr. खाताम्**, an artificial *or* a dug pond, *through an intermediate form* ***खाअम** *or* **खाअंम** (*with doubling or nasalising the cons. to compensate for the shortened vowel; see also Gḍ. Gr.* § 158), *the softening of the consonant being analogous to that of the Shr. Pr. and P. pres. part. suff.* **न्द** *for Skr.* **न्त** (*see Hēm.* iv, 261, *Gḍ. Gr.*, § 301). *In the Skr. Dy. P. the word* **खाताम** *is said to be a mislection for* **खातम**, a natural pond; *but in Pr. the word really occurs and has its proper sense of* an artificial pond; *for the Nām.*, *vs.* 203 *gives its tadbh. form* **खअखाअं** *in the sense of* a pit dug for catching elephants, *while the tadbh. of Skr.* **खात** *is given by Nām.*, *vs.* 130 *as* **खाअ**.]

अखन्बार *akh'bār*, **अखबार** *akhbār*, **Any.**, a newspaper. **Exam.**, *Fam.*, *vs.* 58, **खबर गए अखबार मों, मिथिला के एह हाल, सुनहु फिरङ्गि, कान दे कें मेटहु दुख के जाल**, The news went into the newspapers that this was the condition of Mithilā, saying, 'Hear, O English! give your ears and remove this net of sorrow.'
[*Ar.* اخبار *akhbār*, *properly plur. of* خبر *khabar* news.]

अँख-मुँदन्नी *ākh'mūd'nī*, **Tbh.**, *subst. f.*, the cloth tied over the blinkers for cattle (*Grs.* § 97).
[*A compound of Skr.* **अक्षि** *and* **मुद्रणी** closing *or* covering of the eyes; *Pā. and Pr.* **अक्खि-मुद्दणी**.]

अँख-मुँदन्वा *ākh'mūd'wā*, **Tbh.**, *subst. m.*, blind man's buff (*Āz. Gy.*). **Exam.**, *Coll.* (*Bh.*), **ऊ लरिकन में अँख-मुँदन्वा खेलत, रहल, मुँडन्वा छूवे दौरल**, He was playing blindman's buff with the boys, and ran to touch the goal; (*one of the boys, called the* **चोर** *chōr*, *has to touch one of the others, before they reach the goal.*)
[*Comp. of* **आँखि** (*or* **आँख**) eye *and* **मुँदन्वा** (*lg f. of* **मूँदा**) closed, covered; = *Skr.* **अक्षि-मुद्रित**.]

अखय *akhay* = **अखै** *akhāi*, *q.v.*

अखर *akhar*, **आखर** *ākhar*, **Tbh.**, *subst. m.*, [1]*the same as* **अच्छर**, *q.v.*; [2]that which is imperishable (*in this sense only known to occur in compounds*). **Comp.**, **अखर-तितिजिया** *or* **अखर-तीज** (*Mg.*) *and* **अखर-तीज** (*S. Bh.*), *subst. f.*, *the same as* **अखैतीज**, *q.v.* (*Grs.* § 1444). **Exam.**, *Han.* 39, **सुमिरे सहाय राम लखन अखर दोऊ, जिनके समूह साके जागत जहान हैं**, As in the case of Rām and Lakhan (*the latter of whom in his difficulty called on Rām for help*), so there is help in remembering those two letters (*i.e.* **रा** *rā and* **म** *ma*), the joint powers of which are active throughout the world. *See* **अखै** *akhāi and* **आखिर** *ākhir* (1).
[*Skr.* **अक्षरः** *m. or* **अक्षरम्** *n.*, *Pā.* **अक्खरो** *or* **अक्खरं**, *Pr.* **अक्खरं** (*cf. Hēm.* iii, 134, *nom. pl. n.* **अक्खराइँ**), *old Gḍ.* **अक्खर**. *The forms* **अक्खर** *or* **आखर** *belong to the older usage; they are now less frequent than* **अच्छर**. *But in the works of Tul'sī Dās, they are used almost exclusively, while in Bidyāpati the proportion is equal.* (*In Bid.* 60, *ll.* 2, 5, *both occur side by side*). *In Pā. and Pr. the form* **अच्छर** *only occurs in the sense of* a moment (**अच्छरा** *fem.*, *lit.* the time occupied in pronouncing a letter, *see Aup.* § 136 *and Pā. Dy.*, *s.v.*). *The truth is that the modern* **अच्छर** *is a tats.*, *representing the modern pronunciation of Skr.* **अक्षर**.]

***अखर** *akhar*, (*pr. pts.* **अखन्रैत** *akh'rāit*, *Bh.* **अखन्रत** *akh'rat*, **अखन्रित** *akh'rit*; **अखन्रल** *akh'ral*; **अखन्रब** *akh'rab*; **अखन्रै** *akh'rai*), **Tbh.**, *v. intr.*, [1]to be displeasing, irksome, burdensome, difficult, insupportable; [2]*used also impersonally.* **Exam.**, [1]*Coll.* (*Bh.*), **घाम अखन्रत बा**, The heat is insupportable (*Ās. Gy.*). [2]*Ib.* **मार खेले रैंहें, अब अखन्रत बा**, You have been beaten, are you sorry now (*lit.* is it now displeasing)?

[*Probably the same as H.* √अखड़, *and another form of* √अकड़ *akar, q.v.*]

अखर-तिजिया *akhar'tijiyā*, (*Mg.*), *see under* अखर *akhar*, (*Grs.* § 1444).

अखर-तीज *akhar'tij*, (*Mg.*), *see under* अखर *akhar* (*Grs.* § 1444).

अखर-तीत *akhar'tīt*, (*S. Bh.*), *see under* अखर *akhar* (*Grs.* § 1444).

अखर-वार *akhar'wār*, **Tbh.**, *subst. m.*, a subdivision of Kurmīs or land cultivators in the districts of Gōrakh'-pūr and Banāras (*Ell., vol.* I, *p.* 156).

अखरहा *akh'rahā*, **Tbh.**, *subst. m.*, (*S. Mth.*), the hut of a religious mendicant (*Grs.* § 1234).

[*Probably a bye-form of* अखाड़ा *or* अखाड़ी, *the str. f. of* अखाड़ (1), *q.v. Compare* अखड़वा *as to the shortening of the vowel* a.]

अखरा *akh'rā* (1), **Tbh.**, *subst. m.*, an ear of corn or rice which is empty and yields no grain (*Hd. Dy.*).

[*Probably a negative formed from* खरा genuine; *whence* अखरा a spurious ear, an ear but without grain. *It should not be confused with* अखरा, *which is a* blighted, dried-up ear, *while* अखरा *is an empty one.*]

अखरा *akh'rā* (2), **Tbh.**, *subst. m.*, (*Mg., Bh.*) unhusked barley, barley ground without being first cleaned, coarse flour (*Grs.* § 1272 *and Āz. Gy.*). **Exam.**, *Prov.*, खाय अखरा, रहै निखरा (*with two meanings*) *either* one should eat coarse flour and remain clean, *or* one who eats coarse flour remains robust.

[*Skr.* अ-क्षरित: uncleaned; *the opp.* निखरा *represents either Skr.* निक्षरित: cleaned, *or Skr.* निःक्षरित: *or* निःचरित: not waned, robust.]

अखरी *akh'rī* (1), (*Mg.*), *fem. of* अखरा *akh'rā* (2), *q.v.* (*Grs.* § 1272).

अखरी *akh'rī* (2), **Tbh.**, *subst. f.*, noise, yell, howl, scream. (*It has only been observed in the following*) **Phr.**, अखरी उठाएब, to make a great noise. **Exam.**, *Coll.* (*Mg.*), छौंरा, के अखरी उठाए राखिच है, Boys, who is making such a terrible noise? (*after Fallon.*)

[*Perhaps 1st verb. noun of* √अखर *or* √अखड़, *q.v., meaning properly the noise of wrangling or swaggering, but possibly connected with Skr.* √आखर.]

अखरो *akh'rō*, **Tbh.**, *subst. m.*, (*Mth.-Mg.*), *the same as* अखरा *akh'rā* (2), *q.v.* (*Grs.* § 1272).

अखरोट *akh'rōt*, *the same as* आखोट *ākhōt*, *q.v.*

अखरौटी *akh'rauṭi*, **Tbh.**, *subst. f.*, [1] orthography; [2] a mode of playing on a stringed instrument so as to express the words of a song. **Exam.**, [1] *Coll.* (*Bh.*), ऊ तो अबही अखरौटी सिखैछा, He is only now learning his orthography.

[*Probably Skr.* अक्षरावृत्ति:, *Pr.* (*with pleon.* क) अक्खरावट्टिआ; *hence Gd.* (*contracted*) अखरौटी.]

अखर्ब *akharb*, **Ts.**, *adj. com. gen.*, not short, tall, long, large, big. **Exam.**, *Hindī Mahābhārat, Ban Parbā, p.* 214, *l.* 6 (*Rājā of Banāras edition, sambat* 1887), मत्स्य मत्स्य कौं खात त्यौं, जीव जीव कौं खवै, अखड प्रानी जीव कौं, सर्वदा खर्ब अखर्ब, Thus fish eat fish, everything alive eats everything alive, that which has breath eats that which is alive, the big always devours the little.

[*Skr.* अखर्वः; *as above possibly in all Gds.*].

अखलाक *akh'lāk*, अख़लाक़ *akhlāk*, **Any.**, *subst. m.*, [1] disposition; [2] the good properties of mankind; [3] morals, ethics.

[*Ar.* اخلاق *akhlāq, properly plur. of* خلق *khulq.*]

आँखलगी *ãkh'lagi*,—*see under* आँखि *ãkhi*.

आँखवा *ãkh'wā*, *the same as* अँखुआ *ãkhuā*, *q.v.* (*Grs.* § 1009).

(*It is properly the lg. f. of* आँख *or* आँखि, *q.v. It is now considered incorrect and vulgar as compared with the form* अँखुआ, *though in reality the latter is the less correct form of the lg. f. of* आँख.]

ँअखा *ãkhā*, (*pr. pts.* अँखाइत *ãkhāit*, अँखात *ãkhāt*; अँखाएल *ãkhāël*; अँखाएब *ãkāëb*, अँखाब *ãkhāb*; अँखाए *ãkhāë*), **Tbh.**, *v. intr.*, to eye, look keenly, be sharp, clever, intelligent. **Exam.**, *Coll.* (*Bh.*), को के केहू नत ठग सकौं, ऊ बड़ अँखावौं, No one can swindle him; he is far too sharp.

(*The word has, in Bihār, not the meaning of* 'to be angry,' *given in the H. Dy.*)

[*A den. root derived from* आँखि, *q.v.*].

अखाउत *akhāüt* = अखौत *akhaut*, *q.v.*

अखाड़ *akhār*, (*obl. sg.* अखाड़ा *akhārā or poet.* अखड़ा *akharā*), *the same as* अखार *akhār*, *q.v.* **Exam.**, [1] *Din.*, गुलामी जट एक सौ एकैस दण्ड अँखारत बहि अखाड़ा (*obl.*) पर, Gulāmī Jaṭ is performing one hundred and twenty-one daṇḍ exercises in the palæstra. [2] *Padm., ch.* 115, 6, क्षुद्र घण्ट मोहहिँ नर राजा, इन्द्र अखाड़ साथ जनु बाजा, Their small bells bewitch kings of men, like the music (*of the Apsaras*) on entering Ind'r's court; *ib.*, *ch.* 597, 4, नट नाटक पतुरनि औ बाजा, आय अखाड़ सबै मढ़ें साजा, Jugglers, actors, dancing-women, and musicians came into the arena with all their paraphernalia.

अखाड़ा *akhāṛā*, अखारा *akhārā*, *str. f. of* अखाड़ *akhāṛ or* अखार *akhār*, *q.v.* **Exam.**, *Alh.*, *l.* 126, देखल अखाड़ा इन्दरमन के हृदय बड़ मनुस होय जाय, (*When*) Rūdal saw the palæstra of Indar'man, great was his joy.

अखाढ़ *akhāṛh* (1), (*str. f.* अखाढ़ा *akhāṛhā*), *the same as* अखार *akhār*, *q.v.* **Exam.**, *Hb.* ix, 1, भरि जोजन भए, भवल अखार, For a whole league the palæstra extended (*lit.* was made).

[*This form of the word, though less correct than* अखाड़ *or* अखार, *is the more usual one in Bihārī. Regarding the inorganic aspiration, see Gd. Gr.*, § 131, *p.* 72. *It also occurs in Multānī* (*Ml. Gy.*, *p.* 10), अखाड़ा *or* खाड़ा, *with the following additional special meanings:* [1]an indigo-ground, consisting of one or more sets of indigo-vats; [2]the hole into which the water from the vats is run off; [3]the place where the indigo is dried; *and khāṛhā is also used for* a cattle-road.]

अखाढ़ *akhāṛh* (2), (*lg. f.* अखढ़वा *akhaṛh'wā*, *q.v.*), **Ts.**, *subst. m.*, the name of the tenth month of the Hindū system of the faslī or agric. year, which commences with the month Āsin. It corresponds to part of our June and July, in which the full moon is near the constellation *Ākhāṛhā*, whence the name of the month (*Grs.* § 1082). *It is the first month of the rainy season, and consequently of cultivation* (*Grs.* §§ 1083, 1084, *also* 1009, 1039). **Exam.**, *Krish.* 314, आयल मास अखाढ़, सखी री; जल से भरि गेलें ताल नदी री, The month of Akhāṛh has arrived, O friend; with water have been filled (*all*) tanks and rivers. *See* असाढ़ *asāṛh or* असाढ़ *asāṛh.*

[*Skr.* आषाढः. *The tats. occurs in all Gds. and is in Mth. more usual than the tbh. form* असाढ़ *or* असाढ़, *q.v. The latter is more used in Bhoj'pūrī. The form* आखाढ़ *ākhāṛh is merely a modern unphon. spelling; see the remarks under* अकाढ़.]

अखाढ़ी *akhāṛhī*, **Ts.**, *adj. com. gen.*, relating to the month Akhāṛh, *hence used substantively* (*fem.*) *as* the name of various agricultural [1]products and [2]operations; *thus* [1]grass which grows in Akhāṛh (*see Bih.* ii, 9); [2]the chief hoeing (*koṛ or koṛan*) of sugar-cane done in Akhāṛh (*Grs.* §§ 866 *and* 1009), the second sowing of indigo (*called so in North Bihār, Grs.* § 1039). *See* असाढ़ी *asāṛhī or* असाढ़ी *asāṛhī.*

[*Skr.* आषाढी *āṣāḍhī*. *The tats. occurs in all Gds. A modern unphon. spelling is* आखाढ़ी *ākāṛhī.*]

अखाद्य *akhādy'*, **Ts.**, (I) *adj. com. gen.*, not to be eaten. **Exam.**, *Coll.* (*Bh.*), ई अखाद्य फल था, This is a fruit not to be eaten.

(II) *subst. m.*, forbidden food. **Exam.**, ऊ तो अघोरी थौ, खाद्य अखाद्य किछु बिचार नो से लेखे, He is an Aghōr'panthī and takes no thought of forbidden or unforbidden food.

[*Skr.* अखाद्यः; *as above in all Gds.*]

अखार *akhār*, अखाड़ *akhāṛ*, अखाढ़ *akhāṛh*, (*poet.* अखारा *akhārā*, *mod. obl. f.* अखारा *akhārā*, *mod. loc. sg.* अखारें *akhārẽ*, *old obl. plur.* अखारेन्ह *akharenh*, *str. f.* अखारा *akhārā*), **Tbh.**, *subst. m.*, *properly* [1]a place for wrestling, palæstra; *hence* [2]any court *or* open space for the exhibition of sports or shows *or* for the holding of assemblies, an arena, circus (*used as an epithet of Ind'r's court*). **Phr.**, अखारा खेलब to perform athletic exercises (*lit.* to play in the arena). **Exam.**, [1]*Rām.*, *Su.*, *chh.* 1, 8, नाना अखारेन्ह भिरहिं बहु-बिधि एक एकन्ह तर्जहीं, In different palæstras (*wrestlers*) grapple with one another shouting mutual defiance; *Din.*, कनौजी में सात से मल्ल अखारा (*obl.*) खेलवैत अछि, In Kanaūlī he is causing seven hundred wrestlers to perform athletic exercises. [2]*Padm.*, *ch.* 480, 3, दोउ नवल भर जोबन गाजें, अछर जाहु अखारें (*loc.*) बाजें, The two young women with full bosoms scream and fight like Apsaras in Ind'r's court; *Rām.*, *Ln.*, *ch.* 14, 4, लङ्का सिखर उपर आगारा, तहँ दसकन्धर देख अखारा (*m.c.*), On the top of Laŋkā hill there is a palace where Das'kandhar (*i.e.* Rāban) witnesses the sports of the arena; *ib.*, *ch.* 11, 7, लङ्का-सिखर उपर आगारा, अति बिचित्र तहँ होइ अखारा (*m.c.*); बैठ जाइ तेहि मन्दिर रावन, लागे किंनर गुन गन गावन, बाजहिं ताल पखाउज बीना, नित्य करहिं अपछरा प्रबीना, On the top of Laŋkā hill, in his palace, there was a most handsome courtyard; in its hall Rāban sat himself down, and kinnars and gandharbs began to sing and play on cymbal, drum, and lute, while accomplished apsarases danced (*before him*).

[*Skr.* अक्षपाटः, *Pr.* *अक्खवाडो; *G.* अखाडो, *M.* अखाडा, *P.* अखाड़ा, *H.* अखाड़ा *or* अखारा, *B.* अखाड़ (*q.v.*) *or* अखार *or* अखाड़ (*q.v.*), *but Bg. and O.* आखड़ा, *A.* आखरा (*apparently only in the second meaning*).]

अंखिया *ãkhiyā*, अँखिआ *ãkhiā*, (*old obl. pl.* अँखियनु *ãkhiyanu*), **Tbh.**, *subst. f.*, *lg. f. of* आँखि *ãkhi*, *q.v.*, [1]*with all the meanings of* आँखि, *q.v.*, *e.g. Grs.* § 1009, (*North Tirhut*) a sprout *or* the sprouting eyes of the sugar-cane; [2]a kind of cake made of wheat-flour and rice-flour and boiled in water, *used at Musalmān marriages; it is shaped like an eye, hence* *its name* (*Grs.* § 1376). **Exam.,** [1]*Krish.* 314, **फागुन में फरकै बाईं अँखियाँ, अब कछु आगम जानि परी री,** In (*the month of*) Phagun the left eye throbs, hence I conclude that something is going to happen; *Gōp.*, 19, **जरी रे करमवाँ, कोरिया के टुकड़ा मोहि अँखिया देखौलू, उतरल नगरिया के रे भार,** My luck was burnt (*i.e., I had bad luck*): you showed to my eye pieces of burnt food, (*thereby*) the burden (*i.e., the beggar*) of your city has been removed; *B. Rām.*, *vs.* 30, **चितवनि बसति कनखियनु अँखियनु बीच,** Warning may be seen (*lit.* lives) in the glances of (*lit.* within) his eyes; *Bais.* 13, 1, **सइयाँ अँखियाँ नहिँ लागी** (*sing.*) **रे, समुझि उन की बतियाँ,** I have not yet set eye on my husband, (*though*) I am constantly remembering his promise (*of an early return*); *Alh.*, *l.* 15, **पुतली फिर गैल आँखन के, अँखिया भेल** (*sing.*) **रकत के धार,** The pupils of his eyes were turned up, and his eye became (*red*) like a stream of blood.

(*From this long form should be carefully distinguished the plural form* **अँखियाँ** *or* **अँखिया**, *which not unfrequently occurs in poetic literature (e.g., B. Rām.* 36, **अँखियाँ दोउ** two eyes, *Mag.* 26, **दूनों अँखिया** both eyes). *The latter is an older uncontracted form of the modern* **आँखैं**, *plur. of* **आँखि**, *q.v.*)

अँखियाय *ākhiyāy*, **Tbh.,** *subst. f.*, the sprouting eyes of the sugar-cane (*South Bhagalpur, Grs.* § 1009).

[*Apparently a fem.* **अँखियाइ** *formed from* **अँखिया**.]

अखिल *akhil*, **Ts.,** (1) *adj. com. gen.*, (*lit.* without a gap; *hence*) [1] whole, entire (*used as an epithet of God, Rām, etc.*); [2] all, every (*synonymous with* **सकल**). **Comp.,** **अखिल-भुवन** *or* **अखिल-लोक** *or* **अखिल-जग** *or* **अखिल-विश्व**, the whole world, the universe; **अखिलेसर** (**अखिल** + **ईसर**) lord of all, God (*used as an epithet of Rām, Sib, etc*). **Exam.,** [1]*Rām.*, *Ut.*, *ch.* 87, 7, **अखिल बिस्व यह मम उपजाया,** This whole world is my creation; *San.*, *vs.* 7, **यह बिराग सन्दीपिनी अखिल ग्यान को सार,** This 'Encouragement to Asceticism' (*name of one of Tul'sī Dās's smaller works*) (*contains*) the whole essence of saving knowledge; *Rām.*, *Ut.*, *ch.* 72, 4, **ब्यापक, ब्याप्य, अखण्ड, अनन्ता, अखिल, अमोघ, सक्ति भगवन्ता,** (*Rām is*) the Permeator and the Permeated, the Indivisible, the Eternal, the Insoluble (*lit.* the Entire), the Unerring, the Primeval Energy, the Godhead. [2]*Ag.* iii, 4, **अनरथ, अपसगुन, अघ, असुभ, अनभल, अखिल अकाज,** Disappointments, inauspicious omens, mishaps, misfortunes, bad luck, (*and in short*) every evil; *Dōh.* 35, **हरन अमङ्गल अघ अखिल, करन सकल कल्यान,** Removing all ill and evil, and effecting every thing good; *Bin.* 46, **प्रथि आरति निरत सनकादि सुनि सेस सिव देव रिषि अखिल-मुनि तत्त्व-दरसी,** On this Ārati ceremony deeply intent are Sanak and the rest (*i.e. Brahma's four sons, Sanak, Sanatkumār, Sanandan, Sanātan,*) the Bēds, Sēs-nāg, Sib, the Gods, the Rishis, and all the Munis who philosophise on the 'substance'; *Rām.*, *A.*, *do.*, 253, 1, **मिटहिँ पाप परिपञ्च सब, अखिल अमङ्गल भार,** All sin and delusion, and the burden of every ill, are wiped out (*by the invocation of Bharat's name*); *ib*, *Bā.*, *ch.* 59, 2, **पूजे रिषि अखिलेसर जानी,** The Rikhi, recognising them (*Sib* and *Bhawānī*) as the Deity, worshipped them.

(II) *adv.*, wholly, entirely, completely, (*sometimes used as a mere superlative particle*) most. **Exam.,** *Rām.*, *Su.*, *ch.* 42, 2, **साधु अवग्या तुरत, भवानी, कर कल्यान अखिल कै हानी,** Disrespect to a saint, O Bhawānī, speedily causes the destruction of the most (*lit.* entirely) prosperous (*person*); *Sat.*, iii, 10, **हरन बिपति बर बुद्धि-बरन धरा-धरन बल धाम, सरन चाहु तुलसी अखल, बरन अखिल अभिराम,** The remover of the calamity of death (*i.e. the letter* **र** *ra or Bishnu*), the bearer of a mountain-load of virtue (*i.e. the letter* **अ** *a or Brahmā*), and the abode of power (*i.e. the letter* **म** *ma or Sib*); Tul'sī Dās desires (*to seek*) his protection (*i.e. Rām's*), the letters (*of whose name; i.e.* **राम** *rāma*) are most delightful.

[*Skr.* **अखिलः**, *Pā.* **अखिलो**, *Pr.* * **अखिलो**; *all Gds.* **अखिल**.]

अखिलेसर *akhilēswar*,—*see under* **अखिल** *akhil*.

अँखुआ *ākhuā*, **अँखुवा** *ākh'wā*, **Tbh.,** *subst. m.*, [1] sprout, shoot, blade, scion, plantlet, *esp.* of the sugar-cane (*Grs.* § 1009), *also* (*in South Bihār*) of the small bullrush millet (*holcus spicatus, Grs.* § 987), *and* (*in Pat'nā*) of the pea (*pisum sativum, Grs.* § 1001); [2] (*South Bhagalpūr*) a finger-ring. **Exam.,** [1] *Prov.*, **अँखुए** (**अँखुआ** + **ए**) **बकरी चर गेल, तो पेड़ कहाँ से होत,** A goat has grazed on the shoot, so how can the tree come?

[*Properly long form of* **आँखि** eye, bud, *q.v. In its second meaning the word may have a different* (*unknown*) *derivation.*]

अँखुआ *ākhuā*, (*pr. pts.* **अँखुआइत**, *ākhuāit*, **अँखुआत** *ākhuāt*; **अँखुआएल** *ākhuāēl*; **अँखुआएब** *ākhuāēb or* **अँखुआब** *ākhuāb*; **अँखुआए** *ākhuāē*), **Tbh.,** *v. intr.*, to throw out shoots (*used in South Bihār, esp. of the small bullrush millet, holcus spicatus, sugar-cane, etc.*). **Exam.,** *Coll.*, **ऊख अँखुआइत है,** The sugar-cane is beginning to sprout; **ऊख अँखुआएल भेल,** The sugar-cane has sprouted (*Grs.* §§ 987, 1009).

[*A den. root, derived from* **अँखुआ** *or* **अँखुवा** *q.v. In form it resembles a double caus. root* (= **अँखुवाव**), *the simple caus. root being* √ **अँखा**, *q.v.*]

अखुता *akhutā, the W. Bh. form of* √अकुता *akutā, q.v.* (*Ās. Gy.*)

[*Perhaps der. from Skr.* अतिक्रमण, *the aspiration being transferred from* क *to* ख. *See also the remarks on the der. of* √अकुता.]

अखेता *akhētā*, **Tbh.**, *subst. m.*, (*optionally in Gayā and Paṭ'nā*), the cross-axle of the lever used in raising water (*Grs.* § 933).

[*This is merely a bye-form of* अखौता, *q.v.*]

अखेतीज *akhētīj* = अखैतीज *akhãitīj, q.v.*

अखेद *akhēd*, (*optionally in Gayā and Paṭ'nā*), *the same as* अखौता *akhãutā, in its fourth meaning, q.v.* (*Grs.* § 933.)

अखेना *akhēnā*, (*in Paṭ'nā, Gayā, and South Mungēr*) = अखैना *akhãinā, q.v.* (*Grs.* § 76.)

अखै *akhãi*, अखय *akhay*, **Tbh.**, *the same as* अछै *achhãi, q.v.* (*The forms with* ख *kh occur only in compounds*). **Comp.**, अखैतीज *or* अखैतीज or अखन्तीज, *subst. f.*, a Hindū festival, the third of the second or bright half (*i.e., the 18th day*) of the month Baisākh (*i.e., April–May*), which is the first day of the sat-jug (*or golden age*) and secures (*akhãi or*) permanent rewards of actions then performed (*Skr. Dy. P.*). *On this day the cultivators settle their accounts for the expenses of the* (*rabi or*) *spring-crop and the repayment of advances* (*Ell. vol.* I, *pp.* 193, 194.)

(*This expression is properly Hindī, the more usual Bihārī expressions will be found under* अखर *and* आखिर (1).

[*Skr.* अक्षयम् imperishable, *Pā. and Pr.* अक्खयं; *all Gds.* अखय *or* अखै. *The comp.* अखैतीज *consists of Skr.* अक्षय + तृतीया, *scl.* तिथि, the third (*day*) of Akṣaya; *see der. of* तीज *tīj under that article.*]

अखैतीज *akhãitīj,—see under* अखै *akhãi.*

अखैन *akhãn*, (*S. Bh.*), *wk. f. of* अखैना *akhãinā, q.v.* (*Grs.* § 76.)

अखैना *akhãinā* (*S. Bh., Mg., S. Mth.*), अखैन *akhãn*, अकैना *akãinā*, अखेना *ōkhēnā*, खेना *khēnā*, उखैनो *ukhãinō*, **Tbh.**, *subst. m.*, a kind of hooked stick used for turning up and pushing the corn under the bullock's feet while it is being trodden out (*Grs.* § 76).

[*Properly str. f. of* अखैन; *perhaps from Skr.* अक्षकर्षः; *not met with in other Gds.*]

अखैला *akhãilā* (*Mg.*), **Tbh.**, *the same as* अखौता *akhãutā, q.v.* (*Grs.*, § 431).

[*Skr.* अक्षवेष्टः *or* (*prākritising*) अक्खवेढो, *Pr.* (*with pleon. suff.* क) अक्खवेढअो *or* अक्खपउअो (*cf. Hēm.* iv, 168, 222), *hence Gd.* (*contracted*) अखैला.]

अखोतो *akhōtō*, **Tbh.**, *subst. m.*, (*South Bhagalpūr*), the cross-axle of the lever used in raising water (*Grs.* § 933).

[*This is merely a bye-form of* अखौता, *q.v.*]

अखोर *akhōr*, **Any.**, *subst. f.*, leavings, sweepings, rubbish, refuse; (*agric.*) fodder which cattle leave uneaten (*Cr., p.* 58). **Comp.**, अखोर-बखोर, rubbish and refuse. **Exam.**, *Coll.* (*Muh. Wom.*), तोबा, का अखोर उठा लाया, Good gracious! what rubbish is this you have brought! (*Hd. Dy.*) *Coll.* (*Bh.*), घर मैं तर भर के अखोर-बखोर लागल रहैन, His house is full of sweepings and rubbish.

[*Prs.* آخور *ākhōr, neg. of* خور *khūr, food.*]

अखोह *akhōh*, **Tbh.**, (I) *adj. com. gen.*, inaccessible. **Exam.**, *Coll.* (*Bh.*), एक अखोह पहाड़ मैं आ परल, He found himself on an inaccessible mountain.

(II) *subst. f.* [1] uneven ground (*Ās. Gy.*); [2] an inaccessible place; [3] difficulty, trouble. **Exam.**, [1] *Coll.* (*Bh.*), एगो अखोह मैं कहाँ जाइछ, Why do you go on uneven ground? [2] *Coll.* (*Bh.*), ई गढ़्हा अखोह छा, This cavity is an inaccessible place. [3] *Coll.* (*Bh.*), हम अखोह मैं परल बानीं, I have fallen into difficulties.

[*A compound of* खोह pit, chasm, *and the pleon. pref.* अ (6), *q.v. The word* खोह *represents the Skr.* खात-क a dug out place (*see Skr. Dy.*) *The Skr.* √खा *dig has a tendency in Pr. to change to* √खु (*as shown by Prof. S. Goldschmidt, see Sapt., p.* 101, *footnote*). *Hence Skr.* खात-क *or* *खुत-क, *Pr.* *खाअहू *or* *खुअहू, *B.* (*contr.*) खोह. *Similarly Skr.* आखात-क *would form Pr.* अक्खाअहू *or* अक्खुअहू, *B.* अखोह. *The meaning of* deep *easily passes into that of* steep (*cf. M.* खोल); *hence* अखोह *comes to mean* inaccessible *in a general way, both as regards depths and heights. Compare S.* खुखोड़ो a pit for a water-wheel, खुड़खुड़ो *or* खाडो a hole *or* ditch, *M., H.*, खोल deep *or* steep, a cavity; *and M.* √खोप, *H.* √खुप *or* खुभ penetrate, *etc.*]

अखौत *akhãut*, (*Mg. also*) अखाउत *akhāut*, **Tbh.**, *subst. m.*, the name of various instruments having the form of an axle; *thus* [1] the axle of the apparatus for husking grain (*Grs.* § 611, *also* अखौता, *q.v.*); [2] the axis on which the pulley of a well-rope turns (*Grs.* § 940, *also* अखौता, *q.v.*); [3] the cross-axle on which a well-lever works (*Grs.* § 933, *also* अखौता, *q.v.*)

(*The Hd. Dy. spells this word* अखौता, *which is perhaps merely a misspelling for* अखौता, *q.v.*)

[*Skr.* अक्षावर्तः, *Pr.* अक्खावत्तो; *hence Gd.* अखावत *and* (*contr.*) अखौत; *apparently wanting in the other Gds.*]

अखौता *akhautā*, **Tbh.**, *subst. m.*, the name of various instruments having the form of an axle; *thus* [1](*Mg. and N. Bh.*) the axle on which the pestle for grinding bricks into powder works (*Grs.* § 431, *also* (*Mg.*) अखैला *akhailā or* उखौता *ukhautā*, *q.v.*); [2]the axis-pin on which the lever for crushing tobacco works (*Grs.* § 464); [3]the axle of the apparatus for husking grain (*Grs.* § 611; *also* अखौत *akhaut*, *q.v.*); [4]the cross-axle on which a well-lever works (*Grs.* § 933; *also* अँखौता, अखौत, अखोतो, अखेला, अखेद, *q.v.*); [5]the axis on which the pulley of a well-rope turns (*Grs.* § 940, *also* अखौत, *q.v.*)

[*Properly str. f. of* अखौत, *q.v.*]

अँखौता *ãkhautā*, **Tbh.**, *subst. m.*, (*South Munger*), the cross-axle of the lever used in raising water (*Grs.* § 933).

[*This is merely a bye-form of* अखौता, *q.v.*]

अख्ता *akhtā* = अखता *akh'tā*, *q.v.*

अख्बार *akhbār* = अखबार *akh'bār*, *q.v.*

अख्यात *akhyāt*, **Ts.**, *adj. com. gen.*, (*subst. f.* अख्याता *akhyātā*), famous. **Exam.**, *Coll.* (*Bh.*), ऊ इतन्ने अख्यात नहिंचे, He is not so famous.

[*Skr.* अख्यातः; *the spelling* अख्यात *is a modern unphonetic one. Though a theoretically possible tatsama, the word is not used in the sense of* 'not famous,' 'obscure' (*Skr.* अख्यातः) *as stated in the H. Dy.*]

अख्यान *akhyān*, **Ts.**, *subst. masc.*, knowledge, understanding. **Exam.**, *Coll.* (*Bh.*), एतन्ना नऽ अख्यान कर सकैछ, Cannot you understand this much? *ib.*, ई बात तोहन्ना अख्यान मेँ आएल, Have you understood this?

[*Skr.* आख्यानम्, a saying, *or* story. *In B. the meaning has been changed as above. In this sense not met in other Gds. Possibly there has been a confusion with the Ar.* خيال *khayāl* understanding.]

अख्रोट *akhrōṭ*, आखोट *ākhrōṭ*, *the same as* आखोट *ākhōṭ*, *q.v.*

[*The Gip. has* akhor (*Mik.* vii, *p.* 6).]

अख्लाक *akhlak* = अखलाक *akh'lak*, *q.v.*

अग *ag*, **Ts.**, *subst. m.* (*lit.* that which does not *or* cannot go; *hence*) the immoveable *or* inanimate creation (*incl. the vegetable and mineral world*). **Comp.**, अग-जग (*synonymous with* जड़-चैतन्य) the inanimate and animate creation, the universe; अगजग-नाथ, lord of the universe, god; अगजग-मय, present in all creation (*an epithet of god*) *or* containing all creation (*i.e., the universe*). **Exam.**, *Rām.*, *Ar.*, *chh.* 9, 11, सो प्रगट करुना-कन्द सोभा-ब्रिन्द अग जग मोहई He, manifesting himself as the all-merciful and all-radiant, gives delight to the inanimate and animate (*i.e., the whole*) creation; *ib.*, *Ln.*, *ch.* 54, 2, सेवहिँ सुर नर अग-जग जाही, (*Rām*) whom gods and men and the inanimate and animate creation adore (*here* जग *includes the animals only*); *Gīt.*, *A.*, 27, 2, पायन पनहीँ न चितु मृदुल हैं पद हैँ। रूप की मोहनी मेलि मोहे अग-जग हैँ, On (*Rām's*) feet are no sandals; his feet are sweeter than lotuses; the beauty of form in them (*lit. being added to them*) enchants the whole creation; *Han.*, *vs.* 24, करम, काल, लोक-पाल, अग-जग, जीव-जाल, नाथ, हाथ सब; निज महिमा बिचारिये, Causation, time, the gods, the animate (*i.e., animals and men*) and inanimate creation, (*in short*) the whole mass of living beings, O Lord! are in thy hands; consider thine own glory! *Rām.*, *Ln.*, *ch.* 101, 13, अगजग-नाथ मनुज करि जाना, You took the Lord of the universe to be a (*mere*) man; *ib.*, *Bā.*, *ch.* 197, 7, अगजग-मय सब-रहित बिरागी, (*Hari is*) present in all creation (*inanimate and animate*), passionless, and unbiassed; *ib.*, *Ut.*, *ch.* 61, 5, अगजग-मय सब मम उपराजा, The whole universe is my creation.

(*This word is also said to mean* tree *and* mountain, but it *has never been met with by us except in composition with* जग *jag, which latter word means* that which can go, *i.e.*, the moveable *or* animate creation, *incl. either animals and men, or animals only. With regard to the probable fictitiousness of those two meanings in Sks., see Zach., p.* 24.)

[*Compound of Skr.* अग + जगत, *Pr.* *अगजगो (*cf. Hēm.* iv, 404, जगि *in the world*). *The word is alliterative and belongs to poetic usage, and may probably be thus found in all Gds.*]

अँगऊँ *ãgaū*, अगौँ *agaū*, (*lg. f.* अँगौँयाँ *ãgaũyā̃*), **Tbh.**, *subst. m.*, the first fruits given to Brāhmans (*Grs.* § 1203). *Synonyms are* अगब्बर *ag'bar*, अगेरा *agaira*.

[*Derivation, see under* अगौँ.]

अग-काढ़ना *ag'karh'nā*, **Tbh.**, *subst. m.*, (*Mg.*) the name of the shovel for stoking the fire in a sugar-refinery (*Grs.* § 319, *k*).

[*Properly a compound of* अगि fire *and* काढ़न instrument for pulling, poking, *q.v.*]

अगट, *agaṭ*, **Tbh.**, *subst. m.*, a butcher's stall (*Hd. Dy.*). [*Der.* ?]

अगन्टी *ag'ṭī*, **Tbh.**, *subst. f.*, (*agric.*), an advance of money to buy seeds. (*Cr.*, *p.* 87.) *For synonyms, see under* अगन्ड़ौर *ag'ṛaur.*

[*A corruption of the Skr. compound* अग्र + वृत्ति, advance-wages, *Pr.* अग्गवट्टि, *S.* अगुवाड *or* अगुवार. *This belongs to a very numerous class of words of nearly or quite the same meaning. They all imply* something which is 'before' either with regard to time or place; *such as* first, former; front of a house; top of sugar-cane, ears of a crop; first fruits; advance of money, etc. *They may, for practical purposes, be considered as derived from* अगा former, front, *by means of various pleonastic suffixes. But there is much reason to believe that ultimately they all are more or less disguised representatives of a Sanskrit compound consisting of* अग्र former *and* वृत्त being. *The Skr.* वृत्त (*and its congeners, such as* वर्त्त, वृत्ति, *etc.*) *admit in Prākrit of the alternative forms* वट्ट *and* वत्त (*cf. Hēm.* ii, 29, 30, i, 128, 132). *The former is the more usual form and gives rise to the numerous B. words containing a final* ट *or* ड़ *or* ल *or* र *or* न, *all these consonants being interchangeable in the order here given,* (*see Gd. Gr.* §§ 29-31, 103-106). *The Pr. form* वत्त *is the less usual one and has but few descendants in B., such as* अगोत, अगुत्ती, अगता, *q.v. The full Pr. form* अग्गवट्ट *is best preserved in the S.* अगुवाड, *less so in the S.* अगुवार, *B.* अगुवार, अगवड़, अगवन. *The medial dissyllable* अव ava *is apt to be vocalised to* अउ (*see Gd. Gr.* § 122), *as in B.* अगाउर, *and to be further contracted into* औ *or* ओ *or* ऊ (*see Gd. Gr.* § 122), *as in B.* अगौर, अगोर (*cf. Gip.* agor, *Mik.* vii, 5), अगोड़ो, अगूत, *etc. Or by eliding* व, *the dissyllable may be changed to* अअ, *and contracted to* आ, *as in B.* अगाड़, अगार, *etc.; or an euphonic* य *may be inserted between* अअ (*see Gd. Gr.* §§ 68, 69), *thus making the dissyllable* अय aya, *and this may further be contracted to* ऐ *or* ए *or* ई (*see Gd. Gr.* § 121), *as in B.* अगेरा, अगीन. *Finally the contracted vowel* (औ *or* ओ *or* ऐ *or* ए) may be shortened and *reduced to* उ *or* इ *or* अ *see Gd. Gr.* §§ 26, 66), *as in B.* अगुत्ती, अगिला, अगला, अगरा, अगता, *etc. Other examples of similar shortenings are M.* अँगठा *and* अँगोठा toe-ring, *etc. These observations show that the so called pleon. suffixes occurring in all these words are properly nouns* (वृत्त, *etc.*) *in a more or less advanced state of decay. The process of decay, however, must, in the case of some of them* (*such as* अड, रड, औड़, और, *etc.*) *be of a very old date, because in the form of* अड, रड, उड, अड, *etc., they are already observed to occur in mediæval and perhaps even older Prākrit* (*see Hēm.* ii, 164-166, iv. 429, 430, *cf. Vr.* iv, 25, 26).]

अगड़ *agaṛ*, (*Mth.*), *the same as* अकड़ *akaṛ*, *q.v.* **Comp.**, अगड़ धत्त, *adj. com. gen.*, *or str. f.* अगड़ धत्ता *m.* (*f.* धत्ती *f.*), high, tall, gigantic; अगड़ धैंधैं *or* अगड़ दौंदौं, *adj. com. gen.*, [1] strong, powerful; [2] fleshy, plump, corpulent (*Hd. Dy.*). **Exam.**, *Riddle, Bh.*, एक पेड़ अगड़ धत्ता, जेकरा जड़ न पत्ता? अमर बेल, There is a tree very tall, which has neither roots nor leaves (*what is it*)? the air-creeper. *Coll.* (*Bh.*), ई अदिमी बड़ अगड़ धत्त बा, This is an exceedingly stout and tall man.

अगड़-बगड़ *agaṛ'bagaṛ*, अगर-बगर *agar'bagar*, **Tbh.**, (I) *subst. m.*, [1] *lit.* odds and ends, promiscuous things; *hence* [2] trifling talk, babble; [3] trifles, trumpery, trash. **Exam.**, *see* अगर-बगर *agar'bagar and* अगड़म-बगड़म *agaṛam'bagaṛam.*

(II) *adj. com. gen.*, worthless, useless, good-for-nothing.

[*This is merely another form of* अकट-बकट, *q.v.*; *H. has* अगड़-बगड़, अगड़-तगड़, *P.* अगड़-बगड़, *M.* अगड-बगड, अगड-तगड अगड-बगड. *Note, however, M.* बगड *f.* refuse *or* dregs, worthless, *which appears to be connected with Skr.* अवगत *or* अवगर्त.]

अगड़म-बगड़म *agaṛam'bagaṛam*, *the same as* अगड़-बगड़ *agaṛ'bagaṛ*, *q.v.* **Exam.**, [1] *Prov.*, अगड़म-बगड़म काठ कठ कब्बर, odds and ends, splinters, and rags (*Hd. Prov.*); *Coll.* (*Bh.*), उनकरा फुलवारी में कौनो नीमन चीज नहिं छे; सब अगड़म-बगड़म भेल बा, There is nothing good in his garden; it is all filled with worthless trifles.

अगन्ड़ा *ag'ṛā* (*in South Bhagalpūr*), अगन्ला *ag'lā* (1) (*Mg. and Bh.*), **Tbh.**, *subst. m.*, (*agric.*) [1] the ears of a crop; *hence* [2] the act of cutting the ears without the stalks (*Grs.* § 875). *See* अगन्रा *ag'rā* (1).

[*Der. from Skr.* अग्रं front part, tip, *Pr.* अग्ग (*Nām.*, *vs.* 235), *with the Pr. pleon. suff.* डअ (= ड + अ) *or* डअ *superadded,* अग्गडअं or अग्गलअं (*cf. Hem.* iv, 341), *contr. Gd.* अगड़ा *or* अगला. *See also the remarks under* अगन्टी.]

’अँगन्ड़ा *ãg'ṛā*, (*pr. pts.* अँगन्ड़ाइत *ãg'ṛāit*, अँगन्ड़ात *ãg'ṛāt*; अँगन्ड़ाएल *ãg'ṛāël*; अँगन्ड़ाएब *ãg'ṛāëb*; अँगन्ड़ाए *ãg'ṛāë*), **Tbh.**, *v. intr.*, (*W. Bh. and Bw.*) [1] to yawn, stretch the limbs; [2] to roll about in bed. **Exam.**, *Coll.* (*Bh.*), का, तूँ बड़ अदिमी कोंचौं बैठ के बाँह उठा के अँगन्ड़ाइंड; ई ठिक नाहीं, What, do you sit in the presence of a gentleman, and stretch your arms and yawn? This is not proper.

[*There is a synonymous noun* अँगेठो, a yawn (*B. Gr.*, iii (*Mg.*), *p.* 87, *where it is explained as* अङ्ग का ऐंठना, *the latter being the Skr.* √आवेष्ट), *which points to a derivation from a Skr. comp.* अङ्ग + वेष्ट, twisting *or* rolling about of the body. *The Skr.* वेष्ट *becomes*

Pr. वेढ (*Hēm.* iv, 221), *but Gḍ.* बेढ़ *or* बेढ (*see Gḍ. Gr.* § 145, *exc.* 2). *Hence we should have a der.* √अङ्गवेढ, x*th. cl. Skr.* * अङ्गवेढयति, *Pr.* * अंगवेढावेद *or* अंगवेढावेद, *Gḍ.* * अँगौड़ावै (*with the usual contraction of* अवे *to* औ, *see Gḍ. Gr.* § 122) *or shortened* अँगन्ड़ाव. *There is, however, also another synonymous noun* अँगन्मड़ी (*q.v.*), *which might suggest a derivation from the Skr. comp.* अङ्ग + मर्द shampooing of the body; *whence might come a der.* √अङ्गमर्द, x*th. cl. Skr.* * अङ्गमर्दयति, *Pr.* * अंगमड्डावेद, *Gḍ.* * अँगौड़ावै (*with the contraction of* अम *to* औ, *see Gḍ. Gr.* §§ 122, 127), *or shortened* अँगन्ड़ाव. *On the other hand, the consonants* म *and* व *are liable to be interchanged (see Gḍ. Gr.* §§ 134, 122, *note*); *and hence* अँगन्मड़ी *may stand for* अँगवड़ी (*cf. P.* अगवाड़ी) *and be also referable to the first-mentioned derivation.*]

अँगन्ड़ाई *ãg'ṛãi*, **Tbh.**, *subst. f.*, (*W. Bh. and Bw.*) a stretching of the limbs, yawning = अँगेठी *ãgēṭhī or* अँगन्मड़ी *ãg'maṛī*, *q.v.*, *which are the usual words.* **Exam.**, *Coll.* (*Bh.*), बैठल बैठल अँगन्ड़ाई आवे लागल, ऊ नऽ ऐलँ, While we sat waiting we began to yawn, but he did not come.

[*Properly* 1*st verb. noun of* √ अँगड़ा, *q.v.*]

अगन्ड़ाही *ag'ṛāhī*, **Tbh.**, *subst. f.*, an extensive conflagration (*especially of a forest; see Mth. Ch. Vocabulary*). **Exam.**, *Chan.*, आधा राति अवल निसि भेल। कारी कारी आन्ही भेल। अगड़ाही लागल वन-मोर। जरै लगल गाछ वन मोर॥ When half the night has passed, a heavy black darkness fell; conflagration began all around, and trees and peacocks in the forest burnt excessively.

[*Comp. of Skr.* अग्नि fire *plus* दाहिका conflagration, *Pr.* अग्गिदाहिआ *or* अग्गिडाहिआ; *B.* अगन्डाही *for* अगिडाही; *the change of an initial* ड *ḍ* to ड़ *ṛ is rather unusual. The initial Skr.* द *d may optionally change in Pr. to* ड (*Hēm.* i, 217, *Sapt., vs.* 163, 229, 536, 730). *The H. has* अगवाही.]

अँगडिया *ãgaḍiyā*, अँगड्डिया *ãgaḍḍiyā*, **Tbh.**, *subst. m.*, a man who carries money *or* jewels in his quilted cloth.

[*Properly a long form of* अँगडी *or* अँगड्डी, *formed with the Gḍ. suff.* ई, *implying* possession (*see Gḍ. Gr.* § 252), *from a stem* * अँगड *or* अँगड्ड. *The latter is probably a corruption of the Skr. compound* अङ्ग-वेढ, a body-wrapper *or* something wrapped *or* secreted about the body, (*cf. M.* अँगडें *or* अँगडी a body-garment, *and B.* आगरि *or H.* अँगरी armour). *Skr.* वेढ *becomes Pr.* वेढ, *and Gḍ.* बेढ़ *or* बेड़. *The junction syllables of a comp. word are liable to extreme wear and tear. See also the remarks on the derivation of* √अँगन्ड़ा *and* अगन्डी.]

अगन्ड़ौर *ag'ṛaur*, **Tbh.**, *subst. f.*, the advance of pay to labourers (*Grs.* § 1186). *See* अगवाड़ *ag'war*, अगाउर *agāūr*, अगार *agār*, अगाड़ *agāṛ*, अगौरी *agaūrī*, अगौड़ी *agaūṛī*, अगवान *ag'wan*, अगन्डी *ag'ṭī*, अगौर *agaūr*, अगोर *agōr*, अगेरा *agērā*.

[*Derived from* अगन्ड़ा *or* अगन्रा *by means of the pleon. suff.* और, *see Gḍ. Gr.* § 209. *See also the remarks under* अगन्डी.]

अगत *agat*, *the same as* अगति *agati*, *q.v.*

अगन्ता *ag'tā*, (*f.* अगन्ती *ag'tī* (2)), **Tbh.**, *adj.*, *the same as* अगिला *agilā*, *q.v.* **Phr.**, *loc.* अगन्तेँ *ag'tẽ*, before (*of time*), (*Ās. Gy.*). **Exam.**, **Prov.* (*Mg.*), अगन्ता खेती आगे आगे, पिछन्ता खेती भागे जोगे A field first (*i.e. early prepared*) yields a future return, the field last (*i.e. too late prepared*) is (*as regards a return*) a matter of chance; (*Mg. does not observe gender; for a more correct form of the proverb, see* आगिल).

[*Contracted from Skr.* अग्रतस्, *Pr.* अग्गत्तो; *see the remarks under* अगन्डी; *or possibly a corruption of Skr.* अग्रतः, *Pr.* अग्गतो, *B.* अगत (*with loss of aspiration, as in* अगती (2), *q.v.*), *P.* (*adj.*) अगेता, (*subst. f.*) अगेत, *S.* (*adv.*) अगती *or* अगिती *or* अगुती in future, (*subst. f.*) अगति credit.]

अगति *agati* (1), अगत *agat*, **Ts.**, *subst. f.* [1]evil condition, misfortune, distress; [2]disgrace; [3]damnation; [4]want of resource, necessity. **Exam.**, [1]*Gīt.*, *Bā.*, 82, 2, रिधि, सिधि, विधि चारि सुगति, जा बिनु गति अगति, Success, prosperity, and the four kinds of good conditions, without which (*one's*) condition is an evil condition. [3]*Bin*, *vs.* 112, काल कर्म गति अगति जीव की सब, हरि, हाथ तुम्हारे, Time, fate, salvation, and damnation of (*all*) living beings, all is in thine hand, O Hari! (*the comm. explains* गति *and* अगति *by* वैकुण्ठादि की प्राप्ति *and* नरकादि प्राप्ति). [4]*Coll.* (*Bh.*), उन्हकरा एक मरब अगति भेल बा, से घर बरे पड़ल रहेला, He is altogether without resource, and stays helplessly at home.

[*Skr.* अगतिः; *all Gḍs.* अगति *or* अगत, *but in M. and G. in the sense of* importance, necessity.]

अगति *agati* (2), *Mth. and poet.* = अगती *agatī* (1), *q.v.*

अगती *agatī* (1), **Ts.**, *subst. m.* (*lit.* unfortunate, *hence*), one whose funeral ceremonies have not been performed. **Exam.**, *Coll.* (*Mg.*), ऐसन पापी रहल, के अगती भो गेल, He was such a sinner that he got no funeral.

[*Skr.* अगतिकः, *apparently Pr. tech. tats.* *अगतिओ, *Gḍ.* अगती.]

अगती *agatī* (2), **Tbh.**, *subst. f.*, the agati-tree (*Æschynomene or Sesbana grandiflora or Agati* *grandiflorum*), *the leaves and pods of which are eaten as vegetables.*

[*Skr.* अग्निस्थिः, *Pr.* अगत्थी *or* (*with pleon.* क) अगत्थिअो, *G.* अगथियो, *H. and B.* अगती (*with loss of the aspiration.*]

अगन्ती *ag'tī* (1), **Tbh.**, *subst. f.*, the ceremony of fumigating with incense a bridal pair by the officiating Brāhman, after the circumambulation of the sacrificial fire (*Grs.* § 1332).

[*Perhaps derived from a Skr. comp.* अग्नि-वृत्ति *or* वृत्ति *lit.* encircling with fire. *See also the remarks under* अगन्ता *and* अगन्डौ.]

अगन्ती *ag'tī* (2), **Tbh.**, *adj. fem. of* अगन्ता *ag'tā*, *q.v.*

अगद्-बगद *agad'bagad*, **Tbh.**, *subst. m.*, (*Bh.*) falsehood, fraud (*Āz. Gy.*)

[*Der.? Perhaps connected with Skr.* अवद्य, what is not to be uttered. *Mg. pandits identify it with* अगड़-बगड़, *q.v.*]

अगन्दाइँ *ag'dāī*, (*Mg.*) = अगन्दाइन *ag'dāin*, *q.v.* (*See Grs.* § 889.)

अगन्दाइन *ag'dāin*, (*Mg.*) अगन्दाइँ *ag'dāī*, अगन्दाएँ *ag'dāẽ*, अगन्देँयाँ *ag'dãiyã*, **Tbh.**, *subst. m.*, (*agric.*), the outer *or* fore ox of a team of oxen engaged in treading out corn (*Grs.* § 889).

[*A compound of* अग *and* दाइन ; *the former is the Pr.* अग्ग, *Skr.* अग्र, anterior, foremost ; *the latter is a noun of agency, meaning* one who treads down, *from the* √दाम (*also* दाव *or* दाप), *corresponding to Skr.* √दम्. *The latter probably had a Pr. equivalent* √दम्म (*see H. R., p.* 48), *which accounts for the long* आ *ā in the modern derivatives as compared with the corresponding Skr. derivatives. Thus B.* दाइन, *etc., also* दाउनि (*Mth. Ch. Vocabulary*), *or* दौनी (*Grs.* § 887), *H.* दाएन, दावन, (*Cr., p.* 51), *corresponds to Skr.* दमनं, treading out. *See the remarks on the derivation of* दाउनि.]

अगन्दाएँ *ag'dāẽ*, (*Mth.*), *the same as* अगन्दाइन *ag'dāin*, *q.v.* (*See Grs.* § 889.)

अगन्देँयाँ *ag'dãiyã*, (*Mg.*), *the same as* अगन्दाइन *ag'dāin*, *q.v.* (*See Grs.* § 889.)

अगाधा *agadhā*, **Tbh.**, *adj. com. gen.*, meek, unresisting, inoffensive. **Exam.**, *Padm.*, *ch.* 619, 1, हबसी बन्दवाना जिव-बधा, तेहीं सौंपा राजा अगाधा, To a cruel negro jailor he delivered the unresisting king.

[*From* अ not *and* गधा ass (*q.v.*) *The ass being an animal noted for its obstinacy and troublesomeness, the word* अगधा, *lit.* not having the nature of an ass, *comes to mean* inobstinate, meek, *etc. The Skr. equivalent would be* अगर्दभः, *Pr.* (*with pleon.* क) अगद्दहओ, *Gḍ.* अगदहा *or* (*contr.*) अगधा.]

अगन *agan*, आगन *āgan* = अगनि *aganī*, *the same as* अगिनि *aginī*, *q.v.* *See* अगिन *agin*, आगि *āgī*.

[*Derivation see under* अगिनि. *M., H., G., Ksh. and P., also have this form* अगन.]

अँगन्माँ *ãgan'mã*, **Tbh.**, *a bye-form of* अँगनवा *ãgan'wā* (*q.v.*), *used by Musalmān women.* **Exam.**, *Mars.*, 1, 2, नहाए सोनाए बीबी बैठलि अँगनमाँ, The lady bathed and sat in her courtyard, (*the printed edition wrongly divides* अँगन माँ.)

[*Regarding the change of* व *to* म, *see Gḍ. Gr.* § 134.]

अँगनवा *ãgan'wā*, अगनवाँ *agan'wã*, **Tbh.**, *lg. f. of* आँगन *ãgan*, *q.v.* **Exam.**, *B. Gr.*, II (*Bh.*), xii, 1, ननदि अँगनवा चनन गाछ बिरवा, In my sister-in-law's courtyard there is a sandal-tree ; *ib.*, 18, 1, गरमि का कारन सुतलौँ अँगनवा, On account of the excess of heat I slept in the courtyard ; *Bais.* 7, डेरा डाले सुन्दर के अँगनवा, He took up his lodging in Sundar's courtyard ; *Mag.* 7, चोलिया कसिया, गोरी, सुतलूँ अँगनवाँ, रसिक के फाटल है करेजा, Tightening my bodice, O fair (*lady*), I slept in the courtyard, and the heart of my lover is torn.

अँगनवेँ *ãgan'wẽ*, **Tbh.**, (*Bh.*), *a bye-form of* अँगनवा *ãgan'wā*, *q.v.* **Exam.**, *Prov.* (*Bh.*), नाचे न जाने अँगनवेँ टेढ़, Not knowing how to dance, (*she declares*) the courtyard (*to be*) crooked (*i.e., she blames others for her own fault*) ; *Coll.* (*Bh.*), ऐ छौँड़ि तोर अँगनवेँ कतना बड़, O girl ! how large is thy courtyard ?

अँगन्ना *ãg'nā*, अगन्ना *ag'nā*, **Tbh.**, *subst. m.*, *str. f. of* आँगन *ãgan*, *q.v.* *In addition to the* [1] *meanings of* आँगन, (*see Grs.* § 1237), *it is used in the following senses :* [2] (*in N.-E. Tirhut*) the women's quarters, *which are always situated within the inner court of a native house,* (*see Grs.* § 1254) ; [3] (*derivatively*) a visit of condolence *made by women on the death of friends, so called from the fact of the visitors going to the women's quarters* (*see Āz. Gy.*). **Phr.**, अँगन्ना करब to make a visit of condolence (*the more usual B. phr. is* पुछारि करब). **Exam.**, *Coll.* (*Mg.*), तोहर अँगन्ना टेढ़ा बौ, Your courtyard is uneven.

(*This word is almost entirely limited to the Mg. dialect. It should be carefully distinguished from another* अँगन्ना, *which is an obl. form of* आँगन (*q.v.*), *and which, so far as our knowledge of Bihārī literature* (*esp. Bw. and Mth.*) *extends, never occurs as a direct form; whence it would appear that, in literature at least, it is looked upon as an obl. form of* **आँगन**.)

[*Derivation see under* **आँगन**. *M.* **आँगनैं** *n.*]

अँगन्नाई *ãg'nāi*, **अँगन्ने** *ãg'nāī*, (*lg. f.* **अँगन्नैया** *ãg'nāiyā*, *q.v.*), **Tbh.**, *subst. f., a sort of str. f. of* **आँगन** *ãgan*, *q.v.* **Exam.**, *Rām.*, *Ut.*, *ch.* 76, 3, **बरनि न जाइ रुचिर अँगनाई, जहँ खेलहिं नित चारि उ भाई**, The charming courtyard cannot be described where the four brothers are always playing; *Gīt.*, *Bā.*, 30, 4, **जननि सकल चहु-ओर आलबाल मनि-अँगनाई, दसरथ सुकृत बिबुध-बिरवा बिलसत बिलोकि, जनु बिधि बर बारि बनाई**, It was as if the Creator (**बिधि**), on seeing the kalpa-tree (*lit. tree*, **बिरवा**, *of the gods*, **बिबुध**, *i.e. Rām and his three brothers*) of the good actions of Das'rath sporting, had planted a goodly hedge (**बारि**), (*consisting of*) all their mothers, around its watering-basin (**आलबाल**), (*represented by*) the jewelled courtyard.

[*This form of the word also occurs in P. and H. It is a curious formation, being a fem. abstract noun made by means of the sec. der. suff.* **आई** *or* **आई** (*see Gd. Gr.*, § 220) *from* **अँगना** *or* **आँगन**, *but used as a concrete.*]

अगनि *agani*, **Tbh.**, *subst. f., the Mth. and poet. form of* **अगनी** *ag'nī*, *the same as* **अगिनी** *agini*, *q.v.* **Exam.**, [1] *B. Rām.*, *vs.* 33, **सीतलता ससि की रहि सब जग छाइ, अगनि ताप है हम कहँ स चरत आइ**, The coolness of the moon has overspread the whole earth, but it comes to me like the heat of fire; *Bin.* 187, **बिष पियूष सम करउ, अगनि हिम तारि सकउ बिनु मैरे**, Thou canst make poison equal to nectar, and deliver from heat and cold (*lit.* fire and snow) without delay; *Chh. Rām.*, *vs.* 3, **उठे ततच्छन मेघ-निमिष जल अगनि बुझायो**, Clouds rose up at that moment, and the water of the rain extinguished the fire. [6] *Gīt.*, *Su.*, 10, 3 (*p.* 190), **बिरह अगनि जरि रही लता ज्यों क्रिपा दिष्टि जल पलुहावहिं जे**, Just as the creeper, being consumed in the fire (*i.e.* pain) of separation (*from the beloved tree to which it used to cling*), eagerly longs after the water of a gracious sight (*of the beloved*). *See* **अगिनि** *agini and* **आगि** *āgi*.

(*The word is not unfrequently spelt unphon.* **अग्नि**, *as in Rām.*, *Bā.*, *ch.* 195, 10.)

[*This is prop. the wk. f. of* **अगनी**, *q.v. See the remarks under* **अगिनि** *and* **आगि**.]

अगनित *aganit*, **अगिनित** *aginit*, **Ts.**, *adj. com. gen.*, not reckoned *or* counted, innumerable, countless. **Exam.**, *Rām.*, *Bā.*, *ch.* 49, 7, **ते जलचर अगनित बहु भाँती**, They were innumerable, in varied modes, as fishes (*in the sea*); *ib.*, *A.*, *ch.* 7, 3, **रोम-पाट-पट अगनित** (*fem.*) **जाति**, Garments of wool and silk (*and*) other innumerable kinds; *Gīt.*, *A.*, 5, 2, **दुसह बात, बरखा, हिम, आतप; कैसे सहिबी अगनित दिन राति**? Painful things, rain, snow, heat; how shall I be able to bear them for countless days and nights? *Bin.* 166, **कहँ लगि कहौं दीन अगनित, जिन्ह की तुम बिपति निवारी**, How can I tell the countless wretches whose miseries thou hast relieved? *Padm.*, *ch.* 462, 2, **अगनित दान निछावर कीन्हा, मँगतन दान बहुत कै दीन्हा**, Of innumerable gifts he made offerings, and to beggars he gave manifold gifts.

[*Skr.* **अगणितः**; *as above in all Gds. The tadbh. Pr.* **अगणिओ** (*cf. Sapt.*, *vs.* 102) *has only survived in the pleon. neg. form* **अगनगो**, *Gīt.*, *Bā.* 5.]

अगन्नी *ag'nī*, **Tbh.**, *subst. f., the same as* **अगिनी** *agini*, *q.v.* **Exam.**, [6] *Coll.* (*My.*), **ओकर अगन्नी मन्द भो गेलइ अछि**, His pangs of hunger (*lit. fire*) have become relaxed.

[*Properly str. f. of* **अगनि**, *q.v.*]

अगन्नू *ag'nū*, **Tbh.**, *subst. m., a contraction of* **अगन्नेउ** *ag'neü*, *q.v.* **Exam.**, *Padm.*, *ch.* 410, 2, **तीज एकादस अगनू मारी, चौथ दुआदस नेरित बारी**, On the third and eleventh (*of any month*) the south-east is disastrous (*for making a journey towards it*), and on the fourth and twelfth the south-west is prohibited.

[*Derivation see under* **अगनेउ**.]

अगनेउ *ag'neü*, **Tbh.**, *subst. m.*, the south-east. **Exam.**, *Padm.*, *ch.* 412, 3, **छठएँ नेरत, दखिन सतैं, बसै जाय अगनेउ सो आठैं**, On the sixth (*day of the lunar month, when*) she (*i.e. the moon*) is gone to dwell in the south-west, on the seventh (*when she is*) to the south, and on the eighth (*when she is*) to the south-east. *A synonym of* **अगिनि** *agini* (*q.v.*) *in its thirteenth sense.*

[*Skr.* [*] **आग्नेयः** *scl.* **कोणः** the south-east quarter, *Pr.* * **अग्गनेओ**.]

अगनेता *ag'netā*, *poet. for* **अगन्नेउ** *ag'neü*, *q.v.* **Exam.**, *Padm.*, *ch.* 411, 6, **बुध (= अधिक) काल पछिउ, बुध नरेता, गुरु दखिन, सुकर अगनेता**, Tuesday is fatal (*for a journey*) to the west, Wednesday (*for one*) to the south-west, Thursday (*for one*) to the south, and Friday (*for one*) to the south-east.

[*This is an imaginary form of the word, being simply made to rhyme with* **नरेता**. *The latter is a corruption of the Skr.* **नैरृत**.]

अँगन्नै *ãg'nāi* (*Grs.* § 1237) = **अँगन्नाई** *ãg'nāi*, *q.v.*

अँगन्नैया *ãg'nāiyā*, **अँगनैया** *ãg'nāiā*, **Tbh.**, *subst. f.*, *lg. f. of* **अँगन्नाई** *ãg'nāi*, *q.v.* **Exam.**, *Gīt.*, *Bā.* 9, 3, **मनि-खचित प्रतिबिम्ब झलक छबि छलकिहि भरि अँगनैया**, The courtyard is full to overflowing with the brilliant beauty of the figures (*of Rām and his brothers*) reflected in its jewelled pillars.

[*Uncontracted* अँग॰नइया *ãg'naïyā. The fem. gender is shown by* भरि, *uk. f. of* भरौ.]

अग॰बर *ag'bar*, **Tbh.**, *subst. m.*, [1] (*Mg.*) the gleanings and refuse grain on the threshing-floor (*Grs.* § 901); [2] (*Bh.*) first fruits given for religious purposes (*Grs.* § 1203). *Synonyms see under* अग॰वार *ag'wār and* अँगाऊँ *ãgāū̃*.

अगम *agam* (1), **Tbh.**, (I) *adj. com. gen.*, *lit.* what cannot be walked over (*opp.* सुगम), *hence* (*physically*) [1] inaccessible, unapproachable, impassable, difficult to pass *or* approach; [2] (*generally*) inaccomplishable, unattainable, difficult to attain, difficult; [3] (*mentally*) unbearable, unpleasant, miserable, unlucky; [4] incomprehensible, inconceivable. **Comp.**, अगम-पन्थ, (*lit.* inaccessible path,) the next world. **Exam.**, [1] *Rām., A., ch.* 61, 6, 7, चरन-कमल मृदु मंजु तुम्हारे, मारग अगम भूमिधर भारे, कन्दर खोह नदी नद नारे अगम अगाध न जाहिँ निहारे, Your lotus feet are soft and pretty, (*while*) the road is difficult to pass, and there are huge mountains and chasms, precipices, rivers, streams, and torrents impassable and unfathomable, such as one dare not behold; *Ag.* v., 9, मारग अगम सुगम सुभ होइहि राम पसाउ, The impassable road will become pleasant by the favour of Rām; *Rām., Bā., do.* 47, 2, तिन्ह कहँ मानस अगम अति, जिन्हहिँ न प्रिय रघुनाथ, For those the lake is very difficult to approach who have no love for Raghunāth; *ib., A., ch.* 102, 5, देस अगम गढ गाढ सुहावा, An inaccessible domain and magnificent forts; *Gīt., Bā.*, 81, 1, रामहि नीके कै निरखि, सुनयनी, मनसहु अगम समुझि, यह अवसर कत सकुचत, पिकबयनी, (*Wishing*) to look well at Rām, O fair-eyed one, why are you at this time afraid (*to do so*), thinking him unapproachable in your mind, O cuckoo-voiced one; *Padm., ch.* 435, 4, कहाँ सोँ गुरु पाऊँ उपदेसी, अगम-पन्थ कर होय सँदेसी, Where shall I find so instructive a guru who will give me information about the next world. [2] *Rām., Bā., ch.* 168, 3, तप तेँ अगम न कछु संसारा, Nothing in the world is unattainable to penance; *Gīt., Ut.* 318, 3, राम सीय सनेह बरनत अगम सुकबि सकाहिँ, To describe the love of Rām and Sītā is beyond (*lit.* inaccomplishable to) the power of any poet; *Pārv., vs.* 6, अगम न अस कछु तुम कहँ, मुहि अस सूझइ, Nothing in the world is inaccomplishable by you, so it appears to me; *ib., vs.* 4, लागी करन मुनि अगम तप, तुलसी कहै किमि गाइ कै, She began to perform penances (*such as are*) difficult to do for a Muni, how can Tul'sī Dās describe them in song? *Gīt., A.*, 82, 1, जानिहैँ सङ्कर, हनुमान, लखन, भरत राम-भगति; कहन अगम (*fem.*), करन सुगम, सुनत मीठी लगति, Saṅkar, Hanumān, Lakhan and Bharat know (*what is*) devotion to Rām; it is difficult to describe, (*but it is*) easy to exercise, and it is sweet to hear; *Han., vs.* 15, मन को अगम, तन सुगम किये, कपीस, It (*the conquest of Laṅkā*) seemed difficult to the mind, but in reality it was easy to accomplish, O lord of monkeys. [3] *Rām., A., ch.* 76, 5, घर न सुगम, बन न अगम लागा, Neither home seemed happy (*to Sītā*), nor the woods miserable; *Pārv., vs.* 3, कछु न अगम, सब सुगम भयेउ बिधि दाहिन, Nothing (*fell out*) unlucky, but all chanced to be lucky according to the rule (*of omens*) of the right side; *Gīt., A.*, 80, 3, आपु अवध बिपिनि बन्धु सोच-जरनि जरत, तुलसी सम बिखम सुगम अगम लखि न परत, (*Bharat*) himself, being in Awadh (*while*) his brother is in the wood, is consumed with the fire of anxiety, but Tul'sī Dās (*says*) it cannot be determined whose is the comfort and whose the discomfort, or whose the happiness and whose the misery (*i.e., Bharat, being comfortable at Awadh, is miserable through anxiety for his brother Rām, while the latter, though in the discomforts of the woods, has no anxieties and is happy*). [4] *Rām., A., ch.* 47, 7, नारि सुभाउ सब बिधि अगम अगाध दुराउ, A woman's nature is altogether incomprehensible, unfathomable, and deceptive; *ib., Bā.*, 27, 5, उभय अगम, जुग सुगम नाम तेँ, Both (*the twofold knowledge of God, as immanent and transcendent*) are incomprehensible, but both become intelligible by means of the name (*of Rām*); *Jan., ch.* 32, मुनि-मन अगम अनन्द सुलोचनि पावहिँ, Her eyes enjoy a pleasure inconceivable to a Muni's mind; *Gīt., Ar.*, 17, 1, सेवरी सोर उठी फरकत बाम बिलोचन बाहु, सगुन सुहावने सूचत मुनि-मन अगम उछाहु, Sēwarī, she stood up, and her left eye and arm began to throb, which appeared to her a lucky omen of joy inconceivable to a Muni's mind; *Misc.* 28, अगम अगोचर लीला-धारी सो राधा बस कुञ्ज-बिहारी, (*Hari*), the inconceivable and imperceptible, he (*as Krish'n*) indulges in sports and takes his pleasure in groves under the influence of Radha.

(II) *adv.*, extremely, excessively, exceedingly, (*often practically serving as a superlative particle*). **Exam.**, *Hb.* i. 3, कौन परि होत तकर निरबाह, प्रबल लगैयहि अगम अथाह, How can it be accomplished (*by me*)? it seemeth now extremely difficult; अगम अथाह *in this sense is a common phrase; so also* अगम अपार, exceedingly difficult (*Āz. Gy.*), *and* अगम अलख, exceedingly difficult to distinguish (*Gīt., Ut.*, 317, 4); *Misc.* 49, भव-जल नदिया अगम बहै, सूझै वारो न पार, The river of mundane cares (*lit.* water of existence) flows violently (*lit. so as to be* impassable), the further side of the river is not to be seen; *Din.*, आजु देखैत छी अगम अथाह, To-day I see (*the river*) to be exceedingly deep.

[*Skr.* आगमः, *Pr.* आगमो, *B., H., and G.* आगम; *in the other Gḍs. apparently only tats.* आगम, *q.v.*]

अगम *agam* (2), आगम *āgam*, (*obl. pl.* अगमन *agaman*), **Ts.,** *subst. m.,* [1]arrival, commencement; [2]approach, futurity; [3]any shāst'r *or* holy scripture (*Smṛiti*) as distinguished from the Bēds (*Shruti*, निगम) and the Purāṇs; *esp.* [4]later works, Tāntrik, Baishnab, etc., such as the Nārada Pañcharātra (*comm.* नारद-पञ्चरात्रादिक). **Comp.,** अगम-ग्यानी, (*subst. f.* -ग्यानिनी) *or* अगम-जानी, (*subst. f.* -जानिनी), *adj.,* knowing the future, *hence subst.,* a prophet; अगम-बक्ता, (*subst. f.* -बक्त्री), *adj.,* telling the future *or* expounding the shāst'r, *hence subst.,* a prophet *or* a religious teacher; अगम-बात (*f.*) *or* अगम-बानी (*f.*), prophecy, prediction; अगम-बिद्या, the art *or* science of prophecy; अगम-निगम *or* निगम-अगम the Hindū sacred books, the Bēds and other shāst'rs. **Exam.,** [1]*Bih.*, vii, 3, भादो अगम पन्थ नहिं सूझे, *or B. Gr.*, II (*Bh.*), v, 5, भादों अगम डगरिया ना सूझे, On the arrival, *or* with the commencement of Bhādō̃ the paths can no more be seen (*on account of the floods*); *Krish.* 139, दादुर मोर कोकिला बोलैं पावस अगम जनावै, The frog, peacock, and cuckoo by their cry announce the arrival of the rainy season. [2]*Coll.* (*Bh.*), ऊ जन अगम भाखे में बड़ चोखियार बाड़े, That man is very clever at telling the future. [3]*K. Rām., Ut.*, 54, तुलसी महेस को प्रभाव-भाव ही सुगम, अगम-निगम हू को जानिबो अगम है, Tul'sī Dās (*says*) the understanding of the power of Mahēs is easy, (*but*) it is difficult to know the shāst'rs and the Bēds; *Pārv., chh.* 13, ईसान महिमा अगम-निगम न जानहिं, He does not know the glory of Sib, nor the shāst'rs and Bēds; *Gīt., Bā.*, 2, 24, सारद-सेस-गनेस-गिरीसहिं अगम-निगम अवगाह, The shāst'rs and Bēds are the (*subjects of*) deep study to Sārad (*i.e., Saraswatī*) Sēs, Ganēs, and Girīs (*i.e., Sib*); *Dōh.* 80, निगम-अगम साहेब सुगम राम साँचिलो चाह, अँबु असन अवलोकि यत (= प्रत) सुलभ सबै जग माह, According to the Bēds and shāst'rs the Master is easy to approach for those who truly wish for Rām, just as easy as the drinking of water may be considered to be for every one in the world; *Misc.* 27, गुन-गहि, अगम-निगम जो भाखे, तीन-लोक उदर मैं राखे, The virtuous woman, whom the Bēds and shāst'rs declare, conceived (*the lord of*) the three worlds in her womb; *Padm., ch.* 148, 7, जहँ न सुरज, चाँद न सूझा, चढ़े सोइ जो अगमन बूझा, There neither sun nor moon is visible, (*there*) let him ascend who understands it through the shāst'rs.

(*The word is of rather rare occurrence in this form, the usual and proper spelling being* आगम. *In the third and fourth meanings the word, in this form, has* (*with the exception of the example from Padm., ch.* 148, 7) *never been met with except in combination with* निगम, *and it should be noted that, according to the commentators, this compound* निगम-अगम *always admits both meanings, viz.* '*the Bēds and other shāst'rs*,' *or* '*the Bēds which are difficult to understand.*' *That exceptional case, too, admits of an alternative interpretation, by reading* अगम *and* न *as two words, and translating:* there let him ascend who does not consider (*the feat*) inaccomplishable. *It is probable that the form* अगम *was purposely used by the poets with a view to the double meaning, this being a favorite conceit with Hindū poets. It may be added that in the Rām. it never occurs.*)

[*Skr.* आगमः, *Pā.* आगमो, *Pr.* आगमो (*cf. Sapt., vs.* 581, arrival; *Bhag. p.* 282, shāst'r), *Mg. Pr.* आगमे (*Hēm.* iv, 302); *H. like B.; M. and B.* आगम, *P.* आगम, *S.* अगुमें (prophecy), *G.* अगम (futurity). *The tadbh. Pr.* आगमो *apparently occurs in Sapt., vs.* 476, *but it has not survived in the Gḍs.*]

अँगम्मड़ी *ãg'maṛī*, आँगम्मड़ी *ãg'maṛī*, **Tbh.,** *subst. f.,* [1]a stretching of the limbs; [2]yawning. *See* अँगड़ाई *ãg'ṛāī; also under* आँग *ãg.* **Exam.,** *Coll.* (*Bh.*), रात के अगम्बा से बड़त अँगम्मड़ी चोल था, From lying awake at night, one gets to yawn a great deal.

[*Skr.* अङ्गमर्दिका, (*Pā.* अंगमद्दिका?), *Pr.* अंगमड्डिया (*cf. Hēm.* iv, 126), *B.* अँगमड़ी, *H.* आँगमड़ी, *A.* आँगामुरि, *or* गामुरि, *M.* अँगमोड़ *f. or* आँगमोडा *m., also* अँगवळा *m., P.* अँगवाड़ी. *See, however, also the remarks on the derivation of* √अँगड़ा.]

अगम्मन *ag'man*, (*poet.* अगम्मना *ag'manā*), (*Bw.*) *a shortened form of* अगम्मान *ag'mān or* अगम्वान *ag'wān, q.v.* **Exam.,** [1]*Padm., ch.* 280, 6, धरि पाँच जो अगमन आवे, ते अंगद धर सूँड़ फिरावे, Angad seized the trunks of the five elephants which ran in front, and slung them round; *ib., ch.* 445, 2, रतन-सेन आवै जेहि बाटा, अगमन जाय बैठ तेहि बाटा, On the road by which Ratan'sēn was to come, in that pass she (*i.e. Padmāwatī*), going before, sat down (*to await his arrival*); *Gīt., Su.*, 51, 3, रावन कर परिवार अगमनो (= अगमन + उ) जम-पुर जात बहुत सकुचे हैं, Rāban, placing his retinue in front, is greatly ashamed on going towards Jam'pur; *Padm., ch.* 670, 1, राजा बन्द जेहि के सो पतना, गा गोरा ता पहँ अगमना, He whose prisoner the Rājā is, is Pat'nā; to him the Gorā went first.

(*This word also occurs as a v.l. in Rām., A., ch.* 26, 1, *for* अगङंइ, *in the edition printed in* लखनउ रजाजी. *P.* अगम्मन guide.)

अगम्मना *ag'manā*, *poet. for* अगम्मन *ag'man q.v.*

अगम्मान *ag'mān*, *the same as* अगम्वान *ag'wān, q.v.*

अगम्मानी *ag'mānī*, *the same as* अगम्वानी *ag'wānī, q.v.*

A COMPARATIVE DICTIONARY

OF THE

BIHĀRĪ LANGUAGE.

PART II.

From अंगत्मालिका *āg'mālikā* to अञ्जलि *añjali.*

COMPILED BY

A. F. RUDOLF HŒRNLE,

OF THE BENGAL EDUCATIONAL SERVICE,

AND

GEORGE A. GRIERSON,

OF HER MAJESTY'S BENGAL CIVIL SERVICE.

[Published under the Patronage of the Government of Bengal.]

CALCUTTA:
AT THE BENGAL SECRETARIAT PRESS.

SOLD BY

TRÜBNER & CO., 57 AND 59, LUDGATE HILL, LONDON;

BREITKOPF & HÆRTEL, LEIPZIC;

AND

W. NEWMAN & CO., 4, DALHOUSIE SQUARE, CALCUTTA.

1889.

PREFACE TO PART II.

The authors feel that they owe to the Subscribers of their Dictionary an apology for the long delay in the appearance of the IInd Part.

The difficulties they have met with to a speedy and continuous prosecution of their labours have been beyond their control. Some are inseparable from the conditions of life in India. The latter are such as to leave any one but very small and interrupted leisure for the prosecution of work outside the round of official duties. Moreover, for about a year and-a-half, at different times, both of the authors were compelled, for reasons of health, to be absent from India; and during this time all work was practically discontinued.

Another circumstance that caused very considerable delay, though it has also its counter-balancing advantages, is that from time to time new and important works of Bihārī literature are discovered by the authors. Some of these are very large and important, such as the Maithilī Rāmāyan and the Puruṣa Parīkṣā. They must be read and carefully indexed, while the preparation of the Dictionary progresses, in order to avoid the inconvenient necessity of encumbering the work with numerous supplements or appendices.

There have been also delays at the Printing Office owing to the necessity of procuring fresh or new types.

All these circumstances have co-operated to cause the long delay, which no one can regret more than the authors themselves. They will use their best endeavours to render the interval between the appearance of the several parts as short as possible.

SUPPLEMENTS

to Chapters 14 *and* 16 *of the Introduction.*

14.—BIHĀRĪ LITERATURE.

In Maithilī.

(16) Maithilī Rāmāyan in MS, a version of the legend of Rām, in the Maithilī dialect, composed in various metres for the Mahārāja Bahādur of Dar'bhaṅgā by Kabi Chandra Jhā. Finished in Sāka 1808 (1886 A.D.). *MS.* in Mr. Grierson's possession. An extensive work in the modern dialect, which will shortly, we believe, be printed. *Read.* Index (in *MS.*).

(17) Puruṣa Parīkṣā, a Maithilī translation of Bidyāpati Ṭhākur's Sanskrit work of the same name. The translation was prepared by Kabi Chandra Jhā and printed in the Mahārāja of Dar'bhaṅga's Press, in Sāka 1810 (1888 A.D.). *Read.* Index (in *MS.*).

(18) Ukhā Haran. *MS.* now in Mr. Grierson's possession. *Read.* Index (in *MS.*).

N.B.—(11, 12, 13) Gīt Nebārak, Gīt Dīnā Bhadrīk, Gīt Dīnā Bhadrī Kawand; text and translation now published by Mr. Grierson in J. G. O. S., vol. XXXIX (for 1885). *Read.* Index (in *MS.*).

In Bhoj'pūrī.

(12) Folksongs in modern Bhoj'pūrī, Part II. Text and English translation by G. A. Grierson, PR. (J. R. A. S., vol. XVIII, N. S., Part 2, 1886). *Read.* Index (in *MS.*).

(13) Gīt Nāīkā (or Nāyaka) Banijāra, a Bhoj'pūrī ballad. Text and translation by G. A. Grierson in J. G. O. S., vol. XLIII (for 1889). *Read.* Index (in *MS.*).

In Magahī.

(5) Magahī Bible, translated in 1818 A.D. by the Serampur Missionaries.

16.—LIST OF ABBREVIATIONS EMPLOYED IN THE DICTIONARY.

I.—Names of Languages and Titles of Works.

Āch.	Ācharānga Sūtrā (ed. Jacobi for Pāli Text Society, London, 1882).
Bhoj.	Bhoj'pūrī Folksongs, Part II, (ed. G. A. Grierson, in Journal R. A. S., vol. XVIII, Part 2).
Bih. Tul.	Bihārī Tul'sī Bhūkhan Bōdh, by Bihārī Lāl Chaūbe. A treatise on Hindī Rhetoric. (Bankipur, Khaṛg Bilās Press.)
Dutt	Materia Medica of the Hindus, compiled from Sanskrit Medical Works by Dr. Uday Chand Dutt, with a Glossary of Indian Plants by Dr. G. King and the author. (Calcutta: Thacker, Spink & Co., 1877.)
H. Lit.	The Modern Vernacular Literature of Hindūstān, by George A. Grierson. Extra Number to Journal A. S. B., Part I, for 1888.
Hd. Dy. Sh.	Shakespeare's Hindūstānī Dictionary.
J. A. O. S.	Journal, American Oriental Society.
Mg. Bible	Magahī Bible, translated 1818 A D.
Mth. Rām.	Maithilī Rāmāyan (in MS.).
Nāk.	Gīt Nāikā Banijārā (in MS.).
Piy.	Les Inscriptions de Piyadasi, par E. Senart. (The Ashoka Inscriptions). Vol. I & II (Paris, 1881, 1886).
Pur.	Puruṣa Parīkṣā translated into Maithilī (Mahārāja of Dar'bhaṅga's Press, 1888).
Shāsh.	Shāshvata's Anekārtha Kosha, ed. Th. Zachariae (Berlin, 1882).
Ukh.	Ukhā Haran.
Uv.	Uvāsagadasāo or the Seventh Anga of the Jains (ed. A. F. Rudolf Hœrnle in the Bibliotheca Indica).
Watt	Economic Products of India, exhibited in the Calcutta International Exhibition, 1883-84. By George Watt, M.B.

II.—Grammatical and other Terms.

alg.	algebra.
arith.	arithmetic.
bot.	botanical.
def.	definite.
encl.	enclitic.
excl.	excluding *or* exclusive of.
idiom.	idiomatic.
incl.	including *or* inclusive of.
math.	mathematics *or* mathematical.
per.	perfect.
pluperf.	pluperfect.
pot.	potential.
relig.	religious.
syn.	synonym.

अँगन्मालिका *ãg'mālikā*, **Ts.**, *subst. m.*, the embrace *of men after a wedding at the departure of the bridegroom's party.*

[*Probably a corruption of Skr.* अङ्कपालिका embrace; *the cons.* प *is liable to be softened to* व *and afterwards exchanged with* म; *see Gd. Gr.*, § 134. *It is the custom, however, on the occasion of the departure of guests, to throw garlands made of flowers or tinsel round their necks. This may have led to the confusion of* मालिका *and* पालिका *in the mouth of the people.*]

अगन्यारा *ag'yārā*, (*f.* अगन्यारी *ag'yārī*), **Tbh.**, *adj.*, *the same as* अगियारा *agiyārā* (1), *q.v.* **Exam.**, *Padm.*, *ch.* 666, 5, दृग कटाछ सौं साज सँवारी, औ मुख तेज भाल अगयारी, Of side glances she mustered an army, and from her mouth (*she shot*) fiery-tipped spears, (*said of a lover's intercourse*).

अगर *agar* (1), आगर *āgar* (1), *the same as* आगल *āgal or* आगिल *āgil*, *q.v.* *The form* अगर *agar has only been observed in compounds, such as* अगरपाट *agar'pāṭ*, अगरपरौस *agar'paraūs*, *q.v.*

[*Der. see under* अगला.]

अगर *agar* (2), (*old form* अगरु *agarŭ*), **Tbh.**, *subst. m.*, [1]wood of aloes, agallochum (*aquillaria agallocha*), *a fragrant wood used as incense*; [2]a fragrant powder made of aloe wood; [3]a certain tree which yields bdellium (*Amyris agallocha*); [4]the sisū-tree (*Dalbergia sisoo*). **Comp.**, अगर-धूप incense of aloes. **Exam.**, [1]*Padm.*, *ch.* 37, 6, औ कपूर बेना कस्तूरी चन्दन अगर रहा भरि पूरी, And (*the market*) was always stocked with camphor, bēnā (*a kind of aromatic grass*), musk, sandal wood, and aloe wood; *Rām.*, *Bā.*, *ch.* 14, 9, धूम उ तजै सहज करुआई, अगर प्रसङ्ग सुगन्ध बसाई, Even smoke abandons its natural pungency, and in conjunction with aloes yields a sweet scent; *Rām.*, *Bā.*, *ch.* 207, 5, अगर-धूप बहु जनु अँधियारी उड़ै अबीर मनहु अरुनारी, Incense of aloes rises like the darkness (*of night*) and abīr (*a kind of red powder*) like the redness (*of dawn*). [2]*Padm.*, *ch.* 36, 4, रचि रचि साजैं चन्दन चूरा पोत अगर मेद औ कपूरा, (*The people of Ceylon*) are always preparing and adorning themselves with powder of sandal, turmeric, aloes, mēd (*a kind of fragrant root*), and camphor; *Gīt.*, *Bā.*, 2, 16, कुङ्कुम अगर अरगजा छिरकहिँ भरहिँ गुलाल अबीर, They sprinkle ar'gaja, aloes, and kuṇkum (*a red powder*), and fill (*the air*) with gulāl and abīr (*a red liquid and a red powder, see s.vv.*); *Krish.* 44, चन्दन अगर कुमकुमा मिश्रित तन ते अङ्ग चढावैं ते, They diligently rub on the body (*powdered*) sandal and aloes, mixed with kum'kum (*red powder*). *See* अगरु *agarŭ*, अगुर *agur*, अगुरु *agurŭ*.

[*Skr.* अगुरुः *or* अगरुः, *Pā.* अगरु *or* अगलु, *Pr.* अगरु (*Hēm.* i, 177); *M.*, *G.*, *H.*, *B.* अगरु *or* अगर, *S.* अगरु, *Bg. and O.* अगुरु; *the last also in most other Gds.*]

अगर *agar* (3), **Any.**, *conj.*, [1]if; [2]though, although; [3]when. **Exam.**, [1]*Coll.* (*Bh.*), अगर रेजगी नइ मिले, तउ पैसा ले ले ऐहँऽ, If you can't get small silver, then bring pice. [2]*Prov.*, अगर कोह टले, नउ टले फकीर, Though the mountain move, the faqīr won't (*Hd. Prov.*)

[*Prs.* اگر *agar.*]

√अँगर *ãgar* (1), (*pr. pts.* अँगरैत *ãg'rait*; अँगरल *ãg'ral*; अँगरब *ãg'rab*; अँगरै *ãg'rai*), **Tbh.**, *v. intr.*, to melt, to dissolve, to be eroded, to wear away (*Āz. Gy.*). **Exam.**, *Coll.* (*W. Bh.*), मिसरी पानी मेँ अँगरत बाट, The lump of sugar is melting in the water; *Coll.* (*W. Bh.*), लोनाही लगला से भीत अँगर गेल बा, From the exudation of salt the wall is wearing away; *Coll.* (*Bh.*) ओकरा गोड़ के माँस अँगर अँगर गिरत रहल, The flesh of his leg is melting away.

[*Skr.* √अवगल, *Pr.* ओगल (*cf. Hēm.* i, 172, *and Sapt.*, *vs.* 205, ओगलिय = *Skr.* अवगलित), *G.* ओगळ, *M.* ओगळ *or* ओघर, *B.* अँगर (*with shortening of* ओ *to* अ, *as in* अर *and for* ओर, *etc.*, *see Gd. Gr.* § 26, *the nasalisation serving as a compensation*).]

√अँगर *ãgar* (2), (*pr. pts. see under the preceding root*), **Tbh.**, *v. intr.*, to ache with a burning sensation (*Āz. Gy.*). **Exam.**, *Coll.* (*W. Bh.*), बिछी का मारला से बाँह अँगरत बाट, The arm is aching from the sting of a scorpion.

[*Probably a den. root from* अँगार a live-coal, *Bg.* आँगरा, *S.* अङरु (अँगर), *with the second* a *shortened, as in B.* कुँअर *or* कुँआर prince (*cf. Hēm.* i, 67). *Similarly in P. the noun* अँगिआरा *means both* a coal of fire *and* a painful boil on the palm of the hand; *and in G.* आगरा *means* boils, eruptions caused by heat. *For a similar reason* blight in cereals *is M.* अँगारा, *B.* अँगरा (*with the same shortening of the vowel* a).]

अँगरखा *ãgar'khā*, (*Mth. also*) अँगिरखा *ãgir'khā*, **Tbh.**, *subst. m*, a sort of single-breasted frock-coat *worn by Hindūs buttoning down on the right breast, by Musalmāns on the left, by the advanced of either class and by Christians in the middle. It is sometimes tied at the neck by a string which runs in a hem* (*see Grs.* § 729). **Phr.**, छुटिया अँगरखा (*lit.* a small coat), a jacket (*Grs.* § 728). **Exam.**, *Coll.* (*Bh.*), ऊ सुन के अतिसैं आनन्द भैलैं कि अँगरखा के बन्द टूट गैल, When he heard that, he got so happy that the strings of his coat burst. *See* अङ्गा *aṅgā*.

[*Skr.* अङ्गरक्षकः, *Pr.* अँगरक्खओ, *Bg.* आँगराखा *or* अँगराखा, *M.* अँगरखा *or* अँगरखा *or* आँगराखा *or* आँगरखा,

P. अँगरखा *or* अँगरखा, *H.* अँगरखा *or* अगरखा, *O.* अँगरखा, *S.* अँगरखु (*S. Dy.*, *p.* 54).]

अँगरखी *ãgar'khī, fem. of* अँगरखा *ãgar'khā* (*q.v.*), *used in a dim. sense*, a small coat, a jacket.

अगर-दास *Agar'dās*, अग्र-दास *Agr'dās*, **Tbh.**, *subst. m.*, the name of a well-known Hindū poet, *who flourished in the second half of the sixteenth century A.D. He was one of the eight famous poets of Braj, known collectively as the Ashta Chhāp, and was a disciple of Krish'n Dās, who, together with the celebrated poet Sur'dās, was a disciple of Ballabhāchār'j* (*see Siv.*, *p.* 394, *No.* 59; *cf. As. Res.*, *vol.* XVI, *pp.* 47, 86). *He was himself the guru or preceptor of the poet Nābhā Dās* (*or Nārāyan Das*), *the famous author of the Bhak't Mālā* (*see Bh. Mā.*, *vs.* 151, 166, *and Siv.*, *p.* 379, *No.* 35). *Many of his songs are said to have been included in Krishnānand's great collection, called the Rāg'kalpadrum.* **Exam.**, *Misc.* 1 (*one of his songs*), निबहो नेह जानकी बर से ॥ टेक ॥ सब सिधी नव निधी सदा पल, काम नहिं चारौं फल से । मन चित चाहि मनोरथ मेरो, सनमुख रहौं सत सारँग-धर से । चारौं न और दुवार काहु के, नेह लगो मोरि दसरथ सुत से । अगर दास को चाहो बिनती, राम नाम नहिं बाहौं मन से ॥ Preserve my love with Jān'kī's husband (*Rām*). (*This is the*) burden (*of the song*). May the seven sidhis (*or heavenly powers*) and the nine nidhis (*or heavenly treasures*) always be my prize; I have no concern with the (*so-called*) 'four prizes' (*viz. dhar'm, ar'th, kām, mōksh*); this only is the desire of my heart, that I may remain in the presence of the True, the Sarang'dhar (*Vishnu*); I do not beg at any other's door: my affection is set on Das'rath's son. This only is the prayer of Agar' dās, that Rām's name may never be wiped from his mind.

अगरपरौस *agar'paraus*, **Tbh.**, *subst. m.*, (*Coll.*) neighbourhood, vicinity (*Hd. Dy.*). **Exam.**, *Coll.* (*Bh.*), अगरपरौस का लोगन से मिल के रहब अच्छा है, It is good to be on friendly terms with the people of one's neighbourhood.

[*Comp. of* अगर in front *and* परौस neighbourhood (*q.v.*), *as it were Skr.* अग्रे प्रतिवासः, *Pr.* अग्गे पडिवासो.]

अगरपाट *agar'pāt*, **Tbh.**, *subst. m.*, (*agric.*), flush irrigation, *when the water is at a higher level than the field and the cultivator has only to cut the bank of the water-channel and allow the water to overflow into the field* (*Grs.* § 918).

[*Comp. of* अगर in front *and* पाट a bed *or* channel of irrigation; *lit.* an advanced channel. *A Prākrit synonym appears to be* अग्गवेगो (= *Skr.* अग्र-वेग an advanced current), *mentioned in Hēm. Dy.*, *vs.* 29, *and explained by* नदीपूरः flooding of a river.]

अगरपार *agar'pār*, **Tbh.**, *subst. m.*, name of a Rāj'pūt tribe, *otherwise unknown.* **Exam.**, *Padm.*, *ch.* 542, 3, खत्री औ बछवान, बघेली, अगरपार, चौहान, चंदेली, The Khatrī and Bach'wan, the Baghēl, Agar'par, Chauhan and Chandēl (*Raj'pūts assembled at Chitor*).

अगरबन्धु *agar'bandhū*, अँगेरबन्धु *ãgēr'bandhū*, (*Mg.*), **Tbh.**, *subst. m.*, (*agric.*) sugar-cane ready for cutting (*Grs.* § 1010).

[*Comp. of* अँगेरी *or* अँगारी sugarcane (*q.v.*) *and* बन्धु (*from* √बन्ध *with Gd. suff.* उ, *see Gd. Gr.*, § 330), *lit.* that which has formed itself, *hence* what is mature.]

अगर-बगर *agar'bagar* = अगड़-बगड़ *agar'bagar*, *q.v.* **Exam.**, [2]*Misc.* 27, अगर-बगर का पढ़ावत पण्डित, हम तो पढ़ब राम नाम, What trifles dost thou make me recite, O Pandit? I shall but recite the name of Rām.

अँगरवार *ãgar'wār*, **Tbh.**, *subst. m.*, (*agric.*), the receptacle for sugar-cane ready cut up in pieces for the mill (*used in Shāhābād*; *Grs.* § 281).

[*Derived from* अँगेरी *or* अँगारी (*q.v.*) *by means of the Gd. sec. der. suff.* वार *or* वाल, *implying* possession *or* relation, *lit.* cane-holder. *See Gd. Gr.*, § 293.]

अगरवारा *agar'wārā*, अगरवाला *agar'wālā*, **Tbh.**, *subst. m.*, a race of merchants of the Bais tribe. "*This is by far the most important family of the Vaisya tribes throughout a large portion of Northern, North-Western, and Central India.*" *They are descended from a person called Agar, also Agar Sēn or Agar Nāth, who lived in a place called Agrōhā, now a small town on the confines of Hariānā, not far from Delhi. See Sherring's Hindū Tribes and Castes, vol. I, p.* 283.

[*Derived from* अगर, *the founder's name, by means of the Gd. sec. der. suff.* वारा *or* वाला, *implying* relation. *See Gd. Gr.*, § 293.]

अँगरवाह *ãgar'wāh*, (*Bh.*), **Tbh.**, *subst. m.*, (*agric.*), the man who cuts the sugar-cane into lengths for the mill and boils the juice (*Grs.* § 293).

[*A compound of* अँगेरी *or* अँगारी (*q.v.*) *and* वाह, *lit.* a carrier. *The man is called so from the fact that bringing or taking away the cane in one form or other is necessarily connected with his work. Similarly the driver of the mill is called* कतरिवाह, *lit.* the man who sits on the कातर *or* driving-board (*Grs.* § 278); *see Grs.* § 294, *also* §§ 292, 295. *The element* वाह *practically serves as a suff. expressing a variety of occupations.*]

अँगरस *ãg'ras*, **अगरस** *ag'ras*, **Ts.**, *subst. m.*, [1]the native juice *or* simple, produced from any substance; *espec.* (*Bh.*) [2]the solution of saline earth *or* the mother liquid from which saltpetre is extracted (*Grs.* § 366).

[*Skr.* **अङ्गरसः**, *M.* **अङ्गरस**.]

अगरा *ag'rā* (1), (*f.* **अगरी** *ag'ri* (2)), **Tbh.**, (I) *adj.*, *the same as* **अगला** *ag'lā* (1) *or* **अगिला** *agilā*, *q.v.*

(II) *subst. m.*, [1]the top or tip of a thing; *esp.* [2](*Mg.*) the leaves at the top and the upper part of sugar-cane *which are useless for making sugar, as they possess no juice, but which are used for seed or fodder*, (*Grs.* §§ 1008, 1010, 1012); *fem.* (**अगरी**) [3]sugar-cane leaves *or* grass *collected for thatching purposes* (*this sense, again, being a spec. application of the first meaning*); [4](*Gayā*) the eaves of a house (*lit.* projecting parts, *see Grs.* § 1252, *and synonyms under* **अगुआर** *aguār*). **Exam.**, [3]*Coll.* (*Bh.*), **छावे का बदे अगरी बटोरले बाड़ें**, They have collected leaves for thatching (*Āz. Gy.*). *See* **अगरा** *ag'rā*.

[*Derivation see under* **अगला** (1). *M.* **अगरला** *or* **आगर** (*subst.*) tip, *cf. also* **अगरी** sprouting; *Ml.* **अगरी** pieces of sugar-cane cut for eating. *In the 3rd and 4th meanings the word is evidently connected with Skr.* **अङ्गारिका**, the stalk of the sugar-cane, *which is commonly, though with very little probability, said to be the same in origin as* **अङ्गार** *or* **अङ्गारक** coal. *Similarly Skr.* **अङ्गारित**, *another supposed connection of* **अङ्गार**, *is said to mean a* bud. *There is evidently here some confusion with* **अग्र** *and* **अङ्कुर** *owing to sanskritisation of prākrit words* (*such as* **अग्गार** *and* **अंगुर** = **अंकुर**).]

अगरा *ag'rā* (2) = **अगला** *ag'lā* (2), *q.v.*

√अगरा *ag'rā*, **अगराा** *ag'rā*, (*pr. pts.* **अगराइत** *ag'rāit*, **अगरात** *ag'rāt*; **अगराएल** *ag'rāël*; **अगराएब** *ag'rāëb*; **अगराए** *ag'rāë*), **Tbh.**, *v. intr.*, to be in high spirits, give oneself airs, be arrogant (*Āz. Gy.*). **Exam.**, *Prov.* (*Grs.* § 1089), **हथिया बरिसे, चितरा मेंड़राय, घर बैठे गिरहथ अगराय**, If (*the asterism of*) Hathiyā rains, and the clouds of Chit'rā hover about, the paddy-cultivator sits at home in high spirits; *Coll.* (*Bh.*), **बेटा का बियाह भेला से आज-काल्ह ऊ बड़ अगराइल बाड़े**, Nowadays he is in high spirits on account of the marriage of his son having taken place; *Coll.* (*Bh.*), **जब से इनका नोकरी भैल, तब सें बड़ अगरात रहेले**, Since he got employment, he is in high spirits; *Coll.* (*Bh.*), **नोकरी छूट गेल; अब, सब अगराइल भेल गेल**, His employment is gone, and now all his high spirits have disappeared.

[***Apparently*** *connected with* **√अकड़** (*q.v.*), *which would admit of a bye-form* **अगड़** (*q.v.*), *and of which it would be a pleon. form made after the manner of caus. roots; see Gd. Gr.*, § 349, *and compare* **√अकड़ाव**. *It might, however, also be identical with* **√अगरा** (*q.v.*); *for the meanings of 'twisting' and 'giving oneself airs' are closely connected. S. has the verbal noun* **अगराट** *or* **अगिराट** (*S. Dy.*, *p.* 41).]

अँगरा *ãg'rā*, **Tbh.**, *subst. m.*, (*agric.*), [1](*N. Bh.*) blight in cereals *caused by the sharp west wind* (*Grs.* § 1074); *also* [2](*N. Bh.*) blight in opium (*Grs.* § 1074).

[*Probably from Skr.* **अङ्गार** live coal, *the plants destroyed by blight looking black and carbonised. M. has* **अँगारा**. *See also the remarks under* **√अँगर** (2).]

अगरी *ag'ri* (1) (*Grs.* § 1250) = **अगली** *ag'li*, *q.v.*

अगरी *ag'ri* (2) (*Grs.* § 1252), *fem. of* **अगरा** *ag'rā* (1), *q.v.*

अँगरी *ãg'ri*, *less usual than* **अँगुरी** *ãguri*, *q.v.* **Exam.**, *Misc.* 26, **अँगरी लिये से चली जसोदा, ओरहन देत चली**, Taking (*the little Krish'n*) by the finger Jasōdā went, she went to upbraid (*Rādhā*); *Coll.* (*Mg.*), **ओकरा अँगरी में पोरा-पोर अँगुठी बा**, He has a ring on every joint of his fingers.

अगरु *agarū*, *an older form of* **अगर** *agar* (2), *q.v.* **Exam.**, *Git*, *Bā.*, 1, 8, **बीथिन्ह कुमकुम कीच अरगजा अगर अबीर उड़ाई**, In the streets the mud was (*made up of trampled*) kuŋkums (*or hollow balls made of lac and filled with abir*), and ar'gaja (*a certain yellowish perfume*) and (*incense of*) aloes and abir (*a kind of red powder*) were wafted about.

अगरेज *ag'rēj*, **अँगरेज** *ãg'rēj*, **Any.**, *subst. m*, [1]an Englishman *or* woman; [2]the English nation. **Comp.**, **अगरेज-खाम** England. **Exam.**, [2]*Fam.*, *vs.* 71, **धन्य धन्य अगरेज बहादुर, सभ के जूटल गात**, Twice-blessed be the noble English nation, for every one's limb became fat; *Dēv.*, *p.* 23, **सरकार अँगरेज बहादुर के राज में प्रति-दिन सरबो चोख जाले**, Under the government of the noble English nation (*every one*) is daily becoming more prosperous.

("*This word is often confounded with* **रँगरेज** (*or* **रँगरेजा**); *and in jest, or when speaking facetiously, the English in India are called* **रँगरेज** dyers," *Grs.* § 504, *footnote.*)

[*E. English, through the Portuguese 'Ingleze.' Kn.* **इङ्ग्लेष** *inglez* (*Kn. Dy.*)]

अगरेजी *ag'rēji*, **अँगरेजी** *ãg'rēji*, **Any.**, (I) *adj.* English (*Grs.* § 504). **Exam.**, *Coll.* (*Mg.*), **ऊ दिन राति अँगरेजिए कपड़ा पहिरले रहे बा**, Day and night he wears nothing but English clothes.

(II) *subst. m.*, [1](*scl.* ईंटा *īṭā*) the English brick (*a large table-moulded kind, introduced by the English, Grs.* § 1263); *fem.*, [2](*scl.* भाखा *bhākhā*) the English language. **Exam.**, [2]*Coll.* (*Mg.*), ऊ अँगरेजी पढ़ के किरस्तान भो गेल, He has turned a Christian through reading English.

[*Formed from* अगरेज *by means of the Gd. sec. der. suff.* ई; *see Gd., Gr.*, § 252.]

अगरैल *ag'rāil*, **Tbh.**, *subst. m.*, a pan with straight and short edges (*Grs.* § 679).

[*Derived from* अग edge, *by means of the Gd. sec. der. suff.* ऐल. *See Gd. Gr.* § 245.]

अगरौटा *ag'rauṭā*, a kind of mould *or* press for making cakes (ठेकुआ *or* ठकुआ). (*It is sometimes a board carved with patterns on both sides, and sometimes two carved pieces fitting together between which the dough is pressed, Grs.* § 1272, *p.* 349.). **Exam.**, *Coll.* (*Bh.*), हमार अगरौटवा (*lg. f.*) टूट गेल बा, तूँ तनि आपन अगरौटा मँगनी देबू, ठेकुआ पकावे के बाज बा, My cake-shape is broken, lend me yours for a little, as I have to bake cakes to-day.

[*Derivation see under* अगरौटी.]

अगरौटी *ag'rauṭī*, *Mth.* अगरौटि *ag'rauṭi*, **Tbh.**, *subst. f.*, a box for holding fragrant aloe powder, a scent-box.

[*Derived from* अगर (2), *q.v.*, *by means of the Gd. sec. der. suff.* आवट *or* औटी, *as if it were Skr.* अगरवर्त्ति; *see Gd. Gr.*, § 284. *H.* अगरौटा.]

अगल *agal*, *the same as* आगल *āgal*, *q.v.*

अगल-बगल *agal-bagal*, अगला-बगला *ag'lā-bag'lā*, **Any.**, *adv.*, right and left, on this side and that side. **Phr.**, अगल-बगल राखब, *v. tr.*, to put aside *or* away, to put on one side. **Exam.**, *Misc.* 55, अगल-बगल सुर नर मुनि रोके, मुरचा रोके हनुमान, On this side and on that gods, men, and munis are stationed, in the entrenchment is stationed Hanuman; *Song*, (*Mg.*), अगल्ला-बगल्ला सँखनी सखी अलबेलिया, Right and left, O friend, were wanton damsels (*Hd. Dy.*).

[*Prs.* اغل بغل *aghal baghal*, *a repetition of* بغل *baghal.*]

अगलह *ag'lah*, **Tbh.**, *adj. com. gen.*, (*old poet. f.* अगलहि *ag'lahi*), wicked, vicious. **Exam.**, *Hb.*, 2, 30, तहि अगलहि रहीं पुतना नारि, There was there the very vicious woman Put'na. *See* अगिया *agiyā* (1) *and* अगियाह *agiyāh*.

[*The word is said to mean lit.* an incendiary, *and is clearly a comp. of* आगि *or* आग fire (*Skr.* अग्नि) *and some other word, the identity of which is not quite certain. The corresponding M. word is* आगलावा, *from* आग *and* लावा. *The latter portion is a regular derivative of the M. verb* लावबँ to apply; *the compound meaning lit.* one who applies fire, an incendiary. *The B. equivalent of the M. verb* लावबँ *is* लगाएब (*see s.v.*). *In that case a change of* ग *to* ल *would have to be assumed. But the B. word may have an independent, though synonymous, origin. Its latter portion may be Skr.* दह burning, *Pr.* डह, *whence B.* लह (*through the change of* ड *to* ल, *see Gd. Gr.* § 105); *or it may be Skr.* रथ a vehicle, *Pr.* रह *or Mg. Pr.* लह, *whence B.* लह (*with exceptional preservation of* ह, *see Gd. Gr.* § 110, *exc.*). *Another M. synonym is* अगलाव्या.]

अगला *ag'lā* (1), (*fem.* अगली *ag'li or m.c.* अगलि *ag'li*, *old loc.* अगलहिँ *ag'lahi*, *mod. loc.* अगलेँ *ag'lẽ*), (I), *adj.*, *a less usual form of* अगिला *agilā*, *q.v.* **Exam.**, *B. Gr.*, II (*Bh.*), 14, 2, ए-री! अधि राति अगलि (*fem.*) पहर राति पिछिलि, Hearken, the first half of the night (*had passed*) and the (*first*) quarter of the second half of the night (*had commenced*); *Padm. ch.* 549, 5, चला कटक अस बहा अपूरी, अगलहिँ पानी, पिछलहिँ धूरी, The army marched to the attack (*in*) such extraordinary (*strength*) (*that while there was*) drinking-water for the vanguard, (*there was only*) dust for the rear-guard, (*i.e., the army was so great that the water on the way was, in the course of the march, turned into dust by being drunk up and trampled*); *ib., ch.* 555, 2, अगलेँ दौरैं आगे आरैं, पिछले पाछ कोस दस जारैं, In front the vanguard marched at double quick, behind the rear-guard extended to ten kōs.

(II) *subst. m.*, (*Grs.* § 875) *the same as* अगरा *ag'rā*, *q.v.*

[*Skr.* अग्रः, *Pr.* अग्गो *or* (*with the addition of the two pleon. suff.* ल *and* क, *Hēm.* ii, 164-166) *अग्गलओ, *Ap. Pr.* अग्गलउ (*Hēm.* iv, 341), *hence Gd.* अगला. *The latter form properly belongs to H. and the W. Gds. generally, also to M., which has* अगला; *while B. prefers the form* अगिला. *Gip.* (*adv.*) angle (*Mik.* vii, *p.* 8). *See also the remarks on derivation under* अगिला.]

अगला *ag'lā* (2), अगरा *ag'rā* (2), **Tbh.**, *subst. m.*, a large bolt *or* bar. **Exam.**, *Coll.* (*Bh.*), फाटक के अगला लागल बा, The gate is barred. *See* आगल *āgal*, *of which it is the str. f.*

[*Skr.* अर्गलक, *Pr.* अग्गलओ, *Gd.* अगला *or* अगरा.]

अगली *ag'li*, अगरी *ag'ri* (1), *the fem. form of the preceding word with a diminutive sense*, a small bar or bolt. **Exam.**, *Coll.* (*Bh.*), केवाड़ी के अगली लगाव देऽ, Bolt the door.

[*Skr.* अङ्गेक्षिका, *Pr.* अङ्गच्छिआ, *O. Gd.* अँगछिच, *M. Gd.* अँगछी.]

अँगऽलेच *ãg'lēch*, **Tbh.**, *subst. f.*, physical frame, corporeal frame, personal appearance. **Exam.**, *Coll.* (*Bh.*), ओकर अँगऽलेच बड़ा नीक बा, His general appearance is very good. *See* अँगोट *ãgōṭ*.

[*Derivation is doubtful; the synonym* अँगोट, *H.* अँगेठ, *M.* अँगवठा *or* अँगवटा, *is derived from the Skr. comp.* अङ्ग + अवस्था form of the body, *Pr.* अंगावट्ठा, *hence Gd.* अँगवठ *or* (*with loss of aspiration*) *contr.* अँगोट; *or, eliding* व *and inserting euph.* य, *Pr.* अंगयट्ठा, *hence contr. H.* अँगेठ. *Again to* अङ्ग *might be added the Ap. Pr. pleon. suff.* ल (*Hēm.* iv, 429), *which may change into Gd.* ल (*see Gd. Gr.* § 217), *whence would come, as before, Ap. Pr.* अंगलावट्ठा *or* अंगलायट्ठा, *and contr. Gd.* अँगलोट *or* अँगलेट, *or shortened* (*M.*) अँगलठ. *The difficulty is to account for the substitution of the final* च *of* अँगलेच *in the place of* ठ. *It may be noted, however, that* च *also appears in Pr.* चिट्ठइ *for Pā.* तिट्ठति, *Skr.* तिष्ठति *from* √स्था. *Pr. would admit both forms* अवट्ठा *and* अवत्था, *and according to Hēm.* iii, 32, *also* अवत्थी. *The latter would admit a bye-form* अवच्छी, (*as in Pr.* पिच्छी *for* पित्थी, *Skr.* पृथ्वी), *hence Ap. Pr.* *अँगलावच्छी *or* *अँगलायच्छी, *and thence, contracted and with loss of aspiration, old Gd.* अँगलेचि, *B.* अँगलेच. *Or the form may have arisen through a transposition of the conj.* त्थ *into* च्छ, *which would naturally change into* च (*cf. Hēm.* ii, 21), *as in* √अँगेच, *q.v.*]

√अँगव *ãgaw*, (*pr. pts.* अँगऽवैत *ãg'wãt*, *Bh.* अँगवत *ãgawat*; अँगवल *ãgawal*, *Bw.* अँगऽवा *ãg'wã*; अँगवै *ãgawai*; *Bw. noun of agency* अँगवऽनिहारा *ãgaw'nihārā*), **Tbh.**, *v. tr.*, to bear, to endure, to bear with. **Exam.**, *Padm.*, *do.* 542, 2, जौ लगि जिव काया महँ परै, सो अँगवै भार, So long as the soul is in the body, it has to bear its load; *ib.*, *ch.* 548, 1, आवे डोलत सर्ग पताऽ, धँसि धरति न अँगवे भाऽ, At their coming the heaven and the nether-world shake, the earth quivers and cannot bear the load; *ib.*, *ch.* 621, 6, जो दुख कठिन न सहहि पहाऽ, सो अँगवा मानुष सिर भाऽ, The load of severe pain which mountains cannot bear, man has borne on his head; *Coll.* (*Bh.*), हम तोहऽरा बड़ा अँगवत बानीं, I am bearing with you a good deal; *Rām.*, *A.*, *ch.* 26, 4, सूल कुलिस असि अँगवनिहारे, ते रति-नाथ सुमन-सर मारे, Those who (*are able to*) endure the trident (*of Sib*), the thunderbolt (*of Ind'r*), or the sword (*of Jam*), are slain by the flowery shafts of Rati's spouse (*Kām'dēb*).

(*This is a synonym of* √अँगेज *or* √अँगेव, *q.v.*, *and is more common towards the west, while to the east the latter roots are more usual.*)

[*Clearly connected with Skr.* अङ्ग (*cf.* अङ्गी *in* अङ्गीकार), *from which it is probably formed as a den.* √अङ्गापि, *Pr.* अँगावि, *M.* अँगावि, *B.* अँगव *with shortening of the suffixal vowel* a, *as in Pr.* तोसविअं *for* तोसाविअं (*Hēm.* iii, 150), ठविओ *for* ठाविओ (*Hēm.* i, 67), *etc.*]

अँगऽवछा *ãg'wachhā*, *Bh. for* अँगौछा *ãgãuchhā*, *q.v.*

अगऽवड़ *ag'war*, अगऽवढ़ *ag'warh*, **Tbh.**, *subst. m.*, (*Bh.*), advance wages to labourers (*Grs.* § 1186), *esp.* to ploughmen (*Grs.* § 844). **Phr.**, अगऽवड़ जन *or* अगऽवढ़ जन one who works on advances (*Grs.* § 842). *See synonyms under* अगऽरौर *ag'rãur*.

[*For derivation see the remarks under* अगऽरौ.]

अगऽवढ़ *ag'warh*, **Tbh.**, *subst. m.*, *a corruption of* अगऽवड़ *ag'war*, *q.v.*

अगऽवैन *ag'wan*, **Tbh.**, *subst. m.*, (*Bh.*), [1]*the same as* अगऽवड़ *ag'war*, *q.v.* (*Grs.* § 1186.); [2](*S. Bh.*) interest in kind paid on seed-grain (*Grs.* § 1475).

[*With change of* ड़ *to* न; *see Gd. Gr.*, § 106.]

अँगवऽनिहारा *ãgaw'nihārā*, (*Bw. plur.* अँगवऽनिहारे *ãgaw'nihārē*), **Tbh.**, *subst. m.*, one who is able to bear or endure. *A noun of agency, derived from the* √अँगव *ãgaw*, *q.v.*

अँगऽवरिया *ãg'wariyā*, अगऽवरिया *ag'wariyā*, **Tbh.**, *subst. m.*, (*agric.*) a ploughman who has a share in a plough and cattle, *or* who receives the use of a plough and cattle for one day in three instead of wages in cash or kind (*Grs.*, §§ 842, 846). *See* अँगऽवार *ãg'wār*.

[*Formed with the sec. der. suff.* ई *or* इया (*see Gd., Gr.*, § 252) *from* अँगऽवारा (*q.v.*), *hence* अँगवरिया, one to whom that custom applies.]

अगऽवा *ag'wā*, अँगऽवाँ *ãg'wã*, **Tbh.**, *subst. m*, *a synonym of* अगऽवान *ag'wān*, *q.v.* (*Cr.*, *p.* 105). **Exam.**, [1]*Bij.*, *vs.* 643, अगऽवाँ के डाल पछवाँ डलली, She drew back the foot which she had put forward (*lit.* she threw the foot of the front towards the back); *ib.*, *vs.* 774, अँगऽवाँ के मोँह पाछे फेरली, She turned back her face, which had been to the front; [2]*Padm.*, *ch.* 138, 1, तब लग बोला सुआ सरेखा, अगवा सोई पँथ जेँहि देखा, At that moment said the cunning parrot, let him be guide who has seen the road; *ib.*, *do.* 625, 1, को गुरु अगवा होय, सखि, मुहिँ लावै पँथ माँह, What guru will be my guide, O friend, and bring me into the road? *See* अगुआ *aguā*, अगुवा *aguwā*.

[*Prop. lg. f. of* आगा, *q.v.*, *just as* अगुआ *is lg. f. of* आगू.]

अँगन्वा ăg'wā, Tbh., *lg. f. of* आँग ăg, *q.v.* Phr., अँगन्वा के पातर, slender of body, thin, lean. Exam., [4] *Mag.* 4, जिनके कहैबे, गोरी, अँगवा के पातर, केसिया तोर छोटे भुँइयाँ, जेहिछोडे गे बटिया चलऽ है सुकुआर, तेकरा कोर कैसे जाब, Whose slender-bodied (*wife*) thou art called, O fair one, with thy (*long*) hair trailing on the ground, on which thou treadest as upon a road, how canst thou approach his lap? *ib.*, 83, काहे लिह, गोरियो, अँगन्वा केरी पतरी, काहे लिह दबनवाँ सुकुँआर, Why, O fair one, are you slender of body, why is your body delicate (दबनवाँ *being the lg. f. of* दबन, *an inversion of* बदन)? [3] *Mag.*, 82, जोहि अँगन्वा करनवाँ, गे गोरियो, काहे छोड़े घरवा तो दुआर, For the sake of that person, O fair one, why did you leave the door of your house? *See* अँगिया ăgiyā (1) *and* अङ्ग ayg.

अगन्वाइ ag'wāi, *Mth. and poet. for* अगन्वाई ag'wāī (1) *and* (2), *q.v.*

अगन्वाई ag'wāī (1), Tbh., *subst. f.*, *the same as* अगुआई aguāī *and* अगम्वाही ag'wāhī, *q.v.*

[*An abs. noun derived from* अगन्वा *by means of the sec. der. suff.* आई, *see Gd. Gr.* § 220. *See, however, also the remarks under* अगुआई.]

अगन्वाई ag'wāī (2), Tbh., *subst. f.*, a conflagration (*of a city, forest, &c.*). Exam., *Coll.* (*Bh.*), मिरजापूर मेँ हर साल अगन्वाई होले, There is a conflagration in (*the town of*) Mirzāpūr every year.

[*This is apparently an abstract noun, formed like* जवाई going (*from* √जा go), *from an assumed der.* √अगाव set fire to something, *derived from* आग *or* आगि fire. *This root, however, does not appear to be otherwise in use; but cf.* √अगियाव.]

अगन्वान ag'wān, अगम्मान ag'mān, (*poet.* अगन्वाना ag'wānā, *Bw. pl.* अगन्वानन ag'wānan), Tbh., *subst. m.*, *properly an abstract noun meaning* [1] being in front, advance, *but now commonly used in a concrete sense*, a forerunner; *hence* [2] a guide, conductor, leader; [3] herald, harbinger; *hence again tech.* [4] the person who is deputed to negotiate a marriage, a match-maker, *or* [5] the person who is deputed in advance to welcome and bring in a marriage procession (*in this sense, generally, a deputation consisting of a number of people*). Exam., (*for examples of Nos.* 1 *and* 4 *see* अगन्वा *and* अगुआ); [5] *Rām.*, *Bā*, *ch.* 104, 1, ले अगवान बरातहिँ आये, The deputation brought in the marriage procession; *ib.*, *do.*, 311, 2, सजि गज रथ पदचर तुरग, लेन चले अगवान, Having prepared elephants, chariots, footmen, and horses, the deputation went out to bring in (*the marriage procession*); *ib.*, *ch.* 312, 7, 8, अगवानन्ह जब दीख बराता, उर आनन्द पुलक भर गाता, देखि बनाव सहित अगवाना, मुदित बरातिन्ह हने निसाना, When the deputation saw the marriage procession, their heart was filled with joy and their bodies with excitement (*lit.* horripilation); (*while*) the marriage procession, seeing the deputation (*coming*) with (*so much*) preparation, joyfully beat their drums. *See* अगन्वानी ag'wānī, अगन्वा ag'wā, *and* अगुआ aguā.

(*This word appears to be only used in the Bw. dialect.*)

[*The word is an abstract noun formed from* अगन्वा (*q.v.*), *by means of the sec. der. suff.* आन (*see Gd. Gr.* § 224), *just as* ऊँचान height, *from* ऊँच *or* ऊँचा. *Or it might be derived from the* √अगुआ go forward (*q.v.*) *by means of the prim. der. suff.* आन (*see Gd. Gr.* § 313). *The former derivation appears the more probable, but either gives the same meaning. The P. has* अगेवान, *S.* अगवान guide.]

अगन्वाना ag'wānā, *poet.* (*m.c.*) *for* अगन्वान ag'wān, *q.v.*

अगन्वानी ag'wānī (1), Tbh., *adj. com. gen.*, *the same as* अगन्वान ag'wān *in its concrete sense*, *q.v.* Exam., [5] *Jān.*, *chh.* 29, नियरान नगर बरात, हरषि लेन अगवानी गये, On the approach of the marriage procession to the town, the deputation rejoicing went forth to bring it in; *Coll.* (*Bh.*), जोहि देस मेँ अगन्वानी करन्हा के बड़ चाल बा, In that country there is a general custom of sending marriage deputations.

[*Derived from the abst.* अगन्वान *by means of the Gd. sec. der. suff.* ई (*Gd. Gr.* § 252), *which forms concrete adj.*]

अगन्वानी ag'wānī (2), Tbh., *subst. f.*, [1] guidance, leadership; [2] reception, welcome, the going forward sending forward a person or a deputation to meet a visitor with honour (*especially in the case of marriage processions, see* अगन्वान ag'wān). Phr., अगन्वानी करब to advance to meet a bridegroom *or* visitor on the road, to escort to one's house.

[*This is an abstract noun, derived by means of the Prs. suff.* ई, *from* अगन्वान *in its concrete sense* (*q.v.*). *The latter noun was itself originally an abstract, but having commonly lost its abstract sense and been turned into a concrete, it became necessary to form a new abstract noun from it by means of the Prs. suff.* ई, *like* नादानी foolishness, *from* नादान fool.]

अगन्वार ag'wār, Tbh., *subst. m.*, [1] a portion of corn set apart on the threshing-floor for village-servants, *like the customary 'sharping corn' in England* (*Ell. vol.* II, *p.* 210); [2] the gleanings and refuse grain left on the the threshing-floor (*Grs.* § 901). Exam., [2] *Coll.*

(*Bh.*), **अग॰वार के अन्न नञ पतुआ होआ**, The gleanings are not properly formed grains (**पतुआ** *is spoken of an ear which has no grain*); *ib.*, **अग॰वार फटक के फिग दिँञ, जे अनाज साफ हो जाय**, Winnow off and throw away the refuse grain, so that the corn may be clean. *See synonyms of the first meaning under* **आँगँऊँ** *ãgaũ*. *Synonyms of the second meaning are* **अग॰वारी** *ag'wāri*, **अगाड़** *agāṛ*, **अग॰बर** *ag'bar*.

[*Derived from* **अग = अग्र** front, *by means of the sec. der. suff.* **वार** (*Gḍ. Gr.* § 293), *the latter probably representing Skr.* **वृत्त** (*Skr.* **अग्रवृत्त** *or perhaps* **अग्रवार**), *lit.* advance quantity of corn ; *see the remarks under* **अगउरी**. *It may be so called because much of the refuse consists of the light grain which is carried by the wind in the process of winnowing in advance of the heap of cleaned grain* (*Cr.*, *p.* 88) · *The 'sharping corn' also is a quantity of corn first set apart, before the bulk is removed. The word does not appear to occur in the other Gḍs. The Mṛ. equivalent is* **जरी** (*Hd. Dy.*, *p.* 119), *and the Ml. is* **आँगनी** (*Ml. Gy.*).]

अँग॰वार *ãg'wār*, **Tbh.**, *subst. m.*, [1]the proprietor of a portion of a village, shareholder in a village; [2]*the same as* **आँग॰वरिया** *ãg'wariyā*, *q.v.* (*Grs.* §§ 842). *See* **आँग॰वारा** *ãg'wārā*, **आँग॰वारी** *ãg'wāri*, **आँगौरिया** *ãgauriyā*.

[*Derived from* **अङ्ग** portion, share, *with the Gḍ. sec. der. suff.* **वार** (*Gḍ. Gr.* § 293), *which, in this case, is a modification of the Skr.* **वृत्त** practice *or* **वृत्त:** practising. *Hence* **अङ्गवृत्त** the practice *or* custom of going shares, *and* **अङ्गवृत्त:** one who follows that custom, a shareholder. *The word has both an abstract and a concrete sense. The Pr. would be* **अंगवट्ट** *or* **अंगवट्टो**, *which still appears in the M.* **आँगवाँडा**. *In the B. form* **ट** *has become softened to* **ड़** *and changed to* **र**.]

अँग॰वारा *ãg'wārā*, **Tbh.**, *subst. m.*, the custom of sharing in *or* of lending a plough and cattle for one day in three. (*Grs.* § 846.)

[*Derived by means of the suff.* **आ** *from* **आँग॰वार** *ãg'wār*, *q.v.*]

अग॰वारी *ag'wāri*, **Tbh.**, *subst. f.*, *the same as* **अग॰वार** *ag'wār*, *q.v.* (*Grs.* § 901).

[*Properly a fem. str. form of* **अग॰वार**, *made with the pleon. suff.* **ई** (*see Gḍ. Gr.* § 195).]

अग॰वास *ag'wās*, **Tbh.**, *subst. f.*, (*Bh.*) the space in front of a house (*Grs.* § 1237). *For synonyms, see under* **अगुआर** *aguār*.

[*Skr.* **अग्रवास:**, *Pr.* **अग्गवासो**. *S. has the adv.* **अगुवाय**, in front, before.]

अग॰वाँसी *ag'wãsi*, **अग॰वासी** *ag'wāsi*, **Tbh.**, *subst. f.*, the wedge which holds the share and sole to the body of a plough (*Cr.*, *p.* 2).

[*Skr.* **अङ्ग + वासिका**, *lit.* sticking in the body, *Pr.* **अंगवासिआ**, *B.* **अगवाँसी**. *Not in the other Gḍs.*]

अग॰वाह *ag'wāh*, **Tbh.**, *adj. com. gen.*, (*Mth. fem.* **अग॰वाहि** *ag'wāhi*), first, beforehand. **Exam.**, *Coll.* (*Bh.*), **अग॰वाह मत बोलिँह**, Do not interrupt beforehand; **हर बात मेँ ई अग॰वाहे** (**अग॰वाह + ई**) **बोलत रहेला**, In every affair he is the very first to speak.

[*For derivation, see under* **अग॰वाही**.]

अग॰वाही *ag'wāhi*, **Tbh.**, *subst. f.*, guidance, leadership. **Exam.**, *Coll.* (*Bh.*), **उन॰कर अग॰वाही कैला मेँ किछु मिली, जे एतन्ना जलन्दी कैले बाड़ँह**, Shall you get anything in being a guide (*lit.* doing guidance) to him, that you make so much haste? *Coll.* (*Bh.*), **बन मेँ अग॰वाही करे मेँ जीव के बड़ा डर रहेला**, It is very dangerous (*lit.* there is great fear of mind) to be a guide in a forest.

[*Perhaps an abs. noun derived from* **अग॰वाह** guide, leader (*q.v.*), *with the sec. der. suff.* **ई**; *the noun* **अग॰वाह** *being Skr.* **अग्रवाह:**; *the element* **वाह** *is now not uncommonly used as a general sec. der. suff., synonymous with* **वाल** *or* **वार**, *as in* **असर॰वाह**, **चर॰वाह**, *etc. It is possible, however, that* **अग॰वाही** *may be merely another form of* **अग॰वारि** (1), *with an interpolated euph.* **ह**, *see Gḍ. Gr.*, § 69.]

अग॰सारी *ag'sāri*, **Tbh.**, *adj. com. gen.*, (*subst. f.* **अग॰सारिनी** *ag'sārini*, *Mth. and poet.* **अग॰सारिनि** *ag'sārini*), going in front, forming the vanguard, *also substantively* the vanguard. **Exam.**, *Padm.*, *ch.* 281, 4, **हस्ति की जूह आय अगसारी, हनुमन्त तबै लँगूर पसारी**, A troop of elephants came forming the vanguard, then Hanumān spread out his tail (*and caught them with it*).

[*Skr. comp.* **अग्र-सारी**, *Pr.* **अग्गसारी**.]

अगस्त *agast* (1), *the same as* **अगस्ति** *agasti*, *q.v.* **Exam.**, [1]*Prov.*, **उगे अगस्त बन फूले कास, अब नाहीँ बरखा के आस**, When the (*star*) Canopus appears and the kās (*grass*) flowers in the forest, then there is no more any hope of rain (*Grs.* § 1091); [2]*Padm.*, *ch.* 486, 1, **पण्डितन्ह कहा परा नहिँ धोखा, कौन अगस्त समुँद जेहि सोखा**, Pandits are never mistaken; who (*knows not*) Agast that dried up the ocean?

अगस्त *agast* (2), **Any.**, *subst. m.*, the month of August.

[E. August.]

अगस्त॰वार *agast'wār*, **Tbh.**, *subst. m*, the name of a small clan of Rāj'pūts in Hawēlī Banāras (*Ell.*, *vol.* I, *p.* 2).

अगस्ति *agastī*, **अगस्त** *agast* (1), **अगस्त्य** *agasty'*, **Ts.**, *subst. m.*, [1] a certain star (*Canopus*); [2] name of a celebrated sage (*or rikhi*). *He was brother of Basishth, and both were the offspring of Mit'r and Barun, whose seed fell from them into a water-jar at the sight of Urbasī; being born in the water-jar, he bears the names of Kal'sisut, Kumbh'sambhab, and Ghaṭōdbhab; from his parentage he was called Māitrābarun and Āurvasiy'; and as he was only a span long when born, he was also called Mān. The above is the Vedic story. According to the Purāns, however, he was son of the saint Pulasty'; he is regent of the star Canopus; he swallowed the ocean when it had given him offence, and because he wished to help the gods in their wars with the Dāityas, when the latter had hid themselves in its waters; he is hence called Pītābdhī or Samudra-chuluk; at another time he commanded the Bindhyā hills to prostrate themselves before him, through which they lost their primeval altitude; this miracle obtained for him the name Bindhyākūṭ; he changed king Nahukh into a serpent and afterwards restored him to his proper form; he made his own wife out of the most graceful parts of different animals, hence her name of Lōp'mudrā, as she subjected each to the loss (lōp) of its distinctive beauty. In the Skr. Rāmāyan, Agasty' dwelt in a hermitage on mount Kuñjar, south of the Bindhyā hills, and was chief of the hermits of the south; he kept the Rākhas's of the south under control; one of them, named Bātāpi, who had assumed the form of a ram, he ate up, and he destroyed by a flash of his eye Bātāpi's brother Ilbal, who had attempted to avenge him; he received Rām, Sītā, and Lakhan in his hermitage with the greatest kindness, and became their friend, adviser, and protector from the first; he gave Rām the bow of Bishnu, and when he was restored to his kingdom he accompanied him to Ajōdhyā. He appears in Tul'sī Dās's Rāmāyan most prominently in the Aranya kāṇḍ.* [3] A certain tree (*Æschynomena grandiflora*) = **अगस्ती** *ag'tī*, *q.v.* **Comp.**, **अगस्त्यमुनि** *or* **अगस्त्यऋषि**, the sage Agastī. **Exam.**, [1] *Rām.*, *Ki.*, *ch.*, 16, 3, **उदित अगस्ति पन्थ जल सोखा**, The rising of Canopus has dried up the water on the roads. [2] *Rām.*, *Ar.*, *ch.* 7, 1, **मुनि अगस्ति कर शिष्य सुजाना, नाम सुतीछन रत भगवाना**, The sage Agastī had a learned disciple, by name Sutīchhan, devoted to God; *ib.*, *ch.* 9, 9, **सुनत अगस्ति तुरत उठि धाये, हरि बिलोकि लोचन जल छाये**, Hearing it Agastī quickly rose and ran, and beholding Hari his eyes were dimmed with tears. [3] *Mth. Rām.*, *Bā.* 11, 3, **जिन अगस्तिक निकट पाठ कर, तनि कर पुण्य बड़ भारी**, If a man read it near an agasti tree, great will be the benefits thereof.

[*Skr.* **अगस्तिः**, **अगस्त्यः**; *as above possibly in all Gds.*]

अगस्त्य *agasty'*, *the same as* **अगस्ति** *agastī*, *q.v.* **Exam.**, [1] *Padm.*, *ch.* 656, 5, 6, **उएँ अगस्त्य, हस्ति घन गाजा, औरु बहुरै घर आएँ राजा; बरषीं गयो अगस्त्य की दीठी, परे पलान तुरङ्गम पीठी**, (*When*) Agasty' rises, the elephants are pleased, the waters abate, and the king returns home; the rains cease at the sight of Agasty', and the saddles are placed on the backs of the horses (*see also ib.*, *ch.* 372, 3), [2] *Padm.*, *ch.* 348, 7, **तस जो अपार बिरह दुख दूखा, जनउँ अगस्त्य उदधि जल सूखा**, Woe to him who is suffering the pains of bereavement, just as when the waters of the ocean were dried up by Agasty'.

अगह *agah*, **Tbh.**, *adj. com. gen.*, what cannot be comprehended, incomprehensible, mysterious. **Exam.**, *Gīt.*, *Bā.*, 87, 2, **कहै गाधि-नन्दन मुदित रघु-नन्दन, सो नृप-गति अगह** (*fem.*), **गिरा न जाति गही है**, Says Gadhi's son (*i.e. Bishwāmit'r*) to Raghu's delighted descendant (*i.e. Rām*), the nature of that king (*i.e. Janak*) is incomprehensible, nor can it be expressed in words. *See* **अगाह** *agāh*, **अगाध** *agādh*.

[*The word is probably a shortened form of* **अगाध** (*q.v.*), *of which it is a synonyn, for there is a* √**गाह** = √**गाध** = √**गाध**. *But it might also be derived from Skr.* **अ** + **ग्रहः**, *adj.*, without comprehension, *Pr.* **अगहो**.]

अगहन *ag'han*, **Tbh.**, *subst. m.*, the name of the third month of the Hindū system of the Faṣlī or agric. year, which commences with the month Āsin. It corresponds to part of our November and December, *when the full moon is near the constellation Mir'gasirā (Skr. Mṛigashiras) or 'the head of the antelope' (in Orion), whence the month is also called Mārg'sir. According to another Hindū system it is the first month of the year, whence comes its name ag'han (see below). It is the month of the cold-weather rice-crop, which is hence called ag'hanī (see Grs.* §§ 1082, 1092; *Bih.*, *introd.*). *In this month, on account of its following the festival of the Dēb'uthān (11th of light half of Kātik), generally takes place the first journey (durāgaman, gawan, or gāunā) of the Hindū bride to her husband's house from her father's house. In this month also the preparation and putting on of the new cold-weather clothes take place. Both customs are alluded to in the examples below.* **Comp.**, **अगहन-मास** the month of Ag'han. **Exam.**, *Rām.*, *Bā.*, *ch.* 318, 13, **हिम-रितु अगहन-मास सुहावन**, In the cold season, in the pleasant month of Ag'han; *Padm.*, *ch.* 364, 1, **जाय सिसिर रितु तहाँ न सीउ, अगहन पूस जहाँ घर पीउ**, No trace of any cold season comes there, where the beloved is at home in (*the months of*) Ag'han and Pūs; *Bih.*, v, 6, **अगहन मैं, सखि, जाड़ लगतु है**, In Ag'han, O friend, I feel cold; *ib.*, ii, 2, **कातिक उतरत अगहन लाग, सब सखियन मिलि गवन के आस**, On Kātik passing away Ag'han begins, (*and*) all female friends jointly are escorting brides (*to their husbands' houses*); *B. Gr.*, II (*Bh.*), v, 7, अगहन पथिक कवेस खाम पिछ, नेहर मैं हम बाहर जाएँ, In Ag'han without (*my husband*) Syām great are my troubles; (*hence*) from my parents' (*house*) I will go to my father-in-law's (*house*); *Bih.*, iv, 9, अगहन कुँवरी करत सिँगार, कपड़ा सिजावे सोना के तार, In Ag'han virgins adorn themselves, embroidering their garments with golden threads; *B. Gr.*, II (*Bh.*), iv, 6, अगहन डारि अँगनवा चो, पचिरौं आगरा के चोर, In Ag'han I put on a cloth of Āgra and stand in my courtyard.

[*Skr.* अग्रहायण: *lit.* first (*agra*) of the year (*hāyana*); *Pr.* *अग्गहायणो *or* *अग्गहणो; *the syllable* आय *āy is omitted, analogous to the omission of the syllable* व *va in B.* देवल *temple, Pr.* देउलं (*Sapt.*, *vs.* 109), *for Pr.* देवउलं (*Sapt.*, *vs.* 64), *Skr.* देवकुलं, *etc. In all Gds.* अगहन.]

अगहन्नी *agah'nī*, **Tbh.**, *adj. com. gen.*, appertaining to the month of Ag'han; *hence used substantively as* the name of various agric. [1]operations and [2]products; *thus* [1]the cold-weather harvest (कतिक), *esp.* the main rice-crop of the year. **Exam.**, *Coll.* (*Bh.*), तोहन्ना कइ बिगहा अगहन्नी बा, How many big'has of winter crops have you (*i.e. how much land have you under winter crops*)?

[*Skr.* आग्रहायणिकः. *See under* अगहन.]

अगहनुआ *ag'hanuā*, **Tbh.**, *the same as* अगहन्नी *agah'nī*, *q.v.*; *thus* [1]the cold-weather harvest of rice (*Grs.* §§ 965, 971; [2]the winter rice (अगहनुआ धान), *some kinds of which are sown in the month of Phāgun* (*February–March*) *or Chait* (*March–April*), *while others are sown in the month of Jēṭh* (*May–June*) *and transplanted in Sāwan* (*July–August*), *all being cut in the month of Ag'han* (*November–December*), (*see Grs.* §§ 965, 971); *also* a kind of pulse (*phaseolus Roxburghii or phaseolus radiatus*), which bears in Ag'han (*Grs.* § 996).

[*Properly* अगहनवा, *of which* अगहनुआ *is a bye-form; lg. f. of* अगहन; *it represents Skr.* आग्रहायणक.]

अगहुड़ *agahuṛ*, अगहूँड़ *agahūṛ*, **Tbh.**, *adj. com. gen.*, (*old Bw.*), [1]*lit* moving forward; *hence* [2]*met.* eager. **Exam.**, [1]*Rām.*, *A.*, *ch.* 26, 1, भय-बस अगहुँड़ परै न पाय, Through fear (*of Kaikēyī king Das'rath's*) feet were not able to move forward. [2]*Gīt.*, *A.* 69, 2, मन अगहुड़, तन पुलकि सिथिल भयो, नलिन नयन भरे नीर, (*Bharat's*) mind being eager, his thrilling body became languid, and his lotus-eyes filled with tears.

[*Probably from Skr.* अग्र-हुत (*from* √हु go, *cf. the prākritic Skr.* √हुड *or* √हुड) going forward, *Pr.* *अग्गहुडो, *B.* अगहुड़; *cf. the words* हड़बड़ी haste, हूड़ wrangling, हूड thrust, push हड़ rout, dispersion. *A v.l. of Rām.*, *A.*, *ch.* 26, 1, *gives the synonym* अगमन, *see* अगमनो.]

अगा *agā*, **Tbh.**, *adv.*, before; *only occurring in the comp.* अगा-पीछा *or* अगा-पछा before and behind, one behind another. **Exam.**, *Sal.* 14, अगा-पीछा बनौधिया, बीच मैं सलहेस, Before and behind went the Banaudhiyās, in their midst went Salhēs; *ib.* 17, अगा-पछा बिदा भेल, They went away one behind the other. *See* आगा *āgā*.

[*Derivation, see under* आगा.]

अगाउ *agāu*, (*Bw.*) अगाऊ *agāū*, **Tbh.**, (I) *adj. com. gen.*, being before, being in front (*also* अगारी *agārī and* अगिला *agilā*, *q.v.*).

(II) *subst. m.*, [1]a forerunner, a precursor (*also* अगवान *ag'wān*, *and* अगुआ *aguā*, *q.v.*); [2](*military*) an advance, attack, charge; [3]an advance of money (*esp. takāwī advances to cultivators for implements, digging wells, etc.*), pay given in advance (*for synonyms, see under* अगरौर *ag'ṛaur*). [2]*Padm.*, *ch.* 558, 1, भा संग्राम न भा अस काऊ, लोहे दुहुँ दिस भयो अगाऊ, A fight there was such as there was never before, with the sword on both sides the charge was made.

[*The word is properly W. Gd., whence it is borrowed in B. The M., P., H., have* अगाऊ, *G.* अगाउ.]

अगाउर *agāur*, **Tbh.**, *subst. m.*, (*S. Mth.*) *the same as* अगवड़ *ag'waṛ*, *q.v.*, (*Grs.* § 1186). *See synonyms under* अगरौर *ag'ṛaur*.

अगाऊ *agāū*, *the Bw. form of* अगाउ *agāu*, *q.v.*

अँगाकर *ãgākar*, गाकर *gākar*, गँकर *gaŋkar*, **Tbh.**, *subst. m.*, bread made of chanā (*or* gram), rahar and mūg (*two kinds of pulses*), (*Cr.*, *p.* 72).

[*Perhaps derived from* अँगा (*or* अङ्ग) share, portion, *by means of the Gd. sec. der. suff.* कर made of (*see Gd. Gr.* § 274); *lit.* (*bread*) made of portions. *In that case* गाकर *and* गँकर *must be looked upon as curtailments of* अँगाकर.]

अगाड़ *agāṛ* (*Mg.*), [1]the head-rope for horses (*also* अगार *agār* (1), *q.v.*, *Grs.* § 113); [2]*the same as* अगौँड़ *agõṛ*, *q.v.*, (*Grs.* § 1012); [3]*the same as* अगवार *ag'wār*, *q.v.* (*Grs.* §§ 901, 914). **Exam.**, [1]*Coll.* (*Bh.*), घोड़ा के अगाड़ पछाड़ लगा दैऽ, Tie the horse's head and heel-ropes. [3]*Coll.* (*Bh.*), ओसौनी के अगाड़ के धान हम नाहिँ लेब, I will not take the refuse grain (*lit.* the front grain) of the winnowing heap.

अगाड़ा *agāṛā*, **Tbh.**, *subst. m.*, a certain plant (*Achyranthes aspera*), *said to cure the bite of venomous reptiles.*

[*Skr.* अग्राग्रागेव:; *from the latter pari* आगेव:, *the B.* अगाड़ा *might be derived by means of the pleon. suff.* ड़ा (*Gḍ. Gr.* § 209), *through Pr.* अग्गअड़ओ.]

अगाड़ी *agāṛī* = अगारी *agārī*, *q.v.* (*Grs.* § 113). **Exam.**, ²*Alh.*, *l.* 91, खोले अगाड़ी, खोले पिछाड़ी, गरदनियाँ देल खोलाय, He unloosens the front-heel ropes, he unloosens the hind-heel ropes, he let loose the neck-ropes.

अगाध *agādh*, (*old dir. m.* अगाधु *agādhu*, *old obl.* अगाधहि *agādhahi*; *poet.* अगाधा *agādhā*, अगाधू *agādhū*), **Ts.**, *adj. com. gen.*, ¹*lit.* bottomless, unfathomable, very deep; *hence met.*, ²*intellectually*, inconceivable, mysterious, very great; *and* ³*morally*, *either* most excellent *or* most heinous. **Exam.**, ¹*Rām.*, *Bā.*, *ch.* 171, 8, जलधि अगाध मौलि बह फेनू, On the surface of the unfathomable ocean floats the foam; *ib.*, *A.*, *ch.* 298, 2, सानुज आपु अत्रि-मुनि साधू सहित गये जहँ कूप अगाधू, (*Bharat*) himself with his younger brother (*Satrugh'n*), and accompanied by the sage Atri and (*the other*) saints, went where there was the bottomless well; *Gīt.*, *Ut.*, 24, 2, सकल चाहत रामही, ज्यौं जल अगाधहि मीन, Every one longs for Rām, just as the fish long for very deep water; *Rām.*, *Ki.*, *ch.* 17, 1, सुखी मीन जे नीर अगाधा जिमि, हरि-सरन न एकौ बाधा, Just as the fish are happy where the water is very deep, so the believers in Hari have not one single trouble. ²*Rām.*, *Ut.*, *ch.* 90, 1, प्रभु अगाध सत कोटि पताला, The Lord is as unconceivable as (*the depth of*) seven times ten million hells; *Gīt.*, *Ln.*, 1, 5, एकहि बान बालि मार्यो जेहि जो बल उदधि अगाधु, With one arrow (*Rām*) slew Bali, whose strength was as great as (*the depth of*) the ocean; *Rām.*, *Bā.*, *ch.* 27, 1, अगुन सगुन दोउ ब्रह्म-सरूपा अकथ, अगाध, अनादि, अनूपा, Both forms of Brahm, the absolute and the conditioned, are indescribable, inconceivable, eternal, and incomparable; *ib.*, *Ln.*, *ch.* 111, 3, सुनु खगेस, प्रभु कै यह बानी अति अगाध (*fem.*), जानहिं मुनि ग्यानी, Hear, O king of birds (*Garuṛ*), this word of the Lord is very mysterious, wise sages (*only can*) comprehend it; *ib.*, *A.*, *ch.* 197, 7, तात भरत, तुम सब बिधि साधू, राम-चरन अनुराग अगाधू, Son Bharat, you are altogether upright, your love of Rām's feet is very great. ³*San.*, *vs.* 22, तुलसी ऐसे सद्-गुरु साधु बेद मध गुन बिदित अगाधु, Tul'sī (*says*) thus are the most excellent qualities of a holy preceptor and saint related in the Bēds; *K. Rām.*, *Ut.*, 138, देखि मिटैं अपराध अगाध, निमज्जत साधु समाज भलो रे, By the sight (*of the bathing-places of pilgrimage*) the most heinous sins are wiped away, and (*there*) companies of saints bathe most comfortably. *See* अगाह *agāh*, अगह *agah*.

[*Skr.* अ + गाध, *lit.* without bottom; *M. and G.* अगाध, *and so probably in all Gḍs. The tadbh. Pr. form* अगाह (*Nām.*, *vs.* 133, *Hēm. Dy.*, *vs.* 54) *is represented by* अगाह, *q.v.*]

अगाधा *agādhā*, *poet. for* अगाध *agādh*, *q.v.*

अगाधु *agādhu*, *old dir. f. of* अगाध *agādh*, *q.v.* (*Gīt.*, *Ln.* 1, 5.)

अगाधू *agādhū*, *poet. for* अगाधु *agādhu*; *see* अगाध *agādh*.

अगार *agār*(1), **Tbh.**, (I) *subst. m.*, ¹the front *or* foremost place; ²anything which occupies that place, *thus* a leader, a headman (= अगुआन, *ag'wān*, *q.v.*); (*Mg.*) advances of pay to labourers (*Grs.* § 1186); the head-rope for horses (= अगाड़ *agāṛ*, *q.v.*, *Grs.* § 113); a thin piece of wood spliced to the end of the beam of a (ढेकुल *or*) well-lever (*Grs.* § 931, *also* अगारी *agārī*, *q.v.*) **Exam.**, ¹*Coll.* (*Bh.*), अगार के बरद जोरावर चाही, The leading bullock (*lit.* bullock of the front place) should be a stronger one; *Coll.* (*Bh.*), घोड़ा का अगार में घास लगा दँऽ, Put grass in front of the horse; ²*Coll.* (*Bh.*), गाँव भर के अगार ओही हँवन, He is the headman of the whole village.

(II) *adv.*, ¹before, previously, formerly; ²prematurely. **Exam.**, *Coll.* (*Bh.*), अगारे (= अगार + ए) हम कहले रहीं, के ई बात होई, I told you long ago that this would happen; *Coll.* (*Bh.*), हम बड़ा अगार ऐलौं, I came long before.

[*Derivation see under* अगाड़ी. *It might also be derived from Skr.* अग्र *by the combined addition of the pleon. suffixes* अ + र (*i.e.* क + र); *thus Pr.* अग्गअर, *Gḍ.* अगाड़. *But the existence of parallel forms, such as* अगेर, अगैर, अगोर, अगौर (*q.v.*), *makes the first-mentioned derivation more probable.*]

अगार *agār* (2), आगार *āgār*, (*poet.* अगारा *agārā*), **Tbh.**, *subst. m.*, *lit.* any house, *whether used for purposes of residence or storage*; *hence* ¹a dwelling-house, home, residence, palace; ²warehouse, store, reservoir; *hence, derivatively*, ³those who live together in a house, the people of a house, household, family, relatives (*according to the Hindū joint family system*); ⁴*fig.* (*in construction with another noun*) full of. **Exam.**, ¹*K. Rām.*, *Su.*, 14, बाट बाट कोट-कोट अटनि अगार पौर खोरि खोरि दौरि दौरि दीन्ही अति आगि है, Quickly running from lane to lane he (*Hanumān*) set a great fire to the market-places, streets, lean-to sheds against the city walls, balconied houses, and gateways; *ib.*, *Su.*, 12, मीँजि मीँजि हाथ धुनि माथ दस-माथ तिय, तुलसी, तिलो (= तिल-उ) न भयो बाहिर अगार को, Tul'sī (*says:*) wringing violently their hands and beating their heads the wives of Das'māth (*i.e. Rāban*) (*lament, that*) not so much as a sesame seed has been (*saved*) out of the palace; *Padm.*, *ch.* 528, 7, को मोहिँ ते अस सुर अगारा, चढ़े सरग कुच, परे पतारा, What (*other*) residence (*can anyone find*) so splendid as mine, whether he penetrate up into heaven or descend into the nether world? *Sat.* iii, 24 (*a riddle*), अमर-अधिप बाहन बरन दूसर, अन्त अगार, तुलसी, ईस सब राम भर-तारन, तोर अधार, Tul'sī Dās (*says, let him, i.e. Rām, whose name consists*) of the second letter of (*the name of*) the vehicle (*i.e.* रा *in* *Āirāvat*) of the king of the immortals (*i.e. Ind'r*), and of the last (*letter*) of (*a synonym of*) house (*i.e.* म *in* धाम,), (*and who is*) the powerful saviour of the beings (*engrossed*) with (*worldly*) interests, be thy trust. [2]*Hb.* viii, 29, देखलन्हि अस्त्र-क अस अगार, They saw the storehouse of the arms of Kans; *Gīt.*, *Bā.*, 64, 3, सील-सुधा के अगार सुखमा के पारावार, पावत न पर पार, पैरि पैरि थाके हैं, They are eagerly engaged, though unsuccessfully, in swimming across the ocean of bliss, the reservoir of nectar-like goodness (*referring to people's intense devotion to Rām*). [3]*K. Rām.*, *Ut.*, 30, सुत दार अगार सखा परिवार, Sons, wives, relatives, friends, and followers; *Dōh.*, 475, नारि नगर-भोजन सचिव सेवक सखा अगार सरस परिहरे रङ्ग-रस निरस बिषाद बिकार, Wives, society (*lit. eating in town*), followers, servants, friends, family, pleasures and amusements, let (*the sage*) abandon as resulting only in displeasure and disappointment. [4]*Gīt.*, *Bā.*, 71, 2, रूप के अगार, भूप के कुमार, सुकुमार, गुर के अधार सब सेवकाई है, The beautiful (*lit. abodes of beauty*) boys, sons of the king, fine princes, the darlings of their teacher, together do (*household*) service; *K. Rām.*, *Ut.*, 68, अघम उतार अपकार को अगार, The worst of sinners and full of shortcomings; *see also ib.* 142.

[*Skr.* आगारं *and* (*prākritising*) अगारं, *Pā.* आगारं *or* अगारं, *Pr.* आगारं (*Nāy.*, *vs.* 134, *v.l.*) *or* अगारं (*Nām.*, *vs.* 49, *Nāy.* §§ 111, 134, *Aup.* § 57, *Kalp.* §§ 1, 89, 116). *The tadbh.* अगार *is the usual form; the tats.* आगार *occurs in the Rām. only.*]

अंगार *ãgār*, (*poet.* अँगारा *ãgārā or* अँगारू *ãgārū*, *old obl.* अँगारहिँ *ãgārahĩ in Padm.*, *ch.* 379, 3), **Tbh.**, *subst. m.*, [1]live coal, hot embers, (*never in the sense of* dead coal); [2]sparks, bits of fire; [3]flames, fire, firebrand; [4]meteor; [5]*fig.*, *subst.*, anger, wrath, *or* annoyance, nuisance, *adj.* (*only used predicatively*), angry, wrathful, *or* troublesome, annoying. **Comp.**, अँगार-भौर hot embers and hot ashes, *used in abuse by women with* खाव *or* परव (*Āz. Gy.*). **Exam.**, [1]*Rām. Su.*, *so.* 12, 2, जनु असोक अँगार दीन्ह, As if the asōk-tree had dropped a live coal; *Padm.*, *do.* 477, 1, काह कहूँ ओह पिय, जो मोहि सिर धरेसि अँगार, What shall I say to that beloved, who has placed hot embers on my head; *Coll.* (*Bh.*), तुलसी पर अँगार-भौर परो, May hot embers and ashes fall on Tul'sī. [2]*Rām.*, *Su.*, *ch.* 12, 8, देखियत प्रगट गगन अँगारा, अवनि न आवत एकौ तारा, I see the heaven bright with sparks, (*but*) not a single star drops to the earth. [3]*Padm.*, *ch.* 259, 4, जनहु अगिन के उठहिँ पहारा, वै सब लागहिँ अङ्ग अँगारा, Like the masses (*lit.* mountain) of flames that rise (*in the mundane conflagration*), so fires are burning in all his limbs; *ib.*, *ch.* 396, 5, बिरह साँस तस निकसै झारा, दहि दहि परबत होहिँ अँगारा, The sighs of bereavement are emitted with such ardour as that he becomes like an intensely burning mass (*lit.* mountain) of fire. *Rām.*, *Ln.*, *ch.* 51, 1, नभ चढ़ि बरख बिपुल अँगारा, Mounting up into the sky, he rained down a shower of firebrands. [4]*Padm.*, *ch.* 380, 1, जेठ जरै जग, चलहिँ लुआरा, उठहिँ बौंडर, परहिँ अँगारा, In (*the month of*) Jēṭh the world burns (*i.e.*, *it is hot*), hot winds blow, storms arise, and meteors fall. [5]*Alh.*, *l.* 263, जरल करेजा है बघ रूदल के, तरवा से बरे अँगार, The heart (*lit.* liver) of the tiger-like Rūdal was set on fire and his wrath kindled exceedingly (*lit.* from the soles of his feet); *ib.*, *l.* 235, एतनी बोली सुनल इन्दरमन राजा, जर के भेल अँगार, When Rājā Indr'man heard these words, he fired up and became angry; *Padm.*, *ch.* 532, 5, सूर उठे दहक होइ अँगारू, The hero uprises burning with anger; *Ukh.*, *Act* iv, कि करिय मन गुनि प्रकर बिचारा; राजकुमरि भेल्हि कुलक अँगार, What is the good of deliberately considering the matter; the princess has proved a nuisance to her family. *See* अँगोर *ãgōr and* इँगोर *ĩgōr*; *see also* अगिनि *aginī and its synonyms.*

[*Skr.* अङ्गार, *Pā.* अंगारो, *Pr.* अंगारो *or* इंगालो (*Hēm.* i, 47, *Nām.*, *vs.* 158); *M.* अंगार, *S.* अँगर (*S. Dy.* अङ्गर); *Gip. angār*, *Hungarian Gip. āngara*, *Russian Gip. vangār*, *Italian Gip. li'ngar*, *English Gip. wōngar*, *Spanish Gip. hangar*, *langar* (*Mik.* vii, *p.* 8).]

अगारा *agārā*, *poet. for* अगार *agār* (2), *q.v.*

अँगारा *ãgārā*, *poet. for* अँगार *ãgār*, *q.v.*

अगारी *agārī*, अगाड़ी *agāṛī*, **Tbh.**, (I) *subst. f.*, [1](*locally*) the front *or* fore part; *hence* [2]the rope by which a horse's head *or* his fore-hoofs are fastened (*Grs.* § 113, *also* अगार *agār*, *q.v.*); [3]a thin piece of wood spliced to the end of the beam of a well-lever (*Grs.* § 931, *also* अगार *agār*, *q.v.*); [4]the top of sugar-cane, cut up for seed (*Grs.* § 1008, *see synonyms under* अगौन *agin*, *q.v.*); *also* (*temporally*) [5]first in point of time, early time, the future; *hence* [6]money paid in advance (*especially to field labourers, in which sense* अगौरी *agaurī is more usual, also* अगऱौर *ag'raur*, अगवर *ag'war*, *and* अगाव

agāü, &c., q.v.). **Comp.,** अगारी-पिछारी, the ropes by which a horse's hoofs are tied before and behind. **Phr.,** अगारी-पिछारी लगाएब, to tether a horse. **Exam.,** *Prov., (Hd. Dy.),* फौज को अगारी, आँधी को पिछारी, *lit.* the army's is the front place, the storm's the back place (*i.e. being between two fires*). [2] *Prov., (Hd. Dy.),* कुंजड़ा को अगारी, कसाई को पिछारी *lit.* the greengrocer's is the early time, the butcher's the later (*i.e., buy first of the green grocer, afterwards of the butcher*).

(II) *adv.,* before, in front. onward, forward. **Exam.,** *Coll. (Mth.),* अगारी अगारी चलैंच, go on in front; अगारी मारैंच attack in front (*used of a pitched battle*); *Coll. (Bh.),* अगारिये (= अगारी + ए) हम कहलें रहीं, I told you long ago. *See* आगे *āgē.*

[*Probably Skr.* अग्रकृति *or (with pleon.* क) अग्रकृतिका. *See the remarks under* अगार *and* अगाड़ी. *H., Bg., P.* अगाड़ी, *G.* अगाडी, *M.* अगारी (*in the sense of* sprout). *The adv. is probably a contraction of* अगारहि *or* अगारहिं, *an old loc. of* अगार, *q.v.*]

अँगारी *ăgări* (1), **Tbh.,** *subst. f.,* [1](*S. Bh.*) pieces of sugar-cane, cut up ready for the mill (*Grs.* § 288, *Āz. Settl. Rep.,* p. 125, *also* गँड़ेरी *gĕṛi, q.v.*); [2]the green tops of sugar-cane when chopped up and used as cattle-fodder (*Āz. Settl. Rep.,* p. 101). *For synonyms of the word in its second sense, see* अगोन *agin.*

[*This is merely a bye form of* अगारी, *q.v., the anunāsik being due to the simplification of the original Pr. double consonant of* अग्ग. *The Pr. has* अंगालिअं, *see Hēm. Dy, vs.* 28, *where it is explained by Skr.* इक्षुखण्डम्. *The Skr. has* अङ्गारिका, *which, however, is a mere resuscitation from the vernacular* अँगारी, *and has no connection with the word* अङ्गार: live coal (*see next word and the remarks under* अगेँड़).]

अँगारी *ăgări* (2), **Tbh.,** *subst. f.,* [1]*the same as* अँगार *ăgăr, q.v.; hence* [2](*S. Bh.*) a kind of firework (*Grs.* § 585*f.*); *also* [3](*amongst ascetics*) a ball of dough baked in ashes (*Āz. Gy., No. III*).

[*Skr.* अङ्गारका, *fem.* अङ्गारिका, *a str. f. of* अङ्गारः; *Pr.* अंगारिआ, *B.* अँगारी, *Bg.* आँगारि; *M. has the m.* अँगारा = *Pr.* अंगारओ; *P. has* अँजिआरा *and* अँगिआरी a coal of fire; *G.* अँगारी a frying-pan.]

अँगारू *ăgărū, poet. for* अँगारु *ăgărŭ, the old dir. f. of* अँगार *ăgăr, q.v.*

अगाव *agāu,* **Tbh.,** *subst. m.,* the leaves at the top, and the upper part of the sugar-cane plant (*Cr., p.* 75). *See synonyms under* अगोन *agin.*

[*Probably from* आगा front, top, *with the pleon. suff.* आव (*see Gd. Gr.* § 349), *which is also used to form pleon. roots. In the W. Gds. the word is still used in its proper meaning* front, before; *H., M., P.* अगाव before, a forerunner, an advance; *G.* अगाव first.]

अगास *agās, (Coll.), the same as* अकास *akās, q.v.*

अगासी *agāsi,* **Tbh.,** *subst. f.,* [1]a turban; [2]a terrace in front of an upper room; [3](*in the slang of thags or robbers*) the cry of a kite, *which, if heard between the first watch of the night and daybreak, is unlucky, but in the day it is immaterial* (*Wil.*). *See* अकासी *akāsi.*

[*Skr.* आकाशीया, *lit.* anything raised in the open air, *such as a turban, terrace, etc. naturally is, Pr.* *आगासिआ; *B. and G.* अगासी, *M.* अगाशी *or* अगाशी. *Cf. Ml.* आँगासी, that arrangement of the gear of a Persian wheel by which water is raised to a considerable height above the mouth of the well (*Ml. Gy.*); *S.* अंगास a flagstaff raised by Musalmans during the Muharram; अंगासी one who raises a flag-staff (*S. Dy., p.* 54).]

अगाह *agāh, (old dir. m.* अगाहु *agāhŭ, poet.* अगाहू *agāhū*), **Tbh.,** *adj. com. gen., the same as* अगाध *agādh, q.v.* **Exam.,** [1]*Hindi song,* लाठी ऐसी चीज है, सदा राखिये संग; नदी नार अगाध जल, तहाँ बचावो, अंग, A stick is such a thing as you should always keep with you; (*if*) in river or stream the water is very deep, you may there save yourself (*by it*). [2]*Padm., ch.* 242, 6, जस तुम काया कीन्ह दगदाहू, जो सब गुरु कहँ भयो अगाहू, Such a burning (*desire*) as you have made in your body is inconceivable to all the gurus; *ib., ch.* 253, 3, जबहिं सुरुज कहँ लागा राहू, तबहिं कमल मन भयो अगाहू, Till Rahu (*who is supposed to attack the sun in an eclipse*) should overcome the sun, so long the lotus (*representing princess Padmāwati*) will be a mystery to the mind. [3]*Padm., ch.* 262, 6, अब ले गये देय सब सूरी, तेहि सों अगाह (*fem.*) बिथा तुम पूरी, Now they have taken (*your lover*) away to impale him (सूरी = शूली), hence you are full of grievous distress; *ib., do.* 81, 1, सो जो सुनत घुमत सिर राजहिं प्रीति अगाह, As soon as he (*the king*) hears it (*i.e., the description of Padmāwati*), an intense love will distract the mind (*lit.* beat the head) of the king. *See* अगाध *agādh,* अगह *agah.*

[*Skr.* अगाधकः, *Pr.* अगाहओ (*Nām., vs.* 133, *Hēm. Dy., vs.* 54). *This tadbh. form has only been met with by us in Padm.*]

अगाहू *agāhū, poet. for* अगाहु *agāhŭ, the old dir. f. of* अगाह *agāh, q.v.*

अँगिकार *ăgikăr, (poet.)* = अङ्गीकार *aṅgīkăr, q.v.* **Exam.,** *Hb.* vi, 43, कै अँगिकार सकल सफहर, दृगसम हेतु करत

भेल पूर, When he (*Kans*) agreed, Akrūr laughed and became full of joy at the prospect of gazing (*upon Krish'n*).

अगिन *agin*, अगन *agan*, **Tbh.**, *subst. f.*, *the same as* अगिनि *agini*, *q.v.* **Comp.**, अगिन-पहार *m.*, a mountain or mass of fire, *such as will be seen in the general conflagration at the pralay or end of the world* (*Padm.*, *ch.* 559, 6); अगिन-बान *m.*, a fiery arrow, a rocket (*Padm.*, *ch.* 108, 5, 112, 5); अगिन-बाय *f.*, (*lit.* fiery rheumatism), the farcy in cattle and horses (*Grs.* § 1170); *also* a disease of human beings accompanied by boils. **Exam.**, [1]*Dōh.*, 426, अगनि अगिन लगु नीच घिर, जरत धनिक धन धाम, The fire catches the houses of the small and lowly, it burns the riches and palaces of the rich; *Bais.*, 48, (*Prov.*), बेसा, बानर, अगिन, जल, कुटी, कटक, कलाल, ई दसो नहीं आपना, सुगा, सूर, सोनार, Prostitute, monkey, fire, water, buffoon army, liquor-merchant, (*as well as*) parrot, needle, and goldsmith,—these ten are never one's friend; *Ukh.*, *Act.* iv मन कर गरल करिय पम पाने, अगिन गमन करि तेजिय पराने, I have a mind to drink poison, or give up life by entering into fire; *Padm.*, *ch.* 559, 6, चल कोपित सेना चल धाई, अगिन-पहार जरत जनु आई, The army ran quickly forward, very wrathful, just as a burning mass of fire comes on. [4]*Padm.*, *ch.* 374, 6, बज्र अगिन बिरहिन हिय जारा, सुलग सुलग दगध भए छारा, The hearts of separated (*lovers*) burn like lightning (*lit.* fire of the thunderbolt), and burning intensely are consumed to ashes; *see also ib.*, *ch.* 564, 1. [6]*Padm.*, *ch.* 211, 2, बिरह अगिन बजराग बसूझा, जरे सूर न बुझायें बूझा, The hero burns with the invisible fire (*i.e. pain*) of separation as (*if struck by*) lightning, and does not know how to put it out. *Bih.*, ii, 6, बिरह अगिन मो सेँ सहखो (= सहब + ओ) न जाए, The pain (*lit.* fire) of separation can no longer be even endured by me. [7]*San.*, *vs.* 53, जगहार की अगिन (*fem.*) मेँ जरत सकल संसार, The whole world is moved by the ardour (*lit.* burned with the fire) of self-conceit; *ib.*, *vs.* 54, संत अगिन तेँ नहि दहेँ, (*The saints*) are not troubled with the ardour of (*seeking*) self. *See* आगि *āgi*.

[*Derivation see under* अगनि *and* अगिनि.]

अगिन-बाय *agin'bāy*, **Tbh.**, *subst. f.*, *see under* अगिन *agin* (*Grs.* § 1170).

[*Skr.* अग्नि-वायुः *or* अग्नि-वातः *which is masc.; but the word* बाय *and its compounds are always fem. in B.*]

अगिनि *agini*, अगनि *agani*, अगिन *agin*, अगन *agan*, **Tbh.**, *subst. f.*, [1]fire, flame; *espec.* [2]a sacred flame, *of which there are three kinds*, the perpetual household fire (*called* गार्हपत्य), the sacrificial or eastern fire (*called* आहवनीय), and the southern (*or* दक्षिण); [3]live coal, hot embers; [4]lightning; [5]fiery missiles of war (*as shells, rockets, etc.*); [6]*fig.*, burning sensation, pain, torment (*as of hunger, separation, etc.*); [7]heat, ardour of any emotion *or* action, (*in this sense usually* आगि *āgi*, *q.v.*); [8]*either abs.*, any bad passion, *such as* anger, envy, jealousy, *etc.*, *or concr.* (*only used predicatively*), an angry, envious, jealous (*etc.*) person, (*in this sense usually* आगि *āgi*, *also* अगियाह *agiyāh or* अगिया (1), *q.v.*); [9]the effect of any bad passion, angry disturbance, quarrel, sedition, *etc.*; [10]digestion; [11]*phil.*, fire as one of the five elements (*viz. earth, water, fire, wind, and ether*); [12]*myth.*, the god of fire (*who appears in three forms, as the sun in heaven, as lightning in mid-air, and as ordinary fire on earth; he is described as clothed in black, having smoke for his standard and headpiece, and carrying a flaming javelin; he has four hands, and rides in a chariot drawn by red horses, and the seven winds are the wheels of his car; he is accompanied by a ram, and sometimes he is represented as riding on that animal; he is also the regent of the south-eastern quarter*); *hence* [13]the south-east (*in this sense also* अगन्नू *ag'nū or* अगन्नेउ *ag'neu*, *q.v.*); [14]*med.*, the venereal disease, syphilis; [15]*a symbolical name for* the number three (*because of the three sacred fires, see above*). **Comp.**, अगिनि-अस्त्र *m.* fire-arms, rocket, a fabulous weapon so called; अगिनि-कुण्ड *m.*, a fire-pit, a hollow for kindling fire in; अगिनि-कुल *m.*, fire race (*a tribe of Rāj'pūts, said to have been produced from fire*); अगिनि-कोन *m.*, the south-eastern quarter; अगिनि-क्रिया *f.*, *the same as* अगिनि-संस्कार; अगिनि-गर्भ *m.*, *the same as* अगिनि-मनि; अगिनि-तनु *m.*, the name of a certain demon whose body is of fire; अगिनि-त्रेता *f.*, the three sacred fires of the Hindūs (*see above*); अगिनि-दाह *m.*, ceremony of burning a dead body; अगिनि-दीपक *m.*, a lamp; अगिनि-पात्र *m.*, any vessel set apart for holding fire; अगिनि-परीक्षा *f.*, fiery ordeal (*by a heated iron or boiling oil, etc.*); अगिनि-पुरान *m.*, the name of one of the eighteen great Purans, (*which was communicated by the god of fire to the saint Basishṭh*); अगिनि-पुरुष *m.*, the god of fire; अगिनि-पूजक *m.*, a fire-worshipper; अगिनि-पूजा *f.*, fire-worship; अगिनि-बंसी a Rāj'pūt of the fire race (*see* अगिनि-कुल); अगिनि-बान *m.*, a fiery arrow, a rocket; अगिनि-बाय *f.*, the farcy in horses and cattle, an eruptive disease in men and elephants; अगिनि-भोजक *com. gen.*, a fire-eater; अगिनि-भोजन *m.*, the eating of fire, fire-eating; अगिनि-मनि *m.*, the sunstone, *a fabulous gem supposed to contain and impart solar heat*; अगिनि-सिखा *f.*, a flame of fire; अगिनि-संस्कार *m.*, any ceremony in the performance of which fire is essential, *such as the burning of a dead body, etc.*; अगिनि-होत्र, *m.*, the ceremony of making oblations to fire; अगिनि-होत्रि *or* अगिनि होत्री *m.*, one who keeps a perpetual sacred household fire, one who acts as a priest in the aginī-hōt'r ceremony, one who is conversant with the Rigbēd; अगिनि-होम *m.*, a sacrifice by fire, a burnt offering. Exam., [1]*Rām.*, *A.*, *ch.* 274, 3, अगिनि धूम गिरि सिर तिन धरहीं, Fire carries smoke, and a mountain grass, on its top; *ib.*, *Su.*, *ch.* 12, 11, देहि अगिनि तन करहि निदाना, Supplying fire, do thou consume my body. [2]*Rām.*, *A.*, *ch.*, 180, 5, अरुन्धती अरु अगिनि-समाजू, रथ चढ़ि चले प्रथम मुनि-राजू, The king of sages (*Basishṭh*), mounting his chariot, first went away with (*his spouse*) Arundhatī and (*all*) the materials for (*preparing*) a sacrificial fire; *Jan.*, *ch.* 34, अगिनि थापि मिथिलेस कुसोदक लीन्हेउ, कन्या-दान बिधान सकल्प कीन्हेउ, The Lord of Mithilā having set up the sacrificial fire, took kus (*grass*) and water, and duly performed the ceremony of giving away the bride, (*the ceremony is performed by the father of the bride close to the sacrificial altar; see J. A. S. B., vol.* LIII, *Pt.* I, *p.* 97). [3]*Coll.* (*Bh.*), अगिनि की के चिलम पे रखियो, Clearing the hot embers (*of ashes*) put them on the tobacco-bowl (*of the hukka*). [4]*For an example, see under* अगिन *agin and* अगिया *agiyā* (2). [5]*Bij.*, *ll.* 1080, 1081, रन है के मारउ अगिनि-बनवाँ, छोड़ल चाहे सब अगिनि-बनवाँ, (*Sūraj Mal said,*) 'slay him with fiery arrows'; so the servants discharged fiery arrows. [6]*Rām.*, *Su.*, *ch.* 31, 7, बिरह अगिनि तन-तूल समीरा-स्वास जरै छन माँह सरीरा, My body is within a moment burned in the fire (*i.e., by the pain*) of separation, (*which is fanned*) by my sighs like wind and (*in which*) my body is like (*a heap of*) cotton (*i.e., I am tormented by the pain of separation*). [7]*Rām.*, *Ar.*, *ch.* 6, 1, अस कहि जोग अगिनि तन जारा, Having thus spoken, the ardour of his devotion consumed his body; *San.*, *vs.* 52, ता मैं तन मन रहत सियोरे, अहं अगिनि नहिं दाहै कोरे, Therein (*i.e. in the exercise of quietism*) body and mind become cooled, nor does the ardour of self-consciousness consume them (*i.e., the sages*) any more; *ib.*, *vs.* 60, राम देव की अगिनि (*fem.*) बुझानी, काम क्रोध वासना बिलानी, The ardour of passion (*which is one's*) enemy is quenched, and the tendency to love and anger has vanished; *ib.*, *vs.* 41, यह दिन-रैन नाम उचरै, वह निस मान अगिनि मैं जरै, One (*the ascetic*) repeats the name (*of God*) day and night, the other (*the worldling*) burns continually with the ardour of self-conceit; *Bij.*, *l.* 801, स्वामी आजु मोरि अगिनि (*fem.*) बुझाइँह, O husband, to-day satisfy my ardent desire (*for marital union; lit.* put out my fire); *ib.*, *l.* 804, तिरिया कैसे मैं अगिनि बुझैबौं, O wife, how can I satisfy thy ardent desire (*lit.* put out thy fire); *Krish.* 278, परत सदन अगि कूप, सर, त्यों मदन अगिनि दहियै मैं, Sūr Dās (*says*), I am so consumed by the ardour of love that I shall drown myself in the well (*which is*) dug in my house, [8]*Bu.*, *ch.*, *modern anon.*, सुनतहि अगिनि लगा तन भारी. As soon as he heard it, fierce rage filled his body; *Coll.* (*Bh.*), ज सुनत की अगिनि को गेल, As soon as he heard it, he became furious. [10]*Coll.* (*Bh.*), इनका पेट मैं इतनी अगिनि नहिंखे, कि ई अनाज पचावस; अगिनि जागे किछु दवाइ दीं, His stomach is not strong enough to digest his food; give him some medicine to stimulate (*lit.* waken) his digestion. [11]*Krish.* 34, धर जल अगिनि पवन नभ छाया, पच तत्त मिलि जगत उपाया, (*God*) diffused earth, water, fire, wind, and sky, (*and thus*) having mixed the five elements he produced the world. [12]*Rām.*, *Bā.*, *ch.* 201, 6, भक्ति सहित मुनि आहुति दीन्हे, प्रगटे अगिनि चरु कर लीन्हे, The saint devoutly offered the oblation, and the fire-god appeared (*in the form of ordinary fire*), holding the offering in his hand. [13]*For examples, see under* अगजू, *etc.* [15]*Bw.*, *do.*, *modern anon.*, सम्बत ऋषि अग अगिनि ससि, माघ मास, बुधवार, शुभ दिन, शुभ घर-लगन, प्रन्थ कीन्ह अवतार, In the year 1832, in the month of Māgh, on a Wednesday, on a lucky day, and under a lucky constellation of planets, this book came into the world.

(*This word occurs in a great variety of bye-forms,* अगन, अगनि, अगन्नी, अगन्नू, अगन्नेउ, अगन्नेसा, अगिन, अगिनिया, अगिनी, आगन, *q.v. Synonyms, with all the above given meanings, are* आग, आगि, अगिया (2), *q.v. Synonyms, with certain of the above given meanings, are* अँगार, अँगारी, अगिया (1), अगियार, *q.v. It should be added that the word in this and its bye-forms is rarely used with the seventh and eighth meanings, the usual form being* आगि.)

[*Skr.* अग्निः *m.*; *the dissolution of the Skr. conj.* ग्न *gn occurred already in early times; thus Pā.* अग्गिनि (*Kach.*, *p.* 54, अगिनि ?) *or* गिनि *m.* (*Pā. Gr. K.*, *pp.* 35, 45), *Pr.* अगणी (*Hēm.* ii, 102); *both kinds of dissolution, by means of* इ *i and of* अ *a, are preserved in the modern Gḍs.; thus B.* अगिनि *or* अगिन *and* अगनि *or* अगन (*q.v.*); *M.* अगीन *m. or f.*; *O.* निँया (*O. Vy.*) *or* निआँ (*O. Dy.*). *In Skr. and Pā. the word is masc., so also usually in Pr.* (*cf. Sapt.*, *vs.* 770, सुणो जलइ अग्गी, empty burns the fire), *though an optional fem. use would be justified by Hem.* i, 35. *In all Gḍs. the word is fem. in the form* आगि (*q.v.*), *but there appears to be no uniformity in the case of the forms* अगनि, अगिनि, *etc. In B. and P. the latter are fem.* (*e.g.*, *San.*, *vs.* 60, राम की अगिनि, the fire of passion); *but in M. and H. they are said to be masc. or fem.*]

अगिनित *aginit*, **Ts.**, *adj. com. gen.*, *the same as* अगनित *aganit*, *q.v.* Exam., *Rām.*, *Su.*, *ch.* 5, 5, देखे जहँ तहँ अगिनित जोधा, He saw everywhere innumerable warriors; *ib.*, *Ut.*, *ch.* 38, 6, सन्तन्ह के लच्छन, सुनु भाता, अगिनित स्रुति पुरान बिख्याता, Hear brother, the marks of the good as told in the Bēds and Purāns are countless; *Ag.*, vi, 42, बाजि-मेध अगिनित किए, दिए दान बहु भाँति, He performed countless horse sacrifices, and gave gifts of many kinds. *See* अगनित.

[*A corruption of* अगनित, *analogous to that of* अगिनि *for* अगनि fire.]

अगिनिया *aginiyā*, अगिनियाँ *aginiyā̃*, **Tbh.**, *subst. f.*, *lg. f. of* अगिनि *agini or* अगिनी *aginī*, *q.v.* **Exam.**, [1]*Bij.*, *l.* 800, सामी मोरे देहे उठेला अगिनियाँ, सामी आजु मोरि अगिनि बुझैसँ, O husband, in my body a longing desire (*lit.* fire) is rising up; O husband, to-day satisfy that longing of mine, (*the princess is referring to her longing after the consummation of her marriage with her husband*).

अगिनी *aginī*, **Tbh.**, *subst. f.*, *str. f. of* अगिनि *agini*, *q.v.*

अँगियवा *ãgiyawā*, **Tbh.**, *subst. f.*, *red. f. of* अङ्गी *aṅgī*, *q.v.* **Exam.**, *Bih.*, xv, 3, अँगियवा भीँजल ए को बमारे, My bodice became wet, alas!; *ib.*, xv, 4, अँगियवा भिँजले रे, My bodice was wet.

अगिया *agiyā* (1), अगिआ *agiā*, **Tbh.**, (I) *subst. m.*, *the name of various diseases or destructive insects which attack animals or plants, and cause burning, blistering, &c.; thus of* farcy in cattle (*Cr.*, *p.* 60, *Grs.* § 1170); *of* a disease in cattle in which the skin becomes covered with pimples (*Ās. Gy.*); *of* a kind of fly that causes blisters (*Ās. Gy.*); *of* a kind of grass which blisters (*Andropoyon schoenanthus*, *agya ghas*, *Wat.*, *Ās. Gy.*); *of* a spider which attacks the buds of the millet before the flower forms (*Cr. p.* 81); *of* a weed which burns the rice-plant (*Grs.* § 1075); *of* a disease in rice by which the whole plant is burnt up (*Cr.*, *p.* 18.) **Exam.**, *Coll.* (*Bh.*), अगिया घास में पीस के ई दवाइ लगवैंड, तऽ खजुलाह छूट जाई, Pound this medicine with *agiyā* grass, and when you apply it, your itch will be cured.

(II) *adj. com. gen.*, fiery, irascible, mischievous, violent, very active. (*In this form the word has been met with in the under-mentioned compound; another form of it, in which it is more generally used, is* अगियाह *agiyāh*, *q.v.*). **Comp.**, अगिया-बैताल, *m.*, (*lit.* fiery demon) the name of a demon of an irascible and mischievous character, *also called Dāno or Dān sāhib, a hideous demon, who lurks in trees, lives on dung-beetles, and seizes wayfarers at night* (*Cr.*, *p.* 110, *Grs.* § 1458); *the story of the demon is given in the Singhāsan Battīsī, according to which King Bikramādity' had two Pishāch's under his command, who were respectively called Agiyā and Koïlā; the name agiyā-baitāl, however, is also used as a term of abuse, and figuratively to denote any kind of energy.* **Exam.**, *Coll.*, (*Bh.*), ऊ बड़ अगिया-बैताल बा, एकी दिन में सब काम कर डाँसले बा, He is a most active fellow: in one day he has finished the whole business; ई दवाइ अगिया-बैताल बैड, This medicine is very effective; ई दारू अगिया-बैताल बा, This wine is very strong; ई चले में अगिया-बैताल बैदम, He is a very quick walker.

(*In the subst. sense the word is occasionally confounded with* अगिया *agiyā* (2), *and treated as fem.*)

[*Skr.* अग्निक, *Pr.* अग्गिओ (*Hēm. Dy.*, *vs.* 53). *Hēmachandra's statement is*: अग्गिओ इन्दगोवअम्देड, *with the comment*: अग्गिओ इन्दगोवकीडो मन्दश्चेति द्वार्थः, *i.e.*, aggiō is used in two ways, either substantively as a name of the Indragōpa insect, or adjectively with the meaning of 'mischievous,' 'bad.' *This agrees, in a general way, with the modern usage of the word, though in Bihār at least the word does not appear to be used as a name of the Indragōpa, which is a small, harmless insect, with a bright red, glossy coat, emerging from the soil in the beginning of the rainy season* (*commonly called* बीरबहूटी, *q.v.*). *This insect has its name of aggiō from its red colour, while the modern use of the name agiyā is taken from the burning or blistering property of the insects and diseases so named. The M. has* अग्या *or* आग्या. *G. has* आगियो *in the sense of fire-fly.*]

अगिया *agiyā* (2), अगिआ *agiā*, **Tbh.**, *subst. f.*, *lg. f. of* आगि *āgi*, *q.v.* **Exam.**, [1]*Bih.*, xviii, 5, दिया बाड़े तेलवा बोरसि बाड़ि अगिया (*fem.*), There is oil in the lamp, there is fire in the pan; *Gor.*, v, 9, अगिया लगावोँ, भौजि, बाव के मुनरवा, In the fire I would cast your finger-ring, O sister-in-law. [4]*Misc.* 84, अगिया लगौ, मेघिया, सावन भदौवा, बजर परौ तोरा देहिया, May the lightning strike and the thunderbolt fall on thy body, O Meghiyā, in (*the months of*) Sāwan and Bhadō̃.

√**अगिया** *agiyā*, (*pr. pts.* अगियात *agiyāt*, अगियाइत *agiyāit*; अगियाएल *agiyāēl*; अगियाएब *agiyāēb*; अगियाए *agiyāē*), **Tbh.**, *v. intr.* [1]to be burning (*as of the head in headache*); [2]*fig.* to be very angry. **Exam.**, [2]*Coll.* (*Bh.*), काहें एतना अगिआत बैठें, Why are you in such a rage?

[*A der. root, formed from* आगि, *q.v. Not noted in other Gds. Its tr. form is* अगियाव, *q.v.*]

अँगिया *ãgiyā* (1), **Tbh.**, *subst. f.*, limb, body. **Phr.**, अँगिया के पातर *adj.*, slender of body. **Exam.**, *B. Gr.*, II (*Bh.*), xii, 5, अँगिया के पातर भरे मुख दरदर, Lo, her body is slender and her face is fair. *See* अँगउवा *ãg'wā*, अङ्ग *aṅg*, *and* आँग *ā̃g*.

[*Skr.* अङ्गः *or* (*with pleon.* क) अङ्गकः, *of which a fem. dim. may be formed* अङ्गिका *in an endearing sense, Pr.* अङ्गिआ, *hence Gd.* अङ्गी *or lg. f.* अंगिया.]

अंगिया *ãgiyā* (2), **Tbh.,** *subst. f.,* ¹a bodice, jacket (*for women, short, and only covering the breasts, Grs.* § 744); ²a sieve with a cloth bottom (*for sifting fine. flour, Grs.* § 607). **Exam.,** ¹ *Bais.,* 11, अंगिया मसक गई (*fem.*), चुड़िया तड़क गई, The bodice has got loose, and the bangles have been shivered; *Sudh.,* 28, अंगिया की खिड़िया नित चाभै जोबनवाँ कै माल, The slits of (*thy*) bodice ever suck the wealth of (*thy*) swelling breasts; *Mag.* 72, साँकरि अंगिया, कमरवा बेरी पतरी, धड़िया चलत यो धमसाय, In a tightly-fitting bodice, O slender-waisted one, you are walking in the road with palpitating heart.

[*Properly the lg. f. of* आँगी *or* अङ्गी, *q.v. M. has* अँग्या.]

अगियाब *agiyāb* (*pr. pts.* अगियबैत *agiyabãit, Bh. and My.* अगियावत *agiyāwat,* अगियाबित *agiyāwit, Mg. also* अगियाइत *agiyāit;* अगियाओल *agiyāöl;* अगियाएब *agiyāëb;* अगियाबै *agiyābai,* अगियाए *agiyāë*), **Tbh.,** *v. tr.,* to burn metallic vessels for the purpose of cleaning them, to purify a vessel by passing it through fire. **Exam.,** *Coll.* (*Bh.*), बाँड़ी कैँ अगिया।वैं, Clean the saucepan by fire.

[*A der. root formed from* आगि, *q.v. Not noted in other Gds., except H. which has* √ अगया. *Its intr. form is* √ अगिया, *q.v.*]

अगियारा *agiyārā* (1), (*f.* अगियारी *agiyārī*), **Tbh.,** (I), *adj.* (*lit.* fire-making), fiery. *See* अगन्यारा *ag'yārā.*
(II) *subst. f.,* the kindling of the fire at the time of devotion by Hindūs (*H. Dy.*).

[*Skr.* अग्निकारका *adj.,* अग्निकारिका *subst., Pr.* अग्गि-आरओ, अग्गिआरिआ; *H.* अगियारी *or* अग्यारी (*sometimes spelt wrongly* अघारी, *Hd. Dy., p.* 114), *G.* अगियारी.]

अगियारा *agiyārā* (2), **Tbh.,** *subst. m.,* the place of the sacrificial fire of the Hindūs.

[*Skr.* अग्न्यागारः, *Pr.* अग्गिआआरो *or* (*with pleon. suff.* क) अग्गिआआरओ, *B.* (*contr.*) अगिआरा, *M.* अगियारी *and* अगेरी, *G.* अगिआरी, *both esp. in the sense of* the fire-temple of the Parsis.]

अगियासी *agiyāsī,* **Tbh.,** *subst. f.,* ¹the Hindū ceremony of fumigating with incense a bride and bridegroom (= आरती, *Grs.* § 1332); ²the fire kept burning in a lying-in chamber for ten days after delivery (= पसँगी, *Grs.* § 1398). See अगन्ती *ag'tī* (1).

[*Skr.* अग्निवासः, *fem. dim.* अग्निवासिका, *Pr.* अग्गि-वासिआ, *B.* अगियासी.]

अगियाह *agiyāh,* अगन्याह *ag'yāh,* (*str. f.* अगियाह *agiyāhā, f.* अगियाही *agiyāhī, Mth. and poet.* अगियाहि *agiyāhi*), **Tbh.,** *adj. com. gen.,* fiery (*of temper*), angry, jealous, wicked. **Exam.,** *Coll.* (*Bh.*), ई गुस्से मैं अगियाह उठेला, He quickly turns (*lit.* rises) angry. *See* अगिया *agiyā* (1) *and* अगल्ह *ag'lah.*

[*This appears to be merely a pleon. form of* अगिया (1), *q.v., made by means of the pleon. suff.* ह *or* आह (*see Gd. Gr.* § 206). *The corresponding Pr. word is* अग्गिओ (*Hēm. Dy., vs.* 53), *which is a synonym of Skr.* अन्धः bad, wicked. *There may be some bond of analogy between the final* ह *of this word and of* अगल्ह.]

अंगिर *ãgir,* (*pr. pts.* अँगिरैत *ãgirãit;* अँगिरल *ãgiral;* अँगिरब *ãgirab;* अँगिरै *ãgirai*), **Tbh.,** *v. intr.,* to agree, admit. **Phr.,** अँगिरि लेब, *v. tr.,* to agree to. **Exam.,** *Hb.,* 6, 41, अँगिरि लेलन्हि सब कन्सक कहल, He agreed to all that Kans said; *Prabh., p.* 6, *l.* 8, अँगिरल गरल तेजल नहि सङ्कर, सहब सतत बर दाघे, Saṅkar did not abandon the promise of (*lit.* the agreed to) swallowing (*the poison*), but still bore continually the burning (*pain of the poison*).

[*Skr.* √ अङ्गीकृ, viiith *cl.* अङ्गीकरोति; *Pr.* अंगीकरइ, अंगीअरइ; *hence B.* √ अँगिर (*shortened for* अँगीर). *Not met with in other Gds.*]

अँगिरखा *ãgir'khā, the same as* अँगरखा *ãgar'khā, q.v.* **Exam.,** *Coll.* (*Bh.*), अँगिरखा पेन्ह लेंऽ, नाहिँ तऽ जाड़ लागी, Put on your coat or you will feel cold.

अँगिरखी *ãgir'khī, fem. of the preceding, with a diminutive sense.*

अगिलहि *agilahi,* (*Hb.* iv, 7), *old obl. f. of* आगिल *āgil, q.v.*

अगिला *agilā,* अगला *ag'lā,* (*f.* अगिली *agilī,* अगली *ag'lī, old Bw.* आगिलो *āgilō, wk. f.* आगिल *āgil or* आगल *āgal, q.v.*), **Tbh.,** (I) *adj.,* (*both in place and time*), ¹prior, preceding, former, early; ²foremost, first, chief, best; ³immediately in front, next in order, forthcoming, future. **Phr.,** अगिला जनम *m.,* a former birth *or* a future birth (*tech. term of transmigration of souls*); अगिला बन्द *m.,* the foremast of a ship; अगिला परन्दा *m.,* the foremost sail of a ship; अगिला कराह *m.,* the lower pan of a sugar-refinery, (*as opposed to the* पछिला कराह *or upper pan*); अगिली बात *f.,* a future event, the consequences of any action. **Exam.,** ¹*Prov.* भाड़ा लेखा नहिँ, से अगिला माँगि सवार, He who has no money to pay his fare, asks for the bow seat (*lit.* front seat); *Bih.* xvi, 23, गोड़ तोर लागोँला, अगिला कहरवा, I fell at thy feet, O front bearer (*of the palankeen*); *B. Gr.,* II (*Bh.*), xxiii, 4, आगि राख अगिलि (*m. c. for* अगिली), पछर राख पिछलि रे, (*When*) the former half of the night (*had passed*), and the (*first*) quarter of the latter (*half of the*) night (*had commenced*), (*this is a common phrase in poetry for* soon after midnight, *see the example under* अगन्वा); *Prov.*, अगिला छोपा गया हराया, अब का छोपा आगे आया, Former benefits (*lit. wipings of the hands as an oblation to ancestors*) are gone and have had their praise, the turn for (*conferring*) present benefits has come round (*Hd. Prov.*). ²*Prov.* (*Bh.*), अगिलो भेलो पछिलो, पछिलो परत्वान, The first (*wife*) became last, and the last (*became*) foremost. ³*Phr.*, अगिलो पछिलो करत्नो, The consequence of a future and past life (*i.e. of transmigration of souls*); *see also under* आगिलो āgilō (*Bin.*, *vs.* 261).

(II) *subst. m.*, ¹ancestor, forefather, elder, predecessor; ²descendant, successor; ³chief, superior; *hence* ⁴(*wom.*) husband. Exam., ³*Prov.*, अगिला करे, पछिला पर आवे, The superior does it, (*the evil consequence*) falls on the subordinate (*Hd. Dy.*). ⁴*Coll.* (*Bh.*), अगिला घर मेँ नाहि बा, My husband is not at home.

(*This word has many bye-forms and synonyms, such as* आगल, आगिल, अगन्वा, अगन्रा, अगेला, अग्रठ, अग्रिम, *etc.*)

[*Skr.* अग्रः, *Pr.* अग्गो *and* (*with pleon. suff.* इल, *see Hēm.* ii, 164, *Bhag.*, *p.* 437) अग्गिलो, *and* (*with pleon. suff.* क *superadded, see Hēm.* ii, 164) अग्गिलओ, *hence B. wk. f.* आगिल, *and str. f.* अगिला. *See also the remarks under* अगन्वा *and* अगन्डी.]

अगिवान *agiwān*, Tbh., *subst. m.*, *the same as* अगन्वान *ag'wān*, *q.v.* Exam., *Pārv.*, *ch.* 13, प्रमुदित भे अगिवान विलोकि बरातहिँ, डमरे डमर न रहत, न डमर परात हिँ, Joyous the deputation went forth on seeing the marriage procession, (*but*) alarmed (*at the sight of the spectres*) they could neither stand still nor could they run away.

अँगिशन्ती *āgish'tī*, Any., *subst. f.*, (*vulg. Mg.*) a spark (= चिंगारी *chīgārī*).

[*Apparently connected with the Prs.* انگشت *angisht, though the latter properly means 'dead charcoal,' not 'live coal.'*]

अँगीश *āgish*, Any., *subst. f.*, (*vulg. Mg.*), *the same as* अँगिशन्ती *āgish'tī* (*q.v.*), *of which it appears to be a corruption.*

अगीन *agin*, Tbh., *subst m.*, the leaves at the top and the upper part of sugar-cane (*Cr.*, *p.* 75).

(*This word has numerous synonyms, thus* अगन्रा (1), अगन्ड़ा, अगम्भा (1), अगाड़, अगारी, अँगारी, अगाव, अगेँड़, अगेड़ा, अँगेर, अँगेरा, अँगेरी, अँगोर, अँगोरी, अगौड़ा, अगौरा, आग (2), अँड़, गँड़ो, *etc.*)

[*Skr.* अग्रम् top, *Pr.* अग्गं *or* (*with pleon. suff.* इल, *Hēm.* ii, 164) अग्गिलं; *hence* (*with change of* ल *to* न, *see Gd. Gr.* § 111) *B.* अगीन. *See also the remarks under* अगन्डी.]

अगुअई *aguaī* (*Mth. and poet.* अगुअइ *aguaï*), *the same as* अगुआई *aguāi*, *q.v.*

अगुआ *aguā*, अगुवा *aguwā*, Tbh., *subst. m.*, ¹*with all the meanings of* अगन्वान *ag'wān*, *q.v.* (*Grs.* § 1286); *besides* ²the opening *or* slit in a Hindū woman's chemise (*Hd. Dy.*); ³the pommel of a saddle (= *H.* आगूआ); ⁴the highest brass bangle on the arm (*Grs.* § 558). Phr., अगुएँ *aguē̃ or* अगुवेँ *aguwē̃* (*old loc. used as an adv. and prep.*), in front, before, *used of place and time* (*Ās. Gy.*). Exam., ¹*Alh.*, *l.* 38, समधी बाँधल जब गारत मैं, अगुआ बेड़ी पहिरावल जाय, When the father-in-law was bound in prison, and the matchmaker was made to wear fetters; *Prov.* (*Bh.*), अगुआ दुओ ओर से गारी खेला, The matchmaker hears abuse from both parties (*both being apt to be dissatisfied with his services*); *Coll.* (*Bh.*), हमन्होंका अगुएँ चलौं, Let us go ahead. *See* अगन्वा *ag'wā.*

[*Prop. the lg. f. of* आगू (*q.v.*), *the latter being the same as* आगर, *of which* अगन्वा *is the lg. f.*]

अगुआई *aguāi*, अगन्वाई *ag'wāi*, अगुअई *aguaī*, Tbh., *subst. f.*, ¹guidance, leadership; ²the office *or* the services of a matchmaker. Exam., ¹*Rām.*, *A.*, *ch.* 195, 1, कियेउ निषाद-नाथ अगुआई, He made the lord of the Nikhads lead the van. ²*Coll.* (*Bh.*), हमन्हका अगुआई से है बियाह भेल छँ, The marriage took place through his services as matchmaker. *See* अगन्वाही *ag'wāhī.*

[*Either an abs. noun derived from* अगुआ *with the sec. der. suff.* आई, *see Gd. Gr.* § 220, *or it may be a verbal noun derived from* √ अगुआ. *H. and S.* अगुआई; *the pure B. form is* अगुअई.]

अगुआनी *aguāni*, Tbh., *subst. f.*, (*Mg.*) the space in front of a house (*Grs.* § 1237). *For synonyms see under* अगुआर *aguār.*

[*This is merely a bye-form of* अगन्वानी (*q.v.*) *with a special meaning.*]

√ अगुआब *aguāb*, (*pr. pts.* अगुअबैत *aguabāit*; अगुआएल *aguāēl*; अगुआएब *aguāēb*; अगुआए *aguāē*), Tbh., *v. intr.*, ¹to go before, precede, advance; ²to get in front, hurry forward. Exam., ¹*Hb.* ix, 54, तात, तोहित अब बढ़ अगुआए, Father, do thou go quickly preceding me; *Bid.* 21, 3, सकल सखि अगुआइलि हे, हम एकसर नारी, My female companions have gone ahead, I am a lonely woman.² *Mth. Rām.*, *Bā.* 90, 50, सोरह सहस्र सब धिँ अगुआय, चार्यौ रथम मरत पछताय, (*Each one said to* *himself*) 'I will get in front and break the bow. If I remain behind I shall die of regrets.'

[*Compound root, formed from* आगु *and* √ आब, *q.v.*]

अगुआर *aguār*, (*Mth.-Mg. of South Munger*) अगुआड़ *aguāṛ*, (*obl. and str. f.* अगुआरा *aguārā*, *lg. f.* अगुअरवा *aguar'wā*, *loc. sing.* अगुआरे *aguārē*), **Tbh.**, *subst. m.*, [1]the front, fore part; *espec.* [2]the space in front of a house, (*opp. to* पिछुआरा, *Grs.* § 1237). **Comp.**, अगुआरा-पिछुआरा, the neighbourhood, neighbours. **Exam.**, *Coll.* (*Bh.*), [1]उन का अगुआरा (*obl.*) में गोबर के ढेरी बा, In front of his house is a dung-hill; *Coll.* (*Bh.*), ऊ अगुआरे (*loc.*) बैसल होएँ, He is probably sitting in front of his house; *Coll.* (*Bh.*), उन के घर का अगुआरे एक पीपर के पेड़ बा, There is a pipal-tree in front of his house. *Synonyms are* अगरा *ag'rā* (1), अगवास *ag'wās*, अगुआनी *aguānī*, अगुत्ती *aguttī*, अगूत *agūt*, *q.v.*

[*Derived from* आगु *with Gḍ. suff.* आर, *see Gḍ. Gr.* § 241. *See also the remarks under* अगस्ती. *Cf. H. and P.* अगवाड़ा, *G.* अगवाडो. *S. has an adv.* अगुआरे (*or* अगुआड़) in front, before. *Not noted in other Gḍs.*]

अगुएँ *aguẽ*, *old loc. of* अगुआ *aguā*, *q.v.*

अँगुठवा *ãguṭh'wā*, **Tbh.**, *subst. m.*, *lg. f. of* अँगुठा *ãguṭhā*, *q.v.* **Exam.**, [1]*Nāk.*, *l.* 484, स्वामी, हर देवँ अपना अँगुठवेँ, O husband, touch it (*i.e. the door*) with your thumb.

अँगुठा *ãguṭhā*, *Bw. and Mg.* अँगूठा *ãgūṭhā* (1), **Tbh.**, *subst. m.*, [1]the thumb; [2]the great toe; [3]a toe-ring (Grs. §§ 760, 772) (*esp. one of brass or other baser metal worn by low-caste women*); [4](*among Chāis*) a syringe (*Ās. Gy.*, *No.* VII). **Phr.**, अँगुठा चूमब, *lit.* to kiss the great toe, *hence* to flatter, to fawn; अँगुठा देखाएब, *lit.* to show one's thumb, *hence* to deride, *or* to defy, to brave (*in this sense used by women, in coquetry, as a token of affected unwillingness*), *or* (*obsc.*) to invite to sexual intercourse; अँगुठा मारब, *lit.* to snap one's fingers, *hence* to hold very cheap. *See* अगुण्ठा *aguṇṭhā*.

[*Skr.* अङ्गुष्ठः, *Pā.* अंगुट्ठो, *Pr.* अंगुट्ठो (*see Sapt.*, *vs.* 946, पाअंगुट्ठ॰ great toe of the foot) *or* (*with pleon. suff.* क) अंगुट्ठओ, *hence B.* अँगुठा *or* अगुण्ठा (*q.v.*), *H.* अँगूठा *or* गूँठा, *P.* अँगूठ *or* अँगूठा (*and* अँगूठड़ा a toe-ring), *M.* अँगुठा *or* अँगोठा *or* अँगठा *or* आँगठा, *S.* आङूठो (*or* आँगूठो?), *Ksh.* न्योठ, न्यौठ. *or* न्योट, न्यौट (*spelt nyoṭh, etc., in Ksh. Vy.*), *Kn.* बोट, बोटा; *Gip. has* angusht *in the sense of* finger (*Mik.* vii, *p.* 9).]

अँगुठी *ãguṭhī*, *Mg. and Bw.* अँगूठी *ãgūṭhī*, **Tbh.**, *subst. f.*, [1]a finger-ring (*Grs.* §§ 756, 769); [2]a thimble. **Exam.**, [1]*Alh.*, *l.* 199, पोरे पोरे अँगुठी पड़ गैल, बाहे बुरियन के झनकार, On every joint (*of her fingers*) was a ring, and all her armlets (*gave forth*) a tingling sound; *Nāk.*, *l.* 413, रामा, केंद्र देवे अँगुठी मुँदरिया, O Rām, some gave her finger-rings and seal-rings. [2]*Coll.* (*Bh.*), सिआवनवाला, अँगुठी पेन्ह लेंऽ, तऽ सूई अँगुरी में ना गड़ी, Tailor, put the thimble on, and then the needle will not pierce your finger. *See* अगुण्ठी *aguṇṭhī and* अगुस्ताना *agustānā*.

[*Skr.* अङ्गुष्ठिका, *Pr.* अंगुट्ठिआ, *hence B.* अँगुठी *or* अगुण्ठी, *A. and Bg.* आँगुठी *or* आँगठी, *O.* अँगुठि (*O. Vy.*), *H.* अँगूठी *or* गूठी, *S.* आङूठी, *P.* अँगूठी; *Gip.* angustri, a ring (*Mik.* vii, *p.* 9). *The Pr. has also* अंगुत्थलं, *see Hēm. Dy.*, *vs.* 31.]

अगुण्ठा *aguṇṭhā*, **Tbh.**, *subst. m.*, (*Mth.-Bh.*), a woman's toe-ring. *See* अँगुठा *ãguṭhā*.

अगुण्ठी *aguṇṭhī*, **Tbh.**, *subst. m.*, (*Mth.-Bh.*), a woman's finger-ring. *See* अँगुठी *ãguṭhī*.

[*Properly a fem. dim. of* अगुण्ठा.]

√ **अगुता** *agutā*, (*pr. pts.* अगुताइत *agutāit*, अगुतात *agutāt*; अगुताएल *agutāël*; अगुताएब *agutāëb*, अगुताब *agutāb*; अगुताए *agutāë*), **Tbh.**, *Mth.*, *v. intr.*, [1]to be distressed, worried; [2]to be in a flurry *or* hurry *or* confusion. **Exam.**, [1]*Mth. Rām.*, *A.*, 87, 14, रामचन्द्र मन मन अगुताथि, Rām'chandra's heart is filled with regrets. [2]*Mth. Rām.*, *Ln.*, 95, 11, घुरि कै लङ्का लज्जित जाउ, प्रातहि अबिऔ, जनु अगुताउ, Return now, ashamed as you are, to Laṅkā; come to-morrow morning (*to fight*), and do not be flurried. *This is the Mth. form of* √ अकुता *akutā*, *q.v.*

[*The derivation may be the same as of* √ अकुता, *only substituting Skr.* अग *in the place of* अक.]

अगुताउ *agutāu*, **Tbh.**, *subst. m.*, worry, trouble. **Exam.**, *Mth. Rām.*, *Ln.*, 98, 18, पिबि जल मधुर, मधुर फल खाउ, कपि-दल कुसल, कि अछ अगुताउ, Drink sweet water and eat sweet fruit; is it well with the monkey army, or is it in trouble?

[*Verbal noun derived from* √ अगुता, *q.v.* *See Gḍ. Gr.* §§ 326, 329. *The term.* उ *is a vocalisation of* व. *See the remarks under art.* √ अकुता.]

अगुत्ती *aguttī*, **Tbh.**, *subst. f.*, *a Bh. and Mg. synonym of* अगुआर *aguār*, *q.v.* (*Grs.* § 1237). *See* अगूत *agūt*.

[*Skr.* अग्र-वृत्ति, *Pr.* अग्गवत्ती *or* (*with pleon.* क) अग्गवत्तिआ; *Gḍ. contr.* अगोती, *whence B.* अगुती. *S. has an adv.* अगुतो in future. *See the remarks under* अगस्ती.]

अगुन *agun*, (*old obl.* अगुनहिँ), **Ts.**, (I) *adj. com. gen.*, (*subst. f.* अगुना *agunā*), [1]without any quality, unconditioned, transcendent (*a tech. term of Hindu* *philosophy, used as an epithet of God, synonymous with* निर्गुन, *and opp. to* सगुन conditioned, immanent, phenomenal); [2] incapable of being qualified, indescribably good *or* great, *etc.*; [3] without any good quality, worthless, bad; [4] without any of the three tempers (सत goodness, तमस badness, रजस passion), temperless, passionless, indifferent; [5] unskilful. **Comp.**, अगुन-सगुन transcendent and immanent, unconditioned and conditioned. **Exam.**, *Rām. Bā., ch.* 27, 1, अगुन-सगुन दोउ ब्रह्म सरूपा अकथ अगाध अनादि अनूपा, Both forms of Brahm, the absolute and the conditioned, are indescribable, inconceivable, eternal, and incomparable; *ib., Bā., ch.* 123, 9, 10, सगुनहिँ अगुनहिँ नहिँ कछु भेदा, गावहिँ मुनि पुरान बुध बेदा; अगुन अरूप अलख अज जोई, भगत प्रेम बस सगुन सो होई, There is no difference between (*God in His*) transcendent and (*His*) immanent (*form*), so declare the Munis, Purans, the sages, and the Bēds; (*God*) Who is unconditioned, formless, markless, uncreate, He became conditioned (*as a man, alluding to the incarnation in Rām*) through the influence of His love to the faithful. [2] *Rām., Bā., ch.* 46, 2, रघुपति महिमा अगुन अबाधा, बरनब सोइ बर बारि अगाधा, The glory of Raghupatī (*i.e. Rām*) is indescribably great and cannot be gainsaid; it may be described as the fine unfathomable waters (*of a lake*); *Bin., vs.* 220, देखि प्रीति प्रतीति जन पर अगुन अनघ अमाय, दास तुलसी कहत, मुनि-गन जयति जय उर गाय, Seeing the love and trust (*of Rām*) in man (*to be so*) indescribably great, pure, and unfailing, Tul'sī Dās says, the Munis from their heart declare its great glory. [3] *Rām., Bā., ch.* 77, 7, 8, सैल, सुलच्छनि सुता तुम्हारी, सुनहु जे अब अवगुन दुइ चारी; अगुन, अमान, मातु-पितु-हीना, उदासीन, सब संसय छीना. O Mountain (*Himālaya*), such are the merits of your daughter (*Pārvatī*), but now listen to a few (*lit.* two or four) drawbacks; (*her bridegroom will be a man*) without worth and dignity, having no father and mother, an ascetic, with no thought for anything; *ib., Ln., do.* 31, 1, अगुन अमान जानि तेहि दीन्ह पिता बन बास, Seeing him to be of no worth or dignity, his father has banished him (*i.e. Rām*); *Bin., vs.* 272, अगुन अलायक आलसी जानि अधम अनेरो, Considering them to be bad, worthless, lazy, needy, and not fit to be associated with; *ib., vs.* 274, अधम अगुन आलसनि को पालिबो फबि आयो रघुनायक नवीन को, To care for the mean, worthless, and weak is a (*another*) new beauty of Raghunāth (*i.e. Rām*); *Pārv., ch.* 7, कहहु, काह सुनि रीझिहु बर अकुलीनहिँ अगुन अमान अजाति मातु-पितु हीनहिँ, Say, what have you heard to make you rejoice (*lit.* what having heard do you rejoice) at having for your bridegroom a man without family, without worth, without dignity, without caste, and possessing no father and mother (*said to Pārbatī regarding Sib*). [4] *Bin., vs.* 57, सान्ति निरपेच्छ निर्मम निरामय अगुन सबद ब्रह्म परब्रह्म ग्यानी (*The sādhu or saint is*) tranquil, contented, disinterested, sound (*morally*), unimpassioned, and a proficient in the knowledge of God's word (*i.e. the Bēds*) and of the supreme divine nature.

(II) *subst. m.*, a defect, a fault, a drawback. **Exam.**, *Rām., Bā., ch.* 7, 1, खल अघ अगुन साधु गुन गाहा उभय अपार उदधि अवगाहा, Both to declare the sins and faults of the bad and the virtues of the good is like plunging into a fathomless ocean.

[*Skr.* अगुण; *Gd.* अगुण *or* अगुन.]

अगुनी *aguni*, **Ts.**, *adj. com. gen.*, (*subst. f.* अगुनिनी *agunini*), possessing no merits *or* virtues, worthless, bad. **Exam.**, *K. Rām., Ut.* 11, ऐसे अनूप कहैं तुलसी रघुनायक, कि अगुनी गुन गावैं, Tul'sī Dās describes Raghunāyak (*i.e. Rām*) as so incomparable that (*even*) the bad declare his virtues.

[*Skr.* अगुणी; *Gd.* अगुणी *or* अगुनी.]

अगुर *agur, the same as* अगुरु *agurŭ, q.v.*

अँगुरा *ãgurā, str. f. of* आँगुर *ãgur., q.v. It occurs in Padm., ch.* 543, 5 (*see under* अँगुरी *ãgurī*), *and is chosen to suit the rhyme with* काँगुरा *kãgurā.*

अँगुरिया *ãguriyā*, अँगुरिआ *ãguriā*, अँगुरिआँ *ãguriā̃*, *or* अँगुलिया *ãguliyā, etc.*, **Tbh.**, *subst. f., lg. f. of* अँगुरी *ãgurī, q.v.* **Exam.**, [1] *Gop., (Bh.)* 19, तोहरा अँगुरिया मेँ अमिरित बरवा, चीर के अँगुरिया बहिन के पियाए जोगी रम के चल देले, 'Thy finger contains ambrosia'; (*hearing this*) the ascetic split his finger, and having giving drink to his sister (*and thereby brought her to life again*), he went off on his wanderings; *Gīt., Bā.* 32, 1, कौसल्या कल कनक अजिर महँ सिखवत चलन अँगुरिया लाये, Kausalya, in the beautiful gilt courtyard, taught (*Rām*) to walk, causing him to hold her finger; [3] *Gīt., Bā.* 33, 1, छोटी छोटी गोड़िया, अँगुरियाँ छोटी छबीली, नख जोति मोति मानो कमल दलनि पर, ललित आँगन खेलै, With small small feet and beautiful little toes, and white nails (*glittering*) like pearls on lotus stalks, (*Rām*) used to play in the charming courtyard.

अँगुरी *ãgurī*, अँगुली *ãgulī*, (अँगुरि *ãguri, m.c., obl. plur.* अँगुरिन *ãgurin*), **Tbh.**, *subst. f.*, [1] a finger; [2] a finger's breadth; [3] a toe. **Phr.**, बता अँगुरी the fore-finger (*lit.*, the finger of showing *or* pointing, *from* बताउब to show); डैनी अँगुरी the middle finger (*from* डाइन a witch, *owing to the superstition that any child or animal touched with it will die within six months; rings are not worn on thi finger from* *fear of snakes, and also from a belief that all the blood of one's brother would dry up, Hd. Dy.), also* छिनकी अँगुरी ; कन अँगुरी *or contr.* कनगुरिया (*see* Gōp. (*Mg.*) 19) the little finger (*from Skr.* कन *or* कनिष्ठ small; *it is reckoned as an ōjhā or exorcist, hence women oil the navels of children with this finger at the feast of the Dasah'rā, Hd. Dy.*); पूजा अँगुरी, the ring-finger, (*lit.* ritual finger, *being the finger with which sandal is applied or sprinkled at religious ceremonies*); अँगुरीक नोक, the tip of the finger; पैरक अँगुरी, a toe; अँगुरी उठाएब, *v. tr.*, to point the finger at one; अँगुरी फोड़ब, *v. tr.*, to crack or snap the finger; अँगुरी नचाएब *or* अँगुरी पै नचाएब, *v. tr.*, to jeer one by moving the middle finger before him, (*regarding a supposed derivation of this idiom from the puppet show, see Hd. Dy., p.* 164). **Exam.**, [1] *Din., l.* 135, सलहेस अँगुरी चीरि कै देलन्हि जियाय, Salhēs, splitting his finger (*and extracting ambrosia or* अमिय *from it*) brought (*the jackal Phot'rā*) again to life; *Mag.* 18, अँगुरी ममोरे, दसों अँगुरी ममोरे गे, अलबेलवा, गुलवा ममोरे जैसे गाल, He twists my fingers, he twists (*all*) my ten fingers, O fair lady, and squeezes my cheeks like powdered rice; *Prov.* (*Mth.*), अँगुरी धरैते पहुँचा धरि लेलक, Catching hold of a finger, he took hold of the wrist (= *E.* give an inch, take an ell; *after Fallon*); *Prov.* (*Mth.*) सोझ अँगुरी घीउ नहिँ निकसै, A straight finger will not bring up any ghī (*from the pot*); *in a slightly different form the latter prov. occurs in the following, Padm., ch.* 436, 6, जौ लहि मथे न कोट दै जीउ, सूधी अँगुरि (*m.c.*) न निकसै घीउ, However long one may churn (*milk*) with all one's heart with a straight finger no ghī will be brought up (*from the pot*); *Coll.* (*Mg*). मोरा बबुआ कैं जेठो अँगुरी सँ छू देलक, ओकर बबुआ मरे, He has touched my son with his middle finger, may his son die (*after Fallon*); [2] *Mag.* 25, आठ अँगुरी दस मुँदरी, अलबेलवा, खिरकी में रचल है जंजीर, He fixes, O fair lady, a chain eight finger-breadth long and (*consisting*) of ten links (*lit.* rings) in the window; *Padm., ch.* 543, 5, बैठे धानुक कंगुरन कँगुरा, भूमि न आँटी अँगुरिन अँगुरा, The bowmen sat (*so closely packed*) in all the battlements, that there was not even a finger's breadth room available.

[*Skr.* अङ्गुलिः *or* (*with pleon.* क) अङ्गुलिका, *Pr.* अंगुलिआ *or* अंगुरिआ (*cf. Spt.* 277); *hence B.* आँगुली *or* आँगुरी, *Bg.* आँगुली *or* आँगुरी, *H.* अँगुली *or* उँगली, *P.* अँगुली *or* उँगुली, *M.* आँगोली *or* आँगुली, *O.* अङ्गुलि (*O. Vy.*) *or* अँगुली.]

अँगुरीवा *āguriwā*, अँगुरीआ *āgurīā*, अँगुलीवा *āguliwā*, अँगुलीआ *āgulīā*, **Tbh.**, *subst. f., red. f. of* अँगुरी *āgurī*, *q.v.* **Exam.**, *Mars.*, i, 2, दसो अँगुरीवा केसवा झारे है हाय हाय, She combed her hair with her ten fingers, alas, alas!

[*This is properly the contracted form of the full redundant form* अँगुरियवा; *the more usual form is that which contains* व *w.*]

अगुरु *agurū*, **Ts.**, *subst. m., the same as* अगरु *agarū*, *q.v.* (*This should not be confused with the tats.* अगुरु not heavy, *which is not used.*)

अँगुली *āguli*, *the same as* अँगुरी *āgurī*, *q.v.* **Exam.**, [1] *Gīt., Ut.* 17, 7, सुभग, सुरेख, सुलच्छन अँगुली घन, सुन्दर पानि मुद्रिका राजति, अँगुली-त्रान कमान बान छबि सुरनि सुखद, असुरनि उर सालति, A fine line adorns his thumb joint, fine white nails his fingers, and a beautiful seal-ring his hand; the beauty of his finger-guard (*or thumb-ring*), bow and arrows, causing joy to the gods, pierces the heart of the demons; *Dōh., vs.* 527, प्रभु समीप छोटे बड़े, निबल होत बलवान, तुलसी प्रकट बिलोकिये कर अँगुली अनुमान, Before the Lord the little are great and the weak are strong; Tul'sī (*says*), you may observe this clearly from the analogy of the fingers of the hand (*i.e., though the several fingers are of different sizes and of different usefulness, yet they are alike in being 'fingers' of the hand*). [2] *Gīt., Bā.* 108, 2, चरन अरुन, अँगुली मनोहर, नख दुतिवन्त कछुक अरुनारे, (*Jānakī's*) feet are (*coloured*) red, her toes are charming, and her white nails (*show*) a shade of redness; *ib., Ut.* 17, 3, सुभग अङ्गुष्ठ, अँगुली अविरल, कछुक अरुन नख जोति जगमगति, Beautiful was (*Rām's*) great toe, and his toes were close, and his slightly reddened nails were of glittering brightness.

[*P.* अँगुली, *M.* अँगुळी *or* आँगोळी *or* आँगोळी.]

अगुवा *aguwā*, **Tbh.**, *the same as* अगुआ *aguā*, *q.v.* **Phr.**, अगुवे *aguwē*, (*old loc. used as an adv. and prep.*), in front, before, *used of place and time* (*Āz. Gy*). **Exam.**, *Padm., ch.* 20, 2, अगुवा भयउ सेख बुरहानू, पन्थ लाय मुहि दीन्हों ज्ञानू, Shekh Bur'hān became my (*spiritual*) guide, and bringing (*me*) into the (*right*) way he imparted to me knowledge.

अँगुस्ताना *āgustānā*, अँगुश्ताना *āgushtānā*, **Any.**, *subst. m.*, [1] a thimble; [2] a thumb-ring (*Grs.* § 769). **Exam.**, *Gīt., Ut.* 17, 7, *comm.*, अँगुली त्राण अँगुस्ताना, The finger-guard is a thumb-ring (*which serves to protect the thumb in shooting with a bow*); *Krish.* 261, बाजूबन्द पिजायद बिछुवा छल्ला छाप अँगुस्ताना, मुख भरि पान, नयन भरि सुरमा, लै दरपन, कान्हा मन मुसकाना, (*Adorned*) with armlets, wristlets, toe-rings, (*plain*) rings, seal-rings, and thumb-rings, his mouth filled with pān and his eyes with collyrium, and holding a mirror (*in his hand*), Kānhā (*i.e. Krish'n*) smiled in his heart.

[*Prs.* انگشتانه *aṅgushtānā; also in H.; P. has* अँगुश्ताना (*P. Dy. St.*), *Bg.* अँगुठाना, *S.* अँगुश्तानो, *O.* अँगुठाना, *M.* अँगुस्ताव *or* अँगुस्तान *or* अँगुस्तान.]

अँगूठा *ăgūṭhā* (1), *Bw. and Mg. for* अँगुठा *ăguṭhā, q.v.*

अँगूठा *ăgūṭhā* (2), **Tbh.**, *num. adj.*, (*f.* अँगूठी *ăgūṭhī*), (*Bh.*), *the same as* अँगूँढ़ा *ăgū̃ṛhā, q.v.* (*see B. Gr.*, II (*Bh.*), § 18).

[*This word is simply a corruption of* अँगूँढ़ा (*q.v.*), *the soft cons.* ढ़ *having been hardened by false analogy to* हूँठा (*q.v.*).]

अँगूठी *ăgūṭhī*, **Tbh.**, *subst. f.*, *for Bw. and Mg.* अँगुठी *ăguṭhī, q.v.* **Exam.**, *Padm.*, *ch.* 13, 6, हाथ सुलेमाँ केर अँगूठी, जग कहँ दान दीन्हि भरि मूँठी, In his hand he had Solomon's ring, (*with which*) he gave gifts to the world with a full hand; *Gōp.* (*Mg.*), 17, गोपी चन्द बोलल कि देखऽ बाबा के हाथ के अँगूठी सोभे, Gopī Chand said, behold thy father's ring is shining on thy finger (*lit.* hand).

अगूढ़ *agūṛh*, **Ts.**, *adj. com. gen.*, difficult to understand, mysterious (*see Āz. Gy.*). **Exam.**, *Coll.* (*Bh.*), ऐसन अगूढ़ बात बोलेलन कि समझ में ना आवे, He says such hard things that they cannot be understood; *Bw. ch. anon.*, अति अगूढ़ गति जान न परई, His very mysterious actions cannot be fathomed.

[*From* गूढ़ (*q.v.*) *with intens.* अ; *see art.* अ *a* (5). *The tats. meaning*, 'not mysterious,' *is not known.*]

अँगूँढ़ा *ăgū̃ṛhā*, **Tbh.**, *num. adj.*, (*f.* अँगूँढ़ी *ăgū̃ṛhī*), (*Bh.*), three and one half, (*see B. Gr.*, II (*Bh.*), § 18). **Exam.**, *Coll.* (*Bh.*), हमार लरिका अँगूढ़ा पढ़ेला, My son is learning the multiplication table for 3½: *ib.*, तूँ कह के अँगूढ़ा पढ़ेलऽ? हम चार के अँगूढ़ा पढ़ोला, How far have you got in the multiplication table for 3½? I have got as far as four times 3½. *See* हूँठा *hū̃ṭhā and* अँगूठा *ăgūṭhā.*

[*A compound of* षट् six *and* अढ़ा two and one half, *lit.* six less two and one half, *which is equal to* three and one half. अढ़ा *itself is a comp. of Skr.* अर्ध + तृतीयः, *lit.* third less one half, *i.e.* two and one half (*see Gd. Gr.* § 416). *Fractionals may be formed either by prefixing or by suffixing* अर्ध one half, *in the sense of* 'lessened by one half.' *Thus it is suffixed in the fractionals* डेढ़ा *or* डेढ़ा, one and a half, = *Skr.* द्वि + अर्ध, *lit.* two less one half; *and in* अँगूँढ़ा three and a half, = *Skr.* षट् + अर्धतृतीयः, *lit.* six less two and a half. *It is prefixed in* अढ़ा, two and a half, =*Skr.* अर्ध + तृतीयः, *lit.* three less one half; *also in* हूँठा, three and a half, = *Skr.* अर्ध + चतुर्थः, *lit.* four less one half (*see Gd. Gr.* § 416). *The word should be properly* अँगौढ़ा, *from* षट् + अढ़ा, *and the change to* अँगूँढ़ा *is probably due to false analogy with the alternative form* हूँठा (*q.v.*). *It is possible, however, that* अँगूढ़ा *is equivalent to Skr.* षट् + ऊन + अर्धतृतीयः, six less two and a half, = षडूनार्धतृतीयः, *which might contract into* अँगूँढ़ा, *the element* ऊनार *accounting for the nasalised long* ऊँ *in the Bh. form of the word.*]

अगूत *agūt*, **Tbh.**, *subst. m.*, (*Bh.*) the front part of a house, (*Grs.* § 1245). **Phr.**, अगूत के छाड़ the front thatch of a double thatch-roof house. *For synonyms see* अगुआर *aguār.*

[*Skr.* अग्र-कूटम्, *Pr.* अग्गऊडो, *whence contr. B.* अगूत.]

अँगूर *ăgūr*, (*poet.* अँगूरा *ăgūrā or* अँगूरू *ăgūrū*), (1) **Any.**, *subst. m.*, ¹a grape (*vitis vinifera, Wat.*); ²granulations in a healing sore (*being like little grapes in reddish colour*); ³*fig.* (*sweet as grapes*) sweetness, happiness. **Phr.**, अँगूरक टट्टी *or* टट्टरी, a vinery, a vineyard; fireworks in imitation of clusters of grapes in a vine; अँगूर बन्धब *or* छोड़ब, *v. intr.*, to become sound and healthy (*of a sore*). **Exam.**, ¹*B. G.*, *Fable* 13, अँगूर समह प्रचन गुच्छ सब पाकल टट्टी म लटकि रहल अछि, Bunches of grapes were hanging ripe on the trellis; *ib.*, (*Prov.*) खट्टा अँगूर के खाचो Who eats sour grapes? *Padm.*, *ch.* 69, 3, बिष दाना किन होय अँगूरा, How should poisonous seed become grapes? *ib.*, *ch.* 84, 3, बिष राखेँ नहिं होत अँगूरू, Poison, by being kept, does not turn into grapes (*said with reference to keeping a parrot, a proverbially ungrateful bird*). ³*Padm.*, *do.*, 596, 1, जो पै जाके नयन रस, हिरदे प्रेम अँगूर, He who has the happiness of love in his heart, shows the passion of it in the eyes (*i.e., as juice or* रस *comes from grapes, so if the fruit is in the heart, the juice will be in the eyes*); *ib.*, *ch.* 258, 5, किमि कमलहिँ भा प्रेम अँगूरू, जो पै गहन लेइ दिन सूरू, How can the lotus have the happiness of love, seeing that it can keep possession of the sun only during the day?

[*Prs.*, انگور *aṅgūr; the same in all Gds.; in the second sense perhaps connected with Skr.* अङ्कुर.]

अँगूर *ăgūr* (2), (*poet.* अँगूरू *ăgūrū*), *the same as* अँकूर *ăkūr, q.v.* **Exam.**, *Padm.*, *ch.* 656, 7, रहै न दुख कर मूल अँगूरू, Neither the roots nor the shoots of grief remain; *ib.*, *ch.* 685, 3, नयन जो कुमुदिनि लीन्ह अँगूरू, Her eyes, which were (*like*) water lilies, took (*new*) shoots.

[*S.* अँगूर (*S. Dy.*, *p.* 55). *Compare the P. and Ml.*, अँगूरी (*Ml. Gy.*).]

अंगूरा ãgūrā, *poet. for* आँगूर ãgūr (1), *q.v.*

अंगूरी ãgūrī, **Any.**, *adj. com. gen.*, of *or* belonging to the grape. **Exam.**, *Prov.*, (*Hd. Dy.*), गधा कैं आँगूरी बाग, A vineyard for a donkey!
[*Prs.* انگوری aŋgūrī.]

अंगूरू ãgūrū, *poet. for* आँगूर ãgūr (1) *and* (2), *q.v.*

अगे *age*, आँगे ãge, गे ge, गै gaĩ, **Tbh.**, *voc. ptc.*, *used for the purpose of calling to, or addressing females, and in Mg. also, inferiors of either sex*, Ho! hulloa! hark! oh! (*Mth. Gr.* § 24). **Comp.**, अगे माई *or* अगे मैयो, (*lit.* O Mother!) oh dear, dear me, mercy on us, *etc.* **Exam.**, *Mag.* 4, अगे, सूतल रहिऐ सुगवा लाली गे पलँगिया जेकरे सुगवा बैठी आँचरा फारे, Hark, I was sleeping, O parrot, on a red couch, dear, on which thou, parrot, wast sitting and tearing my bosom-cloth; *ib.*, 75, अगे, हुमुकि हुमुकि चाल चलै न, टैंगिछिया, आँचरा झलपवा देबे आए, Ho, do not walk about with such airs, fine lady, coquetting with your bosom cloth! *ib.*, 78, ओही कारनवाँ, गे गोरिखो, काहे गो नयनवाँ चुवे लोर, Why then, O fair lady, do on that account tears drop from your eyes? *ib.*, 82, ओही आँगवा कारनवाँ, गे गोरिखो, काहे छोड़े घरवा गो दुआर, For the sake of that person, O fair lady, why did you leave the door of your house? *Bid.* 82, 1, आँगे माए प्रबल जमत बर लेलैंह, O dear, such a wilful bridegroom have you brought! *Hb.* ii, 62, आँगे माँए आँगे माँए अद्भुत भेल, Dear me, dear me, a miracle has happened!

[*Derivation doubtful; perhaps connected with Skr.* अये, *Pr.* अम्मे; *cf. English vulgar* 'get along.' *Molesworth* (*M. Dy.*) *suggests a derivation from Skr.* अम्बा mother, *Haughton* (*Bg. Dy.*), *from Skr.* अघो, *voc. of* अघवत् sinful; *the latter seems very improbable, as the Bg.* अगो *or* गो *is said to be used in respectful address.—Bg. and O.* अगो, गो (*respectful*); *H.* अगे, गे; *M.* अगे, अगो, गे, गो (*plur.* अगा).]

अंगेड़ीहा ãgeṛīhā, **Tbh.**, *subst. m.*, (*Bh.*), the man who is engaged at a sugar-mill to cut the standing sugar-cane, (*Grs.* § 292).

[*Probably a contraction of* आँगेड़ *and the sec. der. suff.* वाहा, *as in* आँगरवाह, *q.v.*]

अंगेछ ãgēchh, (*Mg.*), (*pr. pts.* आँगेछैत ãgēchhait; आँगेछल ãgēchhal; आँगेछब ãgēchhab; आँगेछे ãgēchhe). **Tbh.**, *v. tr.*, [1] to accept; *hence* [2] bear, endure. **Exam.**, [2] (*Mg. song in Hd. Dy.*) सौतिन, बिरहिया न अगेछवौं रे को, O co-wife, I will not endure my husband's absence. *See* √आँगेज ãgēj, √आँगव ãgaw, √आँगिर ãgir.

[*The root, as shown by its synonyms, is clearly a derivative of Skr.* अङ्ग, *though the origin of its latter portion is obscure. It may perhaps be traced to Skr.* स्थित *or* अवस्थित, placed, abiding in, *similarly to* आँगवेच, *q.v.*]

अंगेज ãgēj, (*pr. pts.* आँगेजैत ãgejait; आँगेजल ãgējal; आँगेजब ãgējab; आँगेजै ãgējai), **Tbh.**, *v. tr.*, [1] to accept; *hence* [2] to bear, endure. **Exam.**, [2] *Bij.*, *ll.* 851-853, एतन्हे मैं तोहर बकुलैछा? आँति बड़ो छनिये ओयन्या सुमरवा, उहाँ कैसे आँगेजब? Are you distressed at so little as this? When the hour of fighting with weapons comes, then how will you bear it? *See* √आँगेछ ãgēchh, √आँगव ãgaw, √आँगिर ãgir.

[*This is clearly a derivative of Skr.* अङ्ग, *like* √अङ्गीकृ. *It is probably a der. root, from Skr.* अङ्गीकार्य acceptable, endurable; *hence Skr.* *√अङ्गीकार्यि, *Pr.* अंगीअज्जि, *Gḍ.* √आँगेज. *It is usually explained to be a hybrid, Persian-Hindī, root* (*e.g., by Shakespear, Fallon*), *and connected with Prs.* انگیختن aŋgēkhtan to excite, انگیز aŋgēz excited. *But as the meaning of the Prs. and Gḍ. words are so entirely different, there is probably no direct connexion between them. It also occurs in P., M., and H.*]

अंगेठा ãgēṭhā, **Tbh.**, *subst. m.*, *Mg. and Bn. for* आँगैठा ãgaiṭhā, *q.v.* (*Grs.* §§ 529, 567.)

अंगेठी ãgēṭhī (1), **Tbh.**, *feminine of the preceding*; *Mg. and Bh. for* आँगैठी ãgaiṭhī, *q.v.* (*Grs.* §§ 567, 1409).

अंगेठी ãgēṭhī (2), (*Mg.*), the action of stretching the arms, as in yawning (*B. Gr.*, III (*Mg.*), *App.* II).

[*A comp. of* अङ्ग *and* √ऐंठ, a twisting of the limbs; *cf.* आँगन्मड़ी.]

अगेँड़ agẽṛ, आँगेर ãgēr, (*str. f.* आँगेड़ा ãgēṛā *or* आँगेरा ãgērā), **Tbh.**, *subst. m.*, *Mg. and Bh.*, [1] the green leaves at the top with the upper part of the sugar-cane, *cut up for seed or fodder*, (*Grs.* §§ 1008, 1010, 1012, 1144; *for synonyms, see* अगौन agīn); [2] the stalk of sugar-cane (*a synonym of* आँगारी ãgārī *and* आँगेरी ãgērī, *q.v.*; *in this sense the word appears to occur only in certain compounds, such as* आँगेरबन्धू ãgēr'bandhū, आँगरवाह ãgar'wāh, आँगरवार ãgar'wār).

[*With the first meaning, the word is probably a corruption of Skr.* अग्रपत्र, *as explained under* अगन्ही, *q.v. With the second meaning the word is probably a corruption of Skr.* अङ्गपर्व, having limbs *or* joints, *this being a striking feature of the sugar-cane. In Pr. the two words would be represented respectively by* अग्गवत्त *and* अंगवव्व, *etc.*; *and as in Pr. the first member of a double consonant has a tendency to change into a nasal* (*see Hēm.* i, 26), *the two words would naturally tend, in the course of evolution, to be confused,—a state of things which now actually obtains in Bihārī. It may be added that this result would be assisted by the fact that, both in Pr. and in Gḍ., there are identical sets of pleon.* (*or svārthe*) *and sec. der.* (*or bhave*) *suffixes* (*see Hēm.* ii, 163, 164, *and Gḍ. Gr.* §§ 209, 241, 245, 249), *which are equally corruptions of the Skr. word* कर्म *or* कृत. *Thus in* अँगारी *or* अँगेरी *in the sense of* the upper part of the sugar-cane *the suff.* आरी *and* एरी *are pleon., while in the sense of* sugar-cane, *the same suff. are sec. der. It may be added that in the form* अँगारी (*properly representing Skr.* अङ्गपर्विका having joints) *the word has been reintroduced into Sanskrit and sanskritised into* अङ्गारिका, *in which latter form the word is in Skr. dictionaries erroneously connected with Skr.* अङ्गार charcoal.]

अंगेरबन्धू ā̃gēr'bandhū, **Tbh.**, *subst. m., Mg. for* अगरबन्धू agar'bandhū, *q.v.* (*Grs.* §§ 1010).

[*A compound of* अँगेर *or* अँगेरु, *q.v., and* बन्धू. *See the remarks under* अगरबन्धू.]

अंगेरा ā̃gērā, **Tbh.**, *subst. m., Mg., str. f. of* अँगेर ā̃gēr *or* अँगेँरु agẽr, *q.v.* (*Grs.* §§ 1008, 1010, 1012).

अंगेरी ā̃gērī, **Tbh.**, *subst. f., Mg., fem. of the preceding* (*Grs.* §§ 1010, 1012).

अगेला agēlā, **Tbh.**, *subst. m.*, [1]front, foremost (*a synonym of* अगिला agilā, *q.v.*); [2]the gleanings and refuse grain on a threshing-floor (*Cr. p.* 53), *see synonyms under* अगवार ag'wār; [3](*scl.* चौरी) the uppermost bangle on the arm (*synonym* अगुआ aguā, *q.v., Grs.* § 558). **Exam.**, [1]अगेला के खूँटा, the front peg, *a peg at the extreme end of the loom to which the woof is tied by a string* (*Grs.* § 363, 11).

[*Derivation see under* अगाड़ी.]

अगेह agēh, (*poet.* अगेहा agēhā), **Tbh.**, *adj.* without a home or house, a vagabond. **Exam.**, *Rām. Ba., ch.* 89, 6, अकुल अगेह दिगम्बर ब्याली, (*Sib is*) casteless, houseless, naked, and covered with snakes; *ib., ch.* 166, 4, तुम सम अधन भिखारि अगेहा, A poor, homeless beggar such as you.

[*Skr.* अगृह:, *Pr.* अगिहो *or* अगेहो, *B.* अगेह, *and so possibly in all Gḍs. The prākritic form* गेह house *exists, however, also in Skr.*]

अगेहि agēhi, (*subst. f.* अगेहिनि agēhinī), *Mth. and poet. for* अगेही agēhī, *q.v.*

अगेही agēhī, **Tbh.**, *adj. com. gen.*, (*subst. f.* अगेहिनी agehinī) houseless, homeless. **Exam.**, *Dōh.* तुलसी, प्रीति प्रतीत सौं राम नाम जप जागु किये, होय बिधि दाहिनो, देय अगेहो भागु, Tul'sī Dās (*says*), if with love and faith Rām's name be unremittingly (*lit.* wakefully) repeated, the Creator, becoming favorably inclined, gives luck to the homeless.

[*Skr.* अगृही, *Pā. and Pr.* अगिही *or* अगेही (*Bhag., p.* 183). *Skr. admits also the prākritic form* अगेही.]

अंगैठा ā̃gạiṭhā, (*Mg. and Bh.*) अँगेठा ā̃gēṭhā, **Tbh.**, *subst. m.*, an iron or earthen moveable fireplace or furnace, *used by jewellers, glassmakers, etc.* (*Grs.* §§ 529, 1247).

[*Skr.* अग्निष्ठ *or* (*with pleon.* क) अग्निष्ठका, *Pr.* अग्गिट्ठओ *or* अग्गोट्ठओ (*cf. Hēm.* i, 85), *Ap. Pr.* अग्गिट्ठउ (*Hēm.* iv, 429) *or* अग्गोट्ठउ, *hence B.* अँगेठा, (*with compensatory nasal, see Hēm.* i, 26). *The change of* ए *to* ऐ *in the form* अँगैठा *is probably a mere provincialism. Bg. has* आँगठा *or* आँगठ, *P.* अगीठा, *Kn.* आगुठँ *or* आगुठेंया *or* आगठँ *neut.*]

अंगैठी ā̃gạiṭhī (1), (*Mg. and Bh.*) अँगेठी ā̃gēṭhī, **Tbh.**, *the feminine of the preceding word*, [1]the iron or earthen portable fireplace or chafing-dish in a native Indian house (*Grs.* § 1247); *hence tech.* [2]the furnace of a jeweller or glassmaker, *etc.* (*cf. Grs.* § 567); [3]a flower-pot (*from its resemblance to a portable furnace*).

[*M. has* आगठी *or* अगठी, *meaning both* a fire-pot *and* a small fire (*cf. M.* अँगुठा *and* अँगठा); *O.* अँगठि; *S.* आगोठी; *P.* अँगीठी.]

अंगैठी ā̃gạiṭhī (2), **Tbh.**, *subst. f., the same as* अँगेठी ā̃gēṭhī (2), *q.v.*

अगैरा agạirā, **Tbh.**, *subst. m.*, a landlord's due, *consisting of the first sheaves of the tenant's crop.* (*Cr. p.* 89, *and Wils.*). *See* अँगऊँ ā̃gaū̃ *and* अगवार ag'wār.

[*Derivation see under* अगाड़ी.]

अगोरनिहार agor'nihār, **Tbh.**, *subst. m.*, a field watchman (*Grs.* § 870). *See* अगोर agōr (2).

[*Prop. verbal noun of* √अगोर, *q.v.*]

अगोरिया agoriyā (1), **Tbh.**, *subst. f., lg. f. of* अगोरी agōrī (1), *q.v.* (*Grs.* § 870).

अगोरिया agoriyā (2), **Tbh.**, *subst. m., lg. f. of* अगोरी agōrī (2), *q.v.* (*Grs.* § 870).

अगोरैया agorạiyā, **Tbh.**, *subst. m, red. f. of* अगोरी agōrī (2), *q.v.* (*Cr. p.* 50, *Ell. vol.* II, *p.* 210).

अगोचर agōchar, **Ts.**, *adj. com. gen.*, [1] what is beyond the reach of any human faculty *or* activity, *such as sensation, thought, action, speech, etc.*, imperceptible, incomprehensible, indescribable; *hence* [2] *used as an epithet of God.* **Exam.**, [1] *Dōh.* 199, बाम-सरूप तुम्हार बचन अगोचर बुद्धि पर, Like Bām (*i.e. Saraswati*) is thy speech, incomprehensible, past understanding; *Bin.* 203, तेरहि तीनि अवस्था तजहु, भजहु भगवन्त, मन क्रम बचन अगोचर, व्यापक व्याप्य अनन्त, Abandon the three states (*i.e. waking, dreaming, sleeping*) of thirteen kinds and worship the Most High (*who is*) beyond the reach of thought, act, and speech, who pervades the whole world and is eternal; *Rām., Bā., ch.* 215, 5, मन क्रम बचन अगोचर जोई, दसरथ अजिर बिचर प्रभु सोई, The Lord, who is beyond the reach of thought, act, and speech, He plays in Das'rath's courtyard; *ib., chh.* 43, 4, मन बुद्धि बर-बानी अगोचर, प्रगट कबि कैसे करै, (*The mutual love of Sitā and Rām*) exceeds sense, thought, and speech: how can the poet express it? *ib., A., ch.* 119, 7, राम लखन सिय प्रीति सुहाई बचन अगोचर, किमि कहि जाई, The charm of the (*mutual*) love of Rām, Lakhan, and Sita is beyond all telling: how can it be declared? *ib., ch.* 105, 4, मुनि रघुबीर परस्पर नवहीं, बचन अगोचर सुख अनुभवहीं, The sage (*i.e. Bharadwāj*) and Raghubir (*i.e. Rām*) bow to one another, and experience pleasure beyond telling. [2] *Rām., Ar., chh.* 9, 5, प्रभुम् अप्रमेयम् अनादिम् अजम् अव्यक्तम् एकम् अगोचरम् (*Skr., acc. sing. masc.*), The Mighty, Unmeasurable, Eternal, Unborn, Undivisible, One, Incomprehensible (*God*); *Misc.* 28, अगम अगोचर लीला-धारी सो राधा बस कुंज-बिहारी, (*Vishnu*) the incomprehensible and imperceptible—he, under the influence of Radhā, engages in sports and takes his pleasure in bowers.

(*The word is usually said to mean* beyond the reach of the senses, *but its meaning is far more general (see Skr. Dy., s.v.), as shown by the examples.*)

[*Skr.* अ *not* + गोचर accessible, attainable. *As above in all Gds.*]

अँगोछा āgōchhā, *the same as* अँगौछा āgauchhā, *q.v.* (*Grs.* § 733.)

अँगोट āgōt, **Tbh.**, *subst. f.*, the form, mould, contour of the body, personal appearance. *See* अँगलेख āg'lēch.

[*For derivation see the remarks under* अँगलेख. *H. has* अँगोट, *M.* अँगवठा *or* अँगवडा *or* अंगठा, *also* अँगठेवण, अँगलठ, अँगओट. *Not noticed in the other Gds.*]

अगोत agōt, (*poet.* अगोता agōtā), *adj. com. gen., the same as* अगिला agilā, *q.v.* **Exam.**, [2] *Padm., ch.* 696, 5, बाजन बाजहिं, होय अगोता (*fem.*) दोउ कन्त ले चाहैं सोता, The music sounds, and both (*the two queens Nāg'mati and Padmāvati*) stand in front (*of the dead king*) and desire to take their husband to sleep, (*i.e., to be bound with his corpse to be burnt*).

[*This word is merely another and more original form of* अगूत *or* अगुतौ *or* अगता, *q.v., being a contr. of Pr.* अग्गवत्तो, *Skr.* अग्रवर्तः. *See the remarks under* अगाड़ी.]

अगोर agōr (1), (*str. f.* अगोरा agōrā), **Tbh.**, *subst. m.*, an advance of pay to labourers (*Cr., p.* 87). *For synonyms see* अगवार ag'war.

[*For derivation, see remarks under* अगाड़ी. *The Gip. has* agor *in the original sense of* in front.]

अगोर agōr (2), (*str. f.* अगोरा agōrā), **Tbh.**, *subst. m.*, [1] *con.*, a watchman, guard, one who watches over crops (*Grs.* § 870); [2] *abs.*, watching, keeping guard, a watching for, waiting for, expectancy (*Ās. Gy.*). **Exam.**, [1] *Coll.*, (*Bh.*), ओकरा खेत के अगोर के किछु काम नहिंखे, काहे कि ओकरा डर सँ केहु एको दाना ना छुए, There is no use in having a watchman for his field, for through fear of him no one dare touch a single grain belonging to him. [2] *Coll.*, (*Bh.*), तोहार अगोरा होत बा, *lit.* there is a watching for you, *i.e., you are being waited for.*

[*Probably a contraction of the older form* अगऊँव, *q.v., or it may be identical with* अगोर (1), *q.v. In any case it clearly seems to be a derivative of the Skr.* अग्र *or* अग्रा, *which admits the figurative meaning of* being forward, sharp, keen, intent upon *or* attentive to. *Accordingly the Skr. original might be* अग्रमुख *or* अग्रपरः.]

अगोर agōr, (*pr. pts.* अगोरैत agorait, *Bh.* अगोरत agōrat, अगोरित agōrit; अगोरल agōral; अगोरब agōrab; अगोरै agōrai; *verbal noun* अगोर्‌निहार agor'nihār), **Tbh.**, *v. intr.*, [1] to watch, to keep guard; [2] to be in attendance (*as a servant*). **Phr.**, अगोर-बटार, *subst. f.*, a division of the crop on the threshing-floor (*Grs.* §§ 914, 1470, 2; *lit.* division after having watched, अगोर *being the conj. part.; so called because the crop is watched till the division; see also Wil. s.v., for a different meaning*). **Exam.**, [1] *Hb.* iii, 16, की फल भेल सोचि, एतेक अगोरि, What has been the result, after my having watched so much? *Bid.* 37, 4, मालति रसि चलि भार, अगोरथि पुनु रति रङ्गक चाहि, Like a bee roaming over the jasmin, he watches in hope of (*having*) again the pleasures of love. [2] *Padm., ch.* 595, 5, कुँवरि सहस दुइ बार अगोरे, दुहु दिस पँवर ठाढ़ कर जोरे, Two thousand maidens were in attendance at the door, and on both sides janitors stood with joined hands.

[*This is a der. root formed from* अगोर (2). *H. has both* √अगिल *and* √अगोर. *It does not seem to occur in the other Gḍs.*]

अंगोर *ãgōr* (1), **Tbh.**, *subst. f.*, the leafy top of the sugar-cane (*Āz. Gy.*) *See synonyms under* अगोन *agin.*

[*The word is probably identical in origin with* अगोर (1), *see the remarks under* अगाड़ी *and* अगौड़. *It may, however, also be a modification of Skr.* अङ्कुर, *in which the element* कु *is in the Gḍs. apt to change to* गो; *see the remarks under* अंगोरा *and* अंकुरा. *In the former case the anunāsik would be due to compensation for an original conjunct* ग्र; *in the latter case, to the original conj.* ङ्क. *Perhaps the form of the word has been influenced by both possibilities.*]

अंगोर *ãgōr* (2), *the same as* इंगोर *ĩgōr, q.v. See* अंगार *ãgār.*

अगोर-बटाई *agōr'baṭāi*, **Tbh.**, *subst. f., see under* √अगोर *agōr.*

अगोरा *agōrā*, *subst. m., str. f. of* अगोर *agōr* (1) *and* (2), *q.v.* (*Grs.* § 870.)

अगोरी *agōrī* (1), **Tbh.**, *subst. f.*, the watching of crops (*Grs.* § 870). *See* अगोर *agōr* (2).

[*An abs. noun derived from the concrete* अगोर (2), *by means of the Prs. suff.* ई.]

अगोरी *agōrī* (2), **Tbh.**, *subst. m.*, a field-watchman. *See* अगोर *agōr*, अगोरिया *agoriyā.*

[*A concrete noun derived from the abs.* अगोर (2), *by means of the Gḍ. suff.* ई. *See Gḍ. Gr.* § 252.]

अंगोरी *ãgōrī*, **Tbh.**, *subst. f., the same as* अंगोर *ãgōr* (1), *q.v.* (*Cr., p.* 58.) *See* अंगारी *ãgārī and* अंगेरी *ãgērī.*

[*Prop. str. f. of* अंगोरि *ãgōri, the original form of* अंगोर (1), *q.v.*]

अंगोरिया *ãgauriyā*, **Tbh.**, *subst. m.*, (*W. Bh.*), *a contraction of* अंगन्वरिया *ãg'wariyā, q.v.* (*Wil. s.v., and Cr., p.* 47.)

अगौं *agaũ*, **Tbh.**, *subst. m., a synonym of* अगन्वर *ag'bar, q.v.* (*Grs.* § 1203.) *See* अंगाँऊँ *ãgāũ.*

[*A derivative of Skr.* अग्र, *Pr.* अग्ग, *probably containing the pleon. suff.* आप (आपि). *The Ml. equivalent is* अंगवो (*Ml. Gy.*).]

अंगौंआ *ãgaũā*, अंगौंआँ *ãgaũã*, **Tbh.**, *subst. m., str. f. of* अगौं *agaũ, q.v.* (*Grs.* § 1203.)

अंगौंग *ãgaũg*, (*str. f.* अंगौंगा *ãgaũgā*), **Tbh.**, *subst. m.*, (*W. Bh.*), *a synonym of* अगौं *agaũ, q.v.* (*Wil., and Cr., p.* 88.)

[*Apparently a reduplication of* अगौं, *q.v.*]

अंगौछा *ãgaüchhā*, अंगोछा *ãgōchhā*, (*Bh.*) अंगन्वछा *ãg'wachhā*, **Tbh.**, *subst. m.*, a cloth worn by the Hindūs while bathing and used for drying the body afterwards, a towel (*Grs.* § 733). **Exam.**, *Coll.* (*Bh.*), हमार अंगौछा हेरा गेल, देह पोंछे में बड़ा दिक बाड़ीं, I have lost my towel, and feel great inconvenience in drying my body. *See* गमछा *gam'chhā.*

(*Musalmāns call this bathing-cloth* लुङ्गी *or* लूंगी.)

[*Skr.* अङ्गप्रोञ्छः, *Pr.* अंगावच्छो, *hence Bh.* अंगवछा *and contr.* अंगौछा *or* अंगोछा. *H. and P. have* अंगोछा, *S.* अंगोछो, *M.* अंगोछा *or* अंगछा, *also tats.* अंगोछन *or* आंगोछन *or* अङ्गपुछ *or* अंगोछी, *Ksh.* अंगोछा; *but Bg. has* गामछा, *O.* गामछा (*O. Vy.*) *or* गामुछा (*O. Dy.*), *A.* गामोछा, *K.* गोंछा, *which agree with B.* गमछा, *q.v. The M. tats. forms seem to suggest that possibly the tadbh. forms too go back to the Skr.* अङ्गप्रोञ्छनम् *or* (*with pleon.* क) अङ्गप्रोञ्छनकम्. *In that case the change of* च *into* च्छ *or* छ *is probably to be explained by the transposition of* च *into* श्च, *analogous to the Mg. Pr. transposition of* च *into* श्च (*Hēm.* iv, 297). *The Pr. has* अंगुच्छी a veil (*Hēm. Dy., vs.* 6, = *Skr.* शिरोऽवगुण्ठनम्), *perhaps from Skr.* अग्र *and* वस्त्रिका.]

अंगौछी *ãgaüchhī*, **Tbh.**, *subst. fem. of the preceding word, with a diminutive sense*, a smaller kind of bathing-cloth, handkerchief (*Grs.* § 733). **Exam.**, *Coll.* (*Bh.*), लेडिकन के बजार से अंगौछी बनावे के लूगा कीन के लावऽ, Go to market and buy some cloth to make towels for the children.

अगौड़ा *agaüṛā* = अगौरा *agaürā, q.v.*

अगौड़ी *agaüṛī* (*Grs.* § 1186) = अगौरी *agaürī, q.v.*

अगौर *agaür*, **Tbh.**, *subst. m.*, [1]an advance of rent paid by land-cultivators (*asāmīs*) to landowners (*zamīndārs*) in the months of Jēṭh and Akhāṛh, (*Ell., vol.* II, *p.* 3); [2]*the same as* अगोर *agōr* (1), *q.v. For synonyms see* अगन्वड़ *ag'waṛ.*

[*Derivation see under* अगाड़ी. *H. has* अगोर.]

अगौरा *agaürā*, अगौड़ा *agaüṛā*, **Tbh.**, *subst. m.*, the leaves at the top and upper part of a sugar-cane (*Cr., p.* 75). *See synonyms under* अगोन *agin.*

[*Derivation see under* अगउरी. *H. has* अगौरा, अगोरा, गोरा, अगौरा, ओरा (*see Hd. Dy., p.* 108).]

अगौरी *agāuri*, अगौरी *agāuri*, **Tbh.**, *subst. f.*, [1]*the same as* अगौर *agāur*, *q.v.*; [2]advances to agricultural labourers (*Grs.* §§ 844, 1186). *See synonyms under* अगवार *ag'war*.

[*Derivation see under* अगउरी.]

अग्नि *agni*, *unphon. tats. form for* अगनि *agani*, *q.v.*

अग्य॰ *agy'*, **Ts.**, *adj.*, *com. gen.*, (*subst. f.* अग्या *agyā*), [1]unknowing, ignorant; *hence* [2]stupid, silly. **Exam.**, [1]*Bin.* 112, केशव, कारन कवन, गोसाईं, जेंहि, अपराध असाधु जानि, मोहिं तज्यो अग्य की नाईं, O holy Kēsab, what is the reason that, considering me defiled by sin, you abandon me as if you were ignorant (*of my supplications*). [2]*Rām.*, *Bā.*, *ch.* 62, 2, खोजत सो कि अग्य (*fem.*) इव नारी, He is searching about like a silly woman; *ib.*, *Ln.*, *do.* 81, 2, राम विरोध विजय चाहत, सठ हठ-बस अति अग्य, In opposition to Ram, the obstinate and stupid knave (*i.e. Rāban*) desires victory.

(*The word is almost exclusively used with the second meaning.*)

[*Skr.* अज्ञः; *as above in all Gds., with the pronunciation peculiar to each language; see art.* ज्ञ. *The tadbh. form* अन *occurs in Padm. ch.* 186, 6, (अन रानी foolish queen); *in Pr. its tadbh. form is rare. The long form* अयुध (*Skr.* अज्ञक) *occurs in Sapt., vs.* 184; *the short form has not been noted hitherto.*]

अग्यता *agyatā*, **Ts.**, *subst. f.*, ignorance, stupidity, folly. **Exam.**, *Rām.*, *Ut.*, *ch.* 35, 6, तज्ञ चिन्मय अग्यता भञ्जन, The All-wise, the All-generous, the Destroyer of ignorance.

[*Skr.* अज्ञता; *as above in all Gds., with the pronunciation peculiar to each language; see art.* ज्ञ.]

अग्या *agyā*, आग्या *āgyā*, **Ts.**, *subst. f.*, [1]a command, order, precept, injunction; [2](*in polite language*) permission, leave. **Comp.**, अग्या-कार, *adj.*, performing orders, *hence* a servant; अग्या-कारक, *adj.*, making orders, *hence* a commander, ruler, chief; अग्या-कारि *or* अग्या-कारी, *adj.*, acting according to orders, *hence* an obedient person; अग्याधीन (= अग्या-आधीन), *adj.*, submissive to orders, *hence* a manageable person; अग्यानुवर्ति *or* अग्यानुवर्ती (= अग्या-अनु॰), *adj.*, attentive to orders, obedient; अग्यानुसारी (= अग्या-अनु॰), *adj.*, following orders, obedient; अग्या-पत्र, *subst. m.*, written orders; अग्या-पाल *or* अग्या-पालक, *adj.*, law-abiding, obedient; अग्या-पालन, *subst. m.*, observance of orders, obedience; अग्या-विहीन, *adj.*, without orders, without obtaining leave; अग्या-भङ्ग, *subst. m.*, law-breaking, disobedience, insubordination; अग्या-भङ्गी, *adj.*, law-breaking, disobedient, insubordinate; अग्या-भञ्जक, *adj.*, *same as* अग्या-भङ्गी; अग्या-उल्लङ्घन, *subst. m.*, *same as* अग्या-भङ्ग; अग्या-उल्लङ्घनकारी, *adj.*, *same as* अग्या-भङ्गी. **Phr.**, अग्या करब (*lit.* to make an order), to rule, hold sway, command, (*with gen. of the thing ordered*) to command to do a thing; अग्या देब (*with gen. of the thing ordered*), to give the order to do a thing; अग्या पालब, to obey orders. **Exam.**, [1]*Rām.*, *Bā.*, *ch.* 187, 4, एहि बिधि सब ही अग्या दीन्हा, In this wise he gave orders to all; *ib.*, *A.*, *ch.* 290, 4, अग्या सम न सुसाहिब सेवा, सो प्रसाद जन पावै, देवा, There is no service equal to (*that of obeying*) the orders of a kind master, therefore let your servant, sire, obtain the favour (*of an order from you*); *ib.*, *Ki.*, *do.* 25, 1, बदरी बन कहँ सो गई, प्रभु अग्या धरि सीस, She (*i.e. Swayamprabhā*) went to the Bad'ri forest, taking upon her head (*i.e. in obedience to*) the Lord's command; *Gīt.*, *A.* 71, 2, मेटह कुल कलङ्क, कोसल-पति, अग्या देहु नाथ मोहि बन की, Wipe off the stain of (*our royal*) family, O Kōsal'pati (*i.e. Das'rath*), and give me orders, sire, (*to go*) to the forest. [2]*Coll.* (*Bh.*), आप के अग्या पा, Have I permission to go? *Padm.*, *ch.* 670, 6, एक घड़ी जौं अग्या पाऊँ, राजा सौंपि मन्दिर महँ जाऊँ, If I obtain leave for but one half-hour, I will make (*the keys*) over to the king and come to the temple; *also Padm.*, *ch.* 672, 1; *Mth. Rām.*, *Su.*, 55, 2, अग्या-विहीन बहु तोड़ि फल लैले, Without obtaining leave you plucked and ate much fruit.

(*The form* अग्या *agyā represents the common, every-day pronunciation; the pronunciation* आग्या *āgyā also occurs, but is considered affected and stylish. The spelling with a short initial* अ *is the usual one in literature, and though the spelling with initial* आ *does occasionally occur (e.g., in the Rām. four times, Bā., ch.* 87, 4; 238, 6; 362, 6; *A., ch.* 290, 4), *there can be little doubt but that it should be uniformly* अग्या. *Metrically it makes no difference, because the conj. cons.* ग्य *gy causes 'positional length' of the preceding vowel. The spelling* अज्ञा *or* आज्ञा, *with the conj.* ज्ञ *jñ, is a mere unphon. affectation.*)

[*Skr.* आज्ञा; *the word occurs in all Gds., with the pronunciation peculiar to each language, on which subject see the article on* ज्ञ. *The Pr. tadbh. form is* आणा (*Mg. Pr., cf. Hēm.* iv, 293) *or* अणा (*Bhag., p.* 379) *or* आणा (*Hēm.* ii, 83), *which still survives in B.* आन, *q.v. The alternative Pr. tadbh. form* अण्णा (*Hēm.* ii, 83) *does not survive.*]

अग्यात *agyāt*, (*poet.* अग्याता *agyātā*), **Ts.**, (I) *adj.*, *com. gen.*, (*subst. f.* अग्याता *agyātā*), unknown, unfamiliar. **Exam.**, *Mth. Rām.*, *Ki.*, 14, 23, राम अलखक आरा पाय

हिय अग्यान रातिं दिनि जाय, You have got undisturbed rule and Tārā, days and nights have passed unbeknown to you; *ib.*, *Bā.*, 40, 17, एको शाख नहिं तनि अग्यान, Not a single branch of science was unfamiliar to them.

(II) *adv.*, ignorantly, thoughtlessly. **Exam.**, *Rām.*, *Bā.*, *ch.* 293, 6, बहुविधि बड़ाम कहेउँ अग्याना, In my ignorance, I have said much that was unseemly.

[*Skr.* अज्ञानात्; *as above in all Gḍs.*, *with the pronunciation peculiar to each; see art.* ग्य.]

अग्यान *agyān*, (*poet.* अग्याना *agyānā*, *old. dir.* अग्यानु *agyānu*, *poet.* अग्यानू *agyānū*), **Ts.**, (I) *subst. m.*, [1]want of knowledge, ignorance; *hence* [2]stupidity, folly; *espec.* [3]*phil. tech.*, spiritual error, delusion, *preventing the soul from realising its identity with Brahma, causing self to appear a distinct personality, and matter to appear a reality* (*Skr. Dy. W.*); [4]unconsciousness, swooning. **Comp.**, अग्यान-प्रसङ्ग, *adj.*, subject to spiritual error. **Exam.**, [1]*Rām.*, *Bā.*, *ch.* 116, 2, तौ प्रभु हरहु मोर अग्याना, कहि रघुनाथ, कथा बिधि नाना, Therefore, O Lord, remove my ignorance, by telling me in detail the story of Raghunāth (*i.e.* *Rām*). [2]*Rām.*, *Bā.*, *ch.* 64, 1, मैं सङ्कर कर कहा न माना, निज अग्यान राम पहँ आना, I would not accept the advice of Saṇkar, (*but*) in my folly went to Rām; *Dōh.* 490, बड़ मुख, बड़ चहि, बचन बड़, बड़ ब्यवहार-अवचार; इन को भलो मनाइबो, यह अग्यान अपार, Having many faces (*i.e. showing favours without discrimination*), many desires, much talk, many ways and practices; to consider (*all*) these to be good; that is unparalleled folly. [3]*Bin.* 48, भक्त हिरिदि भवन अग्यान तम हारिनी, (*The worship of Rām is*) a remover of the blindness of spiritual error which resides in the heart of believers; *ib.*, 197, सुनिय नाना पुरान मिटत नहि अग्यान, पढ़िय न समुझिय जिमि खग कीर, (*Though*) one may hear many a Purān, (*yet*) his spiritual delusion will not vanish, (*because*) like a parrot he recites but does not understand; *Rām.*, *Bā.*, *ch.* 63, 4, सुमिरत जाहि मिटै अग्याना, सोइ सर्वग्य राम भगवाना, Ram, the omniscient god, is he, by the thought of whom spiritual delusion vanishes; *ib.*, *Ut.*, *ch.* 73, 7, हरि बिषयिक अस मोह बिहङ्गा, सपने हु नहि अग्यान-प्रसङ्गा, In this way (*only*), O Garuṛ, can error be ascribed to Hari, never even in dream is he (*really*) subject to spiritual delusion; *ib.*, *do.* 108, 3, क्रोध कि द्वैत-बुधि बिनु, द्वैत कि बिनु अग्यान, Can there be anger without a notion of duality, or duality without spiritual error? *ib.*, *A.*, *ch.* 280, 2, जोग कुजोग, ग्यान अग्यानू, जहँ न राम प्रेम परधानू, Piety becomes impiety, and spiritual knowledge becomes spiritual delusion, where the love of Rām is not paramount. [4]*Mth. Rām.*, *A.*, 18, 3, खिप नृपति अवसा अग्यान, केकइ कठिन बचन सुनि कान, The king fell fainting in a swoon, as he heard with his ears Kēkayi's cruel words; *ib.*, *Ki.*, 10, 62, बालिक हिरदय हनल प्रभु बान, लगइत तनिका भेल अग्यान, The Lord struck Bāli on the heart with an arrow, and as he received (*the blow*), he became unconscious (*lit.*, unconsciousness was to him.)

(II) *adj.*, *com. gen.*, (*subst. f.* अग्याना *agyānā*), ignorant, foolish. **Exam.**, *Rām.*, *Ki.*, *do.* 2, 1, एक मैं मन्द, मोह-बस, कुटिल-हिरदय, अग्यान, In the first place I was foolish, bewildered, perverse of heart and ignorant.

[*Skr.* अज्ञानम् *subst. or* अज्ञान: *adj. As above in all Gḍs.*, *with the pronunciation peculiar to each language; see art.* ग्य.]

अग्यान-पन *agyān'pan*, **Tbh.**, *subst. m.*, a state of ignorance or folly.

[*A hybrid formation from the tats.* अग्यान *with the tadbh. sec. der. suff.* पन; *see Gḍ. Gr.* § 228. *Similarly in all Gḍs.*]

अग्यानि *agyāni*, (*subst. f.* अग्यानिनि *agyānini*), *Mth. and poet. for* अग्यानी *agyānī*, *q.v.*

अग्यानी *agyānī*, **Ts.**, *adj. com. gen.*, (*subst. f.* अग्यानिनी *agyāninī*), ignorant, stupid, foolish. **Exam.**, *Rām*, *Bā.*, *ch.* 124, 1, निज भ्रम नहिँ समुझहिँ अग्यानी, प्रभु पर मोह धरहिँ जड़-प्रानी, Fools do not perceive their own error, but perversely ascribe delusion to the Lord.

[*Skr.* अज्ञानी; *occurring in all Gḍs.*]

अग्यारी *agyārī*, **Tbh.**, *subst. f.*, the act of kindling the fire at the time of devotion by Hindūs. **Exam.**, *Coll.* (*Bh.*), ऊ पूजा करे का बेरा रोज अग्यारी देला, He kindles the sacrificial fire daily at the time of devotion.

[*Skr.* अग्निकारिका; *Pr.* अग्गिआरिआ; *hence B. and H.* अग्यारी; *not noted in other Gḍs.*]

अग्र० *agra*, **Ts.**, *adj.*, *com. gen.*, *and subst.*, (*f.* अग्रा *agrā*), *the same as* अगिला *agilā*, *q.v.* **Comp.**, अग्र-गामी, *adj.*, preceding; *subst.*, a forerunner, predecessor; अग्र-ग्रास, *subst. m.*, the first mouthful *or* morsel; अग्र-ज (*subst. f.* अग्र-जा), *adj.*, of prior birth, first-born (*Sat.* vi, 18), *subst.*, an elder brother (*or* sister); अग्र-दास, *subst. m.*, *the name of a poet*, *see* अगर-दास; अग्र-भाग, *subst. m.*, the first, chief, front, *or* foremost part *of anything*; अग्र-सर (*subst. f.* °सरा *or* °सरी,), *adj.*, preceding; *subst.*, a chief, leader, guide; अग्र-सोच, *subst. m.*, foresight, forethought, providence, precaution; अग्र-सोची, *adj.*, provident, cautious; *subst.*, one endued with foresight. **Phr.**, अग्र-गामी सेना, the advanced guard of an army; अगे *loc. sg.*, before; moreover, further. **Exam.**, (*of adj.*), *Ram.*, *Ba.*, *ch.* 241, 8, चली अग करि प्रिय सखि सोई, She went, making her beloved friend lead the way; *Krish.* 81, बाल-भाव बहुवरति भरति द्विग अग अम्बुअन थाने, After the manner of a child, with her eyes full (*of tears*), she draws her clothes in front of them; *Git.*, *Ln.* 1, 9, बेगु मिलु सँगि कुसल सारद सिय सहित अग कर मोहि, तुलसि-दास प्रभु सरन सब्द सुनि अभय करैंगे तोहि, (*Mandōdari says to Rāban*) Come quickly and meet him (*i.e. Rām*) with a request for quarter, taking Sītā with you and putting her in front of me, (*then*)—so Tul'sī Dās (*says*)—the Lord, hearing the word 'saran' (*i.e.* quarter), will put you out of fear. (*Of subst.*), *Krish.* 313, अगहन अग सनेह स्याम बस, को पतिया पहुँचारो के जाई, In Ag'han I am under the influence of my love to my husband Syām; who will take my letter (*to him*)? *Sat.* vi, 18, तुलसी पोत बिना नहीं कछु रचित सुगम व्यवहार, तातें ते अगज भयो; सब बिधि तेहि परचार, Tul'sī Dās (*says*), without sons (*i.e. actions*) no business can be done; therefore they are of prior birth (*or* existence); this is altogether evident; (*the meaning of the riddle is this*: करम, *or the actions of men, being produced by them, are, as it were, their sons; at the same time men's present condition is the result of their* '*karm*' *or actions done in a previous existence, according to the Hindū fatalistic doctrine of metempsychosis; hence* '*karm*' *are both before* (*agraja*) *and after* (*suan*), *from different points of view*).

[*Skr.* अग्रः; *the same in all Gds.*]

अग्राँझ्य॰ *agrãjhy'*, (*unphon.* अग्राह्य *agrāhy'*), **Ts.**, *adj.*, *com. gen.*, not to be received, unacceptable. **Exam.**, *Bw.*, *ch. anon.*, मोहि अग्राँझ पर मोर बिचारा, I cannot accept your decision.

[*Skr.* अग्राह्यः; *possibly occurring in all Gds., with the pronunciation peculiar to each language. The Pr. tadbh. form* अगेज्झो (*see Hēm.* i, 78) *has not survived.*]

अग्रासन *agrāsan*, **Ts.**, *subst. m.*, food offered (*in oblations, sacrifices, &c.*) to the gods. **Exam.**, *Coll.* (*Bh.*), अग्रासन काढ़ देऽ तऽ पीछे जैवँऽ, First lay aside a portion for the gods, and then eat.

[*Skr.*, अग्रासनम् (अग्र + असनम्); *not noted in other Gds., except H., which also has* अगास = *Skr.* अग्राशः.]

अग्राह्य॰ *agrāhy'*, *unphon. for* अग्राँझ्य *agrãjhy'*, *q.v.*

अग्रिम *agrim*, **Ts.**, *adj.*, *com. gen.*, (*subst. f.* अग्रिमा *agrimā*), *the same as* अगिला *agilā*, *q.v.* **Exam.**, [1] *Bw.*, *vs. anon.*, अग्रिम बात सुनी तुम तात, अब पिछली सुन लेहु उदार, You have heard the former account, honoured father, now hear the latter, O noble one. [2] *Hb.* ix, 70, मन मनबोध कह्यो सब कंसक अग्रिम सो पुछ कहवाँ रहल, Saith Man'bōdh, I have related Kans' slaughter: what happened subsequently, that remains to be told.

[*Skr.* अग्रिमः; *as above possibly in all Gds.*]

अग्रेज *agrēj*, अँग्रेज *ãgrēj* = अगरेज *ag'rēj*, *q.v.*

अघ *agh*, **Ts.**, *subst. m.*, [1] (*moral*) sin, crime, guilt, wickedness (*exceedingly common in this sense, synonymous with* अवगुन, पातक, *etc., with the former of which it is not uncommonly joined in the phrase* अघ अवगुन sins and demerits); [2] (*physical*) evil, misfortune, calamity (*rarely in this sense, synonymous with* अमङ्गल, *with which it is sometimes joined in the phrase* अघ अमङ्गल evil and misfortune); [3] (*ceremonial, or from the point of view of Hindū caste*) uncleanness, pollution, degradation. **Comp.**, अघ-ओघ, *see* अघौघ *below*; अघ-कारी, *adj.*, sinful, profligate, criminal; अघ-खानि, *subst. f.*, *lit.* a mine of sin, mass of sin (*Sat.* iii, 56), *hence* a thoroughly wicked person (*Ram.*, *Ln.*, *ch.* 31, 4); अघ-गञ्जन, *subst. m.*, an exterminator of sin (*Ram.*, *Ut.*, *ch.* 52, 3; *Sat.* iii, 32); अघ-जन्म, (*lit.* having one's birth in pollution, *hence*) polluted, unclean, degraded (*Ram.*, *Ar.*, *do.* 31, 1); अघ-नासक, *adj.*, sin-destroying, the redeemer; अघ-पुञ्ज, *subst. m.*, an accumulation of sin, the amount of sin debited to a person in God's books (*Ram.*, *Ut.*, *ch.* 90, 2); अघ-मोचन, *subst. m.*, sin-removing, the redeemer (*Git.*, *Ba.*, 16, 3); अघ-राशि, *subst. m.*, *v.* अघ-पुञ्ज (*Ram.*, *Su.*, *ch.* 60, 5); अघ-रूप, *adj.*, *lit.* having the form of sin, an embodiment of sin, a thorough sinner (*Ram.*, *Ba.*, *do.* 180, 2); अघ-लेस, *subst.*, a particle *or* trace of sin (*Ram.*, *Ba.*, *do.*, 157, 2); अघ-हरन, *adj.* (*f.* °नि *or* °नी), sin-removing (*Sat.* i, 6); अघ-हारी, *adj.*, a remover of sin, the redeemer (*Ram.*, *A.*, *ch.* 287, 3); अघारि (= अघ-अरि), *subst.*, enemy of sin, the redeemer; अघासुर (= अघ-असुर), *subst. m.*, *name of a demon who was a general of Kans; he assumed the form of a vast serpent, into whose mouth Krish'n and his companions entered, mistaking it for the cavern of a mountain; but on discovering the truth, Krish'n swelled himself to such a degree that the demon's belly burst and he died*; अघौघ, *subst. m.*, *lit.* the sea of sin, *hence* the whole mass *or* body of sin (= अघ-ओघ; *cf. Ram.*, *A.*, *ch.* 240, 3; *Git.*, *Ut.*, 19, 5). **Exam.**, [1] *Ram.*, *Ba.*, *ch.* 235, 5, परसि जासु पद-पङ्कज धूरी, तरी अहल्या कृत अघ भूरी, through touching of whose (*i.e.*, *Ram's*) lotus-feet Ahalya was delivered from the heinous sin (*of adultery with Indr'*) done (*by her*); *ib.*, *A.*, *ch.* 161, 5, 6, जे अघ मातु पिता गुरु मारे, गाइ-गोठ महिसुर-पुर जारे, जे अघ तिय-बालक बध कीन्हे, मीत महीपति माहुर दीन्हे, जे पातक उपपातक अहहीं, करम-बचन-मन भव, कबि कहहीं, ते पातक मोहि होहु, बिधाता, जौं एहु होइ मोर मत, माता, Whatever crime there is in killing father, mother, or spiritual preceptor—in burning the stalls of cows or the cities of Brāhmans; whatever crime there is in committing murder of wife and children—in giving poison to a friend or a king; whatever sins, great and small, there are, born of thought, word, or deed, as the poets declare,—may those sins be mine, O God, if I give my consent to this, O mother! (*i.e., to Kāikēyī's plot of supplanting Rām*); *ib., A., ch.* 177, 8, **मनि अघ-अवगुन नहि मनि गहइ, हरै गरल, दुख दारिद दहई,** The jewel (*which is fabled to be found in a serpent's head*) does not contract the serpent's sins and demerits, (*but used as medicine*) it cures poison and relieves suffering and poverty; *ib., Ut., ch.* 123, 3, **मन क्रम बचन जनित अघ जाई, सुनहिँ जे कथा स्रवन मन लाई,** His sins, born of thought, word, or deed, pass away, who, with a believing mind, hears the recitation of the story (*of the Rāmāyan*); *Bin.* 194, **सो तन पाइ अघाइ किये अघ अवगुन अधम अभागी,** He who, having received such an (*excellent*) body, contracts sins and demerits to his heart's content, is a mean and wretched fellow; *ib.*, 92, **मेरे अघ सारद अनेक जुग गनत पार नहिँ पावै,** Sārad (*or Saraswatī, the goddess of speech*), counting my sins for many ages, will not reach the end of them; *Sat.* iii, 32, **आदि चन्द चपल मिलि भजु, तुलसी, तजि काम, अघ-गंजन, रंजन, सुजन-भय-भंजन, सुख-धाम,** Worship jointly the first (*syllables*) of the Moon (*i.e.* **राका** *rākā*) and the fickle (*mind, i.e.* **मन** *man*) (*i.e. rā + ma = Rāma*), abandoning evil—(*says*) Tul'sī Dās—, for he is the destroyer of sin, the rejoicer, the breaker of good men's fears, the abode of happiness; *ib.*, iv, 56, **एत बन्स बर बरन जुग सेत अगम-पर जान, चेत सहित सुमिरत करत परत अखिल अघ-खान,** Joining the excellent letters of Sūraj (*a synonym of* ēt) and Bans (*i.e.* Sūraj-bans, *or he who belongs to the solar race, i.e., Rām*), you may recognise the causeway over the sea of existence (*lit.* world); he who remembers (*this*) with (*all*) his heart, destroys his whole mass of sin; *K. Rām., Ut.* 115, **निज अघ-जाल कलि-काल की करालता बिलोकि, होत ब्याकुल करत सोई सोच सौं,** Contemplating the mass of my own sin and the terrible wickedness of Kalī-kāl (*i.e. the fourth or iron age of the Hindūs*), I feel distressed, and can think of nothing else. [2] *Rām., A., ch.* 204, 3, **मातु कुमत बढ़ई अघ-मूला तेहि हमार हित कीन्ह बसूला,** My mother's evil counsel, the root of the (*present*) calamity, like a carpenter, fashioned an adze out of my advantage; *Bin.* 129, **सुमिरत सुख सुकृत बढ़त, अघ अमंगल घटत,** Through hearing (*the name of Rām*), one's happiness and merits increase, (*while*) one's evil and misfortunes decrease; *Dōh.* 35, **हरन अमंगल अघ अखिल, करन सकल कल्यान, राम नाम नित कहत हर, गावत बेद पुरान,** Rām's name, which removes all evil and misfortune and causes every prosperity, Sib is continually repeating, and the Bēds and Purāns are extolling.

[3] *Rām., Ar., do.* 31, 1, **जाति-हीनि अघ-जनम महि-मुक्त कीन्हि असि नारि,** He gave release from the world to such an outcast and polluted woman (*as the Sabarī was; the comm. explains* **हिंसात्मक पापरूप जिसकि नीच-योनी,** a low-born Bhil, given to the sin of killing).

[*Skr.* **अघम्**; *as above in all Gḍs.*]

अघट *aghaṭ*, **Ts.,** *adj., com. gen., the same as* **अघटित** *aghaṭit* (2), *q.v.* (*explained in comm. to Bin.* 25 *by* **जो नहीं घटने योग्य,** what is not likely to happen). **Exam.,** [1] *Bin.* 25, **अघट घटना, सुघट बिघटन, बिकट भूमि पाताल जल गगन गन्ता,** (*Hanumān is*) the accomplisher of what seems impossible, the destroyer of what is well established, the awful traveller over earth, nether-world, sea, and sky.

[*A corruption of Skr.* **अघटितः**.]

अघटित *aghaṭit* (1), **Ts.,** *adj., com. gen., lit.* what cannot be decreased *or* fail, *hence* absolutely certain, unalterable, immutable. **Exam.,** *Rām., A., ch.* 159, 6, **जनि मानहु हिय हानि गलानी, काल-करम-गति अघटित जानी,** Do not think of your (heart's) loss and vexation: remember that the course of time and fate is immutable.

[*Skr.* **अघटितः** *See the remarks on the derivation of* **घट.** *As above possibly in all Gḍs.*]

अघटित *aghaṭit* (2), **Ts.,** *adj., com. gen.,* [1] *lit.* what is not likely to happen, *hence* improbable, impossible (*explained in comm. to Bin.* 30 *by* **जो नहीं घटने योग्य**); [2] *lit.* what should not happen, *hence* unfit, unworthy, shocking. **Exam.,** [1] *Bin.* 30, **अघटित घटन, सुघट बिघटन, ऐसी बिरुदावली नहिँ आन की,** The accomplisher of the improbable and the preventer of the probable, such a contrary experience will not be met with (*in the case of any one else except Hanumān*). [2] *Rām., Bā., ch.* 123, 6, **हरि-माया-बस जगत भ्रमाहीं, तिनहिँ कहत कछु अघटित नाहीं,** Under Hari's delusive influence (*the heretics*) wander about in the world; nothing is (*too*) shocking for them to say. [*The comm. in the Lakh'naū edition interprets:* 'that they should say (*that there is neither agun nor sagun, l.* 7), is nothing improbable, *or* is not to be wondered at,' *thus giving to* **अघटित** *the first meaning.*]

[*Skr.* **अघटितः**; *as above possibly in all Gḍs.*]

अघ॰वाइ *agh'wāi*, **अघ॰वाई** *agh'wāī*, **Tbh.,** *subst. f.,* satiety, fulness. *See* **अघाइ** *aghāī, etc.* **Exam.,** *comm. to Lakh'naū edition of Rām., A., ch.* 289, 5, **कृपा अनुग्रह अमित ते मो को अघ॰वाइ दीन्ह है,** (*Rām's*) mercy and grace has satisfied me (*lit.* has given me satiety) with nectar.

[*First verb. noun in* **इ,** *derived from* √ **अघाव,** *q.v. See also Gḍ. Gr.,* § 308.]

अघा *aghā*, (*pr. pts.* अघाइत *aghāit*, अघात *aghāt*; अघाएल *aghāël*; अघाएब *aghāëb*; अघाए *aghāë*; *Bw. forms:* 1 *sg. pres.* अघाउँ *aghāū̃* (*Rām.*, *Ln.*, *ch.* 56, 7), *or poet.* अघाऊँ *aghāū̃* (*Rām.*, *Ut.*, *ch.* 88, 2); 3 *sg. pres.* अघाइ *aghāi* (*Padm.*, *ch.* 4, 3), *or poet.* अघाई *aghāī* (*Rām.*, *A.*, *ch.* 51, 8); 2 *pl. pres.* अघाहु *aghāhu or poet.* अघाहू *aghāhū* (*Rām.*, *A.*, *ch.* 201, 6); 3 *pl. pres.*, अघाहिँ *aghāhi̐* (*Rām.*, *Ln.*, *do.* 103, 1), *or poet.* अघाहीँ *aghāhī̐* (*Rām.*, *Ut.*, *ch.* 54, 1); 3 *sg. past* अघाउ *aghāu* (*Bin.* 100) *or* अघाने (*Rām.*, *A.*, *ch.* 105, 1); *pres. part. masc.* अघात *aghāt* (*Rām.*, *Ln.*, *do.* 108, 2), *or poet.* अघाता *aghātā* (*Rām.*, *Ar.*, *ch.* 17, 3); *pres. part. fem.* अघाति *aghāti* (*Bin.* 233), *or* अघाती *aghātī* (*Rām.*, *Bā.*, *ch.* 32, 3); *conj. part.* अघाइ *aghāi* (*Rām.*, *Ln.*, *ch.* 85, 9) *or* अघाए *aghāë* (*Kan.* 22); *the pres. and conj. part. are commonly used as adverbs, see* अघात *aghāt* (2) *and* अघाय *aghāy*), **Tbh.**, *v. intr.*, [1]to prevail, to abound (*with this meaning now only found in the pres. and conj. part.*, *used adverbially*, अघात (2) *and* अघाय, *q.v.*); [2]to be full, to be filled, to be replete; [3]to have enough, to be satisfied, to be satiated, *both bodily and mentally*; [4]to have more than enough, to be surfeited, to be sated. (*It is constructed either with the conj. part. or the pres. part. of a dependent verb, and with the postposition* से *and instr. case of a dependent noun.*) **Exam.**, [1]*Git.*, *Ut.* 34, कहत सब रिखि क्रिपा अब भयौ आजु अघाइ, All Rikhis say that to-day they have been abundantly rewarded with mercy; [2]*Rām.*, *A.*, *ch.* 201, 6, राम-भक्ति अब अमिय अघाहू, Now you (*i.e. Bharat*) are full of the nectar-like faith in Rām; *ib.*, *ch.* 105, 1, सुनि मुनि-बचन राम सकुचाने, भाव भक्ति आनन्द अघाने, On hearing the Muni's words Rām was confused, (*but yet*) filled with delight at his display of faith; *ib.*, *ch.* 289, 5, क्रिपा अनुग्रह अङ्ग अघाई, कीन्हि क्रिपा-निधि सब अधिकाई, My whole self is filled with (*Rām's*) mercy and grace, and his wealth of mercy has exceeded everything; *ib.*, *ch.* 203, 1, मुनि-समाज अरु तीरथ-राजू, साँचे हु सपथ अघाइ अकाजू, In an assembly of saints and in such a holy place, an oath, even in (*speaking*) the truth, is replete with sin. [3]*Lit.*, (*of food, etc.*), *Coll.*, *Mth.*, हम एखन नहिँ खाएब, अघाएल छी, I will not eat just now, I am satiated; *ib.*, हम खाए पिबे सँ अघाएल छी, I have taken enough of food and drink; *Prov.*, *Bh.* (*Hd. Dy.*), ऐसन कउ-अक कौन बा, खात जे नाहिँ अघाय, Who is such a fool that he does not get enough in eating (*i.e.*, *who does not beware of surfeiting himself*); *Bh.*, *song*, (*ib.*), भूखल बाबउ कि बाबउ अघाए, कहँउ कउ किछु, देहौँ खिआए, Art thou hungry or art thou full? tell me, (*and*) I will give thee something to eat; *Rām.*, *Ln.*, *ch.* 56, 7, माँगा जल, तेहिँ दीन्ह कमण्डल, कह कपि नहिँ अघाउँ थोरे जल, (*Hanumān*) asked water, (*Kāl'nēmi*) gave him (*some*) in a cup, (*but*) the monkey (*i.e. Hanumān*) said, 'I am not satisfied with so little water'; *ib.*, *ch.* 85, 9, जम्बुक-निकर कटक्कट कट्टहिँ, खाहिँ हुआहिँ, अघाइ दपट्टहिँ, Herds of jackals snap and bite and feed, and, having eaten their full, howl and scamper about; *Kan.* 22, भयौ अघाए गाल गाल सब मुण्ड जोगिनी, The Jōginīs, voraciously feeding on the cheeks and heads (*of the dead warriors*), became satiated. *Fig.*, *Rām.*, *Bā.*, *ch.* 32, 3, जासु क्रिपा नहिँ क्रिपा अघाती, Whose (*i.e. Rām's*) mercy can never get enough in (*showing*) mercy; *Git.*, *Ar.*, 17, 8, दै दै प्रदच्छिन करत प्रनाम, न प्रेम अघात, Eagerly giving presents and making courtesies, she cannot get enough in (*showing*) her love; *Rām.*, *Ut.*, *ch.* 88, 2, प्रभु-बचनामृत सुनि न अघाऊँ, I can never satisfy myself with hearing the nectar-like words of the Lord; *ib.*, *Ln.*, *do.* 108, 2, लोचन-सिन्धु बिलोकत लोचन नहीँ अघात, (*Brahmā's*) eyes could not satisfy themselves in beholding the ocean of beauty; *Git.*, *Su.*, 40, नाम प्रताप पतित पावन किय, जे न अघाने अघ अघे, (*Rām's*) name, by its power has made sinners, who could not get enough of sin and injustice, holy; *Padm.*, *ch.* 4, 3, कीन्हेसि लोभ, अघाइ न कोई, (*God*) made (*the affect of*) desire, (*hence*) no one can be satiated; *Bin.* 100, न हिरदय अघाउ, Their hearts could not be satisfied (*comm.* तृप्त नहीँ भए). [4]*Rām.*, *Ut.*, *ch.* 54, 1, राम चरित जे सुनत अघाहीँ, रस बिसेषि जाना तिन्ह नाहीँ, They who can be surfeited with hearing Ram's history, have no appreciation of its peculiar savour.

(*The word is used in conversation in Bihārī, but in literature we have only met with it in Bw.*)

[*The original of this root is the Skr.* √अघे (1*st cl.* अघेति), *which, however, occurs more commonly in Skr. under the form* अर्घ (1*st cl.* अर्घति). *In the latter form it has both meanings:* (1) to be worth, to cost; (2) to be able, to be equal to,—*hence* to prevail, to abound. *In the form* अर्घ *the root appears to occur in Skr. only with the first meaning. These remarks appear to apply also to Pāli, which has also both forms* अग्घति *and* अग्घति. *In Pr. also both forms occur* अग्घइ (*Hēm.* ii, 104) *and* अग्घइ (*Hēm.* iv, 100); *moreover the latter admits a double form* अग्घइ (1*st cl.*) *and* *अग्घावइ *or* (*shortened by Hēm.* iii, 150) अग्घवइ (*xth cl.* = *Skr.* *अर्घापयति). *In this double form the verb bears all the meanings which it now possesses; thus in Hēm.* iv, 100, *and Nām.*, *vs.* 86, अग्घइ *is said to be a synonym of* अग्घइ (= *Skr.* अर्घति) he is able, राअइ (= *Skr.* राजति) he prevails, सोहइ (= *Skr.* शोभति) *or* विराअइ (= *Skr.* विराजते) he is successful, अग्घइ (= *Skr.* अर्घ्यते, *pass. of* √अर्घ) he is gratified, pleased, satisfied; *and in Hēm.* iv, 169, अग्घवइ *is said to be a synonym of* पूरइ (= *Skr.* पूर्यते) he is full, satisfied, sated. *In Sindhī this double form still survives with the more original meanings* to cost *and* to prevail, to be successful (*S. Dy.*, *pp.* 43,

44). *In Bihārī only the longer of the double forms survives (with loss of* व), *which still occasionally bears the more original meaning of* to prevail, to abound, *while usually it occurs, as in Pr., only with the secondary meaning,* to be full, satisfied, sated. *Skr.* अघेति, *Pā.* ¹अग्घति *or* ²¹अग्घायेति, *Pr.* ¹अग्घइ (*Hēm.* iv, 100) *or* ²¹अग्घाअइ *or* ²अग्घवइ (*Hēm.* iv, 169); *S.* ¹अघवे *or* (*with* म *for* व, *see Gḍ. Gr.* § 134) ²अघाये; *B.* (*with loss of* व, *see Gḍ. Gr.* §§ 33, 123) ²अघाइ. *Not met with in the other Gḍs.*]

अघाइ *aghāi*, (*poet.* अघाई *aghāī*), *adv.*, *the same as* अघाय *aghāy*, *q.v.* Exam., *Ag.* vii, 23 (*see also Dōh.* 420), हित पर बढ़ विरोधु जब, अनहित पर अनुराग; राम विमुख, बिधि बाम-गत, सगुन अघाइ अभागु, When (*a man's*) enmity grows towards (*his own*) good and (*his*) love towards (*his own*) evil, then it is a thoroughly unlucky omen; (*for*) Rām is averse and the Creator disinclined (*from him*); *Rām., A., ch.* 242, 13, लखि सिय सहित सरस दोउ भाई, कुटिल रानि पछितानि अघाई, Looking at the two noble brothers accompanied by Sītā, the wicked queen thoroughly repented. (*The word is properly the conj. part. of the* √अघा *aghā, q.v., as shown by the fuller form* अघाइ कै, *e.g., Gīt., Bā.*, 70, रङ्ग-भूमि भोरे ही जाइ कै, राम लखन लखि लोग बूढ़िहैं लोचन लाह अघाइ कै, Going to the playground very early in the morning, and beholding Rām and Lakhan, the people feast their eyes on them to their hearts' content.)

अघाइल *aghāïl* (*Bh.*), अघाएल *aghāēl* (*Mth. and Mg.*), Tbh., *adj., com. gen.*, ¹satiated, satisfied; ²sated, surfeited. Exam., *Mth. Prov.*, अघाएल बक कैं पोठी तीत, To a satiated crane even the pōṭhī fish is bitter. *Cf.* अघाना *for another version.*

[*P. p. of* √अघा, *q.v.*]

अघाई *aghāī* (1), Tbh., *subst. f., satiety, surfeiting, etc., q.v.* Exam., *Misc.* 81, का दिन छाड़ल नगर अजोध्या, बहुत दिनन पर आजु अघाई, For many days since I left the city of Ajodhyā, I have now (*for the first time*) had my fill (*lit.* satiety).

[*Properly str. f. of* अघाइ, *which is the first verb. noun, formed with the prim. der. suff.* इ, *from the* √अघा, *q.v.*]

अघाई *aghāī* (2), *poet. for* अघाइ *aghāï*, *the same as* अघाय *aghāy*, *q.v. Example, see under* अघाइ *aghāï.*

अघाए *aghāē*, *adv., the same as* अघाय *aghāy*, *q.v.*

अघाएल *aghāēl*, *adj., the Mth. and Mg. form of* अघाइल *aghāïl*, *q.v.*

अघात *aghāt* (1), (*unphon.* आघात *āghāt*), Ts., *subst. m.*, ¹a blow, stroke, knock, kick, shock, gust (*of wind*); ²wounding, a wound; ³killing, murder, destruction; ⁴(*fig.*) blow of fortune, misfortune, trouble. Exam., ¹*K. Rām., Su.* 3, लेखो कपि कौतुको केरात लोचे गात कै कै, लात के अघात सहै, जी मैं कहै, कूर हैं, Thus the cunning monkey (*i.e. Hanumān, when the rākhasas of Laṅkā wanted to bind him*), causing his body to shrink (*as it were*) with fear, patiently bears the kicks of their feet, saying in his heart 'they are bullies.' ²*Coll.* (*Bh.*), ओकरा के बड़ अघात लागल, He received a great wound. ³*Hb.* iii, 12, खसल महातरु, हसल मुरारि, भेल अघात जगत परचारि, The great trees fell and Murāri (*i.e. Krish'n*) laughed, and their destruction made (*his power*) manifest throughout the world; *Coll.* (*Bh.*), ज ओकरा के ऐसन अघात जगह में ले जा के मार-लेलस, कि आज तक किछु पता नाहिँ लागल, He took him to such a lonely place (*lit.* place of murder, *i.e., so lonely as to be fit for the commission of murder*) and killed him there, that to this day no trace of it has been found. ⁴*Coll.*, (*Bh.*), ई ओकरा पर बड़ अघात आ पड़ल, This is a great misfortune which has befallen him.

(*In the sense of* slaughterhouse, place of execution (*H. Dy.*), *the word is not used in Bihār. Compare, however, the second example of the third meaning. The unphon. form has not been met with by us in Bihārī literature. See the remarks under* अघाय *and* अघा.)

[*Skr.* आघातः; *as above possibly in all Gḍs.*]

अघात *aghāt* (2), Tbh., *adv., the same as* अघाय *aghāy*, *q.v.* Phr., अघात करब, *v. tr.*, to do *anything* excessively *or* with a great show. Exam., *Coll.*, *Chhattīs'gaṛhī* एक मनखे, बड़का बीर, चतुरा, अबर अघात डॉठ जीव के रहिस, There was a man, a great hero, intelligent, and of an exceedingly tough heart.

[*Properly the pres. part. of* √अघा, *q.v.*]

अघाना *aghānā*, (*f.* अघानी *aghānī*, *pl. masc.* अघाने *aghānē*), Tbh., *adj.*, (*Bw.*), full, filled, replete; ²satiated, satisfied; sated, surfeited; (*subst.*) one who enjoys a competency, a rich man *or* woman. Exam., ¹*Gīt., Bā.* 4, देत लेत पहिरत पहिरावत, प्रजा प्रमोद अघानी, Giving and receiving, dressing and bestowing dresses, the people are full of joy; *ib.*, 61, बिनय बड़ाई रिखि राउ ज परसपर करत, पुलकि प्रेम आनन्द अघाने हैं, The rikhi and the king, complimenting and extolling each other, were full of intense love and joy; *see also Rām., A., ch.* 105, 1, *under* √अघा. ²*Bh., Prov.* (*Hd. Dy.*), अघाना बगुला पोठिया तीत, A satiated stork considers the pōṭhī fish bitter (*cf.* अघाइल *for another version*).

[*Pr.* अग्घाओ (*Hēm. Dy.*, vs. 19, *where it is explained by Skr.* पूर्ण). *It is derived from the* √अघा *by means of the suff.* अवय (*Hēm.* iv, 443), *Gd.* अवा (*Gd. Gr.* §§ 315, 321). *Forms of this kind are used in Bw. as past participles. See under* √अघा.]

अघाय *aghāy*, अघाइ *aghāï*, अघाए *aghāē*, **Tbh.**, *adv.*, abundantly, to one's heart's content, fully, completely, thoroughly. **Exam.,** *Gīt.*, *Su.*, 16, अब अमिय सरिस खाये अघाय, (*Hanumān*) ate nectar-like fruit in abundance; *Rām.*, *A.*, *do.* 62, 1, 2, सखा सुहिद गुरु स्वामि सिख जो न करै सिर मानि, सो पछिताय अघाय उर, अवसि होइ हित हानि, Whoever does not willingly accept the advice of his friend, preceptor, or husband, he will thoroughly repent, and his interests are sure to suffer (*see Dōh.* 421 *for a less accurate version*); *Bin.* 194, जो तन पाइ अघाय किये अघ-अवगुन, अधम अभागो, When a man, having received that body (*which is a means of salvation to the wise*), works sin and wickedness (*with it*) to his heart's content (*comm.* भरि पेट), he is a wretched and miserable fellow; *ib.*, 41, दीन सब अङ्ग हीन छीन मलीन अघी अघाय, I (*Tul'sī Dās*) am thoroughly poor, destitute of all means of grace, wretched, defiled, and sinful.

[*Properly the conj. part.* (के *being understood*) *of the* √अघा, *q.v. See also under the art.* अघाइ.]

अघारी *aghārī*, *poet. for* अघारि *aghārī*. *See under* अघ *agh*.

अघासुर *aghāsur*,—*see under* अघ *agh*.

अघी *aghī*, **Ts.**, *adj.*, *com. gen.*, (*subst. f.* अघिनी *aghinī Mth. and poet.* अघिनि *aghini*), [1]sinful, guilty, wicked *or subst.*, a sinner, a criminal, a wretch. **Exam.,** *K. Rām.*, *Ut.* 131, ए तें बड़े अपराधी अघी कह, तैं कहु, अम्ब कि मोरे तौं, मो तौं, Therefore admitting myself to be greatly sinful and wicked, tell me, O mother, that I am thine (*lit.* say 'thou art mine' to me); *ib.*, 5, क्रूर कुजाति कपूत अघी, सब की सुधरै, जु करै नर पूजो, The coward, the base, the unfilial, the wicked,—he (*i.e. Rām*) cleanses every man if only he will pray to him; *Bin.* 253, लाले पालन पोषे तोषे आलसी अभागी अघी, नाथ, पै अनाथनि सौं भये न उरिन, Nursing, fostering, comforting the lazy, miserable, and wicked, like dear little children, O Lord, thou dost not keep aloof from those who have no protector; *K. Rām.*, *Ut.* 21, आलसी अभागी अघी आरत अनाथ पाल, साहेब समर्थ एक नीके, मन गुनी मे, Considering in my mind, (*I have heard that Rām is*) the protector of the lazy (*like Ahalyā*), the miserable (*like Guh, the Nikhād*), the sinful (*like Jaṭāyu, the carnivorous vulture*), the afflicted (*like the Sabarī*), and the helpless (*like Sugrīb*), a master powerful, unique, and good.

[*Skr.* अघिन्, *nom. sg.* अघी.]

अघोख *aghōkh*, (*f.* अघोखा *aghōkhā*), **Ts.**, *adj.*, *com. gen.*, *lit.* without noise, without sound; *hence* [1](*Gram.*) the hard (not sonant) consonants; *sometimes fig.* [2]obstinate (*like a mute beast*). **Exam.,** [2]*Coll.* (*Bh.*), ऊ बड़ अघोख बाड़े, कितनो मारैंठ, कबूलत नाहीं, He is very obstinate; however much you may beat him, he won't consent.

[*Skr.* अघोषः; *as above possibly in all Gds.*]

अघोर *aghōr*, **Ts.**, *adj.*, *com. gen.* (*f* अघोरा *aghōrā*), [1]not formidable, not terrible; [2]an euphemistic epithet of Sib. **Comp.** अघोरपन्थ, *subst. m.*, *lit.* the path of Sib, a certain order of religious mendicants amongst Hindūs; *they eat anything, however filthy, even human carcases*; अघोरपन्थि (*f.* -पन्थिनि), अघोरपन्थी (*f.* -पन्थिनी), *subst.*, a follower of the above sect; *hence met.*, any gross *or* filthy feeder.

[*Skr.* अघोरः; *as above possibly in all Gds.*]

अङ्क *ayk*, (*poet.* अङ्का *aykā*, *old dir. f.* अङ्कु *aykŭ*, *poet.* अङ्कू *aykū*), **Ts.**, *subst. m.*, [1]the curve of the human body just above the hip, the hip, the lap (*syn.* गोद, *in this sense esp. found in the phrases mentioned below*); *hence* [2](*lit. any curved line serving as a mark, hence*) a mark, sign, token, symbol (*syn.* चिन्ह); *hence esp.* [3]the numerical symbol of the units, any unit figure, a cipher (*from* 1 *to* 9), *as opposed to* शून *or the* '*zero*'; *and* [4]the graphic symbol of any sound, any (*written*) letter, *as opposed to* आखर *or the* '*pronounced letter*' *or* '*syllable*' (*thus,* क *as a mere written sign is called an* '*ayk,*' *but it is pronounced* '*ka,*' *not* '*k*'; *and as such, i.e. as affected with sound,* क *is called an* '*ākhar*' *or* '*syllable*'; अङ्क *is, however, not uncommonly used in a loose way as a synonym of* आखर *or* अच्छर; *cf. the example below*); *and* [5]a series of numbers *or* letters, writing, written word; *especially the letters which according to Hindū superstition are inscribed by the Creator on the skull of every person at his birth, and which pre-record the course of his life*; *hence* [6]fate, destiny, lot, allotted course of life; *hence further* [7]the fate *or* necessity of reiterated *or* recurrent embodiment *or* transmigration of the soul; *further* [8]a sign, signal, hint, nod; [9]spot, stain; [10](*math.*) a coefficient, the product of the principal into the rate and time. **Comp.** अङ्क-बिद्या, *subst. f.*, the science of numbers, mathematics. **Phr.,** अङ्क आरोपब, to lift to one's lap, to embrace; अङ्क बैठाएब, to take *or* place in one's lap; अङ्क भरब *or* अङ्क लगाएब, to embrace, to hug (*both as a salutation and sexually*); अङ्क भरि भेंटब *or* अङ्क भरि मिलब *or* अङ्क लाए भेंटब, to salute by embracing *or* hugging. **Exam.,** [1]*Mth. Rām.*, *Bā.* 62, 2, दिरेफ झुमि झुमि कै सदा-मदान्ध घूमि कै, प्रफुल्ल पद्मिनीक अङ्क भेरि भेरि चूमि कै, The bees, continually humming, wander about blind with a great intoxication, and lie asleep in the laps of the lotuses after kissing them again and again; *Mth. Rām., Ki.* 22, 1, सेजा पर निसाङ मदातङ मातङ्ग सम, बैसल सिख धरजङ देखल लछुमन काँ सतत, Lying on his bed in Ruma's lap, fearless and like a mad elephant, saw he Lachh'man there; *Mth. Rām., Ut.* 58, 2, तनिकाँ बेस अङ्क आरोपि, देल दिव्य सर रघुवर ओपि, Raghubar embraced him, and made over to him the magic arrow; *Mth. Rām., Ln.* 201, 10, भरत उठाय अङ्क आरोप, चिर वियोग दुखक भेल लोप, Bharat raised and embraced him, and the grief of the long separation disappeared; *Rām., Ln., ch.* 48, 7, सुनि सुत-बचन भरोसा आवा, प्रीति समेत अङ्क बैठावा, On hearing his son's words, (*Rāban's*) confidence returned, and he took him lovingly into his lap; *Gīt., Bā.*, 102, यों कहि, सिथिल सनेह, बन्धु दोउ अम्बु अङ्क भरि लीन्हे, Thus saying, with great affection, the mother took and hugged the two brothers in her lap; *ib., A.* 4, बार बार भरि अङ्क गोद लै ललन कौन सों कहिहौं, To whom shall I (*be able to*) say 'my darling,' constantly hugging him and taking him into my lap; *Sudh.* 13, अङ्क लगावत लाल बाल, सब बार बार सकुचाय, On the lover embracing her, that girl again and again shrank back; *ib.*, 20, अङ्क लगा कै लाल ओढ़ाओ धानी चदरा, O beloved, embrace me and hide me under the green sheet; *Rām., Ln., ch.* 60, 7, अब भरि अङ्क भेंट मोहि, भाई, लोचन सुफल करौं मैं जाई, Now, brother, take leave of me with an embrace, (*for*) I go to feast my eyes (*on Rām*); *Gīt., Ln.* 10, आइ भरत भरि अङ्क भेंटि, निज जीवन दान दियो है, Going up to (*Hanumān*), Bharat saluted him with an embrace, and gave him his own life (*i.e. vowed to die unless Hanumān, whom he had wounded, recovered*); *Bin.* 135, भरि अङ्क भेंट्यो, सजल नयन सनेह सिथिल सरीर सो, He (*i.e. Rām*) saluted him (*i.e. the boatman*) with an embrace, his eyes full of tears and his body transported with love; *Misc.* 43, धिग जीवन है तोहिं के, राधा, जे भरि अङ्क मिलो, Shame on thy conduct, O Rādhā, that thou salutest (*Krish'n*) with an embrace; *Rām., A., ch.* 187, 4, लेहि भरि अङ्क राम लघु भ्राता मिलत, पुलक परिपूरित गाता, Rām's younger brother (*i.e. Bharat*) saluted him (*i.e. Guh*) with an embrace, and his body thrilled all over with delight. [2] *Rām., A., ch.* 229, 3, हरषहिं निरखि राम पद-अङ्का, They rejoice on seeing the footprints of Rām; *ib., Ut., ch.* 76, 7, ललित अङ्क कुलिसादिक चारी, Decorated with the four marks of the thunderbolt, etc. (*i.e., the four symbols of royalty, viz., the thunderbolt, lotus, elephant-goad, and flag*); *Gīt., Ut.* 17, भौंहें बङ्क मयङ्क अङ्क रुचि, कुङ्कुम रेख भाल भलि भ्राजति, (*Rām's*) curved eyebrows are beautiful like the (*dark*) marks of the moon, and the red (*sectarial*) line on his forehead shines out finely (*see also ib.* 4). [3] *Sat.*, ii, 24, 25, तुलसी पति रति अङ्क सम, सकल साधना सून। अङ्क रहित कछु हाथ नहिं, अङ्क सहित दस-गून। तुलसी अपने राम कहँ भजन करहु निरसङ्क। आदि अन्त निरवाहिबो जैसे नव को अङ्क॥ The love of Tul'sī's lord (*i.e. Rām*) is like a cipher, all other resources are like zero; without a cipher there remains nothing, (*but*) with a cipher the value is ten times (*greater*); (*therefore*) Tul'sī (*says*), worship your Rām without fear, (*for*) like the ciphers of the nine (*units*), he will give efficiency (*to your other resources*) from beginning to end, (*i.e.* 1, 2, 3, 4, 5, 6, 7, 8, 9 + 0 = 10, 20, 30, 40, 50, 60, 70, 80, 90) (*for a slightly different version see Dōh.* 10); *ib.* vi, 54, करम खरी कर, मोह थल अङ्क चराचर जाल, हरत, भरत, भर हर गनत, जगत-जोतसी काल, Fate is the chalk in his hand, illusion (*i.e. the world*) is his table, the figures are the mass of moveable and immoveable (*creatures*), and time is the universal (*lit.* world) astrologer who subtracts and adds, and, having subtracted and added, multiplies them. [4] *Dōh.* 252, अङ्क अगुन, आखर सगुन, समुझिय उभय प्रकार, खोये राखे आपु भल, तुलसी चारु बिचार, The Agun (*i.e. the transmundane god or Brahm*) is like a (*written*) letter, the Sagun (*i.e. the incarnate god or Rām*) is like its uttered sound; both (*indeed*) are incomprehensible, (*but of the two*) your true interest is rather in letting go (*the former*) and keeping (*the latter*); this is Tul'sī Dās' well-considered opinion; (*as to the simile, cf. Raghuvaṁsha*, I, 1, वागर्थाविव, *etc.; as to Tul'sī Dās' preference of practical religion to religious philosophy, cf. Rām., Ut., ch.* 112, 1, *et passim*); *Dōh.* 365, जनम जोग मैं जानियत, जग बिचित्र गति देखि। तुलसी आखर अङ्क रस रङ्ग बिभेद बिसेषि॥ आखर जोरि बिचार करु, सुमति अङ्क लिखि लेहु। जोग कुजोग सुजोग मय जग गति समुझि बिसेहु॥, Seeing the diverse conditions (*of men*) in the world, I came to know the reason of their births (*into this or that condition*)—(*says*) Tul'sī Dās—by noticing how the words (*lit.* syllables) differ according to the letters you write (*lit.* you colour with ink); (*therefore*) thoughtfully join syllables together (*i.e. read words*) and carefully trace your letters, (*for*) you must clearly understand that the conditions (*of men*) in the world are the result of bad and good associations; *Bij., l.* 13, अक्षर अक्षर जोर परि जैहैं, देवी, अङ्के अङ्के दोहैं का लेखाए, If any syllables are forgotten, O goddess, bring them together letter by letter (का *is a mere expletive*). [5] *Rām., A., ch.* 171, 7, जाउँ राम पहँ आयसु देहु, एकहि अङ्क मोर हित एहू, Give me permission that I may go to Rām; in that word (*i.e. the name of 'Rām'*) alone centres all my interest; *Sat.* iii, 30, अङ्क दसा, रस आदि जुत, अन्त सुवन सब अन्त, The word 'ten' (*i.e.* दस *das*), joined to the initial (*syllable*) of love (*i.e.* र *ra, of* रस *ras*), together with the final (*letter*) of (*the name of*) the sons of Paṇḍu' (*i.e.* व

th, of पारथ *pār'th, or Judhishṭhir, Bhīm'sēn, and Arjun, the three sons of Prithā, the wife of Paṇḍū*) (*produce the name of Rām's father Das'rath*) ; *Rām., Bā., ch.* 105, 8, तुम सब मिटहिं कि बिधि के अङ्का, What! can the writing of the Creator be effaced by you? *ib., Ln., ch.* 29, 1, जरत बिलोकेउँ जबहिं कपाला बिधि के लिखे अङ्क निज भाला, When I saw the skull burning with the letters traced by the Creator on my forehead. [6]*Padm., ch.* 206, 7, जसो अङ्क नल जैसो दमावत, अयसा अँङ्क छिपी पद्मावत, As it was the fate of Damayantī that Nal should be hid from her (*lit.* as Nal was in the destiny of Damayantī), so Padmāwatī hid herself, avoiding the sight (*of the Rājā*). [7]*Sat.* vi, 71, 72, बर बस करत बिरोध बढि बोल बचन अङ्क-बोल। जदि अति बक बिक स्वान सम, तुलसी, परम प्रबीन। अङ्क करम, भेषज बिदित, जबत नहीं अति-दीन। तुलसी सठ अङ्क-बस बढि, दिन दिन दीन मलीन। Violently and stubbornly struggling (*man*) seeks to become free of the necessity of embodiment, (*herein*)—Tul'sī Dās (*says*)—with all his great cleverness behaving only like a crane or a wolf or a dog; that his embodiment is (*the result of*) his works (*done in a previous existence*), and that the remedy (*for getting delivered from it*) is known,—this, in his dementedness, he does not see, (*but*)—Tul'sī Dās (*says*)—like a fool, under the constraint of his embodiment (*or his fate*) he persists day by day in making himself wretched and stained (*with sin*). [8]*Dōh.* 200, माया जीव सुभाव गुन काल करम महदादि, ईस अङ्क ते बढ़त सब, ईस अङ्क बिनु बादि, The world, life, dispositions, virtues, time, works (*or fate*), they all increase at a sign from God, the great First (*Cause*): without God's sign they are annihilated (*lit.* are mere air). [9]*Gīt., Bā.* 56, केलि अङ्क तनु रेनु पङ्क जनु प्रगटत चरित चुराए, The stains made by the dust and mud on their body betrayed the play in which they had, as it were, stealthily indulged. *For another example see under* अङ्कु *aykū. See* आँक *āk* (2).

[*Skr.* अङ्कः (*in the sense of* unit figure, *see Zach. p.* 48, एकादिसंख्यावाचकः ; *in the sense of* letter, *see the comm. to Sapt. vs.* 191, *where Pr.* चित्तक्खरा *is explained by Skr.* चाटुरेखारचिता:) ; *Pr.* अङ्को (*in the sense of* lap *in Nām.* 237, *where it is given as a synonym of* उच्छङ्गो = *Skr.* उत्सङ्गः, *also in Hēm. Dy. vs.* 33 (= *Skr.* क्रोडः), *also in Āch.* ii, 15, § 13, *Nāy.*, § 117 ; *in the sense of* nearness *in Hēm. Dy., vs.* 5, *where it is explained by Skr.* निकटम् (*a meaning, however, which we have not noted in B.*) ; *in the sense of* mark *in Nām., vs.* 114, *where it is given as a synonym of* चिंधं = *Skr.* चिह्नम्, *also in Sapt. vs.* 233) ; *Gd.* अङ्क. *It is found in all Gds.; only S.* अङ्कु, *with the additional meanings of* a tear in a cloth, a knob on a stick, a piece of branch sticking out (*S. Dy., p.* 54).]

√अङ्क *ayk*, (*pr. pts.* अङ्कैत *aykait* ; अङ्कल *aykal* ; अङ्कब *aykab* ; अङ्कै *aykai*), **Ts.**, (1), *v. tr.*, [1]to mark, distinguish a thing by some mark; [2]to write numbers (*as in paging a book*) or letters (*as in an inscription*); [3]to judge, think, consider, appraise, price, value, calculate, count; [4]to stain, soil. *See* √आँक *āk and* √आँकाब *ākāb*.

(II) *v. intr.*, to be appraised, priced, valued.

[*A den. root from* अङ्क : *Skr.* √अङ्क, 1*st. cl.* अङ्कते, *part.* अङ्कित, *q.v. S. has* √अङ्क to write numbers, (*S. Dy., p.* 55).]

अङ्कक *aykak*, **Ts.**, *subst. m.*, one who calculates nativities *or* predicts one's fortunes, a soothsayer.

(*Sometimes used in Bihār in this sense, but not in the sense of* an accountant.)

[*Skr.* अङ्ककः ; *P.* अङ्कक.]

अङ्कट *aykaṭ*, **Tbh.**, *subst. m.*, the calcareous nodular limestone used for līme-burning. *See* आँकरा *āk'rā*.

अङ्कम *aykam*, **Tbh.**, *subst. m.*, [1]hip, lap, (*in this sense esp. found in the phrases mentioned below*); [2]mark, sign. **Phr.** अङ्कम भरब *or* अङ्कम भरि लेब *or* अङ्कम धरब *or* अङ्कम लागब, *lit.* to take into one's lap, *hence* to embrace, *both as a salutation and sexually*. **Exam.**, [1]*Bid.* xxiii, 3, जब जन पठ कैँ पहुँचि, सजनी रे, पहुकब अङ्कम मारी, I proceeded (*to the bridal chamber*) in the closest proximity of my husband, O friend, (*but*) being a woman my body (*lit.* lap) shrank (*through shame and fear*) ; *Hb.* vii, 28, 29, भरि अङ्कम भरि चप दुइ बाह, पूँछि पूँछि कुसल पुछल ब्रज-नाह ; उठि हलधर उनि अङ्कम लेल, बपन जत तुनि आदर देल, Hari embraced (*Akrūr*) with both arms, and with much smiling the Lord of Braj inquired after his welfare ; (*then*) Hal'dhar rose and embraced him, and, recognising him as his devotee, did honour to him ; *Prabh., p.* 19, *l.* 22, कर धयल, चलु झपुटल सेजा, अङ्कम भरि भरि सयन-सिमारी, Catching hold of her hand, he eagerly goes to the (*bridal*) chamber and seizes and embraces her in the bed chamber ; *Bid.* xxix, 4, अङ्कम भरि भरि सयन सुतायोल, परत बसन अपिहिले, Embracing her, Hari makes her sleep on the bed, having pulled off her garments without exception ; *ib.*, xxvii, 4, मुख हेरि नाकय भमर, झाँपि देल ; अङ्कम भरि मैं कमल-मुखि लेल, Gazing on her face, the lover (*lit.* humble-bee, *which is said to be enamoured of the lotus*) looked, (*but*) she covered it up again ; (*then*) he took the lotus-faced one in his embrace. [2]*Padm., do.* 412, 2, आदि अन्त जुग जो एक दुइ दुइ अङ्कम लाग, According as you recognise it to be the initial (*unit figure, i.e.* 1) or the last (*i.e.* 0), consider it (*lit.* apply it) as the mark of good or evil (*fortune*).

[*Der. uncertain; the word is a synonym of* अङ्क (*cf. its second and fourth meanings*), *and somehow derived from it. Pr. has* अङ्किय *in the sense of* embrace (= *Skr.* परिरम्भ, *Hēm. Dy.*, vs. 11).]

अङ्का *aykā*, *poet. for* अङ्क *ayk*, *q.v.*

अङ्कित *aykit*, **Ts.**, *adj.*, *com. gen.*, (*subst. f.* अङ्किता *aykitā*), [1]marked, distinguished by a mark (*syn.* चिह्नित); [2]numbered (*as the pages of a book*) or lettered or written (*as an inscription*); [3]engraved, stamped, coined; [4]soiled, stained; [5]appraised, calculated, counted. **Exam.**, [1]*Rām.*, *A.*, *ch.* 296, 4, प्रभु पद अङ्कित अवनि बिसेखी, आयसु होइ, तो आवौं देखी, If permission be given, I will go to see the spot specially marked with the foot-prints of the Lord (*i.e. Rām*); *Git.*, *A.*, 46, सीता राम लखन पद अङ्कित अवनि सोहावनि बरनि न जाई, The ground marked with the foot-prints of Sītā, Ram, and Lakhan became (*so*) beautiful (*that*) it cannot be described; *Bin.* 24, भूमि बिलोकि राम पद अङ्कित, बन बिलोकि रघुबर बिहार थल, Beholding the ground marked with the foot-prints of Rām, and the forest which was the place of Raghubar's wanderings; *K. Rām.*, *Ut.* 132, बारिपुर दिगपुर बीच बिलसति भूमि, अङ्कित जो जानकी चरन जल जात की, Between Bāripur and Dig'pur lies the spot which is marked with the foot-prints of Sītā as she crossed the water. [2]*Padm.*, *ch.* 206, 5, मग अङ्कित तेहि करत बिछोवा, The lettered path (*i.e., the row of letters of destiny inscribed on a man's skull*) causes them separation. [3]*Mth. Rām.*, *Ki.* 26, 2, अङ्कित हमार जाहि मैं नाम. (*The ring*) on which my name is engraved.

[*P. p. of Skr.* ✓अङ्क; *used in all Gds. The tadbh. Pr. form* अङ्कियं *in the sense of* embrace *is mentioned in Hēm. Dy., vs.* 11, *but has not survived in the Gḍs.*]

अङ्कु *ayku*, (*poet.* अङ्कू *aykū*), **Ts.**, *subst. m.*, *the old dir. of* अङ्क *ayk*, *q.v.* **Exam.**, [2]*Padm.*, *ch.* 642, 5, कापर महँ न छूट असि अङ्कू, सो असि काय कोहि देह कलङ्कू, Ink of which the stains cannot be taken out of any cloth, such ink (*i.e. disgraceful suggestions*) thou hast brought and stained me with it.

[*It is the older Bw. or H. form of* अङ्क; *see Gḍ. Gr.* § 46.]

अङ्कुर *aykur*, **Ts.**, *subst. m.*, [1]germ, sprout, shoot, scion, blade, seed-bud, germ (*used both literally and figuratively*); [2]bit of plants, herbs (*plucked for eating or seasoning*); [3]growth, product; [4]fate, destiny; [5]a cattle disease. **Exam.**, [1]*Sat.* vi, 56, (*lit.*), अङ्कुर बिटप दल बिपुल साखा फूल फर रितु, तुलसी सब भाँति, From a good root there grow the sprout, the sapling, the stem, and numerous branches, (*then*) flowering it bears fruit according to the seasons; in the same way, Tul'sī Dās (*says*), (*it goes*) with every thing; (*fig.*), *Rām.*, *A.*, *chh.* 7, 2, लोचन-सरोरुह स्रवत सींचत बिरह उर अङ्कुर नये, (*Bharat's*) lotus eyes flowing with tears watered the fresh shoots of desolation in his heart; *Doh.* 568, कीरति राम गुन-गन नयन जल अङ्कुर पुलकालि, (= पुलक-आवलि) सुकिती सुतन सुखेत बर बिलसत, तुलसी, सालि, He who listens to the good deeds (*of Rām*) is (*like*) a fine field—(*says*) Tul'sī Dās—with a bountiful crop of rice, (*for*) Ram's numerous virtues are the seed, from the eyes (*comes*) the water (*of irrigation*), and the rows of hair standing erect (*on the body, from pleasure at hearing Rām's virtues*) are the sprouts. [2]*Rām.*, *A.*, *ch.* 104, 2, कन्द मूल फल अङ्कुर नीके दिये आनि मुनि मनहुँ अमी के, The Muni brought and presented bulbs, roots, fruits, and herbs as delicious as if they were ambrosia; *ib.*, *ch.* 241, 2, भरि भरि परन पुटी रचि रूरी, कन्द मूल फल अङ्कुर जूरी, They filled daintily-made leaf cornets (*or* '*dōnā*') brimful with bulbs, roots, fruits, and herbs; *Git.*, *Ut.* 33, बिरस बृ-क्ष सरस फूलत फलत अति अधिकाई, कन्द मूल अनेक अङ्कुर स्वाद सुधा लजाई, Tasteless (*i.e. wild*) plants bear tasteful flowers and fruits in great abundance, and the taste of many bulbs and roots and herbs puts ambrosia to shame. [4]*Mth. Chr.*, *p.* 4, § 15, अङ्कुर मेटल नहिं जाएत, One's fate cannot be altered. [5]*Coll.*, (*Bh.*), हमरा बरद का गोड़ में अङ्कुर भेल बा, देखौं बचेला कि नाहीं, The aŋkur has got into the feet of my bullock; I wonder (*lit.* see) whether he will live or not. *See* अँकुरा *ãkurā*, अँकूर *ãkūr*, आँकुर *ãkur*.

[*Skr.* अङ्कुरः, *Pr.* अङ्कुरो (*in the sense of sprout, Sapt.* 672), *all Gḍs.* अङ्कुर, *exc. S.* अङ्कुरु, *Kn.* आँकरो.]

✓अङ्कुर *aykur*, (*pr. pts.* अङ्कुरत *aykurat*; अङ्कुरल *aykural*; अङ्कुरब *aykurab*; अङ्कुरै *aykurai*; *Bw. forms*, 3 *sg. past* अङ्कुरेउ *aykureü*, *p. p. pl.* अङ्कुरे *aykurē*, *v. n.* अङ्कुरि *aykuri*), **Ts.**, *v. intr.*, [1]to sprout, shoot, bud; [2]to grow up, rise up; [3]spring up, to make one's appearance. **Exam.**, [1]*Git.*, *Bā.* 6, कन्द सकल आनँद को जनु अङ्कुरि आयो, The root of all happiness had, as it were, sprouted. [2]*Rām.*, *Bā.*, *ch.* 136, 4, उर अङ्कुरेउ गरब तरु भारी, बेगि सो मैं डारिहउँ उखारी, In his heart pride has grown up like a big tree, so I will quickly root it up and throw it away. [3]*Rām.*, *Ln.*, *chh.* 21, 4, मरदहिं दसानन कोटि कोटिन्ह कपट भू भट अङ्कुरे, They (*i.e. Hanuman, etc.*) crush millions upon millions of Dasānans (*i.e. Rābans*), as they by magic sprang up as warriors on the (*battle-*) field.

[*Den. verb derived from* अङ्कुर, *q.v. The Pr. p.p.* अङ्कुरियं *is given in Nām., vs.* 256. *M. inf.* अङ्कुरणें, *S.* अङ्कुरणु.]

अङ्कुस *aykus*, **Ts.**, *subst. m.*, [1]an iron hook with which elephants are driven, a goad (*Grs.* § 102); [2]the mark of an elephant-goad on the soles of the feet, (*considered to be indicative of future royalty of an infant when occurring together with the marks of a flag, a lotus, and a thunderbolt*); [3](*agric., in Sāran and Mungēr*) the hook attached to a harrow (चौकी) to connect it with the chain traces (जोतर *or* जोगन्हवी). **Exam.**, *Rām.*, *Bā.*, *do.* 266, 2 मत्ता-मत गज राज कहँ बस कर अङ्कुस बरव, A little goad can control a big furious elephant. [2]*Gīt.*, *Ut.* 21, कञ कुलिस धज अङ्कुस रेख बरन सुभ चारि, जन मन-मीन धरन कहँ बनसी रची सँवारि, The four beautiful figures of lotus, thunderbolt, flag, and elephant-goad on his foot, are like a fishing line arranged to catch the fish of our hearts, (*the comm. of Baij'nāth remarks on this passage as follows: a fishing line is composed of four parts, the bait* (चारा), *the hook* (काँटा), *the float* (खाडापोड), *and the line* (डोरि). *Of these the first corresponds to the flag, which grants all desires; the second to the elephant-goad, which drags our minds by means of knowledge; the third to the lotus, which stands out of the water; and the fourth to the thunderbolt, which destroys sin and makes the mind pure*); *ib.* 17, पदुम राग-रुचि मिदु पद-तल धज अङ्कुस कुलिस कमल एहि सूरति, On (*Rām's*) soft soles of ruby-like sheen there were those beautiful figures of flag, elephant-goad, thunderbolt, and lotus. *See* आँकुसा *ākusā*, आँकुसी *ākusī*, *and* आँकुस *ākus*.

[*Skr.* अङ्कुशः *or* अङ्कुशम्; *Pr.* अङ्कुसो (*Sapt.* 999, *Hem.* iv, 383); *the same in all Gds.*]

अङ्ग *ayg*, (*poet.* अङ्गा *aygā*, *obl. pl.* अङ्गन *aygan or* अङ्गनि *aygani*), **Ts.**, *subst. m.*, [1]a limb, member of the body (*of which the Hindūs reckon eight*); [2]a side of the body (*the throbbing of the left side is considered a good omen*); [3]the body (*syn.* तन *or* गात); [4]the figure *or* shape of the body (*syn.* रूप *or* आकार); [5]*fig.* being, as it were, some one's body *or* limb, being intimately connected with him, his friend, support, seconder; [6]*met.* soul, self, person; [7]a part *or* point, particular, point of view, respect, aspect, (*syn.* प्रकार); [8]means, expedient, resource, help, assistance, *esp. in the religious sense of* means of grace, means of salvation, service, adoration (*syn* साधन); [9]*the name of* a certain division *or* class of sacred works, (*among Brāhmans the six Vēdaygas or appendixes of the Vedas, see M. Müller's History of Skr. Literature, p.* 108; *among the Jainas the twelve Aygas, see Weber's Indische Studien, vol.* XVI, *p.* 211, *vol.* XVII, *p.* 1); [10]*the name of* a certain division *or* country of North India about Bhagal'pur (*the ancient capital of which was Champā*); [11]*a symbolical name for* the number six (*taken from the six Vēdaygas*). **Comp.** अङ्ग-न्यास, *subst. m.*, a ceremony belonging to the 'sandhyā' or daily prayer of the Brāhmans, which consists in the touching of certain parts of the body according to prescribed rules (*see J. A. S. B., vol.* LIII, *for* 1884); अङ्ग-थिथिरी, *subst. f.*, the ague *or* shivering fit in fever; अङ्ग-चीन, *adj.*, *com. gen.*, without resources, helpless, *or* a scapegrace. **Phr.**, अङ्ग अङ्ग *or* अङ्ग अङ्गन, limb by limb, every limb (*Rām.*, *Bā.*, *do.* 232, 2, *et passim*); अङ्ग पतरी (*Mag.* 34) *or* अङ्ग के साँकरि (*Mag.* 54), *adj. f.*, slender, thin (*said of women*); अङ्ग करब, *v. tr.* (*lit.* to make something one's limb *or* share, *hence*) to make one's own, appropriate, accept (*Bin.* 239, *syn.*, अङ्गीकार करब); अङ्ग भङ्ग करब, *v. tr.*, to mutilate (*Rām.*, *Su.*, *ch.* 24, 9; *ch.* 52, 3); अङ्ग मिलब, *v. intr.*, to come in contact with the body, *hence* to be embraced (*B. Rām.*, *rs.* 12, 13; *Bih.* v, 8); अङ्ग मिलाएब, *v. tr. of the preceding*, to embrace; अङ्ग मोड़ब *or* अङ्ग मोरब, *v. intr.*, (*lit.* to turn the body, *hence*) to shrink from, fly from, avoid, shun, *or* to be modest, retiring (*esp. said of women, whom Indian custom requires to turn away from any man whom they may meet*), *or* to stretch one's self, rest one's self; अङ्ग लागब, *v. intr.*, (*lit.* to be applied to the body, (*hence*) to be embraced, *or* to be assimilated, agree with, nourish (*said of food*), *or* to be spent, be brought into use, *or* to be worn, put on (*Bid.* 44, 4); अङ्ग लगाएब, *v. tr. of the preceding*, to embrace (*Bih.* i, 7), *or* to spend, bring into use, *or* to apply one's self to, give one's attention to, be intent upon, *or* to take into one's heart, take into one's affections (*Gīt.*, *A.* 86); अङ्ग सिथिल होएब, *v. intr.*, to have one's limbs relaxed, be unnerved. **Exam.**, [1]*Rām.*, *A.*, *ch.* 190, 1, भये सनेह-बस अङ्ग सिथिल सब, Then under the influence of love his limbs became relaxed; *ib.*, *ch.* 40, 1, सूखे अधर, जरे सब अङ्गा, His lips were dry and all his limbs were burning (*with anxiety*); *ib.*, *Bā.*, *ch.* 324, 3, सकल सुमङ्गल अङ्ग बनाये, (*The maidens of Ajodhyā*) were rendered beautiful in every limb; *Gīt.*, *Bā.* 22, को कवि जो छवि कहि सकै नख सिख सुन्दर सब अङ्ग, Who is the poet that can describe the beauty of all (*Rām's*) limbs from the nails (*of his toes*) to the top-knot (*on his head*)? *ib.* 73, राजिव नयन, बिधु बदन, टेपारे सिर, नख सिख अङ्गनि ठगौरी ठौर ठौर हैं, (*Rām's*) eyes resemble lotuses, and his face the moon: on his head is a fine cap, and his limbs, from the toe-nails to the top-knot, are ravishing in every part; *Bih.* xii, 9, गँगवा नहैले सिव भसुनि उतरले चाडो (=चाड+ओ) अङ्ग चनन चढ़ाए रे, Having bathed in the Ganges and rubbed off the ashes (*with which, as an ascetic, he had been smeared*), Sib applied sandal-powder to all his eight limbs; *Mag.* 75, भीँजल रसिरि रेसम केरी चोलिया बुँदवा से, भीँजि गे आठो अङ्ग, Your silken bodice is becoming moist from the rain-drops, all your eight limbs are wet; *Bid.* 82, 4, डगर डगर कर अङ्ग, Rattle,

rattle, go (*Sib's*) (*bony*) limbs; *Rām., Su., ch.* 24, 9 (*see also ch.* 52, 3) सुनत बिहँसि बोला दसकंधर, 'अङ्ग भङ्ग करि पठइय बन्दर', On hearing it, Das'kandhar (*i.e. Rāban*) laughed and said: 'Mutilate and dismiss the monkey (*i.e. Hanumān*)'; *Gīt., Bā.* 26, अङ्ग अङ्ग पर मार-निकर मिलि छबि समूह लै लै जनु छाए, (*It seemed*) as if multitudes of Love-gods had met, and taking a mass of beauty spread it over every limb (*of Rām*); *Rām., Ut., chh.* 4, 7, मुकुटाङ्गदादि बिचित्र भूषन अङ्ग अङ्गन्ह प्रति सजे, Diadem, bracelets, and various other ornaments, bedecked his every limb. [2]*Rām., Bā., so.* 24, 2, मञ्जुल मङ्गल मूल बाम अङ्ग फरकन लगे, (*Sītā's*) left side, which was the seat (*lit.* root) of happiness and good luck, began to throb; *ib., A., ch.* 8, 4, राम सीय तन सगुन जनाए, फरकहिँ मङ्गल अङ्ग सुहाए, The bodies of Rām and Sītā showed forth good omens, (*for*) their lucky sides throbbed pleasantly; *ib., Bā., ch.* 243, 4, फरकहिँ सुभग अङ्ग, सुनु भ्राता, Listen, brother, my lucky side is throbbing; *Ag.* v, 12, फरकत मङ्गल अङ्ग सिय, बाम बिलोचन बाहु, Sītā's lucky side is throbbing, her left eye and arm. [3]*Rām, Bā., ch.* 314, 7, पुलक अङ्ग लोचन जल छाये, (*Viswāmitra's*) body thrilled with joy, and his eyes were dimmed with tears (*cf. ib., so.* 29, 1, *p.* 104, पुलक तनु, *and do.* 321, 2, पुलक गात); *ib., ch.* 322, 1, केकि-कण्ठ-दुति-स्यामल अङ्गा, (Rām's) body was of the lustrous darkness of a peacock's neck; *Gīt., Ar.* 4, भुज बिसाल, कमनीय कन्ध उर, स्रम सीकर सोहै साँवरे अङ्ग, His arms were large, and charming his shoulders and chest, and the drops of sweat caused by exertion were glistening on his swarthy body; *K. Rām., Ut.* 143, भस्म अङ्ग, मर्दन अनङ्ग, सन्तत असङ्ग हर, Har (*i.e. Sib*) has ashes (*smeared*) on his body, is the crusher of the Love-god, and lives perpetually as a recluse; *Hn.* 4, 5, सुमरि सुमरि रति रङ्ग छन छन पुलकित अङ्ग, Every moment that I remember those love's delights, my body thrills; *Misc.* 64, खैंचत खैंचत भुज बल हारे, तनिको (= तनिक + उ) न अङ्ग उघरे थे, Though (*the Kāuravas*) exhausted the strength of their arms in diligently pulling (*the clothes of Draupadi*), they could not uncover the smallest part of her body; *Padm., ch.* 676, 2, हौं धौलागिरि गोरा, टरौं न टारे, अङ्ग न मोरा, I Gorā shall play the roll of Dhaulāgir (*or Dēvalagiri*); on their trying to move me, I shall not move, nor turn my body; *H. song,* जब से वह बाँका छबीला दिल को है भाया छबा, अङ्ग लगता नी नहीं, सुइयाँ, मेरा खाया छबा, Since that handsome swain has won my heart, my food, O friends, no more agrees with me; *Coll.* (*Bh.*), अङ्ग लागि गैल, धरल धरल का थोरल, It is already spent, what would have been the good of keeping it (*after Fallon*); *Gīt., A.* 86, अङ्ग अगार सिसु बारे ते करुनामय हम पारे, The dear, kind-hearted children (*i.e. Rām and Lakhan*) have taken (*the horses*) into their affections from their childhood; *Bih.* i, 7, जब जाड़ छुटत, हे सखि, जब कन्त अङ्ग लगावत्नौं, Then the cold will leave me, O friend, when my husband embraces me; *Bid.* 44, 4, आनक भूखन आनक अङ्ग, Thou wearest ornaments of another woman; *B. Rām.*, 12, चम्पक हरवा अङ्ग मिलि अधिक सुहाय, The necklace of champak flowers, as it comes into contact with (*Sītā's*) body, blooms more than ever (*for it knows that when it withers it will die on Sītā's heart*); *Bih.* v, 8, अङ्ग मैं अङ्ग मिलाए बाँहि धरी सिरहानवौं, Embracing each other and placing the arm on the pillow; *Coll.* (*Bh.*), पतोहिया कैँ समुझावँ कि अङ्ग मोड़ के बैठे, Tell the daughter-in-law that she should sit modestly; *Mag.* 34, कहवाँ से अइलू है तू, गोरी, अङ्ग पतरी जैसे कुइयाँ मैं डेवौँ डोर, Whence dost thou come, fair lady (*who art*) as slender as the rope (*which*) I see in the well; *ib.* 54, तोरि तिरियवा तो अङ्ग के साँकरि, कैसे के दिल तो पछताय, Thy wife surely is slender (*enough*), why then is thy heart discontented? [4]*Rām., Bā., chh.* 56, 1, गाँथे महा-मनि मौर मञ्जुल अङ्ग सब चित चोरहीं, (*Rām's*) comely figure, with the large gems knotted in his head-dress (*see Grs.* §. 1326), ravished all hearts; *Gīt., Bā.* 105, मङ्गलमय दोउ अङ्ग मनोहर ग्रथित चूनरी पीत पिछोरी, Delightful were the figures of the two (*i.e. Rām and Sītā, as bridegroom and bride*) and charming, (*as seen*) with his yellow shawl tied (*with the marriage knot, see Grs.* § 1331) to her coloured veil; *K. Rām., A.* 14, जोबन उमङ्ग अङ्ग उदित उदार है, The transport of youth (*i.e. of Rām, Lakhan, and Sītā*) is clearly visible in their figures; *Bih.* xiii, 4, कैसी बियाह, सिव, बड़ निक कैलौं, जे अङ्ग सुभाव बतावँ रे, Thou hast married, O Sib, thou hast done very right, (*but*) describe (*to me*) her figure and disposition. [5]*Rām., A., ch.* 274, 5, तौरे अङ्ग जोग जग को है, Who is there in the world worthy of being your seconder? *Figuratively Bin.* 57, देव, देहि सत सङ्ग निज अङ्ग, श्री-रङ्ग, भवभङ्ग कारन सरन सोक हारी, O God, O Srī-rang, allow me (*to live in*) the company of good men, (*which is*) thy body, (*and*) which causes the severance of (*all*) earthly attachments and removes (*all*) the troubles of those who have taken refuge within it (*comm.* सरन *here* = सरनागत); *Coll.* (*Bh.*) ऊ हमार अङ्ग होए और किछु करियो न करिहैं, He is my friend, and will never do me any (*ill turn*). [6]*Rām., A., ch.* 289, 5, कृपा अनुग्रह अङ्ग अघाई, (*Rām's*) mercy and grace has filled my (*whole*) soul (*or my whole being*); *Coll.* (*Bh.*), अङ्ग लगाय के खा, गिराबैं मत, Eat carefully (*lit.* applying your mind), don't throw (*anything*) down (*Hd. Dy.*). [7]*Rām., Bā., ch.* 12, 6, सूझ न एक उ अङ्ग उपाऊ, मन मति रङ्क, मनोरथ राऊ, I (*i.e. Tul'sī Dās*) know no means of succeeding (*in composing the Rāmāyan*) in any respect, (*for*) my mind is a beggar, (*while*) my purpose is royal; *ib., A., ch.* 226, 8,

सकल अङ्ग उत्तम सुराज, A king perfect at all points; *Git.*, *Bā.* 90, कमठ कोल दिग-दन्ति सकल अङ्ग सजग करहु प्रभु काजु, O tortoise, O boar, and O elephants of the quarters, being on the alert in every respect, do service to the Lord (*by holding the earth steady*); *Bin.* 22, तीरथ सब सुभ अङ्ग (*Kāshī or Banāras is*) a place of pilgrimage well furnished in every respect; *Dōh.* 313, एक अङ्ग जो सनेह, ता निसि दिन चातिक नेह, If one's affection is concentrated on one particular, then his affection is fixed on it night and day, like that of the chatik bird (*which is said to live on rain-drops only; the same idea is expressed in the following*), *Bin.* 65, एक अङ्ग मग अगम, Difficult is the narrow path (*lit.* the one-sided road, *i.e. the single devotion to Rām; comm.*, एकाकार रिति *or* एकाङ्गी रिति, single way of living, *like that of the papīhā bird*); *K. Rām.*, *Ut.* 69, सब अङ्ग हीन, सब साधन बिहीन, मन बचन मलीन, हीन कुल करतूति हौं, I am destitute in all respects, devoid of all resources, defiled in mind and speech, and deprived of caste and business; *ib.* 155, चाहै न अनङ्ग अरि एकौ (= एक + उ) अङ्ग माँगने को, Cupid's foe (*i.e. Sib*) does not desire to beg one particular. ⁹*Bin.* 41, दीन सब अङ्ग हीन छीन मलीन अघी अघाय, I am thoroughly poor, destitute of all grace, wretched, defiled, and sinful; *ib.* 99, कपटी मलीन हीन सब ही अङ्ग तुलसी सो दीन दास को, I Tul'sī Dās am deceitful, defiled, destitute of all grace, and the most wretched of the wretched; *ib.* 170, सकल अङ्ग, पद बिमुख, नाथ, मुख नाम की ओडहुई है, All other service, not directed to thy feet, O Lord, is a taking shelter in names merely with the mouth; *ib.* 225, कै सुनि स्वामि सुभाव, न रहौं चित, जो हित सब अङ्ग थाके, Or though one, hearing of the kindness of the Lord (*i.e. Rām*), should not keep in mind him (*i.e. Rām*) who befriends those that have vainly exhausted all (*other*) means of salvation, (*yet will I, Tul'sī Dās, remember him*). [10]*Hb.* x, 9, सोरठ भोरठ औ गढ़पाल, अङ्ग बङ्ग आयउ नेपाल, From Sōraṭh, Bhōraṭh, and Gaṛh'pāl, from Aŋg (*or Bihār*), Baŋg (*or Bengal*), they came, and from Nēpāl; *ib.* 39, जे जेठ सबल, अबल भेठ भङ्ग, बिथकल अङ्ग बङ्ग तेलङ्ग, The victory was to the strong, to the wicked was the defeat; scattered were (*the men of*) Aŋg, Baŋg, and Tailaŋg.

[*Skr.* अङ्गम् *neut.*, *Pā. and Pr.* अङ्ग *neut.* (*Sapt.*, *vs.* 309, *nom. plur.* अङ्गाइं *Hēm.* i, 93), *Ap. Pr.* अङ्गु *masc.* (*Hēm.* iv, 332, *where it is treated as a neut.*, *but the term.* उ *is a mere shortening of the masc. term.* ओ, *and the change of gender, so common in the Ap. Pr.*, *is accounted for by Hēm.* iv, 445); *most Gds.* अङ्ग, *S.* अङ्गु *masc.*, *but M. and G.* अङ्ग *neut.*, *Kn.* आङ्गु *or* आङ्गा *neut.* (body). *In the sense of the* Jain Aŋga *or* Sacred Book *it occurs in Uv.* § 2, *Nāy.* §§ 8-10. *The Pr. form of the phrase* अङ्ग मिलय to be embraced *occurs in Hēm.* iv, 332, अङ्गहिं अङ्गु न मिलियउ, not embracing one another. *S. has* अँगडु endearment, caress, *and* अँगडी one who shows endearment, loving (*S. Dy.*, *p.* 55), *which seems to be connected with the B. phr.* अङ्ग लगाएब.]

अङ्गकार *ayg'kar*, **Tbh.**, *v. tr.*, to receive, to accept. **Exam.**, *Bin.* 239, जा को हरि दृढ़ करि अङ्गकर्यो, सो सुसिल शरो, Whom Hari (*i.e. Rām*) has definitely made his own, he is full of (*all*) virtues, (*the comm. has* अपनो कियो, made his own). *See* √अँगिर *āgir*.

(*The word has only been met with in the above-cited passage.*)

[*Skr.* अङ्गीक, *base* अङ्गीकर, *whence corrupted* अङ्गकर.]

अङ्गद *aygad*, (*old obl.* अङ्गदहि *aygadahi*), **Ts.**, *subst. m.*, ¹an armlet worn on the upper arm (*syn.* बिजायठ); ²the name of a monkey who assisted Rām. *He was a son of Bāli, the monkey king of Kis'kindā, and a nephew of Sugrīb* (*Rām.*, *Ki.*, *ch.* 6), *whom Bāli had exiled. Rām, having killed Bāli, placed Sugrīb on the throne and made Aygad his co-regent* (*or jub'rāj*, *Rām.*, *Ki.*, *do.* 11, 2, *ch.* 12, 9). *Out of gratitude Aygad went with Hanumān, Nal, Nīl, and other monkeys* (*hence called Aygadādi*) *in search of Sītā* (*Rām.*, *Ki.*, *ch.* 23). *Having discovered her in Laykā, Aygad was sent by Rām as ambassador to Rāban, to demand the restoration of Sītā* (*Rām.*, *Ln.*, *ch.* 18). *In Rāban's court an angry dialogue ensued, which culminated in Aygad's famous wager* (*Rām.*, *Ln.*, *ch.* 33): राम प्रताप सुमिरि कपि कोपा। सभा माँझ पन करि पद रोपा॥ जौं मम चरन सकसि सठ टारी। फिरहिं राम, सीता मैं हारी॥ *i.e.*, As the monkey thought on Rām's power, he waxed wroth; he planted his foot firm in the assembly and offered this wager: 'If thou canst stir my foot, thou wretch, Rām will take flight and I lose Sītā.' *This is a very favourite incident with the poets* (*e.g.*, *Dōh.* 516, *Sat.* vii, 76, *Misc.* 64, *Padm.*, *ch.* 678, 7). *After Rāban's destruction and Rām's return, Aygad went back to his own country* (*Rām.*, *Ut.*, *do.* 19). **Comp.**, अङ्गदादि (=अङ्गद-आदि) Aŋgad and the other monkey heroes (*see above*; *K. Rām.*, *Ki.* 1, *Su.* 31); अङ्गद-पन Aŋgad's wager (*Rām.*, *Ln.*, *ch.* 34, 13). **Exam.**, ¹*Git.*, *Bā.* 43, 2, पहुँची अङ्गद चारु हियहु पदिक-हार, (*Rām wears*) a wristlet, an armlet, and a beautiful neck-chain on his heart. ²*Misc.* 64, रावन सभा मध्य अतिभारी अङ्गद चरन धरे सो, मेघनाद कोटी बल-बीरा तनिको (= तनिक-उ) न चरन चडे सो, When in Rāban's great and very mighty assembly Aŋgad put down his foot, Mēgh'nad and ten millions of powerful heroes could not move his foot one whit; *Padm.*, *ch.* 678, 7, जिन्ह सामहिं मोरा रन कोपा, अङ्गद उरच पावँ

भुइँ रोपा, Gōrā waxed wroth on the battlefield in front of them, and, like Aŋgad, planted his foot firm on the ground; *Rām., Ln., ch.* 37, 3, इहाँ राम अङ्गदहि बुलावा, आइ चरन पङ्कज सिर नावा, Hither Rām called Aŋgad, and he coming bowed his head to (*Rām's*) lotus-like feet.

[*Skr.* अङ्गदः; *as above in all Gds.*]

अङ्गन *aŋgan* (1), **Ts.**, *subst. m.*, (*poet.* आँगन *ãgan*, *m.c.*, *Padm., ch.* 206, 1), *the same as* आँगन *ãgan*, *q.v.* **Exam.**, *Rām., Ln., chh.* 13, 4, सङ्ग्राम-अङ्गन सुभट सोवहिं, राम सर-निकरन्हि हये, On the field of battle the warriors are conspicuous (*through their numbers*), slain by the multitude of Rām's arrows; *ib., chh.* 31, 4, सङ्ग्राम-अङ्गन राम अङ्ग अनङ्ग बहु सोभा लही, On the field of battle Rām's body displayed the beauties of the bodyless one (*i.e., the love-god, a pun*) in manifold ways; *Padm., ch.* 206, 1, जस बिछोह जल मीन दुहेला, जल हुति काढ़ि अँगन महँ मेला, Just as fish are distressed through separation from water, (*when*) being pulled out of the water they are brought into the court-yard.

[*Skr.* अङ्गनम्, *Pr.* अङ्गणं (*Hēm.* i, 30); *as above possibly in all Gds.*]

अङ्गन *aŋgan* (2), *obl. plur. of* अङ्ग *aŋg*, *q.v.*

अङ्गना *aŋg'nā*, **Ts.**, *subst. f.*, a woman. **Exam.**, *K. Rām., Ut.* 145, अरध अङ्ग अङ्गना, नाम जोगीस जोगपति, In one half of his body (*Sib*) is a woman (*i.e. Pārbatī*), and his name is Jōgīs, (*as being*) the lord of the jōgī (*or ascetics*); *ib.* 154, नाम बामदेव, दाहिनो सदा, असङ्ग रङ्ग, अरधङ्ग अङ्गना, अनङ्ग को अनङ्ग है, (*Sib's*) name is Bām'deb, he is always gracious, his delight is solitude, in one half of his body he is a woman, he is the destroyer of Anaŋg (*i.e., the love-god*); *Kan.* 17, घनेरि जहाँ आवि भै आवि माँगैं नवो अङ्गना, सो मनो गीत गावैं, Numerous young women who came there to ask alms sang sweet songs.

[*Skr.* अङ्गना; *as above possibly in all Gds.*]

अङ्गनि *aŋgani*, *old obl. plur. of* अङ्ग *aŋg*, *q.v.*

अङ्गा *aŋgā* (1), *poet. for* अङ्ग *aŋg*, *q.v.*

अङ्गा *aŋgā* (2), **Tbh.**, *subst. m.*, [1]*the same as* अँगरक्खा *ãgar'khā*, *q.v.* (*Grs.* § 729); [2](*N. Bh.*) bits of old cotton padding in a quilt (*Grs.* § 731); [3](*Tirhut*) a kind of black bearded rice (*Grs.* § 972). **Exam.**, [2]*Coll.* (*Bh.*), अङ्गा के दाम होयत आव, Please let me have the price of the old cotton. *See* आँगा *ãga*.

[*Skr.* अङ्गकः, *Pr.* अङ्गओ, *Gd.* अङ्गा. *P. has* अङ्गा coat.]

अङ्गार *aŋgār*, **Ts.**, *subst. m.*, *the same as* आँगार *ãgār*, *q.v.* **Exam.**, *Mth. Rām., Ln.* 60, 5, कपि-दल आएल सागर पार, रिपु-दल तूल-राशि अङ्गार, The army of monkeys has come across the sea upon the army of its foes, like burning coals upon a heap of cotton.

अङ्गि *aŋgi*, (*f.* अङ्गिनि *aŋgini*), *Mth. and poet. for* अङ्गी *aŋgī* (1), *q.v.*

अङ्गिरस *aŋgiras*, *the same as* अङ्गिरा *aŋgirā*, *q.v.*

अङ्गिरा *aŋgirā*, अङ्गिरस *aŋgiras*, **Ts.**, *subst. m.*, the name of a saint to whom many of the hymns of the Rig-bēd are attributed. *He was one of the seven Maharkhis or great Rikhis, and also one of the ten Prajāpatis or progenitors of mankind. As an astronomical personification he is Brihaspati, the regent of the planet Jupiter, or the planet itself. According to one account, he was the son of Uru by Āgnēyī, the daughter of Agni; another account makes him born out of the mouth of Brahmā.* **Exam.**, *Mth. Rām., Ut.* 2, 2, अत्रि अङ्गिरा बामदेव सम बिरतख सकल बिबेक, Atri, Aŋgiras, and Bām'dēb, all (*of whom were*) saints of clear discrimination.

[*Skr.* अङ्गिराः *or* अङ्गिरसः; *as above possibly in all Gds.*]

अङ्गी *aŋgī* (1), **Ts.**, *adj.*, *com. gen.*, (*Mth. and poet.* अङ्गि *aŋgi*, *subst. f.* अङ्गिनी *aŋginī*, *Mth. and poet.* अङ्गिनि *aŋgini*), [1]having a limb *or* limbs; [2]having a body, bodily, corporeal. **Exam.**,[1] *Coll.* (*Bh.*), बिराट-रूप भगवान अङ्गी हैवन, औ, स्वर्ग भूमि समुद्रादि उन्ह के अङ्ग बाटन, God in the form of Birāṭ possesses limbs, and heaven, earth, sea, etc., are his limbs.

[*Skr.* अङ्गी; *as above possibly in all Gds.*]

अङ्गी *aŋgī* (2), **Tbh.**, *subst. f.*, a bodice, jacket. *The word is generally used in its long form* अँगिया *ãgiyā*, *q.v.*

[*Skr.* अङ्गिका, *Pr.* अङ्गिआ, *Gd.* अङ्गी. *S. has* अङ्गी, *both with the meaning of* bodice *and of* an allowance of one anna in the rupee (*S. Dy., p.* 55).]

अङ्गीकार *aŋgīkār*, अङ्गिकार *aŋgikār* (*poet.* अङ्गीकारा *aŋgīkārā*), **Ts.**, *subst. m.*, [1]agreement, acceptance, acquiescence, concession, submission; [2]avowal, confession; [3]promise. **Phr.**, अङ्गीकार करब, *v. tr.*, to accept, receive, agree to, consent, concede, admit, submit, be willing. **Exam.**, *Rām., Bā., ch.* 98, 4, पारबती तप कीन्ह अपारा, करहु तासु अब अङ्गीकारा, Par'batī has performed excessive penance; so do now accept her; *K. Rām., Ut.* 13, नाम तुलसी, पै भोंडे भाग, सो कहायो दास किए अङ्गीकार ऐसे बड़े दगाबाज को, My name is (*the pure*)

Tul'sī, but my condition is impure, yet calling me his servant, he has received me, (*who am*) such a great impostor; *Rām., Bā., do.* 193, 1, सापवि अङ्गीकार करि सब सबं कीन्ह बिचार, Submitting to the curse (*Rāban*) thought within his heart; *Chan.* कुरम-राज धरु धरनी-भार, कालकूट बर-कर बिस्तार, बड़वानल बस जलधि, उदार त्याग न सुपुरुख अङ्गीकार, The king tortoise bears the weight of the earth, the deadly poison is diffused in Sib's throat, the submarine fire floats on the liberal ocean, (*thus*) good men are never willing to desert (*their protégés*).

[*Skr.* अङ्गीकारः; *as above in most Gḍs., but S.* आङ्गिकार *or* अङ्गिहार, *both as a subst. and as a verb* (*S. Dy., p.* 56).]

अङ्गुर *aŋgur*, अङ्गुल *aŋgul*, **Ts.**, *subst. m.*, a finger's breadth, *equal to about two-thirds of an inch, or to the combined thickness of eight barley-corns; four finger-breadths are called a chāũā; twelve finger-breadths make one span* (*bittā*), *and two bittās or four chāũās make one cubit* (*hāth*), (*see Grs.* §§ 1489, 1490). *See* आँगुरी *āguri*.

[*Skr.* अङ्गुलः; *as above possibly in all Gḍs.*]

अङ्गुरि *aŋguri*, अङ्गुलि *aŋguli*, **Ts.**, *subst. f.*, *the short and less commonly used form of* आँगुरी *āguri*, *q.v.* **Exam.**, *Ukh., Act.* 2, निरखि अनिरुध रूप मन गुनि, अङ्गुरि देख देखाय गो, Seeing Anirudh, she thought over his form, and pointed him out with her finger.

[*Skr.* अङ्गुलिः; *as above possibly in all Gḍs.*]

अङ्गुल *aŋgul*, *the same as* अङ्गुर *aŋgur*, *q.v.* (*Grs* § 1489). **Exam.**, *Rām., Ut., do.* 79, 2, जुग अङ्गुल कर बीच सब राम भुजहिँ मोहि तात, Two fingers' breadth, sir, was all the distance between me and the arms of Rām; *K. Rām., Ki.* 1, चारिहूँ चरन के चपेट चाँपे चिपिटि गो, उचके उचकि चारि अङ्गुल अचल गो, Pressed by the pressure of (*Hanumān's*) four feet the earth was flattened down (*to hell*), and as he leaped off (*to Laŋkā*) the mountain sunk (*into the earth*) four finger-breadths.

अङ्गुलि *aŋguli*, *the same as* अङ्गुरि *aŋguri*, *q.v.* **Exam.**, *Rām., Bā., ch.* 124, 3, चितव जो लोचन अङ्गुलि लाँयें, प्रगट जुगल ससि तेहि के भाय, (*Men*) who gaze through their fingers placed before their eyes, and to whom the moon appears to be doubled.

अङ्गुष्ठ *aŋgushṭh*, **Ts.**, *subst. m.*, [1]the thumb; [2]the great toe. **Exam.**, [2]*Mth. Rām., Ki.* 9, 6, सुनि बिहँसि चरन अङ्गुष्ठ लगाय, दस योजन खसल से जाय, As he heard this, he smiled, and applied his great toe (*to the bones, and kicked them, so that*) they fell down at a distance of ten leagues; *Git., Ut.* 17, 3, सुभग अङ्गुष्ठ, आँगुरी अबिरल, कछुक अरुन नख जोति-जगमगति, Beautiful was (*Rām's*) great toe, and his toes were close, and the slightly red sheen of his nails was of glittering brightness.

[*Skr* अङ्गुष्ठः; *as above possibly in all Gḍs.*]

√**अँच** *ãch*, अच *ach*, (*pr. pts.* अँचत *ãchat*; अँचल *ãchal*; अँचब *ãchab*; अँचै *ãchai*), **Tbh.**, *v. intr. and v. tr.*, (*W. Bh. and Bw.*), *the same as* √अँचाव *ãchāb*, *q.v.* **Exam.**, [1]*Rām., Bā., ch.* 361, 2, अँचै पान सब काहू पाये, Having rinsed (*their mouths*) they all and every one received pan (*to chew*); *Git., Ar.* 17, 7, रघुबर अँचइ उठे, सबरी करि प्रनाम कर जोरि, Raghubar (*i.e. Rām*) having rinsed (*his mouth*) arose, (*while*) the Sewari paid reverence with folded hands. [1]*Krish.* 57, मनो मधुकर अचै सुधि है अवि, बालक सोए न जाग्यो री, As a bee does not wake up a little child, (*when*) it eagerly sips the nectar (*from its face*). [2]*Āg.* iii, 45, पैठि बिबर मिलि तापसिहि, अचइ पानि, खइ चार, Having entered the cavern and met with the ascetic (*i.e., the holy woman Swayamprabhā, see Rām., Ki., do.* 24), (*Hanumān*) drinks water and eats fruit.

[*This is a secondary derivative root from the Skr.* √आचम् (= आ + चम्), *cl.* I, आचामति, *which in Gḍ. assumes the form* √अँचाव (*q.v.*; *cf. Hēm.* iv, 226, 397, *and Gḍ. Gr.* § 351). *The latter, happening to coincide in form with Gḍ. causal roots in* आव (*e.g.* √कराव cause to do), *is popularly mistaken for a causal, and from it, by the rejection of the apparently causal suff.* आव, *the new primary root* √अँच *is derived. On the shortening of the initial* आ, *see the remarks under art.* अ *a* (6), आच॰ *being changed to* अच *or* अँच (*see Gḍ. Gr.* §§ 143—146). *See also the remarks on derivation under art.* √अँचव *and* √अँचाव.— *Besides W. Bh. and Bw., this very reduced form of the root occurs only in H.* √अच *and Bg.* √आँच; *the other Gḍs. have only the longer forms* √अँचव *or* √अँचाव, *q.v.*]

अचक *achak*, (*str. f.* अचक्का *achákkā*), **Tbh.**, *subst. m.*, unexpectedness, unpreparedness, suddenness, accident, chance. *It has been only met with by us in the instr. case* अचक सेँ *achak sẽ*, *used adverbially*, unexpectedly, unawares, suddenly, accidentally, by chance (*Mth. Gr.* § 201). *See* अचाका *achākā*, अचाँचक *achãchak*, अचानक *achānak*, अचानचक *achān'chak*.

[*Der.? Apparently a compound of the neg. pref.* अ *and* चक. *The latter is probably a corruption for* चिक, *and apparently derived from a compound root* (*Gḍ. Gr.* § 353) चिक, *connected with Skr.* चित् *and* √क to make known. *G.* अचक *or* अचुक, *M.* अचूक.]

अचक्कन *ach'kan*, **Tbh.**, *subst. m.*, a long loose coat buttoning right down the front (*Grs.* § 729). *It is like a dressing gown, and is worn over the chap'kan.*

[*Der. ? B. and H.* आचकन.]

अचकरी *ach'kari*, **Tbh.**, *subst. f.*, wantonness, lasciviousness, obscenity, indecency (*especially in speech*). *See* अचगरी *ach'gari*.

[*Derived from the Skr. compound* अवाच्य *and* कृत्या, *lit.* doing that which is unspeakable, *i.e.* obscene; *with pleon. suff.* क, *Skr.* अवाच्यकृत्यिका, *Pr.* अवाचकरिआ *or* (*by false analogy*) औचकरिआ (*see Hēm.* i, 172), *hence Gḍ.* * औचकडी *or* (*shortened*) अचकडी (*Gḍ. Gr.* § 26) *or* अचकड़ी *or B.* अचकर (*Gḍ. Gr.* § 103). *The intermediate Gḍ. form with* ड *is still preserved in the M. adj.* अचकड, obscene, indecent.]

अचका *ach'kā*, (*f.* अचकी *ach'kī*), **Tbh.**, *adj.*, *the same as* अचिक *achik*, *q.v.* **Exam.**, अचकी सुरती दे हँउ, Give a little dry tobacco (*Āz. Gy.*).

[*A corruption for* अचिका, *str. f. of* अचिक, *q.v.*]

अचक्का *achákkā*, **Tbh.**, *subst. m.*, *str. f. of* अचक *áchak*, *q.v.* *Only met with in the instr. or loc.* अचकें *or* अचक्का में unexpectedly (*Āz. Gy.*). **Exam.**, *Coll.*, (*Bh.*), अचक्का में पकर लिहलें, They caught him unawares *or* unpreparedly. *See* अचाका *achākā*.

अचगरी *ach'gari*, **Tbh.**, *subst. f.*, *a modification of* अचकरी *ach'kari*, *q.v.* **Exam.**, *Krish.* 235, 'जाति पाँति सों करौं अचगरी' यह कहि हसति खिरावति, (*Jasumati*) upbraids her son (*Krish'n*), saying, 'What (*art thou indulging in*) wanton speech with (*people of thy own*) caste and lineage'!

अचङ्गा *acháṅgā*, **Tbh.**, *subst. m.*, (*Mg.*) a stage, a shelf (*B. Gr.*, III (*Mg.*), *p.* 87).

[*Der. ? Said by Pandits to be a corruption of* अचङ्ग, *from Skr.* अचं-ग.]

अचञ्चल *acháñchal*, **Ts.**, *adj.*, *com. gen.*, (*subst. f* अचञ्चला *achañchalā*), not moving to and fro, immoveable, firm, fixed, steady. **Exam.**, *Rām.*, *Bā.*, *ch.* 242, 4, भये बिलोचन चारु अचञ्चल, मनहुँ सकुचि निमि तजेउ द्रिगञ्चल, His beautiful eyes became immoveable, just as if Nimi, in confusion, had given up the winking of his eyes.

[*Skr.* अचञ्चल: ; *as above in all Gḍs.*]

अचढ़ *acharh*, **Tbh.**, *adj.*, *com. gen.*, unridden, *hence of a horse* unbroken. **Exam.**, *Anon.*, (*Mth.*), बछि कैसन, पिठ बसन न जीन, घोड़ा अचढ़ कहाव नवीन, A young horse which has not been trained (*and*) on whose back a saddle has never been fastened, is called acharh; *Coll.*, (*Mth.*), ओ अचढ़ जकाँ करैत अछि, He acts like an unbroken horse.

[*Derived from* √चढ़ *and neg. suff.* अ *a* (4). *It appears to be the same as the H.* अचचढ़, *spelt* अँचढ़ *in H. Dy.*]

अँचताहर *ăch'tāhar*, **Tbh.**, *subst. m.*, (*E. Mg.*) the man who stokes the fire in a sugar boiling-house (*Grs.* § 303). *See* अँचवाहा *ăch'wāhā*.

[*Derived from* √एँच (*q.v.*) *and the Mg. verbal termination* ताहर (*q.v.*). *See also the remarks under* अँचना.]

अचतुर *achátur*, **Ts.**, *adj.*, *com. gen.*, (*subst. f.* अचतुरा *achaturā*), not dexterous, inapt, inactive, stupid. **Exam.**, *Coll.*, (*Bh.*), तूं बड़ अचतुर देखि परतारैड, कि अपनी हानि आप करत बाड़ँ, You appear to be very stupid, in that you yourself do yourself harm.

[*Skr.* अचतुर: ; *as above possibly in all Gḍs.*]

अँचना *ăch'nā*, **Tbh.**, *subst. m.*, (*E. Bh.*) the stick used as a poker in a sugar boiling-house (*Grs.* § 303).

[*Derived from the Skr.* √आ-कृष्, *through a secondary radical form* आ-कर्ष (*probably the base of the future tense, see H. R.*, *p.* 40), *which appears in Pr. in the form* आअंच *or* आइंच *or* (*contr. and disaspirated*) अंच (3 *pers. sg.* आअंचइ *or* आइंचइ *or* अंचइ, *Hēm.* iv, 187). *Hence the Skr. word* आकर्षणम् *or* (*with pleon.* क) आकर्षणकम्, a stick for pulling about *or* poking, *would take in Pr. the form* अंचणअं, *whence comes the Gḍ.* अँचना. *Similarly the Skr. word* आकर्ष *would turn into Pr.* आइंच *or* अंच *and Gḍ.* ऐंच *or* अँच, *which last, however, is now only met with in compounds, such as* अँचताहर *and* अँचवाहा, one who wields a poker (*q.v.*). *Similarly Skr.* आकर्षक: *becomes Pr.* अंचओ, *Gḍ.* अचा, *which occurs in the compound* चुल्हअचा, one who pokes the fireplace (*q.v.*). *Comp. the B.* √ऐँच to pull, *M.* √आँचव.]

अचम्पल *ách'pal*, **Ts.**, *adj.*, *com. gen.*, [1]wayward, unruly, obstinate; [2]unsteady, restless, inconstant; [3]frisky, sprightly, vivacious. **Exam.**, *Coll.*, (*Bh.*), [1]ओ गौ के बछा इस ओ अचम्पल बन पकड़ रहता, The calf of that cow seems to keep obstinate and dumb. [2]*Coll.*, (*Bh.*), मोर लरिकवा ऐसन अचम्पल बाड़े कि एक ठौर बैसल नाहिं रहता, My boy is so restless that he won't sit still in one place.

(*The word is not commonly used with the second and third meanings.*)

[*From the Skr.* चपल:, *with the intens. pref.* अ *a* (5), *q.v.* *P.* अचपल.]

अचञ्पला *ách'palā*, **Ts.**, *adj.*, (*f.* अचञ्पली *ách'pălī*), *str. f. of* अचञ्पल *ách'pal*, *q.v.*

अचञ्पलाहटि *ach'palāhaṭi*, **Ts.**, *subst. f.*, [1]restlessness, inconstancy, unsteadiness; [2]unruliness, obstinacy, waywardness; [3]friskiness, sprightliness, vivacity.

[*Derived from the Ts.* अचपल *by the Tbh. suff.* आहटि; *therefore a hybrid formation. See Gḍ. Gr.* § 284.]

अचञ्पली *ach'palī* (1), *fem. of* अचञ्पला *ach'palā*, *q.v.*

अचञ्पली *ach'palī* (2), **Ts.**, *subst. f.*, *the same as* अचञ्पलाहटि *ach'palāhaṭi*, *q.v.*

[*Derived from* अचञ्पल *by the Prs. suff.* ई *forming abs. nouns.*]

अचञ्मन *ách'man*, **Tbh.**, *subst. m.*, the act of rinsing the mouth before or after a meal, *or* before a religious ceremony (*by way of purification*). *See* अँचञ्वन *ách'wan and the tats.* आचमन *āchaman.*

[*Skr.* आचमनम्, *Pr.* आचमणं *or* अचमणं, *Gḍ.* अचमन. *See the remarks under art.* अ *a* (6); *also those under* √अँचाव.]

अचञ्मनी *ách'manī*, **Tbh.**, *subst. f.*, (*Bh.*) a spoon for throwing water on the Lingam, *used in worshipping the idol* (*Grs.* § 774).

[*Skr.* आचमनिका, *Pr.* आचमणिआ *or* अचमणिअ, *Gḍ.* अचमनी. *See the remarks under* अ *a* (6). *Cf. S.* आचिमाड़ the palm of the hand full of any liquid (*S. Dy.*, *p.* 15).]

अचम्भव *achambhab*, **Ts.**, *subst. m.*, [1]*concr.*, something wonderful, a wonder, marvel, miracle, prodigy; [2]*abs.*, wonder, astonishment, amazement (*in this sense only in the phr.* अचम्भव करब). **Phr.** अचम्भव मानब *lit.* to consider (*something to be*) a marvel, to be astonished *or* amazed at *something* (*constructed with the acc. of the object of wonder*); अचम्भव करब *lit.* to make a marvel *of something* (*i.e. look upon it as a marvel*), to be astonished *or* amazed at *something* (*constructed with the abl. of the object of wonder*). **Exam.**, [1]*Krish.* 70, सूरदास, प्रभु बड़े अचम्भव तीनि तिलक कहँ पाये, Sūr Dās (*says*), O Lord, this indeed is a wonderful thing, whence did you get the three marks (*on your face*)? *Rām.*, *Ln.*, *ch.* 68, 8, तासु तेज प्रभु बदन समाना, सुर मुनि सबहि अचम्भव माना, His (*i.e. Kumbh'karan's*) soul entered the Lord's mouth, (*and*) all the gods and sages were amazed at it. [2]*Coll.*, (*Bh.*), बड़ अचम्भव के बात भयी कि मछरी बा बेट से मनुख जनम्मे, It is a matter of great astonishment that a fish gives birth to a man. *See* अचम्भो *achambhō*, अचम्हो *achamhō*.

(*The word has not been met with by us as an adj., though it may occasionally be so used by the vulgar.*)

[*Derivation uncertain; possibly identical with Skr.* अद्भुतम् any extraordinary event, *though the change of* द *to* च *is quite exceptional. The nearest analogy is the change of* ध *to* च (*e.g. Pr.* चलचबो *for Skr.* धलधबं: *Hēm.* i, 49, 265, *B.*, *Bg.* चालताँव *for Skr.* धलधाव:). *The opposite change of* च *or* छ *to* ध *is common enough* (*see Gḍ. Gr.* § 11). *Perhaps the S. and Kn. forms point to an influence of the Arabic on the change.*—**H.** *and P.* अचम्भा *or* अचंभा, *G.* अचम्भो, *M.* अचम्बा, *Kn.* अजाप *or* अजापा, *S.* अजब (*Ar.* عجب), *N.* अचम (*N. L.* 2, 47).]

अचम्भो *achámbhō*, *a contr. of* अचम्भव *achambhab*, *q.v.* **Exam.**, *Padm.*, *do.* 280, 1, देखत रहे अचम्भो जोगी हस्ति न आव, The Jōgī kept looking at the miracle, (*but*) the elephants (*which had been whirled up to the sky*) did not come down again. *See* अचम्हो *achamhō.*

अचम्हो *achamhō*, *a Bh. cor. of* अचम्भो *achambhō*, *q.v.* **Exam.**, *Gōp.* 11, मनञ्वाँ मेँ सोचत बाड़े बराम्हन के छोकड़वा, 'कवन रे अचम्हो भोर गेले!' The Brāhman boy thinks in his mind, 'what a wonderful thing has come to pass!'

अचर *áchar* (1), **Ts.**, *adj.*, *com. gen.*, *lit.* immoveable, devoid of the power of locomotion; *in this sense never used, but only in contrast with* चर (*see the compounds below*) *in the sense of* [1]insentient, unconscious, devoid of sensation *or* consciousness (*syn.* जड़); *hence*, [2]unintelligent, devoid of intelligence *or* understanding, foolish, stupid. **Comp.**, चर-अचर (*Sat.* iii, 47) or अचर-चर (*Rām.*, *Bā.*, *do.* 94, 1; *Bin.* 46) or चराचर (= चर-अचर, *Gīt.*, *Ut.* 38, 8), *lit.* moveable and immoveable, *hence* sentient (*men, animals, but excl. superhuman beings*) and insentient (*trees, minerals, etc.*) creation (*syn.* जड़ चेतन्य, *comm. to Bin.* 203), *or* wise and foolish people. **Phr.**, चर अरु अचर the sentient and insentient creation (*Bin.* 91; *Rām.*, *Bā.*, *ch.* 115, 8). **Exam.**, *Rām.*, *A.*, *ch.* 134, 2, परसि चरन रज अचर सुखारी, Touching the dust of (*Rām's*) feet, insentient creatures were gladdened; *Bin.* 203, चौदसि चौदह-भुवन-अचर-चर-रूप गोपाल, The fourteenth lunar day (*reminds us that*) Gōpāl constitutes the fourteen worlds and the insentient creation; *Bin.* 46, अचर-चर-रूप हरि सरब-गत सरबदा बसत इति बासना-धूप दीजे, 'Hari, as constituting the whole insentient and sentient creation, is all pervading and existing at all times,' such fragrant incense (*of praise*) you should offer (*to him*); *Rām.*, *Bā.*, *ch.* 115, 8, चर अरु अचर नाग नर देवा, सकल करहिँ पद पङ्कज सेवा, Sentient and insentient creatures (*i.e., animals as well as trees and* *minerals*), nāgas, men, and dēbs, they all do service to (*Rām's*) lotus-like feet; *Gīt.*, *Ut.* 38, 8, चौदह भुवन चराचर हरषित आए राम राज-धानी, (*All*) the sentient and insentient creatures of (*all*) the fourteen worlds rejoice that Rām has come to his capital. ²*Rām.*, *A.*, *ch.* 229, 8, होत न भूतल भाव भरत को, अचर सचर चर अचर करत को, There is not to be found in the (*whole*) world a disposition like Bharat's, who makes the foolish wise and the wise foolish, (*the comm. of the Lakh'naū edition, however, interprets* who causes the solid to dissolve (द्रवि उठे) and the dissolving to become solid (जड़ीभूत)); *Rām.*, *Bā.*, *do.* 94, 1, 2, जे सजीव जग, अचर चर, नारि पुरुष, अस नाम, ते निज निज मरजाद तजि भये सकल बस काम, Whatever living creatures are in the world, whether fools or wise, whether men or women, or whatever else they may be called, they all, abandoning their own natures, came under the influence of love; *Sat.* iii, 47, भजु, तुलसी, ओघादि कर्ं सहित तत्त्व-गुन धाम, भव आयुलेय जासु बल भव मन चर अचर करन, Do thou worship—(*says*) Tul'sī Dās—(*Rām whose name consists of*) the initial (*letter* रा ra *of* राशि mass, *a syn.*) of (*the word*) 'ōgh' together with the final (*letter* म ma *of* व्योम ether) which belongs to the five elements, whose power renders Bhava (*Sib*) immortal, and the unintelligent mind, intelligent. *See* अचल *achal.*

[*Skr.* अचरः; *as above in all Gds.*]

अचर *áchar* (2), **Ts.**, *adj.*, *com. gen.*, *the same as* अचल *achal*, *q.v.*

[*Skr.* अचलः; *the difference between* अचर (1) *and* अचर (2) *is that the former is derived from the Skr.* √चर्, *but the latter from the Skr.* √चल्; *the* र *of the former is original, while that of the latter is a mere B. provincialism for* ल; *the former occurs only with a specialised technical meaning, but the latter is used with its original and more general meaning. It may be added that the two Skr.* √चर् *and* √चल् *are themselves ultimately identical.*]

अचरज *acharaj*, आचरज्ज *āchar'j*, **Ts.**, (I) *ad.*, *com. gen.*, marvellous, astonishing, wonderful, extraordinary. **Exam.**, *Sat.* iv, 45, खग-सुमन अवतन्स चह चावत अचरज (*fem.*) बात, Oh marvellous thing! the fool wants to obtain an ornament made of the flowers of heaven (*see also Rām.*, *Bā.*, *ch.* 168, 6 आचरज बखानी marvellous accounts).

(II) *subst. m.*, ¹*con.*, a wonderful thing, a wonder, marvel, miracle, prodigy; ²*abs.*, wonder, astonishment, surprise. **Phr.**, ¹अचरज मानब (*San.* 55), *v. tr.*, *lit.* to consider (*something to be*) a wonder, to wonder at, to be astonished at; ²अचरज आएब (*Rām.*, *Bā.*, *ch.* 134, 4) *or* अचरज लागब (*Rām.*, *A.*, *ch.* 38, 1), *or* अचरज होएब (*Padm.* 449), *v. intr.*, (*lit.* the coming *or* being of astonishment, *hence*) to be astonished, to be surprised, to wonder (*with the dat. or obl. f. of the person affected with the feeling*). **Exam.**, *Misc.* 14, जमुना के तीरे तीरे धेनु चरावे, बन्सी में कुछ अचरज गावे, On the banks of Jamunā's stream thou tendest thy cattle and playest something wonderful on thy flute; *Padm.*, *ch.* 68, 3, देखिय कछु अचरज अनभला, तरवर एक आवत है चला, He saw something marvellous and portentous, a large tree was coming along walking; *Rām.*, *Bā.*, *ch.* 131, 8, कह प्रसङ्ग मोहि सकल पुरारी, मुनि-मन मोह भो अचरज भारी, Tell me the whole story, Purārī, for it is a marvel that a saint's mind should be filled with passion; *ib.*, *A.*, *ch.* 188, 1, नहिँ अचरज जुग जुग चलि आईं, केहि न दीन्ह रघुबीर बड़ाईं, It is no wonder, it has been so for ages, who is there whom Raghubīr (*i.e. Rām*) did not exalt? *ib.*, *A.*, *ch.* 200, 2, यह तुम्हार अचरज नहिँ, ताता, It is not wonderful that thou shouldst act thus, O son, (*lit.* this *action* is no miracle of thine); *Misc.* 28, अचरज एक देखा रे भाई, निरगुन भव सगुन भो आई, One miracle I have seen, O brother, the transmundane god has become incarnate; *Sat.* ii, 50, काक-सुता पिय ना करे, यह अचरज बड़ भाय, तुलसी, केहि उपदेस सुनि जनहि पिता घर जाय, This is a great marvel, the cuckoo makes no nest (*in which to lay his eggs*)—(*says*) Tul'sī Das—; by (*lit.* hearing) whose advice, then, does he (*when hatched*) go to the abode of his father and mother? *K. Rām.*, *Su.* 20, तुलसी, सुन्यौ न कान सलिल सरपी समान, अति अचरज कियौ केसरी कुमार हैं, Tul'sī (*says*), we have never heard with our ears (*that*) water (*can be as inflammable*) as clarified butter; Kēsarī's son (*i.e. Hanumān*) has done a great miracle; *ib.*, *Ut.* 72, अति सो अभागे अनुराग न राम पद, मूढ़ एतो बड़ो अचरज देखी सुनी सो, The fool who, hearing or seeing so great a miracle, does not conceive a love for Rām's feet, is utterly wretched; *Rām.*, *Bā.*, *do.* 118, 1, बहुरि कहहु, करुना-यतन, कीन्ह जो अचरज राम, Tell me again, O gracious Lord, what miracles Rām performed; *Rām.*, *Bā.*, *ch.* 176, 2, जागेउ नृप अनभएउ बिहाना, देखि भवन अति, अचरज माना, The king awoke when the morning had not yet broke, and, seeing himself at home, was much astonished; *San.* 55, तेज होत तन तरनि को, अचरज मानत लोग, तुलसी, जो पानी भयो बहुर न पावक जोग, When the fire of the sun (*i.e. passion*) gets into the body (*of a saint*), people are astonished (*for*, *says*) Tul'sī Das, that which has become (*cool like*) water cannot again become (*hot like*) fire? ²*Rām.*, *A.*, *ch.* 215, 8, यह आनन्द अचरज प्रति-ग्रामा, जनु मरु भूमि कलप-तरु जामा, There was the same delight and astonishment in every village, as though the tree of paradise had sprung up in the desert; *Padm.*, *do.* 449,

2, अचरज भयो सबन कहँ, भए ससि कमलहिँ मेल, All were amazed (*on seeing that*) a meeting of the moon with the lotus was taking place; *Rām., Ba., ch.* 134, 4, सुनि सब के मन अचरज लागा, On hearing it, every one's mind was astonished; *ib., A., ch.* 38, 1, आजु हमहिँ बड़ अचरज लागा, To-day we are greatly surprised (*at seeing Das'rath not rise at the usual hour*).

[*Skr.* आश्चर्यः, *with an inorganic sibilant,* (*from* आ *and* √चर), *which perhaps accounts for the loss of it in the modern tats. The Pr. forms are* अच्छरिअं *or* अच्छरीअं *or* अच्छरिज्जं *or* अच्चेरं, (*Hem.* i, 58), *none of which has survived in Gd. As above in all Gds., but S.* अचरजु; *G. also* अचरत one who is astonished, *and* अचरति astonishment.]

अँचरधरुआ *ãchar'dharuā,* अँचरधरौआ *ãchar'dharauā,* —*see under* अँचर *ãchar.*

अचरनवा *acharan'wā, the same as* अँचरवा *ãchar'wā, lg. f. of* अँचर *ãchar, q.v.* Exam., *B. Gr.,* II (*Bh.*). iv, 11, ताहि मैं सोवतै बलमुआ रो, करतौं अचरनवैं बाड़, In it (*i.e., my bungalow*) my husband would have slept, (*while*) I fanned him with the skirt of my body-cloth.

[*This is a very vulgar form derived from* अँचर *by means of the pleon. suff.* न, *identical with the Pr. suff.* ण (*Hem.* ii, 165). *This makes* अँचरना, *of which* अचरनवा *is the long form.*]

अँचरवा *ãchar'wā,* अचरवा *achar'wā,* Tbh., *subst. m., lg. f. of* अँचर *ãchar, q.v.* Exam., *Bais.* 7, अँगना बोढ़ारत मोरा उड़ल अँचरवा, रामा, While sweeping in the yard (*of my house*) the skirts of my cloth flew away, O Rām!

अँचरा *ãch'rā,* अचरा *ach'rā,* Tbh., *subst. m., str. f. of* अँचर *ãchar, q.v.* (*Grs.* § 741). *See also Index to Mth. Ch., s.v.* Exam., *Mag.* 23, काहे लिहु अँचरा ढरके, रँगिलिया, काहे लिहु पतरी सरीर, Why is thy bosom-cloth so loose, fair lady, why is thy body so thin? *ib.* 29, अँचरा खोल गोरी अँगनवाँ सेँ सूते गे, रसिका के फाटैत है करेज, Loosening her bosom-cloth, the fair lady sleeps in the courtyard, and the heart of her lover (*dat. ethicus*) is torn; *B. Gr.,* II (*Bh.*), xxiv, 8, अचरा उघार ओकरावत बा, Raising my bosom-cloth he bawls (*at me*); *Sal.* 2, बालकपन अचरा बान्हलि, From childhood I tied on a bosom-cloth.

[*This word is almost entirely limited to the Mg. dialect. It should be carefully distinguished from another* अँचरा, *which is an obl. form of* अँचर (*q.v.*), *used with or without a postposition; e.g.,* अँचरा पे, On my bosom-cloth (*B. Gr. II, Bh.,* xxiii, 6); मोरे अँचरा से, With my bosom-cloth (*Sudh.* 15); अचरा छिपैतौं, I would have hid under my bosom-cloth (*Bih.* xvii, 1); अचरा बहारितौं, I would have swept with the skirts of my bosom-cloth (*Gōr.* xii, 3). *See the remarks under* अँगना *ãg'nā.*]

[*Skr.* अञ्चलः *or* (*with pleon.* क) अञ्चलकः, *Pr.* अंचलओ, *B.* आँचरा (*with* र *for* ल, *see Gd. Gr.* § 30). *H.* आँचरा, *P.* आँचला, *M.* अचला (a handkerchief), *S.* आँचिरु (a piece of cloth for straining with).]

अँचरिया *ãchariyā,* अचरिया *achariyā,* Tbh., *subst. f, lg f. fem. in a dim. or endearing sense of* अँचरा *ãch'rā, q.v.* Exam., *B. Gr.,* II (*Bh.*), vii, 3, ताहि रे बीचे राधा मोरी धरेला अँचरिया, Between the two (*i.e., Ganges and Jamunā*) Rādhā (*i.e. Krish'n*) seizes hold of my dear little bosom-cloth; *ib.* vii, 4, छाड़ैं छाड़ैं राधा हमरि अँचरिया, Let go, let go, O Rādhā, my dear little bosom-cloth!

अँचरी *ãch'rī,* अचरी *ach'rī,* Tbh., *subst. fem. of* अँचरा *ãch'rā, with the force of a diminutive or of endearment.* (*Grs.* § 766). Phr. अँचरी पाटी *or* अँचरी पटी *or sometimes* (*elliptically*) *only* अँचरी, an ornament tied to the border of the bride's body-cloth (*Grs.* §§ 766, 1331).

अचल *achal,* (*old dir. f.* अचलु *achalu*), Ts., (I) *adj., com. gen.,* (*subst. f* अचला *ach'lā*), *lit.* not moving, immoveable; [2]*met.* immoveable *by opposition, i.e.* unconquerable; *or* unremovable *by death, i.e.* alive; *or* unshaken *by vicissitudes, i.e.* firm, confirmed, established, enduring; *or* unchangeable, unalterable *by fate, and with many other varieties of meaning;* [3]*mentally or morally,* imperturbable, constant, (*syn.* थिर, *opp.* विचल). Exam., [1]*Rām., Ut., ch.*73, 5, नौकारूढ़ चलत जग देखा, अचल मोह-बस आपुहिँ लेखा, People on board a ship see the world moving, and in their delusion suppose themselves to be not moving; *ib., Ar., ch.* 7, 15, मुनि मग माँझ अचल होइ बैसा, The sage, becoming immoveable, sat down in the middle of the road; *ib., Bā., ch.* 30, 5, ध्रुव सगलानि जपेउ हरि-नाऊँ, पायेउ अचल अनूपम ठाऊँ, Dhruva in his trouble called upon the name of Hari, and (*thus*) obtained an immoveable, incomparable station (*in the heavens*). [2]*Rām., Bā., ch.* 157, 6, भुज-बल अतुल अचल संग्रामा, Unequalled in strength of arm, and unconquerable in battle; *ib., Ki., ch.* 10, 2, अचल करौं, तनु राखहु प्राना, I allow thee (*i.e. Bāli*) to live, keep the breath of your body; *ib., Ut., do.* 85, 4, काय बचन मन मम पद करेहु अचल अनुराग, In deed, word, and thought, exercise an unshaken devotion to my feet; *similarly Gīt., Ut.* 35, 2, अचल प्रतीति unshaken faith; *Sat.* iii, 96, अचल बचन unshaken word; *Rām., A., ch.* 68, 8, अचल अहिवात unshaken *or* enduring happy married life; *ib., A., ch.* 29, 9, अचल बिपति enduring calamity; *ib.*, *Bā.*, *do.* 95, 2, अचल समाधि enduring trance; *Git.*, *Su.* 6, 4, अचल असीस enduring blessing; *Hb.* viii, 6, अचल बिचार firm opinion; *Rām.*, *Su.*, *ch.* 23, 1, अचल राज firmly established rule; *Git.*, *Bā.* 2, 1, अचल भयेउ कुल राजु the family and the kingdom have been secured; *Rām.*, *A.*, *ch.* 271, 6, बिधि प्रपंच अस अचल अनादी, The illusion of the Creator is thus unalterable and eternal; *Chan.*, अचल रङ्ग बर पच्छिन पाँखि देख अकल्पित अपनहिँ आँखि, Observe with your own eyes what lasting and inartificial colours are in birds' wings. ³*Rām.*, *Ar.*, *ch.* 40, 7, षट-बिकार-जित अनघ अकामा, अचल अकिंचन सुचि सुख-धामा, Saints are victors over the six disturbing influences, sinless, passionless, imperturbable, poor, chaste, and contented; *ib.*, *Ln.*, *ch.* 77, 9, अमल अचल मन त्रोन समाना, His pure and constant soul stands for a quiver; *Sat.* i, 5, सो देखत तुलसी प्रगट अमल सु-अचल प्रचण्ड, Him (*i.e. Rām*) Tul'sī perceives clearly as the pure, all-constant, and mighty; *Sat.* iii, 96, धरा धराधर सम अचल, बचन न बिचल सु-धीर, (*Rām*) is firm like the earth and the mountains,—not changeable, but constant in his promises.

(II) *subst. m.*, ¹a mountain; ²*a name of* Sib; ³*a symbolical name of* the number seven. **Exam.**, ¹*K. Rām.*, *Ln.* 55, भरत को कुसल अचल ल्यायो चलि कै, (*Hanumān*) has gone and brought back with him good news from Bharat and the mountain (*on which the curing herb grew*); *Pārb.* 8, 4, अचल-सुता मनु अचल बयारि कि डोलइ, The daughter of the mountain (*Himālaya*) remained (*firm*) like a mountain, for can a wind shake it? *Similarly*, *Hb.* v, 28, 46, गोबर्धन अचल the mountain Gobar'dhan; *K. Rām.*, *Ut.* 136, चित्रकूट अचल the mountain Chitrakūṭ. ²*Pārb.*, *chh.* 13, 1, पुर खरभर उर हरषेउ अचल अखण्डलु, Sib, the Destroyer, rejoiced in his heart at the tumult in the city. *See* अचर *achar* (2).

[*This word is also said to have the meaning of* 'an old man' (*Hd. Dy*)., *lit.* decrepit, unable to walk; *but this is doubtful; we have not met with it in that sense.*]

[*Skr.* अचलः; *P.* अचल, *G.* अचळ *or* अचर, *M.* अचल *or* अचळ *or* अचर, *B.* अचल, *S.* अचलु, *H.* अचल *or* अचर.]

अचलु *achalŭ*, *old dir. f. of* अचल *achal*, *q.v.* **Exam.**, *K. Rām.*, *Ki.* 1, चारिहूँ चरन के चपेट चाँपे चिपिटि गो, उचके उचकि चारि अंगुल अचलु गो, Pressed by the pressure of (*Hanumān's*) four feet, the earth was flattened down (*to hell*), and as he leaped off (*to Laṅkā*) the mountain sunk (*into the earth*) four finger-breadths.

[*Skr.* अचलः *Pr.* अचलो, *Ap. Pr.* अचलु (*Hēm.* iv, 331).]

अँचव्ला *ā̆ch'lā*, अचव्ला *ach'lā*, **Tbh.**, *subst. m.*, *str. f. of* आँचल *ā̆chal*, *the same as* आँचर *ā̆char*, *q.v.*

√अँचव *ā̆chaw*, अचव *achaw*, (*pr. pts.* अँचवत *ā̆ch'wat*; अँचवल *ā̆ch'wal*; अँचवब *ā̆ch'wab*; अँचवै *ā̆chaai*; *prec. imper.* अँचइअउ *ā̆chaïya* (*Rām.*, *A.*, *ch.* 111, 1); *Bw. pret.* अँचयो *ā̆chayŏ*), **Tbh.**, *v. tr.*, (*Bw. and W. Bh.*), *the same as* √अँचाव *ā̆chāb*, *q.v.* **Exam.**, ¹*Coll.*, (*W. Bh.*, *Āz.*) रस अँचवत बा, He is sipping the juice; *Rām.*, *A.* 222, 7, जो अँचवत मातहिँ नृप तेई, नाहिन साधु-सभा जिन्ह सेई, Those kings who merely sip (*kingly power*) are maddened by it, unless (*they be guided*) by a council of good men. ²*Rām.*, *A.*, *ch.* 111, 1, एक कलस भरि आनहिँ पानी, 'अँचइअ नाथ,' कहहिँ मिदु बानी, One brought a pitcher full of water, and with tender voice said (*to Rām*), 'Drink, my Lord'; *Dŏh.* 306, व्याध पपीहहि प्रेम की सुन रे तुलसी दास, जो अँचवै जल स्वाति को परिहरि चारि उ मास, Listen ye, (*says*) Tul'sī Dās, to the infatuated thirst of the papīha bird, which, abstaining for four months, drinks only of the rain-water (*that falls*) in Swati, (*the rainy season lasts four months and stops in Swāti, or the latter half of October*; *see Grs.* § 1084; *the rain of Swāti is considered most precious, and fabled to be the only sustenance of the papīha or chātik or the sparrow hawk*; *see another reading of this verse in Sat.* i, 96); *Git.*, *Ln.* 11, 4, यह जल-निधि खन्यो मथ्यो लङ्घ्यो बाँध्यो अँचयो है, This ocean (*the sons of Sagar*) have dug out, (*the dēvas and dāityas*) have churned, (*Hanumān*) has leaped over, (*Rām*) has bridged over, (*and Agasty'*) has drunk up; *Krish.* 74, जे मुख सदा सुधा अँचवत हैँ, ते बिष क्यों अधिकारी, Those who continuously drink nectar with their mouths, how should they carry (*lit. be possessors of*) poison? ²*Coll.*, (*W. Bh.*, *Āz. Gy.*) नरियर अँचवेला, He is smoking his water-pipe (*made of the shell of a cocoanut*). *See* √अँच *ā̆ch*.

[*This is deterioration of the fuller form* √अँचाव (*q.v.*), *produced by a confusion similar to that in the case of* √अँच; *see the remarks s.v. The form* अँचाव *being looked upon as a causal, has been treated as such, and subjected to the shortening process of the element* आव *to which the causal suff.* आव *is liable in* Prākrit (*see Hem.* iii, 150, *also* i, 67). *Thus, just as Pr. admits both* ठाविओ *and* ठविओ set up (*Skr.* स्थापितः, *caus. of* √स्था), तोसविअ *and* तोसाविअं gratified (*caus. of* √तुष), *etc.*, *so from Pr.* आचामिअं *or Ap. Pr.* आचँविअं (*Hēm.* iv, 397) *is formed, by false analogy, the form Ap. Pr.* आचँविअं sipped, *whence comes Ap. Pr.* √आचँव *or Gd.* √अँचव (*see the remarks under art.* अ *a* (6)). *See also the remarks on derivation under art.* √अँच *and* √अँचाव.—*This form of the root also occurs in H. and M., viz. H.* अँचव, *M.* आँचव *or* अँचव. *The proper B.* (*Mth.*) *form is* अँचाव.]

अँचन्वन ăch'wan, Tbh., *subst. m., the same as* अचमन *ách'man, q.v. See* आचमन *āchaman.*
[*Skr.* आचमनम्, *Pr.* आचमणं, *Ap. Pr.* आचँवणं (*see Hēm.* iv, 397) *or* अचँवणं (*see art.* अ *a* (6)), *Gḍ.* अँचवन.]

√**अँचन्वाब** ăch'wāb, (*pr. pts.* अँचन्वबैत *ăch'wabăit, Bh. and Mg.* अँचन्वावत *ăch'wāwat,* अँचन्वावित *ăch'wāwit;* अँचन्वाओल *ăch'wāöl;* अँचन्वाएब *ăch'wāëb;* अँचन्वाबै *ăch'wābai,* अँचन्वाए *ăch'wāë*), Tbh., *caus. v. of* √अँचाब *ăchāb, q.v.* Exam., [1]*Rām., Bā., chh.* 13, 4, अँचवाइ दीन्हे पान, गवने बास जहँ जा को रही, Having helped them (*with water*) to rinse (*their mouths*), they gave them betel, (*after which*) they went each to where his dwelling was. [2]*Pārb.* 15, 2, पूजि दीन्ह, मधु-परक अमिय अँचवाएउ, (*Himāwant*) paid his respects (*to the guests*) and gave them nectar to drink as the honey-offering.

अँचन्वाहा ăch'wāhā, Tbh., *subst. m., Mg., the same as* अँचन्ताहर *ăch'tāhar, q.v.* (*Grs.* § 303.)
[*Derived from* √अँच *and the suff.* वाह. *The latter is the Skr.* वाहक: one who carries, *Pr.* वाहओ, *Gḍ.* वाहा.]

अचाका achākā, *the same as* अचक्का *achakkā, q.v. It is used adverbially,* suddenly, unexpectedly. Exam., *Padm., ch.* 549, 1, दिनहिं रात अस परी अचाका, भा रवि अस्त चन्द रथ हाँका, (*Owing to the dust*) on that day night fell so suddenly that the sun set and the moon hastened on her chariot.

अचाँचक achăchak, Tbh., *adv.,* suddenly, unexpectedly, unawares. *See* अचानक *achānak,* अचक *achak.*
[*Apparently a reduplication of* अचक. *S. has* अचाचेति, *Ml.* अचाचेत *or* अचकचेत, *G.* अचोतूं.]

अचानक achānak (1), Tbh., *adv.,* suddenly, unexpectedly, unawares. Exam., *B. Gr.,* I (*Intr.*), *Fable* 1, अचानक ओहि सँ बड़का मोतीक दाना बहराएल, Suddenly a large pearl (*lit.* seed of pearl) came forth from it; *Hn.* 12, 4, करि धनवान अचानक बधिय, Drawing (*the bow of thy eyebrows*) strike me unexpectedly. *See* अचानचक *achān'chak,* अचाँचक *achăchak,* अचाका *achākā,* अचक *achak.*
[*Derivation doubtful; probably a comp. of the neg. pref.* अ *and* चानक, *and the latter apparently some derivative from the Skr.* √चित *or* √चि *or* √चाय, *such as* चेतन *or* चयन *or* चायन, *which in Pr. would be* चेअण, चअण, चाअण, *and in Gḍ. might contract to* चान. *The final* क *might be a pleon. suff. As above in all Gḍs.*]

अचानक achānak (2), Tbh., *subst. m.,* the name of a place in Tirhut. Exam., *Kan.* 18, रामपटी तैं कूच करि चढ़ौ अचानक जाय, Marching away from Rām'paṭī they arrived at Achānak.

अचानचक achān'chak, Tbh., *adv., the same as* अचानक *achānak or* अचाँचक *achăchak, q.v.*
[*Probably produced by a confusion of the two synonymous forms* अचानक *and* अचाँचक.]

√**अँचाब** ăchāb, अचाब *achāb* (*pr. pts.* अँचन्बैत *ăch'băit, Bh. and Mg.* अँचावत *ăchāwat or* अँचावित *ăchāwit;* अँचाओल *ăchāöl;* अँचाएब *ăchāëb;* अँचाबै *ăchābai or* अँचाए *ăchāë*), Tbh., *v. tr.,* [1]to cleanse *or* rinse the mouth before eating *or* after eating, *or* before a religious ceremony (*by way of purification*); *it is done by sipping a little water from the palm of the hand and spitting it out again;* (*in this sense the verb is used absolutely, 'water' to be understood*); [2]to sip; [3]to drink; [4]*idiom.* (*with* करियर, तमाकू, *etc.*) to smoke. *For examples see under the W. Bh. and Bw. forms* √अँच *ăch and* √अँचव *ăchaw.*
[*Skr.* √आचम् (= आ-चम्), I. *cl.* आचामति, *whence Pr.* √आचाम, *Ap. Pr.* √आचाँव (*see Hēm.* iv, 397) *or* √आचाव (*see Hēm.* iv, 226), *whence Gḍ* √अचाव (*see art.* अ *a* (6)). *From* √अचाव *are formed by false analogy the two der. forms* √अँच *and* √अँचव, *see s.vv. H. has* √अचा *and Bg.* √आँचा.]

अचार achār (1), आचार *āchār,* (*poet.* अचारा *achārā, old dir.* अचारु *achārŭ, poet.* अचारू *achārū*), Ts., *subst. m.,* [1]deed, action, act (*opp.* वचन word *and* विचार thought, *see Dōh.* 411); [2]practice, usage, custom, manner of life, occupation; [3]conduct, morals; [4]religious practice or ceremony; (*from the Hindū point of view there is no essential difference between practices, social, moral, or religious; all being equally regulated by the shāst'rs or sacred books*). Exam., [1]*Dōh.* 411, वचन विचार अचार तन मन करतब छल छूति, तुलसी क्यों सुख पाइये, If what is to be done with the body or the mind be defiled with deceit, in word, thought, or deed, what peace—Tul'sī Dās (*says*)—can you (*expect to*) find? [2]*Sat.* vii, 34, बड़ कुल, बड़ रुचि, वचन बड़, बड़ अचार बेवोहार, इन को भवल अनारबो, यह अन्याय अपार, Having many children, many desires, much talk, many usages and practices,—to consider (*all*) these to be good, that is unparalleled folly, (*see a slightly different version in Dōh.* 490); *Rām., Ut., ch.* 87, 1, एक पिता के बिपुल कुमारा, होहि पृथक गुन सील अचारा, One father has many children, and, theirs are different characters, tempers, and occupations. [3]*Rām., Bā., chh.* 18, 3, अस भ्रष्ट अचारा भा संसारा, धरम सुनिय नहिं काना, So corrupt had morals become in the world, and righteousness was no (*longer*) heard of with the ears; *K. Rām*

Ut. 97, कलि-काल बिचार अचार हरो, नहिं सूझे कछू अघ-पूरर को, The Kali age has destroyed (*all*) good thoughts and good conduct, the (*people being*) blatant fools do not mind anything. [1]*Rām.*, *Ut.*, *ch.* 114, 10, जप तप व्रत जम नियम अपारा, जे श्रुति कहँ सुभ धरम अचारा, Those grand duties of prayer, penance, fasting, and self-restraint, the Sruti (*i.e. the Bēds*) teaches as meritorious religious practices; *Rām.*, *Bā.*, *ch.* 329, 8, दुहुँ कुल-गुरु सब कीन्ह अचारू, The two family priests performed all the ritual ceremonies.

[*Skr.* आचारः; *as above in all Gds. On the shortening of the initial* आ *see art.* अ *a* (6). *The tadbh. Pr.* आयारो (*Aup.* § 78) *has not survived in Gḍ.*]

अचार *achār* (2), **Tbh.**, *subst. m.*, pickles. **Phr.**, अचार करब *or* अचार निकालब, *fig.* to beat to a pickle, to beat severely, beat to a jelly (*Hd. Dy.*). **Exam.**, *B. Gr.*, I. (*Introd.*), *Conversation* 18, (*p.* 31), थोड़ेके टिकोरउँ अचार के देब, Give me a few (*young green mangos*) for pickling.

[*Probably from Skr.* चव hot, pungent, *with the intens. pref.* अ (*see under art.* अ *a* (5)). *Skr.* अतिचव्य:, *Pr.* अइचंचो, *Gḍ.* *ऐचाँड़ *or* *अचाड़, *whence* अचार. *Or it may be connected with B.* चाड़ *or* चाड desire, relish.—*G.*, *P.*, *H.*, अचार, *S.* अचारु, *Sgh.* अचार.]

अचारज *achār'j*, अचार्ज *achārj*, आचारज *āchār'j*, आचार्ज *āchārj*, **Ts.**, *subst. m.*, [1]a spiritual guide, a religious leader; [2]a family priest (*syn.* पुरोहित, *Grs.* § 1347); [3]one learned in sacred lore, a learned paṇdit. **Exam.**, [1]*Coll.*, (*Bh.*), सुकरजी दैतन के अचारज बाड़े, Sukr' is the spiritual guide of the Daityas. [2]*Coll.*, (*Bh.*), आज होम करे के बा, अचारज के बोलावँऽ, To-day I have to perform the hōma (*sacrifice*), call the priest. [3]*Das Kumār Charitr'* (*by Bihārī Lāl*) अचारज जन मिली सिखलाया, निरखि निपति सुत अतिसुख पाया, The learned paṇdits together taught the son, and the king observing him was greatly pleased.

[*Skr.* आचार्य; *as above possibly in all Gḍs.*]

अचारा *achārā*, *poet. for* अचार *achār* (1), *q.v.*

अचारी *achārī*, **Tbh.**, *adj.*, *com. gen.*, fit for pickles; *hence, subst.* (*scl.* मटुक), a pickle-jar (*Cr.*, *p.* 32).

[*Derived from* अचार (2) *by means of the sec. der. suff.* ई (*see Gḍ. Gr.* § 256); *P.* अचारी.]

अचारू *achārū*, *poet. for* अचार *achār* (1), *q.v.*

अचिक *áchik*, (*str. f.* अचिका *áchikā or* अचका *ách'kā* (*q.v.*), *fem.* *की), **Tbh.**, *adj.*, *com. gen.*, very little, inconsiderable (*of quantity*); *see Āz. Gy. For an example see under* अचका *ach'kā*.

[*This word has a strange derivation. Its original form is* रचिक *or* रचिका, *whence by the elision of the initial* र r *it becomes* अचिक *or* अचिका, *and may still further be changed to* इचिक *or* इचिका. *To these forms* एक one *may be added idiomatically; similarly* क *or* का *may be omitted; so that we have the following series of forms*:—रचि एक, रचिका एक, रचिक *or* रचिका; अचि एक, अचि का एक, अचिक *or* अचिका; इचि एक, इचिका एक इचिक *or* इचिका. *The original form* रचि *or* रचि के *is the conj. part. of the* √रच to contrive, *and means* having contrived, having made a shift. *It is commonly used in precative sentences, and thus assumes the meaning of* a little,—*which meaning is emphasised by the addition of* एक. *Thus we have the word used in Bhoj.* 46, 3, रचि एक आपन भैया देहू जगाए, *lit.* contriving a little wake up your brother; *or in Bhoj.* 45, 20, रचि एक जोतिया देखावँऽ, *lit.* contriving a little show me his body. *Similarly Bh. Coll.* अचिकी सुरती दे देँऽ *means lit.* contriving a little give me dry tobacco, *hence* kindly give me a little dry tobacco. *The conj. part.* रचि के *appears to have been gradually turned into an adj.* रचिक *with a regular lg. f.* रचिका, *f.* रचिकी, *meaning* a little. *With regard to the loss of the initial* र r, *which is uncommon in Bihārī, the Rang'pūrī dialect may be compared, in which it is almost always elided, e.g.*, आँधिते *for* राँधिते *to cook. See Rg. Gr.*, *p.* 189. *See also Bhoj.*, *Addenda*, *p.* 61.]

अचिन्त *achint*, **Ts.**, *adj.*, *com. gen.*, what cannot be thought, inconceivable, past comprehension. **Exam.**, *Coll.*, (*Bh.*), परमेसर के सकति अचिन्त बा, The power of God is past comprehension.

(*This word does not occur with the meaning* thoughtless, heedless, *given to it in the H. Dy.*)

[*Skr.* अ-चिन्त्य; *as above possibly in all Gḍs.*]

अचिर *áchir*, (*old obl.* अचिरहि *achirahi*), **Ts.**, *adv.*, not long, before long, soon. **Exam.**, *Hn.* 7, धैरज धरु रउ, अचिर मिलत पउ, Have patience, before long the Lord will meet thee; *Vaish.* xviii, 6, बिपद बिभव दुउ थिर नहिं, अचिर मिलत गुन धारे, Misfortune and wealth are both not enduring, soon the essence of all good (*i.e.*, *the summum bonum, or Krish'n*) will meet thee; *Mth. Rām.*, *Bā.* 119, 4, अचिरहि पुनि सुख हे अवनिपाल, But soon, O king, there will be happiness.

[*Skr.* अ-चिरम्; *as above in all Gds.*]

अचीर *achīr*, **Ts.**, *adj.*, *com. gen.*, without clothes, unclothed, undressed, naked. **Exam.**, *Padm.*, *ch.* 30, 5, कोइ जो दिगम्बर अचीर नाँगे, Some again are Digambars (*a kind of naked Jain monks*), unclothed and naked.

(*The Benares edition of the Padm. has the false reading* अचिरन.)

[*Skr.* अ-चीरः; *as above possibly in all Gds.*]

अचुत *achut*, अच्युत *achyut*, **Ts.**, *subst. m.*, he who cannot fail, the unfailing, imperishable, eternal. (*The word is properly a general adj., but is now used only as an epithet of Krish'n or Bish'n or God.*) **Comp.**, अचुतानन्द (= अचुत-आनन्द), the Eternally-happy-one, *an epithet of Bish'n or Krish'n.* **Exam.**, *Misc.* 28, 5, चौदह भुवन पलक में डाहे, अचुतानन्द रम से न्यारे, (*Krish'n*) overturned the fourteen worlds in the twinkling of an eye, the Eternally-happy-one is removed far above all.

[*Skr.* अ-च्युत: ; *as above possibly in all Gḍs.*]

अचूक *achūk*, **Tbh.**, *adj.*, *com. gen.*, unfailing, unerring, sure. **Exam.**, *Chan.* ससब सबद सरोज-मुखि, निज नयन बान अचूक, Close fast, O lotus-faced one, the unfailing arrows of thy eyes; *ib.*, बाढि बेमाय न जाय कदापि, बिरचि बिरचित देखु अचूक, The natural disposition (*of a person*) and 'bemāy' (*a kind of foot disease*) never disappear; created as they are by the Creator, you see, they are unerring (*in producing their effects*).

[*Comp. of the neg. pref.* अ *and* चूक a failing, error. *The latter is derived from a compound root* चूक, *corresponding to Skr.* च्युत-क ; *see Gḍ. Gr.* § 353. *The word* अचूक *therefore is ultimately identical with* अचुत, *q.v. G. and M.* अचूक ; *not noticed in other Gḍs.*]

अचेत *achēt*, (*poet.* अचेता *achētā*, *old dir.* अचेतु *achētú*), **Ts.**, (I) *adj.*, *com. gen.*, [1] (*naturally and permanently*) devoid of sensation *or* consciousness, insentient, inanimate (*syn.* जड़ *or* अचर *or* थावर, *opp.* चेतन, चर, जङ्गम); [2] (*accidentally and temporarily*) unconscious, senseless, fainting, swooning; [3] (*morbidly or ecstatically*) deprived of one's proper senses, out of one's senses, beside one's self, at one's wit's end, bewildered, confused (*syn.* बिकल, *see Padm.*, *ch.* 457, 2, *or* आकुल); [4] devoid of intelligence *or* experience *or* design, foolish, ignorant, artless, simple (*syn.* अज्ञान); [5] wanting in attention, unmindful, forgetful, thoughtless, heedless, careless. **Exam.**, [1] *Han.* 32, देवी देव दनुज मनुज मुनि सिध नाग, छोटे बड़े जीव जेते, चेतन अचेत हैं, Goddesses, gods, demons, men, sages, saints, and nāgs, whatever beings there are, great or small, sentient or insentient; *Ag.* v, 34, क्रिपा-सिन्धु प्रभु सिन्धु सन माँगेउ पन्थु, न देत ; बिनय न मानहि जीव जड़, डाटे नँवहि अचेत, The Lord (*who is*) the ocean of mercy, asked the ocean to make a way for him, but it refused; (*for*) inanimate creatures pay no heed to prayers,—the insentient only submit to threats. [2] *Rām.*, *Bā.*, *do.* 187, 1, गयो रसातल अचेत ह्वै, अरे न बिप्र प्रसाद, Senseless (*Mēgh'nād*) sunk down into the nether world, (*though*) he was still alive by the Brāhman's blessing; *ib.*, *Bā.*, *do.* 161, 2, खोजत ब्याकुल सरित सर, जल बिनु भयेउ अचेत, They kept searching in distress for a stream or pond, and were fainting for want of water. [3] *Rām.*, *A.*, *do.* 77, 2, बन्दि बिप्र-गुर-चरन प्रभु चले करि सबहि अचेत, Having reverenced the feet of the Brāh'mans and Gurus, the Lord departed, they all being beside themselves (*with grief*); *ib.*, *ch.* 308, 7, चले जाहिँ सब लोग अचेता, All the people went away beside themselves (*with grief*); *ib.*, *Ln.*, *chh.* 26, 10, कपिदल कपीस समेत भये सकल बीर अचेत, All the warriors, including Lachhiman and the monkey chief (*Hanumān*), were at their wits' end; *K. Rām.*, *Ln.* 36, तुलसी, तब हाँक दसानन देत, अचेत भे बीर, को धीर धरे, Tul'sī Dās (*says*), there Dasānan (*i.e. Rāban*) gave a shout, (*whereupon*) all the warriors grew bewildered, none (*lit. who*) could maintain his courage; *Ag.* iii, 18, राम लखनु बन बन बिकल फिरत, सीय सुधि लेत, खरत उछुन बिखाद बड़ सगुन चाहिं अचेत, Rām and Lakhan in bewilderment wander from wood to wood, making search for Sītā, and, beside themselves with grief, by reason of the great misfortune and calamity, they seek for some good omen. [4] *Rām.*, *Bā.*, *do.* 37, 2, समुझ नहीं तसु, बालपन तब अति रहेउँ अचेत, I had no understanding of it (*i.e. of the story of Rām*), (*as*) I was then in my childhood, and was quite unintelligent; *Bin.* 83, लरिकाई बीती अचेत (*fem.*), (*My*) childhood passed in simplicity. [5] *Padm.*, *ch.* 346, 5, चित अचेत जनु बारी भोरी, Her heart was careless as that of an artless girl; *Ag.* v, 43, रावन भाइ जगाइ तब, 'कहाँ प्रभु अचेत,' Rāban then waked up his brother (*Kumbh'karan*), (*saying:*) 'Where is your devotion (*to me*), you fool?' *Coll.*, (*Bh.*), अचेत नाहित काहे करैछँह, देखँह ना ठीक, Why are you acting like a fool; can't you see properly? (*Hd. Dy.*); *Coll.*, (*Mg.*), ऐ हुड़्बक अचेत, जे जो में आएछ, से बकैछक, The heedless fool babbles away just what comes into his head (*Hd. Dy.*).

(II) *adv.*, *with similar meanings to the above*, unconsciously, confusedly, foolishly, heedlessly. **Exam.**, *Coll.*, (*Bh.*), ऐसन अचेत घोड़ा हँकलक कि लरिका पिचा गेल, He drove the horse so heedlessly that the child was run over.

[*Skr.* अ-चेतस् (*nom. sg.* अचेता) ; *as above probably in all Gḍs.*]

अचेतन *achētan*, **Ts.**, *adj.*, *com. gen.*, *a synonym of* अचेत *achēt*, *q.v.*

[*Skr.* अ-चेतन ; *as above probably in all Gḍs.*]

अचेतु *achētú*, *old dir. f. of* अचेत *achēt*, *q.v.* **Exam.**, [3] *Sat.* ii, 99, आपुहि मद मों पान करि आपुहि होत अचेतु, तुलसी, बिबिध प्रकार को दुख उतपति यह हेतु, Having himself taken a draught of wine, (*man*) himself becomes deprived of his senses; this—Tul'sī Dās (*says*)—is the cause of the rise of manifold kinds of trouble. [4] *K. Rām.*, *Ut.* 82, मोह मद मात्यो, रात्यो कुमति कुनारि सों,

बिषारि मैद लोक लाज, चाबरो चचेत है, Intoxicated with the liquor of worldly enjoyment, and strongly attached to the vile women of my wicked intellect, in disregard of the (*dictates of the*) Bēds and the reproach of men, I have become an exceeding fool (*like Ajāmil*).

अचेता *achētā, poet. for* अचेत *achēt, q.v.*

अचेष्ट *achēsht*, **Ts.**, *adj.*, *com. gen.*, motionless, paralysed. **Exam.**, *Mth. Rām.*, *A.*, *ch.* 24, 21, निप अचेष्ट नहि सुनलन्हि घोर, मुन्दल नयन सुगल बह नोर, The king, paralysed (*with sorrow*), did not hear the cries (*of joy*), but tears flowed from his two closed eyes.

[*Skr.* अचेष्टः; *as above possibly in all Gds.*]

अचैतन *achāitan, a corruption of* अचैतन्य० *achāitanya, q.v.*

अचैतन्य० *achāitanya*, **Ts.**, *adj.*, *com. gen.*, *a synonym of* अचेत *achēt, q.v.*

[*Skr.* अ-चैतन्यः ; *as aboce probably in all Gḍs.*]

अचैन *achāin*, **Tbh.**, *adj.*, *com. gen.*, restless, uncomfortable, ill at ease (*used principally in W. Bihār.*). **Exam.**, *Mth. Rām.*, *Ar.* 50, 1, परमानन्द बिछोह अचैन, The Supremely-happy-one (*God*) is inconsolable through separation (*from Sitā*).

[*A comp. of the neg. pref.* अ *and* चैन ease, comfort, *q.v.*]

अँचौना *ăchāunā*, **Tbh.**, *subst. m.*, (*Mg.*), *the masc. form of* अँचौनी *ăchāunī* (*q.v.*), *or* अचमनी *achămani*, *q.v.* (*Grs.* § 774).

[*Skr.* आचमनकः, *Pr.* आचमणओ, *Ap. Pr.* आचँवणउ, *whence contr. and shortened Gḍ.* अँचौना. *See Gḍ. Gr.* § 122. *See also the remarks under* अँचवन.]

अँचौनी *ăchāunī*, **Tbh.**, *subst. f.*, *the contr. N. Bh. form for* अचमनी *ach'mani, q.v.* (*Grs.* § 774).

अच्छ *achchh, for words commencing thus and not mentioned below, see under* अछ *achh. Occasionally these two forms are interchanged with* अक्ख *akkh*, अख *akh*, आख *ākh*, *or* आँख *ăkh. Accordingly certain words not found below should be looked up under the latter forms.*

(*It may be noted as a practical, though not absolute rule, that tats. words are spelt with* च्छ *chchh, while tadbh. words, such as derivatives from the* √अछ *achh, are spelt with* छ *chh.*)

[*The Skr. conj.* क्ष *kṣ is pronounced* छ *chh or* च्छ *chchh, the latter only in the medial position* (*see Gḍ. Gr.* § 36 ; *also Introd., chap.* 4, *a*). *Hence tats. words, unphon. spelt with initial* अक्ष *akṣ, must be looked up under* अच्छ *achchh or* अछ *achh. In Pr. both forms* क्ख *kkh and* च्छ *chh, or* ख *kh and* छ *chh, occur for Skr.* क्ष *kṣ*, (*see Hēm.* ii, 3, 17). *But it is probable that the form* क्ख *kkh* (*or* ख *kh*) *was the proper prākritic form, while* च्छ *chchh* (*or* छ *chh*) *always was a sanskritic form, i.e., an attempt at tatsama pronunciation.*]

अच्छ० *achchha*, **Ts.**, *subst. m.*, name of a son of Rāban *who was killed by Hanumān.* **Comp.**, अच्छ०-कुमार *m.*, the prince Achchha. **Exam.**, *K. Rām.*, *Ln.* 22, कानन उजारि अच्छ मारि धारि धूरि कीन्ही, After devastating the grove and killing Achchha, he (*i.e. Hanumān*) reduced the army (*of Rāban*) to dust (*see also ib.*, *Ln.* 24, *Su.* 28) ; *Han.* 19, अच्छ-विमर्दन कानन भानि दसानन आनन भा नहिं तारो, He (*i.e.*, *Hanumān*) who, by destroying the grove in order to slay Achchha, became the destroyer of the pride (*lit.* the face) of Dasānan (*i.e.*, *of Rāban*) ; *Rām.*, *Su.*, *ch.* 18, 7, पुनि पठयउ तेहि अच्छ-कुमारा, Again (*Rāban*) sent the young prince Achchha.

(*In the compound* अच्छ०-कुमार *the word is occasionally found corrupted into* अच्छ, *q.v.*)

[*Skr.* अक्षः ; *as above probably in all Gḍs.*]

अच्छत *achchhat*, (*poet.* अछत *achhat*, *instr. sg.* अछतैं *achhatē̃*, *Bij. l.* 80), **Ts.**, *subst. m.*, whole grain of rice, (*it is always used of the best fresh rice grain or* अरवा *ar'wā*, *Grs.* § 963, *and it is never used except in connection with religious or semi-religious ceremonies, such as those of sacrifice, marriage, etc.*; *see Grs., division* xii, *chap.* 1—3, *spec.* §§ 1319, 1329). **Exam.**, *Rām.*, *Bā.*, *ch.* 303, 15, 16, धुज पताक-पट चामर चारू, छावा परम बिचित्र बजारू। कनक-कलस तोरन मनि-जाला हरद दूब दधि अच्छत माला, Banners, silken flags, and beautiful 'chāuris' covered the very gay bazar, and golden vases, arches, networks of jewels, (*heaps of*) turmeric, dūb grass, curds and rice, and garlands (*said of the street decorations on the occasion of Rām's marriage*) ; *ib.*, *Bā.*, *ch.*, 351, 4, 5, हरद दूब दधि पल्लव फूला पान पूँगि-फल मङ्गल-मूला। अच्छत अंकुर रोचन लाजा मंजुल मंजरि तुलसि बिराजा, Turmeric, 'dūb' grass, curds, sprigs (*of the mango-tree*), flowers, 'pān,' betelnut (*all of which are*) pledges of good luck, rice, blades of barley, 'gō-rōchan' (*a yellow pigment for marking the 'tilak'*), parched grain, decorated with graceful bunches of the tul'sī flower (*said of Sumitrā's complimentary gift presented in golden vases on the occasion of Rām's marriage*) ; *B. Gr.* II, (*Bh.*), 3, 3, *p.* 114, दधि अच्छत लेह सीता के चढ़ावल, Taking curds and rice we apply them to Sītā's (*forehead*), (*said of a marriage ceremony, see Grs.* § 1304) ; *Bij. l.* 80, अछतैं मनावौं डिहवरवा, With rice I honour the village god (*said* *of an offering*); *Mg., prov.*, चौंड़ी में अच्छत ना, चलैंड समधी जेंवे, In the pot there is not rice (*enough for an offering*), (*and he says*) : 'Come, my Sam'dhī, let us feast!' (*Hd. Dy.*)

[*Skr.* अक्षत: ; *as above possibly in all Gḍs.*]

अच्छम *achchham*, **Ts.**, *adj. or subst., com. gen.*, powerless, helpless, a powerless one, helpless one. **Exam.**, *Dōh.* 74, सब कि समरथकि सुखद प्रिय, अच्छम प्रिय हितकारि, All things to the powerful are pleasant and dear : to the powerless he is dear who helps him.

[*Skr.* अक्षम: ; *as above possibly in all Gḍs.*]

अच्छर *achchhar* (1), आछर *āchhar*, *poet.* अछर *achhar*, (*nom. pl.* अछरैं *achharẽ*, *Padm.* 350, 3), **Ts.**, *subst. m.*, [1]a letter, a syllable, [2]a graphic sign, a character. (*According to the Indian theory the consonantal signs of the alphabet always carry the inherent sound of the vowel* '*a*,' *hence the sign* क *does not signify* '*k*,' *but* '*ka*'; *hence* क '*ka*' *is called an achchhar or* '*syllable*,' *while the mere sign* क् '*k*' *is called an ayk or* '*mark*' ; *see the remarks under art.* अंक *ayk. From this point of view the letters of the alphabet are called achchhar, while mere signs of the alphabet, such as the anuswāra or the visarga, are not called achchhar. Strictly speaking an achchhar is a syllable, i.e., a consonant joined with any vowel, such as* क '*ka*', कि '*ki*', *or any vowel by itself, such as* अ '*a*', इ '*i*' ; *but it is now often used in a looser way to denote a graphic sign or character.*) **Exam.**, [1]*Bid.* 59, 5, भनथिं बिद्यापति अच्छर लेख, Bidyāpatī saith, 'Write the letters (*in proper order*)' ; *Rām., Bā., dō.* 148, 1, द्वादस-अच्छर-मन्त्र बर जपहिं सहित अनुराग, They repeat the excellent twelve-lettered charm with (*great*) devotion, (*the charm referred to are the Skr. words* ओं नमो भगवते वासुदेवाय, *i.e.*, Oṁ, salutation to the blessed Vāsudēva ; *cf. similarly Bid.* 60, 2 लोखि पठाओलि आखर सात, I have written down the seven letters, (*referring to the words* कुसुमित कानन, *i.e.*, a grove full of flowers, *ib.* 60, 1) ; *Sat.* vi, 6, अनुस्वार अच्छर-रहित जानत है सब कोइ, Every one knows that the anuswār is not counted as a letter. [2]*B. Gr.* ii, (*Bh.*), 31, 3, कैथी अच्छर लिखंउ कचहरिया, Write the Kāithī characters in Kachah'rī ; *Dēv., p.* 22, सरकार जो नागरी अच्छर मैं ब्योरवा कै खानापूरी कौर सफाई का हुकुम दे देंय, तो बड़ उपकार होय, If the Government would give an order to fill up clearly all columns (*in settlement-statements, from Prs.* خانه) in the Nāgarī characters, it would be of great benefit. *See* अखर *akhar*, अक्खर *akkhar*, आखर *ākhar*, आँखर *ãkhar*.

[*Skr.* अक्षरम्. *See the remarks under* अक्षर. *As above in most Gḍs.* ; *S. has* अक्खर.]

अच्छर *achchhar* (2), **Tbh.**, *subst. f.*, an Apsaras or courtesan of Ind'r's heaven. *They are the wives of the Gandharbs, and occupy themselves with singing, dancing, and gambling. According to the Skr. Rāmāyan and the Purāns, they were produced from the churning of the ocean. They have the power of changing their forms and imparting good luck. Sometimes they were despatched by Indr' to the earth for the purpose of leading astray some distinguished ascetic. In the ancient and modern Indian epics and ballads it is their duty to carry fallen warriors to heaven and live with them; thus, e.g., in the Skr. Mahābhārata* xii, 3657, *it is said :* "*thousands of handsome Apsarases run up in haste to the hero who has been slain in battle, exclaiming* '*be my husband.*'" *The most beautiful among them is Rambhā.* (*See Dowson's Class. Dy. of Hindū Mythology, s.v., and J. Muir, Skr. Texts, vols.* iv *and* v, *passim*). **Exam.**, *Padm., ch.* 602, 1, सेव करहिं दासी चहुँ पासा, अच्छर जनहु इन्द्र कैलासा, Maid-servants (*stand*) round him (*and*) do him service, as Apsarases attend Indr' in heaven ; *ib., ch.* 557, 7, जूझे बीर, कहौं कहँ ताईं, लेइ अच्छर कैलास सिधाईं, The heroes fought (*in battle*) ; how far shall I describe it ; (*and as they fell,*) Apsarases took them straight to heaven ; *ib., ch.* 102, 7, जोति भौंहहिं सम कोइ न जीता, अछरैं छिपीं, छिपीं गोपीता, No one could surpass her with (*the bows of*) the eyebrows, the Apsarases hide themselves; there hide themselves the Gōpīs (*abashed at seeing the superiority of their rival in their own special art of fascination*; गोपीता *stands for* गोपी *for the sake of the rhyme*). *See* अपच्छर *ap'chhar*.

[*Skr.* अप्सरा: *or* अप्सरा, *Pa.* अच्छरा, *Pr.* अच्छरसा *or* अच्छरा; *as above possibly in all Gḍs.*]

अच्छर अनन्य० *achchhar ananya*, **Ts.**, *subst. m., said to be the name of a poet* (*Siv., pp.* 26, 378). *He is said to have lived about Samvat* 1710 *or A.D.* 1654, *and to have written in the quietistic style* (*shānti-ras*). **Exam.**, *Siv., p.* 26, जीवन की आसा औ मरन की फिकिर जौं लौं चित हरि-भक्ति बगत जा मन की जीरी है। अच्छर अनन्य एती फाटे न फिकिरि जौं लौं, तौं लौं फजिहति, बाबा, झूरे, ना फकीरी है ॥ So long as there is the desire of life and the fear of death in the little mind of him who in this world is without the faith in Hari,—Achchhar Ananya (*says*)—so long as those cares do not cease (*lit.* break away), so long, sir, disgrace flourishes, nor is there any quietism. (*The language of this poetry is a species of vernacular Ūrdū* ; फिकिरि *or* फिकिर *is Ar.* فكر *fikr* ; फजिहति *is Ar.* فضيحت *fazīhat* ; फकीरी *is Ar.-Prs.* فقيري *faqīrī*, the life *or* state of a darwēsh ; झूरे *is the same as* झूठे *or* झूठे ; जीरी *fem. of* जीरा, *lit.* a cummin seed, *hence* anything small.)

[*Skr.* अक्षर *and* अनन्य, *two epithets of Viṣṇu or Shiva.*]

अच्छा *achchhā, poet.* आछा *āchhā,* (*f.* अच्छी *achchhī, poet.* आछी *āchhī*), **Tbh.,** good, excellent, pleasant, proper. **Exam.,** *Grs.* § 1454, अच्छा सगुन a good omen; *Bhōj.* 3, 1, अच्छा काम नाहीं कैलू, प्र केकइ, A good deed hast thou not done, O Kēkaī; *Dēv. p.* 24, जब सरकार उनका अच्छी तरह समझाएब, If the Government will admonish them in a proper manner.

(*This word belongs rather to H. usage; the usual B. word is* नीमन *nīman or* नीक *nīk, q.v. The form* आछा *has only been met with in old Bais'wārī.*)

[*Skr.* अच्छः clear, transparent, *or with pleon.* क, अच्छकः, *Pr.* अच्छओ (*Aup.* § 166 अच्छा clear, *nom. plur.*); *B., P., and H.* अच्छा, *O.* आच्छ, *G.* अच्छो, *S.* अछो white, clear, *but* उछो good, *M. and Bg. deest.*]

अच्छांस *achchhāns,* **Ts.,** *subst. m.,* (*geog.*), a degree of latitude or longitude. **Exam.,** *Coll.,* (*Mg.*), हम सुनले हे कि लङ्का में अच्छांस नइ है, I have heard that Laṅkā does not fall under any degree of longitude (*i.e., Laṅka is beyond the world of the Hindūs*).

[*Skr.* अक्षांशः. *This is the only survival in B. and H. of either the primary word* अक्ष (अच्छ) *in its various meanings of* '*axle*', '*cube*', '*die*', *etc., or of any of its derivatives.*]

अच्छि *achchhi,* **Ts.,** *subst. m.,* the eye. **Comp.** अच्छि-तारा *f.,* the pupil of the eye; अच्छि-सङ्केत *m.,* a sign or wink of the eye. See आँखि *ā̃khi.*

[*Skr.* अक्षि *n., Pr.* अच्छिं *n. or* अच्छी *m. or* अच्छी *f.* (*Hēm.* i, 33, 35); *as above possibly in all Gḍs.*]

अच्छी *achchhī,* **Tbh.,** *subst. f.,* a sneeze. *See* छींक *chhīk.* **Exam.,** *Coll.,* (*Mg.*), जब महाराज अच्छी कैलन, तब सब कोउ सतजीव कहलक, When the king sneezed, every one said 'May you live long.'

[*Cf.* छींक *for der. and cognate words in other languages; the word is probably an onomatop.; compare the Skr.* छिक्का.]

अच्युत *achyut,* **Ts.,** *the same as* अचुत *achut, q.v.* **Exam.,** *Bin.* 10, जय सर्वज्ञ अमेय अच्युत विभो विश्व भवद्वपु सम्भव पुरारी, Hail, Purāri, who knowest truth, who knowest all things, master of sacrifices, imperishable, the Lord, from thy body is the whole universe born.

[*Skr.* अच्युतः; *as above possibly in all Gḍs.*]

अछ *achh, for words commencing thus and not mentioned below, see under* अच्छ *achchh. It should be noted, however, that certain words commencing with* अछ *achh* (*e.g.,* अछए *achhaë* he is, *Bid.* 45, 1; अछइत *achhaït* being, *Bid.* 3, 4, अछत *achhat* being, *Rām., A., dō.* 263, 2, *etc.*) *are inflections of the* √अछ *achh* be, *and must be looked up under that root. See the remarks under* अच्छ *achchh.*

√अछ *achh,* (*pr. pts.; the verb being defective, only the following forms exist, some of which are used in a honorific and others in a non-honorific sense, and regarding which B. Gr. and Mth. Gr. should be further consulted: the pres. exists complete; sing.,* 1. *pers., Mth.-Bhoj.* छौं *chhaũ or* छिकौं *chhikaũ or* छिकों *chhikō̃ or* छतौं *chhataũ or* छतों *chhatō̃;* 2. *pers., Mth.* छैं *chhaĩ* (*Dīn., l.* 357) *or* छें *chhē̃, Mth.-Bh.* छे *chhē or* छिके *chhikē or* छते *chhatē;* 3. *pers., Mth.* अछि *achhi* (*Bid.* 79, 13) *or poet.* अछी *achhī* (*Mth. Rām., Su.* 53, 10) *or* छहु *chhahŭ* (*Sal.* 19) *or* छौ *chhaŭ* (*Dīn., l.* 150) *or* छौक *chhaŭk* (*Dīn., l.* 110) *or* छिक *chhik* (*Dīn., l.* 285) *or* छीक *chhīk* (*Dīn., l.* 284), *Mth. and Mth.-Bh.* छै *chhaï* (*Dīn., l.* 343) *or* छैक *chhaïk* (*Dīn., l.* 335), *Mth.-Bh.* छिकै *chhikaï or* छिके *chhikē or* छिकैक *chhikaïk; plur.,* 1. *pers., Mth. and Mth.-Bh. and Bh.* छी *chhī* (*Dīn., l.* 286), *Mth.* छिअ *chhia* (*Hb.* ix, 66) *or* छिअहु *chhiahŭ or* छिऔ *chhiaŭ* (*B. Gr.* I, *fable* 14, *p.* 37) *or* छिऔक *chhiaŭk* (*Dīn., l.* 359), *or* *छिअहि *chhiahi or* छिऐ *chhiaï or* छिऐक *chhiaïk or* छिऔन्हि *chhiaŭnhi or* छिऐन्हि *chhiaïnhi, Mth.-Bh.* छिऐन्ह *chhiaïnh or* छिकी *chhikī or* छिकिऐन्ह *chhikiaïnh or* छती *chhatī or* छतिऐन्ह *chhatiaïnh;* 2. *pers., Mth.* छिअ *chhia* (*Hb.* v, 22) *or* छी *chhī* (*Dīn., l.* 289) *or* छिऐन्हि *chhiaïnhi* (*Mth. ch., p.* 2) *or* छिऐ *chhiaï or* छिऐक *chhiaïk or* छहक *chhahak or* छहीक *chhahīk or* छहूँन्हि *chhahũnhi, Mth. and Mth.-Bh.* छाह *chhāh* (*Dīn., l.* 127, *Sal.* 14), *Mth.-Bh.* छौ *chhaŭ or* छिकऽ *chhikă or* छिकाह *chhikāh or* छिकौ *chhikaŭ or* छतऽ *chhată or* छताह *chhatāh, Mth.-Bh. and Bh.* छऽ *chhă, Mth. fem.* छहिँ *chhahĩ;* 3. *pers., Mth.* छैन्हि *chhaïnhi* (*Dīn., l.* 282) *or* छथि *chhathi* (*Hb.* iv, 35, *Dīn., l.* 202) *or* छथीन्हि *chhathīnhi* (*Neb., l.* 36) *or* छथून्हि *chhathūnhi, Mth.-Bh.* छैन्ह *chhaïnh or* छथिन्ह *chhathinh or* छिकैन्ह *chhikaïnh or* छिकथ *chhikath or* छिकथिन्ह *chhik'thinh or* छतन्ह *chhatanh, Mth.-Bh. and Bh.* छथ *chhath, Bh. fem.* छतिन्ह *chhatinh. The past tense also exists complete; sing.,* 1. *pers., Mth.* छलहुँ *chhalahũ* (*Sal.* 19), *Mth.-Bh.* छलौं *chhalaũ or* छलों *chhalō̃;* 2. *pers., Mth.* छलाह *chhalāh or* छलैं *chhalaĩ or* छलें *chhalē̃, Mth.-Bh.* छले *chhalē;* 3. *pers., Mth.* छलौ *chhalaŭ or* छलहु *chhalahŭ* (*Dīn., l.* 138) *or* छलौक *chhalaŭk, Mth. and Mth.-Bh.* छल *chhal* (*Hb.* ii, 53, *Dīn., l.* 229) *or* छलै *chhalaï* (*B. Gr.,* I, *fable* 12, *p.* 36) *or* छलैक *chhalaïk* (*Dīn., l.* 353), *Mth.-Bh.* छले *chhalē or* छलक *chhalak, Mth. fem.* छलि *chhali* (*Hb.* vii, 33, *Bid.* 48, 1); *plur.,* 1. *pers., Mth. and Mth.-Bh.* छली *chhalī* (*Dīn., l.* 235), *Mth.* छलिअहु *chhaliahŭ* (*B. Gr.* I, *fable* 15) *or* छलिऔ *chhaliaŭ or* छलिऔक *chhaliaŭk or* छलिऐ *chhaliaï or* छलिऐक *chhaliaïk or* छलिऔन्हि *chhaliaŭnhi or* छलिऐन्हि *chhaliaïnhi, Mth.-Bh.* छलिऐन्ह *chhaliaïnh;* 2. *pers., Mth.* छलहुँ *chhalahũ or* छलहक *chhalahak or* छलहीक *chhalahīk or* छलहूँन्हि *chhalahũnhi or* छलिऐन्हि *chhaliaïnhi, Mth.-Bh.* छलऽ *chhală or* छलाह

chhalâh or छलौ *chhalāū or* छलहोक *chhalahōk or* छली *chhalī, Mth. fem.* छलीह *chhalīh or* छलीहि *chhalīhi; 3. pers., Mth.* छलैन्हि *chhalainhi or* छलाह *chhalăh* (*Dīn., l.* 175) *or* छलथीन्हि *chhalathīnh, or* छलथुन्हि *chhalathunhi, Mth.-Bh.* छलन्ह *chhalanh or* छलैन्ह *chhalainh or* छली *chhalī or* छलौ *chhalāū or* छलथ *chhalath or* छलथिन्ह *chhalathinh or* छलथुन्ह *chhalathunh, Mth. fem.* छलीह *chhalīh. There exists also the pres. part., Mth. and Bh.* अछइत *achhaït* (*Bid.* 3, 4, *B. Gr.* II, *p.* 42) *or* अछैत *achhait* (*Sal.* 15), *fem.* अछैति *achhaiti* (*Bid.* 51, 6), *Bh. and Bw.* अछत (*Rām., A., dō.* 263, 2), *generally used as a part. absolute. The following old forms have also been noted, pres., 3. sg.,* अछए *achhae* (*Hb.* viii, 18, *Bid.* 45, 1), 1. *plur.* अछी *achhī* (*Dīn., l.* 85), 3. *plur.* अछहिँ *achhahī̃* (*Padm., ch.* 515, 2); *pret.,* 3. *plur.* अछलाह *achhalăh* (*Hb.* x, 50)), **Tbh.**, (I.) *v. intr., used as a substantive verb,* [1]to be; [2]to exist. **Exam.**, [1]*Hb.* ix, 66, जसु सेवक हलधर हम अछए, (*He*) whose servants Hal'dhar and myself are; *Bid.* 12, 3, कत अछि बेरि, How much is the time? *Padm., ch.* 515, 2, अछहिँ बिहँस तम्बुल सो राते, (*Her lips*) when she smiles are red (*i.e. beautiful*) like betel; *Dīn., l.* 285, कालू सदा नाम छैक, (*My*) name is Kālū Sadā; *ib., l.* 150, ई छौ लगे मेँ, He is close (*to you*); *ib., l.* 289, केकर बेटा छौ, Whose sons are you? *ib., l.* 235, नान्हिटा छलौ, I was very young; *Hb.* x, 50, अछलाह मोट छोट से भेल, Those who had been so stout and were (*now*) become small. [2]*Bid.* 45, 1, कमल भमर जग अछए अनेक, Lotus (*loving*) bees exist many in the world; *Bid.* 35, 2, गगन मगन छल सेहो अदेखल भेल, The stars (*which*) existed in the sky, they have become invisible; *in this sense it is in common idiomatic use to express the idea of possession, in construction with the personal pronoun or the dative of the person, Bid.* 79, 13, नहिँ मोरा टका अछि नहिँ बेढ़ गाइ, I have neither money nor a milch-cow (*lit.* for me money exists not); *Hb.* vi, 35, करि वर अछि मोहि, I have a fine elephant (*lit.* a fine elephant exists for me); *in this sense it is also used idiomatically in 'participle absolute' constructions, Bid.* 3, 4, अछइत किछु न करिअ निरास, While anything remains (*to thee*) (*lit.* anything existing), do not disappoint (*him*); *Sal.* 15, तोहरा अछैत घर मेँ चोरी भेल, In your presence (*lit.* you existing) a theft occurred in the house; *Rām., Ut., ch.* 88, 17, काम अछत सुख सपने हुँ नाहीँ, While desire exists there is no peace even in dreams; *ib., A., ch.* 5, 3, मोहि अछत यह होउ उछाहू, In my life-time (*lit.* myself existing) let this happy event take place; *Gīt., Su.* 5, 2, बुधि बल साहस पराक्रम अछत राखे गोए, Though wisdom, power, courage, and might were present (*lit.* existed) in him (*Hanumān*), he kept them concealed; *Bin.* 238, तन पर अछत सीस बुधि, Imagining that its head still sits upon its body.

(II) *v. intr., used as an auxiliary verb, to form periphrastic tenses, active, medial and passive; viz.* [1]*personally,* (*a*) *with the dir. form of the pres. part.* (*with or without the final* त *t*), *to form the def. pres. and the imp. tenses of the active voice* (*see* **Mth.** *Gr.* §§ 136, 137, 154, 155, *Introd., chap.* 9), (*b*) *with the instr. case of the past part. in* एँ *ẽ, to form the perf. and pluperf. tenses of the act. voice of trans. verbs, and sometimes* (*in N. Mth. only*) *of intrans. verbs* (*see Mth. Gr.* §§ 141, 142, 157, 158, *Introd., chap.* 9), *and* (*c*) *with the dir. form of the past participle, to form the pres. and pret. tenses of the pass. or medial voices* (*see* **Mth.** *Gr.* § 170, *Introd., chap.* 9); [2]*impersonally, in the forms of the* 3. *sg. pres.* अछि *achhi and the* 3. *sg. pret.* छल *chhal, with the inflected forms of the pret., to form respectively the perf. and* (*in some of the sub-dialects of Mth. only*) *the pluperf. of the active voice* (*see Mth. Gr.* §§ 139, 157, *Introd., chap.* 9). **Exam.**, [1](*a*) *pres.,* 1. *pers., Dīn., l.* 317, हम जाइत छी डौरी गाम, I am going to Daūrī village; *B. Gr.* I, *fable* 9, भाइ चिट्ठी लिखैछी, Brother, I am writing a letter; 2. *pers., Dīn., l.* 289, कहाँ जाइत छौ, Where are you going? *ib., l.* 127, केना के मारैत छँह, How are you hitting (*him*); *B. Gr.* I, *fable* 3, किए नहिँ गबैछँह, Why are you not singing? 3. *pers., Sal.* 16, कर जोरि मिनती कहैति (*fem.*) अछि, With joined hands she is saying her request; *Sal.* 1, कर जोरि मिनती करैछथि, With joined hands she is making her prayer; *similarly, imp.,* 3. *pers., Dīn. l.* 229, दीना भद्री जिबैत छल, उहे गबैत रहै (*When*) Dīnā and Bhadrī were alive, they used to sing that (*air*); *B. Gr.* I, *fable* 4, हाथ मिड़ैत छल, He was wringing his hands; *ib., fable* 9, एक कोमन्सी चिट्ठी लिखैछल, A scribe was writing a letter; *ib., fable* 11, एक गोआरिनि अछि जाइतछि (*fem.*), A milkmaid was walking along. [1](*b*) *trans., perf.,* 1. *pers., B. Gr.* I, *fable* 7, बहुत दौड़ धूप कैलेँ छी, I have done much running and exertion; 2. *pers., B. Gr.* I, *fable* 3, ओँ ई कहिनी नहिँ सुनलेँ छँह, Have you not heard this saying? *and pluperf.* 2. *pers., B. Gr.* I, *fable* 15, जखन ते धेलेँ छलेँ, When you had caught me; 3. *pers., Bid.* 10, 2, जकरा जनि कर लेलेँ (*for* लेलेँ) अछि (*fem.*) सुन्दरि. से सब सोपलक ताही, Whatever the beautiful one had taken from any, all that she made over again to them; *similarly, but in N. Mth. only, perf.,* 2. *pers., Mth. Gr., p.* 85, *note* 2, सुतलेँ छँह, You have slept; *and pluperf.,* 1. *pers., Mth. Gr., p.* 85, सुतलेँ छलौँ, I had slept (*etc.*). [1](*c*) *pres., pass.,* 3. *pers., Hb.,* i, 37, ई जनमल अछि मारत तोहि, He is born who shall slay thee; *ib.,* iv, 59, जनि जनमल अछि आज मुरारि, As if Murāri is born to-day; *or medial* (*i.e., act. verb, intr., with pass. form*), 1. *pers., Sal.* 12, चोरि कै आएल छी, I have committed a theft (*lit.* I am come from committing a theft); 3. *pers.*, *Sal.* 14, कोन विपत्ति भेल अछि, What fault has happened (*lit.* is become)? *Bid.* 77, 2, चान उगल अधि आधा, As if the moon is half risen; *similarly, pret. pass.*, 3. *pers.*, *Bid.* 79, 4, पुरव लिखल अछ भामि अमार, In my former (*life*), it was written (*that he should be*) my husband; *or medial*, 1. *pers.*, *Sal.* 19, राति हम सूतल छलउँ अपन खिरम्की मेँ, At night I was asleep in my tent; 2. *pers.*, *B. Gr.*, I, *p.* 30, कथी लय ओतय गेल छलउँ, Why were you gone there? 3. *pers.*, *Hb.* ii, 53, सबऽ देखलथिन्हि जे जग जागल, All who were awake saw; *Din.*, *l.* 353, सात नीँदे सुतलि (*fem.*) छलैक फेकुनी, काँचे नीँद मेँ उठलैक चिहाय, Phekuni was asleep in a sound (*lit.* seven) sleep, (*but*) in drowsiness (*lit.* slight sleep) she rose up with a start; *B. Gr.* I, *fable* 16, जेठ भाए, जे भिखारि भे गेल छल, कहै लागल, The elder brother, who had (*lit.* was) become beggared, began to say. [a]*Perf.*, 1. *pers.*, *B. Gr.*, I, *p.* 31, कुसियार तँ रोपनेछउँ अछि, I have indeed planted sugar-cane; *Hb.* i, 2, हम हुँ कैल अछि मन बड़ गोट, I also have made my mind a great one; *Mth. Ch.*, *p.* 1, एक बकस पठाओल अछि, I have sent a box; *Sal.* 17, तखन अहाँ केँ छोड़ाओलि (*fem.*) अछि, Then I have got thee freed; 2. *pers.*, *Sal.* 14, हमरा बाँधि देल अछि, You have bound me; *B. Gr.*, I, *p.* 31, एहि बेरि कुसियार रोपनेछउँ अछि, Have you planted any sugar-cane this year? 3. *pers.*, *Bid.* 34, 3, आजुक रैनि सखि कठिन बितलि (*fem.*) अछि, This day's (*i.e.* last) night, O friend, has passed in suffering. (*It should be particularly noted that in the vulgar language of the lower castes the term.* एँ ẽ *of the instr. case of the past part.* (*No.* [b]), *and in the older poetry the term.* क k *or* कै kai *of the* 3. *sg. of the pret.* (*No.* [c]), *are not unfrequently dropped in the formation of the personal and impersonal forms of the periphrastic tenses. Thus,* [b]*Sal.* 8, सुगा बेदुली देल (*for* देलेँ) अछि, The parrot has given (*her*) the 'beduli'; *ib.* 8, दौना मालिनि कुसोथरि देलि (*fem., for* देलेँ) अछि, Dāunā Mālin has lain despairing (*lit* has given *herself* a spread of 'kusa' grass); *again,* [c]*Bid.* 34, 2, अन्य बचन तोहि के न कहल (*for* कहलक) अछि, Has any one said reproachful words to thee? *Hb.* vi, 48, सनि डाबल (*for* डाबलक) छल रावन गरब, He had brought low the pride of Rāban.)

(*This verb, both in its subst. and auxil. uses, is the usual one throughout the Māithil tract. To a limited extent it occurs in the Māithil-Bhoj'pūrī border-lands In Magahī it is almost totally supplanted by the* √अह *ah* (*see* √हो *hō*), *and in Bhoj'pūrī by* √बाट *bāṭ, q.v. With regard to this subject as well as the relative frequency of the various forms of the periphrastic tenses, and other grammatical points, the Mth. Gr. and B. Gr. should be consulted. On the point, more especially of the relative frequency, only practical experience in the various Bihār dialects can afford a safe guide.*)

[*Regarding the origin of this root, there has been much discussion. Its existence both in Pā.* (*see s.v.* अच्छति *in Childer's Dictionary*) *and Pr.* (अच्छइ *Hēm.* iv, 215) *is an undoubted fact. In Pr. the root carries the following meanings:* 1, to exist, *e.g.*, *Hēm*, i, 388, जं अच्छइ तं माणिअइ, Whatever exists that should be appreciated! *Spt.*, *v.* 83, दुक्खं अच्छिअइ, Pain there will exist; 2, to be; *e.g.*, *Spt.*, *v.* 289, तुप्पाणणा किणो अच्छसि, Why hast thou smeared thy face with 'ghi' (*lit.* why art thou greasy-faced)? *Nāy.* § 96, सुणिव्वुय निसण्णे अच्छाहि, Do thou rest (*lit.* be) satisfied. 3, *sometimes it means* to stand still (*expressing apparently the bare fact of existence, without any specific action*); *e.g.*, *Nāy.* § 104, वारामेसु य विवरएसु य अच्छमाणी य पेच्छमाणी य मज्जमाणी य पत्ताणि य पुप्फाणि य गेण्हमाणी य परिभाएमाणी य वेभार-गिरि-पाय-मूले चारिंसइ, She roams about at the foot of the Vebhāra Mountain, standing still and looking about in gardens, or bathing in tanks, or plucking leaves or twigs and scattering them about. 4, *sometimes, only in the* 2. *sg. imper.* अच्छउ, *it has the idiomatic meaning of* let alone, not to speak of; *e.g.*, *Hēm.* iv, 406, *dō.*, जामहिँ विसमी कज्जगइ जीवहँ मज्झे एइ। तामहिँ अच्छउ इयरु जणु, सुअणु वि अन्तरु देइ॥ As long as a bad condition of affairs goes on among the living, so long—let alone the other (*i.e.*, *evil*) people—the good at least keep aloof (*i.e.*, *whatever the evil may do, the good keep aloof*); *Spt.*, *v.* 201, अच्छउ ता जणवाओ, हिअअं चिअ अत्तणो तुह पमाणं, Let alone the talk of men, thy own heart alone be thy guide (*i.e.*, *whatever the people may say, do thou follow thy own heart*). *In the Skr. commentaries the Pr. root* अच्छ *is rendered ad libitum by the Skr. roots* आस् *or* अस् *or* भू, *all which mean to be, to exist; in the vernacular paraphrases it is rendered by the Gd. root* रह to remain. *Hēm.* iv, 215 *makes it an equivalent of the Skr.* √आस् to exist; *Vr.* xii, 19, *of the Skr.* √अस् to be, *so also Ls.*, *p.* 346. *On the other hand Bs.* iii, 183 *suggests the Skr.* √अक्ष *with the meaning* to appear, *given to it ad hoc, while Weber* (*Spt.*, *p.* 41, 1*st ed.*), *Leumann* (*Aup.*, *Index*), *and E. Müller* (*Beiträge*, *p.* 36) *propose the Skr.*, √गम् to go. *Neither of these two latter Skr. roots will do; their meanings make them impossible. Most scholars now declare for the Skr.* √आस्; *so Childers* (*Pā. Dy. s.v.*), *Pischel* (*Transl. of Hēm.* iv, 215), *Steinthal* (*Nāy.*, *p.* 45), *see also Gd. Gr.*, *p.* 366. *Only Pott* (*Zig.* i, 459) *adopts the Skr.* √आ-अस् to exist, to stand by. *The difficulty is the exact connection of the Pr.* √अच्छ *with the Skr.* √आस्; *it is usually explained as an inchoative form* (*orig.* आस्छ, अच्छ) *of the latter* (*see Pischel in Göttingische Gelehrte Anzeigen*, *p.* 628, *of* 1875, *and Beiträge zur* *vergl. Sprachf., vol.* viii, *p.* 144); *Ascoli makes it the future of* √आस्, *and E. Kuhn the inchoative of* √अस् (*see Nāy., p.* 45; *also Gḍ. Gr., p.* 366). *On the whole Pott's suggestion of the* √आ-स्था *offers the fewest difficulties, phonetically as well as with regard to the meaning. In Pr. the* √स्था, *when* '*compounded with prep., is apt to become shortened to* थ *or* ठ (*cf. Hēm.* iv, 16, 17); *moreover the conj. cons.* त्थ *and* च्छ *are apt to be interchanged in Pr.* (*cf. the remarks under art.* चौतच्छेष), *probably through the metathesis of* त्स *the for* स्थ *sth. Thus the 3. sg. pres. of the* √आ-स्था *would be Pr.* अत्थइ *or* अच्छइ (*Skr.* आतिष्ठति), *both which spellings are found in Prākrit manuscripts. This view is supported by the fact that the modern vernaculars have an alternative auxiliary verb, the forms of which commence with* थ *th, and which is undoubtedly a derivative of* √स्था (*see Gḍ. Gr., p.* 367, *Bs.* iii, 208). *Thus Mth. has the two synonymous compound roots* छिक *and* थिक, *both meaning* to exist, to be (*see Mth. Gr.* § 112; *regarding the final* क, *see Gḍ. Gr.* § 353). *Pāli has the compound* √सम्अस to sit together, *which suits the Skr.* √समास्था *as well as the Skr.* √समास्. *It may be worth noting that while in Pā. and Pr. the root is spelt* अच्छ, *in the Gḍs. it is uniformly spelt* अछ, *with a single cons. The* √अछ *has survived in nearly all modern vernaculars with a more or less complete set of inflections. It appears to be entirely lost only in Br. and Mg. In M. and Gyp. it possesses a complete conjugation* (*Man.* §§ 222 *ff., Mik.* vii, 4); *in A., Bg., Mth., Mr., P., Ksh., Km., and Gaṛh. it exists in the pres. and pret. tenses and the pres. part., while in O., N., G. it occurs only in the pres. tense and pres. part. In S. even the pres. is fragmentary, and in Bh. and Bw. there is only the pres. part. In M., P., and S. the cons.* छ *chh is changed to* स *s; in A. and Bg., though* च *ch and* छ *chh respectively are written,* स *s is commonly pronounced; while in Ksh. and Gyp.* च *ch is both written and pronounced. For further particulars the comparative grammars* (*Gḍ. Gr., Bs.*) *and the special grammars of the various languages should be consulted. The following are simply given as specimens of the various forms in existence:* 1. *sg. pres., A.* आचों, *Bg.* आछि *or* छि, *O.* अछि *or* छि, *Mth.* छिऔं *or* छौं (*pl.* छी), *Mr.* छूं, *Km.* छौं *or* छूं, *Gaṛh.* छौं, *G. and N.* छूं, *P.* हाँ, *S.* छि, *M.* असें, *Ksh.* छुस (*J. A. S. B., vol.* xiii, *p.* 415); *again* 1. *sg. pret., Bg.* आछिलाम *or* छिलाम, *Mth.* छलऊँ *or* छलौं *or* छलों, *M.* असलों, *Km.* छियो, *Mr.* छो, *P.* सा. *The corresponding root in Gyp. is* ach to remain, *past part.* achilō (*Mik.* vii, 4), *which becomes* ash *in Rumanian Gyp., and* ach *or* hach *in English Gyp.*]

अछइत *achhaït, pres. part. of the* √अछ *achh, q.v.*

अछए *achhaē, old* 3. *sg. pres. of the* √अछ *achh, q.v.*

अछत *achhat* (1), *poet. for* अछत *achchat, q.v.*

अछत *achhat* (2), *pres. part. of the* √अछ *achh, q.v.*

अछत *achhat* (3), **Tbh.**, *subst. or adj., com. gen.,* being without an umbrella, one who has no umbrella. **Exam.**, *Padm., ch.* 6, 3, छत्रहिं अछत, निछत्रहिं छाया, (*God makes*) those who carry umbrellas (*i.e. kings*) to be without umbrellas (*comm.* बिहून छत्र), (*and*) gives shade to those who are without umbrellas (*i.e. the poor*).

[*Skr.* अ-छत्रः, *Pr.* अच्छत्तो, being without an umbrella (*see* अच्छत्तगं *Aup.* § 116), *opp. Skr.* छत्रः, *Pr.* छत्तो one who has an umbrella. *As above possibly in all Gḍs*).

√अछ्ताब *achh'tāb, sometimes incorrectly spelt* अचताब *ach'tāb,* (*pr. pts.* अछ्तबैत *achh'tabāīt, etc.*). *Only used in phrases such as* अछ्ताब-पछ्ताब *achh'tāb-pachh'tāb; see* √पछ्ताब *pachh'tāb.*

[*A rhyming repetition of* √पछ्ताब, *q.v.*]

अछ्पन *achh'pan,* **Tbh.**, *subst. m., the same as* अछ्वाई *achh'wāī.* **Exam.**, *Coll.,* (*Mg.*), जोब मैं अछ्पन भरल है, It is full of beauty.

[*From* अछ, *sh. f. of* अच्छा, *q.v., and sec. der. suff.* पन. *See Gḍ. Gr.* § 228.]

अछय *achhay* (1) अछै *achhāī,* **Ts.**, *adj., com. gen.,* undecaying, imperishable, permanent, durable. **Comp.**, अछय-बट (*Rām., Bā., ch.* 55, 5) *or* अछय-बर *or* अछय-बिरिछ, *subst. m.,* the undecaying tree, *a mutilated banian-tree situated in the underground remains of an ancient temple inside the fort of Allahābād; it was already known to Hwen Thsang in the seventh century, being then above ground a tree with widespreading branches* (*see Gen. Cunningham's Archæolog. Survey Reports, vol.* I, *pp.* 297, 298); अछय-लोक, *subst. m.,* the imperishable world, heaven; अछै-तिरतिया, (*scl.* तिथि), *subst. f.,* the imperishable third (*day*) (*Grs.* § 1444). *See* अछै-तीज *under* अछै. **Exam.**, *Rām., A., ch.* 102, 7, सङ्गम सिंहासन सुठि सोहा, छत्र अछय-बट मुनि-मन मोहा, The junction of the rivers (*Ganges, Jam'nā, and Saraswatī*) is the most glorious throne (*of Prayāg or Allahābād*), and the 'Imperishable Tree,' the joy of Munis' souls, is its umbrella. *For another example see under* अकलङ्क *akalaṅk. See* अखै *akhāī and* अखय *akhay.*

(*In literature the word is always spelt* अछय. *It has never been found by us spelt with* च्छ.)

[*Skr.* अक्षयः, *Pā.* अक्खयो, *Pr.* अक्खए (*Bhag., p.* 262, *Aup.* § 20); *as above in all Gḍs.*]

अछय *achhay* (2), *a corruption for* अच्छ *achchha* (*q.v.*), *which is occasionally met with in the comp.* अछय-कुमार *achhay-kumār for* अच्छ-कुमार *achchha-kumār*. Exam., *Mth. Rām.*, *Su.* 28, 6, अछय-कुमार कौं पटकि दृट मारलक, The fool has dashed down and killed Achchha-kumār; *ib.* 50, 9, मुरला मुरला अछय-कुमार, Achchha-kumār is dead, is dead. *It occurs also in the Lakhnaū edition of Tul'sī Dās' Rāmāyan, Su., ch.* 18, 7.

अछर *achhar*, *poet. for* अच्छर *achchhar* (1), *q.v.*

अछ्ंरङ्ग *achh'rayg*, Tbh., *subst. m.*, a false accusation, calumny. Phr., अछ्ंरङ्ग लगाएब, *c. tr.*, to bring a false accusation, calumniate. Exam., *B. Gr.* II, *Bh. song* 24, 4, ना हम चोरिनि, ना हम चढनी, झुठ अ अछ्ंरङ्ग लगावत बा, I am not a thief, nor a glutton, still he reproaches (*me*) falsely.

[*Apparently a corruption of Skr.* आचार + अङ्क, mark of calumny? *Not met with elsewhere.*]

अछ्ंरङ्गी *achh'raygī*, (*lg. f.* अछ्ंरङ्गिया *achh'raygiyā*). Tbh., *fem. of the preceding, q.v.* Exam., *Hd. Dy.*, (*Mg.*), बरे भूठें मतो जोड़ अछ्ंरङ्गिया रे को, Now, don't make up false charges, eh!

अछ्ंरौटी *achh'rauṭī*, Tbh., *subst. f.*, *the same as* अख्ंरौटी *akh'rauṭī*, *q.v.*

अछल *achhal*, Ts., *adj.*, *com. gen.*, without guile, sincere. Exam., *Coll.*, (*Mg.*), है हमर बचन अछल है, My words are true.

अछ्ंलाह *achh'lāh*, *old* 3. *plur. pret. of* √अछ *achh*, *q.v.*

अछ्ंवाई *achh'wāī*, Tbh., *subst. f.*, goodness, excellence, elegance. Exam., *Padm.*, *ch.* 503, 2, रूप सरूप, सिंगार सवाई, अछर जैसि रही अछवाई, Her appearance is beautiful, her dress is one (*dress*) and a quarter (*i.e. best of its kind*), and her elegance is like that of a heavenly nymph.

[*Abs. noun derived from* अच्छा (*q.v.*) *or pleon.* अच्छ्ंवा *by means of the sec. der. suff.* आई. *See Gd. Gr.* § 220.]

अछ्ंवानी *achh'wānī*, अछुमानी *achhumānī*, उछ्ंवानी *uchh'wānī*, वछ्ंवानी *wachh'wānī*, Tbh., *subst. f.*, a strengthening mixture, a caudle, *especially given to women after childbirth* (*Grs.* §§ 1399, 1409). *It is an aromatic decoction prepared of long pepper* (*and sometimes the roots of the same plant*), '*aj'wān' seeds, cloves, cinnamon, and some grains of old or last year's rice, boiled down in water till the whole is of the consistence of thin gruel. A dose of this medicine is usually administered in the morning to the lying-in woman on the second or third day after the confinement and continued for two or three days successively* (*Harris Manuscripts, in Shakespeare's Hd. Dy.*). *The number of ingredients, however, varies; sometimes there are twenty-two* (*when it is called* बत्तीसा *battīsā*, *q.v.*), *sometimes even thirty-six* (*called* छत्तीसा *chhattīsā*, *q.v.*). *The form in which it is administered also differs; sometimes it is given as a draught, sometimes as pills* (*or laḍḍū*), *sometimes as a paste* (*or hal'wā*). *See* अजवानी *aj'wānī*.

[*Probably Skr.* उत्पयवी (*or* उत्पयपी) *or* उत्थापयती *strengthening* (*from* √उत् *or* √उत्-थी), *Pr.* उत्थावयवी (*with pleon. suff.* अपि) *or shortened* उत्थवयवी (*see Hēm.* iii, 150) *or* उत्थवयवी, *whence contr. B.* उछवानी, *or* (*with metathesis of vowels*) अछुमानी (*for* अछुमानी) *or* अछवानी. *If this derivation is correct the true B. form is* उछवानी. *Natives derive it from* अजवान. *H.* अछवान, छवान, *or* हुवान.]

अछहिं *achhahī*, *old* 3. *plur. pres. of* √अछ *achh*, *q.v.*

√अछाब *achhāb*, (*pr. pts.* अछ्ंबैत *achh'bait*, *Bh. and Mg.* अछावत *achhāwat*, अछाविन *achhāwit*, अछाइत *achhāit*; अछाओल *achhāöl*; अछाएब *achhāeb*; अछाबै *achhābai*, अछाए *achhāē*), Tbh., *v. tr.*, to spread. Exam., *Mth. Rām.*, *Ln.* 28, 23, ई कहि कहि कुस सेज अछाय, बानर सभ बैसल पछताय, With these words, spreading seats of 'kus' grass, the monkeys sat down lamenting. *See* √ओछाब *ochhāb*.

[*Skr.* √आ-छद्, *xth cl.*, 3. *sg.* आच्छादयति, *Pr.* आच्छाएइ *or* अच्छाएइ (*see art.* अ *a* (6)), *or* (*with pleon.* आपि, *see Gd. Gr.* § 349) अच्छावेइ *or* अच्छावइ, *hence contr. B.* अछाबै. *Possibly the form* अछाब *is a mere corruption of the form* ओछाब, *in which case the corresponding Skr. root would be* अव-छद्.]

अछार *achhār* (1), Tbh., *subst. m.*, an enhancement, increase, rise, addition (*Ās. Gy.*).

[*The M. has* उच्छाल, *which would seem to show that the initial a of the B.* अछार *is a corruption of u, and that the original is Skr.* उच्छाल.]

अछार *achhār* (2), Tbh., *subst. m.*, a heavy shower of rain, driving rain (*Hd. Dy.*, *s.v.* بوچهار *bauchhār*).

[*Probably Skr.* आसारः, *as a synonym of* आसारः a heavy shower; *Pr.* आसारो *or* अच्छारो (*see art.* अ *a* (6)), *B.* अछार. *In classical Skr. the word* आसार *does not appear to have borne that meaning; but the latter is intrinsically probable, as the causal of* √आसार means to cause to flow (*see shorter Skr. Dy. P.*), *and it may have been in use in the Prākrits. If the word is identified with Skr.* आसार, *a change of* स *to* छ *must be assumed, as in* √छुआ to whitewash, *from Skr.* सुधा (*see Hēm.* i, 265). *The H. has* बौछार, *which would seem to point to Skr.* अवधार *or rather* अवधार; *hence possibly the B.* अवधार *may be a mere corruption of* ओधार *for Skr.* अवधार; *see the remarks on* अवधा. *The word has not been observed elsewhere.*]

अछि *achhi*, 3. *sg. pres. of the* √अछ *achh, q.v.*

अँछिया *ãchhiyā, l. f. of* आँखी *ãchhī, q.v.* (*Grs.* § 1248).

अछी *achhī* (1), *old* 1. *plur. pres. of the* √अछ *achh, q.v.*

अछी *achhī* (2), *poet. for* अछि *achhi*, 3. *sg. pres. of the* √अछ *achh, q.v.* Exam., *Mth. Rām., Su.* 53, 10, की काएक अछि, अकी की काज, Why is he come? What is his business?

अछुत्ता *achhuttā, Mg. form of* अछूत *achhūt, q.v.*

अछुमानी *achhumānī, the same as* अछ्वानी *achh'wānī, q.v.*

अछूत *achhūt*, Tbh., *adj., com. gen.,* (*poet. f.* अछूति *achhūti, str. f.* अछूता *achhūtā, f.* अछूती *achhūtī*), [1]untouched; *hence* [2]fresh; [3]holy (*or* what may not be touched, *used of offerings to idols*); *hence* [4]*fig.* (*used of a woman*) undeflowered, unbroached. Phr., [2]अछूत बरतन, *lit.* an untouched vessel; *hence* a virgin. Exam., [1]*Padm., ch.* 634, 1, तब पदमावत उघारी छूती, पदमावत नहिँ छुई अछूती, Then the female messenger uncovered the food, (*but*) Padmawat did not touch it (*but left it*) untouched; *ib., ch.* 667, 3, भीँजे चार और हिय चोली, रही अछूत (*fem.*), कन्त नहिँ खोली, Her necklace, cloths, and the bodice on her breast became wet (*with tears*), but it (*i.e. the bodice*) was untouched, (*for*) her lover had not opened it; *ib., ch.* 105, 5, ओठि के अधर अमी भर राखे, अबहिँ अछूति, न काहू चाखे, Her lips were full of nectar (*lit.* kept nectar brimful), as yet untouched, (*for*) no one had tasted (*it*). [2]*Padm., ch.* 630, 3, लै पूरी भर डाल अछूती, चितउर गई भीतर कै दूती, Taking a basket full of fresh 'pūris' (*a kind of fritters*), the female messenger went inside Chitaur. [3]*Coll.,* (*Bh.*), ई अछूता चँबे, एकरा मती छूवँ, This is holy, touch it not.
[*Skr.* अ-छुप्तः, *Pr.* अछुत्तो; *as above possibly in all Gḍs.*]

अछूता *achhūtā, str. f. of* अछूत *achhūt, q.v.*

अछूति *achhūti, poet. fem. of* अछूत *achhūt, q.v*

अछूती *achhūtī, str. f. fem of* अछूत *achhūt, q.v.*

अछेद *achhed*, Ts., *subst. m.,* absence of differences *or* of secrets, at-oneness, intimacy. Exam., *Padm., dō.* 263, 1, चेला सिध सो पावई, गुरु सौं करइ अछेद। गुरु करै जो किरिपा, कहइ सो चेला भेद॥ That disciple obtains perfection (*who*) is absolutely one with his religious preceptor; if the religious preceptor show favour the disciple can tell his secrets.
[*Skr.* अ *and* छेद, *the latter of which is here used as a synonym of* भेद difference, secret.]

अछै *achhai*, Ts., *the same as* अछय *achhay, q.v. See* अखै *akhai*.

अछैति *achhaiti, fem. of the pres. part. of* √अछ *achh, q.v.*

अछोनी *achhonī, contr. from* अछोहिनी *achhōhinī, q.v.*

अछोप *achhōp*, Ts., *subst., com. gen.,* (*Mth., f.* अछोपि *achhōpi*), a person of very low caste. (*Water touched by him may not be drunk by higher caste Hindūs.*) Exam., *Coll*, (*Bh.*), ई अछोप जात चँबे, This is a man of low caste.
[*Skr.* अ *and* छोप: *Not met with in other Gḍs.*]

अछोभ *achhōbh*, (*poet.* अछोभा *achhōbhā*), Ts., *adj., com. gen.,* (*subst. f.* अछोभा *achhōbhā*), imperturbable, dauntless. Exam., *Rām., Ba., ch.* 282, 8, जौं तुम्ह अउर अछोभा, गारी देत न पावहु सोभा, If you (*i.e. Parasurām*) are really a heroic ascetic and a resolute and dauntless warrior, you will gain no honour by dealing abuse.
[*Skr.* अ-क्षोभः; *as above possibly in all Gḍs.*]

अछोभा *achhōbhā, poet. for* अछोभ *achhōbh, q.v.*

√अछोर *achhōr*, (*pr. pts.* अछोरैत *achhoraīt*; अछोरल *achhoral*; अछोरब *achhōrab*; अछोरै *achhōrai*), Tbh., *v. tr.,* to snatch. Phr., अछोरि लेब, to snatch away. Exam., *Bid.* 31, 1, अबनहिँ लेल हरि कचु अछोरि, कते परजुगुति कैल अङ्ग मोरि, When Hari snatched away my bodice, how many struggles did I make, twisting my limbs?
[*Skr.* √छोड् *with* आ, *xth cl.* आछोडयति, *Pr.* आछोडेइ *or cl.* vi आछोडइ *or* अछोडइ, *B.* अछोड़े *or* अछोरे; *not met with in other Gḍs. The* √छोड् *mean* to throw away, *the addition of the prep.* आ *reverses the meaning, hence* to snatch towards one's self; *cf.* √दा to give *and* √आ-दा to take. *Regarding the shortening of* आ, *see art.* अ *a* (6).]

अछोहनी *achhōhanī*, अछौहनी *achhauhanī*, Ts., *the same as* अछोहिनी *achhohinī, q.v.*

अछोहिनी *achhōhinī*, अछौहिनी *achhauhinī*, Ts., *subst. f.,* a complete army. *Such an army consists of* 10 *anīkinī or corps, each of these again consists of* 27 *vāhinī* or divisions, *and each division contains* 81 *elephants,* 81 *chariots,* 243 *horse, and* 405 *foot; thus the whole army consists of* 21,870 *elephants,* 21,870 *chariots,*

65,610 *horse, and* 109,350 *foot.* **Exam.,** *Comm. to K. Rām., Bā.*, 8, जो अछोहिनी अछोहिनी अर्थात् कुच कुच आवे राजा निमि के भूमि में आयल अछ, They arrived in king Nimi's country, each provided with an 'achhōhinī,' that is, a complete army. *See* अछोनी *achhōnī and* छोनी *chhōnī*.

[*Skr.* अक्षौहिणी, *probably derived from* अक्ष cube *and* वाहिनी a division, 27 *being the cube of* 3. *See M. Williams' Skr. Dy.*]

अछौर *achhaŭr*, **Ts.**, *subst. m.*, ceremonial impurity, *esp. from a death in the family and the like,* (*lit. which stops shaving*). **Exam.,** *Coll.*, (*Mg.*), हमरा घर में अछौर भेल है, My house is impure, (*lit.* impurity is in my house, *i.e.*, *a death has recently occurred in my house*); *Prov.*, (*Mg.*), अछौर भेल अछूती, का निछूता का अछूती, A death has occurred (*in*) my house; what is pure, what is impure? (*lit.* what is untouched food, and what is touched food, *i.e., there is no difference between them*).

[*Skr.* क्षौरम्, *with neg.* अ.]

अछौहिनी *achhaŭhinī*, अछौहनी *achhaŭhanī*, **Ts.,** *the same as* अछोहिनी *achhōhinī*, *q.v.*

अज *aj* (1), (*fem.* अजा *ajā*), **Ts.,** *subst. m.*, a he-goat, **Comp.**, अज-वीथी, *subst. f.*, (*astr.*), the goat's path, *being the name of one of the three divisions of the southern portion of the path of the sun and planets among the lunar asterisms, of which it comprises the three called* '*mūlā*,' '*pūrvākharhā*,' *and* '*uttarākharhā*.' **Exam.,** *Mth. Rām., Bā.*, 121, 8, अजक गोल जहु देखि हुड़ार, As a wolf watches a herd of goats; *Pārb.*, 12, नाचहिं नाना रङ्ग-तरङ्ग बढ़ावहिं, अज-उलूक-वृक-नाद गीत गन गावहिं, The gans (*attendants of Sib*) dance and carry on all sorts of merry sports, and sing songs in the voices of goats, owls, and wolves; *Mth. Rām., Ut.* 61, 5, अजा उचार करय गान्धार, मध्यम स्वर कौं क्रौंच उचार, The she-goat sounds the (*third note of the scale, called*) 'Gāndhar,' and the heron sounds the 'Madhyam' (*i.e.* middle, *or fourth*) note; *K. Rām., A.*, 5, जो सुमिरे रज मेरु सिला सन होत, अजा खुर वारिधि बाढ़े, Through remembering which (*i.e. the name of Rām*) the rocks of Mount Meru became as grains of sand, and the she-goat's hoofs grew as big as the ocean.

[*Skr.* अजः; *Pr. fem.* अआ (*Hēm.* iii, 32). *This tadbh. form has not survived in the Gḍs.*]

अज *aj* (2), (*fem.* अजा *ajā*, *old obl.* अजहिं *ajahĩ*, *Skr. acc. sg. m.* अजम् *ajam or* अजं *ajaṁ in Rām., Ar., chh.* 9, 5; *ib., Ln., chh.* 36, 9), **Ts.,** (I) *adj. m.*, unborn, uncreated, who exists from eternal, everlasting (*syn.* अनादि *anādi*), *only used as a religious term, applied to the Supreme Spirit or Impersonal God* (*Brahm or Bhagawān*), *or to the Personal Gods* (*Brahmā, Sib, Bish'n, and their consorts Pārbatī and Lachhmī, etc.*), *or to the Incarnate Gods* (*e.g. Rām*). **Exam.,** *Rām., Bā., ch.* 18, 3, एक अनीह अरूप अनामा, अज सच्चिदानन्द परधामा, व्यापक विश्व-रूप भगवाना, तेहिं धरि देह चरित कृत नाना, The Bhagawān (*who is*) one, passionless, formless, nameless, uncreated, a blissful spiritual essence, dwelling in the highest heaven, omnipresent, all-pervading,—he taking a body performed all manner of acts; *ib., Ut., ch.* 108, 3, लागे करन ब्रह्म उपदेसा, अज अद्वैत अगुन हृदयेसा, अकल अनीह अनाम अरूपा, अनुभव-गम्य अखण्ड अनूपा, He began to deliver a sermon on Brahm, (*who is*) uncreated, indivisible, immaterial, sovereign of the heart, partless, passionless, nameless, formless, incomprehensible, indestructible, incomparable; (*see also Mth. Rām., A.*, 82, 1); *Bin.* 49, चन्द्र-सेखर सूल-पानि हर अनघ अज अमित अविछिन्न वृष-भेष-गामी, Hara (*i.e. Sib*), who bears the moon on his head and holds the trident in his hand, is sinless, uncreated, immeasurable, indivisible, and rides upon the great bull (*see also Rām., Bā., ch.* 99, 3); *Rām., Ut., ch.* 35, 4, जय इन्दिरा-रमन, जय भू-धर, अनुपम अज अनादि सोभाकर, Hail to Indirā's (*i.e. Lachhmī's*) spouse (*i.e. Bish'n*), hail to the earth's support, (*who is*) incomparable, uncreated, beginningless, full of splendour; *ib., Ln., chh.* 36, 7, अज व्यापकमेकमनादि सदा, करुनाकर राम नमामि मुदा, I always joyfully worship Rām, (*who is*) uncreated, omnipresent, one, beginningless; *ib., Bā., ch.* 106, 3, मयना सत्य सुनहु मम बानी, जगदम्बा तव सुता भवानी, अजा अनादि सकति अविनासिनि, सदा सम्भु-अरधाङ्ग-निवासिनि, O Mainā, hear my true words: thy daughter Bhavānī (*i.e. Pārbatī*) is the mother of the world, the uncreated, beginningless Sakti (*or* female energy), always dwelling in mystic corporeal unity with Sambhu (*referring to Sib's half male and half female form*).

(II) *subst. m.*, a name of the Supreme Spirits or God; [a] a name of Brahmā. **Comp.**, अजादि (= अज-आदि), *subst. m.*, Brahmā and the other gods (*i.e. Bish'n and Sib, etc., Rām., Bā., dō.* 64, 2); अज-धाम, (*poet.* अज-धामा), *subst. m.*, the abode of Brahmā (*Rām., Ln., ch.* 16, 1). **Exam.,** [1]*Rām., Ut., dō.* 26, 1, (*also Dōh.* 114), ग्यान-गिरा-गो-अतीत अज माया-मन-गुन पार, सोइ सच्चिदानन्द घन कर नर-चरित उदार, The Supreme Spirit (*who*) transcends knowledge, speech, and understanding and is unaffected by material phenomena, the workings of the mind, and the properties of things: he, the absolutely blissful spiritual essence, performs the actions of exalted humanity. [2]*Rām., Ki., dō.* 25, 2, उर धरि राम-चरन-जुग, जे बन्दत अज ईस, (*Swayamprabhā went away*) cherishing in her heart

Rām's two feet, which Brahmā and Īs (*i.e. Sib*) **adore ;** *Bin.* 64, **सेबित पद-पङ्कज अज महेस,** (*Rām's*) **lotus-like feet are worshipped by Brahmā and Mahēs** (*i.e. Sib*) ; *Rām., Su., ch.* 23, 8, **सङ्कर सहस बिष्नु अज तोही सकहिँ न राखि राम कर द्रोही,** Saŋkar (*i.e. Sib*), Sahas (*i.e. Sēs'nāg*), Bish'n, and Brahmā cannot protect you (*if you are*) Rām's enemy ; *similarly Gīt., Su.* 11, 3, **हरि-सिव-अज-पूज्य** adored by Hari, Sib, and Aj ; *Rām., Bā., dō.* 197, 2, **अस्तुति कर अज जोरि कर सावधान मति-धीर,** Aj (*i.e.* Brahmā) clasping his hands composedly and deliberately chanted (*Rām's*) praises.

[*Skr.* **अः** *with neg.* **अ** ; *as above in all Gds.*]

अजऽ *aja, poet., a shortened form of* **आज** *āj* (*q.v.*), *which occurs only in combination with the encl. pt.* **हुँ** *hū̃ or* **हूँ** *hū̃, expressing emphasis.* **Exam.,** *Rām., Bā., ch.* 61, 8, **भये मगन छबि तासु बिलोकी, अजहुँ प्रीति उर रहति न रोकी,** (*Sib*) became (*so*) enraptured on seeing (*Rām's*) beauty, (*that it was*) only on that day (*that*) love unhindered arose in his mind ; *ib., Bā., ch.* 117, 5, **अज हूँ कछु संसय मन मोरे,** On this day, too, there is some doubt in my mind ; *Bāis.* 30, **आवन कहि गए, अज हुँ न आए,** He went away promising to return, (*but*) up to this very day he has not returned. *Often the emphasis is very slight, when practically* **अजहुँ** *is equivalent to* **आज.** **Exam.,** *Rām., Bā., ch.* 72, 3, **ब्रह्म-सभा हम सन दुख माना, तेहिँ तेँ अजहुँ करहिँ अपमाना,** In Brahmā's court he took offence at me, for this (*reason*) he shows disrespect (*to me*) this day.

अजऊँ *ajaū̃, the same as* **अजहूँ** *ajahū̃, see under* **अजऽ** *ajahu.*

अजं *ajaṁ, Skr. acc. sg. m. of* **अज** *aj* (2), *q.v. It only occurs in the Rām.*

अजऽगड़ *aj'gaṛ, the same as* **अजगर** *aj'gar, q.v.* **Exam.,** *Mth. Rām., Ar.,* 4, 32, **मुह बबोलै बड़ अजगड़ साँप,** He opened his mouth wide like a python.

अजगव *aj'gab,* **Ts.,** *subst. m.,* [1](*astr.*) the southern portion of the path of the sun and planets among the lunar asterisms; [2] the name of Sib's bow, *which was broken by Rām.* **Exam.,** [2]*Mth. Rām., Ln.,* 62, 1, **अजगव-भञ्जन जल-निधि-बन्धन,** (*Rām*) the breaker of the bow and the builder of the causeway on the sea ; *Rām., Bā., dō.* 283, 2, **अजगव खण्डेउ ऊख जिमि अजहुँ न बूझ अबूझ,** Though (*Rām*) has broken Sib's bow like a piece of sugarcane, still even now the foolish (*Parasurām*) does not understand.

[*Skr.* **अजगवः** *and* **अजकवः** ; *as above in all Gds.*]

अजगर *aj'gar,* **अजगड़** *aj'gaṛ,* **Ts.,** *subst. m.,* a kind of huge serpent, a python. (*It is supposed to be too unwieldy to move, and to devour only such animals as themselves fall into its mouth ; see Growse's Translation of Rām., rev. ed., p.* 551.) **Exam.,** *Rām., Ut., ch.* 104, 7, **बैठि रहेसि अजगर इव पापी, सरप होहि खल मल-मति ब्यापी,** Thou remainest sitting (*immoveable*) like a python, O thou sinner ; (*therefore*) thou shalt become a serpent, O thou wretch, (*who art*) full of impure thoughts ; *Padm., ch.* 421, 2, **अजगर केर आय भुख-भुखी,** He has got enough food to satisfy the hunger of a python ; *Malūk Dās* (*in Growse, Rām. trans.*), **अजगर करै न चाकरी, पंछी करै न काम, दास मलूका कहि गये, सब का दाता राम,** The python does no service, the birds do no work, (*yet*), thus says Malūk Dās, Rām is the supporter of all ; *Bw., ch., anon.,* **जग बहु नर अजगर सम आहीं, सदन छोड़ि कतहुँ नहिं जाहीं,** In the world many men are unwieldy like pythons ; they never leave their throne or go anywhere. *See* **अजन्दह** *aj'dahā,* **अजन्दाह** *aj'dāh.*

(*This serpent is usually said to be the boa constrictor, but the distribution of the latter animal is confined to South America. Of the pythonidæ, however, one species occurs throughout Peninsular India, and is very common in North-Eastern Bengal.*)

[*Skr.* **अज** + **गरः,** *lit.* swallowing a goat ; *see art.* **अज.** *But compare Prs.* ازدر *azhdar and* اژدها *azhdahā.*]

अजगुत *aj'gut,* **अजगूत** *aj'gūt,* **Ts.,** (I) *adj., com. gen.,* unusual, uncommon, strange, surprising, wonderful. **Exam.,** *B. Gr.,* II (*Bh.*), *song* 13, 4, **पूछिय तोहि, कागा अजगुत बतिया,** I ask thee, O crow, a strange matter.

(II) *subst. m.,* [1]*concr.,* something unusual *or* strange *or* wonderful, a marvel, a miracle (*in a physical sense, but sometimes also in a moral sense*) ; [2] something improper, unfit ; [3]*abs.,* wonder, astonishment, amazement. **Phr.,** [1]**अजगुत लागब,** *v. intr., lit.* to attain to (*the nature of*) a wonder, *hence* to appear wonderful ; **अजगुत करब,** *v. tr.,* to consider wonderful ; to perform a wonder ; **अजगुत कै लेखब,** *v. tr., lit.* to write (*something down*) as a wonder, to mark (*it*) as a wonder, *hence* to consider wonderful, to be struck with wonder ; **अजगुत होएब,** *v. intr., lit.* amazement to happen (*to some one*), *hence* to be amazed. **Exam.,** [1]*Mth. Rām., Su.* 40, 24, **अजगुत जिबित छि अछि दस-माथ,** For a wonder, Das'māth (*i.e. Rāban*) is still alive ; *Bw., song, anon.,* **अजगुत कीन्हो, रे रामा, जगाये कोँची प्रीति गये पर-देसवाँ,** I considered it a wonder, O Rām, that thou didst arouse my young love and then didst depart to a far country ; *Hb.* iv, 27, **अजगुत कैलक, बैलक दाँत,** (*The serpent Kāli*) performed wondrous actions, and seized (*Krish'n*) with her teeth ; *ib.,* ii, 62, **माँगे माँर माँगे माँर, अजगुत भेल,** O mother, O mother, a miracle has happened ; *Din., l.* 119, **देखलक सहेस, जे बड़ अजगुत भेल,** Sal'hēs thought (*lit.* saw) that something very wonderful had happened (*see also l.* 124); *Hb.* v, 56, प्रत दिन प्रत बड़ अजगुत लाग, These (*things occurring*) in so few days appear very wonderful (*lit.* attain to a great wonder); *so also Mth. Rām., Bā.* 31, 2, तोड़ब सङ्कर-चाप जनक-पुर, प्रत दिन अजगुत लाग, The breaking of Saṅkar's (*i.e. Sib's*) bow in Janak'pur after so many days appears wonderful; *Hb.*, viii, 2, डुबि कर्ं जल हरि हलधर देखल सेस सहित, अजगुत भै सोचल, As (*Ak'rūr*) dived he saw Hari and Hal'dhar (*i.e. Krish'n and Bal'rām*) in the water together with the (*serpent*) Sēs, and was struck with awe. ² *Coll.*, (*Mg.*), तूँ बड़ अजगुत कैलँह, कि ओकरा कैँ मारलँह, You did a very improper thing that you beat him (*after Hd. Dy.*); *Sabhā Bilās* (*in Hd. Dy.*), जान बूझ अजगुत करए, ता सौँ कथा बसाए, If one do improper things deliberately, what is one to do with him? ³ *Din.*, *l.* 378, फोटरा के देखि अजगुत भेलौंह, (*Gulāmī said to himself*) "on seeing Phoṭ'rā you are amazed."

(*This word is more commonly used as a subst., and with the first meaning of it. Compare the word* अचम्भा *achambhā.*)

[*Skr.* युक्त: *with neg.* अ, *Pā.* अयुत्तो, not connected *or* not in conformity *with correct principles or analogy, either of nature or morals, hence either* unusual, wonderful, *or* improper. *In the latter sense the word is more usual in Skr. and Pā.; the former is the more common one in the Gds. A synonym is* असङ्गत, *lit.* not going together *or* agreeing *with law or analogy. Not met with in other Gds., exc. G.* अजगत accidental, unexpected. *The word is a tats., formed like* भगत *from Skr* भक्त (*see Gḍ. Gr.* §§ 102, 141); *hence Skr.* अयुक्त *becomes* अजुगत, *and, with transfer of the vowel u,* अजगुत; *in G. the vowel u is dropped.*]

अजग्गुतवा *aj'gut'wā, lg. f. of* अजग्गुत *aj'gut, q.v.* **Exam.**, *Bij.*, *l.* 577, सुतल मैं रङ्गों चित्र-सरिया, राति के सपनवाँ अजगुतवा, I was asleep in my painted room, (*and*) in the night (*there came to me*) a strange dream.

अजग्गूत *aj'gūt*, **Tbh.**, *adj., com. gen., the same as* अजग्गुत *aj'gut, q.v.* **Exam.**, *Bh., song, anon.*, सुतलि रङ्गमहलिया सपना देखल अजगूत, I was sleeping in the women's apartments and saw a wondrous dream.

अजग्य *ajagya*, **Ts.**, *adj., com. gen., lit.* not a sacrifice, *hence* not destined for sacrifice. **Exam.**, *Hb.* viii, 31, अजग्यक धनुख कर लेलन्हि उठाए, The bow (*which was*) destined never to become a subject for sacrifice, he lifted up in his hands.

[Skr. यज्ञ: *with neg.* अ; *as above possibly in all Gds.*]

अजण्ट *ajanṭ*, **Any.**, *subst. m.*, an agent.

[*A corruption of the English word.*]

अजण्टी *ajanṭī*, **Any.**, *subst. f.*, ¹agency; ²the office of a Political Agent *or* Resident in a native state (*a term. techn. of the English administration*); ³the Residency (*i.e. the house and court of a political resident*).

[*A corruption of the English word, made analogically; as if* अजण्ट *with Gḍ. suff.* ई, *see Gḍ. Gr.* § 252.]

अजग्दहा *aj'dahā*, अजग्दहा *aj'dā*, **Any.**, *subst. m.*, a large serpent, a python; *hence adj., met.*, very large, very gross, *said of animals and things, and facetiously of men. It is not used colloquially as a subst., except facetiously.* **Exam.**, *Coll.*, (*Bh.*), का उहवाँ अजग्दहा बैसल बा तोहैं निगल जाई, What python is sitting there, will it swallow you? *Coll.*, (*Mg.*), बड़ अजग्दहा साँप है, It is a very large and thick snake; *ib.*, ओकर दूनों बैल अजग्दहा बाटी, खुब मोटा बाटी, Both his bullocks are fine big fellows; they are very fat.

[*Prs.* اژدها, *ashdahā.*]

अजग्दा *aj'dā, the same as* अजग्दहा *aj'dahā, q.v.* **Exam.**, *subst.*, (*fac.*), *Coll.*, (*Mg.*), अजग्दा ऐसन परल है, He has fallen down (*lying helpless*) like a python (*gorged with food*); *adj.*, *Coll.*, (*Mg.*), ई अजग्दा लकड़ी है, This is a great thick piece of wood.

[*Prs.* اژده *azhda; final Prs. inaudible* ه *h becomes in Gḍ.* आ *ā, as in* بنده बन्दा *bandā*, servant.]

अजग्नब *aj'nab*, **Any.**, *adj. and subst., com. gen.*, foreign, strange, unknown; a foreigner, a stranger. **Exam.**, *Chaukīdārī Niyamābalī*, 4, गाँव में अजनब जे पुरुख आवथि कहियो तान असल अहोवल तनिकरा चाओर जहरी बात, If a stranger comes into the village at any time, (*you must tell*) all his real circumstances, and any other important information (*in Urdūized police jargon*).

[*Ar.* اجنب *ajnab.*]

अजग्नबी *aj'nabī, the same as* अजग्नब *aj'nab, q.v.*

अजन्त *ajant*, **Ts.**, *adj., com. gen.*, (*gram.*), ending in a vowel.

[*Skr. comp.* अच् + अन्त; *as above in all Gḍs.*]

अजब *ajab*, **Any.**, (I) *adj., com. gen.*, ¹strange, wonderful; ²exceptionally fine *or* charming. **Phr.**, अजब देखब, *v. tr., lit.* to look upon as strange, *hence* to appear strange (*to some one*); अजब कहब, *v. tr., lit.* to call (*something*) strange, *hence* to appear strange (*to some one*). **Exam.**, ¹*Prov., H.*, अजब तेरी क़ुदरत, अजब तेरे खेल, छुछुन्दर के सिर में चमेली का तेल, (O God,) wondrous thy power, and wondrous are thy illusions. Lo, on a muskrat's head is found the oil of the (*fragrant*) jasmin (*said of a good point found in a churl*); *Fam.* 53, **अजब कार सरकार के, तिरहुत पहुँचल रेल**, Wonderful are the actions of Government, (*for then*) a railway came to Tirhut; *Misc.* 85, **सेल्ही टोपी ग्यान गुदरिया बिभुति रमाए अजब रूप धैलौं**, With a 'sēlhī' (*or mendicant's head-dress consisting of twists of black rope*) for a cap, with knowledge for a (*mendicant's*) pallet, and applying ashes of cowdung (*to my body*), I put on a strange appearance; *Mag.* 28, **तोरी चमकवा तो अजब देखौं, रँगिछिया, बटिया चलल जौ सरधाए**, Thy brilliance appears to me wonderful, O fair lady, (*as*) thou art coquettishly walking in the way, (*see also ib.* 38). [2] *Mag.* 54, **तोरी धरेमियाँ अजब कहौं, गोरिया, नैना तो देखौं मजगूत** (*vulg. cor. for* **मजबूत**), Thine embracings I call very charming, O fair lady, and thine eyes I see to be powerful; *ib.* 38, **तोरी बदनियाँ अजब देखौं, रँगिछिया, सुरती जबनियाँ रे तोर**, Thy limbs appear (*to me*) most charming, O fair lady, and very beautiful thy breasts.

(II) *adv.*, strangely, wonderfully, extravagantly. **Exam.**, *Mag.* 68, **एही तो बटिया मैं अजब सराहौं गे नैना तोर घूँघट देले जाए**, Here in the road I am praising (*thee*) extravagantly, dear, (*as*) thou art going along hiding thy eyes with thy veil.

(*This foreign word is in very common use.*)

[*Ar.* عجب *'ajab.*]

अजब-सालार, *ajab-sālār*, **Any.**, *subst. m.*, *lit.* a wonderful commander, the name of a certain saint, *worshipped by Musalmān drummers, who during an outbreak of cholera act as village Musalmān priests. They go about beating drums with an iron bar wrapped in red cloth and adorned with flowers, which represents the saint Gājī Miyā̃. They are paid in kind by the people at whose doors they stop and drum. Grs.* § 1456, *p.* 405.

[*Ar.* عجب سالار *'ajab sālār; see art.* **अजब**.]

अजन्बीथी *aj'bīthī*, **Ts.**, *subst. f.*; *see under* **अज** *aj* (1).

अजन्बेस *aj'bēs*, **Tbh.**, *subst. m.*, the name of two Hindī poets, *viz.*, [1]the elder (**प्राचीन** *prāchīn*), *who lived, apparently as a bard, at the court of Rājā Bīr'bhān Singh of Bāndhōgaṛh in Rīwā̃, born* 1513 *A.D.*, (*see Gen. Cunningham's Archæol. Survey Rep., vol.* xvii, *p.* 69); [2]the younger, *who, according to Siv., ib., lived at the court of Mahārāja Bisva Nāth Siṅgh of Bāndhōgaṛh, born* 1833 *A.D.; he is quoted in the Sundarī Tilak.* **Exam.**, [1] *Siv.*, *p.* 14, **शेर शाह सलिल प्रबल को बढ़्यो अजबेस बूड़त हुमायूँ के बड़ोई उतपात भो; बल-हीन बालक अकब्बर बचाइबे को बीरभान भूपति अखैबड़ को पात भो**, Shēr Shāh rose like the waters of the great flood—(*says*) Aj'bēs—(*and*) for the drowning Humāyūn it was a great calamity; (*then*) to save the powerless child Akbar, Bīr'bhān, the chief, became like the leaves of the Akhai Bar (*or* the tree of immortality at Allahābad); *the reference is to the tradition, related in Gen. Cunningham's Archæol. Survey Reports, vol.* xxi, *p.* 109, *of the family of Humāyūn, when he was chased out of India, after the disastrous battle at Kanauj, in* 1540 *A.D., finding asylum in the fort of Bāndhōgaṛh, where Akbar is said (though falsely) to have been born; there is a pun on the words 'Akbar' and 'Akhaibar.'* [2] *Siv.*, *p.* 14, **सुख सरसावनो है, पावनो परम, अजबेस, जो जियावनो, प्रसिद्ध सिद्धि अरो है; उमगो उमंग तै वे तरल तरङ्ग भरो, रङ्ग रङ्ग भरो, वे अनेक रङ्ग भरो है**, Hari is of one colour, yet full of many pleasures, filled with rapture as with a spirituous wave; he is the well-known root of 'siddhi,' the giver of life—(*says*) *Aj'bēs*—the supreme purifier, the increaser of happiness, (*there is a play on the words 'hari' and 'siddhi;' the former means both Bish'n and bhang, and the latter, both perfection and a preparation of bhang.*)

अजम *ajam*, *Skr. acc. sg. m. of* **अज** *aj* (2), *q.v. It only occurs in the Rām.*

अजन्मत *aj'mat*, **Any.**, *subst. f.*, testing, temptation (*only used with reference to the deity as an object*). **Exam.**, *Coll.*, (*Mg.*), **जौं चाहँड तौं अजन्मत के लँड बिना चाह अजन्मती नहौं**, If you desire, you may test Him, but except He will it, no one can be His tester (*i.e. have full experience of His power*).

[*Corruption of Prs.* آزمایش]

अजन्मतिया *aj'matiyā*, **Any.**, (*Mg.*), *subst. f.*, *lg. f. of the preceding.* **Exam.**, *Mg. Bible, Mth.* iv, 7, **यिशु ने ओकरा के कहलन्थीन यह, कहु फिर लिखल हैछ, की तौं अपना ईश्वर यिहुह केर अजन्मतिया जहु करञ्ह**, Jesus said unto him, it is written again, thou shalt not tempt the Lord (*yihuh* = *Jehovah*) thy God.

[*The word occurs in the old Mg. Bible of* 1818.]

अजन्मती *aj'matī*, **Any.**, *subst.*, *com. gen.*, one who tests, *hence*, one who has tested and knows the power of God by experience. *For an example, see* **अजन्मत** *aj'mat.*

[*From* **अजन्मत**; *by the sec. der. suff.* **ई**, *see Gd. Gr.* § 252.]

अजन्माइस *aj'māis*, **Any.**, *subst. f.*, [1]examination, proving, testing, trying; [2](*in revenue language*) the testing of a portion of a crop in estimating its produce. **Phr.**, **अजन्माइस देब**, *v. tr.*, to examine or test, *esp.* to test a crop ; अजमैसी पत्री *or* पत्रा, *subst. f. or m.*, a survey statement (*Wil., p.* 570). **Exam.**, [1]*Coll.*, (*Mg.*), ओकर अजमाइस कै लैंह, Examine him. [2]*Coll.*, (*Mg.*), जो तोरा विश्वास नइ हौ, तो ए कै थोरा काट कै अजमाइस कै लैंह, If you don't trust me, then cut a portion of it (*the crop*) and test it.

[*Prs.* آزمایش *āzmāish.*]

अजमाब *aj'māb*, (*pr. pts.*, अजमबैत *aj'mabāit*, *Bh. and Mg.* अजमाबत *aj'mābat*, अजमाबित *aj'mābit*, *Mg. also* अजमाइत *aj'māit* ; अजमाओल *aj'māōl* ; अजमाएब *aj'māēb* ; अजमाबै *aj'mābai*, अजमाए *aj'māē*), **Any.**, *v. tr.*, [1]to examine, prove, test ; *esp.* [2](*in revenue language*) to test a portion of a crop in estimating its produce. *It is synonymous with* अजमाइस लेब, *the examples of which may be consulted.*

अजमूद *aj'mūd*, *str. f.* अजमूदा *aj'mūdā*, *a corruption of* अजमोदा *aj'mōdā*, *q.v.*

अजमोद *aj'mōd*, **Ts.**, *subst. m.*, *more commonly used in its str. f.* अजमोदा *aj'mōdā*, *q.v.*

[*Skr.* अज + मोदः, *lit.* goat's delight.]

अजमोदा *aj'mōdā*, **Ts.**, *subst. m.*, *the name of several herbs*, [1]the common parsley (*Apium graveolens*); [2]the caraway (*Carum Roxburghianum or Apium involucratum*) ; [3]the lovage *or* Bishop's weed, *also called ajowan or ajawa seeds* (*Carum copticum ; see* अजवान *aj'wān*). *See Grs.* § 1073, *p.* 252. *These herbs are extensively cultivated throughout India ; the seeds are used in diet and medicine ; the root is regarded as medicinal. The seeds of caraway are used in flavouring curry, and those of lovage form an ingredient of the preparation known as* '*pān.*' *See Watt, vol.* V, *pp.* 37, 76, *and vol.* VI, *pp.* 16, 45.

[*This word is a masc. str. f. of* अजमोद, *and should not be confounded with the Skr. fem. form* अजमोदा. *In the second sense the Bg. name is* राँधनी; *see Dutt, pp.* 173, 289.]

अजय *ajay*, अजै *ajāi*, अजे *ajē*, **Ts.**, *adj.*, *com. gen.*, (*subst. f.* अजया *ajayā*), one over whom victory cannot be obtained, unvanquished, invincible. **Exam.**, *Rām.*, *Su.*, *ch.* 13, 3, जीति सकै को अजय रघु-राई, Who is able to defeat the invincible Raghu-rāi (*i.e. Rām*) ; *ib.*, *Ln.*, *ch.* 109, 3, जीतेउ अजय निशाचर-राज, The invincible demon-king (*i.e. Rāban*) has been conquered ; *Mth. Rām.*, *Ln.* 116, 3, समर-अजय रघु-नन्दन करता अरि-दल खण्डन, Raghu's son (*i.e. Rām*), (*who is*) unconquerable in the fight, will destroy the enemy's forces ; *Mth. Rām.*, *Ln.*, 123, करइत छलहुँ अजय मख आग, (*Mēgh'nād said :*) 'I was performing the sacrifice which was to confer invincibility on me' (*lit.* the invincible sacrifice) ; *Rām.*, *Ln.*, *ch.* 72, 2, 'करउँ, अजय-मख' अस मन धरा, 'I will perform a sacrifice conferring invincibility,' thus (*Mēgh'nād*) settled in his mind.

(*The meanings subst.* defeat, *adj.* not victorious, unsuccessful (*H. Dy.*) *are possible ; but they have never been met with by us either in literature or intercourse.*)

[*Skr.* जयः *with neg.* अ ; *as above in all Gds.*]

अजर *ajar* (1), **Ts.**, *adj.*, *com. gen.*, (*subst. f.* अजरा *ajarā*), not subject to decay *or* old age, undecaying, ever-young (*in literature always found in combination with* अमर *amar*, *q.v.*). **Exam.**, *Rām.*, *Bā.*, *ch.* 92, 7, अजर अमर सो जीति न जाई, Being subject to neither decay nor death, he could not be vanquished ; *K. Rām.*, *Ut.*, 152, खायो काल-कूट, भयो अजर-अमर-तन, भवन मसान, गथ गाँठरी गरद की, He ate (*the poison called*) 'kāl'kūṭ,' (*yet*) he became of a body free from decay or death ; his dwelling is the cemetery, and his possessions are a bundle of ashes of cowdung (*see also Bin.* 24).

[*Skr.* जरः *with neg.* अ ; *as above in all Gds.*]

अजर *ajar* (2), **Tbh.**, *adj.*, *com. gen.*, unburnt, incombustible. **Exam.**, *Padm.*, *do.*, 564, 2, रावन माथ जो अनल लिखो, कह किमि अजर सो होय, On Rāban's forehead (*i.e. fate*) when 'fire' was written, say how could he remain unburnt ?

[*Skr.* ज्वल: *with neg.* अ, *Pr.* अजलओ, *B.* अजर, *S.* अजरु, incombustible, indigestible.]

अँजरा *ā̃j'rā*, **Tbh.**, *subst. masc. of* अँजरी *ā̃j'rī*, *see* अँजला *ā̃j'lā*.

अँजरी *ā̃j'rī*, **Tbh.**, *subst. f.*, *see* अँजली *ā̃j'lī*.

अजल *ajal* (1), (*str. f.*, *m.* अजला *aj'lā*, *f.* अजली *aj'lī*), **Ts.**, *adj.*, *com. gen.*, free from water, dry. **Exam.**, *Bw.*, *song, anon.*, अजला जजला होतिहैं जगत असाढ़ कैं मास, In the month of Asāṛh (*June–July*) dry places will become covered with water.

[*Skr.* जलम् *with neg.* अ.]

अजल *ajal* (2), **Any.**, *subst. f.*, death. **Exam.**, *H. song, anon.*, अजल जब आन कर तुलती, किसी की कुछ नहिं चलती, चले सब जाते हैं यों ही अजल जब वजह करती है, When death approaches, naught is of avail to any one, so all depart when death shows favour to (*i.e. visits*) them. *See also under* अजलत *aj'lat.*

[*Ar.* اجل]

अजलत *aj'lat*, **Any.**, *subst. f.*, vileness, baseness. **Exam.**, *Mg.*, *song, anon.*, अजलत भरी करैछ, मारे, अजलत

तेरी छौंड़ी जाती है, My darling, be not vile, death is hastening towards thee.

[*Ar.* عزلّة *azallat, fem. f.* عزل *azall; see Hd. Dy. Sh., s.v.*]

अजल्लतिया *aj'latiyā*, **Any.**, *subst. f.*, a vile, rascally woman; *sometimes used as a term of endearment, even with regard to men.* **Exam.**, *Mag.* 17, चुमगइ चुमवा लेवे, अजलतिया, नव दिनवाँ अकवा दुखाय, Even if you kiss (*me*) without touching (*me*), you (*dear*) rascal, (*my*) cheek smarts for nine days; *ib.* 19, कौन अजलतिया ठिकरी चलावे ले, लागत है करेजवा बिचे चोट, Who is the (*dear*) rascal that throws a potsherd (*at me, as a sign of solicitation*), so that a wound is caused in my heart?

[*Probably a lg. f. of* अजलती, *which, however, we have not met with. The latter is derived from* अजलत, *q.v., with the Gd. sec. der. suff.* ई, *see Gd. Gr.* § 252.]

अँजल्ला *ā̃j'lā* (*Bw.*), अँजरा *ā̃j'rā* (*Bh.*), **Tbh.**, *subst. masc. of* अँजली *ā̃j'lī, q.v.; used in a magnifying sense*, a large double-handful (*Ell., vol.* I, *p.* 196).

अजल्ला *aj'lā, str. f. of* अजल *ajal* (1), *q.v.*

अँजली *ā̃j'lī* (*Bw.*), अँजरी *ā̃j'rī* (*Bh.*), **Tbh.**, *subst. f., the same as* अञ्जलि *añjali, q.v.*

[*Regarding derivation see the remarks under* अञ्जलि.]

अँजवनी *ā̃j'wanī*, **Tbh.**, *subst. f.*, collyrium *or* lampblack *for application to the eyes.* **Exam.**, *Bais.* 1, 2, डलिया बरवनी में डलिया लेबों, चाँद अँजवनी सोरा, As a present for the Chhaṭṭhī ceremony, I shall take (*to my sister-in-law*) a plate, (*and*) a cup for (*holding*) lampblack for the eyes. *See* अञ्जन *añjan*.

[*The word is properly a verbal noun derived from the pleonastic* √अँजाव to anoint, *or derived from the* √आँज to anoint *by the suff.* आवनी. *See Gd. Gr.* § 315.]

अजवर्वाव *aj'war'wāb*, **Tbh.**, *v. tr., a causal of* √अजवार *aj'wār, q.v. See Hd. Dy. under art.* उजवाना *uj'wānā, p.* 40.

अजवाइन *aj'wāin*, **Tbh.**, *subst. f.*, [1] (*S. Mth.*), the thick rope at the foot of a native bed, to which its netting is tied (*Grs.* § 639); [2] (*Mg.*), *the same as* अजवान *aj'wān or* जवाइन *jawāin, q.v.* (*Grs.* § 1073, *p.* 252).

[*Derivation see under* अजवान.]

अजवान *aj'wān*, अजवाइन *aj'wāin*, **Tbh.**, *subst. f.*, the true Bishop's weed *or* lovage (*Carum copticum or Ptychotis ajowan or Ptychotis coptica or Ammi copticum*) *cultivated in many parts of India for its seeds, which are used both as a condiment and as a medicine; they also form one of the ingredients of 'pān' and of a caudle* (*see* अछवानी *achh'wānī*); *on distillation with water they yield an oil, which is used medicinally in cholera, colic, and indigestion* (*see Watt, vol.* IV, *p.* 15; V, *p.* 76; VI, *p.* 45). *See* जवाइन *jawāin*.

[*Skr.* यवानी, *Pr.* जवाणी, *whence* (*with metathesis of* अज *aj for* ज *ja*) B. अजवान *aj'wān* (*for* जवान *jawān*). *The form* अजवाइन *is made by the false analogy* (*for* अजवानी) *of the feminines in* आइन, *like* पण्डिताइन the wife of a pandit; *see Gd. Gr.* §§ 256, 260.]

√**अजवार** *aj'wār*, अँजवार *ā̃j'wār*, (*pr. pts.* अजवाँरैत *aj'wā̃rait, Bh. and Mg. also* अजवारत *aj'wārat*, अजवारित *aj'wārit*; अजवारल *aj'wāral*; अजवारब *aj'wārab*; अजवारै *aj'wārai*), **Tbh.**, *v. tr.*, to empty (*a vessel, house, etc.*), to pour (*from one vessel into another*), *see Hd. Dy., s.v.* उजवाना *uj'wānā*. **Exam.**, (*Hd. Dy.*), *Mag. song*, चले तुरते, कोठिया अनार अजवारे रे को, Lo, quickly he began to empty the barn.

[*The H. has* उजवाना, *or cor.* उड़वाना (*Hd. Dy.*), *which shows that the verb is in the double causal form. On the double causal termination* वार (*or* आवार) *see Gd. Gr.* §§ 354, 2, 475, 476. *The primary root, therefore, is* उज, *of which the B. form* अज *appears to be a corruption; see the remarks on* अजवानी, अजाव, *and* अजार. *The root* उज *is probably to be identified with the Skr.* √उद्य, *with a change of* द *to* ज, *as in Pr.* उज्ज *for Skr.* उद्य (*see Hem.* i, 131). *The M. has the same verb in the form* उजविणें *with the meaning of* to conclude, to close. *This points also to the Skr.* √उद्य, *from which both meanings*—to empty, to pour out, *and* to conclude, to close—*can be derived without difficulty.*]

अजस *ajas*, **Ts.**, *subst. m.*, disrepute, infamy, disgrace, (*opp.* सुजस *sujas or simply* जस *jas; often combined with* अघ *agh* sin). **Comp.**, अजस-पिटारी, *subst. f., fig.*, a basket of disrepute (*Rām., A., dō.* 13, 2), *or* अजस-भाजन, *subst. m., fig.*, a vessel of disrepute (*Rām., A., ch.* 139, 5), *hence* a disreputable *or* infamous person. **Phr.**, अजस लेब, *v. tr., lit.*, to take disgrace (*to one's self*), *hence* to disgrace one's self. **Exam.**, *Rām., A., ch.*, 45, 1, अजस होउ, जग सुजस नसाउ, May disrepute ensue, may (*my*) good reputation perish in the world! *Sat.* ii, 55, नीति प्रीति जस-अजस-गति सब कँहँ सुभ पहिचानि, Justice, love, and the state of repute or disrepute, (*these*) are well known to all; *Rām., A., ch.* 168, 8, पितु-आज्ञा अघ अजस न भयेउ, (*Obeying*) a father's order cannot be sin or disgrace; *ib., Bā., ch.* 257, 3,

कु-कवि कवार अँजस को लेत, By description (*at the hands*) of a bad poet she (*i.e. Sītā*) will only take disgrace (*to herself*).

(*This word never occurs in literature with the adj. meaning of* disreputable; *in that sense* अजसी *is used, q.v.*)

[*Skr.* यशः *with the neg.* अ, *neut.*; *Pr. tadbh.* अजसो *or* (*with euph.* व) अवजसो *masc.* (*Spt. v.* 178, *Aup.* § 117) *or tats.* अजसो (*Spt., v.* 525, *Bhag., p.* 235); *the tadbh. has not survived in the Gḍs. As above in all Gḍs.*]

अजसी *ajasi*, **Ts.**, *adj., com. gen.*, disreputable, infamous, disgraceful. **Exam.**, *Rām., Ln., ch.* 31, 2, अति-दरिद्र अजसी अति-बूढ़ा, (*those who are*) very destitute, disreputable, very old (*etc., even while living are like corpses*).

[*Derived from* अजस *with Gḍ. suff.* ई. *See Gḍ. Gr.* § 253.]

अजहु *ajahu*, अजहुँ *ajahũ*, अजहू *ajahū*, अजहूँ *ajahũ*, *poet., more properly spelt* अजऽ हु *aja hu, etc., being two separate words. See under art.* अजऽ *aja. Rustic also* अजऊँ *ajaũ* (*Hd. Dy.*).

अजा *ajā*, *fem. of* अज *aj* (1) *and* (2), *q.v.*

अजाचक *ajāchak*, **Ts.**, *subst. m.*, (*f.* अजाचिका *ajāchikā*), one who is not a beggar, one who does not solicit. **Phr.** अजाचक करब, *v. tr.*, to make one satisfied, to satisfy. **Exam.**, *Rām., Ut., ch.* 13, 7, बिप्रन्ह दान बिबिध बिधि दीन्हे, जाचक सकल अजाचक कीन्हे, To the Brāhmans all sorts of presents were given, and all the beggars were satisfied.

[*Skr.* याचक *with neg.* अ. *As above possibly in all Gḍs.*]

अजाँचा *ajā̃chā*, **Tbh.**, *adj., com. gen.*, untried, untested, unexamined. **Exam.**, *Coll.*, (*Mg.*), ई बिचार अजाँचा है, This account has not been tested.

[*From* जाँचा *p.p. of* √जाँच, *q.v., with neg.* अ (4).]

अजाचित *ajāchit*, **Ts.**, *adj., com. gen.*, what is not begged, unsolicited, unasked. **Exam.**, *Pur., p.* 241, अजाचित (*fem.*) भिच्छा सौं सरीर-थिति राखि, He nourished his body with unsolicited alms.

अजाची *ajāchī*, **Ts.**, *subst. m.*, (*f.* अजाचिनी *ajāchinī*), *the same as* अजाचक *ajāchak, q.v.* **Phr.**, अजाची करब, *v. tr.*, to make satisfied, to satisfy. **Exam.**, *Bin.* 163, कपि सबरी सुग्रीव बिभीखन, को को न कियो अजाची, The monkey, the Sabarī, Sugrīb, Bibhīkhan, yea, whom did (*Rām*) not satisfy?

[*Skr.* याची *with neg.* अ. *As above possibly in all Gḍs.*]

अजात *ajāt*, *the same as* अजाति *ajāti, q.v.*.

अजाति *ajāti*, **Ts.**, *subst., com. gen.*, [1] one who has lost his caste, an outcast; [2] one who has no caste. **Exam.**, [2] *Pārb., ch.* 7, कहहु काह सुनि रीझिहु बर अकुलीनहिँ, अगुन अमान अजाति मातु-पितु-हीनहिँ, Say, what did you hear to make you so pleased with a bridegroom who has no pedigree, no worth, no dignity, no caste, and no father and mother.

[*Skr.* जातिः *with neg.* अ. *As above possibly in all Gḍs.*]

अजाती *ajātī*, *the same as* अजाति *ajāti, q.v.*

अजान *ajān* (1), (*poet.* अजाना *ajānā*), **Tbh.**, *adj., com. gen.*, (*subst. f.* अजानी *ajānī*), [1] not knowing, ignorant; [2] simple, foolish (*from mere lack of knowledge*); [3] without *or* deprived of right *or* sound knowledge, demented, infatuated; [4] unknown. **Exam.**, [1] *Rām., Bā., do.* 277, 2, पूछत जानि अजान जिमि, ब्यापेउ कोप सरीर, Though knowing it, he asked as if not knowing, (*and*) wrath pervaded his (*whole*) body; *Sat.* ii, 23, तुलसी राम-अजान नर किमि पावहि पर धाम, Tul'sī (says) how can a man who is ignorant of Rām obtain heaven. [2] *Sat.* i, 9, जननि जनक तेहि किमि तजैं तुलसी सरिस अजान, How should a mother and father forsake one (*who is a child*) simple like Tul'sī Dās. [3] *See an example under art.* अजाना *ajānā* (2). [4] *Padm., ch.* 194, 7, कोइ चन्दन फूलहिँ जनु फूली, कोइ अजान बिरवा तर भूली, Some are blooming like the flowers of the sandal-tree, others are straying under (*other*) unknown trees (*so according to the Urdū commentary of the Kānh'pūr edition; but see under* अजान *ajān* (2)). *See* अजाना *ajānā*.

(*The act. meaning* not knowing *is the usual one; according to some pandits, the pass. meaning* unknown, *though used, is incorrect. In the Rām. the word is generally spelled* अयान, अयाना, *for which* अजान, अजान *is frequently given as a false reading, as in Bā., ch.* 285, 2; *cf.* अजाना (2)).

[*Skr.* ज्ञानम् *with neg.* अ, *Pr.* अजाणो *or* अयाणो.]

अजान *ajān* (2), **Tbh.**, *subst. m.*, [1] (*S. Mth.-Mg.*), a white variety of rice, *which is sown broadcast* (*Grs.* § 969); [2] a kind of tree (*not identified*). **Exam.**, [2] *Padm., ch.* 194, 7 (*according to the gloss of the Lakh'naū edition*), कोइ अजान बिरवा तर भूली, Some are straying under ajān-trees.

[*Der.* ?]

अजाना *ajānā* (1), *poet. for* अजान *ajān* (1), *q.v.*

अजाना *ajānā* (2), (*f.* अजानी *ajānī*), *str. f. of* अजान *ajān* (1), *q.v.* **Exam.**, [1]*Rām.*, *Bā.*, *ch.* 127, 4, अब मोहि जानहि निज दासी, जदपि सहज जड़ नारि अजानी, Now regarding me as your own servant, though I am by nature a foolish and simple woman, (*reply to me*). [2]*Rām.*, *A.*, *ch.* 199, 6, जो भावी-बस रानि अजानी, करि कु-चालि अन्तहुँ पछितानी, But the queen was demented by the power of fate, and in the end she has repented of the evil she has done.

(*In the best manuscripts the word is spelled* अजाना, अजानी *in the above and other passages; but* अजाना *is still commonly used colloquially in Bihār.*)

[*From Skr.* अज्ञान: *with pleon. suff.* आ; *see Gd. Gr.* § 196.]

अजानि *ajāni*, **Tbh.**, *adv.*, unknowingly, unwittingly, unintentionally (*opp.* जानि *jāni*). **Exam.**, *Bin.* 160, और अधम अनेक तारे जात का पै गने; जानि नाम अजानि लीन्हे, नरक जम-पुर मने, And as to the many wretches that were saved, how can they be counted; whether (*Rām's or Nārāyan's*) name be taken intentionally or unintentionally (*by any one*), the hells of Jam's abode are propitiated (*for him*); (*the reference is to the story of* अजामिल *ajāmil, q.v.*)

अजानी *ajānī* (1), *fem. of* अजाना *ajānā* (2), *q.v.*

अजानी *ajānī* (2), **Tbh.**, *subst. f.*, [1] want of knowledge; [2] simplicity, innocence; [3] heedlessness.

[*Abs. noun, from* अजान (1), *formed with the Prs. suff.* ई.]

अजामिल *ajāmil*, **Ts.**, *subst. m.*, the name of a Brāhman of Kanauj, *of a most dissolute and abandoned life. He had ten sons, the youngest of whom, by a prostitute, was named Nārāyan. When at the point of death, he happened to summon this son by his name. Thereupon the God Nārāyan* (*i.e. Bish'n*), *thus casually invoked, himself came in answer to his call, and rescued him from the demons that were about to carry him off to hell. In Tul'sī Dās's works this story and the mystic power of the 'Name' is generally ascribed to Rām, he being the incarnation of Bish'n or Nārāyan.* **Exam.**, *Bin.* 239, बिप्र अजामिल अरु सुर-पति, ते कहा जो नहिं बिगरेयो, As for the Brāhman Ajāmil and the lord of the gods (*i.e. Ind'r*), what (*law*) is there that they have not broken? *Gīt.*, *Su.*, 42, सुत हित नाम लेत भव-निधि तरि गयो अजामिल सो खलो, Taking the friendly name of his son, Ajāmil, that sinner, passed out of existence (*see also Bin.* 97); *Rām.*, *Bā.*, *ch.* 30, 7, अपर अजामिल गज गनिका ऊ, भए मुकुत हरि-नाम प्रभाऊ, Further Ajāmil, the elephant, and also the harlot (*i.e. Piŋgalā*), were saved through the power of Hari's (*i.e. Nārāyan's*) name; *K. Rām.*, *Ut.*, 89, 'राम' बिहाय 'मरा' जप ते बिगरी सुधरी कबि-कोकिल हू की, नामहि ते गज की गनिका की अजामिल की चलि गै चल चूकी, By repeating '*Marā*' (*the reversed form of Rām*) instead of '*Rāma*' the sinful state of the sweet poet (*i.e. Bāl'mīk*) was made holy, and through the same name the cessation of the depravity of the elephant, of the harlot, and of Ajāmil, was brought about.

[*Skr.* अजामिल:]

अजिऔरा *ajiaurā*, **Tbh.**, *subst. m.*, (*N.B.*) the paternal grandfather's house (*Grs.* § 1301).

[*Probably a comp. of* अजिया, *lg. f. of* आजी, paternal grandfather's wife *or* paternal grandmother, *and* उरा, *lg. f. of* उर (*for* पुर), place; *properly* अजियाउरा, *contr. to* अजिऔरा. *M. has* अजोरा *or* अजोरा. *All words of this kind take their designation from the wife; e.g.* ननिऔरा *from* नानी.]

अजित *ajit*, **Ts.**, *adj.*, *com. gen.*, (*subst. f.* अजिता *ajitā*), *lit.* unconquered; *hence* unconquerable, invincible, irresistible. **Exam.**, *Rām.*, *Ln.*, *ch.* 54, 5, ब्यापक ब्रह्म अजित भुवनेस्वर, लछिमन कहाँ बूझ करुनाकर, (*Rām though being*) the omnipresent Supreme Spirit and the invincible lord of the world, (*yet*) out of his fulness of mercy he asks after Lachhiman (*comm. to Lakhnaū ed.*, अजित कहो 'कोई जीति नहिं सके'); *Bin.* जरत सुर-असुर-नर-लोक सोकाकुल मृदुल-चित अजित कृत गरल पानम्, (*Sib*) the unconquerable (*and*) tender-hearted, moved with pity with the suffering gods, demons and men, drank off the poison (*comm.* अजित नाम 'काहू के जीतने जोग नाहीं').

(*With the literal meaning, though admissible, the word has never been met with by us in literature.*)

[*Skr.* अजित:; *as above in all Gds. The tadbh. form* अजिय, *as in Kalp.* § 114, *has not survived.*]

अजिन *ajin*, **Ts.**, *subst. m.*, the hairy skin of an antelope (*esp. the black antelope*), tiger, elephant, *etc.*, *which serves a religious student for a couch, seat, or covering* (*for an illustration see the photograph, from a native painting of "Siva's Wrath," opp. p.* 46 *of Growse's Translation of the Rāmāyan, 2nd ed.*); *also in South India at weddings* (*Wil.*, *p.* 14). **Exam.**, *Rām.*, *A.*, *do.* 203, 1, अजिन-बसन फल-असन महि-सयन डासि कुस-पात, (*Rām, Sītā, and Lachh'man are wandering in the forest*) having skins for clothes, (*wild*) fruits for food, and the earth spread with kus-grass or leaves for a bed; *Mth. Rām.*, *Ar.*, 10, 23, सबल अजिन-पट सीत सङ्ग, लछुमन छोटो सेवक रङ्ग, (*Rām*) with Sītā clothed in pure garment of antelope skin and Lachhuman like a loving servant; *Pārb.*, *chh.* 7, सब अजिन दिव्य दुकूल जो रत, सबो सब सुख जोरि कै, (*Your*) companions turning away their faces will laugh (*at him*) whose delight is in his handsome garment (*made*) of an elephant's skin, (*on the story alluded to, see Skr. Dy. W.*)

[*Skr.* अजिनम्; *as above in all Gds.*]

अजिया-सासु *ajiyā-sāsu*, (*Bh.*), **Tbh.**, *subst. f.*, the mother-in-law of the wife's *or* husband's mother-in-law (*a comp. of* आजी *ājī*, *q.v.*)

अजिर *ajir*, **Ts.**, *subst. m.*, [1] any open ground, arena; *hence esp.* [2] the court-yard of a house (*syn.* आँगन *ãgan*). **Comp.**, मन्दिराजिर (मन्दिर-अजिर), *subst. m.*, the court-yard of a palace (*Gīt.*, *Ut.*, 19, 1). **Exam.**, [1] *Bin.*, 39, "जयति रन-अजिर" गन्धर्व-गन गर्व-हर, फेरि फिरे राम-गुन-गाथ गाता, "Hail (*to Rām*) on the battle-field," thus the host of the Gandharbs, whose pride has been humbled, again and again sing the praises of Rām's valour; *fig.*, *Rām.*, *Bā.*, *ch.* 113, 6, कबि-उर-अजिर नचावहिँ बानी, He sets Saraswatī to dance (*like a puppet*) in the arena of the poet's heart. [2] *Rām.*, *Bā.*, *ch.* 215, 5, मन क्रम बचन अगोचर जोई, दसरथ-अजिर बिचर प्रभु सोई, The Lord, who is incomprehensible in thoughts, acts, and words, he plays in Das'rath's court-yard; *Gīt.*, *Bā.*, 5, 1, चित्र-अजिर-अटनि बजार बीथिन्ह चारु चौकैं बिधि बनी, In the court-yards and on the terraced roofs of the houses, in the bazars (*and*) the lanes, (*they prepare*) many kinds of beautiful ceremonial squares.

[*Skr.* अजिरम्; *as above in all Gds.*]

अजी *ajī* (1), *the same as* आजी *ājī*, *q.v.*

अजी *ajī* (2), एजी *ejī*, **Tbh.**, *interj.*, [1] *an interjection used for the purpose of calling attention, usually addressed to an inferior*, hallo you! I say! Look here! [2] (*Hd. Dy.*) *a form of address used by a wife in addressing her husband, whose name it is considered disrespectful to take, and vice versâ.*

(*The usage of this interj., as to its honorific character or otherwise, varies in different localities.*)

[*Probably a comp. of* ए *or* अ *and* जी, *the former being the Skr. interj.* अयि, *Pr.* अए *or* ऐ (*Hēm.* i, 169, ii, 205), *the latter, the form of address* जी, *q.v. H., P.* अजी.]

अजीउ *ajīu*, *the same as* अजीव *ajīb*, *q.v.*

अजीज *ajīj*, **Any.**, *adj.*, *com. gen.*, [1] dear, beloved; [2] esteemed, excellent. **Phr.**, अजीज जानब *or* अ॰ करब, *v. tr.*, to esteem highly, love, respect. **Exam.**, *Bw.*, *do.*, *anon.*, मधुर सत्य अब रस सहित चित-हर बड़ो अजीज, अस बानी जो उचरत, सर दिल बसो अजीज, Accompanied by sweetness, truth, and elegance, friendly and very piquant—he who uttereth such words, is dear to every heart.

[*Ar.*, عزيز *'azīz.*]

अजीटन *ajīṭan*, **Any.**, *subst. m.*, an adjutant.

[*Corruption of the English word.*]

अजीत *ajīt*, (*poet.* अजीता *ajītā*), *the same as* अजित *ajit*, *q.v.* **Exam.**, *Rām.*, *Ut.*, *ch.* 72, 5, अगुन अदभ्र गिरा-गो-तीता सबदरसी अनवद्य अजीता, (*Rām is*) unconditioned, unfathomable, beyond the range of speech and perception, all-seeing, irreproachable, unconquerable.

[*It is a popular form, apparently made from neg* अ *with* जीत, *sh. f. of* जीता, *the p. p. p. of the* √जीत to conquer; *cf. the similar formation of* अजोत *or* अजोतल (*q.v.*). *It has only been met with in literature in the single passage above quoted, where its use seems simply to be due to rhyme. As a name, however, the form is common, e.g.* अजीत सिंह *Ajīt Siṅgh*, *H. Lit.* § 195, 370, 647, 731. *It also occurs in M.* अजीत *and in S.* अजीतु (*S. Dy.*, *p.* 13).]

अजीव *ajīb* (1), अजीव *ajīw*, अजीउ *ajīū*, **Ts.**, (I) *adj.*, *com. gen.*, [1] lifeless, inorganic; [2] dead. **Exam.**, [2] *Bw.*, *do.*, *anon.*, तुलसी, एहि संसार मैं भाँति भाँति के जीव, राम नाम नहिं जो रटे, जीवहिं (*loc.*) अछत अजीव, O Tul'sī, in this world there are many kinds of life, but he who repeateth not the name of Rām, even while his life exists, is dead.

(II) *subst. m.*, (*f.* अजीवा *ajībā*), a lifeless thing, (*used by the Jains as a relig. tech. term, opp.* जीव *jīb*, *collectively for*) the inanimate part of the universe.

[*Skr.* अ *and* जीवः; *as above in all Gds.*]

अजीब *ajīb* (2), **Any.**, *adj.*, *com. gen.*, wonderful, surprising. **Exam.**, *W. Bh.*, *Birhā*, *anon.*, सूरत तोरी अजीब, रे गोरिया, जैसे रे सुरुजवा के जोत; जोबना चमक तूनो जोबि के अँजोरवा, मुखवा चनरमा होत, Thy figure is wonderful, O fair one, like the light of the sun; thy two breasts glow with his splendour, (*and thy*) face is the moon.

[*Ar.* عجيب *'ajīb.*]

अजीयत *ajīyat*, **Any.**, *subst. f.*, wanton injury, oppression. **Phr.**, अजीयत देब, *v. tr.*, to oppress, harass. **Exam.**, *Coll.*, (*Bh.*), गरीबन के एतरनी अजीयत मत दीहल करऽ, Do not harass the poor so much.

[*Ar.* اذية *aẕiyyat.*]

अजीर *ajīr*, **Any.**, *subst. m.*, [1] a hired servant *or* labourer, a bondsman, a bond-slave (*one who has entered into an engagement for a stipulated sum to serve another* *for a specific term or until he repay the sum advanced*); [2] a hirer, a lessee (*Wil., p.* 14).

[*Ar.* اجير *ajīr.*]

अंजीर *ãjīr*, (*poet.* अँजीरा *ãjīrā*), Any., *subst. m., the same as* अञ्जीर *añjīr, q.v.* Exam., *Padm., ch.* 34, 2, नारँग नौंबू तुरँज जँजीरा, औ बदाम बहु मेद अँजीरा, There are the orange, the lemon, the citron, the lime, and almonds (*and*) figs of many kinds.

अजीरन *ajīran*, Ts., (I), *adj., com. gen.*, [1] undecayed, unimpaired, undestroyed; *hence* [2] indestructible, unremitting, persistent, (*of a disease*) incurable, (*of a person*) invincible, exceedingly strong; *or* [3] (*of food*) undigested; *hence* [4] indigestible, unwholesome; *or* [5] (*generally*) tiresome, burdensome, disagreeable. Exam., [2] *Hd. Dy.*, यह बुखार तो अजीरन हो गया, This fever has become incurable; *ibid.*, अजीरन कैं अजीरन सो ठेले, नहिं तउ सिर चौपड़े खेले, Let the strong contend with the strong, otherwise thy head will be played with at cross-roads. [4] *Gīt., A.* 33, 1, असन अजीरन को समुझि तिलक तज्यौ, Considering it like indigestible food, he abandoned his tilak (*or mark of royalty*). [5] *Hd. Dy.*, रोज की दाल तो अजीरन हो गई, (*To eat*) dāl every day is become tiresome.

(II) *subst. m.*, indigestion.

(III) *adv.*, too much, excessively. Exam., *Hd. Dy.*, दाल मैं नमक अजीरन है, There is too much salt in the dāl.

[*Skr.* अजीर्णः; *as above in all Gḍs, exc. G.* अजीरण, *S.* अजीरणु].

अजीव *ajīw, the same as* अजीब *ajīb, q.v.*

अजुआ *ajuā*, अजुवा *ajuwā*, (*obl.* अजुए *ajuē or* अजुवे *ajuwē*), *lg. f. of* आजु *āju, q.v.* Exam., *Bīj., l.* 487, भौजो अजुए से भेलू मयमरिया, O sister-in-law, from this day you have become (*to me*) as a mother.

अजुकत *ajuk't*, (*unphon.* अयुक्त *ayukt*), Ts., (I), *adj., com. gen.*, [1] not yoked, not joined; [2] unfit, unsuitable, improper; [3] *with the meanings of* अजगुत *aj'gut, q.v.* Exam., [2] *Coll.*, (*Bh.*), ओकरा अजुकत (*or* अजुगत) बात से ऊ खिसिआइल, He was vexed at his unsuitable language; *ib.*, ऊ बड़ अजुकत (*or* अजुगत) करलन, कि अपना माता पिता के मार बैठलन, He acted most improperly in that he beat his father and mother. *See* अजगुत *aj'gut*, अजुगत *ajugat*, अजुगुत *ajugut*.

(II) *subst. m.*, violence, oppression, compulsion.

[*Skr.* अ *and* युक्त; *as above in all Gḍs. See also the remarks under* अजगुत *aj'gut.*]

अजुकहि *ajukahi*, *old Mth. gen. obl. of* आजु *āju, q.v.* Exam., *Hb.* viii, 40, अजुकहि दिन धरि देल प्रतिपाल, Up to this very day have I cherished you.

अजुगत *ajugat*, अजुगुत *ajugut*, Ts., *adj., com. gen., the same as* अजुकत *ajuk't, q.v.* Exam., [3] *Bw. do., anon.*, जोग लगन ग्रह बार तिथि सब कुछ भलेउ सुजोग, तुलसी, अजुगत करम तें जोग ह होत अजोग, Conjuncture, ascension, planet, solar and lunar day may all be auspicious, but, O Tul'sī, by a wonderful fate even that which is auspicious becomes inauspicious.

[*Regarding the formation, see Gd. Gr.* § 102. *It is an older tats. form, which has come partially under the operation of Prākrit phonetic laws. G.* अजुगत.]

अजुध्या *ajudhyā, coll. for* अजोध्या *ajōdhyā, q.v.*

अजुरन्दा *ajur'dā*, Any., *adj., com. gen.*, afflicted, sad, weary. Exam., *H., Lāonī, anon.*, हम हुए अजुरदा तेरी फिकर के मारे, हम उठते बैठत भरें आह के मारे, I am afflicted when I think of thee; rising and sitting, I sigh from grief.

[*Prs.* آزرده *āzurda.*]

अजुरन्माद *ajur'mād*, अजुरन्माल *ajur'māl*, Any., *adj., com. gen.*, [1] destitute, poor; [2] unprocurable (*Ās. Gy.*).

[*Der. doubtful; it looks like a corruption, perhaps of Prs.* آرمزاد *aramzād* (*see Shakespear's Hd. Dy.*). *If so, the second form* अजुरन्माल *may be founded on a popular etymology,* अजुर *being the B.* अजोर (अजोड़), not joined *and* माल *the much-used Prs. word for* property, *as it were* without property. *The Prs. aramzād is said to mean both* destitute *and* longing; *and perhaps instead of* unprocurable *the second meaning should rather be given as* longing without being able to procure.]

अजुरन्माल *ajur'māl, the same as* अजुरन्माद *ajur'mād, q.v.*

अँजुरा *ãjurā* (*Bh.*), अँजुला *ãjulā* (*Bw.*), *vulg.* ऊँजन्रा *ũj'rā*, ऊँजन्ला *ũj'lā*, Tbh., *subst. m., the same as* अँजुरी *ãjurī, q.v., used in a magnifying sense,* a big handful. *See* अँजन्रा *ãj'rā*, अँजन्ला *ãj'lā*, अँजौरा *ãjaurā*, अँजौला *ãjaulā*, अञ्जुर *añjur*, अञ्जुल *añjul*, अँजुर *ãjur*, अँजुल *ãjul*, उञ्जर *uñjar*, उञ्जल *uñjal*.

[*This is a secondary masc. form made from the fem.* अँजुरी, *and may be considered as a str. f. corresponding to the wk. f.* अञ्जुर. *For further remarks on the derivation, see under* अँजुरी *and* अञ्जुलि. *All the forms with* अ *are more peculiar to the West, Baiswāṛā and Bundēl'khanḍ. As to the transposition of the vowels* अ *and* उ *in the vulg. form, see Gd. Gr.* § 56.]

अँजुरी *ãjuri (Bh.)*, अँजुली *ãjulī (Bw.)*, *vulg.* ईंजुरी *ĩjuri*, Tbh., *subst. f.*, [1] a double handful, as much as can be held in the cavity formed by joining the two hands together in the shape of a bowl (*Ell., vol. I, p.* 196); *hence* [2] a sort of indefinite measure for various kinds of dues, allowances, *or* perquisites; *thus* [a] dues of grain received in Āudh by Brāhman landlords (*Oudh Gazetteer, vol.* I, *p.* 188, *Cr., p.* 88); [b] perquisites of grain claimed by Brāhmans as religious dues (*Cr., p.* 88); [c] allowance in grain of one or two sērs per plough taken by the tenant in Sāran and Paṭ'nā (*Grs.* § 912); [d] allowance in grain of two to ten sērs per plough made to the cultivator (*Oudh Gazetteer, vol.* II, *p.* 160, *Cr., p.* 54); [e] perquisites of village artisans (*carpenters, blacksmiths, etc.*) received at the time of sowing in Gayā (*Grs.* § 1194) and Bundēl'khaṇḍ (*Cr., p.* 88, *also called* अजौली *ajãulī, q.v.*); [f] perquisites of a midwife in grain (*Grs.* § 1401). Exam., [1] *Krish.* 172, सुर-दास कामी सौं कहियो "दे तिल अँजुरी भारी," Sur Dās (*says*), tell (*thy*) husband to give (*thee*) a heaped-up double handful of sesame seed. *See* अँजुरा *ãjurā*, अँजुला *ãjulā*, अँजौरा *ãjãurā*, अँजौला *ãjãulā*, अञ्जुर *añjur*, अञ्जुल *añjul*, अञ्जुरि *añjuri*, अञ्जुलि *añjuli*, आँजुर *ãjur*, आँजुल *ãjul*, आँजुरि *ãjuri* (*Pur., p.* 193), आँजुलि *ãjuli*. *Cf. also* अँजरा *ãj'rā*, अँजला *ãj'lā*, अँजरी *ãj'rī*, अँजली *ãj'lī*, अञ्जर *añjar*, अञ्जल *anjal*, अञ्जरि *añjari*, अञ्जलि *añjali*.

(*The forms with* उ *throughout this series of words are more peculiar to the West, Baiswārā and Bundēl'khaṇḍ.*)

[*There can be no doubt but that this word is a modification of the original form* अँजरी *or* अँजली, *by the substitution of the vowel* उ *for the medial* अ; *though the cause of it is somewhat obscure, there being no mere transposition as in* उँगली *for* अँगुली (*Gd. Gr.* § 56) *or in vulg.* उँगरा *for* अँगुरा (*q.v*). *It may be noted that this curious substitution is practically confined to the case when the word has the meaning of the* indefinite measure of a double handful, *esp. in its more tech. uses for* dues, allowances, *and* perquisites. *Possibly the form may be due to false analogy with* अँगुरी *finger* (*q.v.*), *which is also used as a standard of measure, or with* अजुरा (*q.v.*), *which has the somewhat similar meaning of* wages, reward. *The substitution is carried on a further step in the forms* अँजौरी *or* अँजौली, *where the inorganic* उ *has been further raised to* औ, *possibly by the false analogy of* अजौरी (*q.v.*), *which has the somewhat similar meaning of* advances to labourers (*see under* अजौरी). *The original is Skr.* अञ्जलि: *m.*; *Pr.* अँजली *is both m. and f.* (*Hēm.* i, 35), *B.* अँजली *or* अँजरी *is only f., though the B. tats.* अञ्जलि *or* अञ्जरि *is m. From the fem.* अँजली *or* अँजरी *has been formed a secondary masc.* अँजला *or* अँजरा (*as if there were a Skr. m. form* अञ्जलक:). *Finally the forms* अँजली *or* अँजरी, अँजला *or* अँजरा, *are modified primarily to* अँजुली *or* अँजुरी, अँजुला *or* अँजुरा, *and secondarily to* अँजौली *or* अँजौरी, अँजौला *or* अँजौरा, *and tertiarily to vulg.* ईंजली *or* ईंजरी, ईंजला *or* ईंजरा. *Corresponding forms have only been observed in P.* अञ्जुल, *and M. vulg.* ओंजळ *or* ओंजळ, *which is both m. and f., and* ओंजळी *or* ओंजळी *f. See also the remarks on derivation under* अञ्जलि.]

अँजुला *ãjulā*, Tbh., *subst. m.*, *see* अँजुरा *ãjurā*. Exam., *Coll.*, (*Mth.*), धान के ढेरी सँ चार अँजुला दे देलकै, They gave away four big double handfuls from the heap of rice.

(*The word is rare.*)

अँजुली *ãjulī*, Tbh., *subst. f.*, *see* अँजुरी *ãjuri*.

अजुवे *ajuwē*, *see under* अजुआ *ajuā*.

अजू *ajū*, Tbh., *subst. m.*, (*North B.*) unripe corn (*Grs.* § 984).

[*Skr.* अयव, *from* अ *and* यव, *Pr.* अजवो *or* अअवो, *lit.* not barley.]

अजुरा *ajurā*, Any., *subst. m.*, [1] hire, wages, pay of a labourer (*Grs.* § 1185), *esp. of one employed by the job* (*Wil., p.* 15); [2] the fee *or* percentage charged on a dishonoured bill, *for the expense of returning it to the drawer when residing at a distance* (*Wil., ibid.*). Comp., अजुरा-हार, *subst. m.*, a hired labourer (*whether paid by the day or by the job*).

[*Corruption of Ar.* اجور *ujūr*, *pl. of* اجر *ajr*, *through the Prs.* اجورة *ujūra*.]

अजेआ *ajeā*, Tbh., *subst. m.*, a he-goat. Exam., *Bid.* xviii, 5, अजेआ-सुत-रिपु-वाहन ओसन, ता सन चलु मिलि राती, The beautiful lady walked exactly like him (*a lion*), who is the vehicle of the enemy of the son of the he-goat (*i.e. of Durgā, to whom goats are sacrificed*).

[*The word has been met with by us only in the above passage. According to the pandits it means* he-goat, *in which case it might be a contraction of* अजका *the lg. f. of* अज (*q.v.*). *But it may be suggested that it rather means* she-goat, *and* अजेआ-सुत the son of a she-goat, *i.e.* a he-goat, *in which case* अजेआ *would be a Mth. bye-form of* अजिया, *lg. f. of* अजा (*q.v.*); *the substitution of* ए *for* इ *being common in Mth., e.g.,* कहए *for* कहइ he says, केआरी *for* किआरी a garden-plot].

अजे *ajē*, *the same as* अजै *ajãi or* अजय *ajay*, *q.v.* Exam., *Rām., Ut., tot.* 1, 17, रघु-बीर अजा-रन-बीर अजे, Raghubīr, the invincible mighty warrior.

अजेय *ajēy*, Ts., *adj.*, *com. gen.*, unconquerable, invincible. Exam., *Mth. Rām.*, *Ln.* 40, 4, **रन मेँ सदा अजेय आव जिनका नहि कालक**, In battle they are always unconquerable, they have no fear of death; *ibid.*, 149, 25, **जौँ यो रावन होम समापत, तौँ अजेय रावन रन थापत**, If Rāban's sacrifice is completed, he will be invincible in battle. *See* **अजय** *ajay*, **अजित** *ajit*, **अजीत** *ajit*, **अजै** *ajē*, **अजै** *ajãi*.

[*Skr.* **अ** *and* **जेय:**; *as above in all Gḍs.*]

अजै *ajãi*, Ts., *subst. m.*, *the same as* **अजय** *ajay*, *q.v.* Exam., *Bin.* 89, **हौँ हार्‍यौ करि जतन बिबिध बिधि, अतिसय प्रबल अजै**, (*Tul'sī Dās says:*) I have been unsuccessful (*though*) trying in every possible way (*to overcome my senses*), (*for*) they are exceedingly strong (*and*) invincible.

अजोधया *ajodhayā*, *coll. for* **अजोध्या**, *q.v.* Exam., *Neb.* 10, **अजोधया मेँ देलक भण्डार**, In Ajodhayā he gave a caste feast.

अजोध्या *ajodhyā*, *coll. for* **अजोध्या**, *q.v.* Exam., *Bhoj.* ii, 2, **बाजेला अजोधा मेँ ढोल**, The drums are being beaten in Ajodhyā.

अजोध्या परसाद *ajodhyā par'sād*, Ts., *subst. m.*, the name of two Hindū poets, [1] *surnamed* Sukal (*H. Lit.* § 622), *who flourished in the early part of the present century*; [2] *surnamed* Bāj'pēyī (*H. Lit.* § 693, 674), *who was alive in* 1883, *and was the author of a prosody entitled Chhandānand, a work on rhetoric entitled Sāhitya Sudhā-sāgara, and of a Rām-kabittābalī. The following are specimens of their poetry.* Exam., [1](*Siv.*, *p.* 19), **पूरि रही है अनन्द बिलास, सबै बिधि सोहैँ सुरूप सोभा बिराजै। चौकत है दृग चञ्चल मीन, सो खञ्जन की गति कौन कि राजै। जोधि, सबै अधरान की लाली भनो रवि प्रात उदोत बिराजै। त्यौँ मध्याह्न की साज सबै सहेत-निधान मेँ हाँसि हि राजै।** (*The fair one*) is full of charming coquetry, (*and*) in every way shineth in her pleasing beauty; (*compared with her graceful*) eyes, the nimble fish appears insipid, and what are the wagtail's movements that they should charm (*like hers*); Jōdhi (*i.e. Ajodhyā*) (*says:*) the crimson of her fine lips is glorious like the glow of the rising sun; then at midday she adorns herself with (*all*) her adornments, and in the trysting place (*in the evening*) she shines by her very laughter. [2](*Siv.*, *p.* 14, 15, *from Sāhitya Sudhā-sāgara*) **लखि के चकोर मोर खञ्जन छिपी-मुख ओर. अकुल के उरग तुरङ्ग मिग छिप जाय। भय मारि मन बारि कञ्ज बारि बूड़े बारि, अपर परीन की परीन की परी न जाय ?। औध सकल हौँ बनाय करि बाल, तोल, तौलि बाल बोलचाल बाल भाव चाव चाव। लखन सकल दृगचल ते नवत, भाग सकल सकल, प्यारी-तेरे नयन पादशाह।** (*On seeing thy eyes*) the partridge, peacock, wagtail, and bee quickly depart (*in confusion*); into the jangal depart the snake, the horse, the deer and their lord (*i.e. the lion*) to hide themselves; in grief and distress the lotus, black (*with melancholy*), sinks under in the water; (*and*) do not from the fairest of fairies drop sighs (*of envy*)? Āudh (*i.e. Ajodhyā*) *Par'sād*) (*says:*) in my opinion, O darling, my condition is as happy as that of Hari (*on seeing Rādhā*); thy co-wife, in chagrin, continually cries out in wonder and grief, when she beholds thy indelible (*lit. hard*) signature (*i.e. the amatory marks of her finger nails*) on this throne (*i.e. my body*), (*for my*) condition (*and*) luck are exalted, (*and*) thy eyes, O beloved, are (*my*) king.

अँजोरवा *ãjor'wā*, *lg. f. of* **अँजोरा** *ãjōrā*, *q.v.* Exam., [2](*W. Bh.*), *Bir'hā*, *anon.*, **जोबना जरत दूनो जोति के अँजोरवा**, (*Thy*) two breasts are aglow with his (*i.e. the sun's*) splendour, (*see under* **अजीब** *ajib*(2)).

अजोँ *ajō̃*, **अजौँ** *ajãũ*, *a contr. form of the emph.* **अजहुँ** *ajahũ*, *q.v. See under* **अजहु** *aja*.

अजोग *ajōg*, Tbh., (I) *adj.*, *com. gen.*, unsuitable, unbefitting, improper, unworthy. Exam., *Coll.*, (*Bh.*), **ओकरा का है अजोग बाटे**, That is unworthy of him.

(II) *subst. m.*, [1]an improper or unseasonable occasion; [2] ill-luck, misfortune.

(*This word is rare; the more usual one is* **कुजोग** *kujōg.*)

[*Skr.* **योग्य** *with neg.* **अ**, *Pr.* **अजोग्गो**; *as above in all Gḍs.*]

अजोत *ajōt*, **अजोतल** *ajōtal*, *adj.*, *com. gen.*, untilled or waste (*of land*).

[*Properly neg.* **अ** *with the p.p.p.* **जोत** *or* **जोतल** *of the root* **जोत** to harness, to plough (*q.v.*, *also H. R.*, *p.* 68); *cf. the similar formation of* **अजीत**. *Not observed in other Gḍs.*]

अजोतल *ajōtal*, Tbh., *adj.*, *com. gen.*, *the same as* **अजोत** *ajōt*, *q.v.* Exam., *Coll.*, (*Bh.*), **ई खेत अजोतल बाटे**, This field is untilled.

अजोध्या *ajōdhyā*, **अजोधा** *ajodhyā*, **अजोधया** *ajodhayā*, **अजुधा** *ajudhyā*, Ts., *subst. f.*, the name of a town, *now commonly called Awadh (Oudh), on the river Sar'jū or Ghāg'rā (Gogrā), close to the town of Faizābād, with which together it occupies the site of the original city of Ajōdhyā, the ancient capital of Das'rath and Rām; it is still one of India's sacred cities and a famous place of pilgrimage; it was anciently* *also known by the name of Sākēta, and is generally identified with the town of 'Oyut'o (or Ayuto), visited by Hiuen Tsiang (see Beal's Buddhist Records of the Western World, vol. I, p.* 224); *on its archæology and traditions see Gen. Sir A. Cunningham's Survey Reports, vol. I, pp.* 317—327. **Comp.,** अजोधा काण्ड *ajōdhyā-kāṇḍ*, the name of the second section of the Rāmāyan (*both Skr. and Tul'sī Dās's*); अजोध्या-पुरी *ajōdhyā-purī*, the town of Ajōdhyā. **Exam.,** *Misc.* 21, सरजू के तीर अजोध्या नगरी अपने हाथ बनाई, तीन लोक के सकल सम्पदा अवध-पुरी चलि आई, On Sar'ju's banks (*Das'rath*) built the city of Ajōdhyā with his own hands, all the wealth of the three worlds accumulated in Avadh town; *Bh.* iv, 1, चैत अजोध्या जनमेले राम, In (*the month of*) Chait in Ajōdhyā Rām was born; *ib.* ix, 17, अमरे घर घर है अजोध्या, नाम मोर दसरथ रे, My house is in Ajōdhyā, my name is Das'rath; *Pur. p.* 187, रहाँथ अजोध्या-पुरी मैं बसु-नामक बैस, There was a merchant called Basu in Ajōdhyā town.

(*The name Ajōdhyā is never applied, either in B. or Skr., to the country of Kōsala, of which the city of Ajōdhyā was the capital, though its modern equivalent 'Avadh' has, in comparatively modern times, come to be applied in that way, as in the modern kingdom or province of 'Oudh.' In a verse of the Bhūtashuddhi Tantra (quoted in the new edition of the Shabda Kalpa-druma), Ajōdhyā is enumerated as one of the following seven 'salvation-giving'* (*mōkṣa-dāyikā*) *cities: Ajōdhyā, Mathurā, Māyā (or Gayā), Kāshī (or Banāras), Kānchī (or Kānchīpura, modern Conjeveram), Avantikā (or Ujain), and Dwārawatī (or Dwārakā).*)

[*Skr.* अयोध्या; *as above in all Gḍs.*]

√ अंजोर *ãjŏr*, अजोर *ajŏr*, **Tbh.,** *v. tr.*, to illuminate, light up. **Phr.,** अँजोरि लेब, *v. tr., the same; hence fig.*, to throw light upon, to make conspicuous, to manifest, *or* to search out, to find. **Exam.,** *Bin.* 158, करौं जो कुछ करौं रुचि-पचि सु-क्रिति सिला बटोरि, पैठि उर बर-बस, दया-निधि, दम्भ लेत अँजोरि (*vr.l.* अजोरि), Whatever good deeds I do, if, gathering them up like the gleanings of harvest, I carefully put them away (*in my heart*), pride entering (*my*) heart forcibly, O merciful Lord, searches them out (*to show them to the people*).

(*We have only met with this word in the above-quoted passage, where the comm. explains it by H.* खोजि लेता है it searches out.)

[*Skr.* √उज्ज्वल, (उत्+ज्वल); *caus.* उज्ज्वालयति, *Pr. caus.* √उज्जाले *or* उज्जाल (उज्जालेइ *or* उज्जालइ), *hence Gḍ.* √उँजाल *or* उजाल, *whence by transposition of vowels and concurrent interchange of* ल *and* र, अँजोर *or* अजोर, *which latter forms appear to be peculiar to Bihār. For another instance of the same changes see under* √बखुर *H. and P.* उजाल *tr. or* उजल *intr., M.* उजळ *tr. and intr., S.* उजिर *intr.*]

अंजोर *ãjŏr*, अजोर *ajŏr*, **Tbh.,** *subst. m., uk. f. of* अँजोरा *ãjōrā, q.v. In addition to the meanings there mentioned, it is also used in the sense of* [2]the light half of the month, *both with and without the word* पाख *pākh* (*Āz. Gy.*).

अंजोरा *ãjōrā*, अजोरा *ajōrā*, *Mg.* ईंजोरा *ĩjōrā* (*prop. str. f. of* अँजोर *ãjŏr, q.v., obl.* अजोरे; *lg. f.* अँजोरवा *ãjor'wā, q.v.*), **Tbh.,** *subst. m.*, [1]*con*, light, flame, blaze; [2]*abs.*, splendour, brightness, brilliancy. **Exam.,** [1]*Padm., ch.* 441, 1, बिहँसा समुँद चला उठि अँजोरा The sea smiled (*and*) up rose a (*flash of*) light; *ib., ch.* 575, 5. सोरह लाख कुँवर हैं मोरे, परहिं पतँग जस दीप अजोरे, Sixteen hundred thousand (*warrior*) princes are with me, (*into whose power*) they (*i.e. the enemy*) will fall like moths into the flame of a lamp. [2]*Padm., ch,* 685, 5, रैन गई दिन कीन्ह अँजोरा, The night had gone, (*and*) the day had brought the light. *See* उजारा *ujārā*, उँजारा *ũjārā*, उजाला *ujālā*, उँजाला *ũjālā*, उँचियारा *ũchiyārā*, उचियारा *uchiyārā*, उँचियाला *ũchiyālā*, उचियाला *uchiyālā*.

[*Skr.* उज्ज्वालकः *or* (*with pleon.* क) उज्ज्वालककः, *Pr.* उज्जालअओ. *For further details see under* √अँजोर. *In* ईंजोरा *there is a secondary change of* ल *to* र, *for a similar instance of which see under* √बखुर.]

अंजोरी *ãjōrī*, अजोरी *ajōrī*, **Tbh.,** *subst. f., the same as* अँजोरा *ãjōrā, q.v., of which it is the feminine.* **Exam.,** [1]*Padm., ch.* 492, 2, सरग सूर ससि करहिं अजोरी, तेहि तैं अधिक देउँ केहि जोरी, (*As*) in the heavens the sun and moon give light, (*so shone she*), more than that what comparison can I give? *ib., ch.* 72, 5, पदुम पदारथ लिखी सु-जोरी, चाँद सुरज जस होय अँजोरी, A ruby (*padum=Padmāwat*) and a jewel (*i.e. Ratan Sēn*) have been written (*by fate*) as an excellent match, like the (*joined*) light of the moon and the sun, (*referring to the astrologer's prophecy regarding the marriage of Padmāwat and Ratan Sēn*).

अंजौरा *ãjaurā*, अजौरा *ajaurā*, अँजौला *ãjaulā*, अजौला *ajaulā*, **Tbh.,** *subst. m., used in a magnifying sense for* अँजौरी *ãjaurī, q.v.; the same as* अँजुरा *ãjurā, q.v.*

[*For derivation, see under* अँजुरी.]

अंजौरी *ãjaurī*, अजौरी *ajaurī* (*Bh.*), अँजौली *ãjaulī*, अजौली *ajaulī* (*Bw.*), **Tbh.,** *subst. f.*, [1]*the same as* अँजुरी *ãjurī, q.v.*; [2](*East. Āudh*) *the same as* अगौरी *agaurī in its second sense, q.v.,* (*Ell. vol. II, p.* 3, *Wil. p.* 14.)

[*For derivation see under* अँजुरी. *In its second sense the word is probably a corruption of* अजौरी, *made by false analogy to* अजौरी *in its first sense.*]

अंजौला *ãjãulā*, अजौला *ajãulā* (*Bw.*), *see* अँजौरा, *ãjãurā*.

अंजौली *ãjãuli*, अजौली *ajãuli* (*Bw.*), *the same as* अँजौरी *ãjãurī and* अँजुरी *ãjuri*, *q.v.* *It has been esp. observed in Banāras in the fifth of the second set of meanings of* अँजुरी *ãjuri*, (*Ell.*, *vol.* I, *p.* 193, *Cr. p.* 88, *Wil. p.* 14).

अज्जु *ajju*, *a dialectic and vulgar form for* आजु *āju*, *q.v.*

अञ *ajñ*; *for words commencing thus, see under* अग्य *agy*. *See General Introd., chap.* 4.

√अझुर *ajhur*, अझुरा *ajhurā* (*pr. pts* अझुरैत *ajhurait*; अझुरल *ajhural*; अझुरब *ajhurab*; अझुरै *ajhurai*), **Tbh.**, *v. intr.*, (*Mg. and Bh.*) [1] to be entangled, entwisted (*as thread or hair, Āz. Gy.*); *hence met.* [2] to be complicated, perplexing; [3] to be ensnared, to be caught in a snare *or* net, *etc.*; *hence fig.* [4] to be entangled in a quarrel, to quarrel; *or* [5] to be inveigled *or* entangled in an unlawful connection, to be seduced, to live in illicit intercourse; [6] to be engaged in, to be occupied with (*some business*); *hence met.* [7] to be locked up, invested (*used of capital*). **Phr.**, अझुर जाएब *or* अझुराय जाएब, *v. intr.*, *with the same meanings.* **Exam.**, [1] *Coll.*, (*Bh.*), ई सभ सूता अझुर गेल, All that thread is entangled. [2] *Ib.*, अझुराएल बात मत कहँ, Do not talk about complicated subjects. [3] *Ib.*, चिरईं जाल में अझुर गेल है, The bird has been caught in the net. [4] *Ib.*, ओकरा से मत अझुराह, Do not quarrel with him. [5] *Ib.*, मोहन के मेहरारू नैहरे (नैहर+ए) में अझुराय गेल रहे, Mōhan's wife was seduced in her very father's house. [6] *Ib.*, हम काम में अझुराएल बानी, I am busily occupied with work. [7] *Ib.*, हमार सभ पूँजी एहि में अझुराय गेल बाड़े, All my capital has been locked up in this. *See* अरुझ *arujh* (*Mg. and Bh.*), उझर *ujhar* (*Mth.*), उरझ *urajh* (*Bw.*).

(*The word is the opposite of* सुझर *sujhar*, *q.v.* *With regard to the meanings, compare the nearly synonymous* √अटक *aṭak.*)

[*Skr.* √जट् *with* उत्, उज्जटति he entangles, *Pr.* √उज्झड, उज्झडइ; *hence Mth.* √उझर *and, with transposition of consonants, Bw. and Br.* उरझ, *or, with transposition of vowels, Bh. and Mg.* अझुर *and* अरुझ; *Hindi has* उरझ *or usually, with further change of* र *to* ल, उलझ, *Br.* ररझ *or* रुलझ, *with the rare change to* र, *probably through the intermediate change of* ड *to* ल, *as in* उँजाला, अँजोरा, इँजोरा, *q.v.* (*see Gd. Gr.* § 61); *P. has* उलझ.]

√अझुरा *ajhurā*, (*pr. pts.* अझुराइत *ajhurāit*; अझुराएल *ajhurāël*; अझुराएब *ajhurāëb*; अझुराए *ajhurāë*), **Tbh.**, *v. intr.*, (*Mg. and Bh.*), *the same as* √अझुर *ajhur*, *under which see for examples. See* अरुझा *arujhā* (*Mg. and Bh.*), उझरा *ujh'rā* (*Mth.*), उरझा *ur'jhā* (*Bw.*).

[*See remarks under* √अझुर; *derived from Pr. pleon. by-form* उज्झडावेइ *or* उज्झडावइ (*with pleon. suff.* अवि, *see Gd. Gr.* § 349); *H.* उरझा *or* उलझा, *Br.* ररझा *or* रुलझा, *P.* उलझा.]

√अझुराब *ajhurāb*, (*pr. pts., Mg. and Bh.* अझुरावत *ajhurāwat or* अझुरावित *ajhurāwit*, *Mg. also* अझुराइत *ajhurāit*; अझुराओल *ajhurāöl*; अझुराएब *ajhurāëb*, अझुराबै *ajhurābai or* अझुराए *ajhurāë*), **Tbh.**, *v. tr.*, (*Mg. and Bh.*), *causal of* √अझुर *ajhur*, *under which see for meanings and examples. See* अरुझाब *arujhāb* (*Mg. and Bh.*), उझराब *ujh'rāb* (*Mth.*), उरझाब *ur'jhāb* (*Bw.*).

[*See remarks under* √अझुर; *Skr. caus.* उज्जाटयति, *Pr.* उज्झडावेइ *or* उज्झडावइ, *Gd.* उझरावे. *The opp. of this word is* √सुझराब, *q.v.*]

अञ्चर *añchar* (*Bh.*), *see* अञ्चल *añchal*. *See* आँचरा *ãch'rā and* आँचर *ãchar*.

अञ्चल *añchal*, (*Bh.*) अञ्चर *añchar*, **Ts.**, *subst. m.*, [1] the hem *or* border of a garment, *esp. of a woman's upper garment or veil*; *hence esp.* [2] (*common in erotic poetry*) the border of the veil *or* the cloth with which a woman covers her bosom; *hence transferred to* [3] the bosom, breasts; [4] a symbol of humble supplication *or* adoration (*used by women only, and consisting in taking up the border of the veil and holding it out so as to be slightly hollowed in the shape of a pan or bowl in which the expected favours may, as it were, be received*). **Comp.**, अञ्चल-बात, *subst. m.*, the wind caused by the borders of one's garment, an accidental *or* side puff. **Phr.**, अञ्चल जोरब, *v. tr.*, to join (*the borders of the veil so as to make*) an añchal, to form an añchal; अञ्चल पसारब, *v. tr.*, to hold out (*the border of the veil in the form of*) an añchal; अञ्चल रोपब, *v. tr.*, to set up *or* make an añchal; (*these three phrases are synonymous; an equivalent gesture, for both men and women, is* अञ्जुलि जोरब, *q.v.*;) अञ्चल भरब, *v. tr.*, to take to one's bosom, to embrace, *syn.* अङ्क भरब, *q.v.* **Exam.**, [1] *Hb.* iii, 19, अञ्चल झाँपि भवन ले गेलि, Covering (*the infant Krish'n*) with the border of her veil, (*his mother Jasōdā*) carried him into the house. [2] *Ukh.* 3, 12, रस-मय पहु अञ्चल गहि लेला, लाज बदन मोर अवनत भेला, My amorous bridegroom seized my bosom-cloth (*to remove it*), in modesty I bent my face; *Padm.*, *ch.* 38, 6, कुच कञ्चुक आगरहिँ धुम धारे, अञ्चल दीन्ह हुमायहिँ डारे, Their breasts under their bodice (*the courtesans*) treated (*lit.*

considered) as (*two*) counters of the game of chāūsar, as in their (*wanton*) nature they drew aside their bosom-cloth. [3]*Rām., Bā., ch.* 357, 3, मुदित मातु अञ्चल भरि लेवीं, The matrons in their joy took (*the infant Rām and his brothers*) to their bosom. [4]*Rām., A., ch.* 263, 5, विनवहिँ अञ्जलि अञ्चल जोरी, (*The people of Awadh*) humbly supplicated (*the men*) with folded hands, (*the women*) with folded veil; *ib., Bā., chh.* 34, 3, पुर-नारि सकल पसारि अञ्चल बिधिहि बचन सुनावहीँ, All the women of the city, holding out the borders of their veils (*in supplication*), made prayer to the Creator; *Gīt., Ut.* 18, 4, हिंडोल साल बिलोकि सब अञ्चल पसारि पसारि कारीं असीसन राम-सीतहिँ सुख-समाज निहारि, Seeing the swinging-room and observing all its comforts, all (*the women*) holding out the borders of their veils (*in adoration*), began to bless Rām and Sītā; *Rām., Ln., ch.* 7, 4, चरन नार सिर अञ्चल रोपा "सुनहु बचन पिय परिहरि कोपा" (*Mandōdarī*) bowing her head (*to Rāban's*) feet, put up the border of her veil (*thus humbly supplicating*:) "hear my word, O beloved, (*and*) desist from your wrath (*against Rām*)." (*Cf. K. Rām., Ln.* 27, *where* अञ्चल पसारि *is used in relating the same incident.*)

[*Skr.* अञ्चल: ; *as above in all Gḍs.*]

अञ्चा *añchā*, **Tbh.**, *subst. m.* (*Mg.*), one who stirs a fire, *only used in the* **Comp.** चुल्ह-अञ्चा *chulh-añchā*, the man who stokes the fire in a sugar-boiling house (*Grs.* § 303). *See* आँचवाहा *āch'wahā*.

[*For der. see under* आँचना *āch'nā. Perhaps a more probable der. is from Skr.* आतञ्चक:, one who throws in (*fuel into the stove*), *from* √आ-तञ्च, *Pr.* आयञ्चओ, *Gḍ.** ऐचा, *whence shortened* अञ्चा; *similarly Skr.* आतञ्चनम्, instrument for throwing in (*fuel*), a poker, *Pr.* आयञ्चणं *or* आयञ्चणअं, *Gḍ.** ऐंचना *or shortened* आँचना. *See the remarks under* अञ्ची *añchī.*]

अञ्चित *añchit*, **Ts.**, *adj., com. gen.*, distinguished, adorned. **Exam.**, *Mth. Rām., Ln.* 162, 8, शक्तिक शक्ति चरल प्रभु नाठ, कनकाञ्चित (कनक-अञ्चित) शिर शर सौँ काठ, The Lord took away the power of the Sakti (*arrow*) in its course, and with (*his own*) arrow cut off (*one of Rāban's*) heads which was adorned with gold.

[*Skr.* अञ्चित:, *syn.* पूजित: *or* अलङ्कृत:]

अञ्ची *añchī*, इञ्ची *iñchī*, ऐँची *ãĩchī* (*Mth.-Mg.*), इन्सी *insī* (*Mg.*), **Tbh.**, *subst. m.*, the sediment which accumulates in the stem of an opium pipe, and which is mixed with the smoking opium *or* chaṇḍū, *when it is intended to make the latter extra strong* (*Grs.* § 1034).

[*Skr.** आतञ्चक: *or* * आतञ्चिक:, *Pr.* आयञ्चिओ, *Gḍ.* *ऐची *or B.* ऐँची, *shortened* अञ्ची *and* इञ्ची. *The cognate Pr. word* आयञ्चण (*Skr.* आतञ्चन) *occurs repeatedly in Jain works; see translation of the Uvāsagadasāō in Bibliotheca Indica, note* 238, *p.* 92.]

अञ्छर *añchhar*, **Tbh.**, *subst. m., a vulg. form for* अच्छर *achchhar, q.v. It is sometimes also pronounced* अनछर *an'chhar, and used in the sense of* a magical word, a mysterious *or* cabbalistic saying (*Hd. Dy.*).

√अञ्ज *añj* (*Bw.*), (*pr. pts.* अञ्जत *añjat*; अञ्जल *añjal*; अञ्जब *añjab*; अञ्जै *añjai*), **Tbh.**, *v. tr., the same as* आँज *ā̃j, q.v.* **Exam.**, *Krish.* 47, प्यारी नैननि को अञ्जन कै अपने लोचन अञ्जत है, He takes the collyrium from his darling's eyes, and anoints his own with it.

[*Skr.* √अञ्ज्, VII*th cl.* अनक्ति, *but Pā.* I*st cl.* अञ्जति, *Pr.* अञ्जइ, *Bw.* अञ्जै; *H. the same.*]

अञ्जन *añjan* (1), **Ts.**, *subst. m.*, [1] *abs.* application of any ointment (*esp. to eyes*); *hence* [2] *con.*, any ointment, *esp. for the eyes*; [3] a collyrium *or* ointment applied to the eyelashes *or* inner coat of the eyelids to darken and improve them, *such as antimony, lampblack*; *hence* [4] *fig.* dark eyes; [5] the elephant of the west *or* south-west quarter. **Comp.**, अञ्जन-केश, *adj., com. gen.*, having hair black as collyrium, *hence subst. m.*, fire. **Exam.**, [1] *Pur.* ii, 13, (*p.* 77), द्वितीय बार अञ्जन सौँ नैन पुतरी भेलि, At the second application of the ointment there appeared the pupil of the eye. [2] *Bin.* 265, जानि अन्ध अञ्जन कहै बन-बाघिनि घी को, (*The world*) thinking me blind prescribes an ointment (*made*) of tigress' butter (*i.e., an impossibility*); *Padm., do.*, 549, 2, पिय आवहिँ दिष्टि, नैनहि अञ्जन मैन करेउ, If I applied that (*dust*) to my eyes as an ointment, I would get a sight of my beloved (*cf. the following*); *Rām., Bā., ch.* 2, 1, गुरु-पद-रज मिदु मञ्जुल अञ्जन, नयन-अमिय द्रिग-दोष बिभञ्जन, The dust of one's teacher's feet is a soft and charming ointment, (*as*) ambrosia to the eyes, removing every defect of vision. [3] *Sudh.* 25, जावक लीक कपोल माहन पर, अञ्जन अधर लखात, With the traces of red lac on his cheeks, and with collyrium marking the lips (*the belated gallant returns home*); *see also under* √अञ्ज *añj*; *Bin.* 142, अञ्जन-केश-शिखा जुवती तहँ लोचन सु-लभ पठावौं, If there is a young girl (*dangerous*) like the flame of fire, I (*only to*) easily cast my eyes there; [4] *Hn.* 5, 7 (*also Ukh.* iii, 1) मिग-अञ्जन अञ्जन मद गञ्जन लोचन सम निज काँती, Her eyes, equal in their own brilliancy, destroy the pride of the khañjan (*or wagtail*) and of the dark eye (*lit.* the collyrium) of the deer. *See* आँजन *ā̃jan*.

[*Skr.* अञ्जनम्; *as above in all Gḍs.*]

अञ्जन *añjan* (2), अञ्जनि *añjani*, इञ्जन *iñjan*, इञ्जनि *iñjani*, **Any.**, *subst. f.* (?), an engine.

[*Cor. of the English word.*]

अञ्जना *añjanā*, **Ts.**, *subst. f.*, a kind of domestic lizard (*the jēṭhī*). **Exam.**, *Coll.*, (*Mth.*), देवार पर अञ्जना कैं देखैं, See the lizard on the wall.

[*Skr.* अञ्जना (*noted in the shorter Skr. Dy. P.*); *B.* अञ्जना; *B.* आँजिना *or* आँजनाइ.]

अञ्जनि *añjani, the same as* अञ्जनी *añjanī* (2), *q.v.*

अञ्जनिका *añjanikā*, **Ts.**, *subst. f.*, *the same as* अञ्जनी *añjanī*(1), *q.v.*

[*Skr.* अञ्जनिका.]

अञ्जनी *añjanī* (1), **Ts.**, *subst. f.*, [1] *the same as* अञ्जना *añjanā, q.v.*; [2] a certain medicinal plant used as a sedative and laxative.

[*Skr.* अञ्जनिका, *Pr.* अञ्जणिआ, *Gd* अञ्जनी.]

अञ्जनी *añjanī* (2), **Ts.**, *subst. f.*, a name of the mother of Hanumān, the wife of the monkey Kēsarī. *Hanumān was her son by Pavana* (*or the Wind*). **Exam.**, *Han.*, 40, ओछे ओछे चावरन चावरन अपनायौ अञ्जनी-कुमार, साध्यौ, राम-पानि पाक कीं, When I was living in very base ways, the son of Añjanī (*i.e., Hanumān*) claimed me as his own; he set me on the right way, and by (*the touch of*) Rām's hand I am become pure.

[*A prākritizing modification* (*see Hēm.* iii, 34) *of the Skr.* अञ्जना. *The latter has not been met with in the vernacular, but only* अञ्जनी.]

अञ्जबार *añjabār*, अञ्जुबार *añjubār*, इञ्जिबार *iñjibār*, **Any.**, *subst. m.*, the name of a creeping plant (*Polygonum bistorta*), *introduced from Persia, now growing in the Panjāb Himālaya, from the pulverised rind of which astringent medicaments are prepared for external and internal use* (*for particulars see Watts*, V, *p.* 224; *also Shakespeare's Hd. Dy.*, *s.v*).

[*Prs.* انجبار *anjabār.*]

अञ्जर *añjar* (*Bh.*), अञ्जल *añjal* (*Bw.*), *see* अञ्जरि *añjari*.

अञ्जरि *añjari*, अञ्जर *añjar* (*Bh.*), **Ts.**, *subst. m.*, *see* अञ्जलि *añjali*.

अञ्जल *añjal* (*Bw.*), अञ्जर *añjar* (*Bh.*), *see* अञ्जलि *añjali*.

अञ्जलि *añjali*, अञ्जल *añjal* (*Bw.*), अञ्जरि *añjari*, अञ्जर *añjar* (*Bh.*), (*tadbh. str. f.*, आँजला *ā̃j'lā*, आँजरा *ā̃j'rā*, *m.*, आँजली *ā̃j'lī*, आँजरी *ā̃j'rī*, *f.*, *q.v.*), **Ts.**, *subst. m.*, [1] the two open hands placed side by side (*of which there are two modes, consisting* (*a*) *in placing them edge by edge, palms turned up and hollowed slightly in the shape of a pan, or* (*b*) *in placing them palm to palm*); [2] a symbol of benediction *or* blessing (*the first of the above-mentioned two modes being used, with the hands held in front of the breast, only by brāhman gurus towards their disciples or devotees*); [3] a symbol of reverential supplication *or* worship (*the same mode being used and in the same way as in No.* 2, *only by suppliants or worshippers*); [4] a symbol of respectful salutation (*also the first mode being used, but with the hands carried up to the forehead, only by inferiors towards superiors, or between equals*); [5] a symbol of respectful attention *or* contemplation (*the second of the two modes being used, with the hands either held in front of the breast or raised to the forehead, only by inferiors towards superiors or by devotees towards objects of devotion*); [6] a libation; [7] a double handful *or* as much as can be held in the cavity formed by joining the hands together in the shape of a bowl (*Ell.*, *vol.* I, *p.* 196). **Comp.**, अञ्जलि-गत, *adj.*, *com. gen.*, placed in the two hands (*shaped like a pan or bowl*); अञ्जलि-बद्ध, *adj.*, *com. gen.*, having the two hands joined (*palm to palm*); बद्धाञ्जलि (बद्ध + अञ्जलि), *the same as* अञ्जलि-बद्ध, *q.v.* **Phr.** अञ्जलि जोरब *or* अ॰ जोड़ब, *v. tr.* to join (*the two hands so as to make*) an añjali, to form an añjali; अञ्जलि देब, *v. tr.*, *lit.* to give a double-handful (*of water*), *hence* to make a libation. **Exam.**, [1] *Rām.*, *Bā.*, *do.* 3, 2, अञ्जलि-गत सुभ सुमन जिमि सम सुगन्ध कर दोउ, Just as a fragrant flower, placed in the joined hands, (*communicates*) its sweet scent equally to both hands. [2] *Rām.*, *A.*, *ch.* 263, 5, रमारमन-पद बन्दि बहोरी बिनवहिं अञ्जलि अञ्चल जोरी, Worshipping the feet of Rama's (*i.e., Lakṣmī's*) lord they humbly prayed, (*the men*) with folded hands, (*the women*) with folded veil (*i.e., the end of the veil folded into the shape of a bowl to receive, as it were, the god's favours into it*). [5] *Mth. Rām.*, *Su.* 82, 15, दूरहि सौं हम कैल प्रनाम अञ्जलि-बद्ध ठाढ़ तेहि ठाम, From a distance I made obeisance, standing in that place with folded hands; *ibid.*, *Ln.* 149, 3, बद्धाञ्जलि राजस-रस-हीन, With joined hands and devoid of any feeling of passion; *Hb.* i, 10, अञ्जलि-बद्ध धेयान धरि लेल, With joined hands they assumed the attitude of contemplation (*before Bish'n, whom Brahmā and the other dēbs had gone to interview*). [7] *Pur.*, iv, 35, (*p.* 194), तखन लोभक आधिक्य सौं बहुत बढ़लि तृष्णा अपनाके आठम मध्य पि भाण्ड-देयन अञ्जलि, Then from the excess of his greediness he put both his hands (*Skr.* करौ निक्षिप्तौ) in the very midst of the vessel in order to take out the eighth double-handful of gold. *See for synonyms under* आँजुरा *ā̃jurā and* आँजुरी *ā̃jurī*.

(*The añjali with its fifth meaning is very frequently mentioned in Jain Prākrit works, where the gesture is thus minutely described* (*see Kalp.* § 5, 12, 15, *etc.*, *Bhag. p.* 298, *Nāy.* 823), कर-यल-परिग्गहियं दस-नहं सिरसा-ऽऽवत्तं मत्थए अञ्जलिं कट्टु, *i.e.*, making the añjali

INDEX TO THE RĀMĀYAN.

Preliminary Note.

THIS Index is founded on the text of Rām Jasan's Banāras edition (1869),* as corrected by the emendations given at its close. We believe that it gives a reference to every occurrence of every word in the text thus emended. Every appearance of even such words as अति or अब has been noted and registered. We hope that the number of mistakes is few; and in order to render them as few as possible, we have tested the majority of entries after they have been set up in type. Any mistakes which do occur will not, we believe, cause serious inconvenience, as there is a double reference to each word—one to the page on which it is found, and the other to its situation according to chapter and verse of the poem.

Any purely Sanskrit passages in the Rāmāyan, such as the invocation at the commencement of Book I, are omitted from the Index; but passages partly Sanskṛit and partly Hindī, several instances of which occur in the *Araṇya Kāṇḍ* and elsewhere, have been included.

In Rām Jasan's edition all *dōhās, sor'ṭhās*, and *chhands* are numbered, each class consecutively in its own series. The *chaupāīs* have not been numbered. In referring, therefore, to *chaupāīs* in this Index, we have considered each as bearing the number of the set of *dōhās* immediately following it. Sometimes a set of *dōhās* is preceded by two or more sets of *chaupāīs* separated by a set of *sor'ṭhās* or by a set of *chhands*. In this case, the same system is adhered to, both sets of *chaupāīs* bearing the same number—that of the set of following *dōhās*, and the numbering of the lines of the two sets of *chaupāīs* running on as if it was only one set. Thus on page 8 of Rām Jasan's edition there is a set of 8 *chaupāīs* followed by a set of *sor'ṭhās* No. 3, consisting of two lines, and again by a set of 10 *chaupāīs*; then follows a set of *sor'ṭhas* No. 4, consisting of two lines; then again another set of 10 *chaupāīs*, and finally a set of *dōhās* No. 22. All these three sets of *chaupāīs* are considered for the purposes of this Index to consist of one set of *chaupāīs* No. 22, consisting of 8 + 10 + 10 = 28 lines. The first set commences with line 1, the second with line 9, and the third with line 19.

In the Index is given, after the word itself, first the book or *kāṇḍ* in which it occurs. The Rāmāyan consists of seven books, for which the following contractions are used:—

Book I	...	...	*Bāl Kāṇḍ*	...	*contraction*	BA.
Book II	...	...	*Ajōdhyā Kāṇḍ*	...	„	A.
Book III	...	...	*Araṇyā Kāṇḍ*	...	„	AR.
Book IV	...	...	*Kis'kindā Kāṇḍ*	...	„	KI.
Book V	...	...	*Sundar Kāṇḍ*	...	„	SU.
Book VI	...	...	*Laykā Kāṇḍ*	...	„	LN.
Book VII	...	...	*Uttar Kāṇḍ*	...	„	UT.

* Since the above was written, Paṇḍit Rām Jasan has brought out a new edition (Chandra Prabhā Press, Banāras, 1883), which is much better printed than the first. The text is practically the same in both cases, except that in the second some misprints have been corrected and a return has been made to the old Sanskrit system of spelling. The paging differs slightly in the two editions, but the numbering of the verses is the same except in the *Ajōdhyā Kāṇḍ*. In the *Ajōdhyā Kāṇḍ*, after *chaupāī* No. 107, an extra set of *dōhās* and *chaupāīs* has been inserted. Hence when referring to the second edition, from and after *dōhā* No. 107, the numbers of the *dōhās* and *chaupāīs* given in the index must be increased by one. In this way no difficulty will be experienced in using this index with it also.

The references are given in order, book by book. Thus taking the word आग, first are given in order all the instances in which it occurs in the *Bāl Kāṇḍ;* then all in which it occurs in the *Ajōdhyā Kāṇḍ,* and so on.

Each reference consists of four parts. First a number (in sanserif type), showing the page in Rām Jasan's edition in which the word occurs : thus, 16.

Then is recorded the fact whether the word occurs in a set of *chaupāīs, dōhās, sor'ṭhās, chhands,* or *tōṭaks,* explained by the contractions ch., do., so., chh., or toṭ., respectively.

Then follows the number of the *chaupāī* or *dōhā,* &c., in ordinary Arabic numerals : thus, ch., 47.

Then follows the number of the line in the set in which it occurs : thus, 6. The entry concludes with a colon.

Taking, therefore, the first entry under [illegible], after noticing that it is one of those which belong to the *Bāl Kāṇḍ,* we find it to be 31, ch. 96, 8 : which means that it occurs on page 31, in *chaupāī* No. 96, line 8. If the word occurs more than once on the same page, the page number is not repeated; if it occurs not only in the same page, but also in the same set of *chaupāīs* or *dōhās,* &c., the *chaupāī* (or *dōhā,* &c., as the case may be) number is not repeated. Thus among the *Sundar Kāṇḍ* entries for आग we have 265, ch. 29, 2, 3, which means that the word occurs on page 265, in *chaupāī* No. 29, in lines 2 and 3. If the word occurs in two different sets of *chaupāīs* in the same page, the word ch. is omitted the second time, and the entries are separated by a semicolon. Thus under [illegible] we have the entries 10, ch. 25, 7 ; 26, 2 ; 27, 1 :— which mean that the word occurs on page 10, in *chaupāī* No. 25, line 7, and in *chaupāī* No. 26, line 2, and in *chaupāī* No. 27, line 1.

It is hoped that with the aid of the above instructions no difficulty will be felt in using the index.

INDEX

TO THE

RÁMÁYAN OF TULSÍ DAS.

॥ अ ॥

अकुलानि, A., 146, do. 76, 2.
अकुलानो, BA., 22, ch. 68, 3 : 64, ch. 197, 12 : 70, ch. 213, 8 : 87, ch. 267, 5 : A., 136, ch. 41, 1 : 138, ch. 50, 14 : 140, ch. 57, 1 : 144, ch. 68, 6 : SU., 260, ch. 13, 2 : 267, ch. 36, 4.
अकुलाने, BA., 79, ch. 241, 7 : 85, ch. 261, 6 : KI., 251, ch. 24, 3 : SU., 276, ch. 58, 7 : LN., 296, ch. 51, 5.
अकुलानीं, BA., 47, ch. 142, 2 : A., 146, ch. 74, 13 : 165, ch. 137, 8.

अकेल, BA., 53, ch. 161, 6 : 57, do. 174, 1 : AR., 230, so. 6, 2 : 233, ch. 19, 7 : 239, do. 32, 1 : LN., 292, do. 42, 1 : 310, do. 85, 2.
अकेलि, BA., 21, ch. 63, 8 : UT., 333, chh. 5, 19.
अकेलो, AR., 236, ch. 26, 2.
अकेले, BA., 54, ch. 163, 3.

अकोविद, BA., 41, ch. 123, 1.

अखण्ड, BA., 22, ch. 68, 8 : 49, ch. 149, 4 : 70, do. 213, 1 : AR., 227, ch. 10, 12 : SU., 272, do. 49, 2 : LN., 298, ch. 59, 18 : 321, chh. 36, 15 : UT., 354, ch. 72, 4 : 356, ch. 78, 4 : 370, ch. 108, 4.
अखण्डं, UT., 368, chh. 11, 9.
अखण्डा, UT., 350, ch. 64, 1 : 374, ch. 115, 1.

अखण्डित, UT., 346, ch. 50, 7.

अखारा, LN., 279, ch. 11, 7 : 280, ch. 14, 4.
अखारेन्ह, SU., 256, chh. 1, 8.

अखिल, BA., 67, do. 203, 2 : 69, ch. 209, 6 : 72, so. 23, 2 : SU., 269, ch. 42, 2 : 274, ch. 57, 5 : LN., 308, ch. 83, 9 : 319, chh. 34, 3 : UT., 340, ch. 30, 8 : 354, ch. 72, 4 : 359, ch. 87, 7 : 361, ch. 90, 2. °ब्रह्माण्ड, A., 201, do. 253, 1. °भुवनपति, KI., 243, do. 1, 2. अखिलेश्वर, BA., 19, ch. 59, 2.
अखिलं, AR., 226, ch. 8, 12.

अग, AR., 237, chh. 9, 11 : LN., 296, ch. 54, 2 : UT., 333, chh. 5, 5 : 362, ch. 92, 7. °जगनाथ LN., 289, ch. 35, 8 : 318, ch. 101, 13 : UT., 328, chh. 1, 3. °जगमय BA., 65, ch. 197, 7 : UT., 349, ch. 61, 5.

अगाध, BA., 10, ch. 27, 1 : 56, ch. 171, 8 : A., 137, ch. 47, 7 : 142, ch. 61, 7 : AR., 240, do. 34, 3 : SU., 272, ch. 50, 6 : LN., 322, ch. 111, 3 : UT., 334, tot. 1, 10 : 361, ch. 90, 1.
अगाधा, BA., 15, ch. 46, 2 : 22, ch. 68, 2 : KI., 249, ch. 17, 1.
अगाध, BA., 3, ch. 6, 6 : 15, ch. 45, 3 : A., 136, ch. 42, 7 : 184, ch. 197, 7 : 203, ch. 259, 6 : 215, ch. 298, 2.

अँगनाई, UT., 355, ch. 76, 3.

अगनित, BA., 16, ch. 49, 7 : 33, chh. 7, 3 : 40, ch. 122, 3 : 42, so. 13, 1 : 45, ch. 137, 2, 6 : 51, ch. 153, 3 : 70, ch. 214, 1 : 100, ch. 306, 5 ; 307, 6 : 112, ch. 335, 5 : 118, ch. 354, 2 : A., 188, ch. 213, 2 : 197, ch. 240, 7 : LN., 285, ch. 26, 3 : 289, ch. 35, 10 : UT., 357, ch. 80, 5, 6 : do. 81, 2. °भाति, A., 125, ch. 7, 8. *See* अगिनित.

अगम, BA., 10, ch. 27, 5 : 16, do. 47, 2 : 51, ch. 154, 3, 4 : 53, ch. 161, 8 : 55, ch. 168, 3 : 56, ch. 168, 16 : 60, ch. 184, 6 : 116, ch. 348, 3 : A., 137, ch. 47, 7 : 141, ch. 61, 6 : 142, ch. 61, 7 : 144, ch. 71, 1 : 146, ch. 76, 5 : 152, ch. 96, 7 : 154, ch. 102, 5 : 156, ch. 108, 6 : 159, do. 116, 2 : 160, do. 119, 2 : 163, do. 131, 1 : 190, do. 217, 2 : 192, ch. 224, 2 : 194, ch. 232, 1 : 195, ch. 232, 5 : 197, ch. 241, 7 : 209, ch. 278, 1 : 210, ch. 283, 2 : 215, ch. 298, 6 : 220, chh. 13, 2 : AR., 237, chh. 9, 13 : 240, ch. 37, 1 : SU., 266, do. 33, 1 : UT., 345, ch. 46, 3 : 354, do. 73, 4.

अगर,—°धूप, BA., 68, ch. 207, 5. °प्रसङ्ग, BA., 5, ch. 14, 9.

अंगव,—अँगवनिहारे, A., 130, ch. 26, 4.

अगवान, BA., 34, ch. 104, 1 : 102, do. 311, 2.
अगवानन्ह, BA., 102, ch. 312, 7.
अगवाना, BA., 34, ch. 103, 2 : 102, ch. 312, 8 : 103, ch. 316, 6.

अगस्ति, AR., 225, ch. 7, 1 : 227, ch. 9, 9 : KI., 249, ch. 16, 3 : SU., 274, ch. 57, 11 : UT., 351, do. 66, 2.

अगहन,—°मास, BA., 104, ch. 318, 13.

अगड़बड़, A., 130, ch. 26, 1.

अंगार, SU., 260, do. 12, 2 : LN., 295, do. 52, 2.
अँगारा, A., 171, ch. 155, 5 : SU., 259, ch. 12, 8 : LN., 295, ch. 51, 1.

अगिनि, BA., 66, ch. 201, 6 : A., 208, ch. 274, 3 : AR., 225, ch. 6, 1 : SU., 259, ch. 12, 11 : 266, ch. 31, 7. °समाधू, A., 179, ch. 180, 5. *See* अग्नि.

अगिनित, AR., 231, chh. 7, 10 : SU., 257, ch. 5, 5 : UT., 330, chh. 3, 4 : 342, ch. 38, 6. *See* अगनित.

अगुआई, A., 183, ch. 195, 1.

अगुन, BA., 3, ch. 7, 1 : 9, ch. 23, 2 : 10, ch. 25, 8 ; 27, 1 : 15, ch. 46, 2 : 25, ch. 77, 8 : 39, ch. 116, 8 : 41, ch. 123, 5, 10 : 48, ch. 147, 10 : 49, ch. 149, 4 : 50, ch. 151, 5 : A., 188, ch. 211, 6 : AR., 226,

ch. 8, 19 : LN., 287, do. 31, 1 : 320, ch. 107, 6 : 323, chh. 39, 3 : UT., 354, ch. 72, 5 : 359 do. 85, 2 : 370, ch. 108, 3, 12.
अगुवर्षि, BA., 41, ch. 123, 9.

अगेह, BA., 28, ch. 89, 6.
अगेहा, BA., 54, ch. 166, 4.

अगोचर, BA., 70, ch. 215, 5 : 108, chh. 43, 4 : A., 155, ch. 105, 4 : 159, ch. 119, 7.
अगोचरं, AR., 237, chh. 9, 5.

अग्नि, BA., 63, ch. 195, 10. *See* अगिनि.

अग्य, BA., 20, ch. 62, 2 : 22, do. 67, 2 : 39, ch. 117, 2 : 41, ch. 123, 1 : LN., 308, do. 81, 2.

अग्यताभञ्जन, UT., 341, ch. 35, 6.

अग्या, BA., 61, ch. 187, 4 : KI., 252, do. 25, 1.

अग्याता, BA., 96, ch. 293, 6.

अग्यान, BA., 21, ch. 64, 1 : 72, do. 219, 1 : KI., 244, do. 2, 1 : UT., 354, ch. 73, 9 : 370, do. 108, 3. °प्रसङ्गा, UT., 354, ch. 73, 7.
अग्याना, BA., 20, ch. 63, 4 : 38, ch. 116, 2 : 41, ch. 123, 15.
अग्यानू, BA., 88, ch. 270, 4 : A., ch. 209, ch. 280, 2.

अग्यनी, BA., 41, ch. 124, 1.

अग्र, BA., 79, ch. 241, 8.

अघ, BA., 3, ch. 5, 9 ; 7, 1 : 12, ch. 34, 1 : 17, do. 50, 2 : 37, ch. 112, 7 : 42, ch. 126, 3 : 77, ch. 235, 5 : A., 129, do. 21, 2 : 136, ch. 43, 5 : 166, ch. 139, 5 : 173, ch. 161, 5, 6 : 175, ch. 168, 8 : 178, ch. 177, 8 : 186, ch. 203, 2 : 192, do. 224, 2 : 197, ch. 239, 2 : SU., 268, ch. 39, 7 : LN., 320, ch. 107, 4 : 325, ch. 117, 7 : UT., 337, ch. 22, 3 : 340, ch. 30, 8 ; 32, 4 : 341, ch. 34, 7 : 343, ch. 42, 4 : 367, do. 103, 4 : 370, ch. 109, 6, 7, 10 : 376, ch. 118, 6, 22 : 379, ch. 123, 3. °अवगुणखगवधिक, BA., 3, ch. 5, 5. °खनि, A., 183, ch. 194, 5. °ओघ, A., 197, ch. 240, 3. °खगगनवधिका, AR., 241, ch. 37, 8. °खगवधिक, KI., 254, so. 1, 2. °खानी, LN., 285, ch. 31, 4. °गञ्जन, UT., 346, ch. 52, 3. °जन्म, AR., 238, do. 31, 1. °परिपाक, A., 201, ch. 251, 6. °पुञ्ज, UT., 361, ch. 90, 2. °बृन्दा, A., 186, ch. 204, 3. °राशी, SU., 275, ch. 60, 5 : UT., 378, ch. 121, 8. °रूप, BA., 59, do. 180, 2 : UT., 380, chh. 12, 3. °वेष BA., 52, do. 157, 2. °वाधिकर, KI., 243, so. 1, 1. °हारी, A., 212, ch. 287, 3. अघारी, BA., 65, chh. 22, 2 : AR., 227, ch. 10, 5 : 238, ch. 30, 3.

अघटित, BA., 41, ch. 123, 6 : A., 172, ch. 159, 6.

√ अघा(य),—अघाइ, A., 142, do. 62, 2 : 186, ch. 203, 1 : LN., 309, ch. 85, 9.
अघाई, A., 176, ch. 173, 1.
अघाई, A., 139, ch. 51, 8 : 198, ch. 242, 13 : 200, ch. 250, 1 : 212, ch. 289, 5.
अघाउँ, LN., 296, ch. 56, 7.
अघाऊँ, UT., 359, ch. 88, 2.
अघाती, BA., 11, ch. 32, 3.
अघाने, A., 155, ch. 105, 1.
अघाय A., 185, do. 201, 2.
अघाहिं, LN., 319, do. 103, 1.
अघाहीं, A., 198, ch. 242, 5 : UT., 347, ch. 54, 1.
अघाहू, A., 185, ch. 201, 6.

अघात, SU., 271, ch. 49, 3 : LN., 321, do. 108, 2 : UT., 347, do. 53, 4.
अघाता, AR., 232, ch. 17, 3.

अङ्क, A., 176, ch. 171, 7 : 181, ch. 187, 4 : LN., 286, ch. 29, 1 : 294, ch. 48, 7 : 299, ch. 60, 7 : UT., 355, ch. 76, 7.
अङ्का, BA., 35, ch. 105, 8 : A., 194, ch. 229, 3 : 196, ch. 236, 3.

अङ्कित, A., 215, ch. 296, 4.

अङ्कुर, BA., 117, ch. 351, 5 : A., 130, ch. 24, 6 : 155, ch. 104, 2 : 175, chh. 7, 2 : 197, do. 241, 2. °जूरी, A., 197, ch. 241, 2.

√ अङ्कुर, अङ्कूर,—अङ्कुरेउ, BA., 45, ch. 136, 4.
अङ्कुरे, LN., 313, chh. 21, 4.
अङ्कूरे, UT., 377, ch. 119, 4.

अङ्कुस, BA., 69, ch. 211, 3 : 87, do. 266, 2 : AR., 233, ch. 20, 7 : UT., 333, chh. 5, 15.

अङ्ग, BA., 4, ch. 12, 6 : 76, do. 232, 2 : 79, ch. 243, 4 : 81, so. 24, 2 : 84, ch. 258, 3 : 89, do. 272, 2 : 102, ch. 314, 7 : 104, ch. 318, 4, 7 : 106, ch. 324, 3 : 111, chh. 56, 1 : A., 125, ch. 8, 4 : 156, ch. 108, 4 : 158, ch. 114, 6 : 181, ch. 190, 1 : 190, ch. 217, 4 : 193, ch. 226, 8 : 208, ch. 274, 5 : 212, ch. 289, 5 : 217, do. 303, 2 : AR., 234, ch. 23, 3 : 237, chh. 9, 12 : SU., 263, ch. 24, 9 : 267, ch. 35, 6 : 272, ch. 52, 3 : LN., 281, do. 15, 2 ; ch. 16, 1 : 317, chh. 31, 4 : UT., 332, ch. 12, 8 ; do. 12, 2 : 333, chh. 4, 7 : 355, ch. 76, 5. °अङ्गरागी, BA., 84, ch. 257, 2.
अङ्गा, BA., 96, ch. 293, 4 : 105, ch. 322, 1 : A., 135, ch. 40, 1 : SU., 262, ch. 19, 6.

अङ्गद, KI., 247, do. 11, 2 ; chh. 1, 8 : 248, ch. 12, 9 : 251, do. 22, 2 ; ch. 23, 1 : 252, ch. 26, 3, 6, 7 : 253, ch. 27, 8 : 254, ch. 30, 1 : SU., 265, ch. 28, 7 : 270, do. 44, 2 : 273, do. 54, 1 : LN., 230, ch. 12, 7 : 282, ch. 18, 5, 9, 13 ; so. 3, 1 : 283, ch. 19, 4 ; 21, 3, 4, 5, 7 : 284, ch. 23, 1 : 285, ch. 24, 3 ; 26, 1 : 286, ch. 29, 5 : 287, ch. 32, 6 : 288, do. 32, 4 : 290, ch. 36, 4 : 292, ch. 42, 2 ; do. 42, 1 : 293, ch. 44, 7 ; 45, 3 ; 46, 1, 6 : 294, ch. 49, 2 : 302, ch. 70, 8 : 303, do. 72, 2 : 304, ch. 73, 6 ; do. 73, 2 : 306, do. 77, 5 ; ch. 79, 6 : 308, ch. 82, 4, 8 : 313, ch. 94, 8 ; chh. 21, 3 : 318, ch. 103, 2 : 324, do. 115, 3 : 325, ch. 116, 10 : UT., 329, ch. 5, 2 : 331, ch. 9, 1 : 335, ch. 18, 8 ; do. 18, 3 : 336, ch. 20, 2, 10. °दुम, KI., 252, ch. 26, 11. °पन, LN., 289, ch. 34, 13. °वचन, UT., 336, do. 19, 1. अङ्गरादि, BA., 8, ch. 22, 19 : KI., 250, do. 20, 1 : LN., 295, do. 51, 1 : 299, do. 62, 1 : 303, ch. 72, 6.

अङ्गहरि, LN., 290, ch. 37, 3.

अङ्गन, LN., 309, chh. 13, 4 : 317, chh. 31, 4 : UT., 333, chh. 4, 7.

अङ्गीकार, BA., 63, do. 193, 1.

अङ्गीकारा, BA., 32, ch. 98, 4 : AR., 240, ch. 36, 6.

अङ्गुल, UT., 356, do. 79, 2.

अङ्गुलि, BA., 41, ch. 124, 3.

√अँच,—अँचे, BA., 120, ch. 361, 2.

अचञ्चल, BA., 79, ch. 242, 4.

अचम्भव, LN., 301, ch. 68, 8.

अचर, BA., 30, do. 94, 1 : 38, ch. 115, 8 : 66, do. 202, 2 : A., 164, ch. 134, 2 : 194, ch. 229, 8 : 219, ch. 309, 6.

अचरज, BA., 39, do. 118, 1 : 43, ch. 131, 8 : 44, ch. 134, 4 : 58, ch. 176, 2 : A., 134, ch. 38, 1 : 181, ch. 188, 1 : 185, ch. 200, 2 : 189, ch. 215, 8.

अचल, BA., 2, ch. 2, 11 : 11, ch. 30, 5 : 13, ch. 39, 10 : 25, ch. 77, 4 : 31, do. 95, 2 : 52, ch. 157, 6 : A., 132, ch. 29, 9 : 144, ch. 68, 8 : 162, ch. 128, 4 : 207, ch. 271, 6 : 208, ch. 274, 6 : 220, ch. 313, 6 : AR., 225, ch. 7, 15 : 242, ch. 40, 7 : KI., 247, ch. 10, 2 : 248, ch. 14, 8 : SU., 263, ch. 23, 1 : LN., 279, do. 8, 2 : 306, ch. 77, 9 ; ch. 79, 4 : UT., 330, ch. 8, 2 : 354, ch. 73, 5 : 359, do. 85, 4 : 361, ch. 90, 3.

√अँचव,—अँचवउ A., 157, ch. 111, 1.

अँचवन, A., 192, ch. 222, 7.

√अँचवाव,—अँचवाए, BA., 35, chh. 13, 4.

अचारा, BA., 64, chh. 18, 3 : UT., 359, ch. 87, 1 : 364, ch. 97, 10 : 373, ch. 114, 10. Cf. आचार.

अचारू, BA., 108, ch. 329, 8.

अचेत, BA., 13, do. 37, 2 : 53, do. 161, 2 : 61, do. 187, 1 : A., 147, do. 77, 2 : LN., 316, chh. 26, 10.

अचेता, A., 218, ch. 308, 7.

अच्छ, LN., 289, ch. 35, 5. °कुमारा, SU., 262, ch. 18, 7.

अच्छत, BA., 99, ch. 303, 16 : 117, ch. 351, 5. Cf. अछत.

अच्छर, BA., 49, do. 148, 1.

अछत, BA., 2, do. 2, 2 : 10, ch. 27, 7 : 92, ch. 282, 5 : 94, do. 287, 2 : A., 123, do. 2, 2 : 124, ch. 5, 3 : 204, do. 263, 2 : UT., 360, ch. 88, 17. Cf. अच्छत.

अछय, BA., 18, ch. 55, 5. °बट, A., 154, ch. 102, 7 :

अछोभा, BA., 93, ch. 282, 8.

अज, BA., 6, ch. 18, 3 : 20 do. 61, 1 : 32, ch. 99, 3 ; 100, 7 : 39, ch. 116, 8 : 41, ch. 123, 10 : 48, ch. 147, 10 : 65, do. 197, 2 : 69, do. 210, 2 : 71, do. 217, 1 : 73, chh. 31, 2 : AR., 224, ch. 3, 24 : 236, ch. 62, 17 : 237, chh. 9, 9 : KI., 252, do. 25, 2 ; ch. 26, 12 : SU., 263, ch. 23, 8 : 268, ch. 36, 10 ; 39, 2 : LN., 281, do. 16, 1 : 318, ch. 102, 2 : 320, ch. 107, 6 : 321, chh. 36, 7 : UT., 329, ch. 6, 6 : 333, chh. 5, 13 : 335, ch. 16, 9 : 338, do. 26, 1 : 340, ch. 31, 9 : 341, ch. 35, 4 : 342, ch. 36, 7 : 354, ch. 72, 3 : 359, do. 85, 2 : 366, ch. 103, 4 : 367, ch. 104, 7 : 370, ch. 108, 3 : 377 ch. 119, 12. °नामा, LN., 281, ch. 16, 1. अजादि, BA., 21, do. 64, 2. अजादिदेवविपतिं AR., 222, chh. 1, 9.

अजं, AR., 237, chh. 9, 5 : LN., 321, chh. 36, 9 : UT., 368, chh. 11, 9. अजअद्वैतमहुअवगम, UT., 334, chh. 5, 21.

अजहिं, UT., 377, do. 119, 3.

अजा, BA., 35, ch. 106, 3.

अजगव, BA., 93, do. 283, 2.

अजगर, UT., 367, ch. 104, 7.

अजय, BA., 57, ch. 174, 5 : 62, ch. 191, 2 : 76, ch. 233, 4 : SU., 260, ch. 13, 3 : LN., 303, ch. 72, 2 : 304, ch. 73, 14 : 306, do. 77, 1 : 321, ch. 109, 3.

अजे, UT., 334, tot. 1, 17.

अजर, BA., 29, ch. 92, 7 : SU., 261, ch. 17, 3 : LN., 310, ch. 86, 4.

अजस, BA., 84, ch. 257, 3 : A., 133, ch. 33, 6 ; do. 33, 2 : 136, ch. 43, 5 ; 45, 1 : 188, do. 210, 2 : 175, ch. 168, 8 : UT., 370, ch. 109, 7. °अपवाद, A., 166, ch. 139, 5. °पिटारी, A., 127, do. 13, 2.

अजसी, LN., 287, ch. 31, 2.

अजहिं, *see* आज.

अजऊ, अजऊँ, अजहूँ, *see* आज.

अजाचक, UT., 332, ch. 13, 7.

अजान, BA., 91, do. 277, 2 : A., 185, ch. 199, 7.
अजाना, BA., 93, ch. 285, 2 : UT., 359, ch. 87, 5.

अजानी, BA., 42, ch. 127, 4 : A., 185, ch. 199, 6.

अजामिल, BA., 11, ch. 30, 7 : UT., 380, chh. 12, 2.

अजित, KI., 252, ch. 26, 12 : SU., 268, ch. 39, 2 : LN., 296, ch. 54, 5 : 320, ch. 107, 6.

अजिन,—°बसन, A., 186, do. 203, 1.

अजिर, BA., 38, ch. 113, 6 : 70, ch. 215, 5 : UT., 339, chh. 6, 3 : 355, do. 75, 2 ; ch. 76, 4.

अजीता, UT., 354, ch. 72, 5.

अजे, *see* अजय.

अजोध्या, UT., 339, ch. 28, 2.

अज्ञ, for words commencing thus, *see* under अग्य.

अञ्चल, BA., 104, chh. 34, 3 : 119, ch. 357, 3 : A., 204, ch. 263, 5 : LN., 278, ch. 7, 4. °वार, UT., 374, ch. 115, 8.

अञ्जन, BA., 2, ch. 2, 1.

अञ्जलि, BA., 110, chh. 52, 4 : A., 204, ch. 263, 5. °गत, BA., 3, do. 3, 2.

√ अटक,—अटकि, A., 165, ch. 138, 6.

अटन, A., 206, ch. 269, 7 : 216, ch. 299, 3.

अटन्ह, *see* अटा.

अटपट,—अटपटि, BA., 46, ch. 141, 6.
अटपटे, A., 153, so. 4, 1.

अटा,—अटन्ह, BA., 117, ch. 352, 4.

अटारी, BA., 74, ch. 225, 2 : UT., 339, ch. 28, 3.
अटारिन, BA., 101, ch. 308, 4.
अटारिन्ह, UT., 329, do. 4, 3 : 331, do. 9, 4.

अट्टहास, SU., 264, do. 25, 2 : LN., 291, ch. 39, 4 : 302, do. 69, 2.

अढ़ाई, A., 206, ch. 267, 6 : 216, ch. 300, 8.

अतुल, A., 169, ch. 150, 1 : 208, ch. 276, 3. °कलाप, UT., 357, do. 80, 4 : 362, ch. 92, 8. °कोप, SU., 262, ch. 21, 6 : UT., 357, ch. 81, 5. °बराया, UT., 356, ch. 80, 3.
अतुलित, A., 125, ch. 8, 8.

अतनु, BA., 84, ch. 257, 5.

अतर्क्य, BA., 42, ch. 128, 3.

अति, BA., 2, do. 2, 1 : 3, ch. 6, 2 : 4, ch. 12, 7 : 5, ch. 12, 11 ; 14, 1 : 6, do. 14, 1 ; 15, 1 ; 16, 2 ; ch. 17, 6, 12 : 7, do. 18, 1 ; 19, 3 : 8, ch. 22, 1 : 12, ch. 34, 1 : 13, do. 37, 2 : 14, ch. 44, 2 : 16, ch. 47, 3, 6, 8 ; do. 47, 2 : 17, ch. 55, 1 : 18, ch. 55, 6 ; 56, 5, 6 ; 58, 4 : 19, do. 60, 1 ; ch. 61, 1 ; so. 5, 1 : 20, ch. 62, 9 ; 63, 2 : 21, do. 63, 1 ; ch. 64, 2 ; 65, 5 : 23, ch. 70, 7 : 24, ch. 73, 8 : 27, ch. 84, 2 ; 86, 8 : 28, ch. 88, 5 ; ch. 90, 2 : 30, ch. 93, 7, 8 : 31, ch. 96, 2 ; chh. 6, 3 : 32, ch. 98, 2 : 33, ch. 102, 4, 8, 10 ; chh. 7, 1 ; so. 9, 2 : 34, ch. 103, 3 ; 104, 5 : 35, ch. 107, 2 ; chh. 13, 2 : 36, ch. 108, 3 : 37, ch. 110, 6 ; do. 110, 1 ; 111, 2 ; ch. 112, 1 : 38, ch. 113, 3 ; 114, 4 ; 115, 3 : 39, do. 116, 2 ; ch. 117, 3 ; 118, 3 ; 119, 3 : 40, ch. 122, 5 : 42, ch. 126, 5 : 44, ch. 132, 1, 2 7 ; 133, 1 ; 134, 6 : 45, ch. 135, 8 : 46, ch. 139, 1, 5 ; 140, 6 ; 141, 5 : 47, ch. 142, 5, 8 ; 143, 6 ; 144, 3 : 48, ch. 145, 2 ; 146, 2 : 49, ch. 148, 10 ; do. 148, 2 : 51, do. 153, 1 ; ch. 154, 4 ; 155, 4 : 52, ch. 156, 1 ; do. 157, 2 ; 53, ch. 161, 6, 8 ; 162, 3 ; 54, ch. 163, 4 : 55, ch. 167, 4, 8 ; 168, 4 ; so. 20, 2 : 56, ch. 170, 8 ; ch. 171, 2 : 57, ch. 173, 1 ; ch. 174, 2, 4, 5 : 58, ch. 175, 6 ; 176, 2 ; 178, 4 : 59, do. 178, 2 : 60, ch. 182, 5, 8 ; do. 182, 1 : 61, do. 188, 1 : 62, do. 191, 2 ; ch. 192, 1 : 63, ch. 193, 9 : 64, so. 21, 2 : 65, chh. 21, 3 : 66, ch. 201, 7 ; 203, 2 : 67, chh. 27, 2 : 68, ch. 207, 7 ; 208, 3 : 69, ch. 211, 5, 7, 9 : 70, ch. 214, 3 ; 215, 1 : 71, ch. 216, 1, 7 ; 218, 3 : 72, ch. 219, 3, 4 ; do. 219, 2 ; ch. 220, 1, 6, 9 : 73, chh. 28, 3 ; 29, 2 ; 30, 1 ; 31, 4 : 74, ch. 225, 7 : 75, ch. 228, 5 : 76, ch. 231, 2, 5 : 77, ch. 234, 8 ; 235, 1 ; 236, 2 ; do. 236, 2 : 78, do. 237, 1 : 79, ch. 241, 3, 7 : 80, ch. 246, 4 : 84, ch. 257, 5 : 86, do. 261, 1 ; ch. 264, 5 : 87, ch. 267, 3, 8 : 88, ch. 268, 8, 271, 5 : 89, ch. 272, 3 : 90, ch. 273, 8 : 91, do. 277, 1 ; ch. 278, 3, 5 : 92, ch. 280, 6 ; do. 280, 2 : 94, ch. 286, 3, 5 ; 287, 1 : 95, ch. 291, 2, 7 : 96, ch. 293, 3 ; 294, 1 : 97, do. 295, 2 ; ch. 298, 8 : 98, ch. 302, 1 : 99, ch. 303, 4, 5 ; 304, 8 : 101, ch. 308, 5, 8 : 102, ch. 313, 2, 7 ; 314, 4 : 104, ch. 319, 6 : 105, ch. 323, 2 ; chh. 35, 1 : 106, chh. 36, 1 : 107, ch. 326, 1 ; 327, 7 : 108, do. 329, 1 : 111, chh. 57,

ch. 7, 11. °वीस, LN., 320, do. 107, 2. °चमेचक, BA., 114, ch. 340, 6. °चरिक्रया, *see* अतिचरिक्रिया. °चरिक्रिया, UT., 380 ch. 126, 4.
अतिथि, A., 123, ch. 3, 2.

अतिकाय, BA., 60, do. 185, 1 : LN., 298, ch. 59, 29. अतिकाया, LN., 293, ch. 45, 10.

अतिथि, BA., 13, ch. 40, 8 : A., 160, ch. 121, 3 : A., 186, ch. 206, 2 : 186, do. 204, 1 : 206, do. 268, 2. °प्रियमत, A., 174, ch. 166, 5.

अतिसय, BA., 9, ch. 22, 25 : 64, ch. 197, 12 : 73, chh. 28, 4 : 79, ch. 243, 6 : 85, ch. 260, 5 : A., 213, ch. 290, 12 : AR., 224, ch. 3, 27 : 225, ch. 7, 14 : 228, ch. 12, 5 : 238, ch. 31, 7 : KI., 244, ch. 4, 6 : 247, ch. 9, 9 : 250, ch. 21, 2 : 251, ch. 24, 3 : SU., 261, ch. 17, 7 : 271, ch. 49, 1 : LN., 294, ch. 49, 4 : 303, ch. 72, 6 : 308, ch. 83, 6 : 324, ch. 116, 1 : UT., 344, ch. 43, 6 : 355, do. 75, 3.

अतीवा, A., 194, ch. 229, 5.

अतुल, BA., 52, ch. 157, 6 : KI., 289, ch. 35, 10 : 290, ch. 37, 6 : UT., 341, ch. 34, 2. °बल, BA., 60 do. 183, 2 : 98, ch. 301, 3 : SU., 267, do. 34, 2 : KI., 282, ch. 18, 4 : LN., 289, ch. 35, 8 : 301, chh. 3, 1 : 307, chh. 8, 2. °बलवीर्य, KI., 243, ch. 1, 2.

अतुलित, BA., 84, ch. 258, 2 : A., 186, ch. 206, 2 : SU., 262, ch. 19, 3 : LN., 322, chh. 38, 3. °बल, BA., 66, ch. 200, 3 : 72, ch. 227, 8 : AR., 222, ch. 2, 12 : 239, ch. 32, 1 : SU., 273, ch. 55, 2. °बलं, LN., 322, chh. 38, 3. °बलप्रताप, AR., 232, ch. 18, 7 : UT., 378, ch. 121, 2. °बलधामो, SU., 262, ch. 21, 9. °बलो, LN., 304, ch. 75, 8. °भुजप्रताप, AR., 226, ch. 8, 15.

अत्रि, A., 162, ch. 127, 7 : 215, do. 297, 1 ; ch. 298, 3 ; do. 298, 2 : AR., 222, ch. 2, 18, 19 : UT., 351, ch. 66, 8. °बहुसासन, A., 215, ch. 298, 1. °बाचक, A., 215, ch. 296, 5. °सुबचावल, A., 216, ch. 299, 2. °तीच, A., 162, ch. 127, 5. °मुनि, A., 215, ch. 298, 2.

✓ **अंथव,**—अथरवि, A., 185, ch. 201, 2.
अंथवंच, A., 169, ch. 150, 6.
अंथवे, A., 169, ch. 148, 3.
अंथव, A., 214, ch. 293, 7.

अथवा, BA., 5, ch. 12, 11 : 56, ch. 170, 3 : UT., 379, do. 125, 1.

अथाई, A., 126, ch. 12, 3.

अद्भुत, LN., 293, ch. 46, 7. *See* अद्भुत.

अदर्भ, UT., 354, ch. 72, 5.

अदाया, LN., 281, ch. 17, 3.

अदिति, BA., 13, ch. 39, 14 : 43, ch. 130, 3 : 65, ch. 199, 3.

अदिन, A., 177, ch. 174, 7.

अद्रस्य, *see* अद्रिस्य.

अदेय, BA., 51, ch. 154, 8 : AR., 241, ch. 37, 5.

अदोखा, A., 220, ch. 313, 6.

अद्भुत, BA., 17, ch. 52, 2 : 67, chh. 20, 3 : 70, do. 213, 1 : A., 210, ch. 283, 3 : AR., 235, ch. 25, 22 : UT., 357, do. 80, 2. °करनी, BA., 65, chh. 20, 3. °रूप, BA., 67, chh. 24, 2. *See* अदद्भुत.

अद्रिस्य, BA., 66, do. 201, 1.

अद्वैत, UT., 334, chh. 5, 21 : 370, ch. 108, 3.

अघ,—°गो, LN., 281, ch. 16, 8. °गनि, UT., 367, ch. 104, 8.

अधन, BA., 54, ch. 166, 4.

अधम, BA., 9, ch. 22, 20 : 40, do. 122, 1 : 43, ch. 128, 6 : A., 166, ch. 139, 4 : 176, do. 171, 2 : 185, ch. 199, 7 : 191, do. 219, 2 : AR., 223, ch. 3, 15 : 235, ch. 25, 8 : 237, ch. 28, 2 : 238, ch. 30, 2, 3 : KI., 247, ch. 9, 10 : 11, 4 : SU., 258, do. 7, 1 : ch. 9, 9 : 263, ch. 24, 3 : LN., 285, ch. 24, 11 : 26, 1 : 287, ch. 30, 6 : 31, 7 : 288, so. 4, 4 : 302, do. 68, 1 : 303, ch. 71, 5 : 315, ch. 97, 8 : 320, ch. 107, 10 : 326, chh. 40, 5 : UT., 327, ch. 2, 8 : 343, do. 41, 1 : 366, ch. 103, 6 : 367, ch. 103, 13 : 104, 1 : 376, ch. 118, 20. °सुभाव, SU., 271, ch. 47. 7. अधमाधम, UT., 367, ch. 104, 8.

अधमाई, A., 186, ch. 203, 2 : UT., 343, ch. 42, 1.

अधमारे, SU., 261, ch. 18, 6.

अधमो, AR., 236, ch. 27, 6.

अधर, BA., 47, ch. 143, 2 : 50, ch. 152, 2 : 69, ch. 211, 8 : 83, ch. 254, 4 : A., 135, ch. 40, 1 : 166, ch. 140, 4 : LN., 281, ch. 16, 5 : 287, ch. 31, 6 : UT., 355, ch. 77, 3. °रुचि, A., 128, do. 17, 1.

अधर्म, AR., 238, chh. 10, 3 : UT., 366, ch. 101, 6. °रत, UT., 363, do. 93, 4.

अधार, A., 167, ch. 144, 1 : 217, ch. 304, 2 : LN., 326, do. 118, 4 : UT., 365, ch. 100, 5 : 373, ch. 114, 15.

अधारा BA., 10, ch. 26, 7 : A., 130, ch. 24, 2 : SU., 272, ch. 51, 4 : LN., 298, ch. 59, 14 : UT., 327, ch. 2, 1.

अँधिआरी, *see* अँधियारा.

अधिक, BA., 6, ch. 17, 8 : 22, do. 66, 2 ; 68, 1 : 34, ch. 104, 7 : 38, ch. 115, 5 : 45, do. 136, 2 : 55, ch. 166, 7 : 60, ch. 182, 8 ; do. 184, 2 ; ch. 185, 6 : 69, ch. 210, 6 : 75, ch. 229, 5 : 78, ch. 240, 6 : 80, ch. 244, 6 : 85, do. 260, 2 : 95, ch. 292, 1 : 97, ch. 299, 1 : 98, ch. 302, 6 : 121, ch. 365, 8 ; do. 365, 2 : A., 127, ch. 16, 8 : 141, ch. 60, 5 : 161, ch. 124, 8 : 185, ch. 200, 7 ; 201, 8 : 195, do. 234, 1 : 199, ch. 245, 5 ; 246, 8 : 200, ch. 250, 4 : 201, ch. 254, 7 : 206, ch. 268, 4 : AR., 238, ch. 31, 3 ; 241, ch. 37, 7 : 242, ch. 41, 1 : KI., 254, so. 1, 1 : SU., 267, ch. 36, 4 : LN., 305, ch. 77, 2 : UT., 331, ch. 9, 8 : 335, ch. 17, 8 : 357, ch. 80, 4 : 358, ch. 84, 3 : 359, 86, 4 : 373, ch. 114, 6 : 375, ch. 117, 16. °रथ, BA., 53, ch. 161, 1.

अधिका, AR., 241, ch. 37, 8.

अधिकाइ, BA., 34, do. 102, 2.

अधिकाई, BA., 6, ch. 16, 2 : 22, ch. 68, 4 : 34, ch. 103, 1 : 45, ch. 136, 7 : 46, ch. 141, 1 : 53, ch. 160, 7 : 57, ch. 174, 2 : 60, ch. 185, 2 : 100, ch. 306, 7 : 113, ch. 338, 3 : A., 182, ch. 192, 2 : 188, ch. 211, 2 : 212, ch. 289, 5 : 213, ch. 291, 8 : KI., 251, ch. 22, 4 : SU., 256, ch. 3, 9 : 268, ch. 37, LN., 296, ch. 56, 6 : UT., 338, ch. 26, 1 : 341, ch. 34, 1 : 342, ch. 38, 3 : 362, ch. 93, 7 : 366, ch. 102, 8 : 369, ch. 107, 16 : 379, ch. 125, 2.

अधिका(य),—अधिकाति, BA., 121, do. 365, 2.

अधिकान, A., 138, do. 50, 2.

अधिकार, BA., 23, ch. 70, 7.

अधिकारी, BA., 12, ch. 37, 4 : 15, ch. 47, 2 : 19, ch. 59, 4 : 39, ch. 118, 1, 2 : 63, ch. 195, 10 : 122, chh. 62, 1 : A., 144, ch. 70, 6 ; 71, 2 : 161, ch. 122, 13 : 164, ch. 134, 2 : SU., 275, ch. 59, 6 : LN., 320, ch. 107, 11 : UT., 337, ch. 22, 4 : 344, ch. 43, 8 : 370, ch. 108, 2 : 379, ch. 125, 6, 7.

अधिप, BA., 43, ch. 130, 7.

अँधियारा,—अँधियारी, AR., 241, ch. 39, 7.

अँधियारे, A., 167, ch. 142, 5.

अँधियारा, BA., 54, ch. 163, 8 : LN., 293, ch. 45, 11 : 295, ch. 51, 4.

अँधियारी, BA., 68, ch. 207, 5 : A., 148, ch. 81, 5 : SU., 271, ch. 47, 3.

अधीन, A., 201, ch. 253, 5. Cf. आधीन.

अधीना, BA., 52, ch. 156, 6.

अधीने, BA., 96, ch. 294, 7.

अधीर, A., 180, do. 184, 2 : UT., 355, do. 74, 1.

अधीरा, BA., 73, chh. 28, 3 : A., 144, ch. 69, 2 : 194, ch. 231, 8 : LN., 305, ch. 77, 1.

अनअधिकारी, BA., 39, ch. 118, 1.

अनअहिवात, A., 130, ch. 26, 7.

अनइच्छित, UT., 374, ch. 116, 4.

अनइस, A., 171, ch. 157, 6.

अनखटतुहिं, *see* अनरितुहिं.

अनख, BA., 11, ch. 32, 1 : 61, ch. 187, 11 : AR., 236, ch. 26, 15.

अनघ, BA., 10, ch. 26, 6 : 42, so. 12, 2 : AR., 242, ch. 40, 7 : LN., 320, ch. 107, 6 : UT., 341, ch. 35, 2 : 345, ch. 47, 6.

अनङ्ग, BA., 31, do. 96, 1 : AR., 237, chh. 9, 12 : LN., 317, chh. 31, 4 : UT., 332, ch. 12, 8. °बराती, BA., 39, ch. 116, 7.

अनजानत, BA., 95, ch. 290, 4.

अनट, A., 203, do. 259, 2.

अनत, BA., 6, ch. 16, 3 : 91, ch. 278, 2 : A., 192, ch. 224, 8 : UT., 350, ch. 61, 7. °अनमनरावं, AR., 237, chh. 9, 7.

अनन्त, BA., 14, do. 42, 1 : 40, ch. 122, 4 : 48, ch. 147, 5 : 49, ch. 149, 4 : LN., 302, ch. 70, 11 : 303, do. 72, 1 : 304, ch. 73, 7 ; 74, 4 : 319, do. 104, 2 : UT., 334, tot. 1, 12 : 341, ch. 35, 2 : 347, ch. 53, 3 : 361, ch. 89, 3. °उर, LN., 307, chh. 8, 1.

अनन्ता, BA., 48, ch. 147, 5 : 67 chh. 25, 1 : AR., 227, ch. 10, 12 : SU., 268, ch. 39, 2 : LN., 295, ch. 53, 4 : UT., 354, ch. 72, 4.

अनन्द, BA., 35, chh. 13, 3 : 70, ch. 215, 1 : 101, ch. 308, 5 : 113, ch. 338, 4 : 118, do. 355, 1 : A., 131, ch. 27, 2 : 155, do. 103, 1 : 160, do. 119, 2 : 189, ch. 215, 8 : UT., 327, do. 1, 5. °बधाए, BA., 16, ch. 49, 8. °बधाये, BA., 119, ch. 357, 6. °भरी, BA., 73, chh. 31, 4. Cf. आनन्द.

अनन्दा, BA., 18, ch. 56, 2 : 113, ch. 337, 5 : LN., 295, ch. 52, 8 : UT., 337, ch. 24, 3.

अनन्दु, A., 159, ch. 118, 1.

अनन्दे, BA., 35, ch. 107, 1 : 74, ch. 227, 2 : A., 195, ch. 233, 2.

अनन्दित, AR., 228, ch. 11, 3.

अनन्य, KI., 244, do. 3, 1. °गति, KI., 244, ch. 3, 8.

do. 61, 2 : 184, do. 197, 1 : 200, ch. 250, 1 : AR., 224, do. 3, 2 : SU., 266, do. 33, 1 : UT., 338, ch. 25, 3 : 378, do. 121, 2.

अनुकूला, BA., 8, ch. 21, 7 : 50, ch. 153, 2 : 94, ch. 288, 4 : 102, ch. 311, 8 : 106, ch. 325, 6 : A., 133, ch. 32, 8 ; 34, 4 : 139, ch. 52, 3 : 154, ch. 101, 1 : 197, ch. 240, 2 : 200, ch. 249, 3 : 202, ch. 257, 2 : 206, ch. 268, 3 : 212, ch. 289, 3 : AR., 228, ch. 13, 4 : 239, ch. 34, 4 : KI., 244, ch. 4, 1 : SU., 266, ch. 34, 2 : 271, ch. 47, 6 : LN., 297, ch. 58, 7.

अनुगामी, BA., 9, ch. 25, 1 : 95, ch. 289, 8 : 116, ch. 348, 5 : A., 191, ch. 218, 16 : 210, ch. 282, 4 : 217, ch. 302, 7.

अनुग्रह, BA., 1, so. 1, 2 : 7, ch. 19, 12 : 48, ch. 146, 4 : 51, ch. 156, 3 : 66, chh. 20, 4 : 73, chh. 30, 1 : A., 124, ch. 4, 7 : 139, ch. 52, 8 : 154, ch. 99, 7 : 168, ch. 146, 8 ; chh. 5, 1 : 181, ch. 188, 8 : 184, ch. 197, 2 : 202, do. 256, 1 : 212, ch. 289, 5 : SU., 258, ch. 7, 5 : UT., 344, ch. 45, 7 : 352, ch. 69, 10 : 368, do. 105, 8 ; ch. 106, 10.

अनुचर, BA., 94, ch. 286, 1 : A., 198, ch. 243, 5 : AR., 232, ch. 19, 1 : LN., 290, ch. 36, 4.

अनुचरन्ह, UT., 348, ch. 57, 4.

अनुचरी, SU., 258, ch. 9, 5.

अनुचित, BA., 23, ch. 72, 1 : 81, ch. 249, 3 : 86, ch. 263, 2 : 87, ch. 268, 3 : 92, do. 281, 1 : 93, ch. 284, 8 ; 285, 3 : 94, do. 285, 2 ; ch. 286, 4 : 96, ch. 293, 6 : A., 126, ch. 11, 7 : 136, ch. 45, 6 : 152, ch. 94, 4 ; 95, 8 ; 175, do. 168, 1 : ch. 169, 5 : 176, ch. 170, 12 : 177, ch. 173, 7 : 191, ch. 220, 7 : 192, ch. 222, 3 : 207, ch. 272, 7 : 211, ch. 286, 6 : 214, ch. 294, 7 : LN., 318, ch. 101, 12.

अनुज, BA., 71, ch. 217, 4 : 72, ch. 219, 10 : 73, ch. 222, 5 : 74, ch. 224, 2, 6 : 79, do. 242, 2 ; 243, 1 : 94, ch. 287, 7 : A., 151, ch. 92, 4 : 154, do. 101, 2 : 219, ch. 309, 4 : AR., 224, ch. 4, 2, 8 : 225, do. 5, 1 ; ch. 7, 5 : 226, ch. 7, 20 ; 8, 18 : 227, do. 8, 1 ; ch. 9, 8 ; 10, 10 : 229, ch. 14, 20 : 230, ch. 15, 10 : 232, ch. 18, 10 : 234, chh. 8, 2 : 236, ch. 26, 4, 5 : 240, ch. 36, 2, 4 : KI., 244, ch. 4, 7 : 248, ch. 13, 3, 7 : SU., 260 ch. 14, 3, 9 : 265, ch. 31, 3 : 269, ch. 40, 2 ; 41, 6 : 270, ch. 46, 3 : 273, ch. 54, 2 : 274, do. 56, 3 : LN., 284, ch. 23, 2, 3 : 296, ch. 54, 6 : 297, ch. 58, 9 ; 59, 2 : 299, ch. 61, 4 : 300, do. 64, 1 : 310, ch. 86, 8 : 318, ch. 103, 1, 4 : 319, ch. 104, 6 : 321, ch. 109, 2 ; do. 109, 1 : 322, chh. 37, 15 : 323, chh. 39, 3 : 324, ch. 114, 8 : UT., 328, ch. 3, 5 : 329, do. 4, 1 ; ch. 6, 3 : 330, ch. 7, 1, 2 : 333, chh. 4, 3 : 335, ch. 17, 6 : 336, ch. 20, 1 : 356, ch. 79, 5. °सिवा, KI., 253, ch. 28, 1. °बल, UT., 327, do. 1, 6. °प्रीति, LN., 323, do. 113, 6. °बधू, KI., 247, ch. 9, 7. °जब, BA., 75, ch. 230, 3.

अनुजन्ह, UT., 338, ch. 27, 3.

अनुजहि, BA., 71, ch. 217, 6 : 77, ch. 237, 3 : A., 149, ch. 85, 6 : 165, ch. 137, 1 : KI., 250, do. 18, 1 : UT., 330, chh. 2, 3.

अनुजहिं, A., 155, ch. 103, 3 : AR., 236, ch. 26, 1 : KI., 247, ch. 11, 9 : LN., 318, ch. 102, 5 : UT., 330, chh. 2, 2.

अनुजा, UT., 365, 99, 5.

अनुदिन, A., 184, ch. 197, 2.

अनुपम, BA., 16, do. 48, 2 : 62, do. 192, 1 : 67, ch. 205, 8 : 122, chh. 62, 2 : AR., 224, chh. 2, 3 : 228, ch. 13, 4 : UT., 341, ch. 35, 4. *See* अनूपम.

अनुभव, A., 239, ch. 34, 5 : UT., 360, ch. 88, 13. °गम्य, AR., 227, ch. 10, 12 : UT., 334, chh. 5, 21 : 370, ch. 108, 4.

✓ **अनुभव,**—अनुभवनि, BA., 83, ch. 253, 7.

अनुभवहिं, BA., 10, ch. 26, 2.

अनुभवहीं, A., 155, ch. 105, 4.

अनुमान, BA., 22, do. 67, 1 : KI., 246, ch. 7, 5 : UT., 358, ch. 84, 3 : 370, do. 108, 2.

अनुमाना, BA., 43, ch. 128, 4 : AR., 236, ch. 25, 12 : KI., 251, ch. 24, 4.

✓ **अनुमान,**—अनुमाना, BA., 20, ch. 62, 13 : 64, chh. 19, 8 : A., 149, ch. 87, 4 : 202, ch. 256, 6 : AR., 222, ch. 2, 16 : 233, ch. 22, 3 : LN., 283, ch. 19, 6 : 294, ch. 48, 4 : 295, ch. 53, 6.

अनुमानि, BA., 51, do. 153, 2 : A., 171, ch. 155, 4 : 176, ch. 171, 2 : SU., 270, do. 43, 1 : LN., 297, do. 57, 1.

अनुमानी, BA., 38, ch. 115, 5 : 53, ch. 162, 3 : 58, ch. 176, 3 : 60, ch. 184, 6 : 68, ch. 207, 4 : 116, ch. 346, 7 : 121, ch. 365, 2 : A., 136, ch. 45, 4 : 186, ch. 206, 1.

अनुमाने, BA., 26, ch. 79, 3.

अनुमोदन, UT., 380, ch. 126, 6.

अनुराग, BA., 2, do. 2, 1 : 4, ch. 7, 9 : 6, do. 16, 2 : 49, do. 148, 1 : 53, do. 159, 2 : 122, chh. 62, 3 ; so. 31, 1 : A., 183, do. 195, 2 : 184, ch. 197, 7 : 187, ch. 208, 7 : 196, ch. 236, 5 ; do. 237, 1 : 199, do. 245, 2 : 200, ch. 249, 1 : 202, do. 255, 2 : 206, do. 269, 2 : LN., 298, ch. 59, 5 : UT., 350, do. 62, 2 : 351, ch. 65, 7 : 353, do. 69, 1 : 359, do. 85, 4 : 362, do. 92, 2 : 369, do. 107, 2. °वचन A., 198, chh. 10, 1.

अनुरागा, BA., 7, ch. 1, 1 : 3, ch. 6, 2 : 17, ch. 55, 1 : 24, ch. 75, 5 : 24, ch. 76, 2 : 27, ch. 84, 3 : 31, ch. 95, 16 : 44, ch. 132, 3 : 55, ch. 168, 4 : 73, chh. 30, 4 : 75, ch. 228, 5 : 78, ch. 240, 6 : 87, ch. 265, 4 : 113, ch. 338, 2 : A., 146, ch. 75, 2 : 76, 5 : 151, ch. 91, 5 : 153, ch. 98, 15 : 155, ch. 103, 4 : 158, ch. 116, 5 : 164, ch. 135, 4 : 180, ch. 186, 7 : 185, ch. 200, 5 : 202, 8 : 195, ch. 233, 3 : 235, 5 : 206, ch. 268, 2 : 217, ch. 305, 5 : AR., 225, ch. 7, 7 : 228, ch. 13, 7 : UT., 332, ch. 13, 1 : 348, ch. 58, 4 : 350, ch. 63, 1 : 351, ch. 64, 8 : 362, ch. 93, 1.

अनुरागु, BA., 59, do. 181, 3 : UT., 368 do. 105, 1.

अनुरागू, A., 181, ch. 190, 2 : 187, ch. 208, 5 : 200, ch. 249, 6 : 208, ch. 275, 5 : 212, ch. 289, 4.

अनुरागे, BA., 84, ch. 256, 7 : 98, ch. 301, 7 : 99, ch. 303, 4 : 102, ch. 313, 2 : 105, ch. 320, 4 ; 323, 2 : 107, ch. 326, 4 : 109, ch. 330, 8 : 112, ch. 335, 1 : 118, ch. 353, 3 : 119, ch. 359, 1 : 121, ch. 365, 4 ; 366, 5 : A., 157, ch. 110, 7 : 163, ch. 130, 5 : 173, ch. 162, 5 : 176, ch. 173, 1 : 179, ch. 181, 3 : 194, ch. 229, 7 ; 230, 4 : 195, ch. 234, 3 : 198, ch. 242, 8 : 204, ch. 264, 7 : 205, ch. 265, 6 : 206, ch. 268, 7 : 210, ch. 281, 1 : 215, ch. 297, 5 : UT., 335, so. 18, 2.

अनुराग,—अनुरागउँ, KI., 247, chh. 1, 6. Cf. अनुरागेउँ.

अनुरागवौं, UT., 334, chh. 5, 24.

अनुरागहू, AR., 238, chh. 10, 4.

अनुरागौं, BA., 117, ch. 351, 2 : A., 125, ch. 9, 2.

अनुरागेउँ, UT., 358, ch. 84, 3. Cf. अनुरागउँ.

अनुरागी, BA., 8, ch. 21, 11 : 40, ch. 120, 8 : 43, ch. 130, 2 : 65, chh. 21, 3 : 76, ch. 232, 4 : 84, ch. 257, 2 : 114, ch. 342, 1 : 118, ch. 354, 8 : A., 200, ch. 249, 5 : 220, ch. 312, 8 : AR., 237, ch. 28, 3 : KI., 251, ch. 23, 7 : 252, ch. 26, 13 : SU., 258, ch. 6, 8 : UT., 327, ch. 2, 3 : 346, ch. 51, 8 : 366, ch. 103, 4.

अनुरूप, BA., 21, do. 64, 2 : 78, ch. 240, 6 : 83, do. 252, 1 : 110, chh. 51, 1 : 119, ch. 359, 6 ; AR., 221, ch. 1, 1 : 229, ch. 14, 9 : SU., 268, ch. 38, 4 : LN., 316, do. 98, 2 : UT., 354, do. 72, 2.

अनुरूपा, BA., 26, ch. 81, 3 : 33, ch. 101, 8 : 68, ch. 209, 4 : UT., 377, ch. 120, 1.

अनुरोध,—अनुरोधू, A., 139, ch. 54, 4.

अनुसर,—अनुसर, A., 165, ch. 136, 6.

अनुसरई, BA., 57, ch. 172, 6 : A., 174, ch. 166, 8 : 195, ch. 232, 3 : UT., 338, ch. 25, 6.

अनुसरउँ, UT., 369, ch. 107, 1.

अनुसरवौं, BA., 3, ch. 3, 10 : 71, ch. 217, 4.

अनुसरहू, A., 175, ch. 170, 6.

अनुसरेहू, BA., 114, ch. 340, 5 : UT., 335, ch. 21, 2.

अनुसरै, LN., 320, ch. 107, 12.

अनुसार, BA., 10, do. 27, 2 : 42, so. 13, 2 : A., 215, ch. 297, 5.

अनुसारा, BA., 13, ch. 39, 1 : 49, ch. 147, 14 : A., 188, ch. 211, 5 : 214, ch. 293, 4 : LN., 282, ch. 8, 4.

अनुसारी, A., 128, ch. 17, 8 : 136, ch. 45, 5 : 198, ch. 244, 4 : LN., 297, ch. 59, 1 : 318, ch. 103, 6 : UT., 341, ch. 35, 1 : 352, ch. 69, 9 : 359, ch. 86, 5.

अनुसासन, BA., 33, ch. 102, 5 : 52, ch. 156, 8 : 77, ch. 237, 4 : 86, ch. 263, 4 : 109, ch. 331, 10 : 119, ch. 358, 1 : A., 182, do. 180, 1 : 199, ch. 247, 6 : 215, do. 295, 1 ; ch. 298, 1 : SU., 268, ch. 38, 3 : LN., 303, ch. 72, 11 : 320, ch. 107, 1 : UT., 332, ch. 11, 5 ; 12, 7 : 344, ch. 44, 5.

अनुसुइया, AR., 223, ch. 3, 1.

अनुहर,—अनुहरर, A., 195, ch. 232, 4.

अनुहरइ, BA., 7, ch. 19, 12.

अनुहरत, BA., 76, ch. 231, 4 : A., 149, do. 85, 2 : 176, ch. 170, 15.

अनुहार,—अनुहार, BA., 33, ch. 102, 1.

अनुहारि, BA., 19, do. 58, 1 : 79, do. 242, 2 : 82, do. 251, 2.

अनुहारी, BA., 15, ch. 45, 2 : 77, ch. 236, 7 : 104, ch. 318, 6 : A., 146, ch. 75, 7 : 169, ch. 148, 4 : 190, ch. 218, 6 : 193, ch. 226, 4 : 199, ch. 247, 7 : 204 ch. 264, 3.

अनूप, BA., 15, ch. 46, 6 : 21, do. 64, 1 : 48, ch. 147, 4 : 59, do. 180, 1 : 71, do. 217, 2 : 74, ch. 225, 7 ; 226, 5 : 83, do. 252, 2 : 84, ch. 256, 15 : A., 157, ch. 111, 4 : 215, do. 297, 2 : 218, do. 305, 1 ; AR., 221, ch. 1, 1 : 237, chh. 9, 1 : LN., 321, chh. 36, 3 : UT., 333, chh. 5, 1 : 335, ch. 18, 5 : 340, chh. 8, 1. °रूपअनूपनि, AR., 223, chh. 1, 21.

अनूपा, BA., 10, ch. 26, 2 : 27, 1 : 26, ch. 81, 3 : 33, ch. 101, 8 : 48, ch. 147, 10 : 49, ch. 148, 1 : 149, 5 : 51, ch. 153, 6 : 58, ch. 176, 1 : 67, chh. 27, 2 : 68, ch. 209, 4 : 104, ch. 318, 7 : 109, ch. 331, 4 : 112, ch. 334, 2 : A., 151, ch. 91, 7 : 185, ch. 202, 1 : AR., 227, ch. 9, 5 : 230, ch. 15, 18 : 236, ch. 27a, 1 : 238, ch. 31, 9 : KI., 248, ch. 13, 3 : 249, ch. 17, 3 : LN., 281, ch. 14, 7 : 310, ch. 86, 8 : UT., 351, ch. 67, 3 : 357, ch. 81, 5 : 370, ch. 108, 4, 12 : 373, ch. 113, 2 : 377, ch. 120, 1.

अनुपम, BA., 9, ch. 23, 2 : 11, ch. 30, 5 : 17, ch. 51, 7 : UT., 361, ch. 91, 8. *See* अनूपम.

अनुपान, UT., 377, ch. 119, 7.

अनेक, BA., 5, ch. 13, 9 : 11, ch. 29, 2 : 14, ch. 42, 7 : 15, ch. 46, 15 : 21, ch. 65, 2 : 23, ch. 72, 7 : 26, ch. 80, 6 : 27, ch. 85, 1 : 29, ch. 91, 4 : 35, ch. 107, 4 : 42, ch. 126, 8 : 52, ch. 158, 6 : 68, ch. 209, 4 : 92, ch. 282, 6 : 97, ch. 296, 7; 297, 2 : 100, ch. 307, 3 : 102, ch. 312, 1, 3 : 106, do. 323, 1 : 110, ch. 332, 5 : 112, ch. 335, 2 : 113, ch. 339, 5 : 118, ch. 355, 5 : 120, do. 360, 2 ; ch. 363, 1 : A., 144, do. 68, 1 : 151, ch. 91, 2 : 152, ch. 97, 9 : 156, do. 107, 1 ; ch. 108, 3 : 169, ch. 150, 1, 4 : do. 150, 1 : 172, ch. 161, 2 : 174, ch. 164, 3 : 201, ch. 253, 3 : 206, do. 267, 1 : AR., 227, ch. 10, 6 : 231, chh. 6, 1 : 237, chh. 9, 10 : 239, ch. 32, 2 : LN., 284, do. 23, 12 : 286, ch. 28, 2 : 287, do. 31, 3 : 299, do. 60, 2 : 311, chh. 17, 1 : 315, chh. 24, 2 : 316, chh. 27, 2, 7 : 321, chh. 36, 3 : 322, chh. 38, 2 : 324, do. 114, 2 : UT., 332, do. 11, 2 : 333, chh. 5, 18 : 337, ch. 23, 2 : 338, ch. 25, 1 : 339, chh. 7, 3 : 340, chh. 8, 3 : 341, ch. 35, 2, 6 : 344, do. 42, 1 : 349, ch. 58, 7 : 354, do. 72, 3 : 356, ch. 78, 7 : 357, do. 80, 4 ; ch. 81, 5 : 364, do. 97, 4 : 374, ch. 115, 6 : do. 115, 4.

अनेका, BA., 17, ch. 50, 2 : 21, ch. 64, 7 : 39, ch. 119, 3 : 41, ch. 123, 5 : 43, ch. 129, 2 : 55, ch. 168, 5 : 59, ch. 180, 7 : 98, ch. 300, 4 : A., 125, ch. 7, 4 : 206, ch. 267, 3 : AR., 241, ch. 37, 7 : KI., 248, ch. 13, 7 : 15, 2 : LN., 313, ch. 93, 1 : UT., 332, ch. 11, 7 : 340, ch. 32, 8 : 345, ch. 46, 3 : 346, ch. 50, 3 : 348, ch. 58, 2 : 352, ch. 69, 6 : 357, ch. 80, 4 : 82, 1 : 376, ch. 118, 37.

अनैसे, BA., 94, ch. 287, 7.

अन्त, BA., 4, ch. 8, 6 : 41, ch. 125, 4 : 71, ch. 215, 8 : A., 129, ch. 23, 3 : 134, ch. 36, 8 : 171, ch. 155, 3 : KI., 247, do. 9, 2 : ch. 10, 3 : LN., 293, do. 44, 1 : 302, ch. 69, 1 : UT., 330, chh. 3, 2 : 344, ch. 45, 1. °काल, UT., 335, ch. 16, 4.

अन्तहु, BA., 85, ch. 259, 5 : A., 133, ch. 35, 4 : 140, ch. 55, 4 : 166, ch. 139, 4.

अन्तहुँ, A., 177, ch. 175, 4 : 185, ch. 199, 6.

अन्ता UT., 345, ch. 46, 6 : 361, ch. 89, 5.

अन्तर, BA., 26, ch. 80, 2 : 51, ch. 155, 6 : A., 199, do. 247, 1 : AR., 234, ch. 23, 17 : SU., 274, ch. 58, 6 : LN., 278, ch. 7, 6 : 292, ch. 43, 1 : 3'1, ch. 89, 2 : 315, do. 97, 2 : 319, ch. 105, 14 : 323, chh. 39, 8 : UT., 342, ch. 37, 7 : 346, ch. 50, 6 : 372, ch. 112, 11, 4 : 375, ch. 117, 2. °जामी, BA., 20, ch. 62, 5 : 63, 3 : 31, ch. 97, 8 : 38, ch. 113, 5 : 42, ch. 126, 2 : 51, ch. 154, 7 : A., 143, ch. 65, 8 : 144, ch. 71, 6 : 183, so. 7, 1 : 186, ch. 203, 3 : 199, do. 246, 1 : 202, ch. 256, 5 : 257, 1 : 212, ch. 287, 1 : AR., 224, ch. 3, 28 : 225, ch. 6, 7 : 226, ch. 8, 19 : 239, ch. 34, 1 : 240, ch. 37, 2 : SU., 271, ch. 49, 5 : UT., 342, ch. 37, 4 : 358, ch. 84, 8. °धाना, LN., 304, ch. 73, 12. °धान, LN., 313, ch. 93, 1 : UT., 332, do. 14, 2. °हित, BA., 46, ch. 140, 2 : 119, ch. 357, 3. अन्तर्यामि, BA., 28, ch. 87, 7 : 48, do. 145, 1 : 52, ch. 156, 14.

अन्तावरि, LN., 306, chh. 6, 5.

अन्तचारी, AR., 231, chh. 7, 5.

अन्देसा, BA., 7, ch. 19, 10.

अन्ध, BA., 30, ch. 95, 5 : 41, ch. 123, 1 : 84, ch. 256, 5 : A., 145, ch. 72, 3 : 210, ch. 282, 8 : AR., 223, ch. 3, 8 : LN., 288, so. 4, 2 : UT., 353, ch. 70, 7 : 364, ch. 96, 6. °कार, UT., 377, ch. 119, 18.

अन्धरि, BA., 118, ch. 355, 7.

अन्धौ, LN., 283 do. 21, 2.

अन्न, BA., 36, ch. 109, 8 : 57, ch. 172, 6 : 58, ch. 177, 6 : A., 174, do. 164, 1 : AR., 234, ch. 24, 8 : UT., 365, chh. 10, 10. °दान, LN., 285, ch. 26, 6.

अन्यथा, BA., 26, ch. 81, 8 : 31, ch. 97, 2 : 45, ch. 135, 1 : 59, do. 178, 2 : UT., 377, s'lo. 5, 1.

अन्स (अंस), BA., 49, ch. 149, 6 : 51, ch. 153, 3 : UT., 373, ch. 114, 2.

अन्सन, (अंसन), BA., 52, ch. 156, 10 : 65, ch. 199, 2.

अन्सिक (अंसिक), LN., 322, ch. 111, 8.

√ **अन्हवाव,**—अन्हवार, BA., 17, do. 52, 1.

अन्हवाई, A., 151, ch. 92, 7.

अन्हवाए, UT., 332, ch. 12, 3, 5.

अन्हवाये, BA., 70, ch. 213, 1 : 114, ch. 342, 3 : 119, ch. 358, 3 : A., 196, ch. 236, 5 : AR., 222, ch. 2, 20.

अन्हवावैं, BA., 6, ch. 16, 5.

अन्हवावा, A., 173, ch. 164, 1.

अन्हवावहु, UT., 332, ch. 12, 2.

√ **अन्हाव,**—अन्हार, A., 155, ch. 103, 6 : do. 105, 1 : 160, ch. 120, 4 : 189, ch. 213, 4 : 198, ch. 243, 8.

अन्हात, A., 185, ch. 200, 5.

अन्हान, A., 204, ch. 263, 3.

अन्हाने, BA., 82, ch. 250, 7 : A., 156, do. 106. 2 : 162, do. 127, 2 : 184, ch. 196, 4 : 190, ch. 218, 8.

अन्हाये, BA., 74, ch. 224, 4 : A., 151, ch. 92, 3 : 184, ch. 186, 3 : 192, ch. 224, 4 : 196, ch. 238, 7 : 205, ch. 266, 14 .

अन्हाएँ, A., 197, ch. 240, 3.

अन्हाहु, A., 139, ch. 52, 1.

अपकार, BA., 47, ch. 144, 8.

अपकारा, LN., 285, ch. 24, 6.

अपकारी,—°कार, UT., 363, so. 10, 1.

अपकीरति, BA., 92, ch. 281, 7.

अपछरा, LN., 280, ch. 11, 9 : 297, ch. 57, 3. °न्हि, UT., 333, chh. 4, 2. Cf. अछरा.

अपजस, BA., 4, do. 9, 2 : 34, chh. 10, 4 : A., 132, ch. 30, 5 : 142, ch. 62, 5 : 151, ch. 93, 6 : 174, do. 165, 2 : 177, ch. 173, 4. LN., 298, ch. 59, 12. °भाजन, A., 172, ch. 158, 5. °जाहू, A., 151, ch. 93, 7.

अपडर, BA., 12, ch. 34, 2 : A., 195, ch. 233, 6 : 202, ch. 257, 3.

√अपडर,—अपडरे, LN., 310, chh. 14, 1.

अपन, अपना, अपनि, अपने, *See* आप.

√अपना(य),—अपनाए, BA., 61, do. 186, 2.

अपनाइब, LN., 323, ch. 113, 7.

अपनाई, BA., 55, ch. 166, 7 : 116, ch. 347, 1 : A., 128, ch. 19, 6.

अपनाया, UT., 360, ch. 88, 11.

अपनाये, A., 212, ch. 288, 3.

अपनावा, SU., 272, ch. 50, 2.

अपनपौ, BA., 54, ch. 166, 2 : 80, ch. 246, 8.

अपबाद, UT., 343, do. 40, 1.

अपबादा, BA., 24, ch. 74, 3.

अपबादू, A., 146, ch. 75, 4.

अपबर्ग, BA., 105, ch. 321, 6 : A., 162, ch. 126, 7 : UT., 341, do. 34, 1 : 376, ch. 118, 10. °प्रद, SU., 257, do. 4, 1.

अपबर्गा, UT., 345, ch. 47, 7.

अपभय, BA., 96, ch. 293, 8.

अपमान, BA., 24, ch. 73, 5 ; do. 73, 1.

अपमानहि, LN., 287, ch. 30, 8.

अपमाना, BA., 22, ch. 69, 2 : 23, ch. 72, 3 : 24, ch. 73, 7 : 61, ch. 188, 2 : AR., 223, ch. 3, 9 : SU., 259, ch. 10, 1 : UT., 348, ch. 57, 3.

अपमाने, BA., 92, ch. 279, 6.

अपर, BA., 11, ch. 30, 7 : 18, do. 57, 1 : 31, ch. 97, 3 : 48, ch. 147, 9 : 52, do. 156, 2 ; ch. 157, 6 : 76, ch. 232, 8 : 77, ch. 235, 1, 3 ; ch. 236, 4 : 84, ch. 256, 5, 8 : 99, ch. 303, 2 : 100, ch. 307, 3 : AR., 227, ch. 9, 13 : 228, ch. 12, 4 : 241, do. 37, 2 : KI., 254, ch. 30, 7 : LN., 278, do. 5, 2 : 281, ch. 16, 1 : 298, ch. 59, 30 : 310, chh. 15, 4 : 317, ch. 100, 1 : 324, do. 115, 4 : UT., 353, ch. 71, 8 : 358, do. 83, 4.

अपराध, BA., 23, ch. 71, 7 : 35, chh. 12, 1 : 36, do. 109, 2 : 43, ch. 131, 7 : 48, ch. 146, 3 : 58, ch. 178, 5 : 95, ch. 290, 8 : 111, chh. 54, 2 : A., 136, ch. 43, 3 : 138, ch. 49, 6 : 146, do. 75, 1 : 188, ch. 210, 5, 6 : AR., 235, ch. 25, 1 : SU., 263, do. 22, 2 : 265, ch. 31, 4 : 274, ch. 57, 6 : LN., 283, ch. 20, 6.

अपराधा, BA., 22, ch. 68, 2 : A., 139, ch. 53, 7 : SU., 262, ch. 21, 3 : 266, ch. 31, 6.

अपराधू BA., 9, ch. 25, 3 : 93, ch. 283, 5 : A., 136, ch. 42, 7 : 176, ch. 170, 16 : 185, ch. 199, 7.

अपराधी, BA., 93, ch. 283, 6 : 94, ch. 287, 4 : A., 177, ch. 176, 3.

अपराधिन्ह, A., 200, ch. 250, 5.

अपर्णा, BA., 27, ch. 84, 7.

अपलोक, BA., 3, ch. 6, 7 : LN., 298, ch. 59, 13.

√अपहर,—अपहरई, KI., 249, ch. 17, 6 : UT., 349, ch. 60, 5.

अपहरन, A., 206, ch. 268, 1 : 220, chh. 13, 3.

अपहरयौं, BA., 100, ch. 306, 4.

अपान, BA., 80, do. 245, 2 : 107, chh. 40, 1 : 109, ch. 331, 6 : A., 194, do. 231, 2.

अपार, BA., 3, ch. 7, 1 : 7, do. 18, 1 : 10, do. 27, 1 : 13, ch. 40, 6 : 42, so. 13, 1 : 89, do. 272, 2 : 91, ch. 277, 8 : 113, ch. 339, 5 : 122, chh. 61, 2 : A., 161, so. 4, 2 : 218, do. 305, 1 : KI., 253, do. 28, 1 ; ch. 29, 3 : SU., 262, do. 19, 2 : LN., 297, do. 58, 3 : 309, do. 83, 1 : 310, do. 85, 2 : 311, do. 89, 1 : 318, chh. 33, 4 : 320, do. 106, 3 : 322, chh. 37, 5. °पुंज, LN., 321, chh. 36, 6.

अपारं, AR., 226, ch. 8, 12.

अपारा, BA., 5, ch. 13, 10 : 6, ch. 17, 10 : 14, ch. 42, 6 : 14, ch. 44, 4 : 18, ch. 57, 8 : 20, ch. 62, 4 : 22, ch. 68, 8 : 32, ch. 98, 4 : 39, ch. 118, 7 : 43, ch. 130, 6 : 50, ch. 150, 2 : 52, ch. 158, 3 : 58, ch. 178, 7 : 60, ch. 182, 6 : 63, ch. 193, 7 : 70, ch. 215, 4 : 87, ch. 266, 7 : 88, ch. 270, 8 : 102, ch. 312, 6 : A., 146, ch. 74, 14 : 152, ch. 96, 7 : 153, ch. 98, 11 : 155, ch. 106, 4 : 205, ch. 266, 3 : AR., 229, ch. 15, 5 : KI., 253, ch. 28, 4 : SU., 262, ch. 18, 7 : 267, ch. 35, 8 : 271, ch. 49, 4 : 272, ch. 49, 10 : LN., 281, ch. 16, 3 : 285, ch. 26, 2 : 286, ch. 28, 4 : 291, ch. 40, 3 : 305, ch. 76, 1 : 308, ch. 83, 3 : 309, ch. 84, 6 : UT., 327, ch. 2, 1 : 344, ch. 43, 2 : 346, ch. 49, 4 : 347, ch. 53, 2 : 351, ch. 65, 8 : 352, ch. 68, 3 : 357, ch. 80, 7 ; 81, 8 : 364, ch. 97, 10 : 373, ch. 114, 10 : 374, ch. 115, 3 : 376, ch. 118, 30.

अबल, UT., 372, ch. 112, 16.

अवलम्ब, A., 215, ch. 295, 8 : 217, ch. 304, 8 : AR., 228, ch. 13, 3 : UT., 334, tot. 1, 12. °बिलोका, A., 152, ch. 94, 8.

अवलम्बन, BA., 11, ch. 31, 7 : A., 178, do. 177, 2.

अवलम्बहु, A., 208, ch. 275, 7.

अबला, BA., 30, chh. 4, 3 : 31, chh. 6, 4 : 34, do. 104, 1 : 35, chh. 11, 3 : A., 133, ch. 35, 7 : 137, do. 47, 2 : 159, do. 117, 1 : 199, ch. 247, 2 : UT., 372, ch. 112, 16. °कपकूलन, UT., 365, ch. 99, 1. अबलाजन, UT., 364, chh. 10, 4. °बिबस, A., 137, ch. 48, 3. °बर्ग, BA., 30, chh. 4, 3.

अबलनिउर, BA., 34, ch. 104, 4.

अबलि, BA., 83, ch. 254, 6 : 117, ch. 352, 2.

अबली, A., 195, ch. 235, 6.

अबलीन, BA., 87, ch. 265, 1.

✓ **अवलोका,**—अवलोकत, BA., 113, do. 339, 2 : A., 155, ch. 104, 6 : 206, ch. 268, 1.

अवलोकत, UT., 346, ch. 52, 1.

अवलोकहिँ, BA., 30, ch. 95, 5 : 83, ch. 253, 2.

अवलोकउ, BA., 82, ch. 249, 7.

अवलोकि, BA., 12, ch. 34, 3 : 22, ch. 68, 3 : 33, ch. 102, 16 ; chh. 8, 1 : 36, chh. 14, 4 ; 48, ch. 147, 12 : 90, ch. 273, 8 : 107, chh. 38, 4 ; 40, 4 : 110, ch. 332, 6 : A., 127, ch. 15, 4 : 190, chh. 9, 3 : AR., 231, chh. 5, 3 : 7, 8 : LN., 280, do. 13, 4.

अवलोकी, BA., 42, ch. 126, 1 : 88, ch. 269, 1 : A., 216, ch. 301, 3.

अवलोकेसि, BA., 62, ch. 190, 4.

अवलोके, BA., 21, ch. 65, 4.

अवलोकन, BA., 108, chh. 48, 3.

अवलोकनि, BA., 17, do. 51, 1.

अवसर, BA., 19, ch. 59, 7 : 30, chh. 3, 2 : 32, ch. 98, 7 : 35, do. 105, 1 : 35, chh. 11, 1 : 38, ch. 115, 2 : 46, do. 138, 1 ; ch. 139, 2 : 64, ch. 197, 20 : 66, ch. 202, 8 : 67, ch. 203, 5 : 68, ch. 208, 7 ; 209, 2 : 71, do. 215, 1 : 75, ch. 227, 4 : 78, ch. 240, 2 : 80, do. 244, 1 : 82, ch. 252, 1 : 91, ch. 276, 2 : 104, ch. 320, 1 : 108, ch. 329, 8 : 109, ch. 330, 7 : 114, do. 340, 1 : 117, ch. 350, 1 : A., 125, do. 8, 1 : 126, do. 11, 1 : 132, do. 29, 1 : 136, ch. 45, 5 : 143, ch. 67, 4 : 147, ch. 80, 3 : 159, ch. 117, 6 : 166, ch. 139, 6 : 167, ch. 142, 4 : 168, ch. 147, 1 : 171, ch. 157, 2 : 173, do. 163, 1 : 190, chh. 9, 4 : 193, ch. 225, 7 : 195, ch. 233, 8 : 196, ch. 236, 6 ; 237, 8 : 199, ch. 247, 7 : 203, ch. 260, 4 : 206, do. 267, 1 ; ch. 268, 4 : 207, ch. 273, 1 : 210, ch. 281, 7 : 217, do. 302, 2 : 219, ch. 309, 6 : 214, ch. 293, 4, 7 : AR., 223, ch. 3, 15 : 230, chh. 4, 4 : 240, ch. 36, 7 : KI., 250, ch. 19, 8 : SU., 258, ch. 9, 2 : 264, do. 25, 1 ; ch. 26, 3 : 268, ch. 38, 2 : LN., 294, ch. 49, 6 : 297, ch. 58, 12 : 302, ch. 69, 6 : 321, ch. 109, 1 : 323, do. 111, 2 : UT., 346, do. 51, 1.

अवसाना, BA., 81, ch. 247, 7 : UT., 350, ch. 62, 6.

अवसि, BA., 28, ch. 89, 3 : 32, ch. 99, 8 : 45, ch. 136, 6 : 57, ch. 172, 3 : 79, ch. 241, 6 : A., 132, ch. 31, 7 : 138, ch. 50, 2 : 142, do. 62, 2 : 144, ch. 70, 6 : 153, ch. 98, 8 : 175, ch. 169, 1 ; do. 169, 1 : 176, ch. 170, 10 : 178, do. 177, 1 : 198, ch. 243, 3 : 201, ch. 254, 8 : 215, ch. 296, 5 : 220, so. 12, 2 : UT., 368, ch. 106, 6.

अवसेखा, LN., 295, ch. 53, 5.

अवसेरी, A., 125, ch. 8, 6.

अवस्था, BA., 110, chh. 51, 4 : UT., 374, do. 114, 5.

अवहिं, अवहीं, *see* अब.

अवा, BA., 54, ch. 165, 7.

अवाँ, BA., 22, ch. 68, 4.

अबाधा, BA., 15, ch. 46, 2.

अबाधी, UT., 373, ch. 113, 6.

अबिकारा, BA., 28, ch. 88, 8.

अबिकारी, BA., 10, ch. 27, 7 : LN., 302, ch. 70, 11.

अबिगत, A., 161, so. 4, 2.

अबिगति, A., 151, ch. 91, 7.

अबिचल, BA., 27, ch. 86, 4 : A., 193, ch. 228, 4 : SU., 267, chh. 2, 8 : LN., 319, ch. 104, 8.

अबिद्या, AR., 228, ch. 12, 4 : UT., 340, ch. 32, 3 : 356, ch. 79, 2 : 371, do. 110, 4 : 374, ch. 115, 3 : 375, ch. 116, 8 ; 117, 5 : 380, chh. 12, 8. °बाद, A., 132, do. 29, 2.

अबिनय, A., 142, ch. 63, 5 : 157, ch. 112, 7 : 212, ch. 289, 8.

अबिनासी, BA., 10, ch. 27, 6 : 11, ch. 30, 1 : 18, ch. 57, 3 : 19, ch. 59, 8 : 23, ch. 70, 2 : 42, ch. 127, 6 : 64, chh. 19, 4 : 65, chh. 21, 1 : 116, ch. 346, 6 : AR., 226, ch. 8, 17 : 236, ch. 26, 17 : KI., 247, ch. 10, 4 : LN., 320, ch. 107, 5 : UT., 344, ch. 45, 4 : 354, ch. 72, 7 : 370, ch. 108, 5 : 373, ch. 114, 2 : 378, ch. 121, 8.

अबिनासिनि, BA., 35, ch. 106, 3.
अबिनासिनिँ, UT., 340, ch. 31, 9.

अबिबेक, BA., 28, ch. 88, 8 : 32, ch. 99, 6 : 84, ch. 256, 5 : LN., 281, ch. 17, 3 : UT., 344, do. 42, 2 : 362, do. 91, 3.
अबिबेकहि, BA., 77, ch. 234, 4.
अबिबेका, BA., 8, ch. 21, 2 : UT., 348, ch. 58, 2 : 376, ch. 118, 37.

अबिबेकी, A., 165, ch. 137, 2.

अबिरल, A., 145, chh. 3, 4 : AR., 225, ch. 7, 13 : 227, ch. 8, 26 ; 10, 11 : 237, do. 27, 1 : UT., 358, do. 84, 1 : 366, ch. 103, 2.
अबिरलहि, UT., 371, ch. 110, 16.

अबिरोधा, A., 211, ch. 285, 3.

अबिश्वित, BA., 42, ch. 126, 5.

अबीर, BA., 68, ch. 207, 5.

अबुध, BA., 92, ch. 282, 2 : KI., 249, ch. 16, 8 : UT., 337, ch. 22, 6.

अबूझ, BA., 93, do. 283, 2.
अबूझा, LN., 291, ch. 39, 10.

अब्यक्त, LN., 322, chh. 37, 13 : UT., 333, chh. 5, 17.
अब्यक्तं, AR., 237, chh. 9, 5.

अब्याहत,—°गति, UT., 369, ch. 107, 12.

अभङ्गा, AR., 227, ch. 10, 11 : LN., 325, ch. 118, 9 : UT., 379, ch. 124, 8.
अभङ्ग, BA., 4, ch. 8, 4.

अभय, BA., 65, ch. 199, 9 : 95, ch. 292, 5 : A., 163, do. 129, 1 : AR., 232, ch. 18, 5 : KI., 244, ch. 4, 3 : 250, ch. 20, 1 : 253, ch. 27, 11 : LN., 283, do. 20, 2 : 317, do. 100, 1 : UT., 337, ch. 24, 3.

अभाग, A., 199, do. 245, 1 : 201, ch. 251, 5 : 202, ch. 257, 4.
अभागा, BA., 16, ch. 47, 3 ; 48, 2 : A., 128, ch. 17, 2 : SU., 269, ch. 42, 3 : LN., 285, ch. 26, 4 : 308, ch. 82, 2.
अभागे, BA., 90, ch. 274, 2 : A., 147, ch. 77, 6 : 172, ch. 160, 6 : 173, ch. 162, 5 : 176, ch. 173, 1 : AR., 233, ch. 21, 1 ; 22, 6 : LN., 294, ch. 48, 2.

अभागी, BA., 41, ch. 126. 1 : A., 134, ch. 36, 8 : 137, ch. 47, 4 : 138, ch. 50, 10 : 140, ch. 55, 5 : 143, ch. 68, 3 : 172, ch. 158, 6 : 177, ch. 175, 8 : 183, ch. 194, 5 : AR., 237, ch. 28, 3 : 241, ch. 40, 3 : SU., 273, ch. 53, 5 : LN., 293, ch. 44, 6 : UT., 354, ch. 73, 8 : 364, ch. 96, 4 : 366, ch. 103, 4 : 369, ch. 107, 7 : 376, ch. 118, 15.
अभागिनि, A., 140, ch. 56, 6.

अभाग्य, LN., 314, ch. 96, 6.

अभिअन्तर, UT., 346, ch. 50, 6.

अभिगति,—°गोतीता, BA., 65, chh. 21, 2.

अभिजित, BA., 66, ch. 203, 1.

अभिनन्दन, A., 175, ch. 170, 7.

अभिमत, BA., 101, do. 310, 1 : 109, chh. 45, 3 : A., 195, ch. 233, 2 : 199, ch. 246, 7 : 202, do. 257, 2 : 218, ch. 308, 3. °दाता, BA., 11, ch. 31, 6. °दातार, A., 124, do. 4, 1. °दानि, BA., 13, ch. 40, 11. °फिरत, A., 124, ch. 6, 5.

अभिमान, BA., 23, ch. 70, 7 : 25, do. 79, 1 : AR., 226, ch. 8, 21 : 233, ch. 21, 1 : KI., 253, ch. 28, 6 : SU., 263, do. 23, 1 : LN., 283, ch. 20, 5 : 290, ch. 37, 2 : 322, chh. 37, 11 : UT., 354, ch. 74, 5 : 365, ch. 99, 3 : 367, do. 103, 2. °बस, KI., 247, chh. 1, 3.
अभिमाना, BA., 16, ch. 48, 3 : 41, ch. 123, 15 : 45, ch. 136, 3 : 61, ch. 187, 2 : 92, ch. 281, 4 : 95, ch. 291, 8 : KI., 247, ch. 9, 9 : SU., 266, ch. 33, 6 : LN., 279, ch. 9, 6 : 281, ch. 14, 8 : 291, ch. 39, 6 : 297. ch. 58, 15 : 298, ch. 60, 2 : UT., 350, ch. 63, 8 : 354, ch. 74, 6.
अभिमानू, BA., 86, ch. 263, 3 : 88, ch. 270, 4.

अभिमानी, BA., 43, ch. 128, 6 : 54, ch. 162, 4 : 60, ch. 186. 4 : 84, ch. 256, 5 : KI., 246, ch. 8, 1 : 247, ch. 9, 10 : 253, ch. 28, 3 : SU., 263, ch. 24, 2 : 268, ch. 37, 1 : LN., 285, ch. 24, 11 ; 26, 1 : 288, ch. 33, 8 : 298, ch. 59, 27 : 312, ch. 90, 2 : UT., 356, ch. 78, 6 : 363, ch. 94, 2 : 367, ch. 104, 1 : 376, ch. 118, 25.

√ **अभिरच्छ**,—अभिरच्छय, LN., 323, chh. 39, 1.

अभिराम, BA., 27, do. 85, 2 : UT., 332, ch. 11, 7.
अभिरामा, A., 216, ch. 300, 5 : LN., 308, ch. 83, 9 : UT., 347, ch. 54, 4.

अभिलाख (ष), BA., 5, do. 12, 1 : 49, ch. 149, 3 : 52, ch. 156, 13 : A., 123, do. 2, 1 : 124, ch. 4, 7 ; do. 4, 2 : 126, ch. 12, 4 : 130, ch. 25, 7 : 187, ch. 207, 6.
अभिलाखा, BA., 30, ch. 95, 1 : 49, ch. 149, 8.
अभिलाखे, BA., 85, ch. 260, 5 : 90, ch. 274, 1 : A., 123, ch. 3, 3 : 161, ch. 123, 6 : 187, ch. 206, 5.

अभिलाखी, A., 195, ch. 235, 2.

अभिसेक (षेक), A., 125, ch. 8, 3 : 215, do. 295, 1.
°समाजू, A., 126, ch. 11, 2.

अभिरिवा, A., 125, ch. 7, 4: 126, ch. 11, 7: UT., 332, ch. 11, 7: 335, ch. 16, 2.

अभिरिहु, A., 198, ch. 243, 2: 199, ch. 245, 1.

अभिष्ट, UT., 342, do. 36, 2.

अभूत, UT., 342, ch. 39, 2.

अभेद, BA., 20, do. 61, 1: LN., 306, ch. 77, 10. °वादी, UT., 364, ch. 97, 2.

अभोगी, BA., 32, ch. 99, 3.

अमङ्गल, BA., 11, ch. 30, 1: A., 201, do. 253, 1. °दमनु, A., 126, ch. 10, 5. °भेष (प), BA., 25, do. 77, 1. °मूल, BA., 105, ch. 321, 1. °रूपा, A., 183, ch. 194, 4. °कारी, BA., 5, ch. 14, 2: 40, ch. 120, 4.

अमर, BA., 29, ch. 92, 7: 31, ch. 97, 7: 37, chh. 16, 4: 45, ch. 138, 3: A., 163, ch. 129, 1: 187, ch. 206, 5: 208, ch. 274, 7: SU., 261, ch. 17, 3: LN., 310, ch. 86, 4. °पति, A., 188, do. 210, 1: 217, do. 304, 2. °पतिईस, A., 175, do. 168, 2. °पतिसदन, A., 171, ch. 155, 3. °पद, BA., 4, ch. 7, 6: A., 212, ch. 287, 6. °पुर, A., 165, do. 136, 2: 176, ch. 172, 4: 177, ch. 173, 3: 206, ch. 269, 3.

अमरउँ, A., 131, ch. 26, 11.

अमरता, BA., 3, do. 6, 2.

अमराई, UT., 346, ch. 51, 5.

अमरावति, BA., 52, ch. 156, 16: 60, ch. 182, 7: A., 156, ch. 109, 3: 197, ch. 239, 7: UT., 339, ch. 28, 5. °पालू, A., 182, ch. 192, 7.

अमल, BA., 17, ch. 51, 7: 59, do. 180, 1; 181, 2: A., 145, chh. 3, 4: 169, ch. 150, 1: 215, do. 297, 2: AR., 223, ch. 3, 3: 226, ch. 8, 12: LN., 306, ch. 77, 9: UT., 337, ch. 24, 8: 348, do. 57, 1: 370, ch. 108, 5: 373, ch. 114, 2.

अमान, BA., 25, ch. 77, 8: A., 188, ch. 211, 6: AR., 238, do. 30, 1: LN., 287, do. 31, 1: 321, chh. 36, 9: UT., 341, ch. 35, 5: 371, do. 110, 1.

अमाना, BA., 67, chh. 25, 2.

अमानी, AR., 241, ch. 38, 8: UT., 342, ch. 39, 4: 345, ch. 47, 6.

अमानुष(ष),—°कम BA., 120, ch. 363, 6.

अमाया, A., 187, ch. 208 5: AR., 242, ch. 41, 4: LN., 297, ch. 58, 6: UT., 342, ch. 39, 3.

अमित, BA., 6, ch. 17, 12: 10, ch. 28, 7: 11, do. 28, 2: 14, do. 42, 1; ch. 44, 2: 17, do. 50, 1: 18, ch. 57, 2: 21, ch. 64, 7; do. 64, 1: 22, ch. 68, 1: 38, ch. 113, 3: 40, ch. 119, 8: 42, so. 13, 1: 52, ch. 158, 3: 55, ch. 168, 6: 60, ch. 186, 2: 69, ch. 211, 7: 81, ch. 247, 7: do. 247, 2: 113, do. 339, 1: A., 153, ch. 99, 6: 157, ch. 112, 1: 162, do. 127, 1: 174, ch. 164, 3: 187, ch. 207, 5: 202, do. 256, 1: 205, so. 10, 1: 209, ch. 278, 2: 210, ch. 283, 2: AR., 226, ch. 8, 2: 230, ch. 15, 7: KI., 246, ch. 7, 13: SU., 270, ch. 45, 5: 271, do. 47, 1: 273, ch. 54, 8: LN., 277, ch. 3, 3: 285, ch. 25, 3: 304, ch. 75, 9: 311, ch. 89, 14: 313, ch. 93, 3: 317, chh. 30, 3: 320, do. 106, 3: UT., 330, ch. 7, 5: 346, ch. 49, 5: 347, ch. 54, 7: 349, ch. 61, 4: 353, ch. 71, 7: 361, ch. 89, 3, 7, 8; 90, 2, 5: 362, ch. 92, 8. °गुनसागर, UT., 361, do. 90, 1. °दामि, AR., 223, ch. 3, 6. °बलवीर, LN., 299, do. 62, 2. °बोध, AR., 242, ch. 40, 8.

अमिति, UT., 370, ch. 109, 11.

अमिय, BA., 2, ch. 2, 1: 4, ch. 7, 6; 12, 7: 112, ch. 336, 5: A., 135, ch. 42, 3: 143, ch. 65, 3: 165, ch. 135, 6: 185, ch. 201, 6: 187, ch. 207, 4: 194, do. 229, 1: 206, ch. 269, 7: 214, ch. 295, 1. °मय, A., 179, ch. 182, 8. °मूरिमय, BA., 2, ch. 1, 2. °रसबोरी, A., 161, ch. 123, 2. °रुचिर, A., 167, ch. 143, 4.

अमी, BA., 9, ch. 23, 8: 109, ch. 331, 9: A., 155, ch. 104, 2: 187, ch. 207, 5: 207, ch. 271, 5: 212, ch. 287, 6.

अमृत, *see* अमिय.

अमोघ, SU., 255, ch. 1, 8: 261, ch. 17, 6: 272, ch. 49, 9: LN., 320, ch. 107, 6: UT., 354, ch. 72, 4.

अमोल, A., 123, ch. 2, 4.

अमोले, BA., 51, ch. 155, 1.

अम्ब, BA., 13, ch. 39, 14: A., 135, ch. 42, 5: 196, do. 235, 2; ch. 236, 5.

अम्बक, BA., 106, chh. 37, 4. °पति, BA., 50, ch. 152, 3.

अम्बर, LN., 324, ch. 114, 6: UT., 333, chh. 4, 6.

अम्बरीष(ष), A., 202, ch. 255, 4.

अम्बा, A., 141, ch. 59, 7: 175, ch. 170, 4.

अम्बिका, BA., 25, ch. 77, 2.

अम्बु, BA., 106, chh. 37, 4: A., 140, ch. 56, 2: 197, ch. 239, 5: 202, ch. 257, 1: 210, ch. 282, 3. °धरबरगात, UT., 333, chh. 4, 6. °पति, LN., 281, ch. 16, 6.

अम्बुज, BA., 38, ch. 114, 7: 50, ch. 152, 3: A., 200, ch. 249, 5: SU., 271, ch. 49, 4.

अम्बुधि, BA., 30, ch. 95, 2 : A., 123, ch. 2, 3 : 205, ch. 266, 6 : 208, ch. 275, 5.

अम्भोज, BA., 106, chh. 37, 4. °जघन, UT., 333, chh. 4, 8.

अम्मित, BA., 118, ch. 355, 6. °धारा, BA., 66, ch. 203, 4.

अय, BA., 100, ch. 305, 5.

अयं, BA., 30, chh. 4, 4 ; LN., 318, chh. 32, 3.

अयना, AR., 226, ch. 8, 20.

अयस, *see* अजस.

अयुत, UT., 367, ch. 104, 6.

अरगजा, BA., 117, ch. 349, 5.

✓ **अरगा(य),**—अरगाई, A., 200, ch. 249, 8.
अरगानी, A., 127, ch. 15, 7.

✓ **अरगाब,**—अरगाई, AR., 241, ch. 38, 6.

अरघ, BA., 118, do. 354, 1. Cf. अघे.

अरघड, A., 135, ch. 42, 3.

अरति, A., 211, do. 284, 2,

अरथ, BA., 8, ch. 21, 6 : 15, ch. 46, 6 : A., 203, ch. 258, 5, 6. Cf. अथ.

अरध, A., 199, ch. 246, 2. Cf. अधे.

अरनी, BA., 13, ch. 39, 6 : UT., 341, ch. 33, 8.

अरबिन्दु, UT., 338, do. 25, 2.

अरम्भ, UT., 350, ch. 64, 5.
अरभा, BA., 14, ch. 44, 6 : 96, ch. 295, 8 : LN., 292, ch. 43, 6.

✓ **अरम्भ,**—अरभेउ, A., 170, ch. 151, 5.

अराती, BA., 39, ch. 116, 7 : 54, ch. 165, 7. Cf. आराति.

अरि, BA., 3, do. 5, 1 : 109, chh. 44, 3 : A., 124, ch. 4, 2 : 131, ch. 26, 11 : 180, do. 185, 2 : UT., 346, ch. 52, 2 : 372, ch. 112, 12 : 375, do. 116, 1 ; ch. 117, 7. °करनी, BA., 91, ch. 279, 3. °दलदलन, LN., 300, ch. 65, 1. °बस, A., 129, ch. 22, 2. अरेन, BA., 52, ch. 157, 6 : 59, ch. 180, 3 : UT., 361, ch. 89, 7.
अरिछ, A., 133, ch. 32, 8.
अरिछक, A., 177, ch. 176, 6.
अरी, BA., 20, ch. 62, 2 : 63, ch. 195, 6 : 65, chh. 20, 2 ; 22, 2 : AR., 227, ch. 10, 5 : 229, ch. 14, 5 : 238, ch. 30, 3 : LN., 288, ch. 33, 23 : UT., 334, tot. 1, 18 : 345, ch. 48, 5 : 355, ch. 75, 6 : 356, ch. 79, 7 : 362, ch. 93, 2 : 363, ch. 94, 8 : 366, ch. 102, 1 : 375, ch. 117, 14 : 376, ch. 118, 18 : 377, ch. 120, 2.

अरु, BA., 4, ch. 7, 6 : 5, ch. 12, 9 : 7, ch. 18, 6 : 9, ch. 25, 1 : 14, ch. 44, 1 : 25, ch. 79, 7 : 27, ch. 83, 8 : 33, ch. 101, 5 : 38, ch. 115, 8 : 41, ch. 123, 4 : 43, ch. 129, 4 : 49, ch. 148, 1 : 52, ch. 158, 4 : 56, ch. 171, 4 : 57 ch. 174, 5 : 66, do. 202, 2 : 68, ch. 209, 1 : 71, do. 216, 1 : 85, ch. 259, 1 : 88, ch. 270, 4 : 90, ch. 273, 1 : 92, ch. 281, 6 : 99, ch. 304, 7 : 101, ch. 310, 8 : 103, ch. 316, 5 : 106, ch. 324, 5 ; 325, 2, 7 : 109, ch. 330, 6 : 110, ch. 332, 4 : 111, chh. 55, 2 : 112, ch. 335, 6 ; do. 336, 1 : 113, ch. 339, 6 : A., 124, ch. 4, 6 : 133, ch. 35, 6 : 139, ch. 54, 4 : 142, ch. 64, 3 : 146, ch. 75, 7 : 150, ch. 89, 4 ; 90, 6 : 164, ch. 133, 6 : 165, ch. 136, 8 : 169, ch. 150, 5 : 172, ch. 160, 4 : 173, chh. 6, 2 : 179, ch. 180, 5 : 186, ch. 203, 1 : 201, ch. 252, 5 : 212, ch. 287, 6 : AR., 223, ch. 3, 7 : 225, ch. 7, 11 : 228, ch. 11, 8 ; 12, 2 : 232, ch. 17, 9 : 236, do. 25, 1 : 239, do. 33, 1 : 241, ch. 40, 2 : KI., 245, ch. 6, 1, 11 : 250, ch. 19, 7 : 251, ch. 22, 6 : 254, do. 30, 1 : SU., 260, ch. 15, 6 : 261, ch. 18, 4 : 262, ch. 19, 4 ; 21, 9 : LN., 281, ch. 16, 3 : 283, ch. 19, 6 : 285, ch. 26, 6 : 286, ch. 29, 7 : 287, do. 31, 2 : 290, ch. 37, 9 : 293, ch. 44, 7 ; 45, 10 : 297, ch. 58, 6, 9 : 299, do. 60, 2 ; ch. 62, 4 : 302, ch. 69, 3 : 303, ch. 73, 1 : 311, ch. 88, 2 ; 89, 14 : 313, ch. 93, 3 : 315, ch. 97, 5 : 320, chh. 35, 3 : 322, ch. 111, 8 : 325, do. 116, 1 : UT., 328, ch. 4, 4 : 330, chh. 2, 4 : 331, do. 8, 1 : 335, ch. 16, 5 : 337, ch. 22, 4, 7 : 338, ch. 25, 2 ; 27, 8 : 343, ch. 41, 5 ; 42, 5 : 344, do. 42, 1 : 347, ch. 54, 4 ; 55, 6 : 351, ch. 66, 8 : 352, do. 67, 4 : 358, ch. 84, 7 : 359, ch. 87, 8 ; 88, 3 : 363, do. 93, 4 ; ch. 94, 2 ; ch. 95, 8 : 364, ch. 97, 3 : 365, do. 99, 3 : 369, do. 106, 7 : 372, ch., 111, 10.

अरुझाई, UT., 373, ch. 114, 6.

✓ **अरुझा,**—अरुझानो, AR., 239, ch. 33, 1.

अरूढ़ा, *see* आरूढ़.

अरुन, BA., ch. 38, 114, 7 : 50, ch. 152, 2 : 69, ch. 211, 2 : 72, ch. 221, 1 : 82, ch. 249, 7 : 90, do. 275, 1 : 91, ch. 276, 5 : 109, ch. 331, 9 : KI., 246, ch. 9, 2 : SU., 269, ch. 42, 5 : LN., 308, ch. 83, 9 : UT., 355, ch. 76, 6 ; 77, 1 : 356, ch. 79, 6. °चूड़, BA., 121, ch. 364, 5. °नयनराजीव, AR., 226, ch. 8, 7. °नयराजी, A., 193, ch. 228, 5. °शिखाधुनि, BA., 78, do. 238, 1. अरुनोदय, BA., 82, do. 249, 1. अरुनोपकनिकर, LN., 291, ch. 39, 9.

अरुनारा,—अरुनारो, BA., 68, ch. 207, 5.
अरुनारे, BA., 69, ch. 211, 8: 159, ch. 117, 3: UT., 355, ch. 77, 3.

अरुन्धती, A., 179, ch. 180, 5.

अरूप, BA., 6, ch. 18, 3: 41, ch. 123, 10.
अरूपा, UT., 370, ch. 108, 4.

अरोख(ष), UT., 345, ch. 47, 6.

अर्क, Kl., 248, ch. 15, 3. °फलनि, LN., 299, ch. 62, 6.

अर्घ, BA., 106, ch. 325, 4, 8: 107, ch. 326, 8: A., 125, ch. 10, 3. Cf. अरघ.

अर्थ, BA., 5, ch. 13, 9: 9, do. 22, 1: 55, ch. 167, 8: A., 184, do. 196, 1: 210, ch. 283, 2. °आखरबल, A., 195, ch. 232, 4. °धर्मकामादि, BA., 53, do. 158, 2. °धर्मकामादिक. BA., 15, ch. 46, 9. Cf. अरथ.

अर्ध, BA., 91, ch. 278, 8: LN., 315, ch. 97, 7. °भाग, BA., 66, ch. 202, 2. °अङ्ग, LN., 309, ch. 85, 4. °राति, Kl., 245, ch. 6, 3: LN., 297, ch. 59, 2. °सिंहासन (सिंघ) A., 152, ch. 96, 4. Cf. अरध.

√**अर्प,**—अर्पो, LN., 300, ch. 64, 5.

अर्पित, BA., 53, ch. 160, 2.

अर्भक,—°दशन, BA., 92, do. 280, 2.

अलक,—अलकनि, BA., 63, ch. 193, 6.

अलख, BA., 41, ch. 123, 10: 116, ch. 346, 6: A., 151, ch. 91, 7. °गति, BA., 39, ch. 116, 8.

अलङ्कृत, BA., 5, ch. 13, 9: 100, ch. 306, 6: 110, ch. 332, 4: 113, ch. 337, 3.

अलच्छ, BA., 4, ch. 7, 7.

अलप, BA., 6, ch. 17, 6: 71, ch. 216, 4: A., 185, ch. 199, 7: LN., 284, ch. 23, 8. °लोभ, SU., 268, ch. 38, 8. Cf. अल्प.

अलम्पट, UT., 342, ch. 39, 1.

अलान, A., 138, do. 50, 1.

अलि, A., 193, ch. 225, 7: UT., 337, ch. 24, 4. °अवलि, BA., 83, ch. 254, 6. °गति A., 193, ch. 225, 7. °गन, A., 193, ch. 227, 7. °माला, BA., 15, ch. 46, 7.
अलिनि, BA., 88, ch. 269, 1.

अली, BA., 81, chh. 32, 3. Cf. आलि.
अलीं, BA., 111, chh. 58, 3.

अलीक, LN., 285, ch. 25, 8.
अलीका, BA., 75, ch. 228, 6.

अलीहा, A., 137, ch. 48, 7.

√**अलुज्झ,**—अलुज्झि, LN., 309, chh. 13, 2.

अलेख, A., 188, ch. 211, 6: 211, ch. 283, 8.

अलोला, Kl., 246, ch. 7, 15.

अलौकिक, BA., 2, ch. 2, 13: 14, ch. 42, 4: 42, ch. 125, 8: 51, ch. 156, 3: 79, ch. 243, 3: 90, do. 273, 2: 105, ch. 320, 5; 322, 4: 107, ch. 326, 7.

अल्प,—°मितु, UT., 337, ch. 22, 5. Cf. अलप.

अष्टादस(श), LN., 281, ch. 16, 7.

अवतेङ, *see* √आव.

अवर, BA., 51, ch. 156, 4.

अँवारी, BA., 100, ch. 307, 1.

अस, BA., 4, ch. 8, 1: 6, ch. 16, 6; 18, 2: 7, ch. 18, 8; 19, 10, 12: 10, ch. 27, 7: 14, ch. 42, 4, 5, 8: 16, ch. 48, 9: 18, do. 56, 1, 2; 57, 1: 19, ch. 61, 3: 20, ch. 62, 4, 6, 13, 16: 22, ch. 67, 1, 3, 5; 69, 4: 23, ch. 70, 8: 24, ch. 73, 6; 74, 8: 25, do. 77, 2; 79, 1: 26, do. 80, 1; ch. 81, 1, 7; do. 82, 1, 2; ch. 82, 1, 4: 27, ch. 83, 5; 85, 1; 86, 6: 28, ch. 87, 1, 7; 88, 2: 28, ch. 87, 8; 89, 7: 29, ch. 90, 4: 30, ch. 94, 3, 9: 30, do. 93, 2; ch. 94, 4; do. 94, 1: 32, do. 97, 1; 99, 4: 33, do. 101, 1: 34, ch. 104, 8; 105, 2, 6: 35, chh. 12, 4: 36, ch. 108, 6: 39, ch. 116, 4; 117, 7: 40, do. 121, 2; 122, 1: 41, ch. 124, 4; 125, 3, 4; so. 10, 1: 42, ch. 125, 8; 126, 6; 128, 3: 45, ch. 135, 1, 8: 46, ch. 140, 2: 47, ch. 142, 7: 48, ch. 145, 6, 8; so. 15, 2: 51, ch. 155, 7: 52, ch. 156, 7, 14; 157, 5: 54, do. 163, 2: 56, do. 171, 1; ch. 171, 6: 59, ch. 179, 1: 60, ch. 185, 3: 64, chh. 18, 3: 68, ch. 209, 3: 69, ch. 209, 6, 7: 70, ch. 212, 5: 72, ch. 219, 7: 73, do. 223, 1: 76, ch. 232, 8; 233, 1: 77, ch. 234, 7; 235, 4: 79, ch. 242, 3: 80, ch. 246, 6: 81, ch. 248, 4: 82, ch. 249, 6: 84, ch. 256, 4, 7; 257, 4: 85, ch. 259, 3: 86, ch. 263, 1, 7: 87, ch. 267, 2: 88, ch. 271, 4: 90, ch. 274, 8: 95, do. 291, 2: 100, ch. 305, 7: 101, ch. 311, 3: 103, do. 316, 2; 318, 1: 114, ch. 342, 9: 120, do. 361, 2: 121, ch. 366, 8: A., 123, do. 2, 1: 124, ch. 3, 7; do. 3, 1; ch. 5, 3: 126, ch. 102, 6; do. 10, 2; ch. 11, 4: 127, ch. 14, 7; 15, 8: 129, ch. 22, 4, 5; 130, 25, 7: 132, ch. 30, 1, 4: 133, ch. 34, 1; ch. 35, 4: 135, ch. 42, 4: 136, ch. 45, 3: 137, ch. 46, 5; 48, 8: 138, ch. 50, 1, 4, 11: 140, ch. 56, 3 : 141, ch. 59, 6 : 142, ch. 62, 8 : 143, ch. 65, 7 ; 67, 1 : 144, ch. 70, 1 : 145, ch. 73, 8 : 146, ch. 75, 8 : 147, ch. 77, 5 ; 79, 5 ; 80, 4 : 148, ch. 80, 8 ; 82, 7 : 151, ch. 91, 1 ; 92, 1, 6 ; do. 92, 1 : 155, ch. 103, 2 ; do. 103, 1 ; 158, ch. 116, 4 ; 159, ch. 118, 1 : 160, ch. 121, 8 ; do. 121, 1 ; ch. 122, 5, 8 : 162, ch. 128, 5 : 164, do. 133, 2 : 168, ch. 147, 4 : 170, ch. 151, 1 ; 152, 2 : 171, ch. 155, 4 ; 156, 6 : 173, ch. 163, 4, 5 ; chh. 6, 3 : 174, ch. 166, 1 : 178, ch. 177, 5 ; 179, 6 : 179, ch. 182, 8 ; do. 182, 1 : 180, ch. 185, 6 ; 186, 2 : 182, ch. 193, 1 : 183, ch. 195, 7 : 184, ch. 196, 8 : 185, ch. 200, 6 ; 202, 6 : 186, ch. 206, 4 : 187, do. 206, 1 ; ch. 209, 6 : 188, ch. 211, 8 : 189, ch. 215, 2, 8 : 190, ch. 217, 8 ; 218, 3, 8, 10 : 192, ch. 225, 4 : 197, ch. 239, 3 ; do. 239 1 : 200, ch. 249, 6, 8 ; 251, 3 : 203, ch. 259, 6 ; 261, 2 : 204, ch. 262, 7 ; 263, 2 : 206, ch. 269, 2 : 207, ch. 271, 6 ; 272, 7 : 208, do. 274, 1, 2 : 209, ch. 279, 7 : 210, ch. 283, 3 : 211, ch. 284, 8 : 213, ch. 290, 5 : 215, ch. 298, 3 : 217, ch. 302, 5 ; 303, 6 ; 304, 8 : AR., 222, ch. 2, 16 : 223, ch. 3, 12, 14, 27 : 224, ch. 3, 29 : 225, ch. 6, 1 : 226, ch. 8, 21 : 227, ch. 9, 6 ; 10, 13 : 232, so. 7, 2 : 233, do. 21, 2 ; ch. 22, 7 : 234, ch. 18, 8 : 235, ch. 25, 16 : 237, ch. 29, 1 : 241, ch. 37, 5, 6 ; 40, 3 : 242, chh. 11, 2 : KI., 243, ch. 1, 6 : 244, ch. 3, 5 : 245, ch. 7, 8 : 246, ch. 7, 24 ; 8, 1 : 247, ch. 10, 5 : 247, chh. 1, 4 : 248, ch. 12, 5 : 251, ch. 22, 3 : 252, ch. 26, 8, 10 : 253, ch. 29, 5 : SU., 255, ch. 1, 4 : 258, do. 7, 1 : ch. 8, 1 ; 9, 8 : 259, ch. 10, 4 ; 12, 6 : 260, do. 14, 2 : 261, ch. 17, 4 : 264, ch. 27, 3 : 268, ch. 37, 5 : 269, ch. 40, 5 ; 41, 4, 6, 9 ; 42, 1 : 270, ch. 46, 1, 7 : 271, ch. 48, 7 : 272, ch. 49, 10 ; 50, 1 ; 51, 6 : 273, ch. 55, 3 : 274, ch. 58, 5 : LN., 276, ch. 2, 1 ; so. 1, 1 : 278, ch. 6, 1 ; 8, 3 : 279, ch. 9, 6 ; 10, 4 ; 11, 2 : 281, do. 14, 3 ; ch. 16, 3 : 282, ch. 17, 8 ; so. 3, 4 : 283, do. 21, 2 : 284, ch. 23, 8 ; do. 23, 4 : 285, ch. 24, 9 : 286, ch. 27, 3, 7 ; do. 27, 1 ; ch. 28, 4 : 287, ch. 30, 2, 3, 8 ; 31, 1, 5 : 288, ch. 33, 8, 15 : 290, ch. 37, 10 : 291, ch. 39, 4, 6 : 292, ch. 44, 5 : 293, ch. 44, 6, 7 : 294, ch. 48, 4 ; do. 48, 1 ; ch. 49, 4 : 296, ch. 56, 1 : 297, ch. 57, 3 ; do. 58, 2 : 298, ch. 59, 8, 10 : 302, ch. 71, 2 : 303, ch. 71, 6 ; 72, 2 : 304, ch. 73, 10 ; do. 73, 1 ; ch. 75, 7 : 305, ch. 76, 13 : 306, ch. 77, 11 ; do. 77, 2 : 307, ch. 80, 3 ; 81, 5 : 308, ch. 82, 8 : 310, ch. 87, 1 : 312, ch. 91, 8 : 313, ch. 94, 6 : 315, ch. 97, 1 : 318, ch. 101, 10 : UT., 327, do. 1, 5 : 336, ch. 19, 8 ; ch. 20, 3, 10 ; do. 20, 3, 6 : 337, do. 23, 2 : 343, ch. 42, 6 : 344, do. 45, 1 : 346, ch. 51, 1 : 347, ch. 54, 5 : 349, do. 60, 1 : 350, do. 63, 4 ; ch. 63, 10 : 353, do. 70, 4 ; ch. 71, 5 : 354, ch. 73, 7 : 358, ch. 84, 6 ; 85, 2 : 359, do. 85, 3 ; ch. 86, 10 ; so. 3, 2 : 360, so. 6, 1 : 362, ch. 92, 5 : 363, ch. 94, 5 : 366, do. 101, 2 : 367, ch. 103, 13 : 369, ch. 106, 15 ; 107, 7, 15 : 373, ch. 113, 8 ; 114, 8 : 374, ch. 116, 7 : 375, ch. 116, 10 ; do. 116, 2, 4 ; ch. 117, 16, 19 : 377, do. 119, 4 : 378, ch. 121, 4 : 380, do. 127, 2.

अषा, UT., 365, ch. 99, 4.

अषि, BA., 21, ch. 66, 3 : 24, ch. 74, 3 : 25, do. 77, 2 : 30, ch. 95, 3 : 34, chh. 9, 4 : 37, ch. 112, 7 : 55, so. 20, 1 : 60, ch. 184, 3 : 76, ch. 232, 6 : 82, ch. 251, 5 : 84, ch. 256, 2 : 87, ch. 266, 2 : 92, ch. 279, 7 : 95, ch. 292, 5 : 97, ch. 297, 4 : A., 144, ch. 70, 7 : 158, ch. 116, 4 : 171, ch. 155, 7 : 172, ch. 158, 6 ; 159, 3 : 179, ch. 183, 4 : 199, ch. 245, 7 ; 206, do. 269, 1 : AR., 230, ch. 15, 17 : 232, ch. 17, 11 ; do. 17, 2 : 238, do. 31, 1 : 240, ch. 36, 7 ; 37, 4 : 241, ch. 40, 2 : KI., 244, do. 3, 1 : 245, ch. 7, 3 : 249, ch. 16, 7 : SU., 260, ch. 13, 3 : 268, ch. 37, 7 : 272, ch. 50, 8 : 274, ch. 56, 4 : LN., 284, do. 23, 5 : 285, ch. 24, 9 : 288, ch. 33, 11 : 289, ch. 35, 2 : 295, ch. 52, 7 : UT., 342, ch. 38, 7 : 345, ch. 48, 4 : 354, ch. 73, 1 : 359, do. 86, 2 : 362, so. 9, 1 : 367, ch. 103, 14 : 372, ch. 112, 1 : 375, ch. 116, 10.

असगुन, A., 170 ch. 152, 4 : AR., 230, ch. 15, 7 : SU., 267, ch. 35, 7 : LN., 281, ch. 15, 2, 4 : 294, ch. 47, 7 : 304, ch. 75, 9 : 305, chh. 4, 1.

असङ्ग, BA., 47, ch. 144, 3 : 62, ch. 191, 7 : SU., 262, ch. 21, 2 : LN., 280, do. 12, 4 : 282, do. 17, 2.

असङ्गता, BA., 40, ch. 121, 1 : KI., 253, ch. 28, 11 : SU., 257, ch. 4, 5 : 262, ch. 20, 8 : 273, ch. 55, 8 : LN., 282, ch. 18, 10 : 288, ch. 33, 12 : 289, ch. 35, 4 : 291, ch. 38, 9 : 308, ch. 82, 5.

असङ्गु, BA., 92, ch. 282, 2.

असज्जन, BA., 3, ch. 6, 3.

असत्य, A., 128, ch. 20, 5 : 131, ch. 28, 5.

असन, BA., 55, so. 19, 2 : 58, ch. 178, 7 : 101, ch. 311, 7 : 114, ch. 342, 3 : A., 142, do. 61, 1 : 158, ch. 116, 1 : 165, ch. 135, 6 : 167, ch. 143, 5 : 179, do. 181, 1 : 186, do. 203, 1 : 187, ch. 207, 5 : 206, ch. 267, 7 ; 269, 7 : 219, ch. 312, 4 : UT., 375, ch. 116, 9.

असनि, LN., 287, ch. 32, 9.

असन्त, UT., 342, ch. 38, 5 : 376, ch. 118, 15.

असमान, UT., 343, ch. 42, 8.

असमञ्ज, UT., 343, ch. 40, 1.

असमाप्त, UT., 342, ch. 38, 7.

असत, AR., 237, chh. 9, 13. °बरबाणाप्रवीणा, BAK., 44, ch. 133, 4.

असमय, BAK., 53, ch. 162, 3.

असमञ्जस, BAK., 7, ch. 19, 10 : 29, ch. 93, 4 : 56, ch. 171, 5 : 77, ch. 235, 3 : A., 132, ch. 32, 4 : 201, ch. 254. 5 : 203, ch. 260, 2 : 204, ch. 261, 6. °बस, A., 148, ch. 83, 5. °समन, A., 210, do. 280, 2.

असम्भव, BAK., 12, ch. 32, 8.

असम्भावना, BAK., 42, ch. 126, 8.

असम्मत, BAK., 41, ch. 123, 3.

असरन,—°सरन, UT., 336, ch. 19, 3 : 346, ch. 52, 4.

असवार, A., 100, do. 305, 2.
असवारा, BAK., 34, ch. 103, 8 : 105, ch. 323, 1 : A., 183, ch. 195, 5 : LN., 308, ch. 83, 3.

असहाई, A., 191, ch. 220, 3.

असा, *see* अस.

असाँचा, BAK., 59, ch. 179, 7.
असाँचो, LN., 286, ch. 29, 2.

असाधि, A., 138, ch. 50, 10 : UT., 377, do. 118, 1.

असाधु, BAK., 4, ch. 7, 5 ; 8, 10.
असाधू, BAK., 3, ch. 6, 6 : A., 185, ch. 199, 7.

असाध्य, 133, do. 34, 1.

असि (1), *see* अस.

असि (2) (a sword), BAK., 25, ch. 77, 6 : A., 130, ch. 26, 4 : SU , 259, do. 9, 2 ; ch. 10, 4, 6 : UT., 333, chh. 4, 4 : 375, do. 117, 3. °कला BAK., 100, do. 205, 2.
असिन, A., 214, ch. 294, 8.

असिव, BAK., 33, ch. 101, 4 : UT., 360, so. 4, 1.

असीस, BAK., 26, do. 80, 1 : 37, chh. 16, 1 : 68, do. 208, 1 : 72, do. 220, 1 : 74, ch. 227, 1 : 81, ch. 248, 7, 11 ; chh. 32, 3 : 82, ch. 251, 3 : 91, ch. 277, 7 : 99, ch. 303, 4 : 103, ch. 315, 2, 6 : 107, do. 326, 2 : 108, ch. 329, 5 ; chh. 42, 2 : 111, chh. 59, 1 : 113, ch. 337, 5 ; 340, 3, 4 : 114, ch. 342, 12 : 116, do. 347, 1 : 119, do. 357, 1 ; ch. 358, 4 ; do. 358, 2 : 121, ch. 364, 7 ; 366, 9 : A., 138, ch. 51, 2 : 140, ch. 57, 1 : 144, do. 68, 1 : 146, ch. 75, 3 : 147, ch. 79, 2 : 155, do. 103, 1 ; ch. 105, 8 : 158, do. 113, 1 : 184, ch. 198, 5 : 187, ch. 208, 2 : 195, ch. 233, 5 : 196, ch. 236, 2 ; 237, 1 : 199, ch. 245, 7 : 207, ch. 272, 1 : 216, ch. 300, 7 : 218, do. 306, 2 : 219, do. 311, 1 : LN., 325, ch. 118, 9 : UT., 330, ch. 8, 2 : 331, ch. 10, 5. °जुगि, BAK., 108, ch. 329, 5. Cf. आसिष, आसिर.
असीसा, BAK., 89, ch. 271, 5 : 90, ch. 273, 2 : 115, ch. 344, 7 : A., 154, ch. 100, 8 : 180, ch. 186, 6 : 181, ch. 189, 5 : 218, ch. 307, 3 : LN., 325, ch. 117, 3.

असीस,—असीसहिं, BAK., 107, do. 325, 2 : A., 196, do. 237, 2.

असुभ, BAK., 25, ch. 79, 7 : A., 134, ch. 38, 8 : 146, ch. 75, 7 : 207, ch. 271, 4 : LN., 308, ch. 83, 1 : 316, ch. 99, 7 ; chh. 28, 2 : UT., 343, ch. 42, 5. °बेष, UT., 363, do. 95, 1. °भेष, AR., 229, ch. 15, 6.

असुर, BAK., 9, ch. 22, 21 : 13, ch. 39, 9 : 14, ch. 43, 7 : 29, ch. 92, 5 : 31, ch. 96, 7 : 37, ch. 111, 7 : 43, ch. 128, 6 : do. 128, 1 : 47, do. 143, 1 : 59, ch. 179, 3 : 73, ch. 222, 6 : 75, do. 228, 2 : 76, ch. 232, 6 : 82, ch. 252, 7 : 89, chh. 33, 3 : AR., 224, ch. 4, 6 : 230, ch. 15, 16 : 232, ch. 19, 1 : 234, do. 23, 2 ; ch. 24, 8 : SU., 263, ch. 22, 9 : LN., 278, ch. 8, 2 : UT., 359, ch. 87, 6. °देव, BAK., 43, ch. 129, 5. °निकाया, BAK., 64, ch. 197, 4. °समूह, BAK., 72, ch. 219, 9. असुराधिपति, BAK., 43, ch. 130, 7. असुरारी, BAK., 20, ch. 62, 2 ; 65, chh. 20, 2 : UT., 345, ch. 48, 5.

असेखा(षा), BAK., 42, ch. 125, 7 : 65, chh. 23, 1.

असोक, KI., 253, ch. 28, 12 : SU., 258, ch. 8, 6 : 260, do. 12, 2. °पादप, AR., 236, do. 25, 2. °वाटिका, SU., 261, ch. 18, 3.
असोका, SU., 259, ch. 12, 10 : UT., 352, ch. 69, 2.

असोकी, BAK., 56, ch. 168, 8.

असोच, A., 195, ch. 233, 6 : KI., 244, ch. 3, 4.

असौच, LN., 281, ch. 17, 3.

अस्त्र, BAK., 54, ch. 163, 2 : A., 164, ch. 133, 6 : UT., 331, do. 10, 2.

अस्तु, BAK., 51, ch. 155, 1 : 52, ch. 156, 7 : 56, do. 169, 1 : 59, ch. 181, 5 : AR., 227, ch. 9, 1 : 241, do. 37, 3 : SU., 266, ch. 34, 4 : 272, ch. 49, 8 : UT., 358, ch. 85, 1 : 368, ch. 106, 2 : 369, do. 106, 1 : 372, ch. 111, 6.

अस्तुति, BAK., 30, ch. 93, 8 : 65, do. 197, 2 : 67, ch. 203, 8 ; chh. 25, 1 : 70, ch. 214, 7 : 73, ch. 222, 6 : 73, chh. 29, 2 : AR., 222, so. 3, 2 : 225, ch. 6, 4 : 226, ch. 8, 1 : 231, do. 16, 4 : 236, ch. 27*a*, 2 : 238, ch. 30, 2 : 240, ch. 36, 3 : KI., 244, ch. 2, 7 : SU., 268, ch. 38, 1 : LN., 301, ch. 68, 9 : 304, ch. 74, 5 : 308, ch. 83, 5 : 313, ch. 94, 5 : 318, ch. 103, 6 : 320, do. 107, 2 : 321, do. 109, 2 :

325, ch. 118, 4 : UT., 333, do. 13, 3 : 341, ch. 35, 1 : 342, ch. 36, 1 : 343, do. 39, 1 : 351, do. 64, 4 : 352, ch. 69, 3.

अस्त्र, BA., 100, ch. 306, 8 : AR., 230, do. 15, 2 : LN., 281, ch. 15, 1 : 295, ch. 50, 6 ; 52, 2 : 302, ch. 70, 1 : 311, ch. 89, 3.

अस्थाना, LN., 325, ch. 117, 2.

अस्थि, A., 176, do. 172, 2 : LN., 281, ch. 16, 7. °ताल, Kl., 245, ch. 7, 12. °माल, BA., 50, ch. 150, 4. °समूह, AR., 225, ch. 6, 6.

अस्नाना, BA., 70, ch. 213, 2 : UT., 339, ch. 30, 2.

अस्व, A., 183, ch. 195, 5.

अस्वनी,—°कुमारा, LN., 281, ch. 16, 3.

अह, A., 190, do. 217, 2.

अहई, अहईं, अहऊँ, *see* √अह.

अहङ्कार, LN., 281, do. 16, 1 : 296, ch. 55, 7 : UT., 376, ch. 118, 35.

अहङ्कारी, LN., 291, ch. 39, 1.

अहनिसि, UT., 338, ch. 26, 5.

अहमिति, BA., 41, ch. 123, 15 : 44, ch. 134, 5 : 45, ch. 136, 7 ; 46, ch. 141, 1 : 95, ch. 291, 6 : A., 194, ch. 232, 2 : UT., 366, ch. 102, 8.

अहार, BA., 49, ch. 149, 1 : 60, ch. 185, 5 : A., 179, do. 181, 1 : Kl., 252, ch. 27, 2, 3 : SU., 257, ch. 4, 3 : LN., 279, ch. 9, 9 : 291, ch. 39, 4. *Cf.* आहार.
अहारा, BA., 59, ch. 181, 7 : A., 205, ch. 266, 16 : Kl., 252, ch. 27, 4 : 253, ch. 27, 5 : SU., 256, ch. 2, 3 : 258, ch. 7, 8.
अहारू, A., 143, ch. 65, 3,

अहारी, A., 183, ch. 194, 3 : 197, ch. 239, 5.

अहल्या, BA., 77, ch. 235, 5.

अहसि, अहहु, अहहिं, अहहीं, अहहू, *see* √अह.

अहि, BA., 6, ch. 16, 1 : 32, ch. 101, 1 : 55, so. 19, 2 : 89, chh. 33, 2 : 109, ch. 331, 9 : A., 163, ch. 131, 5 : 178, ch. 177, 8 : AR., 232, so. 7, 1 : 241, ch. 38, 6 : LN., 286, ch. 26, 7 : 308, chh. 11, 4 : UT., 343, ch. 40, 8 : 366, ch. 103, 6 : 376, ch. 118, 18. °कुलनाथा, BA., 60, ch. 182, 7. °गति, Kl., 245, ch. 7, 8. °गन, SU., 262, ch. 20, 8 : 268, do. 36, 1 : LN., 299, ch. 63, 1. °नाथा, BA., 122, ch. 367, 6. °प, A., 199, ch. 244, 7. °पति, A., 209, ch. 277, 6 : SU., 267, chh. 2, 5. °बेलि, BA., 97, ch. 296, 2. °भवन, BA., 40, ch. 121, 2. °भामिनी, AR., 236, ch. 26, 11. °राजा, BA., 68, ch. 207, 2 : AR., 228, ch. 11, 4. °सीस, A., 158, do. 113, 2. °सेष, BA., 25, ch. 79, 5. अहीस, A., 160, chh. 4, 3. अहीसा, BA., 38, ch. 113, 3 : LN., 304, ch. 73, 14 : UT., 361, ch. 90, 8.
अहिनी, AR., 229, ch. 14, 3.

अहिंसा, *see* अहिन्सा.

अहिन्सा, UT., 376, ch. 118, 22.

अहित, A., 171, ch. 156, 7 : SU., 269, do. 40, 2.

अहिवात, BA., 113, ch. 340, 4 : A., 130, ch. 26, 7 : 144, ch. 68, 8 : LN., 279, do. 8, 2 : 281, do. 16, 4 : 325, ch. 118, 9.
अहिवाता, BA., 25, ch. 77, 4 : UT., 330, ch. 8, 2.

अहीर, UT., 373, ch. 114, 12.

अहेर, A., 163, ch. 131, 7 : 164, ch. 133, 2.
अहेरहिं, BA., 54, ch. 163, 6.

अहेरी, A., 162, ch. 128, 4.

अहै, *see* √अह.

अहो, BA., 37, ch. 112, 4 : 92, ch. 281, 1 : SU., 269, ch. 42, 8 : 271, do. 47, 1 : LN., 281, ch. 17, 1.

॥ आ ॥

आइ, आइय, आइअहिं, आइहि, आइहीं, आई, आईं, आउब, आऊं, आएउं, आएऊं, आएहु, आए, *see* √आव.

आक, UT., 372, ch. 112, 2.

आंक, A., 117, ch. 176, 2.

आकर, BA., 4, ch. 12, 1 : 18, ch. 57, 4 : UT., 344. ch. 45, 4.

आकास, BA., 68, ch. 206, 2.

आकृति, *see* आकिति.

आकिति, BA., 47, ch. 144, 7.

आखर, BA., 5, ch. 13, 9 : 8, ch. 21, 6 : 9, ch. 24, 1 : A., 210, ch. 283, 2 : 217, ch. 304, 6. °खड, A., 195, ch. 232, 4.

आँखि, BA., 94, ch. 288, 8 : 98, ch. 301, 1, 5 : A., 129, ch. 21, 6 : 169, do. 148, 1 : 171, ch. 156, 8 : LN., 289, ch. 35, 12 : UT., 364, do. 96, 4.

आँखिन, BA., 94, ch. 288, 7 : A., 159, ch. 117, 5.

आँखिन्ह, A., 172, ch. 160, 6 : 182, ch. 192, 2 : 201, ch. 252, 7.

आँखी, A., 132, ch. 31, 5.

आगम, BA., 6, do. 17, 1 : 20, chh. 2, 2 : 37, ch. 111, 8 : A., 151, ch. 93, 5 : 194, do. 228, 2 : 210, ch. 282, 7 : UT., 346, ch. 50, 3 : 374, ch. 116, 3.

आगमन, BA., 72, ch. 219, 8 : 82, do. 249, 2 : A., 163, do. 130, 2 : 204, do. 262, 1 : AR., 225, ch. 7, 3 : LN., 315, ch. 97, 10 : UT., 327, do. 1, 4.

आगर, BA., 96, ch. 293, 3 : KI., 253, ch. 29, 1.

आगरि, A., 180, ch. 184, 5.

आगरी, BA., 110, chh. 50, 3.

आगार, BA., 8, so. 4, 2 : UT., 334, do. 14, 2.

आगारा, LN., 279, ch. 11, 7 : 280, ch. 14, 4 : UT., 336, ch. 20, 9.

आगि, BA., 64, ch. 197, 6 : LN., 316, chh. 26, 7.

आगी, BA., 65, ch. 197, 7 : A., 137, ch. 47, 4 : 172, ch. 158, 8 : 173, ch. 163, 2 : KI., 251, ch. 23, 4 : SU., 259, ch. 12, 9.

आगिल, BA., 26, ch. 81, 1 : A., 126, ch. 13, 7.

आगिलि, BA., 71, ch. 218, 1 : A., 128, ch. 19, 8.

·आगे, BA., 7, ch. 19, 6 : 20, do. 62, 2 : 21, ch. 64, 4 : 42, so. 12, 1 : 63, ch. 193, 9 : 93, ch. 283, 6 : 95, ch. 289, 7 : 98, ch. 300, 2 : 102, ch. 313, 2 : 105, ch. 321, 3 : 109, ch. 330, 6 : 119, ch. 359, 1 : 121, ch. 366, 5 : A., 132, ch. 31, 1 : 146, ch. 77, 2 : 149, ch. 86, 3 : 152, ch. 96, 4 : 159, ch. 119, 1 : 160, do. 120, 2 : 163, ch. 130, 5 : 172, ch. 160, 6 : 176, ch. 173, 2 : 183, do. 194, 2 : 189, ch. 213, 5 ; ch. 214, 3 : 194, ch. 230, 4 : 205, ch. 265, 1 : 210, ch. 281, 7 : AR., 224, ch. 4, 2 : 225, ch. 6 ; 5 : 226, ch. 7, 20 : 229, ch. 15, 6 : 233, ch. 21, 1 : 236, ch. 26, 18 ; 27, 7 : 238, ch. 30, 1 : KI., 243, ch. 1, 1 : 245, ch. 7, 7 : 246, ch. 9, 1 : 247, ch. 11, 5 : 250, do. 20, 2 : 252, ch. 24, 8 : SU., 256, ch. 3, 8 : 264, do. 26, 2 : 270, ch. 45, 1 : LN., 279, ch. 10, 4 : 283, ch. 20, 8 : 286, ch. 27, 4 ; 29, 4 : 288, ch. 33, 7 : 292, ch. 42, 1 : do. 43, 2 : 299, ch. 61, 3 : 301, ch. 68, 5 : 303, ch. 73, 4 : 313, ch. 94, 7 : 317, ch. 100, 7 : 324, ch. 114. 4 : UT., 330, ch. 7, 8 : 335, ch. 18, 2 : 346, ch. 49, 7.

आग्या, BA., 28, ch. 87, 4 : 78, ch. 238, 6 : 120, ch. 362, 6 : A., 213, ch. 290, 4. Cf. अग्या.

आचमन, BA., 112, ch. 335, 8.

√आचर,—आचरत, A., 176, ch. 170, 13 : 220, chh. 13, 2.

आचरहिं, LN., 304, ch. 75, 2.

आँचर,—आँचरहु, BA., 111, ch. 333, 7.

आचरज, BA., 2, ch. 3, 2 : 14, ch. 42, 3, 4 ; do. 42, 2 : 48, ch. 147, 4 : 55, ch. 168, 1, 6 : 62, ch. 192, 3 : 105, ch. 320, 8 ; do. 320, 1 : A., 165, do. 135, 2 : UT., 349, ch. 61, 5 : 353, ch. 70, 5. Cf. आचर्ज.

आचरन, BA., 49, ch. 148, 2 : 62, ch. 190, 2 : 64, ch. 197, 7, 11 : 66, do. 200, 1 : SU., 271, ch. 47, 7 : UT., 345, ch. 47, 4 : 346, ch. 49, 4 : 366, so. 11, 1.

आचरनु, A., 189, ch. 215, 1 : 220, ch. 314, 5.

आचरनी, UT., 342, ch. 38, 7.

आचर्ज, A., 179, ch. 182, 8. Cf. आचरज.

आँचा, A., 132, ch. 32, 5.

आचार, BA., 30, ch. 94, 8 : 96, do. 294, 2 : 108, chh. 42, 1 : UT., 377, do. 118, 3. Cf. अचारा.

आचारी, UT., 363, ch. 95, 5.

आछा,—आछी, BA., 4, ch. 12, 7 : 63, ch. 194, 6.

आछे, A., 189, ch. 213, 5.

आज,—आजउ, A., 128, ch. 20, 2.

आजहुँ, BA., 20, ch. 61, 8 : 23, ch. 72, 3 : 49, ch. 147, 13 ; 148, 2 : 57, do. 174, 2 : 93, do. 283, 2 : 94, ch. 287, 7 : A., 134, do. 37, 2 : 160, ch. 120, 1 : 166, ch. 139, 6 : 172, ch. 159, 5, 8 : AR., 224, so. 4, 2 : LN., 290, do. 36, 1 : 314, ch. 96, 7.

आजहूँ, BA. 28, ch. 90, 1 : 39, ch. 117, 5 : A., 132, ch. 32, 5 : KI., 247, do. 9, 2 : LN., 285, ch. 25, 4 : 298, ch. 60, 2.

आजु, BA., 62, do. 191, 2 : 189, do. 214, 2 : 202, do. 254, 1 : KI., 252, ch. 27, 3 : LN., 310, ch. 87, 7.

आजू, BA., 38, ch. 113, 2 : 54, do. 163, 2 : 56, ch. 171, 4 : 72, ch. 219, 3 : 220, 3 : 84, ch. 256, 6 : 85, ch. 260, 3 : 87, ch. 267, 7 : 94, ch. 288, 3 : 98, ch. 299, 7 : 104, ch. 318, 5 : 106, ch. 323, 7 : 112, ch. 336, 6 : 113, ch. 337, 4 : 121, ch. 363, 7 : A., 126, ch. 10, 7 ; do. 12, 1 : 129, do. 21, 1 ; ch. 23, 5 : 134, ch. 38, 1 : 138, ch. 49, 6 : 140, ch. 56, 5 : 153, ch. 99, 5 ;

6 : 155, ch. 104, 5 : 169, ch. 150, 6 : 173, do. 163, 1 : 180, do. 184, 1 : 191, ch. 219, 3 ; 220, 4 ; 221, 3 : 200, do. 250, 2 ; ch. 251, 2 : 204, ch. 262, 6 : 207, ch. 272, 7 : 211, ch. 286, 6 : 216, ch. 301, 2 : AR., 225, ch. 7, 9 : 233, ch. 22, 8 : 238, ch. 31, 8 : KI., 252, ch. 27, 4 : 253, ch. 27, 5 : SU., 256, ch. 2, 3 : 266, ch. 34, 2 : 269, do. 42, 2 : LN., 294, ch. 49, 3 : 303, ch. 72, 13 : 307, ch. 80, 2 : 310, ch. 87, 8 : 317, ch. 101, 8 : 319, chh. 34, 8 : UT., 328, ch. 3, 11 : 332, ch. 11, 4 : 341, ch. 34, 7 : 358, ch. 84, 2 : 378, do. 120, 1. °जिय, A., 129, ch. 23, 8.

आजू, BA., 56, ch. 171, 5 : 91, ch. 278, 4 : 107, ch. 326, 6 : 114, ch. 341, 2 : A., 124, ch. 6, 3 : 126, ch. 11, 3 : 127, ch. 15, 2 : 128, ch. 20, 3 : 135, ch. 42, 1 : 143, ch. 67, 4 : 145, ch. 72, 7 : 155, ch. 104, 6 : 163, ch. 129, 3 : 184, ch. 196, 2 : 186, ch. 206, 3 : 191, ch. 221, 5 : 196, ch. 238, 6 : 203, ch. 261, 5 : 210, ch. 282, 3 : AR., 236, ch. 26, 14 : KI., 253, ch. 28, 10 : SU., 265, ch. 30, 4.

√ आँज,—आँजि, BA., 2, do. 1, 1.

आजन्म, LN., 318, chh. 32, 3.

आज्ञा, *see* आग्या.

आठ, LN., 281, ch. 17, 2.

आठे, BA., 106, ch. 323, 4.

आठव, AR., 238, ch. 31, 4.

आँत, LN., 309, ch. 85, 5.

आतप, BA., 17, ch. 51, 4 : KI., 243, ch. 1, 9 : LN., 298, ch. 59, 4 : 321, chh. 36, 16. °जोरे, A., 167, ch. 142, 7. °आकुल, UT., 353, ch. 69, 11.

आतम,—°अनुभव, UT., 374, ch. 115, 2. °आरो, UT., 353, ch. 70, 6.

आतुर, AR., 222, ch. 2, 11, 19 : 225, ch. 7, 3 : 230, ch. 15, 20 : 235, do. 24, 2 : LN., 296, ch. 56, 8 : 297, ch. 58, 2 : 307, ch. 81, 8 ; chh. 9, 1 : 324, ch. 116, 6 : UT., 360, ch. 88, 7.

आत्मा,—°अवगति, UT., 344, do. 45, 2.

आदर, BA., 24, ch. 76, 6 : 37, ch. 111, 2 : 38, ch. 115, 3 : 72, ch. 220, 9 : 110, chh. 52, 1 : 112, ch. 335, 8 : 113, ch. 338, 3 : 119, ch. 358, 4 : A., 130, ch. 24, 4 : 135, ch. 39, 6 : 147, ch. 78, 3 : 155, ch. 105, 3 : 205, ch. 266, 12 : LN., 279, ch. 10, 7 : 282, so. 3, 3 : 290, ch. 37, 4 : UT., 333, do. 13, 5 : 336, ch. 20, 6 : 345, ch. 49, 2 : 351, ch. 64, 7.

आदरतो, UT., 334, tot. 1, 16.

√ आदर,—आदरहिँ, BA., 7, do. 19, 1 : A., 130, ch. 25, 2 : 192, do. 224, 2.

आदरत्यौ, BA., 7, ch. 19, 8 : 208, A., ch. 274, 3.

आदरिय, A., 175, ch. 170, 2.

आदरो, UT., 333, chh. 5, 9.

आदरेउ, UT., 372, ch. 112, 10.

आदि, BA., 7, ch. 19, 2 : 8, ch. 22, 19 : 9, ch. 22, 23 : 23, 5 : 33, ch. 101, 7 : 41, ch. 125, 4 : 49, ch. 148, 6 : 55, do. 167, 1 : 81, ch. 247, 7 : A., 162, ch. 127, 7 : AR., 229, ch. 13, 12 : KI., 250, do. 20, 1 : SU., 258, ch. 9, 4 : LN., 295, do. 51, 1 : 299, do. 62, 1 : 303, ch. 72, 6 : 318, do. 102, 1 : UT., 342, ch. 36, 5 : 348, ch. 58, 2 : 350, ch. 62, 6 : 361, ch. 89, 5. °कवि, BA., 50, ch. 153, 2 : 52, ch. 156, 12.

आदिहि, A., 171, ch. 154, 8.

आदिहु, SU., 260, ch. 13, 6.

आदिक, BA., 10, ch. 26, 4 : 107, do. 326, 1 : A., 164, ch. 133, 7 : 186, ch. 205, 8 : AR., 223, chh. 1, 16 : 229, ch. 13, 8 : LN., 288, ch. 33, 20 : 298, ch. 59, 30 : UT., 340, do. 30, 2 : 358, do. 83, 4.

आधा, LN., 293, ch. 47, 4.

आधे, BA., 66, ch. 202, 2.

आँधी, LN., 304, ch. 75, 8.

आधीन, BA., 56, ch. 171, 3 : A., 196, do. 235, 2 : AR., 228, ch. 13, 3. Cf. अधीन.

आधीना, BA., 10, ch. 25, 4 : 57, ch. 172, 1 : A., 212, ch. 288, 8.

आधे, *see* आधा.

आन, BA., 2, ch. 3, 6 : 10, ch. 26, 8 : 19, do. 60, 2 : 26, ch. 82, 2 : 39, ch. 119, 5 : 46, ch. 139, 6 : do. 139, 2 ; ch. 140, 6 : 56, ch. 170, 4 : 62, do. 191, 2 ; 70, ch. 213, 7 : 72, ch. 220, 10 : A., 129, ch. 20, 8 : 141, ch. 60, 2 : 148, ch. 83, 8 : 176, ch. 171, 2 : 177, ch. 176, 1 : 184, do. 196, 2 : 186, ch. 204, 6 : 190, ch. 218, 5 : 202, ch. 255, 7 : AR., 223, ch. 3, 12 : 225, ch. 7, 2, 8 : 234, do. 22, 2 : SU., 263, ch. 24, 8 : 271, ch. 48, 8 : LN., 277, do. 4, 2 : 286, ch. 29, 4 : 311, ch. 89, 3 : 318, do. 101, 1 : 320, ch. 106, 7 : 326, do. 118, 4 : UT., 346, do. 49, 2 : 350, do. 63, 3 : 356, ch. 78, 2 : 357, do. 81, 2 : 361, chh. 9, 1 : 363, ch. 94, 2 : 365, do. 100, 1 : 372, ch. 112, 3 : 379, do. 122, 3 : 380, chh. 12, 10.

आनन, UT., 357, ch. 81, 4.

आनहिँ, A., 157, ch. 111, 1 : LN., 277, ch. 4, 8 : UT., 343, ch. 41, 5 : 357, ch. 81, 8.

आना, BA., 21, ch. 64, 1 : 22, ch. 67, 5 : 40, ch. 122, 8 : 73, chh. 30, 3 : A., 136, ch. 43, 2 :

179, ch. 86, 8 : 153, ch. 98, 3 : 203, ch. 258, 8 : AR., 224, ch. 3, 21 : 227, ch. 10, 7 : 228, ch. 13, 3 : SU., 266, ch. 34, 5 : 272, ch. 50, 1 : 272, ch. 52, 6 : LN., 292, ch. 42, 8 : 305, ch. 77, 4 : 315, ch. 96, 10 : UT., 356, ch. 78, 3 : 357, ch. 81, 4 : 361, ch. 91, 2 : 370, ch. 109, 10.

√आन,—आनउं, KI., 254, ch. 30, 9.

आनत, BA., 42, ch. 126, 6 : A., 200, 251, 3 : 201, ch. 253, 7.

आनय, BA., 57, ch. 173, 4.

आनवि, BA., 61, ch. 187, 3 : UT., 370, ch. 109, 13.

आनविँ, BA., 55, ch. 168, 10 : UT., 364, chh. 10, 3.

आनइ, BA., 108, ch. 328, 2 : A., 125, ch. 7, 1 : 134, ch. 39, 1 : 186, ch. 205, 5 : AR., 234, ch. 23, 5 : KI., 245, ch. 5, 7 : SU., 261, ch. 15, 10 : LN., 277, ch. 2, 9 : 283, ch. 19, 2 : 319, ch. 105, 11.

आनइँ, SU., 270, do. 44, 1.

आनि, BA., 45, do. 137, 1 : 73, do. 221, 1 : 85, do. 258, 2 : 107, chh. 39, 2 : A., 124, do. 3, 1 : 128, do. 17, 2 : 148, ch. 80, 8 : 153, ch. 98, 10 ; chh. 4, 2 : 155, do. 103, 2 ; ch. 104, 2 : 159, ch. 116, 6 : 165, ch. 138, 5 : 183, do. 7, 2 : 204, ch. 263, 2 : AR., 226, do. 7, 2 : 238, do. 29, 1 : SU., 259, ch. 12, 3 : LN., 277, do. 2, 2 : ch. 3, 1 : 4, 2 : 288, do. 32, 1 : 298, do. 59, 2 : 320, chh. 35, 6.

आनिबो, SU., 266, ch. 32, 4.

आनिय, BA., 93, ch. 284, 4 : A., 188, do. 210, 1.

आनिये, A., 183, chh. 8, 4 : SU., 266, do. 31, 2.

आनियेँ, KI., 254, chh. 2, 1.

आनी, BA., 14, ch. 42, 8 : 29, ch. 90, 4 : 40, ch. 121, 5 : 60, ch. 182, 3 : 71, ch. 217, 2 : 72, ch. 219, 2 : 80, ch. 244, 7 ; 246, 8 : 88, ch. 269, 3 : 107, ch. 326, 3 : 109, ch. 330, 6 : 114, ch. 341, 4 : 115, ch. 342, 13 : A., 146, ch. 77, 2 : 150, ch. 87, 8 : 157, ch. 110, 8 : 162, ch. 127, 5 : 165, ch. 138, 3 : 179, ch. 182, 6 : 185, ch. 201, 7 : 207, ch. 270, 4 ; 271, 7 : AR., 227, ch. 9, 11 : SU., 260, ch. 13, 10 : LN., 278, ch. 7, 3 : 294, ch. 47, 7 : 298, ch. 59, 27 : UT., 344, ch. 44, 3.

आनू, SU., 274, ch. 58, 1.

आनेउ, LN., 296, ch. 54, 8.

आनेउँ, A., 215, do. 295, 2.

आनेवि, SU., 258, ch. 9, 9 : LN., 287, ch. 30, 6.

आनेउ, A., 132, ch. 30, 2 : 151, ch. 92, 7, 8 : 167, ch. 144, 4 : SU., 263, do. 21, 2 : LN., 283, ch. 20, 5.

आने, BA., 101, ch. 308, 7 : 111, chh. 57, 1 : A., 125, ch. 10, 3 : 160, ch. 121, 2 : 180, ch. 186, 3 : 212, ch. 288, 4 : AR., 222, ch. 2, 21 : SU., 272, ch. 52, 2.

आनै, BA., 96, ch. 295, 1.

आनवीँ, BA., 71, ch. 218, 7 : AR., 233, ch. 21, 2 : KI., 249, ch. 18, 2 : 250, ch. 18, 3.

आनन, BA., 38, ch. 114, 8 : 69, ch. 211, 7 : SU., 256, ch. 2, 10 : 270, ch. 45, 5 : LN., 281, ch. 16, 6 : 302, chh. 3, 4 : 317, ch. 100, 9 : UT., 355, ch. 77, 2 : 364, chh. 10, 4. °रविन्द, BA., 42, ch. 126, 6.

आनन्द, BA., 16, ch. 48, 10 : 19, ch. 61, 3 : 99, ch. 303, 8 : 102, ch. 312, 7 ; do. 312, 2 ; ch. 314, 4 : 104, ch. 318, 9 : 108, ch. 329, 4 : 109, chh. 46, 2 : 111, chh. 59, 1 : 120, ch. 360, 5 : 121, ch. 365, 8 ; do. 365, 2 : 122, ch. 367, 5 : A., 126, do. 11, 1 : 138, do. 50, 2 : 139, ch. 52, 8 : 153, ch. 98, 15 : 155, ch. 105, 1 : 160, ch. 121, 5 : 194, do. 230, 2 : 200, ch. 249, 1 : 206, ch. 268, 2 : AR., 239, ch. 32, 6 : UT., 349, ch. 58, 8. °अवधि, A., 204, ch. 263, 6. °कन्द, BA., 106, chh. 37, 3 : 107, chh. 40, 2. °दाता, BA., 75, ch. 229, 2. °घन, BA., 106, chh. 37, 1. °अर्क, BA., 107, chh. 40, 2. °भवन, BA., 67, ch. 205, 2 : 99, ch. 303, 4 : A., 125, ch. 9, 4. °रासौ, BA., 10, ch. 27, 6. °सिन्धु BA., 69, ch. 209, 5. Cf. अनन्द.

आनन्दू, BA., 75, ch. 229, 2.

आप, BA., 28, ch. 89, 4 : 51, ch. 155, 2 : 55, ch. 166, 6 : 97, ch. 298, 3 : UT., 342, ch. 39, 4.

आपन, A., 171, do. 154, 2.

आपना, A., 129, ch. 21, 7 : AR., 239, ch. 34, 5 : SO., 259, ch. 11, 2 : LN., 296, ch. 55, 5.

आपनि, A., 144, ch. 71, 1.

आपने, BA., 6, ch. 17, 5 : 11, ch. 29, 8 ; 30, 6 : 12, ch. 34, 2 : 20, chh. 2, 4 : 59, ch. 182, 1 : 87, ch. 267, 1 : 92, ch. 282, 6 : 110, chh. 48, 2 : A., 129, do. 21, 1 : 183, chh. 8, 4 : 200, ch. 250, 2 : 208, ch. 274, 3, 7 : 212, ch. 288, 6 ; 289, 6 ; 290, 2 : AR., 242, chh. 11, 2 : LN., 294, ch. 48, 4 : UT., 362, do. 91, 3 : 370, do. 108, 2.

आपण, BA., 22, ch. 68, 7 : 30, ch. 94, 5 : 46, ch. 139, 6 : 47, ch. 144, 5 : 53, ch. 162, 3 : 55, ch. 167, 8 ; 168, 7 : 57, ch. 172, 1 : 60, ch. 186, 2 : 95, ch. 289, 8 : 106, ch. 325, 7 : 122, ch. 367, 2 : A., 141, ch. 60, 3 : 168, ch. 147, 3 : 176, do. 170, 2 : 176, ch. 171, 8 : 178, do. 176, 2 : 181, ch. 189, 2 : 200, ch. 248, 1 : 202, ch. 256, 7 ; 257, 5 : 213, ch. 290, 9 : 214, ch. 293, 3 : KI., 244, ch. 2, 4 : 247, chh. 1, 8 : SU., 268, ch. 38, 5 : LN., 286, ch. 29, 2 : 295, ch. 51, 4 : UT., 350, ch. 62, 1.

आपणि, BA., 3, ch. 6, 1 : 42, ch. 127, 4 : 44, ch. 134, 3 : 79, do. 242, 1 : 87, ch. 267, 6 : 92, ch. 282, 6 : A., 171, ch. 154, 8 : 177, do. 175, 1 : 178, ch. 177, 6 : 191, ch. 218, 16 : 200, ch. 251, 2 : 207, ch. 273,

1: AR., 237, ch. 29, 4: KI., 252, ch. 25, 4: SU., 273, ch. 53, 3: 274, ch. 57, 10: UT., 355, ch. 75, 1.

आपनी, A., 192, do. 224, 3: 212, do. 287, 1: UT., 368, ch. 84, 4.

आपने, BA., 105, chh. 35, 2: LN., 317, chh. 31, 8.

आपु, BA., 8, ch. 22, 18: 10, ch. 28, 6: 12, do. 34, 1: 29, ch. 91, 6: 47, do. 143, 1: 62, ch. 157, 8; 158, 2: 54, do. 164, 2: 57, ch. 173, 5: 58, ch. 176, 1: 70, ch. 213, 3: 71, ch. 217, 6: 73, ch. 222, 2: 93, do. 282, 1: 101, do. 308, 2: A., 123, do. 2, 2: 149, ch. 84, 5: 150, ch. 88, 4: 153, ch. 98, 2; do. 98, 1: 158, ch. 116, 2: 164, do. 134, 1: 168, ch. 146, 4: 182, ch. 191, 4: 183, ch. 194, 14; 195, 3: 191, do. 218, 2: 197, ch. 239, 7: 210, ch. 280, 5; 281, 3: 212, ch. 288, 5: 213, ch. 291, 7: 215, ch. 298, 2: AR., 228, do. 12, 1: LN., 289, ch. 34, 1: 291, do. 40, 2: 318, ch. 103, 4: UT., 343, ch. 41, 5: 349, ch. 59, 4: 364, ch. 97, 3.

आपुन, BA., 61, ch. 187, 4: 64, chh. 18, 2: 210, ch. 282, 3: 211, ch. 285, 7: LN., 304, ch. 75, 1: UT., 354, do. 72, 4.

आपुहि, BA., 96, ch. 292, 8: A., 140, ch. 56, 6: 186, ch. 206, 1: SU., 269, do. 9, 1: 354, ch. 73, 5.

आपू, BA., 11, ch. 30, 3: 177, ch. 173, 4: A., 210, ch. 282, 2: 216, ch. 301, 7.

आपद,—°काल, AR., 223, ch. 3, 7.

आपन्नगामी श्री, UT., 368, chh. 11, 16.

आँब,—°जाय, UT., 349, ch. 58, 6.

आवाहन, A., 197, ch. 239, 3.

आभीर, UT., 380, chh. 12, 3.

आमलक, BA., 12, ch. 37, 7.

आमिख(ष), BA., 58, ch. 177, 3. °भोगी, AR., 237, ch. 28, 2.

आय, आयउ, आया, आयेउ, आयो, आयी, *&c., see* √आय.

आयत, BA., 111, ch. 338, 6: AR., 237, chh. 9, 3: SU., 270, ch. 45, 5: UT., 355, do. 76, 2.

आयतन, A., 183, so. 7, 1.

आयस, A., 186, ch. 205, 3.

आयसु BA., 20, ch. 62, 12: 23, ch. 71, 6; do. 71, 1: 48, ch. 87, 2: 44, ch. 134, 2: 54, ch. 165, 1: 57, ch. 172, 6; ch. 174, 1: 63, ch. 195, 13: 64, ch. 197, 2: 66, ch. 200, 2: 71, ch. 217, 8: 75, ch. 230, 6: 78, do. 237, 2; ch. 238, 1: 81, ch. 248, 6; 249, 5: 86, ch. 263, 7: 87, ch. 265, 4: 88, ch. 270, 2: 89, ch. 272, 8: 91, ch. 279, 2: 100, ch. 305, 3: 101, ch. 309, 3: 103, ch. 316, 6: 108, ch. 328, 2: 110, chh. 49, 1: 113, ch. 338, 7: 114, ch. 340, 5; 342, 6; 118, ch. 352, 7: 119, ch. 357, 5; 121, ch. 366, 10: A., 125, do. 6, 1; ch. 8, 1: 126, ch. 10, 8: 135, do. 40, 2: 136, do. 45, 2: 137, ch. 46, 3: 139, ch. 52, 7: 141, ch. 58, 7; 59, 6; 60, 4: 145, chh. 3, 3: 146, ch. 75, 3: 149, ch. 86, 8: 156, ch. 108, 7: 160, ch. 122, 2: 163, ch. 131, 8: 168, chh. 5, 2: 174, ch. 164, 7: 176, ch. 170, 10; 171, 7: 178, ch. 176, 7: 182, ch. 191, 2: 186, ch. 205, 8: 187, do. 206, 1: 196, do. 238, 1: 198, ch. 243, 3; do. 243, 1: 200, ch. 248, 3, 4; 249, 3: 201, ch. 254, 8: 203, do. 259, 1: 206, ch. 268, 6: 208, ch. 275, 3: 210, ch. 280, 4; do. 281, 2; ch. 282, 4: 211, ch. 285, 5: 212, do. 289, 2: 215, ch. 295, 7; 296, 2, 4, 5, 7: 216, ch. 299, 2; 300, 6: 217, ch. 303, 4: 219, ch. 311, 4, 7: 220, do. 313, 2: AR., 224, ch. 3, 21: 228, ch. 10, 18: KI., 247, ch. 11, 8: 251, ch. 22, 5; 23, 8: SU., 267, ch. 34, 9: 273, ch. 55, 5: LN., 278, ch. 5, 9; 6, 3: 283, ch. 19, 3: 284, do. 23, 1: 288, ch. 33, 10, 13: 291, ch. 39, 7: 295, do. 51, 1: 297, do. 58, 2: 318, ch. 102, 5, 8: 322, do. 110, 1: 325, ch. 118, 7: UT., 332, ch. 13, 5: 338, ch. 25, 6: 345, ch. 48, 8: 351, do. 64, 2.

आयु, BA., 91, ch. 277, 3. °हीन, SU., 269, ch. 42, 1.

आयुध, BA., 66, ch. 200, 4: 67, chh. 24, 3: 73, do. 221, 371: AR., 231, do. 15, 3; chh. 6, 1: SU., 267, ch. 35, 9: LN., 292, do. 41, 1: 295, ch. 50, 6: 305, chh. 4, 1: 307, ch. 80, 4.

आरज,—°सुतपदकमल, A., 152, do. 95, 2.

आरत, BA., 10, ch. 26, 5: 39, ch. 118, 2: 44, do. 133, 2: 46, ch. 139, 5: 48, ch. 146, 2: A., 133, do. 34, 2: 139, do. 51, 1: 147, ch. 79, 3: 167, ch. 143, 1: 178, do. 179, 1: 183, ch. 194, 10: 184, ch. 196, 7: 195, ch. 235, 1: 200, ch. 248, 1: 203, ch. 259, 4: 212, ch. 289, 8: LN., 292, ch. 41, 4: UT., 327, do. 1, 1: 330, chh. 2, 7. °गिरा, AR., 234, ch. 24, 2: LN., 283, do. 20, 2. °जनपाला, UT., 358, ch. 83, 2. °बचो, UT., 336, ch. 19, 1, °बस, A., 152, do. 95, 1. °बानी, AR., 222, ch. 2, 14: 235, ch. 25, 7: LN., 301, ch. 67, 2.

आरति(1) (distressed), BA., 39, ch. 118, 3.

आरति(2) (distress), BA., 17, ch. 52, 1: 77, ch. 234, 8: A., 136, ch. 44, 8: 152, ch. 95, 1: 178, ch. 180, 1: 201, ch. 253, 1: 217, ch. 302, 6. °हर, UT., 331, ch. 10, 7. °हरन, BA., 22, ch. 69, 6: AR., 235, ch. 25, 2: SU., 270, do. 45, 2.

आरति (3) (the lustral rite), **BA.**, 111, chh. 56, 3 : 118, ch. 353, 7.

आरतो, **BA.**, 34, ch. 104, 2 : 68, ch. 206, 5 : 90, ch. 273, 14 : 101, ch. 308, 4 : 106, do. 323, 1 ; ch. 325, 4 : 107, chh. 38, 1 : 114, do. 341, 2 : 117, ch. 350, 6 ; 351, 8 : 118, ch. 354, 1 ; 355, 4 : **A.**, 170, ch. 153, 3 : **UT.**, 330, ch. 8, 4 : 331, ch. 10, 6, 7 : 332, ch. 13, 6.

आराति, **AR.**, 230, do. 15, 1. Cf. अराति.

आरातो, **BA.**, 22, ch. 67, 8 : **AR.**, 232, ch. 17, 7 : **UT.**, 349, ch. 59, 6.

आराध,—आराधें, **BA.**, 26, ch. 80, 8.

√**आराध**,—आराधक, **BA.**, 28, ch. 88, 3.

आराध्य, **BA.**, 26, ch. 80, 4.

आराम, **BA.**, 78, do. 239, 2 : **UT.**, 340, chh. 8, 4.

आरामं, **AR.**, 226, ch. 8, 13.

आरूढ़, **SU.**, 259, ch. 11, 4.

आरूढ़ा, **LN.**, 284, ch. 23, 4.

आलवाल, **BA.**, 117, ch. 349, 8.

आलय, **UT.**, 341, ch. 35, 7.

आलस, **BA.**, 29, ch. 91, 4.

आलसएँ, **BA.**, 11, ch. 32, 1.

आलसी, **SU.**, 272, ch. 51, 4.

आलि, **BA.**, 77, ch. 234, 6. Cf. अली.

आली, **BA.**, 79, ch. 241, 4 : 80, ch. 246, 6 : **A.**, 127, ch. 16, 4 : 130, ch. 24, 3 : 189, ch. 214, 2.

√**आव**,—अवलोक, **BA.**, 97, ch. 290, 3.

आए, **BA.**, 16, ch. 47, 6 : 27, do. 83, 1 : 36, do. 107, 1 : 56, ch. 171, 5 : 61, do. 186, 1 : 62, ch. 192, 5, 8 : 63, ch. 193, 9 ; 195, 7, 13 : 70, ch. 213, 6 : 96, ch. 295, 3 : **A.**, 125, ch. 10, 2 : 135, do. 39, 1 : 154, ch. 100, 3 ; do. 100, 1 : 155, ch. 103, 5 : 162, do. 127, 2 : 164, ch. 132, 5 : 190, ch. 218, 10 ; chh. 9, 4 : 191, ch. 221, 5 : 196, ch. 237, 1 : 198, do. 243, 2 : 204, ch. 262, 1 : **AR.**, 221, do. 1, 2 : 230, so. 6, 1 : 235, ch. 24, 14 : 236, do. 26*a*, 2 : **KI.**, 248, do. 12, 2 : 251, ch. 22, 2 : **SU.**, 256, ch. 2, 2 : 265, ch. 29, 2, 3 : **LN.**, 281, do. 14, 3 : 285, ch. 24, 8 : 290, ch. 37, 3 : 291, do. 40, 2 : 294, do. 48, 1 : 296, do. 54, 1 : 298, ch. 60, 1 ; so. 6, 2 : 308, ch. 82, 7 : 318, ch. 103, 1 : 325, do. 117, 3 : **UT.**, 328, do. 2, 2 : 332, do. 11, 4 ; 335, ch. 17, 2.

आएब, **BA.**, 75, ch. 230, 1.

आएबहिँ, **BA.**, 103, do. 317, 2.

आएवि, **A.**, 166, ch. 141, 3 : **AR.**, 233, ch. 21, 8 ; **SU.**, 264, ch. 25, 1.

आएवीँ, **A.**, 168, chh. 5, 2.

आएँ, **BA.**, 24, ch. 75, 7 : 28, ch. 89, 1 : 34, ch. 103, 1 : 36, ch. 108, 5 : 38, ch. 115, 4 : 50, ch. 150, 7 : 51, ch. 155, 2 : 54, ch. 163, 6 : 57, ch. 174, 2 : 58, ch. 175, 5 : 61, ch. 188, 5 : 63, ch. 193, 4, 6, 8 ; 194, 5 : 68, ch. 207, 3 : 70, ch. 213, 4 ; 215, 3 : 73, chh. 29, 4 : 74, ch. 224, 3 : 77, ch. 236, 5 : 78, ch. 240, 2, 8 : 79, ch. 243, 2 : 91, ch. 277, 6 : 95, ch. 291, 3 : 97, ch. 298, 4, 8 : 101, ch. 310, 6 : 102, ch. 313, 8 : 103, ch. 316, 7 : 106, ch. 324, 7 : 108, ch. 329, 7 : **A.**, 123, ch. 2, 3 : 127, ch. 13, 8 : 128, ch. 20, 1 : 131, ch. 28, 4, 7 : 134, ch. 39, 1 : 140, ch. 56, 3 : 143, ch. 67, 6 : 163, ch. 130, 1 : 164, ch. 134, 5 : 165, ch. 137, 5 : 169, ch. 149, 4 : 170, ch. 153, 3 : 171, ch. 157, 2 : 172, ch. 158, 1 : 181, ch. 188, 1 : 186, ch. 205, 8 : 191, ch. 221, 8 : 196, ch. 236, 1 : 201, ch. 252, 7 : 202, ch. 256, 2 : 206, ch. 270, 2 : 207, ch. 270, 3 : 208, ch. 275, 3 : 211, ch. 286, 7 : 216, ch. 300, 8 : **AR.**, 229, ch. 14, 17 : 239, ch. 33, 9 : 240, ch. 36, 7 : **KI.**, 245, ch. 5, 8 ; 6, 8 ; 7, 3 : 248, ch. 12, 8 : 249, ch. 16, 1 ; 18, 1 : 254, ch. 30, 11 : **SU.**, 256, ch. 2, 5 : 262, ch. 19, 8 : 263, ch. 24, 3 : 268, ch. 37, 7 : 268, ch. 36, 9 : 269, ch. 41, 2 : 273, ch. 53, 4, 6 : **LN.**, 282, ch. 18, 12 : 299, ch. 60, 4 : 300, ch. 64, 8 : 309, ch. 84, 1 : **UT.**, 339, ch. 28, 5 : 343, ch. 41, 2 : 352, ch. 68, 8 : 362, ch. 93, 3 : 371, ch. 109, 16 : 373, ch. 114, 9 : 374, ch. 115, 7.

आरै, **BA.**, 66, ch. 202, 1 : 67, ch. 205, 1 : 120, ch. 361, 8 : **A.**, 188, ch. 21, 3, 2 : 317, ch. 101, 2.

आवथ, **BA.**, 57, ch. 173, 3 ; do. 173, 1 : 80, ch. 246, 6 : **LN.**, 323, do. 112, 2.

आवैँ, **BA.**, 75, ch. 230, 6.

आयउ, **UT.**, 336, do. 20, 3 : 350, do. 61, 1 : 367, do. 103, 2.

आयउँ, **UT.**, 349, do. 58, 2 : 351, ch. 65, 1 : 357, ch. 82, 2 ; do. 82, 2 : 360, ch. 88, 10 : 362, do. 92, 1.

आयउँ, **UT.**, 372, ch. 111, 9.

आयउ, **UT.**, 351, do. 64, 2 : 369, do. 107, 6.

आयए, **BA.**, 79, ch. 241, 4 : **SU.**, 257, ch. 6, 5 : 272, ch. 51, 7 : **UT.**, 332, do. 12, 6 : 333, do. 13, 4 : 334, do. 14, 3 : 336, ch. 20, 6 : 341, ch. 38, 3 : 344, ch. 44, 1 : 345, ch. 49, 1 : 346, ch. 51, 1 ; do. 51, 1 : 350, ch. 64, 4 : 351, ch. 66, 7 : 352, ch. 68, 6 ; 69, 5.

आव, **BA.**, 14, ch. 43, 7 : 82, ch. 250, 10 : 91, ch. 277, 4 : 116, do. 348, 2 : **A.**, 139, do. 52, 2 : 163, ch. 130, 4 : 185, do. 201, 1 : 210, ch. 281, 7.

आवत, **BA.**, 101, ch. 310, 8 : **LN.**, 289, ch. 35, 4.

आवत, BA., 5, ch. 14, 8 : 16, ch. 48, 4 : 22, ch. 67, 1 : 28, ch. 70, 7 ; 72, 7 : 39, ch. 117, 4 : 40, ch. 119, 8 : 44, ch. 134, 4 : 47, ch. 143, 1 : 57, ch. 174, 3 : 58, ch. 176, 5, 8 : 60, ch. 184, 8 : 62, ch. 190, 3 ; 191, 3 : 65, ch. 199, 9 : 67, ch. 205, 5 : 68, ch. 208, 7 : 70, ch. 214, 5 : 75, ch. 228, 2 : 79, ch. 242, 5 : 86, ch. 264, 7 : 91, ch. 276, 5 : 104, ch. 318, 13 : 110, ch. 332, 7 : A., 132, ch. 29, 5 : 153, ch. 98, 14 : 165, ch. 137, 4 : 166, ch. 142, 1 : 205, ch. 266, 4 : AR., 230, ch. 15, 11, 13 : 234, ch. 24, 7 : 236, ch. 27, 6 : 238, ch. 29, 9 : KI., 245, ch. 6, 2, 10 : 247, ch. 10, 5 : 248, ch. 14, 7 : 252, ch. 24, 7 : 253, ch. 27, 10 ; 28, 3 : SU., 256, ch. 2, 11 : 258, ch. 9, 2 : 261, ch. 18, 3 : 262, ch. 19, 4 ; 20, 4 : 264, ch. 27, 6 : 265, ch. 28, 2 : 266, ch. 34, 6 : 268, ch. 38, 2 : 270, ch. 43, 4, 7 ; 44, 8 : 271, ch. 47, 8 : 273, do. 52, 2 : LN., 279, ch. 10, 2 : 282, ch. 18, 16 : 284, ch. 23, 6 : 285, ch. 24, 16 : 292, ch. 42, 6 : 294, ch. 48, 7 : 296, ch. 55, 2 : 298, ch. 59, 22, 24 : 301, ch. 68, 3 : 303, ch. 73, 5 : 304, ch. 75, 6 : 308, ch. 82, 7 : 310, ch. 86, 2 : 320, ch. 107, 10 : 325, ch. 117, 1 : UT., 336, ch. 21, 5 : 370, ch. 108, 7 : 375, ch. 117, 4.

आवे, BA., 54, do. 164, 2.

आवै, BA., 16, ch. 48, 3 : 27, ch. 85, 3 : 73, chh. 28, 3 : SU., 268, ch. 37, 3 : 271, ch. 48, 2 : LN., 302, do. 70, 2 : UT., 360, ch. 88, 19 : 374, ch. 116, 4.

आवौं, A., 137, ch. 46, 4 : 215, ch. 296, 4 : KI., 245, ch. 6, 6 : LN., 303, ch. 72, 13 : 318, ch. 108, 4 : UT., 372, ch. 111, 14.

आवहिं, AR., 224, ch. 5, 2.

आवहु, BA., 20, ch. 62, 10.

आवैं, A., 132, ch. 31, 7 : SU., 261, ch. 16, 4.

आवौं, A., 137, ch. 46, 3.

आस, BA., 17, ch. 52, 2 : 86, ch. 262, 4 : A., 127, ch. 17, 1 : 149, ch. 84, 8 : 155, ch. 104, 7 : 217, ch. 305, 1 : 219, do. 310, 2 : AR., 242, chh. 11, 4 : SU., 268, do. 37, 1 : 275, chh. 3, 4 : LN., 308, do. 82, 2 : 313, ch. 93, 6 : UT., 333, chh. 5, 11 : 342, ch. 36, 5 : 345, ch. 47, 5 : 359, so. 3, 2.

आसा(1) (hope), BA., 87, ch. 265, 1 : A., 138, ch. 50, 13 : 169, ch. 149, 5 : KI., 249, ch. 16, 9 : UT., 341, ch. 33, 6 : 345, ch. 47, 3, 5 : 359, ch. 86, 7 : 377, ch. 119, 6.

आसा(2) (region), LN., 280, ch. 14, 1 : 325, ch. 116, 8.

आसन, BA., 18, ch. 56, 5 : 28, ch. 70, 4 : 24, ch. 76, 6 : 36, ch. 108, 1 : 38, ch. 115, 3 : 45, ch. 135, 5 : 46, ch. 140, 5 : 54, ch. 163, 2 : 57, ch. 174, 1 : 72, ch. 219, 2 : 82, ch. 251, 8 : 106, ch. 325, 8 : 107, do. 326, 2 ; ch. 327, 4 ; chh. 38, 1 ; 40, 3 : 109, ch. 331, 10 : 112, ch. 334, 7 : A., 152, ch. 96, 4 : 155, ch. 104, 1 : 160, ch. 121, 3 : 164, ch. 198, 6 : 167, ch. 207, 3 : 207, ch. 270, 4 : 219, ch. 312, 4 : AR., 222, so. 3, 1 : 227, ch. 9, 11 : 238, ch. 29, 10 : SU., 268, ch. 38, 3 : LN., 280, ch. 12, 4.

आसनन, BA., 121, ch. 365, 3.

आसिख(ष), BA., 91, ch. 277, 5 : 99, ch. 303, 8 : 107, chh. 39, 3 : 116, ch. 347, 8 ; 348, 6 : 119, ch. 357, 3 : A., 143, ch. 67, 5 : 144, ch. 68, 7 : 145, chh. 3, 3 : 163, ch. 129, 7 : 178, ch. 176, 7 : 195, ch. 233, 2 : 198, ch. 242, 12 : 208, ch. 276, 6 : 218, ch. 307, 5 ; 308, 3 : AR., 223, ch. 3, 2 : SU., 256, do. 2, 2 : 261, ch. 17, 2, 6 : LN., 325, ch. 118, 4 : UT., 330, do. 7, 3 : 331, do. 9, 2 : 371, ch. 110, 15. Cf. असीस, आसिर.

आसिषा, UT., 369, ch. 106, 16.

आसिर,—¹बचन, A., 196, ch. 237, 8. ²बाद, BA., 116, ch. 346, 1 : 119, ch. 359, 2 : A., 160, ch. 121, 1 : LN., 321, ch. 109, 2. Cf. असीस, आसिष.

आसीन, AR., 222, so. 3, 1 : KI., 248, ch. 13, 6 : LN., 280, ch. 12, 4 ; do. 12, 1 : UT., 369, do. 107, 3.

आसीना, BA., 21, ch. 64, 6 : AR., 228, ch. 11, 5 : 240, ch. 36, 8.

आसुतोष(ष), BA., 26, ch. 80, 4 : 31, chh. 6, 4 : 136, ch. 44, 8.

आसू, LN., 296, ch. 54, 1 : 306, ch. 79, 3.

आँसू, A., 127, ch. 14, 6 : 172, ch. 159, 4.

आश्रम, BA., 18, ch. 55, 6 ; 56, 1, 3 : 19, ch. 60, 6 : 44, ch. 132, 2 : 52, ch. 156, 15 : 53, ch. 162, 1 : 54, ch. 163, 1 : 63, ch. 194, 1 : 71, ch. 218, 2 : 73, do. 221, 1 ; ch. 222, 11 : A., 160, do. 120, 1 : 162, ch. 127, 2 : 187, do. 207, 2 : 193, ch. 226, 1 : 194, ch. 230, 2 : 196, do. 236, 2 : 205, do. 265, 1 ; ch. 266, 6 : AR., 222, ch. 2, 18, 21 : 226, do. 7, 2 : 227, ch. 9, 2, 5 : 236, ch. 26, 3, 5, 6 : 237, ch. 29, 5 : SU., 274, ch. 57, 12 : LN., 277, ch. 4, 5 : 296, ch. 56, 2 : UT., 351, ch. 65, 2 : 357, ch. 82, 2 : 362, do. 92, 1 : 363, ch. 95, 1 : 369, ch. 107, 10 : 371, do. 110, 3 : 372, ch. 111, 9, 14.

आश्रमनि, A., 210, ch. 280, 5.

आश्रमहिं, BA., 44, ch. 133, 1 : A., 160, ch. 121, 2.

आश्रमहि, AR., 225, do. 6, 2.

आश्रमी, KI., 249, do. 16, 2.

आश्रित, BA., 41, ch. 125, 1 : A., 193, ch. 226, 8 : UT., 333, chh. 5, 19.

आहार, BA., 50, do. 149, 1. Cf. अहार.

'आइहिं, आहि(1), 'आही, *see* √अव.

आहि(2), **A.**, 171, ch. 157, 6.

आहृति, **BA.**, 66, ch. 201, 6 : 93, do. 284, 1 : 95, ch. 291, 2 : 108, do. 329, 1 : **A.**, 133, ch. 33, 4 : **LN.**, 303, ch. 73, 1.

॥ इ ॥

इक, *see* एक.

इच्छा, **BA.**, 21, ch. 66, 6 : 35, ch. 106, 4 : 48, ch. 145, 3 : 67, do. 204, 2 : **A.**, 174, ch. 166, 7 : **AR.**, 239, do. 33, 3 : **KI.**, 252, do. 26, 1 : **SU.**, 267, ch. 35, 9 : 271, ch. 48, 6 : 272, ch. 49, 9 : **LN.**, 295, ch. 52, 4 : **UT.**, 362, ch. 93, 13 : 371, ch. 111, 4. Cf. ईसा. °चारी, **A.**, 174, ch. 166, 7 : **SU.**, 267, ch. 35, 9. °भव, **BA.**, 52, ch. 156, 9. °मरन, **UT.**, 371, do. 110, 2.

इच्छित, **BA.**, 26, ch. 80, 8 : 374, ch. 116, 4.

इत, **BA.**, 71, do. 215, 1 : 90, ch. 275, 8 : **A.**, 135, do. 40, 1 : 148, do. 83, 2 : 190, ch. 218, 11 : **AR.**, 234, ch. 24, 9 : **LN.**, 282, do. 18, 2 : 291, ch. 40, 7 : 295, ch. 52, 4 : 302, ch. 69, 10 : 305, do. 76, 2 : 306, do. 77, 5 ; ch. 79, 5.

इतना, इतनी, इतने, इतनेहि, इतनोई, *see* एतना.

इतराई, **KI.**, 248, ch. 14, 5.

इति, **LN.**, 321, chh. 36, 16 : **UT.**, 368, ch. 106, 2 : 369, do. 106, 1 : 374, ch. 115, 1. °हास, **BA.**, 4, ch. 7, 4 : 24, ch. 75, 4 : 52, do. 156, 1 : 55, ch. 168, 5 : 78, ch. 238, 2 : **A.**, 169, do. 150, 1 : 194, do. 228, 2 : 216, ch. 299, 1 : **UT.**, 371, ch. 111, 2. °हासा **BA.**, 22, ch. 68, 6 : 121, ch. 365, 5 : **A.**, 169, ch. 149, 5 : 188, ch. 210, 7 : **SU.**, 265, ch. 28, 6 : **UT.**, 348, ch. 56, 8 : 349, ch. 59, 1 : 379, ch. 123, 1.

इत्थं, **BA.**, 42, ch. 128, 2.

इदं, **AR.**, 223, chh. 1, 23 : **LN.**, 321, chh. 36, 22. इदमित्थं, **BA.**, 42, ch. 128, 2.

इन, इनहि, इनहिं, *see* ए.

इन्दिरा, **BA.**, 21, do. 64, 1 : **LN.**, 320, chh. 35, 6. °पति **AR.**, 222, chh. 1, 11. °रमन, **UT.**, 341, ch. 35, 4.

इन्दु, **BA.**, 38, ch. 114, 6 : 68, ch. 207, 6 : **AR.**, 227, do. 8, 2 : **KI.**, 249, ch. 17, 7 : **UT.**, 376, ch. 118, 21. °प्रकासा, **BA.**, 69, ch. 210, 7. °बर, **LN.**, 280, ch. 13, 8.

इन्द्र,—°कुलिस, **UT.**, 368, ch. 106, 13. °जाल, **AR.**, 239, ch. 34, 4. °जालि, **LN.**, 286, ch. 29, 10. °जित, **SU.**, 262, ch. 19, 3. °जीत, **BA.**, 64, ch. 197, 1 : **LN.**, 288, ch. 33, 20. °जीता, **LN.**, 326, ch. 116, 9. °जीत-बर, **UT.**, 349, ch. 59, 4. °बधू, **LN.**, 309, ch. 84, 5. °बधूप, **LN.**, 316, chh. 27, 2.

इन्द्री,—°द्वार, **UT.**, 374, ch. 115, 11.
इन्द्रिन, **UT.**, 374, ch. 115, 15.
इन्द्रिय, **A.**, 169, ch. 148, 2. °गन, **KI.**, 249, ch. 15, 12.
इन्द्रियातीतं, **AR.**, 223, chh. 1, 16.

इन्धन, **BA.**, 14, do. 40, 2. *See* ईंधन.

इन्ह, इन्हहि, *see* ए.

इब, **BA.**, 8, ch. 22, 12 ; so. 3, 2 : 19, ch. 60, 7 : 20, ch. 62, 2 : 22, ch. 68, 4 : 41, ch. 124, 8 : 42, ch. 126, 4 : 44, ch. 132, 8 : 51, ch. 153, 7 : 54, ch. 165, 7 : 75, ch. 229, 4 : 79, do. 243, 2 : 83, ch. 253, 5 : 86, ch. 263, 4, 5 : **A.**, 133, ch. 35, 7 : 140, ch. 58, 2 : 166, ch. 141, 8 : 178, ch. 180, 1 : 194, ch. 229, 5 : **AR.**, 226, ch. 7, 21 : 227, do. 8, 2 : 239, ch. 32, 2 : **KI.**, 246, ch. 7, 24 : 249, ch. 16, 9 : **SU.**, 274, do. 56, 3 : **LN.**, 277, ch. 3, 1 : 284, do. 22, 4 : 285, ch. 25, 6 : 301, do. 66, 2 : 303, ch. 72, 12 : 310, ch. 87, 5 : **UT.**, 340, ch. 31, 3 : 354, ch. 72, 2 : 356, do. 77, 3 ; ch. 78, 2 : 367, ch. 104, 7 : 370, ch. 108, 6 : 371, ch. 109, 14 : 376, ch. 118, 17, 18 : 380, ch. 126, 6.

इमि, **BA.**, 14, do. 40, 2 : 42, do. 125, 1 : **A.**, 159, do. 117, 2 : **AR.**, 226, ch. 7, 23 : 235, ch. 24, 10 : **LN.**, 285, ch. 25, 7 : 311, chh. 17, 3 : **UT.**, 354, ch. 73, 2.

इरखा (ष), **BA.**, 90, do. 274, 1 : **A.**, 145, ch. 74, 5 : 159, ch. 116, 6 : **UT.**, 365, ch. 99, 7 : 367, ch. 104, 5. इरखादि-निवारक, **UT.**, 342, ch. 36, 5.

इरखाई, **UT.**, 376, ch. 118, 33.

इष्ट, **BA.**, 20, ch. 62, 8. °देव, **BA.**, 20, ch. 62, 8 : 83, ch. 253, 5 : **LN.**, 302, ch. 69, 8 : **UT.**, 355, ch. 75, 5. °देवन, **BA.**, 85, ch. 260, 6.

इहइ, इहि, इहिं, इहै, इहौ, *see* ए.

इहाँ, **BA.**, 16, ch. 47, 4 : 33, ch. 102, 10 : 55, ch. 166, 8 : 57, ch. 173, 5 : 70, ch. 213, 7 : 74, ch. 226, 6 : 77, ch. 234, 6 : 92, ch. 281, 3 : **A.**, 133, ch. 33, 5 : 163, ch. 131, 4 : 188, ch. 210, 2 : 192, ch. 224, 4 : 197, ch. 239, 7 : 206, ch. 267, 7 : 208, ch. 276, 7 : 209, ch. 277, 4 : 210, ch. 281, 2 : 212, ch. 287, 5 :

॥ ई ॥